Emily Post's Etiquette

Also by Elizabeth L. Post

Emily Post's Complete Book of Wedding Etiquette, Revised Edition

Emily Post's Wedding Planner, Revised Edition

Emily Post on Business Etiquette

Emily Post on Entertaining

Emily Post on Etiquette

Emily Post on Invitations and Letters

Emily Post on Second Weddings

Emily Post on Weddings

Please, Say Please

The Complete Book of Entertaining
(with co-author Anthony Staffieri)

Emily Post Talks with Teens About Manners and Etiquette
(with co-author Joan M. Coles)

EMILY POST'S

ETIQUETTE

15TH EDITION

Elizabeth L. Post

📖 HarperCollins*Publishers*

HarperCollins books may be purchased for educational, business, or sales promotional use. For information, please call or write: Special Markets Department, HarperCollins Publishers, Inc., 10 East 53rd Street, New York, NY 10022. Telephone: (212) 207-7528; Fax: (212) 207-7222.

FIRST EDITION

Library of Congress Cataloging-in-Publication Data

Post, Emily, 1873–1960.
    [Etiquette]
    Emily Post's Etiquette / Elizabeth L. Post.—15th ed.
        p.   cm.
    Includes index.
    ISBN 0-06-270047-2—ISBN 0-06-270028-6 (thumb index)
    1. Etiquette.   I. Post, Elizabeth L.   II. Title.
BJ1853.P6   1992
395—dc20   91-58284

93 94 95 96 PS/RRD 10 9 8 7 6 5 4 3
   94 95 96 PS/RRD 10 9 8 7 6   (thumb index)

Contents

IV. COMMUNICATIONS

V. TRAVEL & TIPPING

VI. ENTERTAINING & ENTERTAINMENTS

VII. CELEBRATIONS AND CEREMONIES

I

FORMALITIES

$\mathcal{T}$he first time you greet someone presents an opportunity that will never come your way again: the chance to make a good first impression. Your appearance and your manners play a part in forming this impression, and they continue to do so even when you meet or greet someone you already know.

1
Greetings and Introductions

INFORMAL GREETINGS AND FAREWELLS

"Hello" is the universal form of greeting in America, and it is acceptable in any situation except after a very formal introduction. Even comparative strangers say "Hello" in passing, and it is the friendly response to a first-name introduction: "Sally, I'd like you to meet Liz Northshield." And Sally says, "Hello, Liz, I'm glad (pleased, happy) to meet you." "How do you do Liz" is perfectly correct but somewhat more formal than hello.

Even more informal is "Hi." A friendly greeting for people who already know one another, it should never be said in answer to a formal introduction. Not acceptable are the vernacular "Yo," or "How ya doin?" (used as a greeting, not as a sincere question about one's well-being) or any other phrase beginning with "how." A verbal greeting should be accompanied by direct eye contact which indicates that you actually are paying attention to the person you are acknowledging.

"Good morning" is a friendly greeting, as are "Good afternoon," although that sounds somewhat stilted, and "Good evening," which is also very formal-sounding. The latter two greetings have largely been replaced by "Hello."

Verbal greetings may be accompanied by a handshake, especially during an introduction or when two acquaintances meet one another in passing.

GREETINGS IN PUBLIC

A nod and a smile are all that are necessary when casual acquaintances pass by chance. In theaters, restaurants, shops, or any public place, people stop to speak to acquaintances as long as the greeting does not create a situation that may disturb others around them, as it would in a narrow aisle. If they are too far apart to speak without shouting, they simply smile and wave.

It is safer to nod to someone whose face is familiar than to run the risk of seeming to ignore an acquaintance. Often what is perceived as rudeness is absent-mindedness. Absorbed in their own thoughts, people do not hear the voice or see the motions made by someone trying to greet them. They may walk right by a friend without noticing him or her. Others literally do not see—they are without their contact lenses, or are quite nearsighted. It is important to make allowances for absentmindedness or poor eyesight before believing that a friend or acquaintance is actually snubbing you. One friendship I know of was strained for months because a woman thought she was slighted by a friend who simply was not wearing her glasses and couldn't see beyond her nose.

In places of worship, or during a performance in a theater or at the movies people should only nod and smile. It is thoughtless to engage in conversation until the service or performance is over.

One of the more effusive forms of greeting to arise in recent years has been that of social kissing between casual acquaintances. This can range from tiny bursts of "air kissing" where no lip-to-cheek contact is actually made, to enthusiastic smacks on cheeks or lips, often from virtual strangers. There are very likely some people in your acquaintance who have adopted the European custom of kissing (either in the air or with contact) both cheeks. Some people even utter "kiss kiss" as they perform this rite.

The most common problems are first, if going along with the practice, which cheek to offer first, and second, how to avoid the entire process.

If participating, first put forward your right cheek to the right cheek of the one you are greeting. If he or she is doing this European style, you then pull back slightly and proffer your left cheek. This should help you avoid that embarrassing bobbing of heads as you move toward one another from the wrong side.

If you prefer to avoid the entire process, you can immediately extend your hand with a fairly stiff arm to prevent the other person from pulling you into an embrace, and pat his or her shoulder with your other hand, letting go as quickly as is possible and taking one step backward to create distance.

AT THE OFFICE

It does not serve you well to ignore everyone in the building or on the floor when en route to your office, no matter how important or how busy you are. A friendly "hello," accompanied by a smile, to the security guard, the receptionist, or the president of the company causes people to think of you as warm and thoughtful. "Hello" followed by a name is even friendlier and more personal. There is no need, however, to stop and chat at every desk along the way. You can be friendly, but purposeful on your way to work. Keep in mind that most people are sensitive, and an unintentional snub when you ignore someone because you are in a hurry or preoccupied is more often assumed to be intentional. While waiting for an elevator or while in one, you may initiate a conversation with a co-worker or an employee, but you should not pursue conversation with an employer unless he or she indicates an interest in exchanging more than a greeting with you.

To Household Staff

When arriving at a house with servants, you may be introduced to the servants. All that is expected is that you smile and say hello, or "Hello, Anna," or "Hello, Mrs. Worthington," depending on what name your host or hostess uses in the introduction. You do not offer to shake hands or initiate a conversation.

The Answer to "How Are You?"

Tact produces good manners. To a chronic invalid or someone in great sorrow or anxiety, a cheery "Hello, Mrs. Holton! How *are* you? You look fine!" is really tactless, however well intended, since a truthful answer would make the situation emotional.

"How are you?" too often is used as a greeting with no interest at all in the person's well being. However, it is a widely-used phrase. Since it is not usually accompanied by sincere interest in an answer, the best response is either "Fine, thank you," or "Very well, thank you."

Taking Leave

Very often it is difficult to know how to extricate yourself from a conversation when you must leave. The most cordial way is to say, "Jim, I'm so glad to have had this chance to see you, but I've got to go or I'll be late for my next appointment (my carpool, nursery school pick-up, the dentist, etc.). Say hello to Helen for me—good bye!"

When a guest is ready to leave a party, he or she stands up at a pause in the conversation. To those with whom he or she has been talking he or she says, "Good bye. I hope I'll see you again soon," or simply, "I'm glad to have met you." The others answer that they were delighted to meet him or her, too.

In taking leave of a group of strangers—whether you have been introduced or not—you nod and smile a good-bye to those who happen to be looking at you, but you do not attempt to attract the attention of others who are unaware that you are leaving.

If you must leave a large party early, you find your host and/or hostess and say good bye without calling more attention than necessary to your going. It might suggest leaving to others and so lead to the premature breaking up of the party.

THE BASIC RULES OF INTRODUCTION

Introductions are required on many, many occasions; and especially when two strangers meet in the company of a mutual friend. This may be when two friends are walking down the street or riding on a bus and a third, known to one of the two, approaches. It may be in a business office when an employee is talking to his boss and a client known to only one of them comes in. It could happen in the hall or at school, at a wedding reception, on an airplane, or anyplace you can name. *Whenever* this situation occurs an introduction is in order. Whether you forget a name, put them in the wrong order, or make any other mistake, some form of introduction is better than none at all. It is inexcusably rude of the one who knows the other two to chat with one and leave the other—unacknowledged and left out—standing by as if they did not exist.

When meeting new people, you present yourself as courteous and interested when you overcome your own shyness or put aside whatever else you may be thinking about and really focus on the other person. The attitude of Jennie Grossinger, who wrote, "To me there are no strangers, only friends I haven't met before," is one to emulate. Introductions often make people nervous as they try to remember who should be introduced to whom. Rules of introduction have become more relaxed in recent years, but certain forms should still be followed. Once learned, they come naturally and are nothing to be nervous about ever again.

To begin, one person is always introduced *to* another. This is achieved in two ways. First, by actual use of the word *to*: "Mr. Knowles, I'd like to introduce you *to* Mrs. Sampson." Second, (and most generally used), by saying the name of the person *to whom* the other is being introduced first without using the preposition *to*: "Mrs. Sampson, may I introduce Mr. Knowles."

Now here are the three basic rules:

1. A man is always introduced *to* a woman.
    "Mrs. Barrett, I'd like you to meet Dr. Farnham."
    "Jenny, this is my roommate, Jason Smith. Jason, this is Jenny Atwood."
    "Mr. Noonan, may I introduce you *to* my mother, Mrs. Fitzhugh?"
2. A young person is always introduced *to* an older person.
    "Professor Moore, I'd like you to meet my niece, Ann Johnston."
    "Aunt Meave, this is my roommate, Heather Poole."
3. A less important person is always introduced *to* a more important person. This is often complicated, since it is sometimes difficult to decide who is more important. There are several guidelines to help you. Except for members of your family, no woman is ever presented to a man unless he is:

    *   the head of a country
    *   a member of a royal family

- a church official, or
- an older man in high position, such as a governor.

Members of your family, even though they may be the more prominent, are introduced to the other person as a matter of courtesy.

"Bishop Frost, may I present Miss Grable?"
"Professor Sagan, I'd like you to meet my stepfather, Dr. Simons."
"Governor Franken, my niece, Annette Crowder."

The latter form—simply two names—is of course the simplest, and is perfectly correct, although it seems much friendlier to say, "I'd like you to meet . . ." or "I'd like to introduce . . . ," and so on. Other acceptable phrases are, "Joan, have you met our new neighbor, Sarah Newgaard?," "Marcia, may I introduce Todd Wagner, my brother-in-law?," "Holly, do you know my cousin, Jack Campbell?," and "Jack, this is Holly Funck, my roommate."

When said with enthusiasm, "This is . . ." is the warmest introduction of all. When a youngster introduces his favorite teacher by saying, "*This* is Mrs. Adler, Mom," or a father proudly says to his boss, "John, *this* is our son, Jamie," the pride and affection are there for everyone to see.

Although in all of these cases the name of the woman, the older person, or the more prominent person *should* be said first, if you inadvertently say the wrong name first, you have a way to extricate yourself. When you should have said, "Mrs. Morgan, I'd like you to meet Mr. Stanley," and instead you began, "Mr. Stanley . . ." all you need do to correct your slip is to say, "Mr. Stanley, I'd like to introduce you *to* Mrs. Morgan."

A very common—but most unfortunate—practice today, especially among young people, is that of introducing people by first names only. It is uninformative, often confusing, and even seems insulting, as if the introducer had not taken the trouble to learn the other's name, or as if it didn't matter at all. When one of my young friends brings someone up to me and says, "Mrs. Post, this is Joanne," I promptly say, "Joanne who?" and then I continue, "Hi, Joanne Jordan, I'm glad to meet you."

Although the worst sin of all is to make *no* introduction, there are certain phrases that should be avoided:

- Never phrase your introduction as a command. "Mr. Jones, shake hands with Mr. Brown," or "Dr. Glassman, meet my cousin Joe," is neither friendly nor courteous.
- When introducing two acquaintances don't call one of the people you are introducing "my friend." You may say "my aunt" or "my sister," but to pick out one person as "my friend" implies that the person you are introducing him or her to is not.

- Do not repeat "Mrs. Jones—Mrs. Smith. Mrs. Smith—Mrs. Jones." To say each name once is enough, except when one is foreign or difficult to pronounce, in which case repeating the name a second time, and slowly, is helpful to the other person.
- Do not speak of your spouse as "Mr. Jansen" or "Mrs. Gordon" unless you are speaking to a child. To another adult, this is very rude. Refer to him or her as "my husband," or "my husband, George," or "my wife," or "my wife, Elaine."

To help introductions develop into a few minutes of cordial conversation, the one making the introduction can provide additional information for the two persons being introduced. "My new neighbor, Alicia Cummings," "This is Kathleen McNeila, Chrissy's teacher," or the family relationship, "my brother, Tom," "my cousin, Clay Coleman," etc. all help new acquaintances have something to say after they say hello. Such phrases automatically provide a conversational opening to two people who otherwise would hesitate to start out with, in effect, "Who are you?"

One should always use the name that the newly introduced pair will use in talking to each other. Even though you may call your stepfather by his first name, your roommate should not, so you would introduce the former not as "my step-father, Howard," but as "my stepfather, Mr. Budding." It is up to an older person to tell the younger person to call him or her by his or her first name, not up to the younger person to assume he or she may do so or to the introducer to make this decision for them.

The Use of First Names

In addition to the rule that younger people do not address significantly older people by their first name unless asked by the older person to do so, there are other persons for whom first names may not be used except by specific request:

- A superior in one's business, unless it is obviously the office custom.
- A business client or customer, until requested to do so.
- A person of higher rank (a governor, a diplomat, a senator, for example).
- Professional persons offering you their services, such as doctors and lawyers, who are not personal friends. In turn, these professionals should not use your first name unless you request them to. Dr. Parker should not call you Georgine unless he is happy having you call him Al.

When trying to decide if you should be on a first-name basis with someone you have just met whether or not you are of the same generation is a good general guideline. Suppose you are around thirty. A new neighbor who is ten or fifteen years older than you moves in next door. You like each other and are soon calling each other "Janet" and "Deirdre." But she has a fifteen-year-old daughter, while your children are four and six. Do the youngsters call you and your neighbor by your first names? They do not. Even though your neighbor's teenager is as close to your age as her mother is, you are of different generations.

When speaking about other people, don't just use their first name if the person to whom you are speaking has never met them, or doesn't have any idea who or what you are talking about. Don't say, "I saw Terry the other day and she told me that the pharmacy is opening a new branch . . ." Say, I saw Terry Anderson the other day, who is on the town planning board . . ."

Name Blackouts

When you are talking with someone whose name you are struggling to remember and a friend joins you and looks inquiringly from you to the nameless person, there is nothing you can do but introduce your friend to the stranger by saying to the latter, "Oh, haven't you met Janet Caldwell?"

Hopefully, the stranger will be tactful and understanding enough to announce his own name. If he says nothing, however, and Janet Caldwell makes matters worse by saying, "You didn't tell me your friend's name," the situation reaches the height of embarrassment. The only solution then is to be completely frank, admit you do not remember the name, and ask them to complete the introduction themselves.

If you didn't learn another thing from this book I would consider it a success if I could persuade you, when meeting someone who obviously does not remember your name (or even someone who *might* not remember it), to offer it at once. *Never* say, "You don't remember me, do you?" and then stop. Start right out with: "Hello, I'm Melinda Tobin, I met you at the Hillmans last Memorial Day." I promise you, you will have made a fast friend! If everyone would do this automatically when he met anyone but his closest friends, the world would be a friendlier place.

Family Introductions

Remember, when introducing members of your family, the other person is always courteously given precedence. This is not only polite, but it also makes it easier to explain your family relationship. "Mary, my sister," or "my cousin, Andy North," can only come at the *end* of an introduction. For example, a mother introducing a man and her grown daughter would say, "Mr. Singh, I'd like you to meet my daughter, Mary." If Mary is married, her last name would be added: "My daughter, Mary Rice."

Husbands and Wives

On formal occasions, a man introduces his wife: "Mr. Brown, may I introduce my wife, Carolyn?"

To a younger man or a business acquaintance, a husband would say, "Jim, I would like you to meet my wife," (never "the wife!"). Then he adds, "Carolyn, Jim Francis."

If a woman has retained her maiden name, it is important that it is included in the introduction so that she is not then called "Mrs. Hanover" when she is really "Ms. Vernon." The same is true when she introduces her husband. She includes his last name so others will not call him by her maiden name. June Vernon would introduce her husband as, "My husband, Steve Hanover."

A wife introduces her husband to friends as "John" and to acquaintances as "my husband, John." You may always use the forms "my husband" and "my wife" because they are proper no matter to whom you are talking.

Parents

It is a flagrant violation of good manners for children to call their natural parents by their first names, and furthermore, it undermines the respect that every child should have for his mother and father. It is all very well to want to be "pals" with your child, but you are *not* the same age and you do not have the same abilities and interests. There is little to be gained by pretending that you do. An attitude that accepts and takes advantage of the age difference is far more satisfactory. One simple mark of recognition of this difference is the use of your proper title. If you deny your position by rejecting the use of "Mother," "Father," or their derivatives you are undermining the natural parent-child relationship. You are trying, instead, to be a contemporary of your child. Not only do the terms show your child's respect for you, but they give him the security he needs with real parents who accept the relationship and are proud of it.

Stepparents

The question of what children should call their stepparents is difficult because the circumstances are so variable, and the answer must depend on what seems best in each case.

A child should *never* be forced to call a stepparent "Mother" or "Father" or any nickname having that meaning, especially if his own parent is living. If the child *chooses* to do so, it is a compliment to the stepparent and should be encouraged.

If a child does not, and probably will not, know his own parent, then he would regard a stepparent who has brought him up as a natural parent and say "Mother" or "Father." This is especially true if he has stepbrothers or stepsisters whom he hears using those names. But if the child is older when one parent remarries, the situation is quite different. If he has known the stepparent for some time he may call him or her by a nickname or first name. Actually, a nickname seems to be the best solution, if one can be found that is appropriate and not a derivative of "Mother" or "Father."

When a child has always lived with his stepparents and has been given their name, he almost invariably calls them "Mother" and "Father" (or derivatives of those names) and introduces them in that way. When he has come to live with one stepparent, or two, later in life, the situation is different, because he may well retain his own name. Since this can be extremely confusing when introductions are necessary, the relationship should be made clear at once. There is nothing objectionable or derogatory in the terms "stepmother" or "stepfather," and the simplest form of introduction, said in the warmest tone to indicate an affectionate relationship, is, "Mrs. Jones, I'd like you to meet my stepfather, Mr. Casey," or "Mrs. Jones, do you know my stepmother?" In the latter case it is not necessary, although perfectly proper, to say the stepmother's name, as it would be the same as their father's and their own.

The same rule holds true when the parents are the introducers. A man would correctly introduce his wife's son by a former marriage, "Jack, I'd like you to meet my stepson, Jimmy Winters."

Parents-In-Law

The question of what a bride is to call her parents-in-law has no definite answer, and the choice of names is purely personal. Only in unusually formal families does one hear "Mr." and "Mrs.," which to most of us sounds very cold. Even "Mr. and Mrs. B." seems warmer and more intimate than "Mr. and Mrs. Brown." More often parents-in-law are called by names that mean "Mother" and "Father," but are not the names that the bride uses for her own parents. Or perhaps they are called "Mr." and "Mrs." until a grandchild's nicknames—"Mimi" and "Poppy," for example—gradually become theirs. When a son or daughter has a special nickname for a parent, the new husband or wife usually uses that same name. And this is one case, especially if the parents are young, when a younger person may call the older by a first name.

Whatever name is decided upon, there is often a difficult period, and sometimes hurt feelings, before the solution is found. The new daughter-in-law is too shy and embarrassed to bring up the subject, and her husband's parents, in turn, don't want to "push" her into too much intimacy.

The parents, simply because they are older and have more self-confidence than the bride, should make the move. Rather than sitting back and wondering why Cindy still calls them "Mr. and Mrs. Pool" when they are so fond of her, they should *suggest* that she call them by the name their son uses, or if that is what she calls her parents, another form of "Mother" and "Father." Or they may prefer that she use their first names. All that need be said is, "Now that you and Dick have been married awhile and we know each other so well, we'd love to have you call us Mom and Dad, or would you prefer Kate and George?" In any case it is up to the parents to make the move, and the daughter-(or son-)in-law should, of course, comply.

If the shoe is on the other foot and you are the devoted daughter-in-law whose parents-in-law have given you no hint at all, you are free, if you wish, to break the ice. But don't just start right out with "Kate" and "George"—ask them what they would like you to call them, since you feel "Mr. and Mrs." is much too formal.

When a mother writes to a son and daughter-in-law who call her "Mom" and "Jean" respectively, she signs her letter "Mom." She has been "Mom" to her son for longer than she has been "Jean" to her daughter-in-law, and "Mom" seems less strange to the latter than would "Jean" to the son.

The less intimate relationships of aunts, uncles, and even grandparents need not pose a question, because the bride calls all her husband's relatives exactly what he does, and he in turn does the same.

Whatever terms you decide on to call parents-in-law, they are introduced as "Tom's parents, Ellen and Harold Aable," or "Tom's parents, Mr. and Mrs. Aable," depending on whom it is you are introducing them to. You would also say, "My mother-in-law, Ellen Aable," if you wished to define your relationship in this way.

The introduction of a parent-in-law as "Mom" or "Dad" is well meant, but can be confusing.

Children-In-Law and Your Children's In-Laws

A parent formally introduces her or his son's wife to acquaintances as "my daughter-in-law," but to friends she may say, "Rosalind, Dick's wife." A son-in-law is introduced in the same way. The more formal, "my son-in-law" or "daughter-in-law" depends for its warmth on the tone of voice in which it is spoken. And this is, of course, an extremely important point in all introductions. By tone, the same words can convey every shade of feeling, from cool indifference to affection.

Unfortunately English, unlike several foreign languages, has no single word to describe your son's or daughter's parents-in-law. In Hebrew the word is *macha-toonom,* and in Spanish, *consuegros.* Sue Shymer in her book *Keep Your Mouth Shut and Your Pocketbook Open* suggests that we coin a neuter version of *machatoonom* and call our co-in-laws *mockitoons.* But until Mr. Webster accepts the word we must simply refer to them as "my daughters-in-law's" or "John's" or "my son-in-law's parents."

Aunts, Uncles, Grandparents and Other Family Relationships

Aunts and uncles are often called by those names, but not necessarily. Those who are younger than the parents often prefer to be called by their first names only, and this is perfectly permissible. For example, my children call my brother, who is considerably older than I am, "Uncle." But his children, who are closer to my age than to his, call my husband and me by our first names. However, in introducing an aunt or uncle the term should always be used, both to show respect and to explain the relationship: "My aunt, Mrs. Singer."

With the possible exception of a young stepgrandmother, grandparents are always called "Grandmother," "Grandfather," or a derivative thereof.

Your brother-in-law is either your sister's husband or your husband's or wife's brother. The same holds true in reverse for your sister-in-law. Their spouses are *not* in-laws but are courteously *referred to* as "sister-in-law" or "brother-in-law" when there is a friendly relationship. They are not defined as in-laws legally.

When introducing other relatives-in-law, say "my brother John's wife" or "John's wife." These identifications are clearer than "my sister-in-law." Naturally, these titles are preceded or followed by the person's given name.

The children of siblings are first cousins. The children of first cousins (the grandchildren of siblings) are second cousins. A sister's child and another sister's grandchild are first cousins once removed (or, your first cousin's child). In other words, a cousin once removed is separated by one generation, while second cousins are of the same generation.

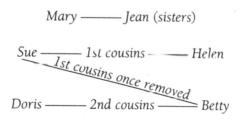

OTHER RELATIONSHIPS

We are inclined to need to give an identification to people in our lives, other than immediate family members, when we are introducing them to others. Although this is not necessary, it does make us feel more comfortable, and there are a few guidelines governing these introductions.

Close Family Friends

The custom of calling family friends "Aunt," "Uncle," or "Cousin" when no such relationship exists has generally gone out of style. When really intimate friends are devoted to your children and feel that "Mr." or "Mrs." does not express the affectionate relationship, they may suggest nicknames for themselves or even specifically request that the youngsters call them by their first names. The children should comply, but the parent should make it clear that this is a special case, and he or she is only to use the first name because it is requested. Otherwise children address all friends of their parents as "Mr." or "Mrs." followed by their surnames.

When children are called upon to introduce these special people in their lives, they will naturally say, "This is Uncle Mark." Uncle Mark should then help out by saying, "Hello, I'm Mark Sessa, a friend of Teddy's," etc.

Ex-Family Members

Many divorced persons retain a close relationship with their ex-husband's or ex-wife's family, even though they remarry. Frequently there are children involved, who love and are loved by their grandparents. The same is often true when a son or daughter dies and the husband or wife remarries. Questions inevitably come up on how these "ex" members of the family should be introduced, or should introduce their former parents-in-law.

If the introduction is *very* casual and there is little chance that any of the people involved will see each other again, there is no need to make any explanation at all. But if that is not so and the new acquaintanceship is likely to continue, it is important to explain the relationship as clearly as possible. The former mother-in-law would say, "I'd like you to meet Mary Dunbar. She is John's [or "my son's"] widow and is now married to Joe Dunbar." Had she been divorced from your son, you would say, "She was John's wife and is now married to. . . ." Her introduction of you would be, "This is Mrs. Judson, Johnny's grandmother," or, "my first husband's mother."

Your Living-Together Partner

A normally poised young man or woman may be heard to say when introducing his or her partner, "I'd like you to meet my . . ." The sentence remains unfinished, swallowed instead by panicky gulps, a quick vocabulary search, and the sudden realization that there is no word for it. What do you call this person you live with? Is he your lover, your boyfriend, your man, your boon companion? Is she your paramour, your lady, your best girl, your roommate, your friend?

Nothing sounds right. I have in the past advocated use of the word "friend" to solve the problem, but it is far from adequate. Others have proposed the word "intime" from the French for "intimate." "Significant other" comes to the rescue of some, whereas "amiable consort" does it for others. Words have been invented— such as "elltee" for Living Together or "POSSLQ" (pronounced "posselque") from the Census Bureau acronym for Persons of the Opposite Sex Sharing Living Quarters. They all sound awkward. And I cannot imagine introducing the man one's daughter is living with as Jane's POSSLQ."

I have come to the conclusion that the best form of introduction under the circumstances is to use no word of definition at all. Merely say, "This is Joan Whitehead," or "I'd like you to meet Bill Adams," when you are at a gathering where relationships make little difference. It is simply not necessary in an introduction to indicate the relationship between two people. In a small group where who relates to whom has more importance, all you need add to the introduction is, "the man [or woman] I live with." Period.

What Your Child Calls Your Living-Together Partner

It is likely that your child calls your living-together partner by her or his first name or by a nickname at home. This is fine for their relationship between one another, but is not appropriate in an introduction to your child's friends. Your child should introduce his or her friend to Mr. or Mrs. [Ms., Miss] Anders. If asked who this person is, a simple reply, "He (or she) lives with us," is all that needs to be said and is more appropriate than having your child define him or her as "my mother's boyfriend" or "my father's girlfriend," since neither of you, at this point is a "boy" or a "girl" yourself.

INTRODUCTIONS AT SOCIAL EVENTS

Introductions are always required when a guest of honor is presented to other guests. If you arrive after the receiving line has dispersed, you must introduce yourself because it is considered very rude to go to an entertainment given in honor of someone and fail to say "How do you do?" to him or her.

In Receiving Lines

If the reception or party is a very big one for a stranger the hostess receives, standing with the special guest. As each guest approaches, the hostess says, "Mrs. Famous, this is my neighbor, Mrs. Johnson"; "Mr. Prominent, our headmaster, Mr. Riley"; or simply "Mrs. Notable, Mrs. Stokes." The guest of honor offers his or her hand, and the other guest says, "How do you do?" or "I'm so glad to meet you," and moves on.

When an invited guest has brought guests of her own to the reception, she precedes them in the line and introduces them to the hostess, who in turn introduces her and her guests to the guest of honor.

On formal occasions when (as a guest) you do not know any of the people in the line, nor could they be expected to know you, you introduce yourself formally: "I am Charles Smith," or a woman would say, "I am Janet Smith," and turning to her husband behind her, "and this is my husband, Charles Smith."

At a smaller, friendlier party given for someone known to most of the people present, the guest of honor does not receive with the hostess, but sits or stands in a convenient place so that everyone can go up and talk to him or her. Whether there is a receiving line or not, a woman introduces herself as "Janet Smith" and her husband as "my husband, Bob."

Even at large balls and receptions, the receiving line should be limited to four whenever possible. It is a necessary formality which is generally endured rather than enjoyed, and the shorter it is, the better.

When a Guest Is Unknown to the Hostess

When you are taking a houseguest who is not known to your friends to a party, remember to introduce him or her to everyone you possibly can. This does not mean that you should make a grand tour of the room—but it is unfair to your hostess to expect her to look after *your* guest and to have a stranger's name at the tip of her tongue in order to introduce him to her other guests.

When at a Formal Dinner

Strangers sitting next to each other at the table should introduce themselves. A man says, "I'm Arthur Robinson," and a woman says "I'm Mary Perkins," and perhaps adds, "Bob Perkins' wife." Your neighbor's place card is a handy reminder if you do not quite catch, or do not remember, the name he or she gives you.

When a woman finds herself next to an unknown man at a dinner party she may start talking to him without telling him her name. But if he introduces himself to her she immediately says, "I'm Fanny Bogart."

Whether they exchange names or not, people who find themselves seated together at any table must accept the obligation of talking. To sit side by side without speaking is a great discourtesy to your hostess, as well as the person next to whom you are sitting. It is equally rude to devote all your time to the person on one side of you and ignore the guest on the other.

Introducing One Person to a Group

On formal occasions when a great many people are present, a stranger is not introduced to every person there. He should be introduced to several people and then he may talk with those near him with or without exchanging names.

It is much more effective to name those already present before naming a new arrival. The one being introduced is paying attention, of course, but one who is chatting with someone else may need to hear his own name before his attention is called to the name of the new arrival.

The well-meant practice of leading a guest on a tour around the room to make sure that he—or more especially she—is introduced to everyone is totally unnecessary and invariably a failure. The poor stranger is hopelessly confused by too many names, and the hostess is often interrupted by the arrival of other guests.

The best procedure is to leave a stranger with a nearby group, introducing her or him to them. Even if the hostess does not complete these introductions the stranger will not be marooned, because in a friend's house people should *always* talk with those near them. The good hostess, however, will make every effort to see that all her guests are introduced during the course of any party of moderate size.

ANNOUNCING ONESELF

When you see someone you would like to meet at a party, or when you find yourself standing next to someone you don't know, and there is no one about to introduce you, don't just say, "What is your name?" which is too abrupt. Start by giving your own name. "Hello, I'm Amelia Coppola." You may add, "I'm a friend of Judy's," or "I'm Judy's next door neighbor." If this does not elicit a response other than "Hello," you may then say, "and you are . . . ?" or "and what is your name?"

At a very large party (a dance or a wedding reception, for example), it is not necessary to speak to people you do not know, unless you and another guest find yourself apart from the others. In such a case you simply make casual conversation and if the other seems happy to talk, you should introduce yourself with an identifying remark: "I'm Sally's cousin," or "I work with Bill."

There are many occasions when you have a good reason for wanting to meet someone, and then it is quite proper to introduce yourself. For instance, you would say, "Mrs. Simms, aren't you a friend of my mother's? I'm Jane, Adelaide Pinkham's daughter."

Arriving at the Door

When an adult member of the family comes to the door in answer to your ring, you never call yourself "Mr." or "Mrs." or "Miss." If he does not know you, identify yourself by a sentence or two: "I'm John Grant, a friend of Jim's at the office. Is he home?" or "Susan and I met at the Barrys' cocktail party. I told her I'd drop by."

If a child answers the door you say, "I'm Mr. Grant," or "Mrs. Smythe," and "Would you please call your mother for me, if she is at home?"

If the door is answered by a maid who does not know you and if you are not expected, you say, "I'm Mr. John Grant. Is Mrs. Jones in?" If you are expected, you merely say, "I'm Mr. Grant," and you may add, "Mrs. Jones is expecting me." A woman uses "Mrs. Grant" in both cases.

WHEN NOT TO INTRODUCE

At a small party it is quite all right for the hostess to introduce as many people as she can, but at a large one such as a wedding reception, repeating never-to-be-remembered names is a mistake—unless there is some good reason for doing so. For instance, a friend might be chagrined if he were not introduced to a celebrity or a person in whom he had a special interest.

An arriving visitor is never introduced to someone who is taking leave. If two people are engaged in conversation, a third should not approach expecting them to interrupt their talk for introductions.

THE "NONINTRODUCTION"

Sometimes it happens that in talking to one person, you want to include another in your conversation without making an introduction. Suppose you are talking in your yard to a gardener, and a friend joins you. You greet her and then casually include her by saying, "Mr. Smith is suggesting that I dig up these daisies and put in delphiniums." Whether or not your friend makes any comment, she has been made part of your conversation.

There are other occasions when a halfway introduction seems most appropriate. Suppose, for example, you wish to make a maid's name known to a guest. "Olga, would you please take Mrs. Jones's coat for her?" Or you might say to your guest, "Mary, this is Olga. She'll be glad to take your coat for you."

In many homes one person is employed who helps in so many ways that she becomes more than a housekeeper. These people frequently are almost members of the family and are treated as such. They are always introduced to guests, especially to houseguests. The hostess might say, "Mary, this is Sally Jones, whom we couldn't manage without. Sally, this is my friend, Mrs. Charles." If Sally is on hand to take wraps from dinner guests she is introduced in the same way. An older woman, especially one whose employers are a young couple, may be called and introduced as "Mrs. Jones."

WHAT TO DO WHEN INTRODUCED

Just as you give a person who is being introduced to you your undivided attention, you look a person to whom you are being introduced in the eye and greet him or her cordially. Repeating the person's name, "Hello, Dr. Wasserman, it is a pleasure to meet you," is a technique that helps you remember the name and is a sign that you are, indeed, paying attention to the introduction.

When Incorrectly Introduced

We have all, at one time or another, been incorrectly introduced. One's title may be wrongly given, the name can be confused or mispronounced, or the identification may be erroneous. It is only sensible and kind that the person being introduced correct the error immediately. If, for example, a hostess introduces a man to a group as "a surgeon who has just moved to Greenwich" when he is really a general practitioner, he should explain this to the new acquaintances—and the hostess, if she remains there—at once. He should also make a correction should she refer to him as "Mr." instead of "Dr.," or call him "Dr. Donald" instead of "Dr. McDonald."

When someone is introducing a stranger to a number of people and consistently says the name wrong, the person being introduced should correct the host as soon as he realizes it is not just a slip of the tongue. He should do so not with annoyance, but if possible, by making light of it. All he need say is, "I know it's confusing, but my name is 'Light,' not 'Bright,' " or "Just so you can find me in the phone book, I'm Bob Lord, not Jim Lord."

If you are introduced by your correct name and someone immediately finds a diminutive or nickname for you, you may say, "Would you mind calling me Jeffrey? For some reason, I've never been called Jeff." If the other person insists on his own version, you may correct him or her one more time, and after that, should ignore his discourtesy the best that you are able.

What to Say

"How do you do?" followed by the name of the person you have just met is a traditional and acceptable response to a formal introduction. However, if you think about it, the phrase "How do you do?" has little meaning. Therefore, except on very formal occasions when tradition is important and desirable, I prefer the less formal responses: "Hello," or "I'm very glad to meet you" (not "Pleased ta meecha"). In the case of an older or prominent person the addition of the name adds a note of respect.

If you have not heard the new name clearly, you may ask to have it repeated. "How do you do?" or "Hello" may be said gladly or casually, and they may be varied in emphasis, depending on the degree of warmth you wish to convey. In any event, when Mrs. Fox has been introduced to Mr. Struthers and replies, "How do you do, Mr. Struthers?" he nods and need not say anything more, or he may say, "I'm very glad to meet you."

When you meet someone whom you have heard a great deal about and have wanted to meet, you might say, "Oh, I am so *glad* to meet you," and then go on to say, "John Brown speaks of you all the time," or whatever may be the reason for your special interest.

When to Rise

Hosts and hostesses always rise to greet each arriving guest. Members of the host's family, including young people, also rise as a guest enters the room, although they do not all necessarily shake hands. With this exception: A youngster who is sitting and chatting with an adult need not rise as each new guest comes in. He should stand up instantly, however, if the guest is brought over to be introduced.

A woman does not stand when being introduced to someone at a distance.

Nor need she rise when shaking hands with anyone, unless that person is much older, or very prominent, is someone she has wanted to meet for some time, or is someone with whom she wants to go on talking. In the first case, think before you leap. Some women would hardly feel complimented if a woman only a few years younger were to jump up for them.

A man should rise when a woman comes into a room *for the first time* and remain standing until she is seated or leaves his vicinity. He does not jump up every time a hostess or another guest goes in and out. A husband rises for his wife when she comes in after they have been apart for a time. This is not a matter of manners but simply of saying, "I'm glad to see you."

When a woman client goes to a man's office on business he should stand up and receive her, offer her a chair, and should not sit down until after she is seated. When she rises to leave he gets up, stands for as long as she remains, and then goes with her as far as the door, which he holds open for her. He does not rise for his secretary or for coworkers in his office. A woman executive follows exactly the same protocol for business clients, whether male or female.

In a restaurant when a woman greets a man in passing, he merely makes the gesture of rising slightly from his chair and nodding or smiling a hello.

HOW AND WHEN TO SHAKE HANDS

A handshake can create a feeling of immediate friendliness or of instant irritation between two strangers. No one likes a "boneless" hand that feels like one is grasping an empty glove, nor does one appreciate a viselike grasp that cuts rings into one's flesh and temporarily paralyzes every finger.

The proper handshake is brief, but there should be firmness and warmth in the clasp. It should always be accompanied by a direct look into the eyes of the person whose hand one is grasping.

Men have traditionally shaken hands when introduced to one another, or even if already acquainted, when meeting on the street, at a function or social occasion, or in business situations. Women have begun to shake hands in like social situations, and generally in business ones.

A child should be prepared to shake hands when introduced to adults who offer their hands to him or her.

When a man is introduced to a woman, she smiles and says, "Hello," or "How do you do?" Strictly speaking, it is her place to offer her hand or not, as she chooses, but if he should extend his hand, she *must* give him hers. Nothing could be ruder than to ignore spontaneous friendliness.

Keeping this in mind, and never ignoring a proffered hand, even if it is technically extended inappropriately, there is a protocol for this form of greeting. The same guidelines that are used for introductions are used for shaking hands:

- A woman offers to shake hands with a man
- An older person extends his or her hand first to a younger one
- A "more important" person proffers his or her hand to a "less important" person

In Other Countries

In many other countries, it is not as usual for women to be as involved in business transactions as they are in the United States. American women, accordingly, should be prepared to have their hands kissed instead of shaken, in some European and South American countries, and to find some Oriental and mid-Eastern business-men who are not prepared to shake hands with women as readily as they do with men.

Additionally, many Europeans shake hands each time they meet, even if they have seen each other several times previously the same day. Americans traveling abroad, male and female, should be prepared for this and be prepared to shake hands enthusiastically and frequently.

Shaking Hands With The Handicapped

When you meet someone whose right arm or hand is missing or is deformed, extend your right hand even though he or she cannot shake hands in the normal way. The handicapped person will appreciate that you have made no unnatural gesture to accommodate his or her disability. He or she will respond by offering his or her left hand, or by saying, "Please forgive me if I don't shake hands, but I'm very glad to meet you."

If you are disabled or are suffering an injury or illness such as arthritis and it is impossible or painful for you to shake hands, you shouldn't feel you must. Simply say, as noted above, "I'm so glad to meet you, please forgive me for not shaking hands. I have arthritis [a sprained finger or whatever the trouble may be]."

*I*f you've ever been called Mrs. when you are a Miss, or have ever been laughed out of court when you called the judge "your honorableness," instead of "your honor," or if someone who you thought cared about who you were called you Linda instead of Lynn, or Tim instead of Tom, you know how important names and titles are. You have also realized this if you have been in a situation where you called someone else "you" or "uh . . ." because you haven't been sure what form to use in addressing them. This may have happened to you when speaking to a minister, not knowing whether to call him "Father" or "Pastor," or when speaking to a government official. For many people, their names and titles are an integral part of their identity. It is worthwhile to review the following information, and that in Chapter Three on Official Protocol, to refresh your memory for those occasions when you will be called upon to address someone whose correct title may be unfamiliar to you.

2
Names and Titles

WOMEN'S NAMES

Traditionally a woman's social title was tied to her marital status. At different times in a woman's life she was known by different social titles. Young girls and unmarried women were referred to as "Miss." At marriage a woman traditionally assumed her husband's surname preceded by the title "Mrs." While many women follow this tradition, others feel their social title need not be tied to their marital status and opt to retain their birthname preceded by the social title "Ms."

The name and social title a woman elects to use is a personal decision, and one others should respect. For instance, if Angela Blake, upon her marriage to Jonathan Adams, decides to continue using her name in both business and social situations, you should not address correspondence to her as Mrs. Jonathan Adams but as Ms Angela Blake. Joint correspondence would be addressed to Mr. Jonathan Adams and Ms Angela Blake.

A Married Woman's Name

A married woman's name usually consists of her given name, her maiden name, and her husband's name. Except in a few instances—for example, on income tax forms—the middle name is shortened to an initial. The title "Mrs." or "Ms" is never used with a *signature,* with the possible exception of a professional woman who wishes it to be known that she is married but does not wish her husband's name to appear. In that case she may put "Mrs." in parentheses before her signature.

Many women are christened with two names and are called by both. Mary-Louise, Elizabeth-Ann, Mary-Beth, are inseparable in some cases. When these girls marry, the requirement that their maiden name be used as their middle name makes the whole thing entirely too long. So the maiden name may be dropped; Mary-Louise Harper, who married Bob Morgan, may call herself Mary-Louise Morgan. But Betsey Hancock Smith, who married James Layton, becomes Betsy Smith Layton—not Betsy Hancock Layton. Susan Jean Franklin, who has always been known as Jean and has never used the "Susan" at all, may, when she marries, drop the Susan and become Jean Franklin Jones. A woman who keeps her own name after marriage continues to use her middle name or initial in her signature. If, however, she hyphenates her name with that of her husband, she drops her middle name. If a woman chooses to hyphenate her maiden name with her husband's name, her birth name is first. Jennifer Ann Burke who marries David Heller is Jennifer Burke-Heller.

A Widow's Name

A widow, until she remarries, keeps her husband's name. She is known, not as Mrs. Mary Scott, but as Mrs. James Scott.

When she remarries she has the option of using her first husband's name as a middle name, or of dropping his name and using her maiden name. If she was married for a long time, and if she had children, she will undoubtedly prefer to keep the name of a man with whom she spent many years, and which identifies her with her children.

A Divorcee's Name

In the past, unless a divorcée took back her maiden name and used the title "Miss," her only possible form of address was her maiden name combined with her ex-husband's last name. Mary Jones, who married John Smith, after divorcing him became Mrs. Jones Smith. This is still absolutely correct, but today many find it stiff or confusing. Divorce was uncommon years ago; and when it occurred the divorcée, who was apt to remain in the same town or city where she was well known, seldom remarried. Therefore her maiden name was known to all of the people around her, and its use identified her and also declared her divorced state. But today many divorcées move; they look for a new life in a community where their maiden names mean nothing and are a source of considerable confusion to people they meet. They are naturally introduced as "Mary Smith," and new acquaintances have no way of making a connection with someone they hear of as "Mrs. Jones Smith." An acceptable alternative now is "Mrs. Mary Smith." With this title she establishes both her identity and her divorced status.

It is quite true that the title "Mrs." should technically be used only in conjunction with one's husband's name, but in the interest of simplifying an awkward custom an allowance may be made for those who prefer this form of address.

When a woman divorces two or three husbands, she drops the previous husband's name each time and retains either her maiden name or her first name with the name of her last husband. Della Smith married Bob White, then Frank Green, and is now divorced from him. She forgets the White entirely and calls herself "Della Green" or "Mrs. Della Green," whichever she prefers.

While childless divorcées frequently revert to use of their maiden name, it is not such a good idea for divorcées with children, for the children will usually retain their mother's *married* name. When your family members use different surnames, for whatever reason, make sure that those who need to know are informed. A child's school should be told, as would your own office staff, for informational purposes only.

Unmarried Woman Living With a Man

A woman who is living with a man but is not married to him does not take his name unless the relationship has gone on for so long that they have become common-law man and wife. She continues to use her maiden name, preceded by "Ms" or no title at all.

Unmarried Mothers

Life will be far easier for you and your child if you both use the same last name—your name. It is not necessary to use any title with your name, but if you wish, "Ms" would be appropriate.

Professional Women in Social Situations

A woman who is a medical doctor, a dentist, etc., is addressed by, and introduced with, her title, socially as well as professionally. She may or may not prefer to be known as "Dr." on an envelope addressed to her and her husband (*see page 260*), but in speaking, the "Dr." is always used.

A woman who has earned a law degree, Ph.D., or any other degree may or may not choose to use the title "Dr." professionally, and generally may use "Mrs.," "Miss," or "Ms" socially. In a formal situation, however, where other people are introduced by title and last name rather than by first names, it is a mark of recognition and respect to use the title "Dr." The distinction, in that case, is in the social setting rather than in the type of degree. In general, it is better to "Dr." a person who would rather be referred to by a social title than to do the reverse. This same guideline is used for men who have earned titles indicating the receipt of a doctorate.

When a woman chooses to retain her maiden name professionally but is "Mrs. Alan Anderson" socially, there is inevitably some confusion about how she and her husband should be addressed in writing, particularly by professional associates who know her only by her professional name. The only correct solution is the use of both names with their titles. A woman doctor and her businessman husband would be addressed as:

Dr. Julia Shaw and Mr. John Sykes

A woman mayor and her physician husband would be:

The Honorable Mary Ann Ilse and Dr. Warren Ilse

An unmarried couple living together would be addressed on an envelope with their names on two separate lines:

Dr. Julia Shaw
Mr. John Sykes

Miss, Mrs., or Ms?

The title "Ms" serves a useful purpose, particularly in the business world, when one is not sure if a client or associate is married or not, or whether she is using a professional name. It is also useful when addressing correspondence to a married woman and not her husband when it is not correct to write either "Mrs. Susan Foltin" (she is not a divorcée) or "Miss Susan Foltin." The first time you write to a professional woman, it is correct to address her as "Ms Susan Foltin" and this is preferable to simply writing "Susan Foltin" with no title. When Ms Foltin replies to you, she can indicate by her signature how she prefers to be addressed. If she is married and wishes this fact to be known, she may precede her signature with "Mrs." given in parentheses: "(Mrs.) Susan Foltin."

"Ms" is still awkward for many people to pronounce. "Mizz" is the sound, and it should be used for all women who prefer it to "Mrs." or "Miss" and when one is uncertain of any woman's title.

NAMES LEGALLY CHANGED

With the exception of persons under a government witness protection program whose names are changed for safety reasons, anyone else who changes the name by which he or she has been known should notify social and business associates of the change to avoid confusion and embarrassing situations. The quickest and simplest way of informing others is to send out formal announcements:

Mr. and Mrs. Brian Malinowsky
Announce that by Permission of the Court
They and Their Children
Have Taken the Family Name of
Malin

THE USE OF "SIR" AND "MADAM"

"Sir" and "Madam" are titles of respect, but they imply an inferior position, in some way, on the part of the speaker. Therefore they are never used between people of equal age and status. No matter how charming a gentleman may be, a woman of the same age does not address him as "Sir," nor does a man address a contemporary as "Ma'am." On rare occasions an older man may say "Sir" to a contemporary, especially if he doesn't know the other's name. It is also used as a means of addressing distinguished people and may be used instead of too many repetitions of a formal name and title.

In the South many youngsters are taught to address their elders as "Ma'am" and "Sir." This is considered correct since it is the local custom, but they should be taught the distinction between using the term for a family friend and using it for a waiter or employee. I have heard young people calling a waiter "Sir" in an effort to be polite, and this is incorrect—they, like adults, should simply say "Waiter."

It is perfectly correct for a salesperson to call a customer "Sir" or "Madam" or for a pupil to so address a teacher—in short, when there is an age difference, or when one is in the position of serving the other.

THE USE OF "JR.," "2ND," AND "3RD"

A man with the same name as his father uses "Jr." after his name as long as his father is alive. He may drop the "Jr." after his father's death, or if he prefers, he may retain it in order not to be confused with his late father. This also helps to differentiate between his wife and his mother if the latter is still living and does not wish to be known as "Mrs. Jones, Sr."

When a man is named after his father who is a "Jr.," he is called "3rd." A man named after his grandfather, uncle, or cousin is called "2nd."

The following diagram may help to clarify these relationships:

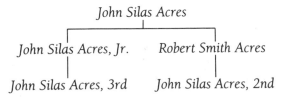

John Silas Acres

John Silas Acres, Jr.   *Robert Smith Acres*

John Silas Acres, 3rd   *John Silas Acres, 2nd*

The wife of each of these men uses the same suffix after her name as her husband does, i.e., "Mrs. John Silas Acres, 3rd."

Some family names are carried on through three to four generations. There is John (Sr.), John Jr., and Johns III, IV, and V. This presents a real problem when John (Sr.) dies. Do they all retain the title they have always been known by or do they all "move up"? There is no rule. Moving up creates a problem of identification, and there is bound to be confusion among acquaintances who used to know John Jr. as John III, or there can be a problem with bank and charge accounts, etc. But moving up does avoid more generations of the same name and thus more confusion. Many people feel the complications outnumber the advantages and prefer to retain their same titles, and I am inclined to agree. However, I feel that too many men having the same name is confusing at best, and after number III the next son should be given a different middle name so that he does not use any numeral at all.

MILITARY TITLES

Commissioned Army officers of all grades are addressed by their title (rank). The officer's name is generally added although it is not wrong to say simply "Captain" or "Lieutenant" when there is no chance of confusion. Noncommissioned officers are addressed officially by their titles although they may use "Mr." socially.

The Air Force follows the same customs as the Army.

Chaplains in all the services are called "Chaplain," regardless of their rank. Catholic chaplains are usually spoken *to* as "Father."

Doctors in the service are generally called by their rank although they may be called "Dr." socially when they are junior officers. Officially, they are addressed by their Army or Navy titles for as long as they remain in the service.

Warrant officers are called "Mr.," or "Ms," both officially and socially.

Naval officers from the rank of lieutenant commander (called "Commander" in conversation) up are called by their titles. Officers below that rank are called "Mr." in conversation but are introduced and referred to by their titles.

Students attending any of the United States military academies are not permitted to be married. Therefore, male students are "Mr." socially, and female students are "Miss." The official title for both male and female students varies by branch of service. All students at the United States Military Academy at West Point, the United States Air Force Academy at Colorado Springs and the United States Coast Guard Academy at New London are called "Cadet" officially. Those at the Naval Academy at Annapolis and the United States Merchant Marine Academy at Kings Point are called "Midshipman" officially.

In speaking to a first or second lieutenant in the Army, or a lieutenant junior grade in the Navy, you say simply "Lieutenant." The rank is made clear by the insignia, but it would be awkward to use the full title in conversation. In the same way, the various grades of colonels, generals, and admirals are spoken to simply as "Colonel," "General," or "Admiral," with their names.

Members of the regular armed services retain their titles after retiring. However, it is not in good taste for reserve officers who served for only a short time or those who held temporary commissions during a war to continue calling themselves "Captain," "Major," or "Colonel." They do, of course, use the titles if they resume an active status in a reserve unit or in the National Guard. When this happens the initials of their service always follow their name. When the rank is used they write "Colonel Harold Gordon, U.S.A.R." (or N.G. or U.S.N.R. or U.S.M.C.R.).

Reserve officers who remain in the service and retire with pay after twenty or more years are, like a member of the regular service, entitled to use their military titles.

In contrast to the abbreviations of "Mr." and "Mrs.," which are *never* written in full, it is both correct and courteous to write out all military and naval titles when addressing a formal social note. However, informal communications may be sent to "2nd Lieut. John Smith," "Lieut. Johnson," "Lt. Cdr. Harris," or "Lt. Col. Graham," because the full titles are so long. Other ranks are more properly written in full.

When introducing or addressing a letter to someone from another country who has both a military and an inherited title, military rank is put first: "Colonel, Lord London."

OTHER TITLES

Every day we run into people who, officially, have a title. The police officer at the desk is Sergeant Flynn; the head of the fire department is Chief Ellmore; the club chef is Chef Touri; the pilot on your plane is Captain Howe; etc. These people are always addressed by their title when they are on the job or when the matter is related to their work. They do not always use their titles socially, although they may. For example, a man who has been village judge for a number of years might well be so universally known as "Judge" that the title sticks, and he is referred to in that way at all times, even into his retirement. The correct titles for various public officials are found in the next chapter.

*I*t is imperative that each new arrival in Washington, D.C.—whether an official or a private citizen who expects to take part in the social life of the capital—learn first of all the proper titles by which each diplomat, government official, and military officer is addressed and the order of his or her rank. When a man or woman has been promoted to high position the respect due his or her office should not be overlooked.

Foreign consulates and embassies provide protocol information to and about their representatives so no mistakes can be made; a "Green Book" of titles, position and protocol is published annually to help ensure those participating in the political and social life revolving around government know how, when and where to address and deal with dignitaries; and other ranks of government, social and clerical hierarchy have their own rules and regulations, as well.

Placing a foreign representative below his proper seat at a dinner table may actually influence diplomatic feelings between nations, and many a host or hostess has paled when not knowing whether a general of the army should outrank the governor of a state, or whether a rear admiral or a justice of a state court should be seated "higher" at the table, or where to seat the Archbishop of X and the Duke of Y.

Because there are so many variables within our own government as well as within diplomatic and international levels, it is a good idea to know further sources of information when planning any event. For United States Government information, in addition to the information in this chapter, you may consult The Department of State, Office of Protocol, Ceremonial Section, a representative of which may be reached by telephone at 1-202/647-1735. The famous "Green Book" is officially called *The Social List of Washington, D.C.,* and is available in most local libraries.

State and local government protocol questions may be addressed to the Governor's Office in each State Capitol and to the mayor's office in local municipalities. Questions regarding military protocol, the answers to which are written in resource documents, may be addressed to each branch of military located nearest you. Telephone numbers can be found in your local telephone directory.

To inquire about further information on United Nations protocol, the U.N. Office of Protocol in New York may be reached by telephone at 1-212/963-7176.

3
Official
Protocol

PRECEDENCE AND RANK

At a dinner party, even though a dinner is given for a guest of medium rank, those present of highest rank have the honor places on either side of the host or hostess. The person for whom the dinner is actually given is merely "among those present," unless those of higher rank agree to waive precedence.

The host or hostess who plans to entertain several government officials, military officers, or foreign diplomats must naturally try to arrange the seating without slighting any of the guests.

In an American house, the ranking foreigner should, insofar as possible, be given precedence.

In a foreign embassy in Washington, the ranking American is given precedence: the President of the United States takes precedence over the representative of the country that is receiving him. In the President's absence, the Vice-President, the Chief Justice, or the Secretary of State—whoever represents the United States on U.S. soil, outranks all foreign ambassadors. In the diplomatic service, the highest ranking ambassador is the one who has been longest in residence in Washington— not longest in the service of his country.

Wives or husbands of officials, whether their spouses are present or not, assume their spouses rank. Widows are given a courtesy position, with the exception of widows of former Presidents, who do have a definite ranking in precedence.

Just the contemplation of all these rules can cause even the most enthusiastic host or hostess to cancel plans to entertain any one of these people, but there are guidelines. Although unofficial, since the Department of State prescribes protocol to be used only for ceremonies of state and does not release a list of rank or precedence, the following list is the order of rank of those in government service, based on what information the Department of State has released. The significance of the rank of cabinet secretaries is based on the date of the establishment of the department and the position:

The President of the United States
The Vice-President of the United States
The Speaker of the House of Representatives
The Chief Justice of the United States
Former Presidents of the United States
The Secretary of State
The Secretary General of the United Nations
Ambassadors of Foreign Powers
Widows of Former Presidents of the United States
Associate Justices of the Supreme Court of the United States
Retired Chief Justice of the Supreme Court of the United States
Retired Associate Justice of the Supreme Court of the United States
The Secretary of the Treasury

The Secretary of Defense

The Attorney General
The Secretary of the Interior
The Secretary of Agriculture
The Secretary of Commerce
The Secretary of Labor
The Secretary of Health and Human Services
The Secretary of Housing and Urban Development
The Secretary of Transportation
The Secretary of Energy
The Secretary of Education
The Secretary of Veterans Affairs
Director, National Drug Control Policy
Director, Office of Management and Budget
President pro Tempore of the Senate
Members of the Senate
Governors of States
Former Vice-Presidents of the United States
Members of the House of Representatives
Assistants to the President
Charges d'Affaires of Foreign Powers
The Under Secretaries of the Executive Departments and the Deputy
    Secretaries
Administrator, Agency for International Development
Director, United States Arms Control and Disarmament Agency
Director, United States Information Agency
United States Ambassador at Large
Secretaries of the Army, the Navy, and the Air Force (ranked according to the
    date of appointment)
Chairman, Board of Governors of the Federal Reserve System
Chairman, Council on Environmental Quality
Chairman, Joint Chiefs of Staff
Chiefs of Staff of the Army, the Navy, the Air Force and Commandant of the
    Marine Corps (ranked according to date of appointment)
(Five-Star) Generals of the Army and Fleet Admirals
The Secretary General, Organization of American States
Representatives to the Organization of American States
Director of Central Intelligence
Director, Office of Personnel Management
Administrator, National Aeronautics and Space Administration
Administrator, Federal Aviation Administration
Administrator, General Services Administration

Chairman, Merit Systems Protection Board
Administrator, Environmental Protection Agency
Deputy Assistants to the President
Deputy Under Secretaries of Executive Departments
Chief of Protocol
Assistant Secretaries of the Executive Departments
Special Assistants to the President
Members of the Council of Economic Advisers
Active or Designate United States Ambassadors and Ministers (career rank, when in the United States)
The Mayor of the District of Columbia
Under Secretaries of the Army, the Navy, and the Air Force (ranked according to date of appointment)
(Four-Star) Generals and Admirals
Assistant Secretaries of the Army, the Navy and the Air Force (ranked according to date of appointment)
(Three-Star) Lieutenant Generals and Vice Admirals
Former United States Ambassadors and Ministers to Foreign Countries
Ministers of Foreign Powers (serving in embassies, not accredited)
Deputy Assistant Secretaries of the Executive Departments
Deputy Chief of Protocol
Counselors of Embassies or Legations of Foreign Powers
(Two-Star) Major Generals and Rear Admirals
(One-Star) Brigadier Generals and Commodores
Assistant Chiefs of Protocol

The rank of rear admiral is divided into two categories: the "upper half" and the "lower half." Those of the upper half are equivalent to two-star major generals. Those of the lower half are equivalent to one-star brigadier generals and may even be, depending on date of rank, outranked by a brigadier general.

OFFICIAL TITLES IN CONVERSATION

Just as there is a certain order of precedence in official circles, so are there specific forms of introduction and address that must be used. If you are introduced to a prominent person and the one making the introduction has not spoken clearly or has not used a title (although he should have), the safest thing for you to say is, "How do you do?" If the conversation continues and the person's title is still not mentioned, you may address any gentleman as "Sir." In fact, to avoid repetition of long titles like, "Your Royal Highness," or "Mr. President," it is preferable to say "Ma'am" or "Sir" occasionally.

For a chart of titles to be used in addressing and introducing important persons, see pages 37–62. The following general rules are some which apply whenever certain officials are spoken to at a public function.

The President of the United States

The correct introduction of a man or a woman is: "Mr. [Madam] President, I have the honor to present Mrs. [or Mr.] King," or "Mrs. King of Ridgefield, Connecticut," if further identification is necessary. Both men and women respond in the same way. They bow slightly but do not reach to shake hands unless the President offers his or her hand first.

The Chief Executive and Vice-President are always spoken to without their surnames as are all cabinet members because only one person holds the position at a time: "I appreciate the honor, Mr. [Madame] President," or "Thank you, Mr. [Madame] Vice-President." If the conversation is prolonged, they, and all the other officials mentioned here, may be addressed as "Sir" or "Ma'am."

Once out of office, the President becomes "Mr.," although he is referred to as "The Honorable."

Senators, Governors, Ambassadors

A senator is always "Senator D'Amato," even when he or she is no longer in office.

Present and former governors and ambassadors are, like a former President of the United States, "The Honorable." On ceremonial occasions, one would present "The Honorable Mavis Wilkins, the former governor of the State of Idaho." It is improper to call governor "Mr." or "Mrs. [Miss, Ms]." He or she is, in public, "The Governor" or, to his face, "Governor Rockefeller," and less formally, he or she may be addressed as "Governor" without his or her surname.

Ambassadors are called "Mr." or "Madame Ambassador" officially rather than "Ambassador Kemp."

Cabinet Members

Members of the Cabinet are usually addressed as "Mr. Secretary," or "Madam Secretary," but if several are present, they are addressed as "Mr. Secretary of State," and "Madam Secretary of Commerce" to avoid confusion as to whom is being addressed.

Justices of the Supreme Court

All Associate Justices are addressed as "Justice Rehnquist," for instance, rather than "Mr." or "Mrs." Justice Lewin. Similarly, the Chief Justice is "Chief Justice Burger" rather than "Mr." or "Mrs." Chief Justice Brown.

Church Dignitaries

To a cardinal, one says, "Your Eminence" [in England it is "Your Grace"], may I present Mrs. Nicolosi?"

A non-Catholic bows slightly, but a Roman Catholic drops on the right knee, places the right hand, palm down, under the cardinal's extended hand, and kisses his ring.

A woman is always presented *to* church dignitaries. Mrs. Nicolosi would reply to these introductions by saying to an archbishop, "How do you do, Your Excellency?" or to a monsignor, "How do you do, Monsignor Ryan?" She would speak to a priest as "Father Kelly" or simply as "Father."

Professional Titles

Doctors and judges are always introduced and addressed by their titles. The titles of Protestant clergy men and women vary according to the denomination, although all are willing to be called "Pastor" or "Reverend." If a protestant member of the clergy holds the title of doctor, dean, or canon, their surname is added to the proper title.

A Catholic priest is "Father," whatever his other titles may be, and Rabbis are called "Rabbi," with or without their last name as in simply "Rabbi," or "Rabbi Rothman."

Academic Degrees

An *earned* title, indicating that a man or a woman has received a doctorate in history, philosophy, literature, etc., is generally used professionally, although it varies according to the feeling of the owner of the degree and the customs of his or her particular institution or academic field. If unsure, follow the general rule of thumb that it is better to "Dr." a person who would rather be referred to by a social title than to do the reverse.

Titles on Place Cards

Place cards present another problem, for at official functions some carry only the title whereas others have title and surname. The following appear without names on all formal occasions:

The President
The Vice-President
The Archbishop of . . .
The Ambassador of . . .
The Minister of . . .

The Chief Justice
The Speaker
The Secretary of . . . or The Attorney General

So, too, at public dinners place cards are inscribed "His Excellency, the Archbishop of New York," "Her Honor, the Mayor of Chicago," etc. "The Assistant Secretary of the Navy" is never used alone, however, because there is more than one assistant secretary in all executive departments. The same is true in the case of the following and similar titles:

Justice O'Connor
Senator Essex
Governor Lansing
Rev. Father Stole
Dr. Sanford

At a private dinner, when the title alone sounds overly stiff and formal, the hostess may modify the official form (except in the cases of the President and Vice-President) by adding the surname: "Ambassador Santorino," "Chief Justice Jay," "Secretary Perkins." For other notables she uses the names by which she would address them in speaking: "Governor Street, will you sit here?" "Father Gaines, I'd like you to meet. . . ." Everyone else appears as "Mr.," "Mrs.," "Miss," or "Ms." Remember that the object of a place card is twofold: to show the owner of the name (or title) where he is to sit and to give his neighbors at the table a clue about how to address him.

Use of "The Honorable"

"The Honorable" is an expression that causes considerable confusion. Federal custom in the United States bestows the title "Honorable," first officially and then by courtesy for life, on the President and Vice-President, United States senators and congressmen, Cabinet members, all federal judges, ministers plenipotentiary, ambassadors, and governors. State senators and mayors are also referred to as "The Honorable" while they are in office. The title is not used by the person on visiting cards, letterhead, or when signing, nor does the individual say it when introducing him- or herself. When an individual is announced as he or she arrives at a large public function, however, the announcer would precede the individual's name with "The Honorable."

Representatives of Other Nations

Because customs vary greatly from country to country, no general rules can be made for the more than one hundred nations in the world. Should you find yourself about to leave for Japan or Finland or Belgium, there are many sources of help. The consulate nearest you, or the embassy for that country in Washington, D.C., or the mission to the United States in New York all are able and willing to provide information to facilitate your communication and dealings with people in their homelands.

There are a few general guidelines, which assist the American social or business traveler or host and hostess:

- The king or queen of most Western European countries is addressed as "Your Majesty" and is referred to as "His" or "Her Majesty." A prince consort to the queen is referred to as "His Royal Highness" and is addressed as "Your Royal Highness."
- A prince or princess is called "Prince" and "Princess" in conversation.
- A duke and duchess are called "Duke" and "Duchess" in conversation, not, for example, Duke of Kent or Duke Charles.
- Countries which were formerly monarchies still attribute the title held by their monarchs to them—a Russian princess, although not recognized by her government as such, is still called, out of courtesy and respect, "Princess" by others.
- European heads of state, ambassadors, cabinet officers, and usually high-ranking members of the clergy, may be referred to as "His Excellency," called "Your Excellency," and would be addressed in correspondence as "His Excellency/Giancarlo Otessi/Ambassador of the Republic of Italy," or "His Excellency/Yoichi Kawasuta/Ambassador of Japan."

Professionals from other countries also are often given titles which, out of courtesy for their custom, should be used by the American traveler. For example, a man who has completed university and earned a degree in Italy is called "Dottore" (Doctor) and a woman "Dottoressa" (also Doctor). This title is used always, formally, and is one of respect for the accomplishment of academic achievement. A male German corporate president is called "Herr Direktor," out of respect for his position, and a French lawyer would be addressed formally as "Monsieur l'Avocat," which means, literally, Mr. Lawyer. Although this is not our custom, it is theirs, and it is only polite to respect it, certainly until bonds of friendship are formed and more personal forms of address may be used.

OFFICIAL AND FORMAL CORRESPONDENCE

At one time or another nearly every one of us either meets or has to write a letter to someone officially, a senator or a judge, or perhaps a clergyman or a professor, and we certainly do not want to appear ignorant because we address him or her improperly. Neither can we remember all the proper forms of address for all the personages we might ever need to speak to or write to. This section has been prepared to cover as many as possible of the situations likely to occur in the ordinary course of events—and some not so ordinary.

As increasing technology makes our world smaller, it is more and more likely we will need to correspond with or perhaps even meet officials of governments besides our own. While this section cannot cover every country and its officials, those of the Canadian government are included. Should the occasion arise when you need to address an official not listed here, a telephone call to that country's embassy or its Mission to the United Nations will provide you with the correct information.

UNITED STATES GOVERNMENT OFFICIALS

The President

Address

Business:	The President, The White House, Washington, DC 20500
Social	
man:	The President and Mrs. Lincoln, The White House, Washington, DC 20500
woman:	The President and Mr. Jenner, The White House, Washington, DC 20500

Correspondence

Business	
opening	
man:	Sir:
woman:	Madam:
closing:	I have the honor to remain, Most respectfully yours,
Social	
opening	
man:	Dear Mr. President:
woman:	Dear Madam President:
closing:	Respectfully yours, *or* Sincerely yours,

Introductions

Formal:	The President *or* The President of the United States
Social and in conversation	
man:	Mr. President *or* Sir (*prolonged conversation*)
woman:	Madam President *or* Madam (*prolonged conversation*)
Place cards	The President

The Vice-President

Address

Business:	The Vice-President, United States Senate, Washington, DC 20510
Social	
man:	The Vice-President and Mrs. Quayle, Home Address
woman:	The Vice-President and Mr. Wagner, Home Address

Correspondence
Business
   opening

man:	Sir:
woman:	Madam:
closing:	Very truly yours, *or* Respectfully yours,

Social
   opening

man:	Dear Mr. Vice-President:
woman:	Dear Madam Vice-President:
closing:	Sincerely yours,

Introductions

Formal:	The Vice-President *or* The Vice-President of the United States
Social and in conversation	
man:	Mr. Vice-President *or* Sir (*prolonged conversation*)
woman:	Madam Vice-President *or* Madam (*prolonged conversation*)
Place Cards:	The Vice-President

The Chief Justice, Supreme Court

Address

Business:	The Chief Justice, The Supreme Court, Washington, DC 20543
Social	
man:	Chief Justice Warren Burger and Mrs. Burger, Home Address
woman:	Chief Justice Elizabeth Seton and Mr. George Seton, Home Address

Correspondence
Business
   opening

man:	Sir:
woman:	Madam:
closing:	Very truly yours, *or* Respectfully yours,

Social

opening:	Dear Chief Justice:
closing:	Sincerely yours,

Introductions

Formal:	The Chief Justice
Social and in conversation	
man:	Chief Justice *or* Sir*
woman:	Chief Justice *or* Madam
Place Cards:	The Chief Justice

    * A woman does not use "sir" in speaking to a man, nor does a man use "madam" or "ma'am" in speaking to a woman. Where indicated a man may use "sir" in place of the title or name in any prolonged conversation.

Associate Justice, Supreme Court

Address

Business:	Justice Thomas, The Supreme Court, Washington, DC 20543
Social	
man:	Justice Clarence Thomas and Mrs. Thomas, Home Address
woman:	Justice Jane Brown and Mr. Michael Brown, Home Address

Correspondence

Business	
opening	
man:	Sir:
woman:	Madam:
closing:	Very truly yours,
Social	
opening:	Justice Brown:
closing:	Sincerely yours,

Introductions

Formal:	Justice Thomas
Social and in conversation	
man:	Justice Thomas *or* Justice Clarence Thomas *or* Sir
woman:	Justice Brown *or* Justice Jane Brown *or* Madam
Place Cards:	Justice Brown

Cabinet Members

Address

Business:	The Honorable James Smith, The Secretary of (*name of department*), Washington, DC
Social	
man:	The Honorable (optional) The Secretary of (*name of department*) and Mrs. Smith, Home Address
woman:	The Honorable (optional) The Secretary of (*name of department*) and Mr. Cook, Home Address

Correspondence

Business	
opening	
man:	Sir:
woman:	Madam:
closing:	Very truly yours,
Social	
opening	
man:	Dear Mr. Secretary:
woman:	Madam Secretary:
closing:	Sincerely yours,

Introductions
Formal
    man: The Secretary of (*name of department*) *or* Mr. Smith
    woman: The Secretary of (*name of department*) *or* Mrs. *or* Miss *or* Ms Cook
Social and in
  conversation
    man: Mr. Secretary *or* Mr. Smith
    woman: Madam Secretary *or* Mrs. *or* Miss *or* Ms Cook
Place Cards: The Secretary of (*name of department*) *or* (*if the only one present*) The
                  Secretary

The Attorney General

Address
Business   The Honorable Andrew Jones, Attorney General, Washington, DC 20503
Social
    man: The Attorney General and Mrs. Andrew Jones, Home Address
    woman: The Attorney General and Mr. Adam Green, Home Address

Correspondence
Business
  opening
    man: Sir:
    woman: Madam:
  closing: Very truly yours,
Social
  opening
    man: Dear Mr. Attorney General:
    woman: Madam Attorney General:
  closing: Sincerely yours,

Introductions
Formal
    man: The Attorney General *or* Mr. Jones
    woman: The Attorney General *or* Mrs. *or* Miss *or* Ms Green
Social and in
  conversation
    man: Mr. Attorney General *or* Mr. Jones
    woman: Madam Attorney General *or* Mrs. *or* Miss *or* Ms Green
Place Cards: The Attorney General

Former President

Address
Business   The Honorable Andrew Jackson, Office Address
Social   The Honorable and Mrs. Andrew Jackson, Home Address

Correspondence
  Business
    opening: Sir:
    closing: Very truly yours,
  Social
    opening: Dear Mr. Jackson:
    closing: Sincerely yours,

Introductions
  Formal: The Honorable Andrew Jackson
  Social and in
    conversation: Mr. Jackson *or* Sir
  Place Cards: Mr. Jackson

United States Senator

Address
  Business   The Honorable Steven Hale, United States Senate, Washington, DC
                    20510
  Social
    man: The Honorable and Mrs. Steven Hale, Home Address
    woman: The Honorable Judith White and Mr. Daniel White, Home Address

Correspondence
  Business
    opening
      man: Sir:
      woman: Madam:
    closing: Very truly yours,
  Social
    opening: Dear Senator Hale:
    closing: Sincerely yours,

Introductions
  Formal: Senator Hale of (*name of state represented*)
  Social and in
    conversation: Senator *or* Senator Hale
  Place Cards: Senator Hale

The Speaker of the House of Representatives

Address
  Business   The Honorable Thomas O'Neil, The Speaker of the House of Representa-
                    tives, Washington, DC 20515
  Social
    man: The Speaker and Mrs. O'Neil, Home Address
    woman: The Speaker and Mr. Tanner, Home Address

Correspondence
Business
  opening
    man: Sir:
    woman: Madam:
  closing: Very truly yours,
Social
  opening:
    man: Dear Mr. Speaker:
    woman: Dear Madam Speaker:
  closing: Sincerely yours,

Introductions
Formal
  man: The Speaker of the House of Representatives *or* Mr. O'Neil
  woman: Madam Speaker *or* Mrs. *or* Miss *or* Ms Tanner
Place Cards: The Speaker

Member of the House of Representatives

Address
Business: The Honorable Anita Lowy, United States House of Representatives, Washington, DC 20515
Social
  man: The Honorable and Mrs. George Lane, Home Address
  woman: The Honorable Anita Lowy and Mr. Samuel Lowy, Home Address

Correspondence
Business
  opening
    man: Sir:
    woman: Madam:
  closing: Very truly yours,
Social
  opening
    man: Dear Mr. Lane:
    woman: Dear Mrs. *or* Miss *or* Ms Lowy:
  closing: Sincerely yours,

Introductions
Formal: Representative Lowy of (*state represented*)
Social and in
  conversation
  man: Mr. Lane
  woman: Mrs. *or* Miss *or* Ms Lowy

Place Cards
man: Mr. Lane
woman: Mrs. *or* Miss *or* Ms Lowy

Ambassador of the United States

Address
Business: The Honorable Jean Kirkpatrick The Ambassador of the United States, American Embassy, (*foreign city, foreign nation*)
Social
man: The Honorable and Mrs. Franklin Clark, Home Address
woman: The Honorable Jean Kirkpatrick and Mr. Timothy Kirkpatrick, Home Address

Correspondence
Business
opening
man: Sir:
woman: Madam:
closing: Very truly yours,
Social
opening
man: Dear Mr. Ambassador:
woman: Dear Madam Ambassador:
closing: Sincerely yours,

Introductions
Formal
man: The American Ambassador *or* Our Ambassador to (*foreign nation*), Mr. Clark
woman: The American Ambassador *or* Our Ambassador to (*foreign nation*), Mrs. *or* Miss *or* Ms Kirkpatrick
Social and in
conversation
man: Mr. Ambassador *or* Mr. Clark *or* Sir
woman: Madam Ambassador *or* Miss *or* Ms Kirkpatrick *or* Madam
Place Cards: The Ambassador of the United States *or* (*if more than one present*) the Ambassador of the United States to (*foreign nation*)

Minister Plenipotentiary of the United States

Address
Business: The Honorable Sherwin Fry, the Minister of the United States, American Legation, (*foreign city, foreign nation*)
Social
man: The Honorable and Mrs. Sherwin Fry, Home Address
woman: The Honorable Susan Graham and Mr. James Graham, Home Address

Correspondence
Business
  opening
    man: Sir:
    woman: Madam:
  closing: Very truly yours,
Social
  opening
    man: Dear Mr. Minister:
    woman: Dear Madam Minister:
  closing: Sincerely yours,

Introductions
Formal
  man: Mr. Fry, the American Minister *or* Mr. Fry, the American Minister to *(foreign nation)*
  woman: Mrs. *or* Miss *or* Ms Graham, the American Minister *or* Mrs. *or* Miss *or* Ms Graham, the American Minister to *(foreign nation)*
Social and in
  conversation
  man: Mr. Minister *or* Mr. Fry
  woman: Madam Minister *or* Mrs. *or* Miss *or* Ms Graham
Place Cards: The Minister of the United States to *(foreign nation)*

Consul of the United States

Address
Business
  man: Mr. Howard Coleman, American Consul, *(foreign city, foreign nation)*
  woman: Mrs. *or* Miss *or* Ms Ann Blank, American Consul, *(foreign city, foreign nation)*
Social: Mr. and Mrs. Howard Coleman, Home Address

Correspondence
Business
  opening
    man: Sir: *or* Dear Sir:
    woman: Madam: *or* Dear Madam:
  closing: Very truly yours,
Social
  opening
    man: Dear Mr. Coleman:
    woman: Dear Mrs. *or* Miss *or* Ms Blank:
  closing: Sincerely yours,

Introductions

Formal

    man: Mr. Coleman

    woman: Mrs. *or* Miss *or* Ms Blank:

Social and in

    conversation

    man: Mr. Coleman

    woman: Mrs. *or* Miss *or* Ms Blank

Place Cards

    man: Mr. Coleman

    woman: Mrs. *or* Miss *or* Ms Blank

Governor of a State

Address

Business: The Honorable Nelson Rockefeller, Governor of (*state*), Office Address

Social

    man: The Honorable and Mrs. Nelson Rockefeller, Home Address

    woman: The Honorable Frances Olson and Mr. Neils Olson, Home Address

Correspondence

Business

    opening

    man: Sir:

    woman: Madam:

    closing: Very truly yours,

Social

    opening: Dear Governor Rockefeller:

    closing: Sincerely yours,

Introductions

Formal: The Governor *or (if necessary)* The Governor of (*state*) *or* Governor Rockefeller

Social and in

    conversation: Governor Rockefeller

Place Cards: The Governor of (*state*)

Mayor

Address

Business: The Honorable Maryanne Ilse, City Hall

Social

    man: The Honorable and Mrs. Bruce Todd, Home Address

    woman: The Honorable Maryanne Ilse and Mr. George Ilse

Correspondence
Business
    opening

man:	Sir:
woman:	Madam:
closing:	Very truly yours,

Social

opening:	Dear Mayor Ilse:
closing:	Sincerely yours,

Introductions
Formal

man:	Mayor Todd, *or* His Honor, the Mayor
woman:	Mayor Ilse, *or* Her Honor, the Mayor

Social and in
conversation

man:	Mr. Mayor *or* Mayor
woman:	Madam Mayor *or* Mayor
Place Cards:	The Mayor of (*city*)

Federal Judge

Address

Business:	The Honorable Frank McCullough, Judge of the (*name of court; if district court, give district*), Office Address

Social

man:	The Honorable and Mrs. Frank McCullough, Home Address
woman:	The Honorable Eva Barber, and Mr. Ralph Barber, Home Address

Correspondence
Business
    opening

man:	Sir:
woman:	Madam:
closing:	Very truly yours,

Social

opening:	Dear Judge McCullough:
closing:	Sincerely yours,

Introductions

Formal:	The Honorable Frank McCullough, Judge of the (*name of court*)

Social and in
conversation

man:	Mr. Justice *or* Judge McCullough
woman:	Madam Justice *or* Judge Barber
Place Cards:	The Honorable Eva Barber

Ambassador of a Foreign Nation

Address
Business
    man: His Excellency Fernando Ferrari, The Ambassador of *(foreign nation)*, Washington, DC
    woman: Her Excellency Regine DuPont, The Ambassador of *(foreign nation)*, Washington, DC
Social
    man: His Excellency, The Ambassador of *(foreign nation)* and Mrs. Fernando Ferrari, Home Address
    woman: Her Excellency, The Ambassador of *(foreign nation)*, Regine DuPont and Mr. Pierre DuPont, Home Address

Correspondence
Business
    opening: Excellency:
    closing: Very truly yours,
Social
    opening
        man: Dear Mr. Ambassador:
        woman: Dear Madam Ambassador:
    closing: Sincerely yours,

Introductions
Formal: The Ambassador of *(foreign nation)*
Social and in
    conversation
        man: Mr. Ambassador *or* Excellency *or* Sir*
        woman: Madam Ambassador *or* Excellency *or* Madam
Place Cards: The Ambassador of *(foreign nation)*

Minister of a Foreign Nation

Address
Business: The Honorable Dietrich Bader, The Minister of *(foreign nation)*, Washington, DC
Social
    man: The Honorable and Mrs. Dietrich Bader, Home Address
    woman: The Honorable Fillipa Ortega and Mr. Raoul Ortega, Home Address

* A woman does not use "sir" in speaking to a man, nor does a man use "madam" or "ma'am" in speaking to a woman. Where indicated a man may use "sir" in place of the title or name in any prolonged conversation.

Correspondence
Business
    opening:
        man: Sir:
        woman: Madam:
    closing: Very truly yours,
  Social
    opening:
        man: Dear Mr. Minister:
        woman: Dear Madam Minister:
    closing: Sincerely yours,

Introductions
Formal: The Minister of (*foreign nation*)
Social and in
  conversation
    man: Mr. Minister *or* Mr. Bader
    woman: Madam Minister *or* Mrs. *or* Miss *or* Ms Ortega
Place Cards: The Minister of (*foreign nation*)

RELIGIOUS OFFICIALS OF THE ROMAN CATHOLIC CHURCH

The Pope

Address
Business: His Holiness, Pope John Paul II *or* His Holiness the Pope, Vatican City
Social: same as business

Correspondence
Business
    opening: Your Holiness:
    closing: Your Holiness' most humble servant,
  Social
    opening: Your Holiness: *or* Most Holy Father
    closing: Your most humble servant,

Introductions
Formal: His Holiness, The Pope
Social and in
  conversation: Your Holiness *or* Most Holy Father
Place Cards: His Holiness, The Pope

Cardinal

Address
Business: His Eminence John Cardinal O'Connor, Archbishop of New York, Office Address
Social: same as business

Correspondence
  Business
    opening: Your Eminence:
    closing: I have the honor to remain, Your Eminence's humble servant,
  Social
    opening: Dear Cardinal O'Connor:
    closing: Your humble servant,

Introductions
  Formal: His Eminence, Cardinal O'Connor
  Social and in
    conversation: Your Eminence *or* Cardinal O'Connor
  Place Cards: His Eminence, Cardinal O'Connor

Archbishop

Address
  Business: The Most Reverend Anthony Ruggerio, D.D., Archbishop of Chicago, Office Address
  Social: same as business

Correspondence
  Business
    opening: Your Excellency *or* Most Reverend Sir:
    closing: I have the honor to remain, Your obedient servant,
  Social
    opening: Dear Archbishop Ruggerio:
    closing: Your obedient servant,

Introductions
  Formal: The Archbishop of Chicago
  Social and in
    conversation: Your Excellency *or* Archbishop Ruggerio
  Place Cards: The Archbishop of Chicago *or* Archbishop Ruggerio

Bishop

Address
  Business: The Most Reverend Joseph Hannigan, D.D., Address of the Church
  Social: same as business

Correspondence
  Business
    opening: Most Reverend Sir:
    closing: I have the honor to remain, Your obedient servant,
  Social
    opening: Dear Bishop Hannigan:
    closing: Respectfully yours, *or* Faithfully yours,

Introductions
Formal:	Bishop Hannigan
Social and in conversation:	Bishop Hannigan
Place Cards:	Bishop Hannigan

Monsignor

Address
Business:	The Right Reverend Monsignor Mestice, Address of the Church
Social:	same as business

Correspondence
Business
opening:	Right Reverend Monsignor:
closing:	I remain, Right Reverend Monsignor, Yours faithfully,

Social
opening:	Dear Monsignor Mestice
closing:	Respectfully yours, *or* Faithfully yours,

Introductions
Formal:	Monsignor Mestice
Social and in conversation:	Monsignor *or* Monsignor Mestice
Place Cards:	The Right Reverend Monsignor Mestice *or* Monsignor Mestice

Priest

Address
Business:	The Reverend Paul Kelly (and the initials of his order), Address of the Church
Social:	same as business

Correspondence
Business
opening:	Reverend Father:
closing:	I remain, Reverend Father, Yours faithfully,
Social:	Dear Father Kelly:
closing:	Faithfully yours,

Introductions
Formal:	Father Kelly
Social and in conversation:	Father Kelly *or* Father
Place Cards:	Father Kelly

Brother

Address
  Business: Brother Richard (and the initials of his order), Address
  Social: same as business

Correspondence
  Business
    opening: Dear Brother:
    closing: Respectfully yours,
  Social
    opening: Dear Brother Richard
    closing: Faithfully yours,

Introductions
  Formal: Brother Richard
  Social and
    in conversation: Brother Richard *or* Brother
  Place Cards: Brother Richard

Nun

Address
  Business: Sister Mary (and the initials of her order), Address
  Social: same as business

Correspondence
  Business
    opening: Dear Sister:
    closing: Respectfully yours,
  Social
    opening: Dear Sister Mary:
    closing: Faithfully yours,

Introductions
  Formal: Sister Mary
  Social and
    in conversation: Sister Mary *or* Sister
  Place Cards: Sister Mary

Note: A Bishop and Priest in the Eastern Orthodox religion are addressed in the same manner as are a Roman Catholic Bishop and Priest.

RELIGIOUS OFFICIALS OF PROTESTANT DENOMINATIONS

Bishops

Address
  Business: The Right Reverend Robert Lazereth, D.D., L.L.D., Bishop of Washington
                     Office Address
  Social: The Right Reverend and Mrs. Robert Lazereth, Home Address

Correspondence
Business
    opening: Right Reverend Sir:
    closing: Respectfully yours,
Social
    opening: Dear Bishop Lazereth:
    closing: Sincerely yours,

Introductions
Formal: Bishop Lazereth
Social and
    in conversation: Bishop Lazereth
Place Cards: Bishop Lazereth

Clergyman or Clergywoman with Doctor's degree

Address
Business: The Reverend William Groth, D.D., (L.L.D., if held) Address of the Church
                 The Reverend Norma Smith, D.D., (L.L.D., if held) Address of the Church
Social: The Reverend Dr. and Mrs. William Groth, Home Address
                 The Reverend Dr. Norma Smith and Mr. Henry Smith

Correspondence
Business
    opening: Dear Dr. Groth:/Dear Dr. Smith:
    closing: Very truly yours,
Social
    opening: same as business
    closing: Sincerely yours,

Introductions
Formal: Dr. Groth *or* The Reverend Dr. William Groth
                 Dr. Smith *or* The Reverend Dr. Norma Smith
Social and
    in conversation: Dr. Groth/Dr. Smith
Place Cards: Dr. Groth/Dr. Smith

Clergyman or Clergywoman without Doctor's degree*

Address
Business: The Reverend Henry Olson, Address of the Church
                 The Reverend Sheila Duke, Address of the Church

     * Different denominations within Protestant churches call members of their clergy by different titles. A Lutheran member of the clergy is called Pastor. A male Episcopal member of the clergy may be called Father. These titles would be used in correspondence, in conversation and on place cards in lieu of "Mr." or "Ms."

Social:	The Reverend and Mrs. Henry Olson, Home Address
	The Reverend Sheila Duke and Mr. Peter Duke, Home Address

Correspondence
Business
  opening: Dear Sir:
                Dear Madam:
  closing: Very truly yours,
Social
  opening: Dear Mr. Olson:
                Dear Ms Duke:
  closing: Sincerely yours,

Introductions
Formal: Mr. Olson *or* The Reverend Henry Olson
                Ms Duke *or* The Reverend Norma Duke
Social and
  in conversation: Mr. Olson/Ms Duke
Place Cards: Mr. Olson/Ms Duke

RELIGIOUS OFFICIALS OF THE JEWISH FAITH

Rabbi

Address
Business: Rabbi Robert Rothman (or if he holds a degree, Rabbi Robert Rothman,
            D.D.), Address of the Synagogue
Social: Rabbi (or Dr.) and Mrs. Robert Rothman, Home Address

Correspondence
Business
  opening: Dear Sir:
  closing: Very truly yours,
Social
  opening: Dear Rabbi (or Dr.) Rothman:
  closing: Sincerely yours,

Introductions
Formal: Rabbi (or Dr.) Rothman
Social and
  in conversation: Rabbi (or Dr.) Rothman
Place Cards: Rabbi Rothman (or if he holds a degree, Dr. Rothman)

Cantor

Address
Business: Cantor David Schwartz, Address of the Synagogue
Social: Cantor and Mrs. David Schwartz, Home Address

Correspondence
  Business
    opening: Dear Cantor Schwartz:
    closing: Sincerely yours,
  Social
    opening: same as business
    closing: Sincerely yours,

Introductions
  Formal: Cantor Schwartz
  Social and
    in conversation: Cantor Schwartz
  Place Cards: Cantor Schwartz

OTHER PROFESSIONALS

Attorney

Address
  Business: Bernard Linden, Esq. (SJD, *if held*), Office Address
  Social: Mr. and Mrs. Bernard Linden, Home Address

Correspondence
  Business
    opening
      man: Dear Sir:
      woman: Dear Madam:
    closing: Very truly yours,
  Social
    opening
      man: Dear Mr. Linden
      woman: Dear Mrs. *or* Miss *or* Ms Rasmusson
    closing: Sincerely yours,

Introductions
  Formal
    man: Mr. Bernard Linden
    woman: Mrs. *or* Miss *or* Ms Jeanette Rasmusson
  Social and in
    conversation
      man: Mr. Linden
      woman: Mrs. *or* Miss *or* Ms Rasmusson
  Place Cards
      man: Mr. Linden
      woman: Mrs. *or* Miss *or* Ms Rasmusson

University Professor

Address
  Business
    man: Professor *or* Mr. *or* (*if he holds a degree*) Dr. Eric Stockmar, Office Address
    woman: Professor *or* Mrs. *or* Miss *or* Ms *or* (*if she holds a degree*) Dr. Lonna Romeo, Office Address
  Social
    man: Professor *or* Mr. *or* (*if he holds a degree*) Dr. and Mrs. Eric Stockmar, Home Address
    woman: Mr. and Mrs. Andrew Romeo *or* Mr. Andrew Romeo and Dr. Lonna Romeo, *or* Mr. Andrew Romeo and Professor Lonna Romeo, Home Address

Correspondence
  Business
    opening
      man: Dear Sir:
      woman: Dear Madam:
    closing: Very truly yours,
  Social
    opening
      man: Dear Professor *or* Mr. *or* Dr. Stockmar:
      woman: Dear Professor *or* Mrs. *or* Miss *or* Ms *or* Dr. Romeo:
    closing: Sincerely yours, *or* Sincerely,

Introductions
  Formal: Professor *or* Dr. Stockmar
  Social and in
    conversation
      man: Professor *or* Dr. Stockmar (*within the university*), Mr. Stockmar (*elsewhere, unless always known as Dr.*)
      woman: Professor *or* Dr. Romeo (*within the university*), Mrs. *or* Miss *or* Ms Romeo (*elsewhere, unless always known as Dr.*)
  Place Cards: Dr. *or* Professor Stockmar

Physician

Address
  Business: Eugene Wasserman, M.D., Office Address
  Social
    man: Dr. and Mrs. Eugene Wasserman, Home Address
    woman: Mr. and Mrs. Mark Josephs, Home Address, *or* (*if she keeps the title socially*) Mr. Mark Josephs and Dr. Lynn Josephs

Correspondence
Business
   opening
      man: Dear Sir:
      woman: Dear Madam:
   closing: Very truly yours,
Social
   opening: Dear Dr. Josephs:
   closing: Sincerely yours, *or* Sincerely,

Introductions
Formal: Dr. Josephs
Social and in
   conversation: Dr. Josephs
Place Cards: Dr. Wasserman

Dentist

Address
Business: John Feuerbach, D.D.S., Office Address
Social
   man: Dr. and Mrs. John Feuerbach, Home Address
   woman: Mr. and Mrs. Ronald Genther, Home Address *or* Mr. Ronald Genther and Dr. Barbara Genther

Correspondence
Business
   opening
      man: Dear Sir:
      woman: Dear Madam:
   closing: Very truly yours,
Social
   opening: Dear Dr. Feuerbach
   closing: Sincerely yours, *or* Sincerely,

Introductions
Formal: Dr. Feuerbach
Social and in
   conversation: Dr. Feuerbach
Place Cards: Dr. Feuerbach

CANADIAN GOVERNMENT OFFICIALS

The Governor General

Address
Business
   man: His Excellency the Right Honourable Pierre Denoyer, Government House, Ottawa, Ontario K1A 0A1

| woman: | Her Excellency the Right Honourable Renée Joué, Government House, Ottawa, Ontario K1A 0A1 | 57
OFFICIAL
PROTOCOL |

Social
| man: | Their Excellencies The Governor General and Mrs. (*or* Dr.) Denoyer |
| woman: | Their Excellencies The Governor General and Mr. (*or* Dr.) Joué |

Correspondence
Business
opening
man:	Sir:
woman:	Madam:
closing:	Yours very truly,

Social
| opening: | Dear Governor General *or* My Dear Governor General: |
| closing: | Yours sincerely, |

Introductions
Formal:	The Governor General of Canada
Social and in	
conversation:	Your Excellency
Place Cards:	The Governor General

The Prime Minister

Address
| Business: | The Right Honourable Adele Racine, P.C., M.P., Prime Minister of Canada, Prime Minister's Office, Ottawa, Ontario K1A 0A2 |

Social
| man: | The Prime Minister and Mrs. Paul Janier |
| woman: | The Prime Minister and Mr. Phillipe Racine |

Correspondence
Business
opening
man:	Dear Sir: *or* Dear Mr. Prime Minister; *or* Dear Prime Minister:
woman:	Dear Madam: *or* Dear Madam Prime Minister: *or* Dear Prime Minister:
closing:	Yours very truly,

Social
| opening: | Dear Prime Minister *or* My Dear Prime Minister: |
| closing: | Yours sincerely, |

Introductions
Formal:	The Prime Minister *or* The Prime Minister of Canada
Social and in	
conversation	
man:	Mr. Prime Minister *or* Sir
woman:	Madam Prime Minister *or* Madam
Place Cards:	The Prime Minister

Address
  Business: The Honourable Donald Crew, P.C., Minister of (*function*), House of Commons, Parliament Buildings, Ottawa, Ontario K1A 0A6

  Social
    man: The Honourable Donald Crew and Mrs. Crew
    woman: The Honourable Margaret Wilson and Mr. William Wilson

Correspondence
  Business
    opening
      man: Dear Sir:
      woman: Dear Madam:
    closing: Yours very truly,
  Social
    opening
      man: Dear Mr. Crew
      woman: Dear Mrs. *or* Miss *or* Ms Wilson
    closing: Yours sincerely,

Introductions
  Formal: The Honourable Margaret Wilson, Minister of (*function*)
  Social and in
    conversation
      man: Mr. Minister *or* Mr. Crew *or* Sir
      woman: Madam Minister *or* Mrs. *or* Miss *or* Ms Wilson
  Place Cards: The Minister of (*function*)

Senator

Address
  Business: The Honourable Brent Adair, Senator, The Senate, Parliament Buildings, Ottawa, Ontario K1A 0A4; *in the case of a Privy Councillor*: Senator the Honourable Clark Firth, P.C.
    man: Senator Brent Adair and Mrs. Adair
    woman: Senator Ann Gray and Mr. Harold Gray

Correspondence
  Business
    opening
      man: Dear Sir: *or* Senator: *or* My Dear Senator:
      woman: Dear Madam: *or* Senator: *or* My Dear Senator:
    closing: Yours very truly,
  Social
    opening: Dear Senator Gray:
    closing: Yours sincerely,

Introductions

Formal:	Senator Adair

Social and in conversation:	Senator *or* Senator Firth
Place Cards:	Senator Firth

Chief Justice of Canada

Address

Business:	The Right Honourable Charles Fitzhugh, P.C., Chief Justice of Canada, Supreme Court Building, Ottawa, Ontario K1A 0J1

Social

man:	The Right Honourable Charles Fitzhugh and Mrs. Fitzhugh
woman:	The Right Honourable Nancy Hill and Mr. Benjamin Hill

Correspondence

Business

opening

man:	Sir: *or* Dear Sir: *or* Dear Mr. Chief Justice:
woman:	Madam: *or* Dear Madam: *or* Dear Madam Chief Justice:
closing:	Yours very truly,

Social

opening:	Dear Chief Justice Fitzhugh:
closing:	Yours sincerely,

Introductions

Formal:	The Chief Justice of Canada

Social and in conversation

man:	Mr. Chief Justice
woman:	Madam Chief Justice
Place Cards:	The Chief Justice

Canadian Ambassador *(when addressed by a non-Canadian citizen)*

Address

Business

man:	His Excellency
woman:	Her Excellency

Social

man:	Ambassador and Mrs. Edward Smythe
woman:	Ambassador Eugenie Reymont and Mr. James Reymont

Correspondence

Business

opening

man:	Your Excellency: *or* Dear Mr. Ambassador: *or* Dear Mr. Smythe:

woman:	Your Excellency: *or* Dear Madam Ambassador: *or* Dear Mrs. *or* Miss *or* Ms Reymont:
closing:	Yours very truly,
Social	
opening	
man:	Dear Mr. Ambassador:
woman:	Dear Madam Ambassador:
closing:	Yours sincerely,

Introductions
Formal

man:	The Canadian Ambassador to (*foreign nation*), Mr. Smythe
woman:	The Canadian Ambassador to (*foreign nation*), Mrs. *or* Miss *or* Ms Reymont
Social and in conversation	
man:	Mr. Ambassador *or* Mr. Smythe *or* Sir
woman:	Madam Ambassador *or* Mrs. *or* Miss *or* Ms Reymont *or* Madam
Place Cards:	The Ambassador of Canada *or* (*if more than one present*) The Ambassador of Canada to (*foreign nation*)

Canadian Ambassador (*when addressed by a Canadian citizen*)

Address

Business:	Mr. Reginald Harrington Canadian Ambassador to (*name of country*)
Social	
man:	Ambassador and Mrs. Reginald Harrington
woman:	Ambassador Sandra Peyton and Mr. Robert Peyton

Correspondence
Business

opening	
man:	Dear Sir:
woman:	Dear Madam:
closing:	Yours very truly,
Social	
opening	
man:	Dear Mr. Harrington:
woman:	Dear Mrs. *or* Miss *or* Ms Peyton:
closing:	Yours sincerely,

Introductions
Formal

man:	The Canadian Ambassador *or* Our Ambassador to (*foreign nation*), Mr. Harrington
woman:	The Canadian Ambassador *or* Our Ambassador to (*foreign nation*), Mrs. *or* Miss *or* Ms Peyton

Social and in conversation	
man:	Mr. Ambassador *or* Mr. Harrington *or* Sir
woman:	Madam Ambassador *or* Mrs. *or* Miss *or* Ms Peyton, *or* Madam
Place Cards:	The Ambassador of Canada *or* (*if more than one present*) The Ambassador of Canada to (*foreign nation*)

The Premier of a Province

Address

Business:	The Honourable Brian Spillane M.L.A.,† Premier of the Province‡ of (*name*)
Social	
man:	Premier and Mrs. Brian Spillane
woman:	Premier Lydia Spelman and Mr. Thomas Spelman

Correspondence

Business	
opening	
man:	Dear Sir: *or* My Dear Premier: *or* Dear Mr. Spillane:
woman:	Dear Madam: *or* My Dear Premier: *or* Dear Mrs. *or* Miss *or* Ms Spelman:
closing:	Yours very truly,
Social	
opening	
man:	Dear Mr. Spillane:
woman:	Dear Mrs. *or* Miss *or* Ms Spelman:
closing:	Yours sincerely,

Introductions

Formal	
man:	The Premier of the Province‡ of (*name*), Mr. Spillane
woman:	The Premier of the Province‡ of (*name*), Mrs. *or* Miss *or* Ms Spelman
Social and in conversation	
man:	Mr. Premier *or* Mr. Spillane *or* Sir
woman:	Madam Premier *or* Mrs. *or* Miss *or* Ms Spelman *or* Madam
Place Cards:	The Premier of the Province‡ of (*name*)

Members of Provincial Governments—Executive Council—Canada

Address

Business:	The Honourable Ryan Verlin, M.L.A.
Social:	Mr. and Mrs. Ryan Verlin

† For Ontario use M.P.P.; for Quebec use M.N.A.
‡ For Quebec use "Prime Minister."

Correspondence
Business
  opening
    man: Dear Sir:
    woman: Dear Madam:
    closing: Yours very truly,
Social
  opening
    man: Dear Mr. Verlin:
    woman: Dear Mrs. *or* Miss *or* Ms Christian:
    closing: Yours sincerely,

Introductions
Formal: The Minister of (*function*)
Social and in
conversation
    man: Mr. Verlin
    woman: Mrs. *or* Miss *or* Ms Christian
Place Cards: The Minister of (*function*)

Mayor

Address
Business
    man: His Worship Christopher Mignone Mayor of (*name of city*), City Hall, (*city, province*)
    woman: Her Worship Amanda Pavelin, Mayor of (*name of city*), City Hall, (*city, province*)

Correspondence
Business
  opening
    man: Dear Sir: *or* Dear Mr. Mayor:
    woman: Dear Madam: *or* Dear Madam Mayor:
    closing: Yours very truly,
Social
  opening: Dear Mayor Pavelin:
  closing: Yours sincerely,

Introductions
Formal
    man: Mayor Mignone, *or* His Worship, the Mayor of (*city*)
    woman: Mayor Pavelin, *or* Her Worship, the Mayor of (*city*)
Social and in
conversation
    man: Mr. Mayor *or* Mayor
    woman: Madam Mayor *or* Mayor
Place Cards: The Mayor of (*city*)

WHITE HOUSE ETIQUETTE

Although customs vary somewhat during different administrations, the following details represent the conventional pattern from which each administration adapts its own procedure.

When you are invited to the White House you must arrive several minutes, at least, before the hour specified. It is an unpardonable breach of etiquette not to be standing in the drawing room when the President makes his entry.

The President, followed by the First Lady, enters at the hour set, and if the group is not too large, makes a tour of the room, shaking hands with each guest. If the occasion is a big reception the President and the First Lady stand in one place and the guests form a line and pass by to be greeted. In this case an aide serves as announcer. Gentlemen precede their wives, unless she is the more prominent one, and they are greeted first by the President and then by the First Lady. If a woman is wearing gloves she *removes* the right one before shaking hands with the President. If the President talks to you, you address him as "Mr. President." In a long conversation it is proper to vary "Mr. President" with "Sir" occasionally. You call the wife of the President "Mrs. Washington" and treat her as you would any formal hostess. You do not sit down so long as either the President or the First Lady remains standing in line.

Requests to see the President on a business matter should be made through one of the presidential aides—the one whose area of responsibility includes the subject you wish to discuss—or through your congressman. Your reason should be a valid one, you should be sure that no one else can solve your problem, and your letter should be stated in such a way that, if possible, the matter can be settled without a personal interview.

If you have a business appointment with the President, it is most important, again, that you arrive a few minutes ahead of the appointed time. No doubt you will be told how much time you are allowed. Make your call brief and, if possible, take less time than that allotted.

If a buzzer should ring when you are in a corridor of the White House, an attendant will ask you to step behind a closed door. The buzzer means that the President or members of his family are leaving or entering. This precaution is for their safety and their privacy.

Don't smoke unless you are invited to.

Gentlemen always remove their hats as they reach the White House portico.

Not only should you avoid taking a present to the President unless it has been cleared with an aide, but you should not *send* anything to the White House without receiving permission from his secretary or one of his aides. For security reasons, the gift must be cleared with the proper authority; otherwise he will never have the opportunity to enjoy it.

Furthermore, the President cannot accept personal gifts worth more than fifty dollars, and there is a strict rule against the gift of an animal. The only exception is a gift from a foreign country or ruler—for example, the pandas sent to Washington from China, following President Richard Nixon's visit there in 1972—because this is in fact a gift to the entire nation.

A Formal Invitation to the White House

An invitation to lunch or dinner at the White House is somewhat of a command and automatically cancels almost any other engagement that is not of the utmost importance. The reply must be written by hand within a day of the invitation's arrival. If the recipient is not near Washington, his reply should be sent by express mail or special delivery to insure arrival. There are very few acceptable excuses for refusing an invitation to the White House, and the reason must be stated in the note of regret. Unavoidable absence from Washington, the recent death of a close relative, or actual illness used to be the only possible excuses. Today "a wedding in the family" or "a vacation trip" reflects a less rigid attitude.

The correct forms for replies are:

Mr. and Mrs. John Jay
accept with pleasure
the kind invitation of
The President and Mrs. Washington
for dinner on Thursday, the eighth of May
at eight o'clock

Mr. and Mrs. Benjamin Franklin
regret extremely
that owing to Mr. Franklin's illness
they will be unable to accept
the kind invitation of
The President and Mrs. Madison
for dinner on Friday, the first of May

An engraved invitation to an evening at the White House means black tie unless white tie is specified on the invitation. Women wear conservative evening dresses, not pants, and if it is a white-tie dinner they wear long gloves.

All the names of guests expected at the White House are posted with the guards at the gate. You announce your name, present your invitation or admittance card, and wait a few seconds until you are recognized.

After the guests arrive, the President and the First Lady enter and speak to each guest and shake hands. Guests, of course, remain standing.

At a formal dinner the President goes into the dining room first with the highest-ranking woman guest. The First Lady follows with the highest-ranking man.

An Informal Invitation to the White House

Informal invitations to dinner or luncheon at the White House are now used more frequently than formerly. They are sent by letter or may be extended by telephone by the President's secretary or by the First Lady's secretary. The replies should be sent in the same form to whoever issued the invitations. Written acceptances (or regrets, when the reasons are valid) are sent on personal stationery, either engraved or plain.

A typical invitation might be worded something like this:

Dear Mrs. Adams,

Mrs. Washington has asked me to invite you to have lunch with her at the White House on Thursday, the sixteenth of May. Luncheon will be at one o'clock.

Yours truly,
Eleanor Smithers
Secretary to Mrs. Washington

The reply might read:

Dear Miss Smithers,

Will you please thank Mrs. Washington for her kind invitation and tell her that I shall be delighted to lunch with her at the White House on Thursday, the sixteenth of May. Thank you very much.

Sincerely,
Frances Adams

AN AUDIENCE WITH THE POPE

Any American tourist visiting Rome can be granted an audience with the Pope, for although there are often hundreds of people in a day who wish an audience no one with a proper introduction is denied. Obviously only relatively few can be granted one of the three types of audience that are considered to be personal; group or collective audiences are arranged for the great majority.

Requests by Americans for these group audiences as well as for the personal ones are cleared by the North American College and then sent to the Office of the Master of the Chamber (*l'Uffizio del Maestro di Camera di Sua Santità*), which is in the Vatican. Your request should be mailed well ahead of your departure date, so that you will have your acknowledgment in hand before you go. On your arrival in Rome, your request and the approval you have received should be presented in person or mailed to the monsignor in charge, whose name, and the address, can be obtained from the concierge of your hotel. Each applicant must fill out a form requesting the kind of audience desired and show his or her credentials; which for a Roman Catholic may be simply a letter of introduction from his parish priest or a prominent layman. The length of your stay in Rome along with your address and telephone number are also included on the form so that you can be notified of the day and hour of the audience. Non-Catholics as well as Catholics are granted audiences, but their requests must be arranged through prominent Catholic laymen or members of the Catholic clergy.

The reply, and the invitation if the answer is favorable, will be sent to you within a few days. You may receive a general admission ticket, meaning no reserved seat, or if you are considered sufficiently important, a reserved seat in a special section.

The concierge will also give you any other information you may need about the procedure.

The General Audience

General audiences are held at 11:00 A.M. on Wednesdays at St. Peter's. During the summer months they take place at 10:00 A.M. People without reserved seats should arrive very early if they want a location with a good view. Choice places are often filled early in the morning.

Everyone rises as the Pope appears, seated on a portable throne called the *Sedia Gestatoria*, carried by eight Swiss Guards. At the end of the aisle he leaves the portable throne for a fixed one, and when he sits down the people may be seated also. He delivers a short address, and then everyone kneels as he gives his benediction to all those present as well as to all the articles they have brought to be blessed. The group rises, and if the Pope has time, he greets each person in the special area. The audience is over when he mounts his portable throne and is carried out.

For general audiences it is only required that everybody be dressed in a sober and suitable manner. Women must have their hair covered, must wear black or dark everyday dresses with necklines that are not too low and skirts that are not too short. They may not have bare arms or legs, but pants are permitted. Men in the general audience wear business suits and white shirts. In the reserved section some men will be seen in formal daytime wear, and women in long-sleeved black dresses and mantillas, but this is no longer obligatory, and sober, conservative daytime wear is acceptable.

Other Audiences

The "private" audience is reserved for cardinals, heads of state, ambassadors, or others in important positions. Another type, the "special," is granted to people of slightly lower rank or to those who have an important subject to present to the Pope. The third type, the "*baciomano*," is the only special audience to which laymen are invited. At the *baciomano* each visitor comes into the personal presence of the Pope, kisses his ring, and exchanges a few words with him, addressing him as "Your Holiness."

In this third type of audience visitors stand in a single file around the room until the Pope enters. They then kneel and do not stand again until he leaves the audience chamber or makes a sign for them to rise. He passes from one visitor to another, extending his hand so that all may kiss his ring. He also may ask a question and exchange a few words with each. As in the general audience, visitors customarily take with them one or more rosaries or other small religious objects, which are also considered to have been blessed when the visitor has received the papal blessing.

The rules of dress are not so strict as they once were, but even now for a private or special audience many men wear evening dress with tails or a morning coat, and women long-sleeved, high-necked black dresses and veils or mantillas over their hair. However, male visitors who do not have formal clothes with them are admitted in very dark blue or gray business suits. No one may wear any but the most functional jewelry—wedding rings, watches, etc.

Non-Catholics

At a general audience every person present must kneel, rise, and sit at the prescribed time. Non-Catholics, if they do not ordinarily do so, need not make the sign of the cross.

At the *baciomano* non-Catholics on their arrival will be told the proper manner of kneeling and kissing the Pope's ring. If they object to these requirements on the grounds of their own religion, there may be some slight modification. But since the procedures are strictly followed, these people would be wiser to forgo the private audience than to make an issue.

THE FLAG OF THE UNITED STATES

There are certain rules and customs connected with the flag of the United States that all citizens should know and follow to show respect for the country and our patriotism.

It is proper to fly the flag every day in the year between sunrise and sunset, although customarily it is not flown in inclement weather unless there is a particular occasion that requires its display. It may also be displayed at night as part of a patriotic display.

On Memorial Day, May 30 (or whatever day it is legally observed), the flag is displayed at half staff until noon and at full staff thereafter until sunset. Flag Day is June 14—the day when we especially celebrate this emblem by displaying the flag. Many of us display the flag on other national holidays too.

There are certain clear-cut situations in which the flag should never be used— on an article of clothing, on a portion of a costume or in any way that is disrespectful to the flag. When a statue or monument is unveiled, the flag should never be used as a covering for the object to be displayed. It is unlawful to use the flag in a registered trademark that comprises "the flag, coat of arms, or other insignia of the United States or any simulation thereof."

Displaying the Flag

When displayed over the middle of a street, the flag should be suspended vertically with the union (the blue field) to the north in an east-west street, or to the east in a north-south street.

When displayed with another flag from crossed staffs, the flag of the United States should be on the right (the flag's own right), and its staff should be in front of the staff of the other flag.

Displaying flags crossed

The flag should be raised briskly and lowered slowly and solemnly.

When flown at half-mast, the flag should be hoisted to the peak for a moment and then lowered to the half-mast position. And the flag should again be raised to the peak before being lowered for the day.

When flags of states or cities or pennants of societies are flown on the same halyard with the flag of the United States, the latter should always be at the peak. When flown from adjacent staffs, the national flag should be hoisted first and lowered last.

When the flag is suspended over a sidewalk from a rope extending from house to pole at the edge of the sidewalk, the flag should be hoisted union first.

When the flag is displayed from a staff projecting horizontally or at an angle from a window sill, balcony, or the front of a building, the union of the flag should go all the way to the peak of the staff (except when at half-mast).

On a power boat the flag is flown from 8:00 A.M. until sunset. It flies from a staff at the stern when the boat is anchored, or if the boat has a gaff, may be flown from the gaff when under way.

The flag is flown from the stern of a sailboat in the harbor or under power, and now may be flown while the boat is under sail.

When used to cover a casket the flag should be placed so that the union is at the head and over the left shoulder. The flag should not be lowered into the grave or allowed to touch the ground.

Displaying a flag out a window *Displaying a flag across a wall*

When the flag is displayed in a manner other than flown from a staff, it should be flat, not tucked or draped, whether indoors or out. When displayed vertically against a wall, the union should be uppermost and to the observer's left. When displayed in a window it should be displayed in the same way, with the union to the left of the observer in the street.

When carried in a procession with another flag or flags, either the American flag should be on the marching right, or when there is a line of other flags, it may be in front of the center of that line.

When a number of flags of states or cities are grouped and displayed from staffs, our national flag should be at the center or at the highest point of the group. If the flags of two or more nations are displayed, they should be flown from separate staffs of the same height, and the flags should be of approximately equal size. International usage forbids the display of the flag of one nation above that of another nation in time of peace.

Displaying a number of flags grouped together

When the flag is used in a church—on the chancel or on a platform—it should be placed on a staff on the clergyman's right; other flags are on his left. When displayed in the body of the church, the flag should be on the congregation's right as it faces the chancel.

As an identifying symbol on an automobile the flag is flown on a small staff affixed to the end of the front bumper, on the right looking forward and within the line of the fender. When used this way, the staff should be tall enough so that the flag clears the car hood. If the flag has become soiled or torn, it should be promptly removed and replaced.

The flag should *never* be hung upside down except as a signal of distress.

Care of the Flag

The flag of our country should be carefully protected in storage and in use so that it will not be damaged. Every precaution should be taken to prevent it from becoming soiled or torn. It should not be permitted to touch the ground, or water, or a floor. In handling the flag do not let it brush against other objects.

If it should get wet it should be hung smoothly until dry—never rolled or folded while still damp.

Flags should be dry-cleaned, not washed.

Saluting the Flag

Whenever the flag passes by, as in a parade, men and women pay it their respects. Women stand quietly with hands at their sides, or they may place their right hands over their hearts if they wish. Men remove their hats and hold them, in their right hands, over their hearts. Men and women in the armed forces give the military salute as the flag passes.

When the salute to the flag is spoken at a public dinner or in church, men and women both stand quietly at attention while they repeat it or listen to the person giving the salute.

The National Anthem

Everyone, even very young children, should rise and remain standing during the playing of "The Star-Spangled Banner." It is not easy to sing, and you need not do so if you do not have the necessary range or "ear," but you must stand quietly until you hear "O'er the land of the free, and the home of the brave."

If you are on the way to your seat at a sports event, or in any public place, when the strain, "Oh say, can you see, by the dawn's early light," sounds, stop where you are and stand at attention until the end. Don't talk, chew gum loudly, eat, or smoke during the rendition.

At home, in private, when it is played on television or radio, it is *not* necessary

to rise. But if at a large private party the orchestra plays the anthem at the start of the dancing, the guests *do* rise and show their respect.

The anthem is never played as dance music, nor are improvisations permissible.

When the anthem of a foreign country is played officially—as, for instance, in honor of a visiting team of athletes—everyone rises and stands at attention, and men remove their hats but they do not salute.

Rules for Those of Other Nationalities

When "The Star-Spangled Banner" is played, foreigners as well as American citizens stand. It is up to them whether they sing or not.

When the pledge of allegiance to the flag is said, foreigners stand, but they do not repeat the words.

Foreigners may display the flag of their own country on its national holidays. Out of courtesy, they should display the American flag also.

On *our* national holidays a foreigner should display the American flag or none—not his own.

When a foreigner attends a parade or other patriotic event he stands respectfully while the flag passes by, but he need not salute in any way.

II

YOUR PERSONAL LIFE

*T*he cardinal principle of etiquette is thoughtfulness, and the guiding rule of thoughtfulness is the Golden Rule. If you always do unto others as you would have done unto you, it is likely that you will never offend, bore or intrude, and that your actions will be courteous and indeed thoughtful.

Although many reasons for thoughtful actions, particularly those between the sexes, no longer exist, the customs that were attached to them have lasted but sometimes in different forms. For example, it used to be that a man escorting a woman on the street walked on the street side to keep her from being splashed by mud thrown up by carriage wheels or horses hooves. Technology has paved our streets and replaced carriages as the primary source of travel, but in the inner cities at night modern manners have men walking on the building side of a woman in order to protect her from muggers and purse snatchers lurking in doorways.

Other courtesies—never intentionally embarrassing another, never talking only about oneself, not gossiping, not prying, not asking personal questions, and not staring or pointing at someone, for example, are as old as time and I fervently hope, will last in perpetuity.

LADIES—OR GENTLEMEN—FIRST

Society generally recognizes that women are not, as earlier presumed, frail creatures that can hardly exit their front door without the consul and services of a man to guide them. There is nothing wrong, however, with the continuing customs that allow a man to extend social amenities and instinctive consideration to a woman he is with.

In most circumstances, indoors and out, when a couple walks together the woman precedes the man, through a door, a narrow passageway, etc. But over rough ground he goes first and offers his hand if she is wearing high heels or needs assistance. He steps ahead of her to open a car door for her but he need not rush around to open the door for her to get out especially if there is passing traffic on his side of the car. Of course, he would offer to help her out if she needed a hand. He precedes her down a steep ramp or slippery stairway, but follows her up *or* down an escalator, unless she asks him to go first to help her on or off. He may also step into a boat first, or off a bus first, for example, to be ready to help her.

4
Everyday Manners

Walking Together

As mentioned before, a man generally walks on the street or curb side of a woman in daytime or in safe areas. This doesn't mean he must hop back and forth each time they cross the street, but when they are continuing in the same relative position for some time, he should walk on the outside. Otherwise, if he prefers to ignore the curbside tradition entirely, he should always walk on the woman's left.

When walking or sitting with two women, a man should not sandwich himself between them. From one side he can look in the direction of both while talking with either one.

A man rarely offers his arm to a woman anymore, unless she is old and infirm. In the evening, however, if she is wearing high heels and going down steps, a ramp, or is walking on broken pavement, she is wise to accept his arm to help keep her balance.

A man also offers his arm to a woman when he is her partner at a formal dinner, or when he is an usher at a wedding.

Never should a man grab a woman by the elbow or the arm and shove her along. It is only when he is helping her into a car, a taxi, or a bus, or up steep stairs, that he should put his hand under her elbow. He may also take her hand and precede her through a crowd to clear a path for her.

Going Through Doors

It is customary for a man to stand aside and allow a woman to pass through an open door ahead of him. If the door is closed, and it is a heavy door however, it is far more practical and simpler if he goes ahead and pulls or pushes the door open and then holds it for the woman. Allow me to interject here that this is a guideline for accepted manners. I am perfectly capable of opening doors for myself, as are most women, but if I am with a man who is used to extending these courtesies, I see no reason to be belligerent and remind him that I know how to open a door, thank you! And I am always grateful for this courtesy, no matter who extends it—man, woman, or child—when I have my arms full of packages.

Traditionally, a woman steps into a revolving door ahead of a man if it is already moving. If it is stationery, he steps in first and gets it moving slowly so that she may step into the section behind him.

Any courteous person holds a door open for the person following him or her, unless that person is some distance behind. It is extremely rude to let a door slam shut in someone's face. Anyone seeing someone with a baby in a stroller, struggling up stairs or toward a door, should certainly offer assistance either by taking an end of the stroller and helping to carry it on stairs, and by holding a door so adult and stroller can enter or exit without a struggle.

On Public Transportation

As any woman who has ever been pregnant knows, to be offered a seat on a crowded bus or train is a wonderful gift. Any man, woman or child should also give up his or her seat to someone who is handicapped and obviously having difficulty standing, and to an older person, or to a man or woman carrying a baby, a small child, or struggling with a heavy burden of any sort. If you would welcome the chance to be seated, smile and say "thank you." If you are having no problem standing or are getting off shortly, refuse graciously. Again with a smile, say, "Thank you so much, but I'd rather stand," or "Thank you very much, but I'm getting off shortly."

Young people should offer their seats to older people, both men and women, and a youngster traveling with his or her mother or father should offer the parent the empty seat, not grab it for him or herself.

Anyone traveling with a very small child should keep the child on his or her lap to free a seat for someone else. In fact, there were signs on many New York City buses for years which read, "Little enough to ride for free? Little enough to ride your knee," to remind parents not to take up a seat they didn't pay for that would be very much appreciated by another adult, particularly after a long day at work.

Elevator Etiquette

It is interesting to me that I still receive a great number of letters from people asking who should precede whom on and off elevators. The answer is very simple: The person nearest the door steps on first and holds the "door open" button for those following, and the person nearest the door steps off first when exiting. It is ridiculous, particularly in a crowded elevator, to have men trying to squeeze to the side to permit women to precede them.

It is only common courtesy that someone who has moved to the back of an elevator to allow room for others to enter be given a clear path to exit when she or he has to get off. Those in front should step to the side, or out if necessary, to let others exit.

In a private elevator, or when a man and a woman are riding alone, tradition has the man letting the woman go first, just as through any other door.

A Word About Hats

Long gone are the days when the well-dressed man always wore a felt fedora in cool months and a straw boater in the summer, necessitating an entire page of "hat etiquette." More men today are bare headed than are behatted, although the preponderance of baseball and "Raiders of the Lost Ark" hats today still recommend a few words about hats. They should always be removed indoors unless religious custom dictates that they be kept in place. Indoors means out of the elements, whether a house, a store, or an elevator, unless the elevator is crowded. If this is the case, it is better for a man to leave his hat on, since the amount of elbow room required for him to remove it and the resultant problem of where to hold it so it does not get squashed is just too cumbersome. These same suggestions apply to young boys and include school buildings and, most particularly, classrooms within schools. However, small boys in fast food restaurants may keep their caps on. As there is no place to put hats they would soon be lost if left on a chair or booth. As a rule, hats of any sort on men and boys are outdoor, not indoor apparel.

Women don't wear hats with evening clothes. Women who wear daytime hats may keep them on outdoors or in, except in places like theaters and auditoriums where the hat blocks the view of those seated behind them. In these situations, it is thoughtful to remove one's hat and check it or hold it for the duration of the event or performance.

Umbrellas

Anyone who has been speared by the point or the spokes of an umbrella knows that care must be taken with these potentially dangerous accessories. They should always be carried close to the body, point down, when closed and held so as not to block one's vision when open, either high or low enough to avoid the eyes of other pedestrians. An umbrella shared by a couple walking together should be held by the taller of the two, both for safety and for comfort.

Personal Habits

We would probably all be amazed if we viewed a videotape of ourselves performing basically unconscious acts as we go about the business of the day. These unconscious acts are comprised of all the little personal habits we don't even think about, but definitely should. These are some of the things that present an image of who we are to others, and if we are sloppy in performing them, this image may well be other than we would like it to be.

Parents who insist that their children practice courtesy and good habits at home are doing them a great service, for these habits then become lifelong and the natural way they do things. It is then unlikely that they will ever embarrass themselves socially or in business, for their unconscious actions will reflect a well-mannered person.

People who, for example, eat with both arms on the table at home will likely do so when out. Those who slouch in private will certainly do so in public. Children who are permitted to be disrespectful to their parents will follow suit with other adults, and will, most likely, become adults who are disrespectful of others. This is an area where the adage "practice makes perfect" may be applied.

I recall reading an article about the actress, Audrey Hepburn, known for her
beautiful carriage and posture. According to her biographer, her grandmother tied her neck to the back of her chair, at table, so that she would not slump over her food, but rather would learn to put only small amounts of food on her spoon or fork and bring them to her mouth. This is a rather extreme "at home" method for the development of erect posture, but it does illustrate the effectiveness of practicing good habits so that, when in public, they are instinctive.

Posture

There is no doubt that a person who stands and sits erect looks best. A round-shouldered slouch, with head thrust forward and stomach sticking out, certainly does little to make one appealing.

Graceful standing and walking posture includes the following components: Shoulders back, chin in and slightly up, abdomen and stomach in, back straight, and knees relaxed. When left to their own devices, the arms are relaxed and swing naturally during walking.

When one is seated, feet should be on the floor or one knee may be crossed over the other. Women in skirts should keep their knees together, not just for modesty, but out of politeness since few people really want a view of the undergarments of women sitting across from them.

Men have less difficulty sitting properly, simply because they don't have to deal with skirts, but they still should make an effort not to slump, and they should not cross their ankle on the opposite knee if it means they are taking up two seats on a couch or on public transportation.

Anyone sinking into an easy chair should pull him- or herself up and sit somewhat sideways to keep from sprawling into the chair.

Chewing Gum

It is hard to understand why so many otherwise attractive people totally destroy their appearance by chewing gum like a cow chewing a cud. There are people who chew it for therapeutic reasons as well as because they like the taste, and others just chew because it's a habit. Chewing gum, in itself, if it is done quietly and unobtrusively, is not unattractive. But when one does it with grimaces, open mouth, smacks, crackles and pops, and worst of all with bubbles, it is in the worst of taste.

It should be unnecessary to remind people not to dispose of gum where anyone can possibly sit on it, step on it, or touch it. But is there anyone who has not been a victim of this thoughtlessness? When you are through with your gum, wrap it in any scrap of paper and throw it in a trash can. If no trash basket is available, keep the gum, wrapped, in your pocket or handbag until you find an appropriate receptacle.

Smoking in Public Places

Smoking has finally become a socially unacceptable personal habit. Laws governing smoking in public places take care of any question of where one may, and may not smoke. Where it is permitted, there still will be those who will let you know that they would prefer you didn't. However one feels, suffice it to say that one should not sit in a smoking section of any public place and then raise a hue and cry because someone nearby is smoking. Suffice it to say, as well, that both the law and the rules of etiquette mandate that one does not smoke where it is prohibited to do so.

If You Do Smoke . . .

When in someone's home, do not smoke unless he or she does, or unless you ask first, if your host does not smoke. If smoking is permitted, keep in mind that it is unforgivable to lay a cigarette or cigar on the edge of a table. Find an ashtray, or ask for one.

Don't strike a match toward someone. The head may fly off and cause a burn.

Never put a cigarette out other than in an ash tray. Saucers or decorative ornaments could be ruined. Always do put a cigarette out completely. The smell of a cigarette burning itself out is nauseating.

Don't litter lawns, parks, or gardens with your cigarette butts. Pick them up and dispose of them properly.

Be careful that your smoke does not drift into anyone else's face. If you are the victim of a thoughtless smoker, you are free to say, "Would you please hold your cigarette on the other side? The smoke is blowing right into my face."

Never throw a lighted cigarette out a car window. Millions of acres of our forests have been destroyed through this kind of carelessness. And never smoke in a car unless you have the permission of the other occupants to do so.

Carry your own cigarettes. People who smoke only O.P.'s (Other People's) are never popular. If you do take out your cigarettes, you should first offer one to the person near you or in your immediate group.

It is polite to light the cigarette of the person near you, but not if he or she is across the table or if it would be awkward to do so.

Whether it is proper to smoke at the table depends on whether places are set with ashtrays. If they are, it is obviously permissible to smoke, not throughout the meal, but after dessert, unless your host indicates otherwise.

Cigar smokers are the least popular of all smokers. Cigars do have a smell that is offensive to many people. Don't leave cigar butts in ashtrays, for the smell lingers. When your cigar is thoroughly extinguished, remove the ashtray and dispose of the butt.

There is no need to post "no smoking" signs in your living room if you prefer that people not smoke in your house. It is your right to say, "I'm sorry, but we don't smoke in the house. There's an ashtray on the deck [outside the door, on the front porch, etc.]. Please feel free to go out there any time you need a cigarette."

If you do permit smoking but have as a guest a careless or sloppy smoker, it is your right to hand him or her an ashtray, with a smile, saying, "Let me give you this," if you see he or she is about to flick ashes onto your great grandmother's porcelain ornamental plate or into your favorite potted palm.

The sensible solution is to see that there is an ashtray within reach of any smokers from the start.

Public Displays of Affection

Lovemaking is a personal matter that does not belong in public. Displays of affection or attraction are often embarrassing to others, are not appropriate in the presence of children, and belong in a private setting.

Holding hands, affectionate greetings accompanied by a kiss on the cheek, or a quick hug are perfectly acceptable in public. Passion is not.

GOOD NEIGHBORLINESS

Again, as in all other aspects of etiquette, the Golden Rule is the guiding one when it comes to thoughtful, cooperative living. Just as you do not want to hear your neighbors arguing, they do not want to hear you. Just as you would be appalled to hear someone talking about your financial difficulties, another would be hurt to hear you gossiping about her's. The closer the quarters, the smaller the town, the more involved we are in the lives of others—the more important it is to practice, at all times, the art of good neighborliness.

Apartment Living

Consideration of others is essential for apartment dwellers since sounds made by one family can often be heard by several others. Children's play may not seem overly loud when you are in the same room with them, nor does the radio or television set when we are engrossed in the program. But to the family living on the floor below, the patter of little feet sounds like a herd of antelope. The theme from "Sesame Street" crashes through each convolution of a tired neighbor's brain. As for a musician's practicing—what manager of an apartment house has not been at his wits' end to solve this cause of complaint?

There are certain annoyances that can't be helped: Babies must sometimes cry, children scream, dogs bark, or someone gets a hacking cough. The best that considerate people can do is try to soften such sounds as much as possible by shutting a window temporarily and by trying to train both children and pets.

In nearly all apartment buildings there are always those who seem to have no feelings for others because their own sensitivity is on another wavelength. We must keep in mind that there can be sounds that greatly annoy some people—the unceasing sound of a television set, for example, or a stereo—but that do not disturb others at all, whereas some of the things that we don't mind can quite possibly be unbearable to our neighbors. Only by being aware of this, and doing our best to minimize these irritations, can we make apartment living bearable.

When an annoyance or problem is on-going and unresolved, you should first knock on your neighbor's door and ask if he could please, for example, lower his television after 10 or 11 P.M., or ask his children to wear slippers or rubber-soled shoes when running through the apartment. If he does not respond to this request, give him one more chance, adding that you fear you will have to complain to the building manager, superintendent, or co-op board if the noise continues. And then do so. You should never do this if it is noise that is a part of daily living—only if it is an extreme intrusion that could be resolved by thoughtful behavior.

Should anyone make the same request of you, you should immediately take steps to cooperate, to the best of your ability. If a neighbor, for example, complains about your piano playing at 10 P.M., ask him what time would be more convenient for him for you to practice, and do your best to respect this.

If you are planning a party, it is not only considerate but also smart to alert your immediate neighbors, assuring them that you plan to lower the noise level by 11 P.M., or whatever the outside time of your local "noise" ordinance, so that they do not immediately complain about you.

Around the Neighborhood

The fact that two families live close to each other does not mean that each should be included in all the other's activities. It is important to recognize that your neighbors have other friends, other commitments, and other things that they like to do, and you should not expect to be included in all their entertainments and activities—nor should you try to involve them in all of yours.

Privacy is essential too. Good neighbors do not pry, do not push, and in no way invade the other's privacy.

To be able to live in close proximity with others, you must have tolerance. Perhaps your neighbors are members of another religion, a different nationality, or come from different surroundings. They will do things differently, and you must accept, and teach your children to accept, their ways. You can learn a great deal from people with different backgrounds if you have an open mind and are willing to study rather than criticize.

There will inevitably be irritations—the neighbor who constantly borrows a cup of sugar, or drops in every morning when you are busiest, or runs the power mower at seven o'clock on Sunday mornings when you are trying to sleep. Don't let these annoyances blow up out of all proportion. Tell your friends how you feel about them. Nine times out of ten, they won't have realized that they were bothering you and will be happy to call before dropping in, or to mow the lawn in the evening. It is all a matter of give-and-take, and remember, the neighbor who upsets you by a trivial act today may be the one who takes care of the kids when you are sick in bed tomorrow.

Impositions

Sometimes neighbors impose on your good nature or good will. My readers have written to me about such situations as neighbors who regularly parked their car directly across the street from their driveway, or so close to the edge that they could not easily get their own car in or out; and about neighbors who imposed on their fields of expertise—an accountant who was expected to give free tax advice—a doctor who was called to check the cause of earaches or to dispense antibiotics.

In these instances, before taking drastic action, keep tempers under control and talk to your neighbors. If someone is regularly invading your space or throwing his grass clippings on your property, for example, ask him over for a cup of coffee or a drink and discuss your concerns rationally. Whether his child is setting off firecrackers every day during your baby's nap time or he is blocking your driveway, he may not even realize he is causing you a problem. Only if he refuses to change his behavior or ignores your request for cooperation should you even consider calling the police or making an official complaint. The same is true for a neighbor whose pack rat instincts or hazardous practices threaten your safety. If your neighbor has a trash heap in his yard, or stores flammable materials in an unsafe way, ask him to clean up before going to your town's sanitary officers. If he doesn't, then you have to report him.

In the case of neighbors who impose on your professional abilities or personal time, you must simply, and gently, refuse. Respect for another's privacy is a cardinal principle of etiquette. The professional person, like any other, needs to escape from business, and common courtesy demands that he or she be allowed to enjoy leisure hours without constant requests for professional advice or performance. If it is just too difficult to refuse on these grounds, say, "My partner [accountant, attorney] has said that I must only advise [consult, provide services] during regular hours and for the fees established by our practice—I'm really sorry I can't help you off-hours, but I have to abide by the terms of our agreement."

It also should be remembered that people with specialties in various fields have other interests. Many doctors I know become social hermits just because they can't go to a cocktail party or other casual gathering without being accosted by people describing their ailments or asking them for advice. Even discussing the weather is a relief to them. Save your questions for your own physician, accountant or attorney and give your friend or neighbor a break.

Neighborhood Children

While it is lovely to be in a neighborhood filled with children, situations arise that call for diplomacy for their resolution. One such situation involved neighborhood children using a neighbor's property as a shortcut to school. She didn't mind their cutting through, but was dismayed by the fact that they left litter in her yard. She resolved the problem with no confrontation by placing a trash can at both ends of her yard with a funny reminder sign, and asked the children to respect not only her yard but the environment, as well, by using it for their debris.

Another woman who was not amenable to having her yard used as the neighborhood shortcut, made the effort to be outside at the times that the gang came through. The first day she was very friendly, asking how their families were, and mentioned that she was sorry, but that her yard was not a public thoroughfare. The second day she said, "I am sorry, but you can't cut through here anymore. Say hi to your mom for me . . ." Her subtlety and tact got the message across with no need for a confrontation with the parents of the children or a fence.

Had she not been so fortunate in the positive response she received, she would have had to call the children's parents and request their intervention.

When a child harms something on your property, whether a flower garden or a window, it would be hoped that he or she would promptly let you know, apologize, and offer to pay for the damage. If this doesn't happen, however, you should call his or her parents and explain, requesting that they make whatever repairs are necessary.

On Borrowing

"Neither a borrower nor a lender be" is a safe rule for neighbors. Unless you want to lend an appliance to a friend you know will take good care of it, you need not do so. If you refuse firmly, pleasantly, and consistently, neighbors will soon give up asking. To keep things amicable, try to soften your refusal with a logical excuse: "I'll be needing it myself tonight," or "I promised to let my daughter use it this weekend," etc.

New Neighbors

When new neighbors move in, don't hesitate for a minute about welcoming them. DO IT. When you see that they have arrived, or perhaps when the moving van leaves, go over with a casserole prepared for their dinner. They will be tired, dirty, and will not only be unprepared to cook a meal, but will probably not feel like getting dressed up to go out. I know of nothing that can get you off to a better start with new neighbors than to greet them with dinner—and a pot of coffee if you wish—in hand.

Swimming Pools

As anyone who has one can tell you, the luxury of an at-home swimming pool has attached to it many costs beyond that of pool upkeep. This is the expense of entertaining friends and neighbors.

Anyone invited to enjoy a friend's pool should bring his or her own towels. Most hosts and hostesses keep a supply on hand, as well as an extra swimsuit or two, but the work of laundering and providing towels for guests can be extensive and the thoughtful guest keeps this in mind.

Children's pool parties, even those of teens, should be supervised. Water accidents do happen and few children are equipped to handle them competently.

The problem of neighborhood children who would love to be able to swim in your pool can be handled beautifully by installing a small flagpole at the gate to the pool. Tell the children, or adult neighbors, for that matter, that they are invited to swim whenever the flag is raised. This means that an adult will be there to supervise. When you have guests, or simply want the pool to yourselves, keep the flag down and the neighborhood will know that it is "off-limits" time.

If you find, in your hospitality, that you are providing refreshments as well as swimming privileges to the neighborhood on a regular basis, tell them, quite firmly, that although you'd love to, you cannot go on providing snacks and drinks. You might suggest that if they make their visits B.Y.O.B. parties, you will provide chips or another simple snack. Close neighbors, in return for your hospitality, should, from time to time, bring sandwiches for the group and help you out by offering soft drinks, beer, or iced tea. Pools are great fun to have, but you must stand firm in some ways, or thoughtless neighbors will immediately impose on you.

When You Have Pets

A dog may be man's best friend and a cat by the hearth a very cozy sight, but their owners are responsible for seeing that they behave in such a way as to make them the real friends of everyone with whom they come in contact. Pets other than dogs and cats may be fewer in number, but their good manners are just as important. And if your children's rabbit or hamster cannot be trained not to make a nuisance of itself, *your* good manners take over, and you must insist that it be kept in its pen when visitors are in the house.

When company comes, unless you know they are absolutely devoted to Fido or Fluffy, it is preferable that animals are put in another room or outside. Although these pets may be important members of your family, no one else is going to think they are as cute as you do. A dog circling the dinner table and begging is not only annoying but also may be offensive to some guests, and a cat, shedding hair, jumping into a guest's lap may be both startling and unwelcome.

When you visit, unless the invitation specifically includes your pets, leave them home and arrange for a neighbor to care for them or board them in a kennel.

Leash laws are common in many areas and should be observed. If a loose dog is bothering you or even attacking you when you are walking your own dog, and you know who the dog's owner is, you will avoid an unpleasant situation by telling your neighbor and asking him to keep the dog at home before reporting him to authorities.

Many towns have "pooper scooper" ordinances, which should be respected. It is only good manners to clean up after your dog.

Cats present similar problems, lurking under neighboring bird feeders, munching on tulips, or digging in gardens. If your cat is guilty of these offenses, expect to hear about it or to receive a cold shoulder from neighbors. It is really required, should this occur, that you keep the cat indoors. If yours is the property under siege, you certainly may call the owner to complain. Often something as simple as a bell around the cat's neck keeps birds safe, and a penned-in area, for dogs or cats, keeps digging an at-home activity.

If you are a visitor who has an allergy or an aversion to pets, it is only sensible that you tell your host or hostess. No one would wish you to suffer while you are a guest in his or her house, and a few words can usually prevent much discomfort and possibly an unpleasant misunderstanding.

On the other hand, if you love animals, you should respect their training and not feed them table scraps or thump the couch cushions inviting them to jump up beside you without first asking if it is all right to do so.

At Public Beaches, Parks and Playgrounds

Guidelines for behavior at public places of recreation are simple:

Don't crowd others
Supervise your children
Clean up after yourself
Confine noise to your own space, including radios

No sunbather is charmed to have sand kicked on him by the feet of running children, nor to have icy water splashed on his back from the bucket of a child busy carrying it to the moat surrounding her sand castle. Logic dictates that families with children sit as close to the water as is possible to avoid these occurrences.

In parks and playgrounds, don't spread your picnic baskets and personal belongings over two or three tables when your share is one.

Help your children learn to take turns on playground equipment, and intervene on their behalf when others don't follow this practice. Don't, however, demand that they share their toys with strangers. I would bet that the last time you got a new lawnmower, your husband or wife did not insist that you share it with your next door neighbor. By the same token, do not insist that another child share with your child, and if you see your toddler helping himself to another's toys, firmly insist that he give it right back.

And it cannot be said too many times, leave public grounds as clean as or cleaner than you found them. If each of us did his share by picking up his own mess, *and one item more*, our countryside would soon regain the beauty it has, in many places, lost.

Public Cleanliness

The subject is not a pleasant one, but no one can be unaware of the increasing messiness (at times actual filthiness) of the lounges and powder and dressing rooms of hotels, theaters, and movie houses. As for such places as waiting rooms in railroad and airline terminals and rest rooms in overcrowded department stores or sports stadiums, the problem is becoming overwhelming!

Discarders of food containers and newspapers have always been conspicuous offenders, and the gum-scatterers have ranked with the graffiti artists in doing permanent damage. But in former years their destructiveness was held in check by employees whose present scarcity makes the orderliness of these places the responsibility of the public—in other words, each one of us.

In writing this, there are certain persons to whom I want to make a special appeal. At one extreme there are those who are really untidy. We all know people who throw ashes no matter where, set wet tumblers down on no matter what, drop wet raincoats on the nearest upholstered chair, and burn table edges with forgotten cigarettes. Women shake face powder on whatever is near them and leave hairs in the sink. Their behavior suggests that in their own homes they would not object if their beds were never made! In other words those who live in disorder can hardly be keenly aware of the disorder they make others endure.

In the second group are those who are careless because they take it for granted that someone will come along after them with dustpan and brush. These people, if made to realize there is no one other than themselves to tidy up, would ordinarily be more careful.

If only all of us who care about our surroundings would become sufficiently conscious of our obligation to act as deputy wardens, the situation would be improved. In short, instead of refraining from showing criticism of others, it is sometimes our obligation to do what we have been trained not to do—frankly to correct them. For example, when a woman tosses a used paper towel at a receptacle and leaves it lying on the floor when it misses its mark, suggest that she make more effort by picking it up yourself, saying, "Didn't you notice that you missed the basket?" It would help, perhaps, if the signs seen in many rest rooms saying: PLEASE LEAVE THIS REST ROOM AS YOU FOUND IT, read, instead: PLEASE LEAVE THIS REST ROOM CLEANER THAN YOU FOUND IT. But signs seem to do little good. Having an attendant on duty seems to be the greatest help—people apparently take a little more care if they feel they are being watched. This is a sad commentary, but in the case of rest rooms—true!

Familiar and troublesome to all who have the care of public places is the discarding of chewing gum. I was told by a railroad official that the chewing gum ground into the marble floor of a crowded terminal meant hours of scraping that cost the building maintenance department a small fortune.

Perhaps the most flagrant examples of sheer thoughtlessness are the people who carelessly throw all manner of trash into toilets. In washrooms that have no attendants conditions are sometimes so bad that there is no answer other than a locked door. The owner of a department store was forced to hang a large sign on the door to the customers' rest room that read: THIS WASHROOM CAN REMAIN OPEN FOR YOUR CONVENIENCE ONLY FOR SO LONG AS YOU COOPERATE IN HELPING TO KEEP IT IN ORDER.

Every city has the same problem in keeping its streets clean. All the campaigns, the special "Keep Our City Clean" weeks, the signs, the trash cans on corners, and the fines imposed for littering fail to solve the problem completely. As in the public washroom it is the duty of each and every one of us to take pride in keeping our cities and towns places of cleanliness and beauty and to impress others with the importance of the problem.

Consideration For Those Who Serve You

Only the lowest type of boor is rude to or inconsiderate of the people who serve him in restaurants, stores, or any public places. It can safely be said that this sort of discourtesy is a sure sign of insecurity. Those who have self-confidence do not need to act in that way in an effort to prove themselves superior. Good manners and thoughtfulness are so much a part of their nature that they treat everyone they come in contact with with the same courtesy, whether there is anything to be gained by doing so or not.

Accordingly, it is insufferable to snap your fingers for the attention of waiters or waitresses, make unreasonable demands of flight attendants, or be rude to anyone, whether a food server in a fast food restaurant or a gas station attendant, just because you aren't being served as fast as you would like to be. Naturally, rudeness or insubordination on their part should be reported to the manager, just as superb service should be remembered or commended. But very often it is someone else along the line who is responsible for delays and it is not only poor manners but also unfair to take out your displeasure on someone whose fault it most likely is not.

Another form of inconsideration is shown by people who go shopping ten minutes before closing time. The sales people have had a long day and have routine chores to do before they leave. The same is true of restaurant personnel who want to go home but cannot because of customers who linger well beyond closing time.

Is the customer always right? It would not seem likely. Unfailing patience and good temper are required of everyone in a service occupation, whereas there is nothing to restrain the ill humor or unreasonableness of a customer—except his or her own good manners.

Consideration for Strangers

Whether on the road or going through a door, respecting the rights and sensitivity of others, even total strangers, is part of what civilized behavior entails.

When in the checkout line at the supermarket, unless you are in a raging hurry, it is courteous to let the person behind you who has only three items go ahead of you and your loaded cart. You only need do this once, however, for to let everyone who is purchasing less than you go first could leave you in line for hours! It is also extremely discourteous to try to go through the Express lanes when you have more than the "10 items or less" in your basket.

After leaving and locking your car, return the grocery cart to the shopping cart station or the store entrance. Shoving it over into another parking space is inconsiderate to someone else who needs to park his car, too.

When driving, don't block intersections or entrances or exits to driveways or side roads when waiting for a traffic light or in a traffic jam. If someone is waiting to exit a side road when traffic is at a standstill, let him into the flow of traffic—don't belligerently inch your car ahead, forbidding them entry.

Dealing With Prejudice

We still hear the voice of prejudice from time to time—ethnic jokes, name calling, sweeping generalizations. What do you do upon finding yourself in such a situation?

If alone, you should feel no need to laugh or silently support such a display of poor taste. You may quietly say, "I don't go along with what you're saying," or "I don't like jokes that belittle people." If you prefer, you may simply get up and take your leave.

If, however, you have with you friends of a minority group about whom the jokes and slurs are being made, your situation is embarrassing. Try to change the conversation if you can. If you cannot, avoid the urge to rise to the defense; it might evoke an onslaught even more embarrassing to your friends. Keep your silence. Break away as soon as possible and apologize to them profusely in private.

If you yourself belong to a minority group under attack, you have two courses. One, you can ignore it, registering in your mind that these are people to be avoided in the future. Or two, you can teach them a lesson that may temper their prejudice in the future. Just say, "You must be talking about me. I'm a [whatever it is]." Their shocked embarrassment will be almost as rewarding as their limp efforts to make amends.

Courtesies Toward Those With Handicaps

It is probably true that a majority of the people in the world have little contact with those unfortunate persons who are handicapped or disabled. If we have a handicapped person in our homes, or in the home of a relative or friend, we quickly become accustomed to the situation and learn how to act so as to be most helpful. Should the disabled person be a member of our own family, we make every effort to learn all that we can about his or her problem, to seek professional advice, and to make family life as normal as possible. This section, therefore, is devoted to people who meet the handicapped only from time to time and who, in making an effort to be helpful, may go about it in the wrong way, through a lack of knowledge. Their intentions may be the very best, but an act of kindness tendered in the wrong way may be a cause of much embarrassment and even actual harm to the very person they are trying to help.

There are certain rules that apply to your behavior in regard to all handicapped people, and by far the most important is this: NEVER stare or indicate that you are conscious that the person is different from others in any way. People who are getting themselves about in wheelchairs, who have mastered the use of crutch or brace, or who can manipulate a mechanical hand dexterously take great pride in their independence and approach to normalcy. The last thing they wish is to be reminded by curious or overly solicitous persons that they have not achieved their goal. An offer of help to a man in a wheelchair who must navigate a steep curb in order to cross the street, or an arm proffered to a woman with a cane and a leg brace who is trying to get down a railless set of steps is, of course, in order. But before grabbing the wheelchair or seizing an arm, ask politely if, and in what way, you can be of assistance.

Another important rule is never to make personal remarks or ask personal questions of one with an obvious disability. If the disabled person wishes to talk about the accident that caused it or discuss the condition, let him or her introduce the subject, but never, never pry into feelings or clinical symptoms—subjects that disabled people may be doing their best to forget.

Deafness and Hearing Loss

There are, of course, all degrees of deafness, from partial loss of hearing in one ear to the more unusual extreme of complete deafness, which cannot be helped even by a hearing aid. It may only be necessary to speak a little more distinctly to one who is partially deaf or to repeat a remark that may have been missed. If you know that the hearing loss is in one ear, it is considerate to sit on the side of the good ear in movies, restaurants, or any other place where you may not be face to face. In the case of total hearing loss, the only means of contact is visual—through lip-reading—so the rules are quite different from those applying to someone with partial hearing.

You must speak distinctly and reasonably slowly. Don't use exaggerated mouth movements. Distorted lip motions may be confusing since those who have been taught to lip-read can read normal lip movement.

It is useless to shout to attract the person's attention. If he or she is not facing you, a gentle tap on the arm or shoulder will do. Be patient while talking and be willing to repeat or make your statement in words that are easier to understand.

Encourage participation in family and social activities. Persons with severe handicaps tend to withdraw into themselves; this is not good for them and upsets their family and friends. A little extra urging and enthusiasm over their presence can make the handicapped feel much more like leading a normal life. On the other hand, try to be sensitive to their reactions, because too much pressure can have the opposite effect from that desired.

Between the slightly deaf and the totally deaf fall the many thousands with intermediate degrees of the disability. The first thing to be recommended for them is that they wear a hearing aid. There is no more stigma or embarrassment in this than in wearing glasses, and the family and friends of the hard-of-hearing who are reluctant should do their best to encourage them to overcome their hesitation. Once persuaded, they will find that their life will attain a normality they never thought possible. Here are some rules that should be observed for conversation with those who suffer from some degree of hearing loss:

Don't raise your voice or shout—hearing aids are usually adjusted to the normal tone of voice.

Call the person by name to attract his or her attention.

As with the more severely handicapped, be patient—willing to repeat if necessary. And if you must repeat, don't shout or appear annoyed. This will only embarrass him or her and make understanding harder.

Don't exclude the hard-of-hearing person from conversation, but make sure that he or she can see you or the group. Even normal people read lips unconsciously, and seeing your lips is a great help to one handicapped by some hearing loss.

If you are one of those handicapped by deafness, a few of the following suggestions may add to your comfort and that of your friends:

DO wear a hearing aid—they are now made in such a way as to be almost invisible, and even if they weren't, loss of hearing is no more "shameful" than loss of sight, and few people refuse to wear glasses.

Having gotten a hearing aid, use it! A strained expression of concentration, a constant "What did you say?" and answers that make no sense may cause you to appear inattentive or stupid. Keep your hearing aid turned on and gain the admiration of your friends for so capably overcoming your handicap.

With or without your aid, do listen attentively and concentrate on what people are saying. Even people with normal hearing miss many remarks through inattention.

Look at the people talking to you—their expression and their lips will help you to "hear" them.

Don't take advantage of your impairment by trying to arouse sympathy. There is no justifiable reason for sympathy—with a little extra effort a deaf person can lead a perfectly normal life.

Blindness

The most important thing to remember when coming in contact with someone handicapped by blindness is that in every other respect this person is probably exactly like you. Blind people's other faculties are in no way impaired, and compensating for this handicap, these faculties may in fact be more sensitively developed than yours. A blind person certainly has a problem to overcome that a sighted person does not face, but it is a problem with which one can learn to live, and most blind people have done so with considerable success.

Therefore the cardinal rule is this: Treat the blind person as you would anyone else. When talking, use a normal voice and talk about the same subjects that would interest your other friends, including blindness, if it should come up. Don't avoid the use of the word *see*. A blind person uses it as much as anyone else. There is no reason to show surprise at his or her ability to dial telephone numbers, light cigarettes, get dressed, or perform any of the other daily chores that we all do. A blind person has simply made a little more effort to learn to do them by touch or sound.

Aside from your attitude, there are several specific suggestions that will make your contacts with a blind person more pleasurable to you both.

When you are with, or pass by, a blind person on a street corner, you are perfectly correct in asking if you can help him or her to cross; but never grasp his arm or try to give assistance without first asking whether it is desired. If the blind person wants help, let him or her take *your* arm, which will give this person far more confidence than being propelled forward by you. If you should be asked for directions, be sure to use left and right from the blind person's viewpoint—the direction he or she is facing.

If you go to a restaurant with a blind person, do not hesitate to read the menu out loud, including the prices if the occasion demands. You certainly may quietly

indicate where the salt and pepper are and help with the sugar and cream. You may
explain how the items on the plate are arranged and help cut the meat if necessary. But much of this he or she will prefer to do unaided.

When a blind person visits your home lead him or her to a chair and then just place his or her hand on the arm or back. If this person is staying with you for any length of time, remember to indicate where the furniture is and if anything is rearranged. Keep doors completely—never halfway—open or closed.

When taking a blind person to a strange place, tell him or her quietly where the furniture is located and who is present. And before you leave your blind guest alone, be sure that there is someone to talk to. One thing a blind person cannot do (unless there are good friends whose voices are recognizable) is single out a person who would, from appearance, be congenial.

When there is a blind person in a room you have just entered, make your presence known and if he or she does not recognize your voice, introduce yourself. When ready to leave, say "I'm leaving now," so he or she will not be left talking to no one.

Last of all, if the blind person has a guide dog, do not attempt to play with or distract the dog in any way. Its attention must remain fully on its master, whose safety and well-being may depend entirely on its strict adherence to its training.

Loss or Paralysis of a Limb

While loss or paralysis of a leg is a tragic thing, it does not necessarily affect the handicapped person's relationship to others. Those in a wheelchair may need help in certain situations, but if they walk on crutches or have an artificial leg they undoubtedly lead a reasonably "normal" life with just a few limitations—which may not even be obvious to those around them.

Loss or paralysis of an arm is in some ways more difficult. If the arm is paralyzed, it may not be obvious, and the handicapped person suffers agonies of embarrassment thinking that people may expect help with heavy packages, or performing other such deeds. A person to whom this happens should say "I'm sorry, I can't help you—I've got a bad arm."

Perhaps the most common difficulty occurs when someone who has lost a right hand, or has an artificial one, is introduced to someone else. What to do next is up to the injured person; he or she may simply smile and say "Hello" without offering a hand, may offer an artificial right hand, or may offer the "good" left hand.

The person being introduced lets the handicapped person take the lead. If the latter offers the left hand, the other takes it with *his* left, which is less awkward than using the right. If an artificial hand is offered, naturally the other person would shake it as he or she ordinarily would—saying nothing and showing no surprise, if possible.

If by chance the nonhandicapped person does *not* notice and offers his or her own right hand first, the handicapped person takes it with his or her left, rather than leave the other standing awkwardly, hand extended in the air.

When Calling or Visiting

Visits to friends, acquaintances, and even relative strangers range from spontaneous, very informal "drop-in" visits to formal calls, with their own protocol and etiquette. Whatever the degree of formality, both visitor and host are anxious that things go smoothly. The following guidelines help ensure a degree of comfortableness for both the visitor and the one being visited.

There is really no need to discuss casual visits between very close friends, where the only etiquette involved is that they be considerate of each other, and that they never abuse the special bond of their friendship.

Beyond the close relationship of good friends, there are a few general guidelines for both visitors and those being visited:

Whether close friends or not, it is the height of thoughtlessness for people with colds or other infectious illnesses to drop in on friends. No matter how bored one is with staying home alone with a cold or cough, home is indeed where one must stay. If you're home sick and desire companionship, telephone someone you haven't seen in a while; it will make you both feel better.

When entering anyone's home, always use the doormat to wipe your feet. If a hostess sees that a guest is not going to do this and the day is a rainy one, she may say, "Would you mind giving your shoes an extra wipe? I've just had the rug cleaned," or "I've just waxed the hall," or whatever is appropriate. Some hostesses today go so far as to ask their visitors to remove their shoes, a request that is offensive to many. If you are one of these hostesses, and you do not permit shoes in your house, then you should consider providing paper slippers for your guests who are embarrassed by the request—whether because they have a hole in their socks that they thought no one would know about, or simply because they are not comfortable without their shoes.

A host has the right to protect his possessions and can do so without seeming obsessive or rude. If your table tops cannot withstand a glass being placed upon them, be sure to have coasters out. If it appears as though a guest is not intending to use the coaster, offer it to her saying, "would you mind using a coaster? This table stains so quickly."

If guests practice the habit of tucking their feet under themselves while sitting on upholstered furniture, there is not much you can do. If they are good friends, however, you may say, "why don't you kick off your shoes? I'm trying to keep that chair from having to be recovered for awhile."

Naturally, a guest, whether a close friend or a more casual acquaintance, does not snoop. It is very rude to tour through someone's house uninvited to do so. Should this happen to you, sit down and ask your visitor to sit down, too. If she asks to see your house, say, "Sorry, it's not in shape today—another time." Surely she won't have the gall to snoop by herself while you remain seated!

A hostess should have guest towels hanging in plain view. Many people hesitate to use a linen hand towel, thinking they are decorative only. Terry hand towels are somehow more reassuring, as are a small stack of paper hand towels which can be thrown into a wastebasket afterward. If linen or terry hand towels are what is provided, a guest should replace the towel she uses on the rack, unfolded, so that it is obvious that it has been used.

It is courteous to offer refreshment to guests, even when they are unexpected; it is not appropriate for a guest to ask to be fed. Of course, if you are absolutely parched, you may certainly say, "Would you mind if I got myself a glass of water? I'm suddenly very thirsty!" You should not request any other specific beverage, such as coffee or a soft drink.

When a host says only, "What would you like to drink?" a guest may say, "What are you offering?" A host should not say, "Would you like something to drink [eat, etc.] since most guests say, "Oh, no thank you," feeling uncomfortable saying "Yes, indeed!" It is easier for a guest to respond to, "Would you like coffee or do you prefer tea," or "We have lemonade and iced tea, which may I get you?"

The Unexpected Visitor

No one, with the exception of closest friends and immediate family, should ever be an "unexpected visitor." (In military circles, since the hours for calls are strictly prescribed, the callers are always welcome.) While occasionally an unannounced "drop-in" works out well, more often it is most inconvenient to the one visited. He or she may have previous plans, may not be feeling well, may be in the middle of preparing dinner, or may simply be resting or relaxing. The sight of an eager visitor at the door, ready for an hour or two of conversation, is rarely an undiluted pleasure.

Therefore do not make a visit without making your intentions known, and agree to a time convenient for both of you. It may be done by a telephone call, or if you live some distance away, by a note. In the latter case it should be written far enough in advance so that there is time for a reply. It should not say, "We are coming on Saturday, etc.," but rather, "If you and John are free Saturday, may we drop by . . . ?"

When you are on the receiving end of one of these unannounced visits you have every right to carry on with any previous plans you might have made. If Aunt Mary arrives unexpectedly from three hundred miles away, and you had been planning to go to a church supper, you might suggest that she go along with you. If, however, you are expected at the Petersons' for bridge, you simply ask her to make herself at home until your return. You should, if possible, find something in the refrigerator or the cupboard that will serve as a snack or light meal. But you need not make yourself late for your appointment by taking the time to prepare a full dinner, although you should get out the ingredients for her if she wishes to do so herself.

When the visitor is a friend or acquaintance from nearby, you merely say quite frankly, "I'm terribly sorry, but we were just leaving for the theater. Could you come back another time?" *And make the future date definite then and there.* "Another time" left at that means little, but a firm invitation proves that you would really enjoy a visit at a more convenient moment. If your earlier plans were such that they could be carried out on another day, it would, of course, be more polite to postpone them and stay at home with your visitor.

If by chance you are just about to start your dinner when a couple drop in, you must try to make the meal stretch to include them. If they say, "Oh, no thank you— we've just eaten," pull up a chair for them, offer them a cup of coffee or a cold drink, and ask their forgiveness while you finish your meal. No one who drops in unannounced can expect you to postpone your meal and let it get cold while you visit or to produce two more portions unexpectedly.

Into everyone's life at some point comes a friend or neighbor who thinks nothing of walking right in without knocking. You may not mind, but your husband or wife might, feeling that he or she has no privacy, even in his or her own home. A cordial way to deal with this is to say, "We love to have you drop in, but you've startled John a few times, so would you mind giving us a warning knock?" Or you might lock your doors for a week or two, explaining, if asked, that you are nervous about leaving the house open.

Television and Guests

Whether a visit is between best friends or more casual acquaintances, the television should never be the third member of the party, unless it is part of the original invitation. If your friend suggests renting a video and watching it together, or getting together to watch a football or basketball game, then it is understood from the beginning that the focus will not be on conversation.

When friends walk in uninvited, however, and you are right in the middle of a movie or program in which you have already invested time, you may properly say, "We're watching a great movie [the second half of the hockey game, etc.], will you join us—and then when it's over we can visit?" Since the visitors were unexpected, they should not expect you to give up what you were enjoying to entertain them. If you have a VCR, of course you may ask them to wait a minute while you find a tape to record the end of the program and watch it later so you can visit with them.

When someone drops by to visit one half of a couple, or one member of a household, everyone else does not need to drop what he or she is doing and entertain the guest. Each person in the room should, of course, greet the friend, chat for a few minutes, and then may excuse him or herself to return to a television program, housework or whatever. If it is a television program that is being interrupted, the guest and his or her friend should have the courtesy to go to another room so that everyone else is not disturbed by their conversation.

Visiting With Children

Unless they are specifically invited it is best, if possible, to leave children—and pets—home when you visit friends. This is not always practical, however, and couples with young children should think carefully about their visiting manners.

People who know that they will have young visitors from time to time—whether children of friends, nieces, nephews, or grandchildren—make preparations in advance. They remove breakable articles and those which might be dangerous from low tables. They shut the doors to rooms they wish to make "off limits," and they see that doors to cellar steps and low windows are tightly closed. Then, when safety precautions are taken care of, they check the supply of recreational materials. A basket or sack of simple toys—coloring books, blocks and comic books; or if you have a VCR rent a children's videotape—goes a long way toward making the visit enjoyable for both parent and host. And of course these same clever people have a supply of cookies and milk or soft drinks ready to fill in when the novelty of the toys wears off.

Parents can make their children welcome guests in many ways. Toddlers should not be taken on visits until they learn the meaning of "No." Parents also may bring a basket of favorite toys to keep a child occupied. And above all, parents should set a time limit for the visit, knowing that no toddler has a very long span of attention. It is best that the visit end before that limit is reached.

When you are not sure whether an invitation includes your children, ask. "Is this invitation adults only, or are the children included?" If this is too difficult, say, "We'd love to come, but I have to see if I can get a sitter. I'll call you back tomorrow and let you know for sure." They can then reply, "Oh, no, please bring the children," if they intended for them to be included.

Calling on a Friend Who Is Hospitalized

We all find a time in our lives when we must go to a hospital when members of our families or our close friends are ill. The same general rules apply to visiting a sick person at home, although if he or she is well on the way to recovery they may be slightly relaxed.

The whole routine of a hospital is highly organized and kept in smooth running order by the medical staff. When visiting a friend in the hospital you should try to make your presence there fit into an orderly pattern so that the hospital's staff can do its best for the patients.

Far too often visitors are thoughtless and careless. One should think of the problems that a visitor makes under the busy, crowded hospital conditions of today.

Courtesy to nurses and the other hospital personnel, quietness of manner and approach in the hospital buildings, avoidance of asking for special attention from busy people, are obvious requirements—and above all, you must not act in any way that will be tiring or harmful to the patient you are visiting. Make your visit short and friendly, leave any small gift without fuss or any expectancy of more than a simple thank you for it. You should not engage the patient in long discussions or ask questions about his or her illness that properly are in the sphere of the doctor and the nurse or that the patient does not wish to talk about. Time your visits so that the patient becomes neither tired nor anxious and of course you must always follow the rules as they are given to us by the staff. A surgeon I know claims that visitors kill more patients than do operations, certainly an overstatement but one with more than a kernel of truth. Here are a few do's and don'ts that may be helpful for visitor and patient.

Don't bring as your gift foods such as chocolates or cakes that the patient may not be permitted to have.

Don't worry a patient about anything that you feel might be upsetting or disturbing. The fact that Bobby is failing algebra, or that someone smashed the window in the family car, is not news calculated to improve the mental outlook of the patient. In any case he or she can do nothing about these problems. The best thing you can do, if you wish to encourage a speedy return home, is to bring cheerful news and talk in a supporting way.

Remember that the average patient is not his or her normal self and the burden of good behavior is on your side, not the patient's. Those who are ill may show little enthusiasm for the things that usually interest them, or they may react overexcitedly to a minor incident. If this happens, simply tell yourself that this reaction is only temporary and change the subject to a safer one. But it is up to you to lead the way.

Don't overstay your welcome. Visit briefly, cheerfully, and leave the patient rested and encouraged. Make up your mind before you arrive that you will stay no more than fifteen or twenty minutes, and stick to it, no matter how much your friend may beg you to stay. If other visitors arrive while you are there, leave sooner so that they may have their share of the patient's time without overtiring him or her. Nothing is more exhausting to a person in bed than to have to try to follow a conversation among several people who may be seated on all sides of the room. If it is possible, when two or three people are present, stand or put your chairs on the same side of the bed.

If, possibly because of the shortage of nurses in many hospitals, the doctor or a member of the family asks you, as a close friend, to stay with the patient, do not let the patient feel that he or she must entertain you or even talk. Take a book along, attend to any simple things required, and settle yourself where he or she may know that you are there, but at the same time indicate that you are quite happy to have an hour or two in which to enjoy your book quietly.

Don't think that the hospital routine has been devised to bedevil you as a

visitor, or the patient. It is only part of a long-range plan carefully worked out to
serve everyone in the best way possible. Limited visiting hours, early meals, and rules governing smoking may seem unreasonable to you, but you must remember that they have not been made just for the benefit of your sister Maureen, who may have nothing more than a broken leg, but rather for the sicker patients, who without a carefully planned routine and the best possible conditions for rest and quiet might not recover at all.

Flowers

Flowers, according to Dr. George Jacobsen, former professor of psychiatry at the University of Miami Medical School, can be "good medicine" for people in hospitals. He says, "Sick people, especially those in hospitals, definitely respond to tender, loving care. Flowers mean that someone cares for them—that someone loves them. That's an important incentive to get better."

Whenever it is possible, bring flowers in their own container and let them be of a size that can easily be handled. Hospitals are invariably short of (or do not provide) containers, and it is an additional chore for the nurses to have to hunt for a suitable vase. Florists know this, and if you mention that your purchase is to go to a hospital, they will arrange the flowers in inexpensive (sometimes even disposable) containers at no additional charge.

Patients often prefer potted plants to cut flowers. They are easy to care for, last longer, and can be taken home by a member of the family if more space is needed for those that arrive at a later date. There they continue to give the patient many further moments of pleasure. Plants, as opposed to cut flowers, continue to live and thrive, and this, too, seems to encourage some patients who identify with the living plant and, therefore, with life.

Semiprivate Rooms and Wards

The number of private rooms in every hospital has been greatly decreased, partly because of the shortage of nurses, partly because they are too costly for most people, and partly because there always seems to be a need for more hospital beds than exist. The vast majority of hospital patients today find themselves in semiprivate rooms or large wards.

The rules governing visitors to these rooms must be stricter than those for visitors to patients in private rooms.

Voices must naturally be kept lower, not only for privacy's sake, but in order not to disturb the other sick people who may badly need their rest.

If you are going to the snack bar or restaurant to bring a dish of ice cream or a candy bar to your friend, it is only thoughtful to ask the other person in a semiprivate room if you can bring him or her anything at the same time. This would not be necessary in a larger ward, unless one of the patients actually asked you to do an errand for him.

If there is a television set in the room—and this rule applies between patients as well as visitor and patient—do not turn it on without asking the other's permission and asking about a choice of program. Unless the other patient shows real enthusiasm, keep the volume very low.

If another patient in a room wishes to rest, draw the curtains between the beds to afford as much privacy and quiet as possible. On the other hand, if the person you are visiting and his or her roommate have become friendly, including the other patient in the conversation and your visit will be doubly appreciated.

Calling on New Parents

When a new mother comes home from the hospital, relatives and friends are expected to call to see the baby. It is customary to take a gift at this time, although the present may also be sent later, after the visitor has had a chance to see what might be needed.

Prospective visitors should always call the mother to find out what time would be convenient. Not only is she busy with the feedings, baths, etc., at certain hours but she will also be able to suggest a time when the baby is apt to be awake.

Calling on a New Neighbor

When strangers move into an established neighborhood it is courteous and friendly of the residents nearby to call on them. The newcomers wait for old residents to issue the first "formal" invitation to a meal, but if contact has been established casually through gardening activities, through children, or in the laundry of an apartment house, the new arrival could further the acquaintance by suggesting the other's child come over to play, by inviting the neighbor to join her for coffee, or by asking advice on stores, doctors, etc. These openings may well lead to an invitation to dine at the older resident's home, after which the newcomer may reciprocate with any form of entertainment.

If you are planning to visit with a new neighbor, stop by first with a bouquet of flowers, a plate of cookies, or some other small welcoming gift. Because your arrival may be inconvenient, after introducing yourself say, "I'd love to come back and visit later this week, when you have time, but wanted to let you know how pleased we are that you have moved in and to give you our number in case you need any help or have any questions." Unless the new neighbor insists that you stay for awhile, make a date for a later, lengthier visit and depart.

If you are passing by before you have a chance to do this and your new neighbor is planting flowers or working outside, say "Hello—I'm Nancy Jones. I live in the brick house across the street."

The new neighbor says, "Hi, I'm glad to meet you." She may also invite you
into her house for a soda or a cup of coffee, and you sit for a few minutes and talk.

You need only stay for ten or fifteen minutes on this first visit, unless your hostess says, "Oh, do stay a little longer," or "Let's have another glass of iced tea." Then you may stay for a few minutes longer if you wish, or reply, "I'm sorry, but I can't today. Do come and see me soon!" She says, "Thanks, I'd love to," you both say, "Good-bye," and that's all.

Returning a First Visit

People who are old friends pay no attention to how often or how seldom one goes to see the other, unless there is an illness, a death, or a birth in the family. Nor do they ever consider whose turn it is to invite whom. But first visits should be returned with considerable punctuality—especially after a *first* invitation to lunch or dine. The casual "first visit" described above allows the newcomer to "drop in" on her neighbor but not to issue a formal invitation to lunch or dinner. To do that too soon makes the newcomer seem "pushy," and older residents may tend to resent being pushed into intimacy too quickly.

The House With a Maid

Today, when a maid who knows you opens the door, she simply says, "Please come in. Mrs. Franklin is in the living room"; and if you know the way, you walk in by yourself. Or she may say, "Mrs. Franklin is upstairs. I'll tell her you're here." If you are unfamiliar with the house, she should show you to the living room to wait while she takes the message. When the visitor is not known to the maid she says, "May I tell Mrs. Franklin who is calling?" and the guest simply gives her name.

If the person on whom you are calling is home and greets you herself, she obviously knows that you have made the effort to see her. If no one is home you may leave a note in her mailbox: "So sorry to have missed you, Joanne." If she does not know you well, you sign it "Joanne Green."

When the door is opened by a maid who tells you that Mrs. Franklin is not at home or cannot see you, you may ask for a pencil and paper and leave her a note or ask the maid to tell her that you have called.

The Visit Ends

When guests leave, it is courteous to escort them to their car, if you live in a house and they are parked in your driveway or in the street nearby, and to stay there until they drive off. If it is raining or cold, say good-bye at the door, leaving the door open if it isn't winter, until they reach their car, wave a last "good-bye" and then shut the door.

If you live in an apartment with an elevator, either escort your guests to the elevator, or wait at your open apartment door until the elevator arrives. Give a final wave and then shut your door when they enter the elevator.

IN PLACES OF WORSHIP

Whether attending a special ceremony or celebration in a church, temple or synagogue, or simply attending services; the basic guidelines for what to do are to respect the customs of that place of worship.

Behavior During Services

Reverence is the quality that guides one's behavior at all religious services, and while it is expressed in various ways, in most faiths quiet, attentiveness, and dignity are the ingredients.

It is perfectly correct to nod, smile, wave at acquaintances before a service starts, and if a friend sits down next to you or in front of you, you may certainly lean over and whisper "Hello." You should not, however, carry on a prolonged conversation, giggle, gossip, or otherwise make yourself objectionable to others around you. Introductions, too, should wait until after the service.

What to Wear

Although clothing restrictions for church have relaxed over the years, the correct dress is still conservative. Skirts or conservative pants and jackets are preferable to jeans or shorts for conventional church or synagogue services.

Hats are no longer required in any of the Christian churches, but in Orthodox Jewish synagogues married women are required to wear some form of head covering—even a wig. Many women still feel more at ease wearing a hat or veil at regular services, and older Catholic women, who grew up in the days when hats were required, rarely enter a church without at least a scarf over their heads. In any case it is *always* correct to wear a hat to church, and if you like to wear them and feel that they are becoming to you, by all means do so. Don't let the fact that you are in the minority make you uncomfortable.

Men *never* wear hats in Christian churches—they *always* do in orthodox synagogues.

Gloves are worn less often than they used to be and generally only when the weather is cold, but wearing them is always correct. In the past gloves were kept on all during the service—today they are removed. It is far easier to turn the pages of the hymnal or prayer book without gloves on, and in those faiths where the communion wafer is placed on the palm, gloves *must* be removed before going to the altar.

Where to Sit

When there are ushers at a service, all members of the congregation are escorted to a pew, although the women do not take the usher's arm as they do at a wedding. The usher leads the way to a vacant seat and stands aside while the arrival—whether single or a couple—steps in. Women precede their husbands into the pew, going in far enough to allow room for him—and for children or others who may be with them. Early arrivals at a wedding or first communion may keep the choice seats on the aisle so that they can see the proceedings, but at weekly services, those who are already in the pews should move over to make room for later arrivals, rather than force the newcomers to climb over them.

When a couple leaves their pew to go to the altar for communion, they need not "switch." The man steps out and walks to the communion rail; the woman follows. They return in whichever order is most practical.

The Offering

Although there is no fixed rule about it, a husband generally puts the offering into the plate for both himself and his wife. When a man takes a woman friend to his church he may or may not contribute for both of them, but when a woman asks a man to go to a service with her they generally each make a contribution.

Attending the Services of Another Faith

Unless some part of the service is opposed to your religious convictions you should attempt to follow the lead of the congregation. Stand when they stand, sing when they sing, pray when they pray. If there is a part in which you do not wish to participate, simply sit quietly until that portion of the service is over.

A Protestant need not cross himself or genuflect when entering a pew in a Catholic church. Nor must you kneel if your custom is to pray seated in the pew—just bend forward and bow your head. But insofar as the proceedings are not objectionable to you, you will get more from the service, and perhaps be more comfortable, if you do as the others are doing.

If you are receiving communion in a church that is strange to you, watch what the congregation does and follow their lead.

You should make a contribution when the offering plate is passed. Even though you have contributed your full share to your home parish your donation is a way of saying "Thank you" to the church you are visiting.

Changing Your Place of Worship

When you are changing from one parish to another or from a church of one faith to another, it is only courteous to inform the clergyman of your old church, or at least the parish secretary. In some denominations each parish is assessed according to the number of registered members, and therefore its financial condition can be harmed if a member who moves away is still enrolled but not contributing.

If your desire to make a change is due to the fact that you are not getting what you think you should from your particular faith, or perhaps your views are not compatible with those of the clergyman, your problem is more difficult. You owe him an explanation of your reasons for changing parishes, either by letter or in person. Although it may be difficult, try to be very honest and clear, because while he may be hurt or upset at the time, your criticisms and comments may help him to see some of his failings and to serve his congregation better.

*M*any a budding executive has been passed over for a promotion because his or her table manners were less than desirable, even though his job performance was exemplary. Whether she waved her fork in the air to make a point, or he talked with a mouth full of food, these were signs that this person would not make a good impression on clients, or would not fit in with the other senior types in the corporate dining room. Table manners should, as will be repeated below, be practiced whether alone or at dinner with family members. When always used in private, they will always be used in public.

5

Mealtime Manners

AT THE TABLE

Whether the mealtime table is in the kitchen at home or at the White House, good manners are part of what makes the experience pleasurable. Just because one is at home does not mean that sprawling posture, elbows akimbo, or talking with a full mouth are acceptable. We shouldn't save our best manners for the outside world anyway—surely the people with whom we live deserve our best efforts!

Mealtime, usually dinner time, is the hour of the day that a family can—and should make every effort to—get together. It is the time when children learn the basics of good manners—not only table manners, but consideration and the importance of courtesy toward one another, and conversational manners as well.

Your Posture

Ideal posture at the table is to sit straight, but not stiffly, leaning slightly against the back of the chair. Your hands, when you are not actually eating, may lie in your lap, which will automatically prevent you from fussing with implements, playing with bread crumbs, drawing on the tablecloth, and so forth. However, if you can't resist the temptation to fidget, you may rest your hands and wrists—but *not* your entire forearm—on the edge of the table, which may seem more comfortable and less stiff. Hands should also be kept away from the face, from nervous scratching, and from twisting or touching the hair.

For all we hear about "elbows *off* the table," there are some situations when elbows are not only permitted on the table but are actually necessary. This is true in restaurants where to make oneself heard above music or conversation, one must lean far forward. A woman is far more graceful leaning forward supported by her elbows than doubled forward over her hands in her lap as though she were in pain! *At home,* when there is no reason for leaning across the table, there is no reason for elbows. At a formal dinner, elbows may be on the table because again one has to lean forward in order to talk to a companion at a distance across the table. But even in these special situations elbows are *never* on the table *when one is eating.*

Slouching or slumping at the table is most unattractive too. Tipping one's chair—a most unfortunate habit—is unforgivable. It not only looks dreadfully sloppy, but is fatal to the back legs of the chair.

Grace Before Meals

Giving thanks before meals—saying grace—is done before the meal is begun. Some people remain standing for the grace, some are seated. Many people hold hands around the table, others fold their hands in their laps or on the edge of the table. Often families say a prayer together. Sometimes one person says the grace. If a minister or rabbi is present, he or she is always asked to give the blessing. Although it is well-intentioned to ask a guest to give the blessing, it may be embarrassing if he or she is not accustomed to doing so. It is more thoughtful not to put a guest on the spot unless you have warned him in advance. When dining in a restaurant with friends whom you know ordinarily say grace it is perfectly all right to do so, but if you are part of a group of people of mixed faiths you should refrain from saying grace.

There are a number of shorter and longer variations, but the following three are typical examples of prayers which could be offered before a meal:

> *Bless us, O Lord, and these Thy gifts, which we are about to receive from Thy bounty. Through Christ our Lord, Amen.*

> *For what we are about to receive, may the Lord make us truly thankful. Amen.*

> *Bless, O Lord, this food to our use, and us to Thy service. Make us ever mindful of the needs of others. Amen.*

The Napkin

Ordinarily, as soon as you are seated you put your napkin on your lap. At a formal dinner, however, you wait for your hostess to put hers on her lap first. It does not matter how you do it, so long as you do not give it a violent shake to open it up. You take it from the table, place it on your lap (if it is large enough, you may tuck a corner under you to keep it from sliding off, or if it is not, you arrange it as safely as you can), and unfold it as much as necessary with both hands.

A man should never tuck his napkin into his collar, his belt, or between the buttons of his shirt.

When using the napkin avoid wiping your mouth as if with a washcloth. Blotting or patting the lips is much more attractive.

When the meal is finished, or if you leave the table during the meal, put the napkin on the left side of your place, or if the plates have been removed, in the center. It should not be refolded, nor should it be crumpled up; rather it is laid on the table in loose folds so that it does not spread itself out. At a dinner party the hostess lays her napkin on the table as a signal that the meal is over, and the guests then lay their napkins on the table—not before.

If a family uses napkin rings, the napkins are refolded and placed in the rings and reused once or twice.

When To Start Eating

At a small table of two, four, or even six people, when the delay will not be sufficient to cause the food to become cold or the soufflé to fall, it is certainly polite to wait to start eating until all have been served. In this case the hostess should pick up her implement first, and the others follow suit.

If the group is larger, however, it is *not* necessary to wait until all have been served. The hostess, if she is at all aware of her guests' comfort, will say, as soon as the first two or three guests have their food, "Please start—your dinner will get cold if you wait," and the guests take her at her word and start immediately. If the hostess says nothing, and you realize that her attention has been devoted to serving or supervising, or that she has simply forgotten to say anything, it is not incorrect to pick up your spoon or fork after five or six people have been served. The others will soon follow your lead. At family meals, as Mother or Father fills and passes the plates, the children should say, "May I please begin?" if they are not old enough to be expected to wait until one or two adults have started.

"Please Pass the Jelly"

It is correct to reach for anything on the table that does not necessitate stretching across your neighbor or leaning far across the table yourself. When something is out of reach, simply ask the person nearest to it, "Would you please pass the jelly, Peter?" When an accompaniment that is ordinarily served—butter for the bread, mustard for the ham, salt and pepper, etc.—is not on the table, it is undoubtedly an oversight. You may ask your hostess, "Do you have any mustard, Anne?" or "Could we have a little butter for the rolls?" You should not, however, ask for anything unusual, or something that your hostess might not have in her larder.

Items should be passed from person to person or if they are awkward to pass, put down on the table so that the next person can easily pick them up. Some people, in fact, will not receive a saltcellar from the hands of another and insist that it be put down before they will receive it and pass it on. Serving dishes with handles and such items as cream pitchers should be passed with the handle toward the person receiving it to facilitate their taking it.

Serving Yourself and Being Served

When helping yourself to any food the most important thing is to pay attention to what you are doing and not handle a serving fork or spoon in such a way as to spill food on the floor, the table, your neighbor, or yourself.

Anything served on a piece of toast should be lifted from the platter on the toast. Squab or quail might be lifted, leaving the toast on the plate, but foods such as mushrooms, sweetbreads, or asparagus must remain on the toast. Otherwise, it would be difficult to serve them, and a soggy, unattractive piece of toast would be left on the platter. The toast with its topping is lifted on the spoon and held in place with the fork. If you don't want to eat the toast simply put it to one side of your plate. If a fork and spoon are presented with the food, one is used to scoop a portion and the other is placed on top to balance it on its way to the plate. When there is only a serving spoon and no fork in the dish, you must balance the food with great care.

Gravy should be put *on* the meat, potatoes, or rice, and the condiment, pickles, and jelly *at the side* of whatever they accompany. Olives, nuts, radishes, or celery are put on the bread-and-butter plate if there is one, otherwise on the edge of the plate from which one is eating.

When passing your plate to the head of the table for a second helping, always leave the knife and fork on the plate and be sure they are far enough on not to topple off.

When the host fills the plates and sends them around the table, they are started counterclockwise. Each diner on the right side of the table takes the plate from the person on his left and passes it on to the person on his right. If there is a woman guest on the host's right she keeps the first plate, but the second is passed on to the person at the end of the table. The third goes to the person farthest down on the right side, the next to the person on *his* left, etc. When all the people on the host's right are served, the plates are sent down the left side, and the host serves himself last. If the hostess is serving, the same order is followed from her end.

Often "family style" means that the host or hostess serves the meat and the other dishes are passed around with each diner helping himself. These dishes, too, are passed counterclockwise. Men do not offer the dish to the women on their right first, but help themselves when the dish reaches them. They may then, if they wish, hold the dish while the woman next to them serves herself. When someone at the far end of the table asks to have a dish passed to him for a second helping, it is only sensible for someone in between, who also would like more, to say as the dish is passed to him on its way down the table, "Do you mind if I help myself so that it needn't come all the way back?" Naturally you would not do that if there were only one portion left!

At a family meal where Mother knows what, and how much, each member will want, she may serve the plates in the kitchen and bring them herself, or with the help of one or two of the children, to the table. This should never be done when guests are present, however. They should have the prerogative of serving themselves. Exceptions are individual "arranged" dishes, such as eggs Benedict, which must be "put together" in the kitchen.

When there is a maid serving food to guests, she presents the platter or bowl to the guest's left. The guest may say, "No, thank you" if he doesn't care for any of that offering.

Refusing A Dish

If you are served a food you are allergic to, or especially dislike, and if you are among friends, you may refuse with a polite "No, thank you." Otherwise it is good manners to take at least a little of every dish that is offered to you, which can be spread out on your plate so that it is barely noticeable that you have not eaten much. The old rule that one must not leave anything on his plate is outdated, but it would be wasteful and upsetting to your hostess if you took a large portion and left it untouched. You need not give your reason for refusing a dish, but if it is because of an allergy, diet, or other physical cause, you may avoid hurting your hostess's feelings if you quietly tell her your problem, always without drawing the attention of the entire table.

When declining a dish offered by a waiter, you say, "No, thank you," quietly, and in fact a negative shake of the head and "No thanks" more nearly describe the usual refusal.

At a buffet dinner, where there are a number of dishes offered, you need only help yourself to those that appeal to you.

When there are servers behind the buffet line, hold your plate forward for those items you would like. Simply smile and say, "No, thank you" when offered items you don't want.

The Silver

From the Outside In

There should never be any question of which silver to use: *You always start with the implement of each type that is farthest from the plate.* This question arises again and again, and the answer is always the same, with one exception. If the table is incorrectly set, and you realize that you cannot use the implement for the course that its position indicates, you must, of course, choose the next one that is appropriate. For example, if the small shellfish fork has been put next to the plate, you would not use the dinner fork for the shrimp cocktail and leave the little fork for the main course, even though they were placed in that order. Otherwise, you assume that the table is correctly set, and starting at the outside, you work your way with each course toward the center.

When you have finished the main course the knife and fork are placed beside each other on the dinner plate diagonally from upper left to lower right. The handles extend slightly over the edge of the plate. The dessert spoon or fork is placed in the same position. If dessert is served in a stemmed bowl or in a small, deep bowl on another plate, the dessert spoon is put down on the plate when you are finished. If the bowl is shallow and wide, the spoon may be left in it, or on the plate below it, as you wish.

Using the Knife and Fork

The proper way to use the knife and fork can best be explained by the accompanying illustrations. Study them carefully and you will see that they depict easy and graceful ways of cutting food and bringing it to your mouth.

American style of using a knife and fork

The American custom of "zigzag" eating (changing the fork from left to right hand after cutting meat) is perfectly correct, but I feel that it is unnecessarily complicated. Therefore it does not have so pleasing an appearance as the simpler European method of leaving the fork in your left hand after you have cut your meat. You eat the meat from your fork while it is still in the left hand, rather than turning the fork over and switching it to your right hand. Although some people feel that it is "putting on airs" to adopt this "foreign" way of eating, I can see nothing wrong in adopting a custom that seems more practical than your own.

European style of using a knife and fork

Pushers

There is no better pusher than a piece of bread crust. Lacking this, the knife is also correct—if properly used. It is held in the left hand in the same position as when cutting with the right hand, and the tip of the blade helps to guide and push the food onto the fork. It is a natural motion and in no way incorrect.

Using knife as a pusher

THE ETIQUETTE OF EATING

Although the basic etiquette of eating all foods is that they only be transported to the mouth in manageable, bite-sized pieces, there are several tips for certain courses and for specific foods which require dexterity in handling. When presented with something you have never eaten before, such as escargots, what you do depends on the company you are in. If among friends, there is nothing embarrassing about saying, "I've never had escargots before. Show me how to do this!" If at a formal function or among strangers, however, you may not want to admit to this. In this case, it is best to delay beginning, by having a sip of water or wine, and watch what others are doing.

Artichokes

Artichoke leaves are always eaten with the fingers; a leaf at a time is pulled off, and the edible portion dipped in melted butter or hollandaise sauce and then bitten off. When the center is reached, the thistlelike part is scraped away with a knife, and the heart eaten with a knife and fork.

Asparagus

By reputation this is a finger food, but the ungraceful appearance of a bent stalk of asparagus falling limply into someone's mouth and the fact that moisture is also likely to drip from the end cause most fastidious people to eat it—at least in part—with the fork. That is, cut the stalks with the fork to where they become harder, and then pick up the ends in the fingers if you choose. But don't squeeze the stalks or let juice run down your fingers.

Asparagus that has no hard end is eaten entirely with a fork. All hard ends should be cut off asparagus before serving it at a dinner party, since picking up stalks in the fingers is scarcely compatible with formal table manners.

Bacon

Breakfast bacon should, when it is limp, be eaten with a fork. But when it is dry and crisp, so that it scatters into fragments when broken by the fork, fingers are permitted.

Bread and Butter

Bread should always be broken into moderate-sized pieces—but not necessarily single-mouthful bits—with the fingers before being eaten. To butter it, hold a piece on the edge of the bread-and-butter plate, or the place plate, and with a butter knife spread enough butter on it for a mouthful or two at a time. If there is no butter knife use any other knife you find available.

This buttering of bread is not an important rule. There are always common-sense exceptions. For instance, hot biscuits or toast can of course be buttered all over immediately, since they are most delicious when the butter is quickly and thoroughly melted. Bread should never, however, be held flat on the palm and buttered with the hand held in the air. If a table knife is used, care must be taken not to smear food particles from the knife onto the butter.

Butter

Every sort of bread, biscuit, toast, and also hot griddle cakes and corn on the cob are buttered with a knife. But corn that has been cut off the cob, or rice, or potato—or anything else on your dinner plate—has seasoning or butter mixed in it with a fork.

If you are serving butter at the table it may be cut in small squares and arranged on a decorative plate. Diners should lift these pats of butter with the utensil provided and transfer them to their own plates, or, if there is no accompanying utensil, with a clean knife. When it is presented in a tub, scoop up a portion on your knife and put it on your plate.

In a restaurant, when butter is offered in individual wrapped squares you should open the wrapper and use your knife to push the square onto your plate, or butter plate, if there is one.

Cheese

Cheese is one food that may be spread with either a knife or a fork: If eaten with a salad with which one is using no knife, a piece of cheese may be broken off and put on lettuce or a cracker with one's fork. Runny or soft cheeses, such as Brie, Camembert, or Liederkranz, are spread with a salad knife or butter knife if there is one. Served as an hors d'oeuvre, cheese is always spread with a knife.

Cherry Tomatoes

Except when served in a salad or other dish, cherry tomatoes are eaten with the fingers. And they *squirt!* The best thing to do is try to select one small enough to be put in your mouth whole. Even then, clamp your lips tightly before chewing it. If you must bite into a big one, make a little break in the skin with your front teeth before biting it in half.

Chicken, Other Fowl, and Frogs' Legs

At a formal dinner no part of a bird is picked up with the fingers. However, among family and friends and in "family style" or informal restaurants, it is permissible to eat it as follows:

The main body of the bird is not eaten with the fingers. You cut off as much meat as you can and leave the rest on your plate. To eat the small bones, such as joint or wing, or the second joint of a squab, you hold the piece of bone with meat on it up to your mouth, and eat it clean. Larger joints, too, such as the drumstick of a roast chicken, may be picked up after the first few easily cut off pieces have been eaten.

Frogs' legs are eaten in the same way.

Chops, Lamb, Pork, and Veal

At a dinner party or in a formal restaurant lamb chops must be eaten with knife and fork. The center, or "eye," of the chop is cut off the bone, and cut into two or three pieces. If the chop has a frilled paper "skirt" around the end of the bone, you may hold that in your hand and cut the tasty meat from the side of the bone. If there is no "skirt" you must do the best you can with your knife and fork. At the family table or in an informal group of friends, the center may be cut out and eaten with the fork, and the bone picked up and eaten clean with the teeth. This is permissible, too, with veal or pork chops, but only when they are broiled or otherwise cooked without gravy or sauce.

Clams and Oysters on the Half Shell

Clams and oysters on the half shell are generally served on cracked ice, arranged around a container of cocktail sauce. The clam is speared with the small shellfish fork (or smallest fork provided), dipped into the sauce, and eaten in one bite. Neither clams nor oysters served on the half shell are ever cut up. They may also be eaten by taking a little of the sauce on the fork and dropping it onto the clam, if only a little sauce is desired. Some people enjoy them with nothing more than a few drops of lemon, and lemon wedges should be offered as well as the sauce.

If oyster crackers are served they may be crumpled up in the fingers and mixed into the sauce. Horseradish, too, is mixed into the sauce, or a drop may be put directly onto the shellfish if you like the very "hot" taste.

When clams are eaten on a picnic, when they are opened fresh and served as an hors d'oeuvre informally, or when they are ordered at a clam bar, the shell is picked up in the fingers and the clam and its delicious juice are sucked right off the shell.

Cocktail Trimmings

If you want to eat the olives, cherries, or onions served in cocktails, by all means do. If they are served on a toothpick or cocktail pick, simply remove them from the drink with it and enjoy them. If there is no pick, drink enough of the cocktail so that you will not wet your fingers, and then you can lift out the olive or onion and eat it in your fingers. Slices of oranges in old-fashioneds are not usually eaten as it is too messy to chew the pulp off the rind.

Condiments

Smearing condiments with a knife on food already impaled on a fork is quite unpleasant if more than a small amount is taken. The proper way to manage a quantity of cranberry sauce, dressing, jelly, pickle, etc., is to lift it onto the fork and either eat it as a separate mouthful or take some of it with a small piece of meat on the tips of the tines.

Corn on the Cob

To attack corn on the cob with as little ferocity as possible is perhaps the only direction to be given, and the only maxim to bear in mind when eating this pleasant-to-taste but not-very-easy-to-manage vegetable is to eat it as neatly as possible. It doesn't matter whether you break the ear in half, or whether you hold it by its own ends or by special little handles. The real thing to avoid is too much buttering all at once and too greedy eating. If you like a lot of butter, spread it across only half the length of two rows at a time. If you take a moderate amount of butter, you can spread it across the whole length of two rows, add salt and pepper, hold the ends in both hands, and eat those two rows. Repeat the buttering and eating until it is finished.

Considerate hostesses should supply small, sharp vegetable knives (steak knives would do nicely) to guests who like to, or must, cut the corn off the cob. Corn served at a formal dinner party should always be cut off the cob in the kitchen and creamed or buttered.

Crackers or Croutons with Soup

Croustades, which are very small forcemeat pastries, are scattered on soup after it has been ladled into the plate to be served. Croutons (tiny French-fried cubes of bread) are either floated on the soup or else passed separately in a dish with a small serving spoon so that each person may put a spoonful in his soup. Oyster crackers, as well as any others, are put on the bread-and-butter plate— or on the tablecloth— and dropped two or three pieces at a time into the soup. Larger soda crackers, served with chowders, are broken, and then, a few pieces at a time, crumbled up and scattered over the soup.

Crudités

When fresh vegetables and dip are offered, only dip the vegetable once, never a second time after taking a bite of the vegetable. If fresh vegetables are passed as a relish at the table, place them on your butter plate or, if no butter plate, salad plate or on the edge of whatever plate is in front of you. Never transfer a relish directly from the serving plate to your mouth.

Dessert

Dessert may be eaten with spoon or fork or both. Stewed fruit is held in place with the fork and cut and eaten with the spoon. Peaches or other very juicy fruits are peeled and then eaten with knife and fork, but dry fruits, such as apples, may be cut and eaten with the fingers.

Pie is eaten with a fork; if it is "a la mode," the spoon is used also. Ice cream is generally eaten with a spoon, but when accompanied by cake, either the spoon alone or both the spoon and fork may be used.

Soft cakes are best eaten with a fork; in most cases it is a matter of dexterity rather than rule. If you are able to eat a plum or ripe pear in your fingers and not smear your face or make a sucking noise, you are the one in a thousand who *may,* with utmost propriety, continue to do so. If you can eat a Napoleon or a cream puff in your fingers and not let the cream ooze out on the far side, you need not use a fork. But if you cannot eat something—no matter what it is—without getting it all over your fingers, you must use a fork, and when necessary, a spoon or a knife also.

Fondues

Cheese fondue is served in a fondue pot that is kept warm by Sterno heat or by electric heat. It is accompanied by a bowl of bite-sized squares of French bread. A piece of bread is speared on a long fondue fork and dipped into the hot cheese. When coated, it is removed, held over the pot for a moment to drip and cool, and then taken from the fork with the front teeth. Lips and tongue should not touch the fork, as it goes back into the fondue pot for the next bite.

Meat fondue, in which pieces of meat, on the fondue fork, are plunged into very hot oil to cook, is eaten differently. Each diner has a plate onto which he removes the cooked meat to let it cool. It is then eaten with a regular fork while his next piece of meat is sizzling in the pot on the end of the fondue fork.

Fruit, Fresh

The equipment for eating raw fruit at table consists of a sharp-bladed fruit knife, a fork, and a finger bowl. In a restaurant, when no knife is given you, it is proper to ask for one.

Raw apples and *firm pears* are quartered, with a knife. The core is then cut away from each quarter, and the fruit is eaten in the fingers. Those who do not like the skin, pare each quarter separately. If the pears are very juicy they must be cut up with the knife and eaten with the fork.

Bananas may be peeled halfway down and eaten bite by bite at the family table, but when dining out it is better to peel the skin all the way off, lay the fruit on your plate, cut it in slices, and eat it with a fork.

Berries are usually hulled or stemmed ahead of time, served with cream and sugar, and eaten with a spoon. When especially fine and freshly picked, strawberries are often served with their hulls on and sugar placed at one side of each person's plate. The hull of each berry is held in the fingers, and the fruit is dipped in the sugar and then eaten.

Cantaloupes and *muskmelons* are served in halves, or sometimes quarters, and eaten with a spoon.

Honeydew, Persian, and *casaba* melons are cut into new-moon-shaped quarters or eighths, depending on size, and eaten with either spoon or knife and fork—whichever you prefer.

Watermelon is cut into large-sized pieces or slices and usually eaten in the fingers. If using a fork, remove the seeds with the tines and then cut the pieces with the side of the fork.

Raw cherries and *plums* are eaten in the fingers, of course. The pit of the cherry should be made as clean as possible in your mouth and dropped into your almost-closed, cupped hand and thence to your plate. The plum is held in your fingers and eaten as close to the pit as possible. When you remove a pit with your fingers, you should do it with your thumb underneath and your first two fingers across your mouth, and not with your fingertips pointing into your mouth.

Grapes should never be pulled off the bunch one at a time. Choose a branch with several grapes on it and break it off, or if scissors are provided, cut the branch off close to the main stem.

Hothouse grapes are eaten in two ways: One, lay a grape on its side, hold it with the fingers of one hand, cut into the center with the point of your knife, and remove the seeds. Two, put a whole grape in your mouth, chew it, swallow the pulp and juice, and drop the bare seeds into your almost-closed fist.

With *garden* or *Concord grapes* you press the stem end of the grape between your lips and against your almost-closed teeth, so that the juice and pulp will be drawn into your mouth and the skin left to be discarded.

Little *seedless grapes* are no problem, since they are eaten whole.

Navel oranges, often served at the table, are rather rough-skinned, firm, and usually seedless. A practical way to eat them is to slice the two ends of the rind off first, and cut the peel off in vertical strips with the knife. You then cut the peeled orange in half at its equator. After this, each half is easily cut and eaten mouthful by mouthful with knife and fork together. Oranges can also be halved, the sections loosened with a curved grapefruit knife, and then eaten with an orange spoon or teaspoon.

A thin-skinned orange, filled with seeds, is more difficult to eat. The best way is to peel it, cut it into eighths, take out the seeds from the center with the tip of the knife, and eat the new-moon-shaped pieces as daintily as you can with the fingers.

Tangerines present no problem because the skin is removed easily and the segments separate readily. But the seeds and fibers must be removed from the mouth neatly with the thumb and first two fingers (fingers above and thumb underneath).

A *freestone peach* or a *nectarine* is cut to the pit, then broken in half and eaten. You can't break a *clingstone* apart; therefore it is eaten whole, or quartered as best you can with a knife. Since most people do not like the fuzz, peaches are almost always peeled before eating.

Fruit, Stewed

Stewed prunes, cherries, etc., are eaten with a spoon. The fruit is put into the mouth whole, and when the meat is eaten off the pit, it is dropped directly onto the spoon from the lips and deposited on the edge of the plate or saucer.

Jellies and Jams

Jellies and jams as well as butter are spread on bread or toast with a knife, never with a fork, though you do put butter on vegetables and jelly on meat with a fork. A small portion is taken from the container with a spoon and put on the butter plate or edge of the large plate. If no spoon is provided, you must use your own knife. In this case be sure that you wipe all butter and crumbs off it carefully, on the edge of your plate, before touching the jelly in the jar or dish.

Gravies and Sauces

You may sop bread into gravy, but it must be done properly—by putting a small piece down on the gravy and then eating it with your fork as though it were any other helping on your plate. You may put it into your mouth "continental" fashion, with the tines pointed down as they were when you sopped up the gravy. A good sauce may also be finished in this way—in fact to do so is a compliment to the cook.

Lobster

Lobster claws should be cracked in the kitchen before being served, but nutcrackers or clam crackers should also be available for the diners' use. The additional cracking of the claws should be done slowly, so that the juice does not squirt when the shell breaks. The meat is removed from the large claw ends and from each joint with a pick or shellfish fork. The tail meat is pulled out of the shell in two solid pieces—one side at a time. It is then cut into bite-sized pieces with a knife or the side of a dinner fork, and dipped into melted butter if hot, or mayonnaise if cold. The red roe and the green "fat" are not only edible but delectable, and a small bit of one or both may be put on the fork with each bite of meat.

Real lobster-lovers get an additional morsel out of the legs by breaking off one at a time, putting it into the mouth, and chewing up the shell, squeezing the meat out of the broken end. A bit of work, but worth it if you care!

Properly, a big paper napkin (or bib) is provided for the lobster-eater. Finger bowls with hot water and lemon slices should be put at the side of each place as soon as people are finished eating. These are carried away after the dinner plates have been removed.

A large bowl for the empty shells and inedible parts is a necessity. If a receptacle is not provided in a restaurant the diners may, and should, ask for one.

Mussels

Mussels, and occasionally clams, may be served in their shells in the broth in which they are steamed. Mussels prepared in this way are called moules marinières. The mussel may be removed from its shell with a fork, dipped into the sauce, and eaten in one bite. But I much prefer to pick up the shell, scooping a little of the juice with it, and suck the mussel and juice directly off the shell. The empty shells are placed in a bowl or plate, which should always be provided for them. The juice or broth remaining in the bowl may be eaten with a spoon, or you may sop it up with pieces of roll or French bread speared on the tines of your fork.

Olives

Eat them with your fingers. Bite off the meat, but don't nibble too avidly around the stone. Remove the stone from your mouth with your fingers. Bite a large stuffed olive in half. Put only a very small one in your mouth whole. When the olive is in a salad, pick it up with your fork and eat it in the same way.

Pizza

Pizza is cut into manageable wedges with a knife, and then picked up and eaten with the fingers.

Potatoes

Baked potato, whether white or sweet, is usually eaten by breaking it in half with the fingers (cutting a slit with a knife first if necessary), scooping all the inside of the potato onto the plate with a fork, and then mixing butter, salt, and pepper in it with a fork.

Another way to eat baked potato is to break it in half with the fingers and lay both halves, skin down, on the plate. Mix a little butter in part of one half with a fork and eat that. Then mix a little more, and so on, eating it out of the skin without turning it out onto the plate.

A third way—for those who like to eat the skin as well as the inside—is to cut the baked potato into two halves and then cut them again into pieces, a few at a time, of eatable size. If you wish to eat the skins separately, scrape the inside part onto your plate, put the skins on the side of the plate, or on the butter plate, and eat a small piece at a time, exactly as you would bread and butter.

When French-fried potatoes accompany a hamburger, hot dog, or other sandwich, they may be eaten with the fingers. At other times they should be cut into reasonable lengths and eaten with a fork.

Salad

Why one should not cut one's salad in small pieces—if one wants to—makes little sense unless, that is, one cuts up a whole plateful and makes the plate messy. Until stainless steel was invented, a steel knife blade was not usable for salad or fruit, since the metal turned black; but silver-bladed knives have always been used for salads as well as for fruits, and stainless steel is not affected in the slightest by the vinegar in the dressing. So there's no possible reason why anyone should be denied the use of a salad or dinner knife. Anything more difficult than managing leafy salad with a fork alone—especially the fresh, crisp, springing variety—is difficult to imagine. At all events, beware of rolling the fork and wrapping springy leaves around the tines in a spiral. Remember what a spring that lets go can do!

Whether salad is ordered specially or comes with the meal it is generally—to my consternation—served before the entrée. I believe that this custom has taken hold because restaurants wished to keep the customer happy while his entrée was being prepared, and people simply became accustomed to it. In private homes salad generally was—and is—served with or after the main course, and as far as I am concerned that is where it belongs.

If you do not wish to eat your salad before your entrée don't ask the waiter to take it back, because this will upset him and you may never see it again. Simply put it to one side, and if you have the willpower, leave it alone. But keep an eagle eye on it! Many a diner has looked away for a moment and looked back to find that the salad has been removed by the waiter. To forestall this you may say to the waiter when he brings it, "Please leave my salad here on the side—I'll eat it later."

Salt in a Saltcellar

If there is no spoon in the saltcellar (a tiny open bowl), use the tip of a clean knife. If the saltcellar is for you alone, you may either use the tip of your knife or you may take a pinch with your fingers. Salt that is to be dipped into should be put on the bread-and-butter plate or on the rim of whatever plate is before you.

If you do not wish to risk insulting your hostess—or the chef—don't sprinkle salt and pepper over your food before tasting it. Furthermore, it is foolish. When dining out you cannot possibly know how much salt was added during the preparation of the food.

Sandwiches

All ordinary sandwiches, not only at picnics but everywhere, are eaten with the fingers. Club sandwiches and other inch-and-thicker sandwiches are best cut in small portions before being picked up and held tightly in the fingers of both hands, or if literally dripping with mayonnaise they should be served on a plate with a knife and fork. If you are not sitting at a table and you have no knife, you bite into an overlarge and hugely thick piece as nicely as you can, and following the previous advice on eating corn on the cob, attack it with as little ferocity as possible.

Shish kabob

Except for shish kabob served as a hors d'oeuvre you do not eat directly from the skewer. When shish kabob is served as a main course, lift the skewer with your fork, and beginning with the pieces at the bottom, push and slide the meat and vegetables off the skewer and onto your plate.

Shrimp

Shrimp as a first course present one of the most difficult problems encountered by the diner. If not too impossibly large each shrimp should be eaten in one bite. But when they are of jumbo size, the diner has no alternative but to grasp the cup firmly in one hand and cut the shrimp as neatly as possible with the edge of his fork. It is impractical to use a knife because the stemmed shrimp cup will tip over unless held with one hand. At home the problem can be avoided by arranging the shrimp attractively on a small plate—where they can easily be cut with knife or fork—and I see no reason why restaurants should not do the same. Among family and friends it is permissible to spear a large shrimp with your fork and bite off a piece. But you must never dip the remainder back in a bowl of sauce that is being used by anyone but yourself.

Snails (Escargots)

Snail shells are grasped with a special holder, in one hand, or with the fingers if no holder is provided. The meat is removed with a pick or oyster fork. The garlic butter that remains in the dish is sopped up with small pieces of French bread and eaten with the fork.

Soups

Either clear soup or thick soup may be served in a cup with one handle or with handles on both sides. After taking a spoonful or two you may pick up the cup if the soup is cool enough. Use both hands if the cup has two handles, or continue to use your spoon if you prefer.

Clear soups are sometimes served in a shallow soup plate rather than in a cup. When the level of the soup is so low that you must tip the plate to avoid scraping the bottom noisily, lift the near edge with one hand and tip the plate away from you. Then the soup may be spooned away from you or toward you, whichever is less awkward.

Both soup cups and soup plates should be served with a saucer or plate beneath them. The spoon, when not in use or when the soup is finished, is laid on the saucer when a soup cup is used, but it is left in the soup *plate* rather than on the dish under it.

Spaghetti

Some restaurants, and hostesses, that feature pasta provide guests with a large spoon as well as the knife and fork. The fork is used to spear a few strands of spaghetti, the tips are placed against the bowl of the spoon, which is held in the left hand and the fork is twirled, wrapping the spaghetti around itself as it turns. If no spoon is provided, the tips of the fork may be rested against the curve of the plate.

Sushi

Sushi is served in small portions which may be eaten whole. If eaten with a fork and the portions are too large, they may be cut with the fork or with a fork and knife. If eaten with chopsticks, they are picked up whole and eaten from the chopsticks, or the ends of the chopsticks may be used to cut the portions into smaller pieces.

Tacos

Tacos and tortillas are meant to be eaten with the hand, since it is impossible to cut into the crisp shell with a knife and fork without having it crack and crumble. However, any filling that falls out should be eaten with a fork, not picked up with the hands.

Toothpicks in Food

When hors d'oeuvres are served with toothpicks, the problem of what to do with the toothpick afterward is a universal one. Thoughtful hostesses provide a small plate near the hors d'oeuvres tray for the used picks. Never put them back on the serving platter or in an ashtray—ashtrays are for cigarette ashes and butts only. Hold the toothpick (or several you have collected) with your cocktail napkin until you can find a wastebasket. Toothpicks in such foods as club sandwiches should be removed and placed at the edge of the plate.

Finger Bowls

Finger bowls are seen most often at formal dinners and when seafood, such as lobster or crab legs which are eaten with the hands, are served. They are placed at the side of each diner's place at the end of a "hands on" dinner, or just before dessert at a formal dinner.

Dip your fingers, one hand at a time, into the water and then dry your fingers on your napkin. If a finger bowl is brought directly before dessert, it is often placed on a doily on the dessert plate. To remove it, lift it, with the doily underneath, and move it to the upper left of your place setting.

A slice of lemon is never used in a finger bowl at a formal dinner, but flowers may be floated in it. Lemon may be floated in a finger bowl used after a lobster dinner.

Serving and Handling Beverages

Hot Beverages

Many people today are using mugs instead of cups and saucers for coffee, tea, or hot chocolate. They are pleasant to hold, and retain the heat better than thin china cups. Since saucers are not used with mugs, the problem arises of what to do with the spoon—which should never be left in the mug. Mugs are not proper on a formal table and are rarely seen on any table covered with a damask or lace cloth, so the solution depends somewhat on the table covering. If the mats (or a cloth) are informal, of paper or plastic perhaps, the spoon may be wiped clean with the lips and laid on the mat or on the table beside the mug. If the mats are of fine quality it would be thoughtless to risk staining them. The bowl of the spoon, face down, should be rested on the edge of the butter plate or dinner plate, with the spoon handle on the table.

When dining informally one may use a teaspoon to put a small piece of ice from the water glass into a steaming beverage to cool it slightly. This may only be done, however, with a clean, unused spoon.

Tea bags are naturally placed on the edge of the saucer, but they should be pressed gently against the side of the cup with the spoon to remove excess liquid. Should the tea be served in a glass or china mug without a saucer, you may ask for a dish on which to place the bag. Otherwise you must put it on the edge of the butter or dinner plate, where it inevitably leaks drops of tea into the food on the plate.

In spite of an outdated idea to the contrary, tea that is too hot to drink from the cup may be sipped from the spoon, as may coffee or any other hot beverage.

When coffee slops into the saucer, the best course is to replace the saucer with a clean one. This is always true at home, where one may get the replacement oneself, or when dining at a friend's house or in a fine restaurant where one may request the exchange. It is sometimes impossible, however, in some restaurants or in a cafeteria. Rather than drip coffee each time you lift the cup to your mouth, it is permissible to pour the liquid back into the cup and use a paper napkin (if one is available) to dry the bottom of the cup.

Iced Tea and Iced Coffee

If iced tea or coffee has been served in a glass with a saucer under it, the spoon used to stir the drink is placed in this saucer. But when there is no saucer the problem arises as to what to do with the spoon. If paper napkins are available put one on the table next to your glass and then put the spoon on the napkin. If no paper napkins are available the spoon should be placed with the bowl upside down on the edge of your butter plate, or dinner plate if necessary. A used piece of silver should not be put on the table, especially when there is a tablecloth. Some people like to leave the spoon in the glass and hold it back with a finger when they drink but I find this awkward and unattractive.

Drinking from Stemware

Wine and champagne glasses with long stems should be held by the stem. This keeps the heat of the hand from warming the beverage. Heavy water goblets or glasses with shorter stems must be held by the bowl of the glass to keep the glass balanced when raising it to the mouth.

Handling Eating Difficulties

Food That Is Too Hot or Spoiled

If a bite of food is too hot, quickly take a swallow of water. Only if there is no beverage at all, and your mouth is scalding, should you spit it out. And then it should be spit onto your fork or into your fingers, and quickly put on the edge of the plate. The same is true of spoiled food. Should you put a "bad" oyster or clam, for example, into your mouth, don't swallow it, but remove it as quickly and unobtrusively as you can. To spit anything whatsoever into the corner of your napkin is unnecessary and not permissible.

Choking on Meat or Bones

Although we occasionally hear of someone choking to death on a piece of meat, the ordinary "choke" or "swallowing the wrong way" is not serious. If a sip of water does not help, but you think you can dislodge the offending bit by a good cough, cover your mouth with your napkin and do it. Remove the fish bone or abrasive morsel from your mouth with your fingers and put it on the edge of your plate. If you need a more prolonged cough excuse yourself and leave the table.

In the event that you are really choking, don't hesitate to get someone to help you. When a person is choking they are unable to speak, cough or make any sound whatsoever. Do whatever is necessary to attract attention to yourself if you find yourself in this position. The seriousness of your condition will quickly be recognized, and it is no time to worry about manners. Keeping calm and acting quickly might well save your life.

Coughing, Sneezing, and Blowing Your Nose

It is not necessary to leave the table to perform any of these functions, unless the bout turns out to be prolonged. In that case you should excuse yourself until the seizure has passed. When you feel a sneeze or a cough coming on, cover your mouth and nose with your handkerchief, or if you do not have one, or time to get it out, use your napkin. In an emergency your hand will do better than nothing at all. Never use your napkin to blow your nose. If you are caught short without a handkerchief or a tissue, excuse yourself and head for the nearest bathroom.

Stones, Bugs, Hairs, Etc.

When you get something that doesn't belong there into your mouth, there is no remedy but to remove it. This you do as inconspicuously as possible—spitting it quietly into your fingers. But occasionally you notice the foreign matter before you eat it—a hair in the butter, a worm on the lettuce, or a fly in the soup. If it is not too upsetting to you, remove the object without calling attention to it and go on eating. If it is such that it upsets your stomach (as a hair does to many people) leave the dish untouched rather than embarrass your hostess in a private home. At a restaurant you may—and should—point out the error to your waiter and ask for a replacement. Of course an observant host or hostess will spot the problem when he or she notices that you are not eating something, and will see that the dish is replaced.

Food Stuck in a Tooth

Toothpicks should not be used at the table, and certainly you should not pick at food in your teeth with your finger. If it is actually hurting, excuse yourself and go to the bathroom to remove it. Otherwise wait until the end of the meal and then go to take care of it, asking for a toothpick if necessary.

The same holds true for food caught in dentures. If it is unbearable, you must excuse yourself and go to the nearest bathroom to rinse them.

Spills

If you should spill jelly or a bit of vegetable or other solid food on the table, pick up as much as you can neatly with a clean spoon or the blade of your knife. If it has caused a stain dab a little water from your glass on it with a corner of your napkin. Apologize to your hostess, who, in turn, should not add to your embarrassment by calling attention to the accident.

If you spill wine or water at a formal dinner or in a restaurant, try quietly to attract the attention of the butler or waiter, who will bring a cloth to cover the spot. At the family table or at an informal dinner without servants, offer to get a cloth or sponge to mop up the liquid and help the hostess clean up in any way you can.

SOME DINING DON'TS

While I much prefer to emphasize the affirmative approach to good manners, there are a number of dining rules that are better expressed by the negative. Here are the most important ones:

Don't encircle a plate with one arm while eating with the other hand.

Don't push back your plate when finished. It remains exactly where it is until the person serving you removes it. If you wait on yourself, get up and carry it to the kitchen.

Don't lean back and announce, "I'm through," or "I'm stuffed." The fact that you have put your fork or spoon down shows that you have finished.

Don't *ever* put liquid into your mouth if it is already filled with food. You might have a little toast in your mouth when you drink your coffee, if it be so little as to be undetectable by others. But a good habit is *never*.

Don't wipe off the tableware in a restaurant. If you do happen to find a dirty piece of silver at your place, call a waiter or waitress, show him the soiled article, and ask for a clean one.

Don't, if you are a woman, wear an excessive amount of lipstick to the table, out of consideration for your hostess's napkin, and also because it is very unattractive on the rim of a glass or on the silver.

Don't crook your finger when picking up your cup. It's an affected mannerism.

Don't—ever—leave your spoon in your cup. Not only does it look unattractive; it is almost certain to result in an accident.

Don't leave half of the food on your spoon or fork to be waved about during conversation. One often sees this done with ice cream, but the coldness is no excuse. One should put less on the spoon and eat it in one bite.

Don't cut up your entire meal before you start to eat; it only makes a mess on your plate.

Don't pile mashed potatoes and peas on top of the meat on your fork—in short, don't take huge mouthfuls of *any* food.

DINING IN RESTAURANTS

Restaurant dining has become a regular rather than a special event for many couples and families in the 90's, with more and more women working outside the home and having less time to grocery shop and prepare meals. Eating in fast food restaurants seldom requires more than every day good manners, while dining in more formal restaurants requires some additional knowledge, simply because it involves more dining room staff and more courses. Children should be taught to speak quietly, and to use their best manners so that this experience is as pleasurable for other restaurant patrons as it is for your family.

Reservations

Reservations are made in one name only. When calling for a reservation, advise the restaurant how many will be in your party, what time you expect to arrive. If you have any questions about the dress rules of the restaurant, or whether it accepts your credit card, this is the time to ask. In addition, mention any special seating preferences you may have: by the window, or in a booth; and whether you wish to be seated in the smoking or non-smoking section. Naturally, if you are going to be delayed or if you must cancel, you should call the restaurant to communicate this.

Checking Coats, Hats and Parcels

Where coat checkrooms exist, men are always expected to check their coats and any accessories. Women generally check their coats as well, although they may keep them if they tend to get chilled easily. Some checkrooms do not accept fur coats because they don't want to be responsible for them. In this case, a woman would wear her coat until she is seated and then throw the shoulders of the coat back over her chair. A man never wears a hat indoors. A woman may keep her hat on in a restaurant. Unless a folder of papers is required for discussion during the meal, it is best to check all parcels, umbrellas, etc., since there is nowhere to put them conveniently at the table. A woman keeps her handbag in her lap or places it on the floor at her feet, never on the table.

Waiting for People in a Restaurant

When members of a group arrive separately at a restaurant, the first arrival should wait for the second rather than go in and sit alone, unless the first arrival sees that the restaurant is filling up and there may shortly be no tables left. When two arrive together they should ask to be seated, explaining to the headwaiter that others are joining them and asking him to see they are promptly directed to the table. This avoids overcrowding the entry and sometimes is the only way of holding a reservation. Some restaurants, however, will not seat a group until all members are present.

When a woman is meeting a man at a restaurant and arrives first, she may do one of several things. If she knows he has made a reservation but does not see him, she may say to the headwaiter, "I believe Mr. Rodgers made a reservation for us. Please show me to the table and tell him I'm here when he arrives." If no reservation has been made, however, it is better for her to wait in the entry for him rather than assume the responsibility of choosing the table—although, again, she may sit down if she sees that there are few tables left. Finally, if it is a nice day, she may prefer to walk down the street, window-shopping for a few moments, and return when she is sure he has arrived. This, however, is really a question of tactics rather than of etiquette.

Ideally a man waits for a woman in the entry, after first making sure she has not been seated. However, many city restaurants have tiny halls or entryways, and if all the people waiting for others stood there, no one could possibly get through. So if the area is crowded, or if there is danger of losing his reservation, a man may ask to be seated—especially if his companion, either male or female, is late. He should keep his eye on the door, ready to wave and rise as the other approaches, and he should tell the headwaiter that he is expecting a lady—or a man—and to please be sure that his guest is brought in at once. The person who is waiting at the table, or at a bar in the entry, may order a cocktail before the other arrives, and may even order for his companion if he knows what he, or she, will want, and that he will arrive very shortly.

Being Seated

When dining alone or when hosting another person or a group, one announces oneself to the restaurant host or hostess: "Good evening. I made a reservation for O'Donnell, a party of four." Or, if you have no reservation, you state how many are in your party. If it is a restaurant with smoking and non-smoking sections, you should, at this time, indicate your preference.

In a group, one person, even though he or she is not paying for everyone else's meal, should serve as spokesperson and handle these arrangements.

When the table is ready the host or maitre 'd leads the way. When a man and a woman are dining together, she walks directly behind the host. The man she is with follows her. In a mixed group, all the women precede all the men.

When one person is hosting a group, he or she should go first to arrange seating. This precludes leaving all the guests standing and waiting for him or her to bring up the rear.

The headwaiter generally pulls out one chair to seat the woman if a couple is dining together.

If you don't like the table that has been offered you, you may always say, "We would prefer a table with a banquette (built-in seating) if there is one free," or "Could we be seated a little farther from the door, please?" If this isn't possible, you may say, "All right then, this will be fine," or, if you are really displeased, "Thanks, but I think we'll try another restaurant that isn't so crowded."

Where there is no waiter at hand to seat people, the man seats his women guests.

When one couple invites another to dine, the host and hostess generally sit opposite one another. If neither couple is giving the party, the two women usually sit opposite each other. In larger groups, the guest of honor is seated to the host's or hostess's right with men and women alternating around the table. Ordinarily, men do not sit next to their wives.

When two men and a woman dine together, she is seated between them, as is one man seated between two women.

At a table with a banquette, a couple is usually seated side-by-side facing the room. Otherwise, women are seated on the banquette and men on chairs opposite them.

In a restaurant with booths, women slide in first and sit against the wall, facing one another. Men sit next to them on the outside.

Hosting a Restaurant Dinner

The first thing a host must consider is the choice of restaurant. Do the guests like exotic food or good plain cooking? If they are from out of town do they have the proper clothes with them for an elaborate restaurant? Do they wish to see a place with a worldwide reputation? If a man is taking a woman to dinner would she like a small, intimate spot, or would she prefer to dance to a good band?

Having reached a decision, the host must make every effort to see that the restaurant chosen meets the expectations of his or her guests. At a well-known restaurant always reserve a table ahead of time; and even in an ordinary restaurant it is always safer to make a reservation in advance.

If the host has ordered the dinner ahead of time he or she must try to check the dishes as they are served to make sure that everything is as requested. If there are any omissions quietly call them to the attention of the waiter and make sure that the missing items are supplied.

If dinner has not been ordered beforehand, it is the host's duty to take the guests' orders and give them to the waiter, or if the party is large, to make sure that the waiter gets the order correctly from each person. Again, if there are mistakes the host must tactfully and politely see that they are corrected, without embarrassing the guests.

When paying the check do not display the total but put the money (or the signed form if paying by credit card) quietly on the plate and nod to the waiter to remove it. If you do not have the exact amount, including the tip, wait for the waiter to bring the change, but if the sum includes both bill and tip, thank the waiter and indicate that you are ready to leave by rising or by making some such remark as, "Well, let's move along or we'll never make the first act."

If the headwaiter has been especially helpful, the host unobtrusively slips a tip (from five dollars, depending on the size of the group) into his hand and thanks him as the party is leaving the restaurant.

Ordering Cocktails and Wine

Hosts should not urge guests to drink cocktails once they have refused, but no guest should feel uncomfortable because he or she would like a drink when the host does not. In fact if the host, or one member of a couple dining together, does not drink, the host should say to the other(s), "I don't think I'll have a cocktail, but please do—I'll have some mineral water while you're having your gin and tonic." If there are some guests who say "No" to liquor, the host should suggest that they have a soft drink while the others are having cocktails. It is impolite to order more than one or two cocktails when others are left with nothing in front of them and only the hope of a meal to sustain them.

If desired, wine should be ordered after the choices for the meal have been made, from the wine steward if there is one, or from the waiter if there is not. The host, or whoever may be best qualified, should choose a wine that goes well with the greatest number of choices of food. For instance, if more people have ordered chicken or fish, choose a white wine; but if more are having a steak dinner, pick a red. Or a bottle of each may be ordered. There are many people who enjoy a vin rosé, or pink wine, and it is often a happy compromise, as it goes well with many menus. Most restaurants also offer wine by the glass, and that is an ideal solution when two people dining together want different wines or they do not want as much as a bottle contains.

If you have a definite preference for red or white wine it is not incorrect to order either with any food. The choices stated above are simply those which, for the majority, result in the most pleasing combination of flavors.

You may choose imported wines if you wish, but there are many excellent domestic wines available. One should not feel it necessary to spend a great deal to enjoy a good wine with dinner. If you do not recognize the names on the wine list, by all means ask your headwaiter's advice, giving him an idea of the type you prefer, and whether domestic or imported.

Ordering the Meal

For many years the rule was that the woman told the man what she would like and he gave the order—she never so much as spoke to the waiter herself. Presumably, the man was supposed to be the protector of his "shrinking violet," and besides, no woman ever spoke to any strange man. Today this is obviously ridiculous. When a couple is dining in a restaurant they may choose to follow the old rule, but when there are more than two people and the waiter asks each one for his choice, there is every reason for the women to give him their orders directly. It is certainly less confusing, and there will be fewer mistakes made, especially if the group is large. When the waiter looks straight at a woman and asks, "What kind of dressing would you like on your salad?" it is insulting if she turns away and relays her message through her escort. Many waiters ask the woman for her order first in an effort to be polite, and there is no reason why she should not answer directly.

When one member of the party knows the restaurant and its specialties well, and sometimes when foreign food is served with which the others are not acquainted, the knowledgeable one should suggest some choices. If all are unfamiliar with the type of food served, there should be no hesitation about asking the waiter to recommend one of the specialties of the restaurant.

Unless a guest knows the host is very well off, he or she should show some consideration for the host's wallet and avoid ordering the most expensive items on the menu. Neither should a guest order the cheapest item, implying that he or she thinks the host can't afford more. The guest should ask for a table d'hôte dinner if one is offered, or choose only a main course, a salad, and a dessert, if it is not. The host may always add more, with the guest's approval. A host who wishes to indicate that he or she doesn't need to spare expenses may say, "The filet mignon is excellent here—wouldn't you like to try it?"

The Difference Between Table d'Hôte and A La Carte

Table d'hote means a set price for a complete meal, irrespective of how many courses are ordered. "Club" breakfasts and lunches, "blue-plate" dinners, or any meals at fixed prices are table d'hôte.

A la carte means that you order from a list of dishes and you pay the price listed beside each dish—even your salad and coffee.

Usually it is very easy to know which is which, because a price follows each item on an à la carte menu. No prices are listed on some table d'hôte bills of fare except at the top where the price for the complete dinner may be printed.

Another type of table d'hôte menu is the one that has a price beside each entrée. This price includes the choice of an hors d'oeuvre or a soup, a salad, and a dessert, and choice of coffee, tea, or milk. If any other items on the menu are followed by a price, there is an additional charge for them.

Very often a separate card or a box inset on the à la carte menu reads, "Special dinner $12.00," or whatever the price may be, and informs you that you can order whatever you choose on this special for twelve dollars, but that any item taken from the regular bill of fare will be charged for as an extra.

A few very exclusive restaurants hand a guest a menu that has no prices on it. Presumably, if the host has chosen the restaurant, he is prepared to pay for whatever the guest selects. Although many guests are made very uncomfortable when this occurs, there is little to do except order what you like. However, if you suspect the host or hostess had not realized that the restaurant made a practice of doing this, you can select an item that is ordinarily lower-priced—a chicken dish instead of filet mignon, for example.

When a waiter or waitress recites a list of daily specials (as many restaurants do today) without telling you the prices, be very sure to ask the cost of each item you are interested in. Otherwise, when the bill arrives you will probably find that you have been charged more than any item on the regular menu. If you are someone's guest, however, it might embarrass your host if you were to ask the price, so it is up to the host to ask (possibly embarrassing *you*) or to take the consequences.

Restaurant Table Manners

Although table manners are much the same whether you are eating at home or in a restaurant, there are a few special problems that do arise when dining out.

In an apparent effort to cut costs or labor, a most unfortunate and deplorable habit is being instituted at many restaurants. Only one knife and, sometimes, one fork is placed on the table, and when the waiter removes the used first-course plate, he hands the dirty knife and/or fork to the diner, or lays it on the tablecloth. I find this disgusting, and I urge every one of my readers to hand the utensil back and say "I'd like a clean knife [or fork] please." If enough of us do that, perhaps restaurant managers will get the message and will find it simpler to put out enough silver for each course.

Individual Side Dishes

Many restaurants serve vegetables and potatoes in small individual side dishes, which the waiter places strategically around your dinner plate. You may eat these vegetables directly from the small dishes, or you may (as I prefer to do) put them on your dinner plate by using a serving spoon or sliding them directly out of the small dish. You then ask the waiter to remove the empty dishes, thus avoiding an overcrowded table.

Cutting Bread and Pouring Coffee

When an uncut loaf of bread is placed on the table the host slices or breaks off two or three individual portions and offers them with the rest of the loaf in the breadbasket or on the plate to the people beside him. This is then passed around the table, and each man should cut or break off a portion for himself and the woman next to him.

If coffee or tea is placed on the table without first having been poured by the waiter, the person nearest the pot should offer to pour, filling his or her own cup last.

Paper Containers

Many accompaniments to meals in restaurants are unfortunately served with paper wrappers or in cardboard or plastic containers. The question of what to do with, for instance, paper sugar packets, comes up frequently. They should be crumpled up tightly and either tucked under the rim of your plate or placed on the edge of the saucer or butter plate. This is preferable to putting them in the ashtray unless there are no smokers at the table.

When jelly or marmalade is served in a paper or plastic container it should be taken out with the butter knife (or dinner knife if there is no butter knife) and put on the butter plate. The top is put back in the empty container, which is left on the table beside the butter plate.

Pouring Wine

When the wine steward or waiter does not return to pour wine after initially opening the bottle and pouring the first glass, the host or hostess may remove the bottle from the wine bucket, wiping off any water from the outside, and refill glasses, beginning with guests.

Grooming at the Table

At the end of a meal a woman may quickly powder her nose and put on a little lipstick, but to look in a mirror and daub at the face for any length of time is in bad taste.

The one never-to-be-broken rule is: Never use a comb at a restaurant table—or in any public place. Never rearrange or put your hands to your hair in any place where food is served. These rules apply to both men and women.

Tasting Another's Food

Occasionally a couple will order different dishes, and each wishes to try a taste of the other's. This is permissible if done unobtrusively. Let's suppose Leeann wants to try Jon's moussaka. She hands her fork to Jon, who picks up a bit of the moussaka and hands it back to her carefully. She should not reach over and spear it herself, nor should he use his fork to give her the taste, unless he does so before he has used it himself. He could, however, before starting to eat, put a small portion of the moussaka on the edge of her plate.

Visiting and Table-Hopping

When a group enters a restaurant and sees people whom some know and others do not, they continue directly to their table, nodding "Hello" as they pass. A public restaurant is scarcely the place for mass introductions.

On the other hand, there are occasions when one or two introductions are suitable. All men at a small table rise when a woman is being introduced, as they do whenever a woman stops to talk. When the group is large only those closest to the visitor rise. If a woman stopping at a table is introduced to other women seated there, the latter never rise—even though they be young and the visitor quite old.

All the men at the table do not rise when another man stops on his way by. When someone comes up to speak to one of the diners, that man only should stand to shake hands. The visitor should then ask him please to be seated while he finishes what he has come to say. If he intends to say more than a few words of greeting he might ask a waiter for a chair (although table-hopping of this sort is not in good taste), or better yet, quickly arrange to meet later.

When a man is seated on a banquette and someone—man *or* woman—stops by to say "Hello," he merely nods and extends his hand. He need not rise. If he did he would either get cramps from the crouched position or he would upset the table trying to straighten up!

One husband solved this problem quite effectively. Gustav Gourmet, just about to eat a perfect soufflé, was forced to stand for a friend of his wife's who stopped at their table. "Oh *please* sit down! You mustn't let your soufflé fall!" said she. Reluctant to sit down, he solved the problem by lifting the plate and eating—standing.

Let us hope that long-talking standees will take this anecdote to heart and pass the tables of their friends without pausing for too long a time.

Too Much Food!

Frequently so much food is served that no one can possibly eat it all. Many restaurants recognize this, but feel they must offer enough for the largest, rather than the smallest, appetite. So they offer the customer a bag called a doggy bag to take home the remainder of the steak or chicken or whatever. Originally the idea was that these "scraps" would be given to the dog, but today the scraps are often so delicious and so expensive that they are fit for human—not canine—consumption.

For some years I resisted the temptation to approve these doggy bags—on the theory that while it was all right to ask to take home a bone for the dog, it did seem rather degrading to ask to take home a "bone" for the family. Until suddenly I realized that I had quite happily done just what I had advised others not to do. I was in Alaska where "men are men" and the portions are, to say the least, man-sized. I was served a steak that *three* New Yorkers could never consume at one sitting.

Neither I—nor my companions—even thought of saying "No" when the waiter arrived and said, "Here's a bag to take home the meat for tomorrow's sandwiches."

Summoning a Waiter

There is no hard or fixed rule for the best way to summon a waiter. In fact ways that are considered proper in some countries are downright insulting in others. For example a waiter who is hissed, whistled, or clapped at in the United States would probably run in the other direction, and yet those gestures are perfectly correct in certain other nations. The usual way here is to catch his eye and then raise your hand, finger pointing up, as if to say "Attention" or "Listen." If he refuses to look in your direction you may call "Waiter" quietly, or if he is too far away to hear you, ask any other waiter nearby, "Please call our waiter." "Miss" is also a correct term for a waitress, but "Sir" is *not* correct for a waiter, whether used by a woman, man, or youngster. Writing this paragraph reminds me of one of my favorite stories—that of the waiter whose tombstone was marked: GOD FINALLY CAUGHT HIS EYE.

Paying the Check

When everyone has finished eating, the host or spokesman catches the eye of the waiter or headwaiter and says, "The check, please." The check is brought, usually face down on a small plate or tray, and is presented to the person who ordered the dinner. He or she looks at it, checks it quickly for mistakes, and returns it to the plate with the necessary money. When the change is returned the host or hostess leaves the correct amount for the tip on the tray. If an error has been found, the waiter is called and the error quietly pointed out; the waiter or the headwaiter makes the adjustment. In no circumstances should a "scene" be made.

Many restaurants ask their customers to pay a cashier on the way out. This practice is especially common in large city restaurants and in those which are used mostly at the lunch hour. It is a great time-saver, as very often a waiter, when he has finished serving a table, gives his attention to other customers, and those waiting for their checks find it difficult to attract his attention. When you read at the bottom of your check "Please pay cashier," put the tip on the table, collect your belongings, and leave, with the host following the group, who wait in the entry while he pays the bill. If he needs change in order to have the right amount for a tip, he pays the check and quickly returns to the table so that the waiter knows he has not been forgotten.

Credit Cards

Credit cards are a great convenience for those who dine out or entertain frequently but do not wish to carry large amounts of cash, and for those who wish to have a record of meals and amounts spent. When making a reservation, find out which credit cards the restaurant accepts. At the time the check is presented, sign it and give the signed check and the credit card to the waiter for processing. Add the tip to the voucher, after making sure that the bill is correct. Make sure to specify how much of the tip is for the waiter and how much for the captain, if you intend your tip to be so divided.

Splitting the Check

The very best way of doing this is to ask for separate checks. When you order with two, three, or four others this causes very little problem. However, in a larger group, separate checks are a nuisance for the waiter, and can become terribly confused. Then, when the one who has acted as host or spokesman (getting the table, ordering, etc.) gets the bill, he or she asks the others for a sum large enough to cover their own share of the meal and the tip. If everyone has chosen items that cost more or less the same amount, it is best to ask each for the same amount of money. But if some have only had a soup or a salad, while others dined on steak and lobster, the spokesman should make appropriate allowances.

Men and women who go out together regularly very often share the cost of meals, especially when she is a wage earner. This is sensible and practical, but a man taking a woman out for the first time, or the first few times, pays the bill. When the woman feels that it is time to suggest that they share and share alike, she should bring it up *before* they get to the restaurant. She should *not,* when the check arrives, say, "Oh, let me pay half." The man asks for the check and pays the full amount. She gives him her share at the time if he needs it, or later if he does not. When a man and woman who customarily share expenses join a group, she should ask him how he wants to handle it. Some men who are willing to accept a woman's share of expenses when they are alone would hesitate to do so in front of their friends.

When a Woman Invites a Man

This is rarely a problem among people who are accustomed to this relationship between men and women, but it is a matter of concern to older men who were brought up to feel that paying a woman's expenses was not only an obligation but a pleasure and privilege.

When a woman invites a man to dine with her for personal rather than business reasons and it is understood that she is paying the bill, the man may be embarrassed at the time the check is presented. He need not be. The best solution is for the woman to have a credit card, or possibly a charge account at the restaurant. If the man is sensitive about it at all, the act of signing a slip of paper does not somehow seem so objectionable as having the woman check over the bill and count out the money while he sits by.

When a Woman Invites a Couple

A woman may invite a couple to have dinner with her, but when she does she should make it clear that it's her party. She does this by saying when she invites them, "I'd like to *take* you to dinner." If the man offers to pay, as he might, she should be firm, saying, "No, this was *my* invitation, and I am treating." She should then proceed to pay the bill.

Special Types of Restaurants

Smorgasbord

The smorgasbord, an import from Sweden originally, has gained tremendous popularity in the United States. Actually it is a buffet, but a buffet of such variety and interest that it is more than worth the effort of serving yourself.

When a man invites a woman to dine at a smorgasbord restaurant, she accompanies him to the buffet so that she may see the delectable displays of food and choose a little of everything that appeals to her.

At this type of meal the individual tables are set as usual. The smorgasbord, which literally translated means "sandwich table," has one or more stacks of small plates to be filled with reasonable amounts of food. Since you are expected to make as many trips as you wish from your seat to the smorgasbord and back, you should never overload your plate and you should only choose foods that go well together each time you serve yourself. Leave your used plate and silver at your table for the waiter to remove while you are helping yourself to your next selection. You are intended to take your time. Start with fish, which should whet your appetite, then cold cuts and salad, followed if you wish by cheeses and a bit of fresh fruit or Jell-O. You then choose your hot food, and end with dessert and coffee if your appetite is still there.

Oriental Restaurants

Japanese and Chinese restaurants offer interesting variations in service and food. Some Japanese restaurants have sections where the guests may remove their shoes, if they choose to, and sit on cushions on the floor at low tables, Japanese style. If you have very long legs, like my husband, or if you are taking older or crippled people to such a restaurant, you would not sit in that section, but you would request a regular table, which is always available for those who prefer it. Chinese restaurants have regular seating arrangements. If you find chopsticks at your place and wish to use them to eat, do so. But if you feel awkward with them or cannot manage them, do not hesitate to ask for a fork and knife. In Chinese restaurants the people at the table may order different dishes, which are placed in the center of the table so that the diners may serve themselves from any or all of them. This is a delightful way to experiment with various dishes—and one that may be helpful in ordering the next time you go to a similar restaurant.

Cafeterias

When the restaurant is crowded and there are no empty tables it is perfectly all right to take an empty chair at a table already occupied, but one should say, "Is this seat taken?" or "Do you mind if I sit here?" When there are busboys who carry the trays to the tables they are generally given a tip depending on the particular cafeteria and the amount of food on the tray. Diners who join a stranger are under no obligation to talk, but it is all right to open a casual conversation if the other person seems to be receptive. If he or she does not respond after an opening gambit don't continue with further remarks.

Lunch Counters

When a couple goes to a lunch counter that is so crowded that there are not two seats together, it is permissible to ask a person sitting between two empty stools if he or she would mind moving down one place. Conversely, a person in this position should offer to move before being asked.

Unless there is a sign saying: NO TIPPING, tips are expected. The minimum—for a cup of coffee only—is fifteen cents. When food is served the tip should not be less than fifty cents.

Coffee Shops and Delicatessens

Most coffee shops have both booths and tables or counters for customers. These are served by waiters or waitresses. Delicatessens often have tables for customers but no waiters. In this case, the order is placed at the counter by the customer and then picked up when ready and taken to the table, or delivered by a counter person. The customer is expected to clear the table and dispose of paper plates, plastic utensils, etc. upon leaving. No tips are expected in this instance.

Appreciation and Complaints

For some reason people voice their complaints much more often—and more loudly—than they voice their appreciation. One *should* complain in a restaurant—when the service is bad, when a waiter is rude or careless, or when the food comes in badly prepared or not as ordered. These are legitimate reasons for speaking up, and it is to the restaurant's advantage that you do so. Its livelihood depends on customers' approval, and if its faults are not called to the management's attention they cannot be corrected.

Complaints should be made quietly, without making a fuss or attracting the attention of other diners. They should be made first to the waiter (or person who commits the error), and if he makes no effort to correct the situation, the headwaiter or whoever is in charge of the dining room should be notified. Food that is cold should be taken back to be heated; meat that is not done as you requested should be replaced. Rudeness and laziness should be reported, but laziness or inattention should not be confused with pure inability to serve too many people. Often a waiter or waitress, because the tables are poorly allotted, or because another waiter is absent, works as hard and fast as possible but still cannot keep up with the requests of the patrons. Diners should recognize this and make allowances. They may complain to the manager, so that more help can be sent to their area, but they should be careful not to put the blame on the waiter, who is no happier about the situation than they are.

If, after making a legitimate complaint, you receive no satisfaction from anyone, you may reduce the tip or leave none at all, and avoid that restaurant in the future.

On the other side of the coin, appreciative comments, as well as appreciation shown by a generous tip, are more than welcome. The tip is expected, but the extra "Thank you," "The food was really outstanding," or "The service was especially good," mean a great deal to someone who is trying to do his best. They also mean a great deal to the management, whose reputation is greatly enhanced by the customer who is satisfied and doesn't hesitate to say so.

(*For information on tipping in restaurants, see pages 338–341.*)

*O*ften we save our best manners for company and even for strangers, giving less than our best to our families and friends, even though these are the relationships that matter most in our lives.

This can happen when good manners are not made a habit, beginning at home, and beginning with young children.

Children can scarcely be too young to be taught the rudiments of good manners, nor can the teaching be too patiently or too conscientiously carried out. As long as the parents set a good example, any child can be taught to be well-behaved through parental patience and perseverance, whereas to break bad habits once they are acquired is a herculean task.

6
Interrelationships

YOUNG CHILDREN

All youngsters must be taught from their earliest years that there are certain rules that have to be obeyed. I firmly believe that too much permissiveness can contribute to delinquency. Young people, no matter what they may say aloud, want and need direction and correction, and the more honest ones will even admit it. I have actually heard one youngster say, "I wish my mother would say 'No'—then I wouldn't have to make up my mind."

The Validity of "No"

Obedience to "No" is perhaps the earliest lesson a youngster must learn. "No's" fall into various categories—from very important, which requires instant response, to "probably not," which may be discussed. The most important "No" is the one that will prevent your child from getting hurt or hurting someone else. This "No" requires instant, unquestioning obedience. If Christopher goes too far out on thin ice, or goes right on touching a match to her sister Joannie's dress while he decides whether or not to obey, it will be too late. The tone of your voice, reserved for this real emergency "No," is usually enough to enforce it.

The next "No" in importance is that which prevents destruction of property. This "No" is used continually with small children—"No, Christopher, don't touch," "No, Eddie, don't step on the flowers," and so on and on. It is a vital part of teaching respect for possessions, and as the child gets older, will become less necessary.

From there on "No" is used for an infinite number of reasons—some good, some bad. It is important that you recognize your motive for saying "No." Is it for Christopher's good or for your own satisfaction? Are you simply feeling too lazy to get him dressed to take him to meet Mommy, or should he *really* be in bed and asleep before Mommy's plane comes in? The good reasons for a firm "No" are:

Protection of Christopher's safety or health
Protection of your own—or someone else's—property
Christopher's education—to help him differentiate between right and wrong
Any legitimate reason—for example, he wants you to buy a toy that he doesn't need and/or you cannot afford. Or he wants to go out and play when he is tired and it is time for his nap.

The bad reasons for a "No" are:

Vindictiveness—because you are angry
Laziness and/or selfishness—It is simply less trouble for you to say "No" at the time.

Having learned to respond to "No" the child must then learn that "No" is inviolable. Temper tantrums, refusal to eat, begging, or feigning sickness will not change "No" to "Yes."

There are only two exceptions to the rule. "No" *should be changed to "Yes"* when:

The reason for the original "No" is gone.
You realize that the "No" was wrong or unfair.

Fair Play

Fair play among children is really good sportsmanship. It includes the practice of kindness, taking turns, and sharing. Amy's insistence on bossing a group of children throughout the play period has to be changed to cooperative agreement where the majority decide what to play, or each child has the chance to suggest a game or activity. If her mother sees that she is being bossy and demanding that everyone do what she wants to do, Amy must be taught that she can't always have her way. Tim's mother shouldn't allow him to brag only about his own achievements or to tell her how inferior other children are. If he wins a medal at school, the family naturally praises him, and it is proper that they should; but wise parents teach their child that boasting and conceit will get him nowhere.

Fair play has to be practiced by parents, too. Parents have to realize that each child is an individual and as such, must be treated with respect. If you don't treat your children with respect, it is quite unlikely that they will ever learn how to treat others with the respect that they deserve, including you.

Don't talk about other people in disrespectful ways, and don't talk about your own child's shortcomings or "funny ways" to others in your child's presence.

Interrupting

Children should not be allowed to get into the habit of interrupting. This is part of learning to respect other people's rights. It is up to you to teach Susan to wait for a break in the conversation before butting in. The mother who invariably stops and says, "What is it, dear?" when her daughter interrupts is helping her to establish a habit that will do her a disservice all her life.

The first "lesson" is to say to Susan, every time she breaks into your conversation, "Susan, Mrs. Smith is talking. Wait until she is finished, please." Some children react to this well; others seem to be deaf to it. It may help to discuss it before your visitor comes. Explain that you expect Susan to stay outside or to play in her room for half an hour, so that you can talk to your friend. You can also make a bargain—if she will give you one hour uninterrupted, you will devote one hour to her later in the day.

But most important, when she does barge in, don't answer her—just keep insisting, "Susan, I'll talk to you when Mrs. Smith and I are through." If she is very small you must help her out by saying to your friend after a few minutes, "Excuse me, Betsy, Susan is waiting to tell me something . . . etc." It is not fair or reasonable to keep a two- or three-year-old waiting while you and Betsy catch up on an hour's worth of neighborhood news.

"Please" and "Thank You"

"Please" and "Thank you" are still the "magic" words, and you will be doing Susan a favor if you insist that she use them until they become a habit. Everyone likes to be appreciated, and "Thank you" is the accepted way of showing appreciation. "Please" turns a demand into a request and indicates an option—it turns an unpopular request into a more palatable one.

The essential requirement in teaching Susan to use the "magic" words is—use them yourself. Too many parents say, "Hand me that hammer," "Go get my knitting," "Put on your jacket," without even a "Would you?" let alone a "Please." Then they consistently respond to their youngsters' demands by saying, "What do you say?" or "If you say 'please.'" You must do this constantly with both "Please" and "Thank you" when Susan is small, as a reminder, but she will get the point much faster if you use them consistently when speaking to her.

Greetings

Teach your children, as soon as they are old enough to understand, to greet people by name. Learning early on to look someone in the eye to say, "Hello, Mr. Barrett," instead of a "Hi" mumbled while looking at the ground is a valuable lesson for the future.

Shyness is not an acceptable substitute for politeness: It is only polite to acknowledge another's presence, even when very young.

To help your children overcome the obstacle of uncomfortableness when greeting others, practice. Show your child how to shake hands and practice exchanging greetings. Have her be the adult and you be first the shy child and then the polite child, looking her in the eye, calling her by name, and responding to an offered handshake. Then ask her which response makes her feel better. Seeing the difference will help her to think about the feelings of others.

Table Manners

Table manners for children should be the same as they are for adults, with one exception: Children should be permitted to be excused from the table, when very young, if the meal is an extended one. Expecting a young child to sit quietly through a protracted meal when his food is gone is an unreasonable demand on his patience and ability to sit still without wiggling, fiddling and noisemaking to help pass the time.

"May I please be excused?" should be asked of parents, or of the hostess when dining with friends and relatives.

OLDER CHILDREN

Perhaps the overwhelming topic of concern that is manners-related for older children is that of privacy. Just as they have been taught to respect yours, you must respect theirs.

- Don't try to involve yourself in their conversations
- Don't listen in on their telephone conversations
- Don't go through their belongings
- Don't pry
- Knock and wait for a "come in" before entering their room

Doing any of these things is either just plain nosy, or an indication of lack of trust. If you indeed are concerned that they are involved in something they shouldn't be, talk to them about your concerns before attempting to monitor every moment of their lives. Serious problems call for serious remedies, but general snoopiness is no solution.

Appearance

Cleanliness and neatness have everything to do with good manners no matter what the fashion trend of the moment is. Insisting on good grooming helps to remind your older children that they should care for their own bodies and their appearance and suggest to them that a neat appearance shows respect for others.

Learning to Entertain

Whether children have one or two friends over or have a party with many friends, they need help in learning how to be a good host or hostess.

Talk to both very young and older children about planning. They should have some activities in mind for those friends who, when asked "What would you like to do?" have no idea.

They should be helped to learn negotiating skills—when one friend wants to play badminton and the other wants to watch television, the young host or hostess must be able to say, "Let's play badminton for an hour and then have a snack and relax in front of the TV."

They should, if refreshments will be in order, know how to serve them, and not expect their parents to drop everything and entertain their guests.

When a party is planned, it is incumbent upon parents to be present and to make their presence known without being in attendance every minute. No child, even a teenager, has the skills to deal with peers when a situation gets out of hand, when "crashers" appear at the door, or in ending a party gracefully.

Dating

Aside from going on a date with your child, there is little you can do about what actually takes place. You can only hope that your early teaching has instilled not only good manners but a sense of self-respect in your child and that he or she is prepared to handle him- or herself with grace and dignity. You can, however, and should, set and enforce guidelines. Setting limits is your prerogative—no parties without an adult chaperon, and reasonable curfews—are two.

Accepting or Refusing a Date

Ordinarily, accepting a date presents no problem. If she wants to go, the girl simply says, "I'd love to!" The worst mistake she can make is to be evasive. If she has promised to baby-sit and doesn't know whether she can get a substitute, or if she is not sure whether the family is going to the country for the weekend, she must say so. But it must be true, and she must be sincere, or he will surely know it. No one should ever say, "Can I let you know tomorrow?" without saying why.

Once a girl has accepted, she must keep the date unless a real emergency arises. One should *never* break one date to accept another.

To refuse a date a girl need only say, "I'm so sorry, but I have a date for Saturday night." As long as she doesn't make the mistake of saying, "I'm sorry, I can't go out that night," she is free to accept if someone else calls. If, however, she would really like the boy to ask her again, she should give him a more detailed excuse that sounds, and is, true.

When girls ask boys, the same rules of courtesy apply.

In either case, etiquette calls for clear communication. The one asking should state:

- What time he or she will call for the other
- Their means of transportation
- What kind of date it will be—movies, a party, etc.
- Who, if anyone else, will be with them

If the asker doesn't offer this information, the askee may and should ask for it. The timeline for planning dates is:

> *One to four days ahead for an ordinary date*
> *At least two weeks ahead for a dance or a party*
> *A month ahead for a prom or college weekend*

There are exceptions, such as when a party is planned on the spur of the moment, but these are good general rules.

Other Dating Data

A girl should introduce a new friend to her parents the first time he comes to her house. She should brief her parents a little before he arrives so that they can carry on a conversation easily. Five minutes or so is enough for the visit, and the girl should be ready to say, "We'd better go now—the others are waiting for us."

Men—and boys—usually call for their dates at their homes. Only if the boy knows the girl well and has a good reason (a late class or hockey practice, for example) should he meet her at a movie house or a snack bar.

Unless a couple has been going steady and they have agreed to share at times, the boy pays all expenses on a date except when the girl asked the boy for the date. The girl may help considerably by suggesting inexpensive entertainment or choosing the lower-priced items on a menu. If after a few dates she wishes to pay for their next dinner or to share the costs, she should bring it up in advance and not surprise him with the offer in front of the waiter.

On a first date, or when a couple dates infrequently, the boy usually plans the entertainment in advance and asks the girl to go to a rock concert, to bowl, or whatever. When they go out together often they generally discuss what they would like to do and plan it together.

The boy should arrive for his date on time, and the girl should be ready. There is no truth in the old idea that she makes herself more desirable by keeping him waiting. Quite the opposite!

If a boy hasn't told his date what they are going to do, she should, as mentioned, call and ask him, so that she can dress appropriately.

The Telephone

Teenagers are absolutely *compulsive* about using the telephone! Arlene leaves Pat at her gate, walks across the street into her house, and picks up the telephone to call—Pat. It is a phenomenon that adults cannot understand, but it's there, and "if you can't fight 'em, join 'em!"

To avoid knock-down, drag-out fights with your youngsters, you must, with their agreement, establish some rules. There should be hours when they can make and receive calls and hours when they cannot. Dinnertime and after a certain hour at night should be taboo. So should any hours at which you are apt to receive important calls—if, for instance, Grandmother regularly calls from California at about eight o'clock on Wednesday nights.

If you can afford to have a separate telephone for your teenagers, you are in luck. But if you cannot, you must all make some concessions. You might ask your friends to call during the afternoon, or early in the evening when your youngsters are doing their homework. After eight or eight-thirty, perhaps, they might be allowed free use of the phone.

Finally, the length of call should be limited. Nothing is more frustrating than trying to get an important call through, only to get a busy signal hour after hour. Settle on a reasonable time with your children—shorter than they want and longer than you want. Something in the neighborhood of fifteen minutes will give them time to say and resay everything they can think of, and will leave your callers short of apoplexy.

Call Waiting

Call waiting is often a solution to teen telephone tie-ups. If you have it, you have to make some rules about using it, particularly when your calls are business ones, or you are active in the community and people need to reach you. Teens should be expected to interrupt a strictly social call to respond to the call-waiting beep and, if the call is for their parents, end their own call and let you know you have a call. Although they may feel this is unreasonable, your rights to receive calls do supersede theirs—if only because you are the one paying the bills! If you prefer, you can instruct them to interrupt their call, answer the waiting call and take a message for you.

(See pages 294–305 for the rules of telephone etiquette.)

Visiting

When a teenager—whether a boy or a girl—goes to spend a weekend with friends, the same basic rules apply as do for adults. The visitor should take a gift, preferably a "house" present rather than a "hostess" present. A game, a plant, a tape or anything that can be enjoyed by the whole family is the best choice.

As a visitor, Mike should be especially careful to pick up after himself, to make his bed, and to leave the bathroom clean. He should *not* leave socks, shoes, sweaters, etc., lying around the house, and he should be reminded, before going, to be polite and helpful—not only to the young host or hostess, but to his or her parents. Even though the menus do not offer the foods to which he is accustomed, he should try everything and keep his feelings to himself if he is disappointed. He must, of course, obey any household rules laid down by the host's or hostess's parents.

Finally, Mike must write a thank-you letter to the host's or hostess's mother. He need not write his friend if they will see one another soon, but the bread-and-butter letter to the mother is a must. This is not necessary at all, of course, for the casual "sleep-over" at a neighbor's. Then verbal thanks in the morning is all that is necessary.

WHEN GROWN CHILDREN RETURN HOME TO LIVE

Quite often today parents have scarcely launched their children into the world than they're back, bag and baggage. Housing in the 90's is prohibitively expensive, and many grown children simply cannot afford to live on their own directly after school or while beginning their careers. The fact that this was the way of the world for generations does not make it any easier today on either parents or their adult children, who have both grown up in eras where everyone lived separately. This rejoining of the old family unit is not easy, and diplomacy and tact and a great deal of readjusting is required for it to work without tempers flaring.

Once again, clear communication helps pave the way for harmonious living. Parents who have just begun to enjoy time alone are faced with a full house, and children who are used to total independence are faced with someone else's rules, as they were when they were children. It is difficult for parents to stop being parents, and for children to act like adults when the living situation has reverted to the way it used to be.

Parents and their grown children, before the latter moves back in, have to have a family meeting to discuss such things as the following:

- Rent—if at all, how much and when will it be paid
- Household chores—whether everyone will assume the responsibility or whether they must be assigned on a weekly basis
- Snacking—how will "off-limits" food items be indicated so that no one raids the refrigerator of tomorrow night's dinner
- Privacy—an absolute must on both sides
- Noise—the reasonable cut off for music, loud television, etc.
- Laundry—will everyone do his/her own, or will good old mom gather it all up like in the good old days
- Cars—a clear understanding of whose car it is and when and how it may be borrowed, if adult children arrive without one
- Dinner—is everyone expected to eat together, and if so, communication guidelines for being late or not present—and if not, how will this be worked out
- Entertaining—who, where, and when; are there off-limits times and rooms?

If these basic communal guidelines are established and everyone lives up to his or her agreement, the entire experience can be a very happy and even joyous one as family members learn to love and support one another in new ways.

SPOUSES, EX-SPOUSES, IN-LAWS AND OTHER RELATIVES

The traditional marriage was composed of a husband and a wife in sharply defined roles with the "right" number of children (determined by the times in which they lived). The husband was income earner, major decision maker and protector; the wife was homemaker, bearer of children, nurturer and acquiescer to her husband's will. By filling these roles men and women built the family into a strong American resource. The Second World War, in sending women from the home into factories, is charged with the first step in changing our perception of what a "normal" family is.

Today marriage comes in a variety of shapes and sizes and can be tailor-made to fit every need. For instance:

- The husband and wife both live at home and work full time.
- The husband and wife both work and live in different cities, meeting on weekends.
- The wife works, and the husband keeps house at home.
- Husband and wife take the option of remaining childless.
- The husband and wife live together but take separate vacations.

- The husband and wife marry under conditions set down by contract.
- The husband and wife elect to review their marriage at regular intervals with the choice of renewing the option or seeking divorce.
- The marriage is open, with both partners free to form sexual liaisons whenever and with whomever they wish.
- The husband and wife both bring children from a previous marriage.

The list is without end, for taste and individual needs may expand it as time proceeds. Although many people are critical of such innovations, it is wise to remember that marriage is a personal agreement between two people. While we may not choose to follow their choices, we must remain open-minded enough to refrain from judging them.

As different as these varied forms of marriage may appear—and in practice are—successful ones of any kind have much in common. Whatever form of marriage two people choose, they can make it fulfilling by applying similar principles:

- Following the rules they agreed to before entering marriage.
- Showing consideration for each other.
- Developing common interests.
- Communicating.
- Having a sense of humor.
- Believing strongly enough in the relationship to work at it, and keep working at it.

It is this last point which makes the difference between marriage and living together.

Husbands and Wives

Neither a husband nor a wife should make social engagements without consulting the other.

Both should work hard to air their problems or differences in a clear and calm way. It is unreasonable, no matter how long they have been married, for one to assume that the other should know what he or she is thinking or what is upsetting him or her.

The Importance of "Our"

Of all the advice one could give a young bride or groom, perhaps the best would be to use the words *we* and *our*. How many times have you heard a wife say, "Yes, *I* have three children," instead of "Bill and I . . ." or "We have: . . ." Or a husband introducing his son: "I'd like you to meet *my* son, Billy."

When a man and woman marry they become a unit made up of two parts.

Their major possessions, whether their children or their worldly goods, become *theirs*, not *his* and *hers*. To refuse to recognize this by using *I* and *my*, instead of *we* and *our*, is not only discourteous but indicates a dangerous attitude toward the marriage itself.

Invasion of Privacy

While, possessions are "pooled" in a good marriage, some things are not. Each member of the couple has a right to his own opinions, to his own interests, and to his privacy. *No one* has a right to pry into the personal correspondence of another person or to listen in on his phone calls or private conversations. Neither a husband nor a wife should *ever* open a letter addressed to the other unless it is obviously an advertisement or unsolicited "nuisance" mail.

Elderly Parents

Elderly people frequently complain that their grown children, their grandchildren or their nieces or nephews don't come to see them often enough. This can be very sad, especially if the elderly person is alone. It is particularly hard at holiday seasons, and I can only urge children of elderly parents to remember their loneliness and to have them visit at those times, no matter how busy the household may be. Other ways to keep in touch are through tape cassettes and videotapes—especially when parents live a distance away from their children and aren't able to see their grandchildren more than once a year or so. The old-fashioned skill of letter-writing may certainly be put to use here, as well, both by children and grandchildren.

On the other hand, elderly parents should do their best to understand how busy their children are and not be selfishly demanding. The older person who stays young by keeping busy himself, by keeping up his interest in what is going on in the world, by participating in as many activities as he can and as he enjoys, will not be sitting around feeling sorry for himself.

They should also remember that we all have to learn things ourselves, and a grown child, unless he or she solicits advice, would prefer not to be told that he or she is doing everything wrong. They surely heard enough of that growing up, and would welcome an adult-to-adult relationship with their parents.

When Parents Live With Their Adult Children

When your parents need to move in with you, either for financial or health reasons, or simply because you would feel more comfortable than having them live alone, there are as many co-habitation manners and courtesies to work out as their are when children move back home after school or between jobs.

I believe, in fact, that there are more. The elderly parent has probably given up most of his or her material possessions in order to move into your house, and this loss is acute, usually representing a lifetime of collecting, and always having to do with a sense of security and belonging. You are asking him or her to fit into your schedule, when he or she may be quite used to his or her own. You might have dinner at seven; she may be used to dining at five. You may do your laundry whenever you have a chance to throw it into the washer; she might have spent a lifetime doing it on Monday. You probably eat quickly, since mealtime is not the sole focus of your day. He might eat slowly, savoring every mouthful as a great pleasure. You might whiz through the drive-in window at the bank; he might look forward to depositing his Social Security check in person and chatting with the teller. Etcetera, etcetera. The differences can be vast.

The best advice I can give you is to remember that your parent (or parent-in-law) has given up not only his "things," but also his independence when he moved in with you. This is usually frightening to an older person, and the least you can do is to make occasional outings fun and at his convenience, not yours, and to set aside some time every day to have a real conversation. As much as you can do to make him feel needed is also tremendously helpful. Ask his advice. Depend on him to complete certain chores or tasks. Be thankful. Tell him you don't know what you would have done without him. Help him to make this radical transition.

And to parents moving in with their children, I can only stress the importance of a positive outlook and noninterference. As much as you are itching to right what you see as wrongs; to tell your daughter a better way to whiten whites; to instruct your grandchild to wear a hat or drink her orange juice—don't. At least not at the beginning, and certainly not in "instructional" tones. Everyone's sensitivities are at an all-time high in making this adjustment, and your family wants most for you to be happy. Suggesting change can often sound like complaining, even if you are only trying to help, and it is best to take this slowly, and then only in the most cheerful way.

Privacy is important to both. Neither should pry, and each should allow the other to entertain without feeling guilty for not including Mom, or Daughter, each time. Some occasions are happier with everyone present, but each should be allowed time with friends without the other there. If the "children" are having friends over for dinner and bridge, a word to "Grandma" that friends are expected and this time it's just dinner for four, accompanied by a special dinner-on-a-tray for her and a rented movie or a good book, should not hurt her feelings or make you feel guilty. This does not mean, however, that she should be locked in her room every time company comes.

When Elderly Parents are In Nursing Homes

There are times when the mental or physical health of an older parent requires that he or she receive full time care which you cannot provide in your home. There are also times when, because of the personalities involved, that living together simply wouldn't work. When this occurs, finding the best facility possible is the joint responsibility of the older parent and his or her children. Again, this decision should not be accompanied by guilt on the part of the children or resentment on the part of the parent, although it often is.

To make the best of the situation, it is important to help make the parent's room as comfortable and "homey" as possible, and to visit cheerfully and often. It is good to check in with staff regularly for a report on how things are going, and to communicate to them some of the things your parent has always enjoyed doing. A good nursing home will try hard to provide craft materials, find a second, third and fourth for bridge, or make piano playing time available, for example, if you ask them to.

In-Law Situations

One is likely to overlook the fact that when John Jones marries Mary Smith, a number of Smiths and Joneses are suddenly forced into the closeness of a family relationship. Even when a man or woman has no family, he or she becomes son or daughter, sister or brother, to those who hitherto may have been total strangers.

The two most difficult situations to meet happily and successfully are that between the husband and his father-in-law and that between the wife and her mother-in-law. The other positions are easier, and there is little reason for failure. In any case the very first rule that every father-in-law—*and* every mother-in-law—must learn is DON'T INTERFERE. Never mind what small blunders your daughter or daughter-in-law or your son or son-in-law may make; remember that it is the individual's right to live and do and think as he or she pleases. If you are asked what you think, answer truthfully, of course; but don't, upon being given one opening, cram in every item of good advice you've been storing up for just this chance—or you will risk never being asked again.

In spite of all the mother-in-law jokes one hears, a great many couples—perhaps a majority—establish very happy relationships with their in-laws—not only the parents, but also the brothers and sisters. The ties may be as strong or stronger than those with their own families, and often continue long after the death of the husband or wife, or even after a divorce.

Unfortunately, however, there are people who feel that the blood relationship is the only important one, and when the blood relative dies they feel no responsibility toward the widowed in-law or his or her children. It is very sad when this happens, as it seems to indicate that the fondness shown before either was very shallow or existed only for the benefit of the one who has died. This is so wrong! People should be loved—or disliked—for themselves, not because they married someone's relative. And the affection should not die because the spouse has passed away, unless of course the bereaved in-law kills it herself (or himself) by becoming demanding, omnipresent, or self-pitying. Sisters—or brothers—in-law should remember that *their* in-laws need just as much support in their loneliness as would any member of their "own" family.

A brother-in-law, according to the dictionary, is "a brother of a husband or wife, a sister's husband, or loosely, a *wife's sister's husband*." Someone in this "looser" relationship merits the same affection and consideration as his wife. He is called "Uncle" by the children in the family and continues to be called by that name even after his spouse dies.

Stepparents

The cruel stepparents of fairy tales have luckily vanished and in their place, with rising statistics on second marriages, we find men and women trying to fill their role as affectionately and effectively as possible. A few guidelines may help.

Understanding the Feelings of Children

When a second marriage involving children takes place, the feelings of everyone require considerate understanding—those of the children most of all. When you bring a stepparent into your children's lives, you may notice hostility and defensive behavior, especially if they see the person as a father or mother replacement. They may act rude and surly toward the stepparent and grow inordinately protective of their own mother or father. Try to respond without anger, with continual reassurances of love, but with the same demands for standards of behavior that have existed prior to the second marriage: Do not let children use the situation for manipulative purposes.

When your new spouse also has children, complications develop. Those children will bring their own hostilities into the home and add to them jealousy as acute as any sibling rivalry. At best the situation is fraught with mixed emotions and potential explosions. Expect them. Try to understand the reasons for them. Handle them with an attitude that says, "We are a family now, all together. Let's deal with our feelings and work things out so that we will all be happy."

One added possibility is that your new spouse may feel out of joint in competing with your children for your attention. Be sure you set aside enough private time for the two of you to forestall trouble.

Finally, do not be surprised to find your own nerves strained to the limit: You are emceeing a difficult act. Communicate your feelings; do not deny and try to hide them. Do not dwell on them, however; think instead of the benefits your new marriage is bringing to you, your new spouse, and everyone's children.

Handling Family Problems

Keeping open lines of communication among family members is the best way to avoid problems and to solve them when they do arise. When the dynamics of a family are not working for any single member, the entire system falls apart, and everyone must be involved in reconstruction. Even children can learn to present complaints without hostility when they have good examples to follow. Remember, however, that a good communications system requires a receiver as well as a sender. Listen to your children when they express their concerns; do *not* do all the talking.

If children in the new marriage begin to act out their upset through academic or behavioral problems at school, the solution is the same: communication. You, your new spouse, and the children can uncover many hidden problems in conferences with teachers, and by discussing them help alleviate them.

If time and conversation fail to heal the hurts that a second marriage may inflict on your children, you may want to seek outside help. Family therapy is available in even small towns these days and has proven highly successful.

One word of warning: Do not try to force your children to accept a stepparent as a new mother or father. Let them be the judge in time of whether parent or stepparent is the major person in their life.

Parent or Stepparent?

One question inevitably arises when children attend an affair requiring the presence of a father or mother: "Whom shall I invite, my real parent or my stepparent?" While etiquette dictates no single answer, common sense does: Let the choice be the child's.

The only events which your child's father (and his wife if he has remarried) *and* you and your present husband should all attend are special occasions such as graduations and weddings.

SINGLE PARENTS

Whether a parent becomes a solo act through divorce or through the death of a spouse, it is important to help children with the many adjustments they must make toward this new family status.

Explaining a Divorce or Breakup

Divorce should be explained to a child in terms of the parents, not in terms of the child. Although the level of explanation depends on the age and understanding of the child, the gist is that Mother and Father have habits and personalities that make it impossible for them to live together any longer. Avoid saying that you no longer love each other, because children will be quick to assume that since their parents can stop loving each other, they can also stop loving them. "We both love you" and "You are in no way responsible for the problem" are important messages to convey. Books for all age levels are readily available to help you explain the mysterious happening of divorce.

Even when proper explanations have been made to a child, negative messages may come across. You both should be especially careful to avoid derogatory remarks about each other in the child's presence. Even emphasis and inflection can speak negatively where words do not: "Your mother let you catch cold *again*?" Children's ears and feelings are keenly attuned, and *sub rosa* hostility creates unendurable stress for them.

If you have been living with a man (or woman) for a long time before the breakup, your partner and your children may have grown close, and they may want to continue seeing each other. Let them: Continuity helps children adjust. If your partner makes a clean break with no effort to see the children again, you will have to explain that too. It is not easy, but try something like this: "We lived together as long as we were able to help each other be happy, but when Joan [or Bill] and I couldn't do that any more, we had to leave each other. Since you live with me and I love you more than anybody in the world, you have to leave too [or, we'll still be living here together]. Let's try to remember how nice it was for a while and find other ways to be happy now."

Divorced Singles With Children

When a divorce occurs and one or the other of the partners simply removes him- or herself from relationships with the children of the previous union, it falls to the remaining and therefore truly "single" parent to do and be all things to the children.

When the parent who leaves the family home is still nearby, however, it is often only manners that make difficult situations bearable.

The non-custodial parent's rights should be scrupulously respected, but when they interfere with the school or social lives of the children, accommodations must be made. A non-custodial parent who demands that children keep their weekend commitment to her, three hours away, when they have softball practice or are starring in the school play, must re-think her demands. Usually all that is accomplished is resentment from the children. In other words, respect and open communication are a must if relationships are to be effectively rebuilt in new situations.

Special occasions and holidays cause a problem because both of you will want to share them with your child, and the child in turn may want to be with you both. One solution is to alternate special days—Thanksgiving with father, Christmas with mother; this year's birthday with father, next year's with mother. Another possibility is to split the holiday, the child spending the morning with father and the afternoon with mother. Many child psychologists suggest that the mothers and fathers of very young children do not plan to spend those days together with them. Having you together again tends to reawaken your child's fantasy of reconciliation, making his adjustment more difficult and painful. When children are older, however, both of you may safely share the important events in their lives—bar mitzvah, graduation, engagement party, wedding, and such.

You should keep in mind the value to a child of an extended family, especially to a child of divorce, whose family suddenly diminishes by half. Since grandparents are the second most significant adults in the life of a child, even those on the side of the noncustodial parent should be encouraged to continue the relationship previously established with the child.

Uncles, aunts, and cousins on the side of the noncustodial as well as the custodial parent can also play a supportive role and should be invited to do so. Anyone who can reinforce a child's conviction that despite the divorce, he or she is still wanted and loved will provide a benefit. It should be made clear that any negative comments concerning either parent are deeply destructive.

In discussing a child's contact with the noncustodial parent and the family of that parent, I am assuming that both of you are able to control any hostility you may feel. You need not be more than agreeable to each other; but since you do have to make various arrangements and see each other on visits, it is essential that you follow the rules of courtesy applicable to others and maintain as cordial a relationship as you possibly can. If this cannot be, and the noncustodial parent is out of control, then visits should be temporarily terminated until that parent is able to act in a manner more conducive to the child's well-being.

In general, the following guidelines help both parents and children deal with particular difficulties.

School

Both you and your former husband or wife should become involved in your children's school to the degree that you can. Report cards can be mailed to both; both should attend teacher conferences, though separately if your relationship is less than cordial. Both of you should attend school functions and PTA meetings, though you may choose to sit apart. The degree of involvement of the noncustodial parent at special school events should depend less on the parent's wishes and far more on the child's. In all cases, the school should know of your divorce, whether it happened prior to the children's attendance or during their time at school, and teachers should be advised to alert the custodial parent of any problem that might be attributable to it.

Your Child's Friends

Friends of young single-parent children inevitably remark on the fact: "You have no daddy [or mommy]." If your child is small and unable to handle the situation, you might intercede with, "Yes she has; only he [or she] lives somewhere else." Confidence that she really *has* a mommy [or daddy] who lives somewhere else will grow from the degree of stability both parents contribute to her life. With that, she will soon be able to handle questions and remarks herself.

If possible, include among your child's playmates other children whose parents are also divorced. It will make her feel less "different."

If your child's friends are attending an affair involving one parent—such as a Father-Daughter or Mother-Daughter party—which happens to be the parent you are *not,* urge the noncustodial parent to accompany your child. If this is not possible, try to secure an aunt or uncle substitute.

Children and a New Relationship

When a "date" becomes a more lasting relationship, children cannot avoid being involved, nor should they: What affects you affects them. Many a new relationship has been severed by children unprepared to share their parent with another adult. Careful planning can help avoid disappointments on both sides.

When you have been dating the same person regularly, it is time to introduce the children. "This is Glen Andrews, a friend of Mommy's," or "Daddy's friend Jennifer Peters has wanted to meet you," should be adequate. Handled as casually as introducing your children to dinner guests, it should pose no problems.

When children sense a more than casual friendship, they may become fearful of their place in your affections and behave with the defensiveness about which parents have nightmares: sulking, rudeness, tears. While embarrassing, this reaction is normal . . . and understandable when you put yourself in the children's situation: "Am I going to lose this parent too?" The best approach is to explain to your date ahead of time what might happen and then handle the scene with as much calm as you can muster. You might want to excuse yourself and speak to the children alone, reassuring them of your love.

After your children and potential partner have met, the relationship takes on a new dimension: Although you are still a parent-child team on most occasions, you are slowly becoming a threesome. You can help your date feel at ease and your children grow secure by sharing outings—picnics, drives, trips to the museum or zoo, maybe a movie or ballet, for example. These experiences will lay the groundwork for the other two sides of your newly formed triangle to become friends on their own and for all of you to feel comfortable in the new pattern.

The Widowed Parent

Feelings About Death

While many situations are similar for widowed and divorced parents, areas of difference should be pointed out.

First, the divorced parent may leave marriage with feelings of resentment and hostility that need controlling. The widowed parent, on the other hand, must handle feelings of grief. It is important for the surviving parent to realize that grief frequently shuts out others, seeking healing in solitude. While this is acceptable therapy for a childless widow or widower, where children are concerned, it must be avoided. Shutting a child out of the remaining parent's life after the death of the other will do lifelong damage. A child must be helped to express his grief and to share it with his parent, receiving love and support as he works through it.

Second, death should be explained to children at the level of their understanding. Books about this are available as an aid to parents. It should be made clear to even young children that Mommy or Daddy is dead and will not return: pretense and game playing are ineffective. The deceased parent should be discussed in a natural way and photographs kept in evidence.

What often adds to the hurt of widowhood is the surprise response of children. Instead of weeping and expressing grief as adults do, they may become angry: "What right had Mommy [or Daddy] to leave me?" They may become fearful of losing the remaining parent and perhaps of dying themselves. Or they may feel guilt, that in some way they are responsible for their parent's death. Love and understanding will in time help children heal, along with repeated explanations when needed as to the cause of death: Accident or illness eliminates implications of the child's involvement.

Finding a Substitute Parent

Suddenly deprived of a mother or father—and even slowly deprived over the period of a long illness—children feel an enormous void which another man or woman may help to fill. A close relative or godparent will probably feel honored to act as surrogate parent during the period of readjustment. The responsibility of such a person is to be on hand—to drop by in the evening or after school, to plan an activity for part of the weekend, to phone frequently. The surrogate parent is also expected to be on call when needed by the child for a function previously shared with the deceased parent or simply to talk. While in no way attempting to replace the deceased parent, the surrogate offers additional support during a painful period.

Rebuilding a Social Life

Long periods of mourning are no longer expected. Widows or widowers may begin to attend small gatherings when they feel emotionally able to handle them. If they have children, however, they may want to extend a nonsocial period somewhat longer so that their presence will lend added support. Occasions which parents and children can attend together are the best route back into social life.

Becoming a Single Parent by Choice

An increasing number of single men and women who have elected the option of parenthood do so by adopting children. Single adoptive parents enter a new life-style and face the same problems of child rearing as all single parents face.

Women who wish to have children but do not find themselves in a traditional relationship sometimes choose to bear a child on their own. While not prevalent, an increasing number of unmarried women are electing this path to parenthood.

If You've Chosen Adoption

A child should know from the start that he is adopted. You may implant the idea as you cuddle him with words to this effect: "Mommy [or Daddy] is so lucky to have found such a wonderful baby." Later on, when a friend or relative becomes pregnant and has a baby, your toddler will undoubtedly ask, "Was I once in your tummy?" if the adoptive parent is a woman, or "Whose tummy was I in?" if he is a man. This provides your opportunity to explain that you chose him because you wanted and loved him—especially him—so much.

The difficult question arises, if not verbally, surely emotionally, when the child asks, "Why did my first Mommy and Daddy give me away?" Your explanation—and it will have to be given more than once—can ease feelings of rejection and help the child reach eventual understanding. I advise you to read some of the many books on adoption to help you deal with this critical issue.

If You've Chosen to Bear a Child on Your Own

Until children are mature, a mother's explanations should be kept simple: "Your daddy lives somewhere else." When children are older and the questions demand an answer, you run two risks. One, if you explain your having a baby out of wedlock as a mistake, you might make your child feel unwanted. Two, if you explain it as a deliberate choice, you offer your child license to follow suit. Either way is Scylla or Charybdis.

I feel the best approach in presenting the fact that you and the child's father never married is something like this: "When I got pregnant I loved your father. We couldn't get married, though life would have been far easier if we could have. I wanted you so much, though, that I had you and kept you. I am glad because I love you more than anything in the world; and whatever problems come up, we'll face them together."

Explaining Your Choice to Others

You need feel no responsibility to explain the absence of a spouse to anyone. Alert your child's school, but go no further. If people who have no involvement ask, all you need reply is, "I have no husband [wife] now," or "Her father [or mother] doesn't live with us."

On the other hand, if you want to explain to some people, prepare yourself for their possible reactions. While many will accept your decision without a qualm, others may react with everything from curiosity to shock. Don't let them undermine your self-confidence: if they can't accept you and your child as the individuals you are, then *they,* not *you,* have a problem.

You may want to inform certain people in your child's life. For instance, you may want to fill in the school guidance counselor. Finally, if you are becoming seriously interested in someone, you should explain the situation in order to prevent later surprises that might shatter what could have developed into a lasting relationship.

When a Single Parent Has a Living-Together Partner

While most parents have their children call their partner by the first name, some urge "Mommy" or "Daddy." This may be cozy, but it can be very unsettling for children because they are quite aware of having a Mommy or Daddy elsewhere. If the real parent is deceased or has disappeared, then the living-together partner may properly assume the "Mommy" or "Daddy" name. Even then, though, do not rush into it. Wait to be sure the relationship is stable and appears to have a good chance of lasting, with marriage a possible eventuality. If the relationship breaks up and a new Joan or Bill replaces the first and perhaps the second, a series of Mommys and Daddies can do your child serious emotional damage.

If you and your living-together partner have children yourselves, of course you are Mommy and Daddy.

Once the new arrangement is underway, you should inform your child's school. All you need say is, "I want you to know that Jenny's home situation has changed. Don Phelps is living with us. You may hear Jenny talk about him. If you notice any change in her behavior or any kind of upset, please let me know." The older the child is, the less necessary this is.

SINGLES

Although we live in a global world and know more about other's customs and lifestyles than ever before, single people still find themselves isolated. Meeting new people is difficult, at best. Singles bars, although well-populated, seldom encourage lasting friendships, and the single person is often hard-pressed to find new friends.

Once met, the next step is developing relationships. Just as customs have changed for teens who are beginning to date, they have changed for adults facing fewer restrictions and "rules" than in the days when etiquette provided the procedures for everything from a social visit and a glass of lemonade to the omnipresence of a chaperon. There still are, however, some guidelines that make easier the often awkward process of getting to know someone.

Extending Invitations

From Single Women

Equality characterizes social communication today, at least as far as logic and intellect are concerned: Women know it is socially acceptable to ask a man for a date. How comfortable they feel doing it, however, may be another matter. If you feel too embarrassed to telephone a man you have just met and ask him out, write him a short, informal note instead:

Dear Bill, I have thought a lot about our talk the night we met—some interesting ideas there. Would you like to pursue them over dinner one night next week?

You will probably have little difficulty in extending a phone invitation to a man you know and see regularly, but what about a man you know and wish you saw regularly? Again, write a note:

Dear Carl, I haven't seen you in far too long. Jill and Joe Simms are coming for dinner on Saturday, March 20th. Won't you join us?

A written invitation for a larger gathering may be a fill-in card that you buy at a stationery store, giving details of time and place.

Even today's face to face invitations may be interpreted as an afterthought and so should be limited to the most informal kind of get-togethers—a drink after work or the familiar, "Drop by for a cup of coffee."

The social events that you might invite a man to are largely determined by your relationship to him. Even in our liberated world, it is difficult to ask a man to your home for an evening alone without risking his belief that sexual overtures are expected with the after-dinner brandy. Only if he is a relative or an old friend can you safely venture into a platonic *tête-à-tête*.

When the man is a new friend or someone you hope will become a better friend, you will find it more comfortable to plan the date with other people around. You might ask him to join a small group for dinner, either at home or at a restaurant. If you have received an invitation to someone else's party and been asked to bring a date, you may use the opportunity to ask him to accompany you. You can always telephone and say, "I have symphony tickets for next Tuesday. I'd love to have you share an evening of Mozart with me." Especially effective and appropriate is an invitation that evolves from a mutual interest: for instance, "Would you like to be my guest at the antiques fair at the Coliseum on Thursday? Maybe we can settle the argument we had over Chippendale."

If you are asked to the home of a man you would like to be with, but feel you do not want to much intimacy you need not blatantly refuse. You can suggest an alternative: "Why don't we have Jim and Sue join us?" or "I owe Jim and Sue a dinner. Why don't we all come to my place?" or more frankly, "I'd really rather go out somewhere if you don't mind."

From Single Men

Men extend invitations to women in much the same way they always have. They mail fill-in invitations to formal and semi-formal affairs; they telephone for informal dates. Like women, they may also extend invitations in person for spontaneous occasions.

Let me offer two words of caution to single men. One, do not extend an invitation by saying, "Give me a call sometime and we'll get together." It is arrogant and rude and highly ineffective with the kind of woman you hope will accept. Two, do not invite a woman for an intimate twosome in your home unless you know— and even more important, *she* knows what it might lead to. If she accepts naively, you might put her in an embarrassing situation and probably destroy a friendship. If she accepts your invitation with her eyes open, she is on her own.

A man who does not want to accept a woman's suggestive invitation has an easy escape route. He can simply say: "I don't want you to go to that bother. Let me take you out instead."

Replying to Invitations

Every invitation should be answered promptly. Whereas written replies were considered the only proper form in years past, time and informality have combined to make telephone replies acceptable today for all but formal invitations. Many written invitations list a phone number next to the R.S.V.P.

Accepting invitations is rarely a problem: all of us enjoying saying "Yes." Sometimes, however, an immediate "Yes" is impossible because of tentative conflicts. If the gathering to which you have been invited is informal and you know the hostess well, you may feel free to phone and explain: "I'd love to be there, but I *may* have to go to Chicago. Can I let you know in a day or two?" If however, it is a formal party and your delayed reply will disrupt the hostess's well-laid plans, then you owe it to her to decline the invitation at the start: "I hate to miss the evening, but I expect to be in Chicago. I hope I will be more fortunate the next time."

Not all invitations make you hope for a next time. Declining invitations you do not want to accept need not be the ordeal some people make it by struggling to invent a believable excuse. Honesty is the best policy. When you invent elaborate

tales to disguise the fact that you simply do not want to accept, you often find
yourself ensnared in them at a later date. The best way to say no is a courteous,
"Thank you, but I can't make it on the fifteenth," or "I'm busy on the fifteenth."

Dating

Who Calls for Whom?

In the past there was no question about whether the man called for the
woman. He *always* called for her and saw her home, even when she extended the
invitation, unless, of course, the occasion was at her home.

Fortunately, times have changed. If you live in the suburbs and have a car,
there is no reason why you cannot meet your date at the party and drive yourself
home afterward. He is expected to escort you to your car and make sure you are
safely in it with the doors locked before a final "Good night." Naturally you would
offer to drop him off at his apartment before continuing on your way if he does not
live too far afield.

If you do not drive or prefer to avoid city traffic, your date is not expected to
travel the thirty miles to your home in order to pick you up. You may come into the
city alone on the train and have him meet you at the station upon your arrival.

Whether he should see you to the commuter train when your date is over or
ride home with you and return again is questionable. You may safely board the train
alone if the hour is early and the train filled with other travelers. If you are with other
people you know, even at a late hour, he could be spared the commute to the
suburbs and back. On the other hand, if it is late and you are alone, he cannot leave
you on the train and go home: It is his responsibility to get you home or to a safe
alternative.

A little thought ahead of time may ease the long-distance dating problem. You
may have friends in the city with whom you can plan ahead to spend the night. Or he
may have suburban friends with whom he can spend the night after taking you
home. If you live with parents or relatives, you may invite him to spend the night at
your home. In each case, you would be safe and he would be spared a night of train
riding.

If the distance is greater than suburb to city and you have no friends with
whom to stay, the man may suggest you stay at a hotel at his expense. You may
accept his offer, or you may insist on paying for your own lodging.

When both the man and the woman live in the same city, logistics pose no
problem. If a man extends you an invitation, he calls for you and takes you home—
with the exception of a lunch date or an after-business drink and dinner. In such
cases it is proper for you to meet him at a specified time and place. Since most
women still feel ill at ease waiting at an empty table, I urge men to be prompt. It is

equally proper after that kind of get-together for the man to see you into a taxi and go his own way.

If the invitation has been extended by you, the man may still wish to pick you up and take you home afterward, especially if he is using his car. However, you may properly call for him in your car or stop by to pick him up in a taxi. An almost universal rule in cities is for the man to take the woman home after all but the most casual after-business meeting, even when the date has been at her invitation. When she is driving her own car, he is still expected to ride to her garage with her and to see her to her apartment building after she has parked. Safety has become an even greater determinant of etiquette than custom.

Expenses

When a man asks you to dinner, he generally expects to pay for the evening. Similarly, when you ask a man, you expect to pay. However, many young singles have developed the habit of sharing expenses in order to alleviate financial burdens and make frequent dating more possible. No matter who initiates the date, if expenses are to be shared, the arrangement must be made clear at the time the invitation is extended. Surprises when the check arrives lead to embarrassment and destroyed friendships.

Many people have not yet overcome the awkwardness of having a woman pick up the check. Women themselves often suffer from not knowing how to do it gracefully. Men tend to fumble with their wallets and look ill at ease. Waiters are the worst offenders: They still automatically hand the check to the man, even when a woman has acted as hostess by ordering the meal.

A woman may clarify and ease the situation for everybody by using a credit card to eliminate handling money. Some women give their credit card to the headwaiter ahead of time with an explanation so that the waiter will make no mistake about who gets the bill. As you and your guest sit down at the table, you may quietly tell the waiter, "I'll take the check please." The safest way to assure that you will receive the check is to patronize the same restaurant repeatedly so that the head-waiter will know you and your custom.

If the inevitable happens, though, and your embarrassed date is presented with the tab, he will probably reach politely into his pocket to pay. You should come to the rescue—and your own—by taking the check from him firmly with a few casual words such as, "Don't be silly. You're my guest."

The Etiquette of Intimacy

Perhaps the most difficult topic facing singles today is that of sexual intimacy. The discovery of AIDS and its rapid spread across all geographical, cultural and social boundaries should be reason enough to defer sexual intimacy until one has discussed, with honesty, one's sexual past. After centuries of sexual abstinence until marriage, followed by years of free and open sex, we have reached an era where caution must be the byword.

It is very difficult, however, and extremely embarrassing to most people to ask, "What have you been doing, and with whom, and when." My opinion is that if you are willing to bare all with someone else, you should also be able to bare your thoughts.

Some sexually transmitted diseases (STD's) have cures. Others do not. A moment of passion, no matter how blissful, is not worth the ending of your life, prematurely and painfully.

With someone you have only recently met, there is absolutely nothing wrong with saying, "I'm sorry, but until we know each other better and feel more comfortable talking about sex, we just can't get involved in a sexual relationship. I'm really worried about STD's."

If she or he becomes insulted, so be it. You aren't after all, casting aspersions upon his or her character, but neither you nor he or she, have any idea with whom each other's previous sexual partners have been intimate, and that is how disease is spread—from one person, to the next, to the next.

With someone whom you are considering establishing a long-term relationship, you must talk openly. Never name names, but if you or he or she has had an active sex life, it is only fair to the other to have or to request a simple blood test to make sure you are healthy and not carrying disease.

And, as often as people eschew condoms, they are, while not a guarantee, a protection against disease. A woman has every right to insist that her partner wear one; a man has every right to wear one. It is not a sign of true love to throw precaution to the wind, just to avoid insulting a sexual partner.

Protecting not only one's self, but also one's sexual partner, is not just courtesy, it can be life-saving.

LIVING TOGETHER

In the early 1970s the practice of two young unmarried people sharing a home emerged from behind locked shutters and became simply—living together. While at first, it shocked parents and often even friends, it found a place in our society, took on a degree of respectability, and has proven that it is here to stay. Indeed, living together is no longer only the province of the young. Financial considerations often play a part in the decision of some senior citizens to forgo marriage in favor of living together. Millions of couples across the country are living together and otherwise conducting lives that fit into more traditional patterns of culture as gracefully as their married neighbors. While living together has not replaced marriage it presents an alternative, giving testimony to the fact that marriage is not the only structure held together by love.

The important issue, however, is not a trend in living together or marriage, but what each means to you personally. Couples have to work at both.

Moving In

"Your place or mine?" That is the question. If both of you live alone and one has a larger apartment or home your question is answered: Move into the roomier one. If one of you lives alone and the other has a roommate, your question is also answered: Move into the solo apartment, unless it is too small for two. In that case, you have to either unseat the existing roommate and take over the larger apartment or turn it over and locate a larger one for yourselves. If you both have roommates, one may relinquish the apartment; if not, you find your own.

Whom to Tell

When a living arrangement is undertaken, probably the first to know is the letter carrier. Simply inform him that William Archer or Alice Jameson will also be receiving mail in your box from now on. There is no need for further explanation.

Family, of course, are the first to really be given the news. Where young children are involved, they must be told before the move takes place. Since young children cannot differentiate between marriage and living together, the impact of your new living arrangement upon them will be as strong as if you were marrying.

Informing parents of your living-together arrangement is the next consideration. Most parents, even those who disapprove, are generally able to accept it and should, therefore, be told. To exclude them from a new relationship in your life is not only unfair but selfish.

Even if you feel your parents will respond with anger and disappointment, telling them is still the wiser course. If you try to hide your living arrangement from them, you will be under constant tension. Will they visit you and discover the truth for themselves? Will they phone and suspect when a strange voice answers? Will mutual friends say something to them? Suspicion of living together may be more painful to them than actually confronting the reality, especially if you are sensitive to their viewpoint.

The gist of what you say may be something like this: "I know you don't approve of living together outside of marriage, and I am sorry to upset you. But Bill [or Alice] and I love each other. We have made a real commitment. The only difference is that we don't feel ready to commit ourselves for life. If we grow in that direction, we'll get married; and if I find that Bill [or Alice] is not what I want for the rest of my life, we'll split up. But right now it is good for us together. I want you to understand and accept it because I love you. The relationship you and I have means a great deal in my happiness."

Relatives need be informed of your new situation only as they are involved in your life: siblings whom you see or correspond with—yes; aunts, uncles, and cousins with whom you are in close contact—yes; but the "funeral and wedding relations"—no need.

Obviously, tell the friends you see and those to whom you write. In short, tell anybody who will meet your new partner on more than a casual basis and anyone with whom you regularly share news of your life. You need not announce your relationship to business associates unless you see them socially, but if it comes up in conversation, do not hide it.

Tell your landlord so that he will not be surprised to see a new name on the rent check. Tell the superintendent and doormen if you have them, so that they will treat your new roommate as another tenant, not as a visitor.

Unless you know your neighbors, there is no need to say anything to them, other than a casual introduction if you meet. Nor is there any need to alert local shops. When your partner orders purchases to be delivered, the address given will be adequate.

What to Call Your Living-Together Partner

Introducing your living-together partner is covered on pages 14–15. Other situations in which the name for your living-together partner arise includes the mailbox, and in correspondence. On the mailbox you simply add your new partner's name. In the telephone book you may list both names: Karen Clark under C and Peter Doern under D, for which you pay an additional charge. Most stores and credit cards, should you decide to share accounts, accept the names of both partners on the account.

Letters pose little difficulty—when both of you are writing a formal letter, such as a complaint or a request for information, or are making a reservation, both sign it with your full names.

When writing to a living-together couple, you merely write Dear Ms Clark and Mr. Doern." or simply Karen Clark and Peter Doern with no titles. Naturally a personal letter would be addressed "Dear Karen and Peter."

In all cases the envelope is addressed "Ms Karen Clark, Mr. Peter Doern" on separate lines.

Sharing

Since living together is a sharing experience—but not 100 percent sharing—it is important to its success to determine what items are to be shared and specifically how.

Expenses

The first question to decide is whether expenses are to be shared equally or disproportionately. If both partners earn roughly similar salaries, a 50 percent split seems equitable. If one partner earns somewhat more than the other, he or she may elect to pick up more than half the tab, although in most instances fifty-fifty remains the rule. However, when one partner earns a great deal more than the other, expenses are usually worked out on a different basis, with that partner underwriting a sizable share of their joint expenses.

The mechanics of sharing finances vary. Some maintain separate bank accounts from which they pay bills previously decided upon between them. For instance, one may pay for food, telephone and gas; the other for rent and electricity. Others, while retaining private bank accounts, open a joint account as well. They calculate expenses and at the start of each month deposit a predetermined share to cover bills and maintain a balance. I feel that this system works more efficiently since it enables both partners to write checks when necessary. Should an extra-lavish party or a trip drain the coffers, each partner makes an additional contribution from his or her personal bank account.

Housework

Since living-together couples generally split everything fifty-fifty, they fall naturally into shared housework, especially when both of the partners are employed. How you divide chores depends on your tastes and abilities. For instance, if Bill likes to cook and you don't, you may settle for his being chef and your being house cleaner. If neither of you has a preference, alternating jobs by the week or month seems to work for most couples. However, you will share your lives more closely by doing both jobs together—one vacuuming while the other dusts, one paring while the other sautés.

Although rules are made to be followed, they are also made to be broken, and there arise times when housework is not to be shared evenly. If one partner's work is more demanding or hours more erratic, the other partner may help out by assuming additional household responsibilities. Living together is, after all, a relationship in which giving, not demanding, brings fulfillment.

Retaining One's Privacy

Respect for privacy is important. In living together (as in marriage), it is essential to success. Being aware of the need is not adequate: You must build it into the structure of your life or it may easily be neglected and both partners hurt. For instance, if you hadn't discussed it ahead of time, you might consider your partner's refusal to have dinner with you one night as a rejection; your partner might feel the same when you choose to spend a Saturday alone. In all probability, there is no reason for resentment—both of you simply need privacy.

To avoid misunderstandings, present your needs to each other before moving in together so that expectations will be clear: "I go crazy if I can't have a couple of

hours alone every day," or, "I need Saturdays by myself to stay on an even keel."
Partners can understand only when needs are expressed.

Once you make each other aware you are faced with the question, "Where can we go to be alone?" If you share a house, you may have an extra room. If not, you can work out a way for one partner to use the living room and the other the bedroom. In a studio apartment you may have to settle for a screened-off area. All else being impossible, you may have to catch your private times on walks, at a library, or in a museum, alternating the procedure with your partner so that each of you has hours at home while the other is out.

Private Friends

Although you will share many friends, some of your personal friends may have little in common with your new partner. Fine. Keep them for yourself. There will be occasions when talking and sharing activities with them will reinforce the independence you are striving to retain in a living-together relationship. You will come back stronger in yourself and, therefore, more able to contribute to your relationship.

It goes without saying that when you are living together, the private friendships you have are never expected to extend beyond the platonic into the sexual. Sexual intimacy grows alongside a commitment; when it becomes experimentation or game playing, the commitment shatters in living together as well as in marriage.

Separate Vacations

Many partners take separate vacations. Some feel that being apart renews their enthusiasm for the absent partner, keeping the relationship alive and at the same time helping each to maintain an independent identity. Others merely find their tastes in vacation pleasures so different from their partner's that they go their own ways.

This is all very well; but couples living together in a bond of love and mutual enjoyment may find joint vacations the best way after all. The sacrifice of two weeks' independence or of a favorite vacation spot may well be worth the adventure or leisure they do share. *Relationships thrive on shared experiences.*

Private Finances

While living-together couples may and should open joint bank accounts, they also should maintain private ones as well. This will give you your own account to draw on to pay for personal expenses such as clothing, medical bills, carfare, etc. Above all, a private account reinforces your own independence, allowing freedom that depositing all of your income in a joint account cannot. Similarly, although you and your partner may have a joint credit card for household expenses, you will find having your own personal credit cards useful.

The Legal Aspect of Living Together

The law is catching up to the nation's trend in living together, adding additional complexity to an already complex field. Since nothing short of a volume would enable me to do justice to the subject, I suggest you seek legal counsel on any of the following areas into which you and your partner are entering. What holds today may be outdated tomorrow; what is legal in one state may be cause for a suit in another. Be sure that you get *competent* advice on:

Obtaining a joint lease on an apartment or house.
Jointly purchasing a condominium, a cooperative apartment, or a home.
Jointly purchasing an automobile.
Taking out insurance—life, homeowners, automobile, any kind.
Writing a will that involves your partner.
Determining a financial settlement (palimony) if you break up.
Determining disposal of joint properties if you break up.
Assigning child custody and child support of children you have parented together if you break up.

If you have neither children nor possessions of great value, legal counsel may seem unwarranted. It is still wise, however, to face the possibility of a breakup by determining at the start who will get what. You and your partner may play the role of attorney yourselves by drawing up a simple contract which clearly states the disposition of your joint possessions: furniture, appliances, pictures, books, housewares, musical instruments, automobile, bicycles, joint bank account, the apartment or house. When you have both signed the contract, you may put it away, like a will, out of sight and mind. Rest assured, however, that having made it, you have spared yourselves the anger and hostility couples rarely anticipate but inevitably face over property settlements.

Family Visits

Even parents who accept your living-together arrangement from a distance may be thrown for a loss when you visit home. For their unmarried son or daughter to share a bedroom and probably a bed with someone of the opposite sex in their own home makes them terribly uncomfortable. Do not demand it or force it. "Everyone does it," or "Don't be hypocrites; you know we do it at home," will not change their minds. Your parents have developed their own set of values, which they have a right to enforce in their own home. If you insist on sharing a bedroom as the terms on which you visit, you may lose their love and respect and wind up not even sharing visits anymore. If you cannot bear to give in to your parents' wishes, rather than cut off visits, you might suggest spending days at their home and nights in a hotel.

On the other hand, when your parents visit you, the situation is reversed.
They know that you and your partner live together, sharing more than a kitchen. When they accept your invitation to stay overnight, they accept the fact that you and your partner sleep together, and they must graciously say nothing. If they can't face up to that, then they should decline the invitation or spend the night at a nearby hotel. They are certainly free to say, "You know, Dad and I will feel more comfortable at a hotel, but count on us for breakfast."

When Family Disapprove

If after you have explained your feelings and your reasons for choosing to live together, your parents still cannot accept it, you must go your own way. (I am assuming you are of legal age and self-supporting.) They may retain the anger and hostility which are expressions of the deep hurt they feel, but you should try not to respond in kind. If you do, all communications will be cut off, leaving both you and your parents deprived of one of life's greatest joys: the relationship between parents and adult offspring. Continue to make contact with your parents, even when they do not respond: phone them, write, remember birthdays and anniversaries. Time and repeated evidence of your love may enable them to relent.

Older Couples Living Together

We have more middle-aged single people in the United States now than ever before, not only because more are living longer, but also because more are getting divorced at a later age. Actually, the highest increase in the divorce rate is in the over-forty age group. Many of these singles, both widowed and divorced, establish relationships, with more and more taking the option of living together over marriage.

Financial Benefits

Until recently the financial benefits of living together on Social Security have been far greater than those of being married, although these regulations are changing so rapidly that I dare not make a generalization. Even without Social Security, however, many middle-aged singles have incomes from pensions, investments, savings, and bequests which are sufficient for comfortable living. The traditional hunt for a "rich widow" or a "comfortably-off widower" is not the popular sport it used to be because the "game" has alternatives to marriage.

When a middle-aged couple decides to live together, her income remains hers, and his remains his, with just enough pooling of resources to fund their joint venture. Since in most cases both of them have living quarters, they move in to one of them together and rent the other; they rarely sell it, preferring to retain ownership in case the new relationship dissolves. After an accumulation of household items over thirty years or so, they have everything they need with no further expense. Materially life continues for them exactly as before; they do not even have to make new wills.

The main change and greatest benefit is companionship. Without the legal fuss of marriage, they have each other and can turn hours of loneliness into belonging again.

Even love blooms anew in a middle-aged relationship, a fact frequently overlooked by the young, who consider themselves its sole possessor.

Difficulties

Parents entering a living-together relationship may run into a blockade set up by their children: "Mother, how could you!" "Dad, what will people say!" It is almost to be expected from young people who have difficulty seeing their parents as individuals in their own right, though fortunately not all young people suffer from this failing.

Life has a funny way of coming full circle, and living-together partners facing disapproval from their children must explain their position in the same way their children years ago may have had to explain to them. If your arguments are convincing, well and good. If not and your children remain adamantly opposed, don't feel that you must dissolve your relationship in order to appease them; after all, it is *your* life, not theirs. You should pursue your living-together plans, hoping that time will reverse the negative attitudes. Let me advise you as I advised your children earlier: Don't let anger cut off communications. Continue to see and call and write your children despite their disapproval.

While children may cause as much trouble as parents over living together, the community will not. Neighbors will probably not care or will simply assume you are married. There is no need to inform them otherwise.

Outside of your family, the only ones who matter are your friends. Tell them of your new relationship. Chances are they will rejoice with you.

Traveling With a Living-Together Partner

Hotels

Reception clerks at hotels in most places in the United States no longer even look up when an unmarried man and woman register for the same room. They are used to it.

It is possible that in some small-town motels and in little inns, you may run into raised eyebrows and possibly even refusals. The safest way to avoid them is to make the room reservation ahead of time in both names. That way, if the hotel objects, it can tell you so; if you do not hear to the contrary, you can register with an easy mind. Of one thing you may rest assured: staff in the big motel chains, no matter how small the town, will pay no attention at all.

Traveling abroad is a different story. Some countries accept unmarried couples with ease—Sweden, for instance; some, like Spain, allow them reluctantly; Arab countries strictly forbid them. In fact, cohabitation in most Arab countries is taken very seriously. It is illegal and can result in jail and execution. Before making travel plans, check with your travel agent or with the tourist bureau of the country you plan to visit to determine how you will be received. If you are told to expect a negative reaction, you have three choices: Plan to register in separate rooms; switch your trip to countries more receptive to your life-style; or pretend to be married.

Sharing Expenses

Travel expenses between living-together partners may be shared exactly as household expenses are: either evenly or disproportionately depending on each partner's income. The easiest method is to divide the expense of transportation at the time you buy tickets. That out of the way, chip in cash or buy travelers' checks jointly to carry you through the trip. Take your own funds as well so that you can buy souvenirs or enliven the trip with an occasional surprise: "I'm taking you to dinner tonight!"

DISSOLVING A RELATIONSHIP

Whether the relationship is between a married couple or two people who have been living together outside of marriage, the dissolving of the relationship requires sensitivity and consideration.

Separation

When a married couple separates, it is never publicly announced, although the news generally spreads quickly. Because they are still legally married, the woman continues to use her husband's name and wear her wedding ring. He quietly moves out of their home, or she may take the children for a visit to her family. They refuse invitations that come to "Mr. and Mrs.," although if they do meet, they should act as friendly and normal as possible. They may even attend certain family functions or holiday gatherings together. Friends, of course, should respect the situation and never invite them both to the same party without their knowledge and consent.

Whether or how much they see each other while they are separated depends on their feelings and the situation. A couple with no children might feel it would do them the most good to sever all ties for a certain period. A wife with small children might, on the contrary, need her husband's presence at times to enable her to fulfill appointments or obligations. There are no rules—each couple must work out their own separation agreement to their mutual satisfaction.

Men and women who are separated are, of course, free to go out with members of the opposite sex, but if they are sincerely trying to save their marriage, they will scrupulously avoid any serious entanglements.

If they decide that life together was better than life apart is, they simply move back together and make as little of the separation as they can. For this reason, it is wise for the wife or husband—whichever has remained there—to keep the home and other property intact, rather than sell or rent it in a moment of bitterness.

Divorce

Even when a couple no longer care about one another, cannot find anything to agree about, or have no interests in common, they may still want to preserve their marriage—often because neither one wants to lose the children. Aside from their own private efforts to communicate and to reevaluate their marriage, they may and should look for outside help. It is no admission of failure to seek the help of a marriage counselor, an experienced lawyer, or a clergyman. It is only evidence that you are willing to do all you can to save your marriage, and many marriages *have* been saved by discussing the problems with an experienced and disinterested person.

However, even the best of help is not always successful and the problems remain insurmountable. In that case, the only solution is divorce.

When a divorce is finally and irrevocably decided upon, both parties must accept the fact that their marriage no longer exists. The husband who insists on "dropping in" to see the children, or the wife who keeps calling his office to ask his advice on this or that, is only prolonging the agony. People who have made the decision to part should have done so with enough serious thought so that once it is accomplished all ties are severed and they can start to make new lives for themselves and leave their ex-partners to do the same.

A divorced couple does not give back any wedding gifts, although a woman whose marriage was annulled, and who never lived with her husband, should do so.

The divorced couple's friends, and if possible their families, should extend their sympathetic support—never criticism or censure—but at the same time respect their privacy and avoid prying or questioning the reasons for or the mechanics of the divorce, unless their advice is asked for.

Letting People Know

The same rule of informing people applies to your breakup as it did to your coming together: Tell those to whom it makes a difference. Tell your parents and close family and your good friends. Tell your business associates only if they are also

friends. Tell the landlord or superintendent and doorman if one of you is keeping the
apartment. You need not tell the mailman; he will know when you remove one of
your names from the door or the mailbox. And, of course, you will be forwarding
mail that continues to arrive for your ex.

A divorce is almost always a tragic experience for at least one of the couple.
Therefore it should not be announced publicly, and under no circumstances should
printed announcements be sent out. Certain people have done it and are doing it, but
it is in the worst of taste. In the first place, a divorce *is* a failure, even though both
people may agree that it is best, and there is little reason to be proud of a failure.
Second, as mentioned above, there is almost invariably one injured party, and it is
surely rubbing salt in his wound for the other to shout publicly, "Hooray! I'm free!"

The situation will become public knowledge very quickly, as soon as one
member of the couple moves out. The one who moves may have change-of-name-
and-address cards printed, and of course his or her Christmas cards will serve as
announcements. A note may be added to them—"As you can see, Bob and I were,
unfortunately, divorced last August. Hope to hear from you at my new address." To
those who might not recognize "Susan Smith," a woman may add in parentheses,
"Formerly Mrs. James Smith." Naturally, either the man or the woman may send as
many personal notes telling of the divorce as he or she wishes.

After the Divorce

Whether you are separated or divorced, you must hold up your head and face
the situation openly. There is no stigma attached to divorce as there once was, and
even though you may feel that you have failed or been betrayed, that is no one's
business but your own. Don't dwell on your problems with everyone you see, but
don't be ashamed to mention your state. When you run into someone who says,
"Where's Ann?" or "How is Joe doing these days?" just say, "I honestly don't know—
we were divorced in April." The first few times it will be hard, but you will find that
you will soon think nothing of it.

Most divorcées today use "Mrs. Sandra Jacobs" rather than, as was true in the
past, Mrs. Rothschild [maiden name] Jacobs" and I feel that this is sensible and
acceptable. However, she is free to choose whichever name she wishes or to take
back her maiden name if she prefers. A woman whose marriage has been annulled
almost invariably uses her maiden name, since an annulment rejects the fact that a
marriage ever existed.

A divorcée, unlike a widow, does not necessarily continue to wear her wedding ring. If she has children, she may do so for their sake, or she may transfer it to
her right hand to indicate that she is no longer married. Her engagement ring may be
kept for their use later, or she may have the stones reset into something that she can
use herself.

Divorce and Your In-Laws

The parents-in-law of a man or woman who has been divorced from their child are often terrified that they will "lose" their grandchildren, and yet they hesitate to contact their ex-son- or ex-daughter-in-law, fearing this will seem disloyal to their child. If you should find yourself in this position, do not hesitate. You need not "take sides" or even discuss the divorce if you do not want to, but the grandparent-grandchild relationship is one that should not be abandoned. Actually this attitude, far from being disloyal, is unprejudiced and commendable, and is often a tremendous help to a newly divorced man or woman, who may be very unhappy.

Your friendship with your child's ex-spouse need not end because he or she remarries. The new spouse may be a fine addition to the family and a wonderful parent to your grandchildren. If your affection for your former son- or daughter-in-law has remained steadfast, any children he or she may have with his or her new spouse, although in no way related to you, may make happy additions to your circle of grandchildren.

ROOMMATES

Living with another person when your bond is either friendship or convenience requires all the same elements I have discussed in the relationships above, and one more—extra patience. Without the tie of love which carries with it additional forgiveness when differences occur, roommate situations with either the same or the opposite sex demand scrupulous attention to the following:

- Respect for privacy
- Personal tidiness and cleanliness
- Cooperation when entertaining
- Prompt and complete financial responsibility
- Sharing of housework

Perhaps the greatest hostility can occur between roommates when one or other abuses entertaining privileges. In this situation, as with all others, clear communication is necessary. If your roommate is seeing someone regularly and they have taken over the living room so that you feel uncomfortable wandering around in your nightclothes or can't get to the kitchen or the television because they are constantly engaged in passionate embraces, you have to speak up and say that, while you know they need a place to be, it is your apartment too, and you feel like a prisoner in the bedroom in your efforts to give them privacy. Suggest that two or three nights a week are off-limits to guests, or simply tell them that you have things to do and cannot stay locked in the bedroom, so they should expect you to be in and out of the living room without having to knock or wait for permission to enter.

The other area which generates anger between roommates is financial—if you share everything 50-50 and your roommate is always bringing someone home for dinner, or is eating all the yogurt the day you buy it and not sharing, or drinking the entire six-pack of the beer you bought to share, you might consider splitting the basics, like cleaning items and paper goods, and buying your own food. Or, the person with the healthier appetite could be asked to pay a little more.

There is no reason to walk around feeling abused in any roommate situation. While extra diplomacy is required, talking out your difficulties usually brings understanding and accord and enables you to enjoy the benefits of this shared living arrangement. As in any other relationship, it is patently unfair to assume that the other knows what you are thinking, what is bothering you, or what you want him or her to do if you don't say so.

*T*oday a large household staff is rare indeed. A moderate number of households have one housekeeper or maid who lives in, but the most that a great majority of people expect is to have help with household cleaning once a week. Other types of household workers today include child care givers, companions, and sometimes nurses and other medical care givers.

(See pages 349–350 for advice on tips and gifts for household helpers.)

LIVE-IN AND FULL TIME EMPLOYEES

Attitude and clear communication of your expectations are everything in successful employee management. It is not right to be too lenient, any more than it is just to be unreasonably demanding. To allow impertinence or sloppy work is a mistake, but it is also inexcusable to show unwarranted irritability or to be overbearing or rude. And there is no greater example of injustice than to reprimand people near you because you happen to be in a bad humor, and at another time to overlook offenses that are greater because you are in an amiable mood. Nor is there ever any excuse for correcting an employee (or any family member, for that matter) in front of anyone else.

If you require that a uniform be worn all uniforms as well as aprons and collars and cuffs are furnished by the employer, with the exception, possibly, of those worn by a cook, for whom the employer furnishes only the aprons.

Live-In Couples

A live-in couple can be a happy solution for a large household. Their duties should be delineated precisely so that you are all under the same understanding as to what they are and are not to do.

The couple must have an apartment of at least two rooms, preferably with a private entrance. Some employers do not object if a child lives with the parents, but it must be understood in advance that he or she will not be disturbing in any way and will not be allowed the run of the house except when playing with the children of the employer.

Their working hours must be carefully scheduled so that they will be able to have at least one day off a week together, even though they alternate being off at other times.

The Chauffeur

Chauffeurs are given quarters if they live in, otherwise they are hired for specific hours, clearly defined in advance and never abused. The chauffeur may also double as handyman and/or gardener, and is generally in charge of keeping the car, or cars, in top condition.

A goodly number of older people who cannot or do not wish to drive themselves have chauffeurs, as do professionals and officials who use the time they are driven to and from their offices to work on papers, dictate, etc.

Chauffeurs no longer wear livery. Even those driving diplomatic cars are most often seen in plain black or dark gray suits, with soft hats.

As with all servants, the chauffeur's duties, his hours, and his salary must be fully agreed upon in advance.

Nurses or Medical Care-Givers

When a household includes someone who is ill or who is recovering from an illness that person, or his or her family or physician, often feel it is important to have around-the-clock or part-time health assistance. The health care giver may be a practical or registered nurse who lives in, or who rotates shifts with family members or other professionals.

A live-in medical care giver always eats with the family or is served a tray in his or her room. When on duty, he or she generally wears a uniform.

Other health care workers may include health aides, physical therapists, and visiting nurses who spend several hours with the ill person tending to personal care or therapeutic needs.

None of these people is a servant and the only expectation of them is to care for the ill person, with the exception of the health care aide, whose duties may include light cleaning, bed-making and laundry for the ill person, only. None of them should be asked or expected to clean, do laundry, or respond to the needs or wants of other household members.

Paid Companions

One of the most upsetting things about getting old is the consequent loss of independence. This makes the job of being a companion to an older person one of the hardest—in some ways—there is. The elderly man or woman resents having to be taken care of, resents his or her loss of privacy, and resents having someone around who is generally hired by another member of the family or perhaps a doctor. Added to all this is the fact that there is sometimes mental failure as well as physical, and the old person may be senile, crotchety, repetitive, and vindictive. To handle all this, certain considerations must be given to a companion, who, to hold the job at all, must often be something of a saint. Of course there are companions who have been known to neglect their charges shamelessly, to physically abuse them, and to rob them blind. This is a real danger if no other member of the family lives in the home or nearby. To guard against this, it is best to hire a companion through a reputable agency and even then to check the references carefully. In cases where a companion is hired through a personal ad in the paper, you must be extra careful, talking to previous employers in person, if possible, and if not, by correspondence.

Because of the confining nature of the work, it is essential that companions have more than the ordinary day and a half a week off. Two days, either consecutively, or if she prefers, one midweek and one during the weekend, allow her enough time away from the monotony and irritations of the job. She should also have two or three hours during the day—perhaps when her charge is resting—to go to her room, read, watch television, write letters, or to do whatever else she chooses. Although she often must accompany her charge when he or she goes out socially, she need not stay in attendance when friends come to visit at the home. She should, however, remain within call in case she is needed.

As in choosing a children's nurse, a companion must be sympathetic, patient, and understanding. It is far more important that she have these qualities, and that the older person be reasonably content with her, than that she be a superb cook and housekeeper. Often she must do those chores too, as well as order food and keep accounts of household expenses. If possible, it is ideal to have the person who takes her place on her days off agree to do some of the cleaning chores, to relieve the companion of all that responsibility.

When you hire a companion you must, as you would with any servant, make very clear what she will and will not be expected to do. In a servantless home she may have to do almost everything, and should be paid accordingly. In a house where there are other servants she may have nothing to do except entertain her charge and take care of his or her physical needs.

The companion generally eats with her patient—from trays or in the dining room. If they live with the older person's children, both she and her charge may eat with the family, but the companion, unless she chooses to do so, would not eat with the servants if the household employs servants.

She ordinarily wears a white uniform if her duties include any nursing. Many women prefer to do this to save their own clothes. When she and her charge go out or travel together, however, she generally wears her own appropriate clothing. Companions to more active people, who need no nursing, are often very refined older women who need a little extra money or who want company themselves. In this case they dress as, and are treated as, good friends.

Child Care-Givers

Au Pair girls and nannies or nursemaids are becoming the predominant household helpers in the United States, next to cleaning services, as more and more women with children are working full time outside the house. They ensure reliable and consistent child care for the working mother, who otherwise has to depend on part-time, hired babysitters or babysitting services, or on daycare facilities which sometimes do not operate during hours required by the mother's work schedule.

Nannies and Au Pair Girls

A reliable, strong, and kind nanny or au pair is the most important servant in the household, whether there are other servants or not. On her depends your child's health, safety, development, and happiness. Therefore it is extremely important to hire only someone with the best of references, or who comes highly recommended through a reputable agency. You may advertise in papers, on store bulletin boards, in your church, or in a civic center, but if you get responses, do not rely on a written reference. Talk personally with former employers, and interview the applicant carefully. Find out why she left her previous job and what her future plans are: How long does she plan to be a nanny? Introduce her to your children, and if possible, leave them alone for a short while, so that you can find out how *they* like her. Ask her how she would handle certain emergencies, how she feels about discipline, and whether she has had or has children of her own.

Some nannies and au pairs have nothing to do with housework or meals, other than the children's. Others will help out in whatever way you specify, but this *must* be established *before* she is hired. Otherwise, if you add duties she had not expected, you will soon find yourself in the market for another nanny. Make it absolutely clear exactly what you expect, and if you stick to your part of the bargain, you have every right to insist that she stick to hers.

It is worth going to a lot of trouble and giving up a lot of time to find the right nursemaid. Only if you are sure that your children are well taken care of at home can you possibly give your full and undivided attention to your job.

Unlike nannies, au pairs are part of the family, even though they are paid a salary. They are usually young women between the ages of 17 and 21 or 22, most often from another part of the country or from another country, who take care of the children, their primary responsibility, and also assist with housecleaning, laundry, and other chores. In return, they have a position in the family as a sort of adopted daughter, in addition to their salaries and any benefits paid to them. They accompany the family on vacation, often eat meals with the family, and are included in other family events. Naturally, whether on vacation with the family or participating in a family party or gathering, they continue to be responsible for the care of the children.

If you expect an au pair to assume more than child care duties, you should clearly delineate what they are at the time of the initial interview so that you both understand what is expected.

All too often in the recent past, parents have tended to treat au pairs as indentured servants rather than as family members, and because of their youth and because they have either signed a contract or haven't the plane fare home, they have been trapped in an unhappy situation. Within the past several years, a great number of agencies for au pairs and nannies have come into being, which serve to match the au pair to the family. These agencies also arrange for such things as Social Security, workman's compensation, etc. and ensure that the rights of the young woman are protected. If you hire outside of an agency, it is important that you check with your state's labor board to be sure you are providing all the benefits you are supposed to, both for your own protection and for that of your au pair or nanny.

Part-Time Baby-sitters

With smaller family homes and small-apartment living and with the tremendous increase in domestics' salaries, the absence of a "live-in" staff has created a special demand—and baby-sitters have achieved both amateur and professional standing. Sitters come in all shapes and sizes from teenagers to senior citizens. Many high-school and college students are glad to supplement their allowances or salaries by baby-sitting a few times a week.

The student employment office of a nearby college or university often lists the names of students available for baby-sitting, and parents in the neighborhood may avail themselves of this service. In many communities there are agencies that provide approved sitters at standard rates.

As the rate of payment varies in different localities no set schedule can be fixed. But the customary rate of the community should be observed, and the sitter should be paid at the end of the evening. It should be clearly understood *ahead of time* what the hourly rate will be. The sitter should be told that after the children are asleep she or he may use the television, stereo, or radio, read, or do homework. In some households a sitter is permitted to ask a friend to keep him or her company, but should never entertain a member of the opposite sex or a group of friends when "sitting," and although it may seem unnecessary you should make that perfectly clear. Otherwise you may run into a situation like this: One evening when our children were young my husband and I returned home an hour or so earlier than we had anticipated. The lights were snapped on as we opened the door, and a very red-faced and rumpled young lady ran out of the bedroom. As she was stuttering and stammering, an even more red-faced young man squeezed out the door—as she muttered, "Er, er, Mrs. Post, this is Moose!" In other words, it should be clearly understood what your sitter is expected to do and what he or she may not do. It is thoughtful to leave a snack in the refrigerator or to tell your sitter what he or she is welcome to as a beverage. Be specific about where you are going—leave the address and telephone number, as well as the name, address, and telephone number of the children's doctor. Always tell the sitter when you expect to be back—and try to be on time.

Adequate transportation must be provided for the sitter's safe return home, and this applies for sitters of any age.

Youngsters of twelve or thirteen are often responsible enough to sit for a toddler or preschooler for a short time. They should never be left alone with an infant, however, or left in a situation where the mother or another adult is not immediately available. It is hard to set age limits because a thirteen-year-old with three or four younger brothers and sisters is far more capable than a seventeen-year-old who has never been around a young child. You must know a young sitter personally before hiring her or him or else have excellent personal recommendations from a friend who has used this sitter's services.

Young adults—married or single—or experienced older persons make the best sitters for very young children, and a married couple ideal if you are leaving your children for several days or even weeks. A couple is unlikely to get restless and bored as would a single person—especially if your home is at all isolated.

If two families wish to share a sitter his or her pay should be adjusted in recognition of the extra responsibility. It need not be double—sitters don't charge twice as much for two children in a family as they do for one—but it would not be fair to ask anyone to sit for two separate families for the price of one. This, too, should be settled ahead of time. It is entirely wrong to hire a sitter to take care of your little Brian and then to say, as the sitter arrives, "Oh, by the way, Mrs. Goodwin is bringing Constance over for the day."

"Baby-sitter-snatching" is perhaps the eighth deadly sin. If you have a neighbor who has a regular sitter and generously "lends" the sitter to you in an emergency, don't try to lure the sitter away no matter how much you like him or her. This is true of all household help of course, but because they are far more prevalent than others, it happens most with sitters. If you wish to discuss it with your neighbor, and perhaps make a sharing arrangement, that is fine, but *never* sitter-snatch behind someone's back if you wish to have a friend left in town.

When someone comes to pick you up, or arrives to spend the evening, your sitter is introduced just as a friend would be—if he or she is present. You need not call your sitter away from the children or from another activity, however, unless it is someone to whom you especially want to introduce him or her.

Mother's Helpers

Mother's Helpers are most often young girls aged 12-16 or so, who are hired to do just what the title implies—help the mother. They really are baby-sitters, but usually in the company of the mother. They entertain and play with the children at home while the mother tends to other things. Often parents with young children have a mother's helper to accompany them on vacation so that the parents can have some time to swim, play tennis, etc., knowing that their children are being cared for.

A mother's helper should be given time to do these things, too, and it is important that the parents give her free time every day and that they don't relegate their children's care to her, treating her as a handy slave.

CLEANING SERVICE

The cleaning woman who comes by the hour or day should be treated with the same courtesy that is expected by the permanent servant. She should be paid promptly—daily, weekly, or in any other way agreed upon.

If your house is far from public transportation, you must see that she is transported to bus or train, or if she is not, that her pay is augmented to cover taxi fare.

If you wish her to wear uniforms, you naturally provide them for her. The part-time cleaning woman often prefers to wear her own clothes covered by a large apron, but if she wishes to wear a uniform in order to save her clothes, she may ask you to buy one or two.

The cleaning woman's duties should be carefully outlined in advance. Are washing and ironing expected, and what about heavy cleaning like waxing floors and washing windows? All these points should be clearly understood on both sides, and if you ask her to do any unusual work or stay on late—to help with a dinner party, for example—her hourly rate for this extra service should be agreed upon before-hand.

Unlike the case of other household employees, it is best to hire part-time cleaning women through friends rather than agencies. The turnover is much higher than it is for live-in help, and many agencies that handle temporary help do not have the opportunity to know very much about them. A good recommendation from a friend who has employed your prospective help for a reasonable length of time is by far the most reliable recommendation you can have.

Since your cleaning woman does not have a room of her own in your house, there must be some space allotted to her to hang her coat, change her clothes, use the bathroom, etc. If your kitchen is too small to hold a table and chairs, she must feel free to sit in your living room or dining area for her noontime break and meal. If she stays all day, you must be prepared to provide a lunch for her. Discuss what sort of a noontime meal she is accustomed to when you hire her, and either be sure to buy something for her or tell her what she is—or is not—free to help herself to from your refrigerator, freezer, or cupboard shelves.

If you work full time and must hire a cleaning service who will come and go while you are out of the house, you must, of course, be doubly sure that he or she is reliable and honest. Using a cleaning service whose employees are bonded and whose contract provides for compensation in case of theft or breakage is perhaps the best solution. However, if you have a cleaning person you know you can trust, your house and possessions will receive far more tender loving care than any commercial service can render.

In any case, you must make arrangements for your cleaning service to get into the house in your absence. Either you must hide a key and tell the service where it is, leave a key with a neighbor who is sure to be home, or leave a key with the doorman if you live in an apartment. Review with the service where all your cleaning equipment is kept, which chores you expect will be done routinely every week, and where you will leave further instructions by note. Be sure to leave your office telephone number where you can be reached in case of an emergency or if your instructions are unclear.

If you are pleased with the work, don't keep it to yourself. A brief note—"The house looked lovely when I came home Tuesday"—will be much appreciated, and will also make any complaints you may have more palatable. When you use a cleaning service it is also a good idea to let the company know when you are pleased with a specific cleaner's work.

Hiring Employees

Whether you are hiring a live-in nanny or maid, or a part-time babysitter or cleaning woman, the rules are the same:

- Check references personally
- Be fair and honest about what the job entails
- Be clear about your expectations
- Be accurate about salary, benefits, and days/time off

If you are hiring a companion for an elderly person or for your children, it is a good idea to have a trial period to make sure the two parties who will be spending the most time together are happy with the arrangement, and that as the employer, you are satisfied with performance, attitude and compatibility.

Live-in employees should be given the opportunity to entertain friends and it is courteous to make a space available for them to do this. If the employee's room is big enough, a part of it may be decorated as a sitting room. If not, one end of the kitchen or, when not in use by the family, a den or the living room, may be made available. Naturally, she or he and any friends should not abuse the privilege by helping themselves to household food or liquor, and should make sure the room is immaculate when they leave.

Legal Requirements

Every person who employs domestic help is responsible for filing a return and paying at least one-half of the employee's Social Security tax. Even though your cleaning woman is a part-time worker, she must, if you pay her wages of over $50 in any quarter (three-month period) of the year, pay a Social Security tax. The employer is responsible for deducting half of the tax due from the employee's wages. The employer adds the other half from his or her own pocket and sends in the total amount to the government. This must be clearly understood by the employee at the time of hiring, so that there will be no question of why the salary is lower than had been promised. Be sure that she *has* a Social Security number and gives it to you when you hire her, as you are *both* legally liable if you do not comply with the regulations. Many employers, instead of paying a higher weekly sum, pay the full amount of the Social Security tax themselves. This is both legal—since the government does not care so long as it receives its percentage of the wages—and simpler, if the arrangement is clearly understood by the employee, who may *not* get the same "break" from her next employer. You will be sent a tax return automatically each quarter, and you will be fined if it is not returned within the specified time. You must of course furnish the employee with a yearly record of how much you have withheld for her, so that she may file a correct income tax return.

Be sure to check the laws within your state for your responsibility for paying state unemployment insurance and/or state Workmen's Compensation insurance. Often these payments depend upon the amount you spend within a three-month calendar period. Further, if you currently spend $1000 a quarter for *any* domestic employee then you are liable for federal unemployment tax. It is important to comply with these regulations both because there are penalties for noncompliance and also because the federal tax code provides single or married working parents with tax credits for child-care payments based on both your income and your yearly child-care expenses. You should also check your state tax code for possible tax credits.

The sensible employer carries sufficient liability insurance to cover any accident that might occur to anyone in his employ. This should be discussed with your insurance company before anyone comes to live in your home.

COMMON COURTESIES

Years ago the butler was "Hastings" and the chauffeur, "Campbell." Today, where households still employ them, they are called "John" or "Jim." Young maids are called by their first names, but an older woman—a nanny or housekeeper—is often called "Mrs. Sykes." In a large, formal household with many servants, chambermaids and waitresses are called by their first names, although the cook's title is sometimes used. When hiring someone for a one-servant household, or as a part-time helper, it is thoughtful to ask her what she would like to be called. Older employees who are called "Mrs. Sykes" or "Miss Stanley" automatically seem to be accorded more respect—especially by children—than if the familiar first name is used.

Household employees, whether young or old, in a large house or a small apartment, call their employers "Mrs. Grant" and "Mr. Grant." The only exception might be an old family nurse who stayed on to help out in her charge's household after the latter married. Children in the family are called by their first names or nicknames by all employees older than themselves. A maid in a very formal household would, however, call adolescent—or older—sons or daughters "Mr. Bob" or "Miss Jill."

Every courteous employer says "Please" in asking that something be brought to her or him: "Would you turn on the lights, please," or "Some more bread, please." One is equally careful to say "Thank you" for any service rendered. No lady or gentleman barks, "Turn on the lights!" or "Give me the bread!" In refusing a dish at the table one says, "No, thank you," or "No, thanks." Children *must* be taught these courtesies with relation to servants as well as friends at the earliest possible age.

A new servant in any capacity is always introduced *to* the members of the household: "Bobby, this is Mary McCormack—she is going to be our new cook."

If you have live-in servants, and guests come to your house for dinner or a party of any sort, it is not necessary to introduce your servant(s) to them. However, when someone comes to stay overnight, or longer, and they will have occasion to talk to each other, introductions are in order. Again, the employee is introduced *to* the guest, and only the name by which the maid is known to the household is used. For example, when your friend Marion comes in, and your maid-of-all-work, Sally, is in the hall to take her bag, you say, "Marion, this is Sally, our housekeeper. Sally, will you take Mrs. Harmon's bag to the guest room, please?" If Sally is normally called Mrs. Loveman, that is the name you use in introducing her.

When it is necessary to write a note to your live-in or part-time help, the rules are slightly different from those for your other correspondence. Although you may start it "Dear Barbara," just "Barbara" is sufficient. The signature, rather than the usual "Sarah Carnes," may be either "S.L.C." or "Mrs. Carnes." Notes left to deliverymen are also signed "Mrs. Carnes."

Your employee's private life is her own business—not yours. As long as her problems do not interfere with her work, there is no reason for you to be "in" on them. Her mail, her telephone calls, and what she does with her spare time are just as inviolate as your children's or your friends'.

Naturally, if she *comes* to you with her problems, you must do your best to help her. It may be advice she needs, or it may be financial help, and you may want to assist with either one. If it is money that is the problem, you are free to advance her a sum or not, as you see fit, but if you do, be sure that it is clearly understood that you will take a certain amount out of future salaries to pay it back—or whatever arrangement you care to make.

Her room is her own domain, and you should not "snoop" when she is on her day off, but you *do* have a right to knock on her door occasionally when she is in, to be sure that she is keeping it in at least reasonably good order.

DISMISSAL

There are several reasons for instant dismissal, with no accompanying reference or special consideration. They are robbery, dishonesty of other kinds, cruelty to children, drunkenness, or use of drugs. When a servant is caught in any of these acts, the sooner he or she is out of the house, the better.

In almost all other circumstances a degree of tolerance and understanding pays off. Even a "second chance" if the misbehavior is not too severe is often better than the necessity of finding and training a new employee. I have, over the years, put up with plates being broken carelessly, with oversleeping, with mops or dust rags being left in the living room, cobwebs on the lampshades, and a variety of other situations, because the mistakes were unintentional, the perpetrator was truly sorry, or simply because I liked her, and she liked me. Having someone who is pleasant and *simpática* in the household, and especially someone who is trustworthy with your children and your possessions, more than makes up for all the little slips that are relatively so unimportant.

When it is necessary to dismiss a household employee it is best to do it promptly, immediately after the episode causing the dismissal takes place, and firmly. You must have a good reason—it is very difficult to tell someone you just don't like her, or her looks, or the way she walks. If these are the reasons, try, in order to leave her her self-respect, to find a more specific reason, even by putting the blame on your financial situation, your future plans, or whatever. Of course, if your reason is more legitimate and definite, you must tell her that too.

If you do not feel that your household employee is achieving the standards you set you should consider trying to correct the faults or changing the conditions that bring on the faults—overwork, overlong hours, etc.—before you decide on dismissal. Of course if you feel there is no rapport between you, no hope for training, nor any possibility of changing the routine, then you must face up to it and "fire" your employee as tactfully and kindly as you can. If circumstances warrant it, offer to provide as good a letter of reference as you can, and you might also offer help in finding another job.

The most considerate letter points out all the good points of the employee and does not mention the bad. The omission will, of course, speak for itself, but the good points will at least prompt a prospective employer to call you, and you can then give a full and honest explanation.

An excellent recommendation—written by hand—might read:

> *Angela Peters has been my general housekeeper for four years. She is completely reliable, honest, and responsible. She is also neat, efficient, and pleasant. Her duties included keeping the downstairs clean, preparing and serving breakfast and dinner. She is an excellent cook and enjoys cooking. My children are devoted to her, and the whole family will miss her terribly. She is*

only leaving because we are moving to Oregon and she does not wish to go so far from her family, who live in New Hampshire.

I will be happy to answer any questions about Angela personally, at 603-555-6343.

An adequate but less enthusiastic reference could be worded:

Arlene Weston has been in my employ for two years as a nanny. I found her at all times honest and good with the children. She cooked simple meals for them and kept their rooms in order. Arlene is leaving because the children have now reached school age, and I no longer need help with them. For further reference, you may call me at 303-555-7274.

When someone does call to check on a written reference, you must be honest, but again, try not to emphasize the drawbacks unless they are serious ones.

*T*here are basically two kinds of clubs and associations— those which you must be invited or nominated to join, and those you may join simply by paying fees or dues. The latter often has residency requirements (a municipal pool or club, for example) or credential requirements (you must be a chef to join the chef's association). If there are no specific requirements once a member, then your money and your good behavior are all that are necessary.

PRIVATE CLUBS

Country clubs, yacht clubs, men's clubs, women's clubs, and often such organizations as garden clubs and fundraising organizations for hospitals welcome new members on an invitation-only basis. Members vote to admit new members, after meeting them at a function held for that purpose. At these coffees, teas or cocktail parties, members make a point of meeting all would-be members and chatting with them for a few minutes. The conversation is usually general, and unfortunately, the would-be member finds him- or herself answering the same questions over and over again: "Yes, I have two children." "Yes, they're both in high school." "Oh, we live on Lavender Lane." "Yes, we have a small sailboat and love to be on the water whenever possible." "Yes, George is an avid golfer and I'm just learning to play." etc.

Although repetitive, the exchanges do enable current and potential members to make a surface judgment as to whether they feel the other would be congenial.

There usually is also an opportunity for the potential member to determine whether the facilities are what she or he wants. Before taking the step of being "interviewed," a potential member should determine what the membership fees are, and what the assessments usually are so that he or she isn't accepted only to have to refuse the invitation because of financial considerations.

If there is a club you would like to join, you may bring up the subject with a friend who you know is a member and ask her if she would be willing to propose you for membership. There may be an application form which needs to be completed or a nominating letter can be written.

8
Clubs
and
Associations

June 10, 1992
Arbor Lane
Madison, WI 99008

Board of Governors
The Shore Club
Milwaukee, Wisconsin

Dear Sirs:

I am delighted to propose Jennifer Hullson for membership in the Shore-side Club. I have known her for many years and consider her qualified in every way for membership.

She is a graduate of Radcliffe, class of 1985, where she was president of Delta Psi and secretary of the senior class. She is a member of the Howard Club in Chicago. She is marketing manager of the firm of Fairbanks & Co.

I know that Jennifer would be a great addition to our membership and hope that you will agree.

Yours very truly,
Rosa Parks

Being asked to support someone's nomination for membership can be difficult if you don't believe the person would fit in, or for whatever reason, are not comfortable sponsoring him or her. In this case, you must refuse. You can simply say, "I'm sorry, I can't sponsor any one right now . . . you'd better ask someone else." If pressed, you have to be firm and refuse. Don't lie and say that there is a long waiting list, because it is fairly easy for someone to discover that there is no waiting list at all, and then you have caused more hurt than if you had simply but kindly refused in the first place.

Most clubs have, if not dress codes, dress customs. These may include tennis whites, no uncovered swimming suits at the terrace restaurant, and jacket and tie for men in the dining room. If there is nothing written in the membership rules, ask or observe. The person who recommended you is a natural resource for information of this sort.

Guests in Clubs

While there is no limit on bringing guests to the restaurants of most clubs—in fact they welcome the added revenue—your common sense should dictate the frequency. If one person returns with you again and again, it is inevitable that you *and* he will be criticized: "If Joe likes our club so much, it's about time he became a member." Also, when a member couple invite guests to play tennis or paddle tennis they are using a court that might otherwise be shared with another member. While everyone is happy to see outsiders enjoying the club facilities no one likes to be told time and time again, "Sorry, there are no courts—the Joneses and their guests are signed up."

When you do invite guests to your club they should be people who are compatible with the membership. No matter what your particular feelings are about politics, race, or religion, you should not make your club the place to launch a crusade. If you don't like the limitations or policies of a particular club and are not willing to abide by them, think twice before joining that club.

Most clubs that have residential facilities will extend club privileges to a stranger—one who lives beyond a specified distance—for a varying length of time determined by the bylaws of the club. In some clubs guests may be put up for a day only; in others the privilege extends for two weeks or more. Many clubs allow each member a certain number of visitors a year; in other visitors are unlimited. In some city clubs the same guest cannot be introduced twice within the year. In country clubs members usually may have an unlimited number of visitors. When these are golf or tennis players the host is responsible for greens fees or court charges. If the guest wishes to repay his host, the matter is settled between them in private.

As a rule, when a member requests club privileges for a friend, the member takes him or her to the club personally, writes the guest's name in the visitors' book, and introduces him or her to those who may be present at the time. If for some reason it is not possible for the host to take the guest to the club, he or she asks the secretary to send a card of introduction:

February 4, 1992
12 Fuller Street
Ellicott City, Maryland 21000

Secretary
The Town Club
Baltimore, Maryland

Dear Sir [or: Dear Mr. Jones]:
I would appreciate it greatly if you would send Mr. A. M. Stanton, of Wilkes-Barre, Pennsylvania, a card extending the privileges of the club for one week.
Mr. Stanton is staying at the Carlton House.

Yours very truly,
Henry Bancroft

Note the degree of formality. One does not write "Dear Jim," because this is not a personal letter but a formal request to be put on file.

The secretary then sends a card to Mr. Stanton:

The Town Club
Extends its privileges to
Mr. Stanton
from Jan. 7 to Jan. 14
Through the courtesy of
Mr. Henry Bancroft

A guest who has been granted club privileges behaves just as he or she would in a private home. He or she does not force him- or herself on the members, nor criticize the personnel, rules, or organization of the club.

Resigning From a Club

When one wishes to resign from a club it is necessary to write a letter of resignation to the secretary well before the date on which the next yearly dues will be due.

Failure to pay one's debts or objectionable behavior is cause for expulsion from any club.

If a member cannot afford to belong to a club, he or she must resign before any fees and bills are overdue. If later on he or she is able to rejoin, the former member's name is put at the head of the waiting list; if this person was considered a desirable member, he or she is reelected at the next meeting of the governors. But a member who has been expelled—unless able to show that the expulsion was unjust—can never again belong to that club. In fact it would probably be difficult for him or her to be elected to any other equivalent club, since expulsion from one will almost certainly come to the attention of another considering him or her for membership.

(For guidance on tipping in private clubs, see page 346.)

Private Associations

Clubs or associations whose prime goal is to provide services or projects which benefit the community or specific organizations, usually collect nominal dues but expect members to join in more than name only. Such organizations as Rotary International, Lion's Club, Junior League, women's clubs, fire department or hospital auxiliaries have several projects a year which are designed to raise funds to support scholarships, to provide for others, or to support the organizations in whose name they meet.

These associations generally nominate persons for membership and make arrangements for members to meet potential members in a similar fashion as do private clubs, and like the membership of private clubs, welcome new members who will work for the best interest of the organization. It is very poor form indeed to join any such association if one does not intend to participate as fully as possible, thus leaving the brunt of the work to be done by others.

City-Owned Clubs

City-owned or municipal clubs generally have residency and membership fees as the only requirements for joining, with no nominations necessary. They have their own rules and codes, which should be followed to the letter by members in order for the club to be enjoyable for all.

Usually this type of club has more members and a smaller staff than does a private club. It is therefore up to the members to be fastidious in their personal habits and not expect someone else to clean up after them.

As in private clubs, children should not be set loose to run rampant through the club, and courtesies on the tennis court or poolside should be maintained at all times.

Health Clubs

Gyms and health clubs are proliferating and with them, new guidelines for courtesy and thoughtfulness, not only on the racquetball court or the workout equipment, but also in the locker room. Unlike private clubs that generally have booths or cabanas for members to change, health clubs have open locker rooms for men and for women.

While it is impossible not to catch the sight of someone undressing out of the corner of your eye, it is impolite to stare, even if they are marching around in the buff for what seems a very long time. If a naked person who thinks nothing of his bareness insists on engaging you in conversation and you are too embarrassed for words, just look him or her in the eye while talking. There's not much else you can do.

The same uncomfortableness can occur in saunas, where many strip off swimsuits or drop towels. If your modesty doesn't allow this, keep your towel up and around you and close your eyes. There is nothing that says you have to bare all just because everyone else does.

Be thoughtful when powdering, deodorizing, toothbrushing, etc. and clean up after yourself. No one wants to walk through your excess powder or wash her face over your spit out toothpaste. Don't spread your cosmetics or personal care items over entire surfaces. Keep your things in a bag and take out only what you need. And please do not shed your hair around the sink or on the shower floor—a damp tissue is a good picker-upper, and leave the facilities spotless for the next person.

Even if half-hour showers are your favorite form of relaxation, save them for home. Keeping others waiting while you lather up and sing an entire aria three times through is not considerate.

The same is true for equipment. Take your turn and no longer. And if you work with a trainer, keep in mind that she has others to help and don't detain her with extra chatter, no matter how much you like her. Out of politeness, she will wait for you to finish talking, but in the meantime is causing others to wait and possibly losing income.

In the same fashion, don't extend your court time, even by just a few minutes, when others are waiting. Even if you haven't finished your tennis or racquetball game, when your time is up, it is up. It is a wrong assumption that others will be pleased to let you go on when they have taken the trouble to make a reservation and are expecting to begin their own game.

In pools, whether at private, municipal or health clubs, respect the lap lanes and use them only for swimming laps. The lifeguard might suggest you leave if he sees you, but more to the point is the lack of courtesy toward those who want to swim laps and can't because you are standing in the middle and talking to a friend.

If you are the one whose patience and goodwill is being abused, a friendly, "I believe we have the court reserved for this hour," or "Excuse me, but this is the lap lane and I have to get ten more laps in before I leave—could you please move to the side if you're not going to be swimming?" is preferable to running for the manager. If another member refuses to respect your rights, however, rather than engaging in fisticuffs it is preferable to find the manager and quietly explain your situation. It is seldom necessary to make a public scene, which does nothing for your image and causes embarrassment to those around you.

III

YOUR PROFESSIONAL LIFE

*I*t may well be that to know you is to love you, but that is not good enough when you are looking for a job. Few employers today have the time to devote to long interviews enabling them to get to know you, so use the premise that what they see is what they get.

What they see first is often your resume. If it is excellent in presentation and content, it goes in the "keep" pile and what they see next is you. Your appearance definitely counts here, as does your ability to be poised and handle tough questions or situations.

For example, a young friend of mine had survived a series of interviews and had made it to the president's office for final approval. The president directed her to a low, upholstered chair at an angle to his desk, putting her almost at his feet instead of at eye level, directly in front of a row of track lighting which shone in her eyes. He asked her a series of questions, and intermittently asked her if she was nervous. She was not nervous, and asked him why he was asking that question. He replied that she had been blinking rapidly throughout the interview, to him a sign of acute anxiety. She huffily replied that his dreadful lights were shining in her eyes and ANYBODY would blink in that situation. She then proceeded to tell him how uncomfortable he had made her, forcing her to sit in that chair and endure the glare. Needless to say, her response, although from the heart, was not expressed in a way that made him react favorably to her. Instead, she should have immediately located a straight-backed chair and said, "If you don't mind, I'd prefer to sit here so that I can see you better and so that the lights aren't shining in my eyes." He could hardly refuse, and she would have been more in control of her end of the interview.

9
Getting and Starting Your Job

JOB HUNTING

Whether you are a newcomer to the job market, or a seasoned professional, you need to draw upon several resources when seeking a job. You should prepare yourself by determining a realistic idea of the salary range for the job you would like to find, and check the classified ads to see what areas within your expertise are being advertised.

Use the classified section, employment agencies and head hunters, as well as personal networking contacts to begin your search. Using the first requires dynamic cover letters and an excellent resume. The second and third options require strong personal skills and professionals who would be willing to recommend you or refer you for a job, based on their personal or professional knowledge of you. People are unwilling to recommend someone who is unproven, who has demonstrated less than reliable job performance, or whose overall appearance or demeanor is embarrassing, and rightly so—their own credibility is at stake.

Even without a personal contact, you may write directly to a company for which you would like to work. If possible, secure the name of the person to whom your letter will be addressed, since a personally directed letter has a better chance than one addressed "Dear Sir or Madam." The letter should explain your reason for writing and ask for an appointment. If a reply by telephone or letter does not follow within two weeks, you may properly call the person's office, refer to your letter, and ask if you may make an appointment.

YOUR RESUME

If you haven't a clue as to how to write a resume, check your library for a reference book or use the expertise of a professional resume writer or company. Again, this document is most often the first introduction a potential employer receives, and it should be strong and represent you well. It should be completely accurate, and should not, unless your background is so extensive that it doesn't fit on two pages, exceed that maximum. Among the items your resume should include are:

> your name, address and telephone number
> the kind of position you are looking for
> your previous work experience
> your educational background

In addition, you may include any special skills or knowledge you have which would be useful to a potential employer. You need not list specific references on your resume, but you should indicate that they will be supplied upon request. Be totally honest on your resume. Do not exaggerate your experience or lie about your education. The truth may not always get you the job; but a lie uncovered will inevitably lose it.

You need not dwell on the negative aspects of your background and experience, but should emphasize what is positive. For instance, instead of downgrading what you might consider an insignificant job you held in retail sales, you can point out the expertise you gained in meeting the public and in accurate account-keeping. Rather than apologize for not having worked in ten or twenty years, you can itemize the skills you have acquired during that time in whatever you were doing— parenting, housekeeping, or serving as a volunteer.

Don't try to be clever or humorous on a resume. Be direct and clear, stating your assets with confidence, but not boastfulness.

Your resume should be printed on a good quality paper and be very neat and attractive in appearance.

REQUESTING REFERENCES

References are to be treasured and guarded. This means that you must first, before ever giving someone's name as a reference, ask that person if you may do so. If she or he agrees, send him a copy of your resume and a brief note detailing any other activities which would give that person an update on your activities, successes or achievements. Having this information in hand, your reference is able to answer any professional questions about you that a potential employer may ask. With these enclosures, include a cover note thanking this person for agreeing to refer you for a job.

Treasuring your reference also means that you do not give out his or her name indiscriminately. The pleasure of doing you a good turn and giving you a glowing recommendation pales quickly if too many people call.

Do have the names and the telephone number your reference has given you to use readily available.

Your references should be professional people who can speak about your on-the-job performance, for the most part. This includes those for whom you have done volunteer work as well as an immediate supervisor or executive in the company you worked in before. Your brother-in-law, although he may think you are simply wonderful, will not carry much credibility as a reference.

For a young person just starting out, a professor, teacher, dean, counselor, or summer job employer, as well as a minister or rabbi are all excellent references if they can attest to your good character, willingness to work hard, scholastic achievement, etc.

Once you have found a job, it is thoughtful to write a thank you note to those people who agreed to give a reference for you, whether they were ever called or not. In the note, mention briefly your new job and how pleased you are to be starting it.

THE INTERVIEW

You may set up an interview by letter or by phone. In the former case, you write asking for an appointment and receive a reply with a time and date. In the latter, you phone, setting up the interview through the secretary or personnel department of the prospective employer. You may combine both ways by suggesting in a letter to a prospective employer that you will phone his or her office for a specific appointment.

Walking into an interview without preparation may limit your chances of getting the job. First, learn all you can about the company where you are seeking employment: you can look it up in Dun and Bradstreet or secure a copy of the company's annual report from the president's office. Business magazines such as *Fortune, Business Week,* and *Forbes* may have written articles on the company or its competitors; a look through *Readers' Guide to Periodical Literature* in the public library will tell you. In addition, trade publications in the company's field may have material: try a phone call to their library.

Second, learn all you can about yourself. Instead of merely wanting a job, think about your professional goals and how this job might lead you toward them. Consider ways in which your previous experience has qualified you for this job. Ask yourself what the employer may be seeking in a prospective employee, and make a mental checklist of the requirements you fill. Thus armed, you will approach the employer prepared for the interview.

Be sure you know the name of the person interviewing you and pronounce it correctly. If you are uncertain, check ahead of time with the secretary. Unless invited to call the interviewer by his or her given name, if it is a man, call him "Mr."; if it is a woman, ask her secretary whether she prefers "Miss," "Mrs." or "Ms."

The following suggestions can make an interview more productive:

- Be on time. Never keep an interviewer waiting.
- Do not sit until you are asked. Then sit in the chair indicated or, if none is, in a chair across from the interviewer. Do not slouch.
- Dress conservatively. Suits are appropriate for both men and women. A woman should wear nothing sheer or tight fitting; she is not being judged on glamour.
- Be neat. Make sure your shirt is tucked in, your shoes polished. No hems or cuffs should be frayed or raveling. Your hair should be combed and not falling over your face. Women should avoid excessive jewelry and makeup.
- Do not smoke.
- Go alone. Do not go to an interview in a group even when there are several openings. Instead of being one in a crowd, go by yourself and stand out alone.
- Take what papers you need in a case. You may have an extra resume or samples of work you have done. Be able to pull out what you need quickly, without riffling through a stack.
- Speak with self-confidence. Answer the interviewer's questions fully so that you may amplify the facts of your resume with specific details. Let the interviewer lead you into subjects of discussion; do not waste time on unsolicited information. Do not be afraid to ask questions about the job, but remember that "What opportunities are there for career growth?" will impress the interviewer far more than "How much vacation do I get?"
- Don't discuss your family or pull your husband's or wife's name into the conversation.
- Don't name-drop if you know important people.

- Don't apologize for your lack of a particular skill. Instead, admit that you don't have it, but that you are a quick study and would be more than willing to learn.
- Don't flirt.
- Know when to leave. Some interviewers rise to indicate the termination of the interview; others wind up verbally with phrases such as "I have enjoyed talking with you," or "Thank you for coming." Be sensitive to this and rise promptly to take your leave.
- Be courteous. Throughout the interview follow the rules of common courtesy. Shake hands when you leave. Thank the interviewer for the time spent and interest shown. Smile. Thank the interviewer's secretary on the way out.

After the interview write a thank-you letter. Not only is this good manners, but it helps the interviewer keep you in mind when another job opening appears.

If you have not heard from the company two or three weeks after your interview, you may write a letter or phone the interviewer, expressing your continued interest in the position. If you still receive no reply, let it rest. Persistent inquiries serve only to irritate.

Questions You Needn't Answer

Even today, women can be at a disadvantage with a potential employer who immediately assumes that if they are young, they will quit and have children, and that if they are older, they are just killing time until their husbands retire and they move to Florida. If they are of an age where they might already have young children, some employers are convinced that the children will take first place over a job, and that excessive absenteeism might be likely. Often these potential employers have had a bad experience which they transfer to every eligible female applicant.

They may not, by law, ask you questions about your marital status and the disposition of your children during working hours. You would be wise, however, to have an answer ready should you be willing to discuss these questions. If you feel the interview is going well and that you are anxious to get the job, you may say, "My husband and I are planning to have children at some point, but I would want to keep working, after a brief maternity leave. We have excellent child care opportunities where we live, and I am dedicated to continuing my career." Or, "I have two small children who are cared for by a wonderful nanny when I am working." These statements impart your seriousness in the way you view your career.

Age is a factor in anyone's finding work, despite the federal law that prohibits age discrimination. Again, your appearance, your vitality, and your experience are strong contributors to overcoming age prejudice.

A woman who has been out of the job market for several years should be sure to draw upon all the areas of skills she has practiced in volunteer and community activities to show that she is capable and energetic. A man should focus on his maturity in decision-making and the wealth of skills he has acquired.

If you are older and concerned that this will be a deterrent to your being hired, it is not necessary to put the years of your high school or college graduations on your resume, and it is never necessary, or recommended, to include such personal information as your age or your marital status.

YOUR ATTIRE

The clothing you wear and your overall appearance makes an immediate impression on a potential employer. An investment in one superb "interview suit" is a worthwhile one. In addition:

- Shoes should be well-heeled, clean, and shined.
- Hair should be neat.
- Jewelry should be at a minimum, tasteful, and not noisy.
- Fingernails should be scrupulously clean and shaped.
- Stockings should not have runs; men's socks should be long enough to cover their legs should their pant legs ride up when they are sitting down.
- Accessories should be practical and neat. This is not the time to carry a bulging briefcase or a handbag stuffed with a pacifier, old tissues and your child's squirt gun.
- In the winter, outerwear should be clean and in very good condition. Whether a secretary takes your coat and hangs it up or you carry it over your arm into the interview, a ripped lining, a dirty collar or spots do not make a good impression.

STARTING THE JOB

Thorough knowledge of company rules makes the first weeks on a new job less painful and more productive. You can learn them through the personnel office, which may have an information handbook to give you, through orientation sessions which some companies hold for new employees, or merely through asking fellow workers. You should learn about work hours, lunch hour, vacations, company policy on sick and personal days. You'll need to know how to requisition supplies. And of course you should find out when and how often you are paid, what deductions are taken out, what benefits you are entitled to, and how salary raises are awarded.

When beginning a job, it is important to know who is in charge of various areas of the operation—know their names and their duties. In this way you will be able to turn to the proper person for help when you need it and also to direct the work you are doing into proper channels. Do not be afraid to ask for help when you are new on a job. People are far more willing to accept your lack of knowledge than your errors.

The first day on the job, your new boss or perhaps his or her secretary or assistant will take you through the office, introducing you to your co-workers. Make a point of listening to their names so that you can remember them. Repeating the name during the introduction helps: "How do you do, Miss Jones." As you become familiar with the staff, you may find that first names are used, but at the beginning you do not know. Therefore, to be safe, when introduced use "Mr.," "Mrs.," "Miss," or "Ms." If they say, "Oh, please call me Mary [or Jim]," then you may feel free to do so. In return you should suggest that they call you by your first name as well.

Shake hands as you are introduced. If you are seated, rise, even if you are older: you are, after all, newer at the job.

If you have been hired at the management level, you will probably want to walk through the office on your first day to meet members of your staff. If while seated at your desk, you are greeted by a staff member whom you have not yet met, you should rise and shake hands. You will benefit far more by showing courtesy than by showing rank.

The first day of work, like the first day of anything else, is always the hardest. When lunchtime rolls around and no one has invited you to join them, you shouldn't invite yourself along. Instead, leave the office for a while, if just to walk around the block or drive home or to a coffee shop, depending on how close to the office you live. To sit alone at your desk feeling lonely and sorry for yourself will not do.

Don't watch the clock and race out the door at closing time on your first day. You also should not hang around indefinitely, but giving the work day an extra fifteen minutes or so will also give you the opportunity to see what people do. Use the time to tidy your desk, arrange a file, etc.

It is also a good idea not to make an immediate and fast friend until you have a better understanding of the politics of the office. Be polite and responsive to everyone, but withhold establishing personal relationships, particularly at the beginning. And most important, do not engage in gossip or ask personal questions of anyone. As a newcomer, you will be resented and labeled a "snoop," even if your intention is honorable and all you want to do is understand who is who and what is what.

"*L*ife is not so short but that there is always time enough for courtesy," that New England gentleman Ralph Waldo Emerson told us. We might well add, "Nor is business so busy." Etiquette enables people in the social world to move in and out of common situations with ease and comfort; in the business world it does no less. The human needs that arise when groups of people meet in social situations are similar to those that arise in business—the need for respect and sensitivity to feelings.

There is also, however, an additional set of needs— business needs, we might call them. Not only must we follow a code that smoothes personal encounters, but we must conform to standards of behavior that make professional encounters pleasant and productive. Intrinsically bound together, they are essential to comfortable working conditions and to personal success.

While certain procedures may seem awkward or wasteful to you as you begin work in a new situation, resist the urge to make immediate changes. Discover how things are done and why: answering the telephone, dressing, decorating desks or office space, snacking on the job, circulating memos, etc. Establish in your mind other people's priorities before asserting your own. Any changes you initiate will have more validity after you have familiarized yourself with customary procedures.

10
On the Job

What to Call Whom

Every office has its own protocol for who is called by his or her first name and who is called by his or her title. New employees should follow suit, after listening carefully to how people are addressed.

If yours is a "title" office, but you call your boss Charlie when meeting alone, you should still call him Mr. Jeppeson when others are around.

If yours is an informal office, you still should wait for the other person to say, "Please call me Steve," before doing so, if he has been introduced to you as "Mr. Feeney."

Everyone, no matter whether the office is formal or informal, has a name. No secretary should ever be referred to as "my girl." She is, if a possessive must be used, "Jean Verrilli, my secretary," or "Tony Anders, my assistant."

Asking for Help

Whether you have a large staff or have no one reporting to you, there are times and situations where you must seek the assistance of others. These "others" may be the people who report to you, or they may be co-workers. Whatever your position, there is never any need to bark orders or make a request sound like a demand. You'll receive more willing help if you pepper your requests with "pleases" and "thank you's."

Requests from the Boss

Part of the daily routine of most executives is to spend a period of time with his or her secretary, going over mail, dictating letters, discussing appointments to be made, etc. It is easy to forget the niceties of human relations that make these meetings more pleasant when they occur daily, but shouting, "Susan! Come in here!" or running through the litany of things to do without a smile is inexcusable. "Susan, when you're finished with that letter could you please come in for some dictation," shows recognition that Susan is busy and turns an order into a request.

At a meeting of project managers saying, "Jim, the Kraus project needs some attention—do you think you could fit it into your schedule within the next two days?" shows acknowledgement that Jim has a schedule and again makes a request out of your order.

By making these requests "you" rather than "I" statements or questions, you are implying that Susan or Jim have a participatory place in the process. If you said, "*I* want you to come in here . . ." "*I* want you to work on the Kraus project," the *tone* of your request would be very different.

Among Co-Workers

Office protocol can make it difficult for one employee to ask another for help. While no one likes the work-shirker who never seems to be able to quite get his own projects finished and turns helplessly to peers for assistance, most will willingly volunteer to lend a hand to someone who has helped him or her.

If you know a co-worker is working through lunch to collate a large client packet, your *volunteering* to stay and help will be gratefully received and most often returned when it's you who is stuck. I say voluntarily because your offer is not to add up paid overtime hours. It is to help a peer in need.

If your offer is accepted, you do not, however, store it away in your mental favor bank or ever remind everyone what a good person you were for helping—you simply hope the favor will be returned when it's you who is overloaded.

Whatever your position, a big "Thank you" is in order, no matter how small the task or favor.

APPOINTMENTS IN YOUR OFFICE

There are frequent occasions when visitors come to your office: salespersons, representatives of other firms, your secretary, prospective employees on an interview, fellow workers of equal or different rank, clients, would-be clients, and outsiders with requests, complaints, and suggestions.

Early Arrivals

If visitors arrive early for an appointment, your secretary should be instructed to greet them graciously, hang up coats, and offer chairs. If you must keep visitors waiting, there is even greater need for courtesy. You should be alerted to their arrival and do everything possible to cut short the business that is holding you up. I know one executive who personally greets a visitor whom he has to keep waiting, offering his apologies with an indication of the time when he will be free to see him. His secretary provides current magazines and tea or coffee while he waits.

Greetings

When do you rise? Whatever your sex, you rise when a superior or an older person, whether male or female, enters. You rise for a client or a customer. In order to save time, you do not rise when your secretary comes in, unless the secretary is new and you are introducing yourself. Nor do you rise when a co-worker of either sex, older or younger, approaches your desk, unless again it is for the first, introductory, time.

At one time etiquette dictated that a woman always be the first to offer her hand when greeting a male business associate. This is no longer the case: both men and women offer their hand to clients, customers, people outside the company, and anyone they are meeting for the first time.

Business greetings traditionally begin with a handshake. In recent years some greetings have started with a kiss which may or may not be appropriate to the situation. Kissing is a very personal way of saying hello, so you have to be careful about using it in business situations. Don't kiss someone you don't know well. They might recoil in surprise or embarrassment, which is awkward for both of you. Generally speaking, the longer you have known a person and the more established your social and business relationships, the more appropriate a friendly peck on the cheek is likely to be for both parties. Take into consideration the occasion and the setting. Kisses exchanged in the context of business meetings that are social in nature or those which are also attended with spouses, such as banquets and conventions, may be acceptable. Those exchanged in pure business settings such as conference rooms or offices should be replaced with a handshake. Avoid kissing up or down the ranks. A junior person kissing a senior executive appears to be currying favor. The opposite can suggest that you're taking advantage of your position to make inappropriate advances toward a subordinate.

Don't ever feel obligated to give or receive kisses. Good feelings can be extended with a smile and words such as "It's really great to see you," accompanied by a warm handshake. If you've been kissed by someone at a previous meeting and prefer that it not happen again keep your distance and extend your hand before the kisser has a chance to get too close.

Giving Your Undivided Attention

While speaking with a visitor during an appointment, you should bear in mind that listening is as essential as talking. The visitor came in order to communicate something; you must let him say it and also let him see your interest. Your body listens as well as your ears: look at the speaker, and do not lean away. When you respond, speak with candor and control. If you disagree, restrain your anger and negative comments; "No" can be said with courtesy. If you are in accord with the visitor, temper your enthusiasm, especially if ensuing action rests on authority higher than yours; do not make promises you cannot be sure of keeping.

Nothing is more irritating and insulting to a visitor than to have an appointment interrupted by continual phone calls. If this seems likely, instruct your secretary to hold all calls except emergencies until the termination of the appointment. Where this is not feasible, keep the calls you take short and to the point. Inform the caller that someone is in your office and offer to call back.

Certain situations may arise during an appointment which can cause embarrassment if you have not armed yourself for them.

For instance, how do you say no to a request? You answer straightforwardly, "I'm sorry, but I really can't do that." You may want to explain, "It is against company policy," or "I don't feel comfortable doing that," or whatever the reason is. However, you are not required to give an explanation.

How do you end a sales pitch? Simply reply, "I understand what you have said; it is interesting, and you present it well. I can't give you any more time now, though; so let me think about it, and I'll get back to you."

How do you avoid a conversation you would rather not have? This situation may be brought about by a personal question or by one relating to a company decision not yet released to the public. You may answer, "I'm sorry, but I really don't want to [or don't feel free to] discuss that now. I hope you understand."

How do you handle a question to which you do not know the answer? There is no stigma attached to saying, "I am sorry. I don't know." Politeness requires that you go further, however, and add, "I'll connect you with someone who can answer that question." If a person nearby or a mere phone call away can provide the answer, transfer the caller right away. If it requires more time and research, offer to contact the person with the answer at a later date.

Ending the Appointment

Many people find winding up an appointment difficult since they do not want to hurt the feelings of their visitors. As a result, they let it drag on long past its productivity.

If you see that a caller is veering away from the subject matter for which the appointment was arranged, you may wish not to terminate the interview, but merely to shorten it. In this case you might say, "Since I have another appointment in a few minutes, I'd like to discuss our primary concern so that we won't have to stop before resolving it." If there is no "primary concern," but the person is merely chatting and wasting your time, suggest that you postpone the conversation to another time. "I'd love to chat now, but I'm too busy," you might conclude.

The least awkward way to wind up an appointment when you feel the time has come is to have your secretary enter the office and say, "I'm sorry, Mrs. Phillips, but your next appointment is due any minute." Mrs. Phillips then uses the remaining few minutes to bring the conversation to an unhurried close, summarizing the points made and any future action to be taken. Mrs. Phillips rises, with her visitors following suit. She escorts them from her office, where her secretary returns their coats and bids them a polite good-bye. The visitors depart feeling that Mrs. Phillips, the company, and they themselves are wonderful.

If you do not have a secretary to help you close a visit, you yourself may alert your visitors to your next appointment, or you can merely find an opportunity to summarize the meeting and hope your visitors get the point. If they do not, as a last resort you can rise.

Appointments in Other Offices

Courtesy dictates much of the visitor's behavior as well as the host's. The first rule is to be on time. If an emergency forces you to be late, telephone promptly to alert the person whom you are to meet. If you cannot phone, ask someone to make the call for you. If you are tied up in traffic, and have a car phone, make the best use of it to alert your appointment to the delay.

When you arrive for an appointment, give your name to the receptionist or secretary and the time designated for your appointment: "I am Susan Arthur. I have an appointment with Mrs. Barnes at three-thirty." Present your business card (if you have one) for the secretary to convey to Mrs. Barnes. If the secretary does not offer to take your coat, you may ask where to hang it.

While waiting, you are expected to sit quietly and not bother the employees with conversation in order to pass time. Do not display impatience with obvious glances at your watch, although if you are kept waiting over twenty minutes, you may ask, "Could you tell me when Mrs. Barnes will be free?" If you are unable to wait until that time, you may explain to the secretary and set up another appointment.

Courtesy to the secretary, no matter how angry you are at her employer, is demanded.

When you are ushered into the executive's office, introduce yourself if you have not met before: "Good afternoon, Mrs. Barnes. I am Susan Arthur. I appreciate your seeing me." If you already know each other, you need only exchange greetings and handshakes.

Since the executive is undoubtedly busy, it behooves you to get to the point of your meeting as quickly as possible. Present what you have to say clearly and directly, avoiding jokes, anecdotes, and references to your personal life. When you have finished, let the executive speak, and that means *listen* to her. Do not interrupt with arguments or additional information; you may offer them after she has finished.

Be sensitive to your host's efforts to wind up the meeting. Rise. Offer your hand. Say, "Thank you" and "Good-bye." Retrieve your coat on the way out, and be sure to thank the secretary. If it was your first meeting write a letter of thanks by the following day. If you have an on-going business relationship you should follow up with a letter or memo reiterating any further action generated by the meeting.

Business Dress and Grooming

Most of us dislike the implications of the old axiom that clothes make the man; yet we know it contains more than a grain of truth, especially in business, where clothes make the woman as well. Reflect on people you see receiving promotions. As often as not, when there are two equally qualified candidates for a new position, the one who "looks the part" will be chosen over the one whose appearance is less than professional. As unfair as you may feel this is, keep in mind that an employee represents not him- or herself, but the company he or she works for. And no company management wants its image to be unprofessional, as would be reflected in the appearance of its inappropriately dressed employees. If you feel you should be allowed to wear jeans at any job level, you may be right, but being right will not further your career.

General Guidelines

For both men and women, appropriate is first of all clean—squeaky clean. Clean nails, clean hair, and clean clothes. Appropriate is also pressed—even clothes of natural fibers which wrinkle immediately should be pressed to start—not look as though the wearer had slept with them crumpled under his pillow.

Perfume, cologne and after shave are lovely when a mere hint of fragrance is apparent. They are ghastly when co-workers are forced to run to open windows for air after you walk by.

Suffice it to say, other grooming aids should be applied with vigor. Toothbrushes, mouthwash, and deodorant are a prerequisite to working in close quarters with others.

When Co-Workers Offend

A question I am asked often is what to do or say about employees or co-workers with offensive breath, body odor, apparent dandruff, etc. The answer really depends on your relationship to the offender. It is never easy, but it is likely this person truly doesn't know he has a problem and even if he is initially embarrassed, he will ultimately be grateful for your helping him. You can say, "Ted, I don't think you realize it, but your breath is pretty strong up close and I thought you might like to know before anyone else noticed," or "Ann, I've noticed that you have the same problem I do with perspiring—I didn't know what to do until I found Brand X deodorant, but its made a difference for me and it might work for you, too." Even if you have never perspired in your life, you will make Ann feel better to think you share a problem than to think that she has gone around offending the entire office on her own.

The supervisor of a person who needs some personal hygiene help should do the same thing, as she should with a candidate for promotion whose attire needs attention. "George, you are doing exemplary work and I'd like to throw your name in as a candidate for the vice presidency, but you have to do something about your body odor [breath, hair, table manners, clothing, etc.] before I can ask the Board to consider you."

Of course we should all help a person who has an unzipped fly, or unbuttoned blouse, who has spinach in his teeth or a stain on the back of her skirt, or labels sticking out from the back of her sweater, whether best friend or nodding acquaintance. No one intentionally walks around the office with food in his teeth or his fly unzipped and when others "politely" say nothing, his embarrassment is greater when he discovers his calamity than if someone had taken him aside right away and told him. Simply and quietly say, "Excuse me John, but your zipper has come undone," or "Jane, here's my mirror—you seem to have something caught in your teeth." Wouldn't you rather be told than spend the day unknowingly undone in front of the whole office? So would anyone else.

Attire for Women

Appropriate attire depends in part on the industry you work in. What is appropriate in a design studio may not be appropriate for a brokerage house. Inappropriate means several things. For women, it means overly dressy clothes in the daytime, too much hair, too much makeup, too much jewelry, too casual an appearance, and such things as glow-in-the-dark colors or patterns that hurt the eye.

Even if slinky and sexy is your after-hours look, keep it out of the office. The way you dress tells your co-workers, your employers, and your customers or clients not only how you feel about yourself, but how you want them to feel about you. If you want them to feel you are a business professional, then great lengths of leg or plunges of décolleté do not belong in the office.

When attending conferences and conventions held at resort hotels or clubs, women need assorted casual clothes plus sports outfits for tennis or golf, swimwear, etc. Most conventions have a relaxed dress code and attenders are expected to shun their suits for comfortable clothing. Again, however, this does not necessarily mean jeans or short shorts. It does mean pulled-together ensembles that still reflect your professional status—crisp, pleated pants with jackets, skirts and blouses, more casual knit dresses, etc., which help bridge the gap between office wear and sportswear. At conferences held within a city, office wear is usually worn instead of sports wear. Women should check on what will be required for evening wear before packing—some conferences have more formal evenings as part of their agenda, others hold luaus, picnics, and more casual events.

Attire for Men

Menswear that is inappropriate is clothing that is too casual, patterning that doesn't "go," such as too many different stripes on suits, shirts and ties worn at once, socks that allow leg to show between pant hem and shoe, socks that don't coordinate with suits, and out-of-date collar, lapel, or trouser width or style. Also inappropriate is obvious or noisy jewelry, chest hair showing through unbuttoned shirts or thin-fabric shirts, and hair that is overstyled, oversprayed, or greasy. Facial hair should be trimmed and neat, and shoes should be of soft leather or a lookalike, not patent leather or otherwise shiny; nor are cowboy boots, woodsman's boots, or rubber-soled shoes appropriate with dress suits.

Attendance at conferences and conventions poses no clothing problems for men. Office wear is customary at city-based conferences, and sport shirts and slacks with sport jackets are fine for conventions outside the city. For activities, men take sports clothes as they would on a vacation, and wear either a dark suit or dinner jacket in the evening, as the occasion requires. They should determine what evening wear will be required before packing to go.

OFFICE COURTESIES

Nowhere are people more confused about manners than in the office. Men who are used to being courtly with women are uncertain whether to let the door slam or hold it open; women who are anxious to prove that they are "as good as any man" may tend to eschew any sign or attention that singles them out as a woman, often with an aggressive, "I am perfectly capable of doing that myself!"

Situations of Gender

If everyone would assume equal gender status and focus on simple courtesy there would be no problem or confusion about who should do what for whom.

- Whoever gets to the door first should open it.
- Whoever is closest to the elevator door should enter or exit first.

- Whoever has the lighter handy should light the other's cigarette.
- Both men and women should rise to greet a client or office guest, whether the guest is male or female.
- Both men and women should shake hands with the other; there is no protocol in the office for who offers his or her hand first.
- Whichever gender is hosting a business lunch pays for it.
- If everyone drinks the coffee in the department coffee pot, everyone should take turns making it and cleaning it afterward, male and female. Nothing is a greater carryover of gender stereotyping than coffee-making, and women can be just as guilty of perpetrating this as men can be, when they assume "household" jobs in the office.
- Personal chores, such as sending a secretary to the dry cleaner or to buy a gift for the boss's spouse are not part of the job, unless so specified at the time of hiring. If one really needs a favor done, the request for someone else to run a personal errand is just that, personal.
- Neither men nor women should use terms of endearment in the office. Joan is not "Honey," Stan is not "Sweetie." When someone persists, simply say, "My name is Joan, not Honey," over and over again until he gets the message.

Even if your instinct, whether man or woman, is to practice your outside-the-office manners in the office, don't. For example a business luncheon is not a date. A woman should not expect her companion to race to seat her, nor should he feel compelled to do so. She fends for herself, just as he does.

Food

In offices where food and beverages are permitted at desks, simple rules of neatness must be followed. Leave no dirty cups or plates around. Wipe up crumbs or spilled liquids. Watching someone eat falls far short of pleasurable entertainment. If you must eat at your desk and have an office door, close it. If your desk is in a common area try to do it when those around you have gone out. Pay strict attention to your eating manners, and do not answer the telephone with your mouth full. Throw everything away as soon as you have finished, preferably in a trash container that is secluded or sealed, rather than in the wastebasket beside your or someone else's desk. The sight, not to mention the redolence of your discarded cantaloupe or tuna and onion does not belong in the office.

Office Collections

If office policy allows it, collections for new baby gifts, funeral flowers or charitable donations, wedding gifts, etc., should be organized so they don't get out of hand. In some offices, these collections can occur almost daily and are often

resented. When this happens, discuss the possibility of a yearly department "kitty"
where everyone chips in $5 or $10 at the beginning of the year, to be allocated as need arises. Guidelines should be established at the same time. The group might, decide for example, that get well flowers would be sent to an employee who was in the hospital, and to his or her spouse, but not to his or her mother or great aunt. Or the group might determine that a birthday card would be purchased and signed by all for co-workers, but that birthday gifts, which would deplete the kitty rapidly, would not be given.

If you choose not to participate, or feel you cannot afford to participate, be honest and say so. If you find your situation changes you may decide to participate in the future.

MEETINGS

A business meeting may be called by anyone whose work requires the input and exchange of ideas with co-workers. Although a higher-level executive usually calls a business meeting, there are occasions when a person of lower rank calls it and includes his or her superior.

Conducting Meetings

Almost all of us attend several kinds of meetings each year, and many of us find ourselves from time to time in the position of having to take charge. Situations vary, of course, but some rather generalized suggestions may be useful. Certain rules apply to all meetings, no matter what kind; when adhered to, they enable a meeting to run smoothly, efficiently and on time.

- Prepare an agenda beforehand and follow it closely.
- Alert attendees to the purpose of the meeting and stay on course toward fulfilling it.
- State the time at which the meeting is to start and set a limit for concluding it. Start on time and end on time.
- Even if you do not follow Robert's Rules, call on people to speak in turn, and forbid interruptions.

It is up to those invited to meetings to be on time, not up to the one who called the meeting to wait for everyone to arrive. Waiting for latecomers inconveniences those who have arrived promptly and who should not be penalized for their courtesy and professionalism.

Serving Refreshments

Coffee or tea breaks may be offered at lengthy meetings. A break is called and the participants may go to the coffee machine or simply stretch their legs. When the meeting extends through lunch without a break, the person who called the meeting should arrange for lunch to be sent in, along with beverages. Someone not involved in the meeting should be alerted to watch for the arrival of lunch and to see that it is delivered to the meeting room. Depending on his or her job responsibilities, this person may set the lunch up and help serve it, or may simply alert the meeting organizer that it has arrived so that he or she can call a break in the meeting and ask those present to help themselves. When a working lunch meeting concludes, everyone who attends is responsible for helping straighten up the conference room and disposing of trash properly.

Meetings Held in a Restaurant

Very often, two or more people from a company, or from different companies, will find it more convenient to meet in a restaurant to conduct their business, away from the constant barrage of telephones and those who feel free to pop in and ask just one question. The person who calls the meeting is responsible for making reservations, no matter whether he or she is paying or they each are sharing the cost, and should be sure that it is a restaurant where it will be quiet or private enough for business to be conducted without shouting or without too many distractions.

Many executives today find it more convenient to meet at breakfast time, since restaurants are so often crowded at lunch. Lunch meetings also tend to interrupt the flow of the day in the office, while starting or ending the day with an outside meeting eliminates this interruption. Rather than ending the day with a dinner meeting, late afternoon meetings at tea time are often efficient. Tea time meetings in restaurants enable executives to clear off their desks and conduct business during the transition between office and home, getting home at a much more reasonable hour than a dinner meeting permits.

Videoconferencing

With more and more companies having branch offices around the country, or in some cases, around the world, a videoconference may be a helpful and cost-efficient way to conduct some of your company's business. You may find yourself in a meeting of two or three participants at each site with a stationary camera, or a large group meeting at multiple sites with a camera that focuses on each person as he or she speaks. The range of equipment your company uses determines the exact features and capabilities of the videoconference system.

There are a few differences between videoconferences and in-person meetings. What follows are general guidelines. It is more important to avoid side conversations at a videoconference than it is at an in-person meeting, for instance, as the unintended conversation may be broadcast to the other sites. Make a point of glancing at the screen occasionally as it gives the appearance that you are making eye contact with those at the other sites.

Circulating a meeting agenda ahead of time is vital to a videoconference.

Should any last minute changes occur be sure to telephone the attendees at all sites to
update the agenda, or send the revised agenda by fax. Before the meeting gets
underway confirm that everyone has received the revised agenda.

When the meeting is ready to begin, each site should make sure that volume
and picture are working properly. If the volume is turned up too high you may get
feedback at the other site. Adjust the volume to a level that allows everyone to be
heard, but which avoids feedback. It is possible that the videoconference call's signal
can be lost at any time, resulting in the loss of sound, picture, or both. Determine
ahead of time how you wish to proceed: does the meeting continue while the signal is
reestablished and then the material covered summarized, or does the meeting recess
until the signal is reestablished? There is no correct solution here. Time constraints,
the availability of the participants to reconvene, and the speed with which the signal
can be reestablished may all play a part in how you choose to proceed.

Depending upon the arrangement of the videoconference room and the
number of people attending the meeting, not everyone at every site may be visible at
all times. This is certainly true when you are working with a stationary camera. All
participants should remember that it is important to speak loudly and clearly,
especially when you are not sitting immediately in front of a microphone and/or you
are out of the stationary camera's range. Since the microphones work much like a
speaker telephone, only one person can speak at a time. Participants speaking at one
site cannot be heard until the person speaking at another site stops talking. If you are
at an ancillary site rather than the main meeting site it is sometimes necessary to use
what amount to hand signals to get the attention of the chair, and to be recognized,
before you begin speaking.

When the agenda has been covered and any new business dealt with, conclude your videoconference as you would any other meeting.

Meetings Held in the Home

Coffee is usually served before or during a morning meeting, and tea or coffee
or a cold drink in the afternoon. The person at whose house the meeting is held may
provide the refreshments, or various others may volunteer to bring them.

Other than the setting, which is generally more informal than a boardroom or
office, the meeting is conducted as any other, with the chairperson calling the group
to order and the agenda addressed, item by item. Often the informality of the setting
induces people to linger and socialize afterward. If the person who is hosting the
meeting really wants the group to depart after the meeting has been officially
adjourned, he or she may rise and say, "Thank you all for coming—I think we got a
lot accomplished," or words to that effect. This is the signal for the group to thank
the host and depart promptly.

Ending a Meeting

Other than in the situation described above where there is both a host and a chair, the one who calls the meeting is responsible for its close. When he or she feels that everyone has spoken to the point and general agreement has been reached as to future actions to be taken, a summary is in order: "We have covered the following points . . . ," or "We have decided to pursue the matter through these steps. . . ." It is useful to state what has been agreed upon, and if further information is needed, to remind those who are responsible for securing it. The meeting ends by thanking those who attended for coming and providing help or information and by thanking any staff members who aided in organizing the meeting.

The notes or tapes compiled during the meeting are used to write a follow-up report, which the person who called the meeting distributes to all who attended. The report should contain a somewhat more detailed recap of the closing statements and serve the dual purpose of reminding and authenticating.

PRESENTATIONS AND SPEAKING IN PUBLIC

There is one guiding rule for public speakers—keep it brief and to the point. This is particularly true for those who introduce keynote or main speakers—the audience has come to hear him or her, not you. Having made the introduction, sit down until the speech is over. When completed, rise, shake hands with and thank the speaker for his or her time and excellent speech.

When You Are the Speaker

The greatest asset to a successful speech is having it well prepared and rehearsed in advance. It may be long or short, serious or humorous, but the confidence gained from the knowledge that your material is good and your presentation smooth is worth hours of preparation and practice.

Unless it is absolutely necessary, don't write your speech out in full and then read it. No matter how familiar you are with the material, reading it makes it sound sterile, and you will rapidly lose your audience's interest. It is possible to use a written speech and refer to it only as you would to notes, but the number of words on the page makes it difficult to keep your place. If you feel uncomfortable using only notes and must write it out in full, practice it often enough that you almost have it memorized and can look up frequently to keep your listeners' attention.

Despite what books on great speeches tell you, no jokes are better than bad jokes, and while your opening remarks should be dynamic in order to seize the attention of the audience, they should not be tasteless or ridiculous. Few people can tell a joke really well, and if you are one who can't, don't worry about it. Serious can be just as effective as hilarious, particularly when you are addressing an issue dear to the hearts of your audience.

Other guidelines for speaking at meetings or in public include:

- Keep your voice well-modulated and low-pitched.
- Practice the best distance for your mouth to be from the microphone so that you can be heard in the back but so that there are no squeals and screeches from being too close to it. Do not whistle into or tap on the microphone; simply ask in a normal speaking voice whether or not you can be heard in the back.
- Make sure the microphone is the right height so that you can stand naturally. Nothing looks more absurd than a six-footer hunched over a microphone, or a petite person on tiptoe with lips tilted up to reach.
- Stay to the point. Even if you are a great extemporaneous speaker, adding unrehearsed illustrations may tend to cause you to ramble or drift from the point.
- Practice what to do with your hands. At a podium, you may grasp the side edges and hold on, or use them to make a few gestures or to turn pages. Don't fiddle with things, do not jingle things in your pockets, and don't hold them trembling in front of you, papers rattling and shaking. If there is no support available, concentrate on keeping your hands still. Gestures can be important to add emphasis to your speech, but throwing your arms around or moving about is distracting and your listeners are diverted from what you are saying. Never grab the microphone. It will pick up the sound of your hands and does give the appearance that you are nervous and hanging on for dear life.
- If you feel the urge to sneeze or cough, do it. If a prolonged fit of coughing occurs, apologize. Pause, take a drink of water, and relax your throat. You should always have a handkerchief available to cough or sneeze into.
- When your time is up or you have said all that you have to say, a brief summary prepares the audience for the ending. Your listeners will go away thinking you are a wonderful speaker if you end your speech before they become restless and while they are still hoping that you have more to say.

When Called on Unexpectedly

Don't ever say, "I'm not used to speaking in public," or "You'll have to bear with me, I really hate this . . ." More people are nervous speaking in front of others than aren't, and you diminish what you have to say or impart if you are an immediate apologist. Just do your best: take a deep breath, speak loudly enough to be heard, but do not shout.

If someone asks you to "say a few words" after another has spoken, it is in very poor taste to contradict him or her by saying, "I'm afraid the chairwoman has greatly exaggerated my abilities." It is an impulse of modesty, but beside being discourteous to the chair, it all too seldom rings true.

Instead, smile and say, "What a wonderful introduction! Thank you, Henry," and then make at least a few remarks.

Answering Questions

Frequently a speech is followed by questions from the floor. You will be better able to orchestrate a question-and-answer period by adhering to a few simple rules. First, call on people in all sections of the room, and do not allow them to speak unless called on. Ask them to rise and, if appropriate, state their name and professional affiliation before asking their question. Repeat their question so the others in the room will hear it.

If someone begins to orate rather than ask a question, you may cut in and ask politely, "What is your question please?"

If someone asks a question that you are unable to answer, you need not be embarrassed to admit it. You might suggest, "Perhaps someone in the audience is more knowledgeable than I and would be good enough to answer your question."

If someone asks a hostile question, you may evade answering by pointing out that this is not the place for a confrontation. You may postpone answering by suggesting that the speaker see you privately afterward. Or you may handle it on the spot by saying, "I can see you are angry over this. Let me try to explain my viewpoint."

If someone asks a question that clearly shows a lack of factual information, you may say, "I don't think you have the facts here. Let me straighten them out before answering."

If someone follows up each question with another, to the exclusion of others, you may suggest that the speaker see you privately afterward, and say, "I appreciate your interest but it's only fair that others be allowed to ask their questions as well."

APPEARING ON TELEVISION AND RADIO

With the proliferation of cable and satellite broadcasting has come new and varied programming at the local, national and international level. At some time in your career you may be asked to represent your company on either television or radio. The most important thing to remember is that you are really a guest in the home of the listener or viewer. Your manners, therefore, should be the same as if you were in their houses in person. You should speak in a well-modulated voice, just as if you were in the same room with your audience. Remember, too, that a pocketful of jingling coins and a rattle of notes will sound far louder through the microphone than they would across a room, so check before the program begins to make certain you have eliminated all distracting and unnecessary noisemakers. If you are being interviewed one-on-one look at the interviewer most of the time and not directly into the camera. However, when you have a point you wish to get across to your audience you should look directly at the camera.

If the program is aired live, act natural and try not to show off. If other people
on the program become noisy or the discussion becomes heated, don't compete. By waiting until the moderator calms them down or changes the subject you retain your dignity.

If you are appearing on behalf of a charitable cause or on a discussion program, be sure that the interviewer knows exactly what your subject is and also let him know of any particular story or incident that you want him to ask you about. Otherwise you may have difficulty in bringing out the points you wish to stress. If you are a participant in a discussion group or on a panel show, listen to the views of the other members and don't concentrate on pushing only your own opinions. But prepare yourself thoroughly and be sure you have enough to say. Nothing is more disconcerting to a moderator or interviewer than to have a guest who can say no more than "Yes," "No," or "Maybe."

Don't talk down to or patronize your audience. You are a guest in the homes of people from every walk of life and you cannot possibly know more than each and every one of them. In other words don't *under*estimate the intelligence of your listeners. On the other hand, simply because they have chosen to listen to you, don't *over*estimate their knowledge of your subject.

11
Getting Ahead in Business

Things to Remember

There are people who make a strong first impression and are hired with hopes of steady advancement, yet never rise. Why? They may have obvious qualifications such as intelligence and creativity but may fail through inattention to smaller´details. An employee who gets ahead in business pays attention to:

Speech

Poor speech does not help an employee get ahead in business. There has been a great deal of controversy over whether or not English lessons should be included as part of the school curriculum, opponents fearing that they would deprive students of a cultural heritage. True or false though this may be, it is a fact that corporations will not place personnel with poor speech into positions where they come into contact with outsiders. My advice to those in the corporate marketplace is to work to improve your speech or your accent, taking lessons if need be, and retain your cultural heritage at home. Poor speech is a handicap in business.

Attitude

A positive attitude will get you much further than will complaints and rebelliousness. Though you may disapprove of your company's dress code or vacation policy, rallying co-workers to your cause will not lead to promotions. What you must do is make a decision: do you want to challenge the company's rights, or do you want to get ahead? Then act in accordance with your decision.

Deadlines

Get to work on time; be prompt for meetings; turn in reports when they are due; and do not watch the clock to see when it is time to go home. If it is impossible to meet a deadline, tell your boss when you accept the assignment and have good reasons to support your statement.

Accuracy

Corporate executives continually express their concern over the lack of accuracy among their staff—spelling and punctuation errors, misspelled names, incorrect addresses, faulty grammar, incoherent sentences and paragraphs. It appears that schools are not training students in these areas as they should, but passing the buck will not protect your job. If your skills are inadequate, take a refresher course. If you are merely careless, realize the importance to you of each of your errors and pay more attention.

Good Use of Time

No matter how diligent you are, you may run into others in your office who use you as an excuse to waste time—both theirs and yours. While they find a variety of ways to occupy you, you need not fall victim, but may get rid of them politely.

If you have a telephone chatterer, summarize the purpose of the call and sign off: "I understand, and I'll mail you the proper forms. Thank you for calling, but I must go now."

If you have completed an appointment with someone who will not leave, rise and say, "I'm terribly sorry, but I have some work that I must complete."

If someone asks, "Do you have a minute?" when you really don't or when you know the "minute" will last an hour, you have to be firm. "A minute is all I have right now," you might say. "If you need longer, we'll have to make it another time."

Thoughtfulness

Try to be aware of the people around you. An office, like a family, brings personalities into close and continual contact. You can improve the dynamics of your working group by paying attention to their needs and avoiding their irritations. A flower on someone's birthday, an offer of help, quiet when someone is concentrating—all these can go a long way toward creating a pleasant atmosphere around you and building a reputation for knowing how to work with people.

Thoughtfulness also enables you to avoid awkward situations that arise in an office. For instance, when you are in someone's office and the phone rings, although you do not know whether the call is personal or not, you could rise and ask softly, "Shall I wait outside?" If a person enters the office looking for someone who is not there, you could suggest, "Perhaps there is something I can do for you." In short, thoughtfulness is following rules that are not written and answering needs before they are asked.

Taking Initiative

Aggressiveness is deplored in an office by both boss and peers. Initiative, on the other hand, is welcomed. Where does the difference lie? Aggressiveness intrudes, pushing for self-aggrandizement; initiative motivates, developing leadership toward group achievement.

THINGS TO AVOID

Just as there are details that should be followed in order to get ahead in business, so are there details which if not avoided, can hold you back on the ladder climb.

Gossip

Do not talk about company personnel with co-workers either at work or outside. Word easily gets back.

Absence/Tardiness

Be at work whenever you possibly can. If you are allowed three personal holidays or ten sick days, do not take them because they are there; use them only if you need them. Avoid being a hypochondriac: a headache or sniffle should not keep you from work. Your absences become a part of your personnel file and a part of the reputation you build.

Arrive at work a few minutes *before* the time you are scheduled to begin working. Allow yourself a few minutes to get settled before you begin your workday.

Messiness

Keep yourself personally neat—hair combed, shirt tucked in, shoes polished, clothes pressed. Keep your desk and the papers you turn in neat as well. Messiness communicates lack of caring.

Discussing Personal Problems

Keep personal problems at home. Even when your co-workers are your friends, keep discussions of personal matters out of the office; you can share them outside without alerting the entire staff. Professionalism leads to promotion, and nothing is less professional than bringing your personal life to work.

Breaking Confidences

When you have access to information that is confidential, keep it confidential. You may be involved in unannounced plans, be privy to financial data, or handle personnel papers; do not divulge the information. If you are in doubt as to its confidentiality, ask. Remember too that your salary, along with everyone else's, is confidential; keep it that way.

Having Your Family Visit

While it may be exciting for your spouse and young children to see you at work, it will not further your career. If they have to see your office, bring them in on a weekend when no one is around.

Personal Calls

Limit private phone calls to only the most urgent. Constant phone chatting about trivia is always overheard. It bothers others who are trying to work and brands you as a "lightweight."

Wasting Time

Phone conversations are not the only way to waste time: wandering and reading magazines and talking to fellow workers are equally popular. Keep at your work, and if you have none, perhaps you can help someone else. Can you imagine the impression you make on your boss by wasting time which is really the company's?

Borrowing

As Shakespeare said, "Neither a borrower nor a lender be." Although you cannot very well say no to a fellow worker who asks for Scotch tape or a stamp, you can avoid being the co-worker who does the asking. Constant borrowing wastes the time of others and depletes their supplies. There is no reason for you to do it; plan ahead and have the materials you need. Borrowing money is even more hazardous since it can actually destroy a good working relationship. With the availability of 24-hour cash machines tap your own account before asking others for money. If you don't have a cash machine card credit cards should preclude the necessity of borrowing or lending money.

Obscene Language

Avoid it. No matter who else in the office uses it, obscenity will do nothing to advance your career.

Gum Chewing

Save this for your home. In an office gum chewing is disconcerting, sometimes noisy, and frequently abhorrent to an employer. I have never seen a rising manager chew gum, nor a successful salesperson either.

Smoking

Smoking should be avoided in the office. However, if you are an inveterate smoker and there is an area set aside for smoking you may go there to have your cigarette break.

Drinking

One drink at lunch, if your client is having one and you choose to join in is acceptable, but obviously more than one can lead to disaster. Drinking in the office is never acceptable.

RAISES AND PROMOTIONS

A raise is an increase in salary for the job you have. A promotion is step up to another job, often accompanied by an increase in pay, but not always.

Getting a Raise

Most companies have systems in place for awarding raises to employees on an annual basis. Where they are in place, cost of living increases are given most often in amounts concomitant with the cost of living index reported regionally and nationally. In essence, they keep a rate of pay at the same level so that an employee is not earning the equivalent of less money as the cost of living increases. Merit increases are given for a job well done. They are based on an employee's job performance. Most jobs have a minimum and maximum salary with a pay scale in between which serves as a guideline for raises. When a company is doing well financially, and an employee is doing an excellent job, merit increases are generally given annually. During difficult economic times, however, merit increases may be deferred or simply not given and cannot be demanded. The rate of pay one agrees to accept at the time of hiring is one's pay, and an increase is not to be expected, although it is usually assumed that it will be given.

People in union jobs, on the other hand, almost always have, as part of the union contract, automatic increases written in and these must be paid. These jobs generally have pay scales which define exactly how much an increase will be during each year of the contract. These increases include cost of living amounts as well as negotiated merit amounts. Union employees abide by the terms of the contract and individual members may not demand a greater increase than was negotiated.

Non-union employees, however, may sometimes have to ask for a raise in pay if it is not given automatically. If you feel you deserve a raise, you may ask your boss for one, but have convincing arguments on hand. Needing more money is not a convincing argument; everyone could use more money. Earning less than a co-worker in the same job is not convincing either, unless you have documented evidence that the other person has equal or lesser qualifications and experience than you and is doing the same kind of work. The only truly convincing argument is your worth to the company. If you have found ways to save the company money, have put systems in place that have generated greater efficiency, or have significantly in-creased your workload beyond your job description when you were hired, for example, you have increased your worth.

To discuss a raise with your employer, it is best to request an appointment at a time when you may speak privately. Don't accost him or her in the hall—make an appointment. You may say the appointment is to discuss your job, but you needn't tell the secretary it is to discuss a raise—that is between you and your boss.

When you meet, have on hand a brief outline of the rationale for your request. For example, if you were hired to handle consumer service for two products the company manufactures and are now handling four products, your workload has increased. If you originally had a staff of ten, but because of a merger of departments now have a staff of twenty and increased responsibility, your workload has in-creased. Delineate the specifics to make it easy for your boss to see the basis for your request.

Do not attack or demand. State your case in an open and relaxed way. Begin with the fact that you would like to be considered for a raise. Proceed with describing the rationale for your request. Mention that you really enjoy the job, that you have even more ideas for better ways to do it and that you hope your discussion has illustrated why you think you deserve consideration for an increase in pay. If your supervisor does not have the authority to grant a raise, but must consult with his or her boss, or with the personnel department, be sure to ask when you can expect to hear if the raise will be granted.

If your supervisor is not convinced or does not follow up with an increase, you either have to settle for your current salary or begin a search for a new job.

When you do receive a raise a thank you to the person responsible for giving it to you is in order, either verbally or by note.

Getting a Promotion

One of the greatest rewards in your career can be a promotion. It recognizes that you have done an outstanding job in the position you have held, and it is very nice to be recognized. While the preceding chapters have discussed ways to ensure that you are promotable, there are additional steps those who wish to move ahead should take:

- Learn other areas of the business, not limiting yourself to the department in which you work. There are many avenues of learning open: volunteering for extra assignments in related fields, observing company operation, asking questions, reading books, attending conferences, taking courses.
- Make suggestions for improvements in your area of operation, but only when they are well thought out and supported.
- Develop a career plan as you learn about the company, outlining the direction in which you hope to progress and the steps you must take to get there.
- Discuss the possibilities of promotion with your immediate supervisors alerting them both to your aims and to your professional development.
- Discuss promotion possibilities with someone in Personnel who is able to coordinate your professional growth with higher-level job openings elsewhere in the company.

If a salary raise does not automatically accompany your promotion, you may ask why not, and when you would be eligible for an increase if not. Although an increase in responsibility is an asset to your resume, fair compensation for an added workload is a reasonable expectation and you are not out of line in asking to discuss this factor.

Once promoted, it is important to work even harder than you have to prove your value in your new position. Part of the work you may have to do is to re-establish relationships with former peers. When you are promoted above those you have been equal to in status, there may be resentment and those who look for ways to criticize, primarily because they wanted the job, too. While most people will support you, there may be some who try to undermine what you are doing simply to promote their own candidacy or to prove that they, not you, should have been selected. Should this occur, inviting this person to meet with you to discuss the hostility or disappointment may be helpful. During the discussion, you may say that you understand how he or she feels, but that, since the decision was made, you hope you can work together amicably in the future and that you would like to help him or her to be considered for the next opportunity that arises. Do not explain your credentials or defend yourself as the choice of management. Do encourage him or her to continue to grow and learn and to maintain a positive attitude, since disgruntlement and unhappiness show and do not place one in the most favorable light for future promotions.

SEX IN THE WORKPLACE

Working closely with others is a natural way for all kinds of bonds to occur. Mutual respect, strong friendship, mutual attraction, and even feelings of love are often an outgrowth of spending many hours a day in the company of someone else. Very often, you spend more hours a day with a workmate than you do with your spouse, and those hours usually include personal as well as professional moments. The spark of humor between two compatible people, the shared goal of a completed project, the joint stress and anxiety of making something work—all these things can lay the groundwork for a deeper relationship if both parties aren't careful to define a relationship as primarily a professional one.

When a single man and woman work together and become attracted to one another, a love affair made in heaven may be budding. However, they should relate to each other as professionals from nine to five for the sake of everyone around them and for their own sake. What they do after hours is their own business and should not be discussed in the office, or be present in any form in the office.

Neither sex nor sexual attraction belong in the office. It interferes with routine; it embarrasses the staff; and it can ruin the personal lives of the people involved. Not only will sex not serve as a rung up the ladder of promotion in the long run, it puts one in the precarious position of possibly destroying a career.

If the single couple's romance is but a brief fling and they part unhappily, it is difficult for them to continue to work together professionally and usually one has to leave.

If one of the couple or both of them are married, even an after-hours romance is not advisable. Men and women have the intelligence to recognize a growing love affair; let them then have the self-discipline to prevent it. If they do not, chances are their employer will and will put them in a far worse light than if they had handled the situation themselves. Some employers may give a man or woman the opportunity of a transfer when they see an office romance of this kind developing; others may fire one of them. All generally agree, however, that the best solution is avoidance, nipping the affair in the bud.

Sexual Harassment

When an employer, be it man or woman, expresses a sexual interest in a lower-ranking member of the staff, no matter how appealing the prospect may appear, it must be discouraged. A straightforward explanation should put a stop to it gracefully: "This makes me feel uncomfortable. Can't we please keep our friendship on a business basis?" This will probably prevent hostility from the boss, embarrassment of the employee, and gossip among the office staff if the matter ends there.

If advances continue despite clear evidence of their unacceptability, you are into something more serious: sexual harassment. Sexual harassment is defined as unwelcome sexual advances, requests for sexual favors, and other verbal or physical conduct of a sexual nature. In some cases of sexual harassment, promotion or retaining a position is dependent upon returning sexual favors: an employee's job or career is at stake. In other cases the advances merely interfere with an employee's personal comfort or work or create an unpleasant environment in the office. In either case, sexual harassment is illegal and not to be tolerated.

If you find yourself a victim of sexual harassment, whether you are a man or a woman, there are steps you can take to eliminate it:

- Make it clear to the person that you do not want sexual advances. Explain that you take your job seriously and expect everyone in the office to treat you as a professional.
- If harassment continues, speak about it to your superior. If your boss is the guilty one, speak to your boss's superior. Have specific times and dates at hand and examples of exactly what was said and done. Write it in a memo, reserving a copy for yourself.
- If this does not solve your problem, speak to the personnel director with a copy of the memo you wrote to your superior and any new documentation of harassment. The personnel department should intercede for you. They are in a position to warn or even fire the offender or to file a complaint with the Equal Employment Opportunities Commission in your area.
- If the personnel department does not put an end to the sexual harassment and does not file a complaint, you have the legal right to file a complaint with the EEOC yourself.

Since employers are now held responsible for sexual harassment in their company, it is probable that the executives to whom you turn will come to your aid at the start, making official complaints unnecessary.

*F*rom the early 1900's through World War II, a gold watch given after 25 years of service to one company was more the rule than the exception. Today, it is more the exception than the rule. Job mobility is frequently internal—promotions and lateral moves from one department to another—but equally as frequently, it is from one company to another. Whether you resign or are fired, how you conduct yourself involves both good manners and good strategy.

12

Leaving Your Job

RESIGNING

A variety of reasons may lead to the decision to leave a job. Some of them stem from the job, which may be too stressful, boring, not adequately remunerative, or lacking opportunity for advancement. Other reasons may be personal—deciding to return to school, a new baby and a desire to stay home, a move away, or the offer of a better position with another firm. How you resign may affect your business career for your entire future. There is a ritual of Do's and Don'ts.

How to Resign

- Notify your employer of your resignation as soon as you have decided on the date you will leave. You may inform your employer in person or write a letter, explaining your reason for leaving, suggesting a terminal date, and expressing appreciation to your boss and to the company for the help and opportunities you have received. After reading the letter, your boss will speak to you, at which time you may repeat orally what you have written. If you have not written a letter of resignation, some companies may request that you do so after you inform them of your intention to leave.
- Check if your company has regulations specifying how much notice is required. In any case do not give any less than two weeks' notice. If you have a highly responsible job, it is better to give the company a month in which to find a replacement.
- Some companies may ask you to help interview for your replacement. Do so with a positive attitude, no matter what your reason for leaving.

- If you are job hunting while still employed, keep it quiet. Only in rare cases should you tell your boss: when you and your boss both agree that the company holds no future for you, or when you are moving to another city and seeking a job there. Otherwise, arrange for interviews during lunch, or before or after work so they will not interfere with your job, thus necessitating your informing your employer.
- Before leaving, bid good-bye to all those with whom you have worked and indicate a wish to keep in touch with them.
- You may be called in for an interview with a company executive, or you may want to write a letter of appreciation before you leave. In either case, keep your statements short and positive.

How Not to Resign

- Don't tell your employer you are leaving for another job until the job is absolutely certain.
- Don't use an offer of another job as a means of manipulating your employer into giving you a raise.
- Don't speak against the company you are leaving, either within it or outside. You never know when you'll need to be in touch with your former employer so don't burn your bridges behind you.
- Don't complain about your former boss to your new employer.
- Don't brag about your new job to your co-workers.
- Don't let down on the job because you are leaving; continue to be cooperative and hard working.
- Don't tell company secrets after you leave.

Adhering to these Do's and Don'ts assures you of a pleasant departure, a positive recommendation, and consideration for rehiring at a higher level in the future should the opportunity appear.

BEING FIRED OR LAID OFF

Unfortunately, not every parting of the ways between employer and employee is a resignation; some people are fired. Worse still is when someone is laid off through no fault of their own. Economic conditions, a merger of two companies, or a relocation of the employer to another part of the country can result in a loss of jobs. Anger, resentment, and threats do not reverse the fact that you have lost your job; they do assure a negative recommendation for future jobs and create a tense environment for all staff members.

There are some positive steps you can take when you lose a job:

- Remain as objective as possible. Your anger will only ignite your boss.

- Ask for an explanation. If you are fired, a review of your shortcomings may enable you to improve yourself for future opportunities. If you are laid off because a merger has resulted in more employees than positions, ask how the decisions were made for who kept their job and who did not. What you learn will help you explain to new employers why you are looking for a job.
- Ask whether you have any recourse: is there a way for you to appeal your employer's decision? If there is, prepare a sound argument with specific details of support for your hearing.
- When firing is inevitable, ask about the terms of severance—date of leaving, pay, benefits, etc. When laying off employees, some companies aid in securing them new jobs; check to see whether yours does.
- Ask what kind of references you may expect.
- Work out with your employer a way of announcing your departure that will let you leave with dignity. Submitting a resignation is the common way, when you are fired.
- If you feel that your firing is due to discrimination, discuss the possibility with your employer. Do not make accusations without detailed evidence to support your claim.
- Refrain from speaking against your boss or the company to anyone. Vituperative remarks have a way of backfiring.
- Keep a positive attitude. If you look at the experience as a way to learn and grow professionally, chances are you will find other business opportunities. If you react with immaturity and petulance, you will not only create a negative image, but will go into a new job making the same old errors.

LETTING AN EMPLOYEE GO

An employer who must dismiss a staff member is often even more distressed than the unfortunate employee. Firing is a difficult assignment that has made many a top executive pace the office floor for an hour before facing the moment of truth. Will the employer be accused of unfairness? Will the rest of the staff support the decision? Will the employer be drawn into a legal squabble? Laying off staff members is no easier.

Just as being fired can be handled constructively, so can the task of firing:

- Be specific. If your company has decided to close down a division and lay off all of the staff, say so. If a merger creates an excess number of employees, cite the criteria used in determining who gets laid off and who doesn't: seniority, special skills, willingness to relocate, etc. It is slightly more palatable to learn you are losing your job through no fault of your own, or because of conditions over which you have no control. Firing someone is different. There are many other reasons for having to fire an employee: inefficiency, dishonesty, trouble making, poor personal relations, refusal to take orders, lack of initiative, weak problem-solving skills, laziness, lack of dedication, inability to follow through; the list could continue for pages. Although any number of these reasons may underlie the firing, do not use them: they are too general. Instead, cite particular examples of these failings: "You turn in false expense accounts," or "You continue to take two-hour lunches," or "You refuse to accompany sales representatives on calls." Nonspecific reasons are disputable.

- Build a case over a period of time so that when you actually fire an employee, the reasons are documented and it is clear that warnings were received. A solid case for firing is built by reviewing the job with the employee over a period of time and sending written warnings and suggestions for improvement. Copies of everything should be kept in the employee's file and used during the final confrontation.
- When you decide there is no hope of rehabilitating the employee, it is time for firing. Do not let the employee stay on, but offer severance pay and ask him or her to leave immediately.
- Many executives suggest that you do not fire an employee in your office, but do it on neutral ground or in their office so that you may easily leave afterward to avoid prolonged wrangling.
- Keep calm even in the face of accusations. Do not attempt to answer them; merely say, "I am sorry you feel that way."
- Be specific about the conditions of severance.
- Do not apologize.
- Do not speak against the employee to others after firing him or her.
- Give the employee an opportunity to save face—i.e., to resign.

REQUESTING REFERENCES

If you resigned from your job or were laid off because of company cutbacks, you will probably feel comfortable asking your former employer if she or he would be willing to serve as a reference for you in your future job hunt. It is preferable that a former employer be contacted by a potential employer rather than asking your previous boss to write a general "To Whom It May Concern" letter. These letters tend not to be taken too seriously, and most potential employers prefer direct contact so they may ask questions specifically pertaining to your abilities as they would be used in a new job.

To respond to an outside reference, it is helpful to leave your former employer with an outline of your job description and duties so he has a reminder of your responsibilities and accomplishments if contacted.

Once you have secured a new position, even though you may have written a note to your former employer at the time of your departure, another thank you for his or her help is in order. Include a brief mention of what your new job is and note again how much you enjoyed working for him or her, or if you didn't, at least thanks for the opportunities he or she gave you.

GIVING A REFERENCE

When you agree to serve as a reference for a present or former employee, you should be familiar with his or her strengths and contributions to you, your department, or your company. In this way, you can find many positive things to say, even if he or she did not work out in your job, for whatever reason.

Most requests for a reference are made by telephone. While they may come at an difficult time for you, they are of great importance to your former employee. Accordingly, be sure you are not in the middle of a meeting or dashing to an appointment when you take the call. Devote a few minutes of undivided attention to the caller. Don't volunteer negative information; you should not agree to give a reference if you don't have positive things to say. Nor should you lie, however, so if asked a question that has nothing but a negative answer, you may simply say, "I prefer not to answer that question," or "I am not prepared to answer that question."

When a former employee has not requested permission to use you as a reference and a company has found your name and contacted you on their own, there is no problem if your responses are favorable. If they are unfavorable, however, you have to be as constructively honest as possible, separating your own personal feelings from the former employee's actual job performance. For example, if you fired John Jones because of persistent tardiness which infuriated you, a consistently prompt person, but he was otherwise a hard worker, you should say so, noting that punctuality is extremely important to you. This gives the caller the tools to evaluate what you are saying and why.

Letters of Reference

When you agree to write a letter of reference, as when you agree to give an oral reference, you accept the fact that the recipient is relying on you as a responsible business person to provide an honest evaluation.

Letters of reference fulfill a specific function: to provide an honest evaluation of an individual whom you have come to know through your business or personal life. In general a letter of reference should give the circumstances through which you know the person you are writing about and provide an evaluation of the qualities and abilities this person possesses. Relay any facts you think necessary to substantiate your evaluation.

If you prefer not to write a letter of reference, for whatever reason, simply decline the request to do so. You may offer instead that your telephone number be given to those requesting a letter of reference. This gives you the opportunity to personally discuss the qualities of the person you have agreed to recommend as well as answer any questions others may have.

When the Reference Is Not Favorable

Requests for job recommendations follow an employer for years, often far into retirement. It is easy and pleasurable to write a positive letter—to point out all those professional qualities that make people valuable to a company and those personal qualities that endear them to fellow workers. Writing a recommendation for a former employee whom you fired poses problems, however.

First, be open-minded and realize the good qualities the employee has. Emphasize these in your letter. Explain that although he was unable to perform as expected in your company's position, he might do well somewhere else.

Next, be tactful. Employees have the right to the letters of reference in their files, and what you write could trigger a lawsuit. Avoid making sweeping statements of condemnation or drawing unwarranted conclusions. The safest way to write a negative reference is to say as little as possible but make it clear to the prospective employer that you will be glad to answer any questions about the person on the phone.

IV

COMMUNICATIONS

*I*deal conversation is an exchange of thought and not necessarily an eloquent exhibition of wit or oratory. Fortunately for most of us, it is not essential to have a special gift of cleverness to be someone with whom others are delighted to talk. An ability to express our thoughts and feelings clearly and simply is sufficient for ordinary conversation among friends.

Conversation should be a matter of equal give-and-take, but unhappily it is frequently all "take." The voluble talker monopolizes the conversation without giving anyone else a chance to do anything other than wait for the turn that never comes. Only on rare occasions does one meet a brilliant person whose continuous talk is a delight.

There is a simple rule by which one who is inclined to "run on" can at least refrain from being a pest or a bore: Stop and think.

13
The Good Conversationalist

DON'T PANIC

If you dread meeting strangers because you are afraid you won't be able to think of anything to say, remember that most conversational errors are committed not by those who talk too little but by those who talk too much.

Many people for some reason are terrified of silence, and they generally have great difficulty in carrying on a conversation. This terror is something like the terror felt by those who are learning to swim. It is not just the first stroke that overwhelms them, but the thought of all the strokes that must follow. The frightened talker doesn't hear a word that is said by others because he or she is trying so desperately to think of what to say next. So the practical rule for continuing a conversation is the same as that for swimming: Don't panic. Just take it one stroke (or word) at a time.

The old sign at railroad crossings—STOP, LOOK, LISTEN—is excellent advice in many circumstances other than when you are waiting to cross the tracks. In conversation *stop* means not to rush ahead without thinking; *look* means to pay attention to the expression of the person with whom you are talking; and *listen*—meaning exactly that—is the best advice possible, because everyone loves to talk to a sympathetic listener. Remember, though, that a sympathetic listener *really* listens. A fixed expression of sympathy while your mind wanders far away won't fool anyone but the most self-centered conversationalist.

THINK BEFORE YOU SPEAK

Nearly all the faults or mistakes commonly made in conversation are caused by not thinking or by lack of consideration. For example, would a computer programmer talk about the latest software to a professor of literature sitting next to her at dinner if she *thought*? No, she would realize that as enjoyable as her work is, not everyone wishes to hear such a lengthy discourse on the subject. The same can be said for new parents who talk of their child as if no one else had ever borne children. I remember the advice I once received from an older and wiser friend: "My dear, there is no point in discussing your children with new acquaintances—they either have some of their own, or they don't."

Many of us do not have anyone to remind us about our thoughtless and inconsiderate talk. Only by careful listening to our own words and strict attention to the reactions of our listeners can we discover our personal inadequacies. The burden of thinking before speaking is our own. Dorothy Sarnoff wrote: " 'I' is the smallest letter in the alphabet. Don't make it the largest word in your vocabulary. Say, with Socrates, not 'I think,' but 'What do you think?' "

CONVERSATIONAL CONTENT

There are those who can tell a group of people that their train broke down, or that they had a flat tire, and make everyone burst into laughter. But the storyteller who constantly *tries* to be funny is generally a bore, and the majority of us, if we wish to be considered attractive, are safer if we rely on sincerity, clarity, and an intelligent choice of subject.

If your friend Alan is both interesting and amusing, you will, if you are wise, do everything you can to lure him to your house frequently, for he can "make" your party. His subject is unimportant; it is the twist he gives to it, the personality he puts into it, that delights his hearers.

In talking to a person you have just met and about whom you are in complete ignorance, the best approach is to try one topic after another just as a fisherman searches for the right fly. You "try for nibbles" by asking a few questions. When one subject runs down, you try another. Or perhaps you take your turn and describe something you have been doing or thinking about—planting a garden, planning a trip, or an interesting article you have read. Don't snatch at a period of silence. Let it go for a little while. Conversation is not a race that must be continued at breakneck pace to the finish line.

When you find yourself seated next to a stranger at a party, introduce yourself before starting your "fishing." Then there are all manner of openings, and if you are shy, have some of them fixed in your mind before you go to the party: If your hostess has told you something about your dinner partner, you might say, "I understand you crewed for Robert in the race last week. That must have been exciting." If you know nothing about him at all, you could ask, "Do you live in Homeville, or are you visiting?" From his answer, hopefully, you can carry on a conversation. He will probably ask where you live and what you do. It's simple enough, but be sure to give him the opportunity to talk.

Another helpful gambit—and one that wins instant popularity—is to ask advice. "We are planning to drive through the South. Do you know any particularly good places to stop on the way?" or "I'm thinking of buying a fax machine. Do you have any suggestions?" In fact it is safe to ask his or her opinion on almost anything: politics, sports, the stock market, a current fad—anything.

The food or the wine provides another good opener at the dinner table: "Isn't this delicious—what do you think Sue put into this sauce to make it so unusual?"

And don't avoid a controversial subject. In an election year "Who are you going to vote for?" or "What do you think of the vice-presidential candidates?" will start the ball rolling with no effort at all.

Compliments

We all love to receive compliments and tend to love those who offer them. Therefore I often wonder why so few people give them. I suspect it is sometimes because most people have an inborn aversion toward being too personal, and some are shy or embarrassed. Still others are simply thoughtless and don't stop to think how a complimentary word can brighten someone's day. But if you are one who finds it hard to give a firsthand compliment, you need not hesitate to give a "compliment once removed." "I saw Margie May yesterday and she told me how successful the fund raiser you organized turned out." This gets you double credit—once with the person you're talking to, and again when it gets back to Margie.

So let me urge you to speak up. The next time you have a nice thought about someone, tell him or her. If we all did it more frequently the world would be a happier place.

Be sure, however, a compliment is sincere. Archbishop Fulton Sheen once remarked that "a compliment is baloney sliced so thin that it is delectable. Flattery is baloney sliced so thick that it is indigestible."

If you are the one being complimented you will want to show your appreciation and pleasure. Don't simper and don't belittle whatever the compliment referred to. For instance if someone says, "What a lovely dress," don't say, "Oh, well, it was very inexpensive, and I don't think it fits very well." The appropriate way to respond to any compliment is to say "Thank you," or "I'm so glad you like it," or "Aren't you nice to say so."

Personal Remarks

Compliments and other favorable personal remarks are not only permissible but desirable. But unpleasant remarks, or remarks that make another person uncomfortable, are definitely in bad taste. The old adage "If you can't say something nice, don't say anything at all" is very good advice.

There are occasions, however, when one wonders whether or not to make what might be construed as a critical remark. This might occur, for example, when you don't know whether you should tell your friend that she has a run in her panty hose. The answer depends on whether she can correct the situation or not. If there is a place where she can buy a new pair of panty hose, by all means tell her. If not, calling attention to her problem will only make her self-conscious and aware of a fault of which she might otherwise have been unaware, or at least have thought was unnoticed.

Women frequently ask whether they should call an unzipped fly to the wearer's attention. Unless you are total strangers, do. The slight embarrassment to you and the man at the time is nothing compared to the mortification he will feel when he discovers the condition and wonders how long it existed. If, however, you have just been introduced, leave it to someone who knows him better.

UNKIND REMARKS

Conversation should never be *about* someone else, especially in a group, even a group of close friends. "Whew," remarked a friend of mine once after a cocktail party where a woman we both knew dissected the life of another friend, "if she talked like that about Jane, I wonder what she says about me!"

One of the kindest people I know, when faced with this situation, immediately halts the speaker by saying, "Goodness, Barbara, Adrian always says such nice things about you!" and then immediately changes the topic. When confronted with a question about someone she doesn't particularly care for, she finds something positive to say, even if it is about the condition of his front lawn or the high polish on his car. She knows that public gossip about others is a forbidden topic and consequently is known as someone who *never* says a mean thing about another.

No matter how strongly tempted you are to pass along a nasty comment or to join in a group talking unkindly about another, don't do it. It doesn't just defame the character of the other, it makes you look bad.

Using Tact

Tactful people keep their prejudices to themselves. A tactful person involved in a discussion says, "It *seems* to me," not "That's not so!" which is tantamount to calling the other a liar.

If you find another's opinion totally unacceptable, try to change the subject as soon as possible. If you care too intensely about a subject, it is dangerous to allow yourself to say anything. That is, if you can only expound your own fixed point of view, then you should never mention the subject except as a platform speaker. But if, on the other hand, you are able to listen with an open mind, you may safely speak on any topic. After all, any mutually interesting topic may lead to one about which you don't agree. Then take care! Much better to withdraw unless you can argue without bitterness or bigotry. Argument between coolheaded, skillful opponents may be an amusing game, but it can be very, very dangerous for those who become hotheaded and ill-tempered.

Tactless Blunders

It's like rubbing salt into an open wound to make such remarks as "What happened to Bobby's complexion since he went away to school?" or "Are you and Joan really getting a divorce?" or even "What's the matter with your baby?" when the child is handicapped. These questions may sound unbelievable but they, and worse, are constantly being asked by people who should know better.

If you have any sense, you won't talk to your grandmother about how you dread getting old, to a handicapped person about what fun skating is, or to a city dweller about your thriving garden.

It is not only unkind to ridicule or criticize others, but the tables can well be turned on those who do. A young girl asked a boy she hoped to date, "How can you possibly go out with *that* drip?" "Because," he replied, "she's my sister!"

UNPLEASANT TYPES

They are all around us, and often a most fervent hope is that we aren't one of them. It is a good idea to listen to yourself talk, once in awhile, to hear, for example, whether you indeed are a conversational bully, monopolizing, insisting you are right, and never giving another a chance to agree or disagree. Or to notice if others seem to nod off when listening to you, or appear to look desperately around the room for the closest escape route away from you. It is possible to correct these flaws, even though they may seem like part of our personalities and therefore firmly entrenched. If you find yourself monopolizing the conversation, simply zip your lip and listen next time, no matter how much you have to say. If you fear you are boring, make every effort to read current magazines, or to find a topic of general interest to study—such things as environmental issues, for example, should be of concern to everyone and your increased knowledge will enable you to not only participate generally in conversation, but to impart interesting information, as well.

There is not much you can do about unpleasant conversational traits in others, except to keep your talks with them to a minimum!

The Bore

One definition of a bore is "one who talks about himself when you want to talk about yourself." This is superficially true, but a bore might more accurately be described as one who insists on telling you at length something that you don't want to hear about at all. He or she insists that you listen to the bitter end in spite of your obvious boredom.

The Wailer

One of the fundamental and commonsense rules of all conversation is that you talk about things that will be interesting and agreeable to the listener. It seems unbelievable, therefore, that so many people can talk about nothing but misfortunes, sickness, and other unpleasantness. Don't dwell on your own problems. Your audience has them, too, and won't be entertained by yours. Only your nearest and dearest care how many times you have been in the operating room.

The Sentence-Finisher

Some people are quicker to find a word or phrase than others. They have an irresistible urge to supply that word or to finish a sentence for one who is slow in finding the exact expression to complete a thought. If you are inclined to do this use all your strength to resist the temptation. It makes the other speaker feel inadequate, and you might appear to be trying to steal the limelight.

The Contradicter

There was a popular song some years ago that went, "It ain't what you say but the way that you say it," and that is true of contradictions, too. Everyone has a right to express his or her viewpoint. If you wish to express an opposing view, or contradict, say, "I *think* it is this way or that way," not "You're wrong and I'm right." Give your reasons for your point of view and then listen carefully to the other person's side.

The Wandering Eye

Nothing is more disconcerting than talking with someone who does not look directly at you. Some people do this while they are talking; others only while listening. Both are lacking in that primary obligation of a good conversationalist— being a good listener. When you are talking to *anyone*, look at him or her, not with a fixed stare but constantly enough so that it is obvious your fellow conversationalist has your undivided attention.

The Story-Snatcher

We all know people who can't let anyone else tell a story to the end. They must jump in and correct the details and then finish the story. This is particularly common between husband and wife, and also between parent and child. It is a habit that is particularly annoying if it happens frequently, and it has been the cause of many a marital battle. Avoid it yourself, and if you are the victim of a story-snatcher don't suffer in silence. Many people don't even realize they are doing it and even less do they realize how annoying it is to everyone who is listening. If, after a gentle hint from you, the offender continues to steal your stories, break in, each time with, "All right, *you* tell it." This will stop all but the thickest-skinned story-snatcher.

The Secret-Teller

Another social pariah is the one who, when part of a group, is constantly whispering or talking in low asides to one person alone. The others cannot fail to feel that either the whisperer is talking about them or that they are missing some especially juicy tidbit. This also applies to speaking a foreign language that most of the group does not know. It is exactly like telling a secret and is equally rude.

The Non-Stop Talker

There are seldom regrets for what you have left unsaid. "Better to keep your mouth closed and be thought a fool than open it and remove all doubt." Don't pretend to know more than you do. No person of real intelligence hesitates to say, "I don't know."

People who talk too easily are likely to talk too much and at times imprudently. Those who have vivid imaginations are often unreliable in their statements. On the other hand, the "man of silence" who rarely speaks tends to wear well among his intimates, but he is not likely to add much to the gaiety of a party. In conversation, as in most things, the middle road is best. Know when to listen to others, but know also when it is your turn to carry the conversation.

Try not to repeat yourself, either by telling the same story again and again or by going back over details of your narrative that seemed to interest or amuse your hearer. Many things are interesting when told briefly and for the first time; few bear repeating.

DEALING WITH AWKWARD SITUATIONS

Snoops

How do you answer personal questions about the cost of a gift, a furnishing, or a piece of clothing?

You are under no obligation to give out this sort of information if you do not wish to. You can simply resort to "I don't know [or remember] what it costs." Or if you wish to play up the value of the article, say, "More than I probably should have paid," and if you wish to play it down, "Not as much as you'd think."

Inquiries about money matters are usually in poor taste and should be given short shrift. You cannot quite say, "None of your business," but you can say, "I'd rather not talk about that, if you don't mind. With the cost of living what it is, the whole subject is too depressing . . ." and change the subject.

"How Old Are You?"

Many people over thirty do not like to be asked their age, and it is a very thoughtless question. However, it *is* frequently asked, and there are a number of ways of parrying the question. You might say, "Old enough to know better," you can be as indefinite as "Over twenty-one," or you can use my particular favorite, "Thirty-nine [or forty-nine, or whatever] and holding."

Ethnic and Other Insults

What can you say when someone makes derogatory remarks about a group, a person, or a nationality, in your presence?

There is no excuse for remarks of that nature, and you should make that clear. Tell the speaker quite frankly that you find their remarks objectionable and do not wish to listen to them, and then walk away. If you do not feel *that* strongly, just say, "Let's get off that subject," and introduce another.

Corrections

When a person pronounces a word incorrectly, or makes a grammatical error, should you correct the error or should you repeat the error to avoid making the speaker uncomfortable?

Two wrongs don't make a right. Don't correct him or her, but when the opportunity arises, use the same word or phrase correctly and hope that the mistake will be recognized.

14

Correspondence

*W*hile it is true that I would be glad to receive a note scribbled on the back of a grocery list from old friends who have been incommunicado for years, and while some of my most cherished letters are pages of news, confidences, and insights dashed off on paper torn from a spiral notebook, it is also true that I would not particularly admire a dinner invitation or a letter of condolence written so haphazardly. When we are unable to talk to someone face to face, our correspondence speaks for us. The impression it makes perhaps doesn't matter to dear friends, but it is very important to potential employers, places with which we do business, and acquaintances whom we hope will become friends.

This chapter is designed to help you make the best on-paper impression possible. In this day of instant electronic mail, computerized desk-to-desk memos, and the convenience of the telephone, a well-written letter, personalized stationery, and traditionally and beautifully crafted invitations are truly a pleasure to the recipient. A sincere letter of condolence to a bereaved friend, a formal reply to a formal wedding invitation, a thank-you note instead of a commercial thank-you card—these are all ways of communicating that are especially meaningful.

Electronic mail and the FAX are forms of correspondence, too, and, represent us as a substitute for an in-person conversation. By following accepted forms of communication, you have a much better chance of getting the response and/or the results you desire. Your correspondence, whether on personalized note paper or via E-mail, will reveal you as a man or a woman who takes the time to communicate the right way and who expects to be taken seriously.

APPEARANCE AND STYLE OF PERSONAL LETTERS

There are three types of letters that should always be handwritten unless you are actually disabled and must use a typewriter or word processor. They are:

Notes of condolence
Formal invitations and replies
Thank-you notes

In the case of the last mentioned, if your thanks are simply part of a longer personal letter, the rule can be waived, and you could, if you customarily do so, type the letter.

Personal Stationery

Suitability should be a factor in choosing your stationery, just as it is in choosing your wardrobe. The texture of the paper—whether it is rough or smooth—is a matter of personal choice. However, everyone should have one box of good-quality paper in a conservative color and shape to be used for condolence notes, answers to invitations, etc. This "good" paper need not be personalized if that seems extravagant, but all leading writing-paper companies sell high-quality solid-color or bordered paper in excellent taste.

If the paper is thin (airmail paper, for instance), envelopes with colored linings should be used so the writing cannot be read through the envelope, or you may fold a blank sheet outside the pages. The monogram or address may be stamped on the paper in a color to match the lining.

A Man's Personal Paper

The most practical man's paper is a single sheet 7 or 7¼ inches by 10 or 10½ inches marked in plain block or Roman letters at the top center. His name (without title), his address, including zip code, all appear. His telephone number is optional. This paper can be used for typewriting or handwriting and for all types of correspondence. It is folded in thirds to fit into a 7¼- or 7½-by-4-inch envelope. For purely social correspondence he may also have a family crest—if he has one—engraved in the top center or the upper-left-hand corner. If it is engraved in the corner his address and telephone number may appear at the right.

A Woman's Personal Paper

White, cream, light blue, gray, or light green are the proper colors for the "conservative" paper for *formal* correspondence, and also for business letters. For personal letters there are no longer many restrictions, and a woman may choose any pattern or combination of colors that pleases her. It may be marked with a monogram, initials, or her name and address—in the center or upper-left corner—in a contrasting shade, or a color to match a border. Ink should match the printing or engraving, or should be chosen to complement the color of the paper.

The paper is smaller than a man's, approximately 5½ by 6½ inches, and it may be single or double. Those who type most of their letters should buy single sheets, which may be used for both typewritten and handwritten letters.

A married woman's formal social paper is engraved "Mrs. William Frost," rather than "Mrs. Mary Frost." However, for informal personal letters she may also have paper marked "Mary Frost" if she wishes. A professional woman may use her professional name without title—"Jane Author" rather than "Mrs. Robert Author"—for business correspondence.

The name engraved on an unmarried woman's paper is written without title,
"Barbara Rodgers." The envelope includes "Miss" or, if she prefers the title, "Ms." A
divorcee's name is preceded by whatever title she is using on the envelope.

Paper for Everyone in the Family

Stationery suitable for use by all the members of a family has the address engraved or printed in plain letters at the top. Frequently the telephone number is put in small letters under the address or in the upper-left-hand corner with the address in the center. This paper is especially practical if you have a country or vacation home, as it can also be used by your guests.

For short notes, for acceptances or regrets, and for invitations, a supply of fold-over notepaper is invaluable. It may be of any color or design you wish or may be engraved or printed with initials or with your name and address and telephone number. If not marked with initials or a name, it is useful for every female member of the family. The notepaper must measure at least 3½ by 5 inches or it will not be accepted by the post office.

For the Young Correspondent

Paper for very young children is widely available. It is ruled, usually has an illustration of animals, toys, or something from a familiar story or nursery rhyme, and may come in a variety of shapes. It is designed to amuse the young child and make him or her consider letter-writing a pleasure rather than a chore.

Using a first name—either Elizabeth in full or Betty—is popular for a young girl's personal correspondence, but it should not be used by an older woman. If the younger girl prefers, she may wish to use her surname also. Available, too, are attractive papers with designs in the upper-left-hand corners or along the left or in borders; usually flowers, birds, or perhaps a kitten or puppy. A name or monogram is not used, and the style of the picture varies with the age of the girl.

Return Addresses

Although the U.S. Postal Service prefers that the return address appear in the upper-left-hand corner of the envelope, that is not particularly attractive on personal stationery and is impossible if the lettering is engraved. Therefore addresses are almost invariably stamped on the back flap. If, however, your paper is not personalized you will find printed address labels very useful. These can be stuck in the preferred place on the front of unmarked envelopes and may even be used when the address is on the back, for business letters or others where it is important that the address be noticed.

Printing or Engraving?

Years ago writing paper was engraved or it was not marked at all. Today the cost of engraving and the amount of correspondence carried on by busy people has changed that entirely: If one can afford it a supply of paper with an engraved initial, monogram, or crest, to be used for special or formal correspondence, is practical and beautiful. For ordinary purposes, however, and for those who find the cost of engraving prohibitive, printed stationery serves very well.

All the fine stationery companies also use a process called thermography, even, in some cases, to the exclusion of real engraving. The type is raised, and to the unpracticed eye is undistinguishable from engraving. It is far less expensive than engraving, although more than plain printing, and is an excellent choice for those who wish their paper to be handsome and of good quality.

Crests

Heraldry, with its medieval origins, is not an American institution, so the use of a coat of arms is a foreign custom. But when a family has used its family arms (or crest) continuously since the days when they brought the device from Europe—and their right to it is certified by the colleges of heraldry—its use is proper, if somewhat conspicuous.

It must be remembered, however, that the crest is the exclusive property of male members of a family, although it may be used jointly by husband and wife on some occasions. Its appearance on the paper of a widow or an unmarried woman is as absurd as it would be to put "Esq." at the end of her name. Surprisingly few Americans, however, seem to be aware of this heraldic rule. A widow has no right to use her husband's crest on her letter paper. She may properly use the device on the shield of his coat of arms, transferred to a diamond-shaped device called a lozenge. She may also, if she chooses, divide the lozenge perpendicularly into two parts and crowd the device from her husband's shield into the left half and the device from her father's shield into the right half. An unmarried woman uses her paternal arms on a lozenge without crest or motto.

Seals

We are all familiar with a variety of seals—Christmas seals, Easter seals, Boys' Town seals, etc.—all of which help to raise money for the organizations that distribute them. They provide a painless way of supporting a worthy cause and at the same time make our correspondence gayer and more attractive.

Seals should not be used on notes of condolence, or on formal invitations and replies. Otherwise, they may be used on all personal letters and on business letters, too. Their appearance on your correspondence calls attention to the organization that sponsors the seal and gives proof of your support—thus encouraging others to contribute, too.

Informals

The small fold-over cards known as informals are convenient when you want, for example, to write a very brief note, but one that requires more space than is afforded by a visiting card.

Plain white informals of good quality are available at all stationers and are perfectly acceptable. If you wish, however, you may have them engraved, thermographed, or printed. Or you may simply have your monogram in the upper left corner. If you use them, visiting cards would be engraved in the same way.

Informals cannot be substituted for visiting cards when you make a formal call. They may be enclosed with a gift *only* if you wish to write a personal message on the inner page.

Mailing envelopes must be large enough to meet the postal service minimum requirement of 3½ inches by 5 inches. Because of this, fold-over notepaper has largely replaced informals.

Mr. and Mrs. William Goadby Post

Mr. William Goadby Post

M B T

Miss Brittany Amendolia

The Form of a Personal Letter

When stationery has a fold, it is customary to use the first and third pages for a shorter letter, leaving the fourth, or outside, page blank to prevent the writing from showing through the envelope. For longer letters one may write first, second, third, fourth, in regular order; or first and fourth, then opening the sheet and turning it sideways, write across the two inside pages as one. The sequence is not important, and there is no fixed rule.

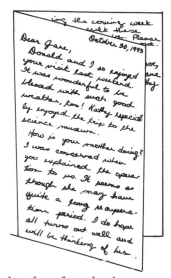

One may write on both sides of single-sheet stationery, but not if it is airmail weight, as the writing shows through and makes the letter hard to read.

On fold-over or informal notepaper, when the address is at the top and there is nothing in the center, the letter or note begins on the first page and follows into the center pages. The paper is opened flat and written on vertically as if it were a single page. If there is an initial, or design, or name in the center of the front page, the note begins at the top of the opened center pages if it is long enough to cover more than half, and on the lower half if it is to be only a few words. In either case, the note would continue on the fourth side, beginning at the cut side and ending at the fold. Although this seems to be upside down, it enables the reader to simply fold up the note paper and continue reading in one direction instead of having to turn it around.

Your Home Address and the Date

If your stationery is not marked with your address, it is a good idea to provide it for your correspondent's convenience in replying even though it also appears on the envelope. Envelopes are often thrown away before the receiver realizes that he or she does not have the return address. The upper-right-hand corner of the first page

ELP

d
it

ida
g her
ly. She
well with
eems to
good friends

December 9, 1992

Dear Bob,

I apologize for not having written sooner. These days have been so busy with my new job and the renovations on the house. You wouldn't recognize the place! Jack and I have really worked to get it in shape.

Mary called from Florida yesterday. She's enjoying her spring break immensely. She is doing quite well with her classes and seems to have made several good friends of your letter is the usual place for the return address. Although the placement of the return address in the lower-left-hand part of the page, just below the level of your signature, is more appropriate for business letters than for social correspondence, it may be included there, especially on a short note. In either case, the date goes below the address.

> Sincerely,
> Mary Swenson
> (Mrs. John Swenson)

45 Barton Street
Racine, Wisconsin
May 19, 1992

When your address is already engraved or printed on the stationery the date only is placed in the upper-right-hand corner of the first page or at the end and to the far left of the signature. The form "May 19, 1992" is preferable to "5-19-92."

On a friendly note "Thursday" is sufficient unless the note is an invitation for more than a week ahead, in which case you write "Thursday, January 9." The year is not essential except in business letters.

The Closing

It is too bad that for personal letters and notes, the English language does not permit the charming closing of letters in the French manner, those little flowers of compliment that leave such a pleasant glow. But ever since the eighteenth century, English-speaking people have been busy pruning away all ornamental expressions; even the last remaining graces—"Kindest regards," "With kindest remembrances"—are fast disappearing, leaving us little but an abrupt "Sincerely yours."

The best ending to a formal social note is "Sincerely," "Sincerely yours," "Very sincerely," or "Very sincerely yours."

"I have the honor to remain . . ." followed by "respectfully yours" is used only in correspondence to very prominent people in the government, diplomatic corps, or church.

"Faithfully" or "Faithfully yours" is rarely used but is appropriate on very formal social correspondence, such as a letter to the President of the United States, a member of the Cabinet, an ambassador, a clergyman, etc.

"As always" or "as ever" is useful to someone with whom you may not be on intimate terms, especially when you have not seen the person for some time.

"Sincerely" in formal notes and "Affectionately" or "Fondly" or "Love" in friendly notes are the most frequently used closings at present. Between the first and last two there is a blank; in English we have no adequate expression to fit sentiment more friendly than the first and less intimate than the others. "Cordially" was brought into use no doubt to fill this need.

"Yours in haste" and "Hastily yours" are not so much bad form as rather carelessly rude, unless for some reason your communication indicates real and necessary haste and "Yours" alone is too abrupt.

"Gratefully" is used only when a benefit has been received, as to a lawyer who has skillfully handled a case or to a friend who has gone to unusual trouble to do you a favor.

In an ordinary letter of thanks the signature is "Sincerely," "Affectionately," "Fondly," "Much love"—whatever your usual close may be.

Signatures

A married woman or a widow always *signs* a letter to a stranger, or a business letter, with her legal name, but her married name should appear too. If her stationery is marked with her full married name and address, "Mrs. Henry Mathews," her signature—"Mary Jones Mathews" or "Mary J. Mathews"—needs no further explanation. But if it is not, she should give her married name (to which the reply will be sent) in one of the several ways. When she writes by hand she adds her married name below her signature (her legal name), in parentheses.

> *Very truly yours,*
> *Mary Jones Mathews*
> *(Mrs. John Mathews)*

When the letter is typed, her married name is typed beneath the space left for her signature, where it need not be enclosed in parentheses.

> *Very truly yours,*
> *Mary Jones Mathews*
> Mrs. John Mathews

If a woman does not want to indicate her marital status she may use "Ms." When writing by hand, a single woman, a divorcée, or a widow may use one of these signatures:

> *Sincerely,*
> *(Miss) Mary Mathews*
> [*or*] *(Mrs.) Mary Mathews*
> [*or*] *(Ms) Mary Mathews*

When the letter is typed, her name is typed beneath the space left for her signature, where it need not be enclosed in parentheses.

> *Sincerely,*
> *Mary Mathews*
> Miss Mary Mathews

On ordinary friendly letters you sign the name by which your correspondent thinks of you. If that name is a special nickname, use that as a signature rather than what you generally call yourself.

If your name is a common one and you are writing to someone who might not recognize you by your handwriting or by the contents of your letter, you must use your last name as well as your first. You may, if it seems friendlier, put the last name in parentheses.

When you are writing a letter for you *and* your spouse (or sister, or whoever it may be) sign your own name only. It is not a sin to sign "Flo and Jack," but Jack is *not* writing the letter, and it is preferable to include him by referring to him in the text. "Jack and I had such a terrific time last weekend, and he especially asked me to tell you again how much he liked the golf course," "Jack joins me in sending thanks and love to everyone," etc. On Christmas cards and other greeting cards joint signatures are permissible.

A final word about the signature: Avoid the unrecognizable flourish. While the reader may be able to decipher a word in a sentence because of its context, the recipient of your letter cannot possibly make sense of an illegible signature if he or she does not already know who wrote the letter.

A BUSINESS OR PROFESSIONAL WOMAN'S SIGNATURE

When an unmarried woman starts her career using her maiden name she generally continues to do so throughout her professional life. She uses "Ms" or "Miss" in combination with that name even after she marries.

But many women start their careers after their marriage or marry after they are established and wish to have it known that they are married. Professionally called Mary T. Forsyth or Helen Horton Hughes, they use business stationery with their names printed that way. This can be most confusing to a correspondent. In order to make it clear what title he should use in addressing a reply, Mary or Helen may precede her signature with (Mrs.). This should *never* be done except on business correspondence—in all other cases their husbands' names are used below the handwritten signature when it is necessary.

OTHER SIGNATURES

The only times a woman actually uses "Mrs." in her *signature* are in a hotel register, on a business telegram, or on a charge account (if the account is in her husband's name), and then it must be "Mrs. John Smith." A note to a household employee is signed "Mrs. Smith."

In the past, a married woman was always listed as a member of a club or organization as "Mrs. William Franklin," not as "Nancy Franklin." Today, however, many women's organizations list their members by their first names with their husband's name in parentheses: "Elizabeth Post (Mrs. William G.)." If the organization is a professional one she uses her professional name and signature, whatever that may be. In all other cases—checks, legal documents of any sort, and as her signature on letters, she uses "Nancy Maiden-name Franklin," which is her legal signature.

Husbands and wives sign most registers as "Mr. and Mrs. William Franklin." However, when asked to sign a guest book, always sign "Jean and Bill Franklin," using your last name.

A man registers at a hotel as "Robert Huff," without title, unless he is accompanied by his wife, when, naturally, he signs "Mr. and Mrs. Robert Huff." If their children are with them he may sign the register "Robert Huff and family."

On social lists, such as patrons or sponsors of a fund-raising party, a man's name is listed with his title. On professional or business listings he is simply "James Regent," and that is also the correct signature if he is signing reports, diplomas, etc.

Folding a Letter

It is not very important which edge of a letter is inserted first into the envelope, but for those who wish to be strictly proper—insert the open, or unfolded edge, first. It should be placed so that when the recipient withdraws and opens it the writing will be right side up. The paper should be folded neatly—once for the envelope that is as deep as half the length of the paper, and twice for the envelope that is a third as deep. The paper that must be folded into thirds is used only as personal stationery for men or for business purposes. Women's personal letter paper should fold only once and fit into its envelope. Notepaper is the same size as the envelope and goes into it flat with only the original fold.

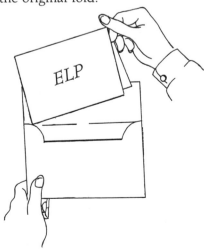

The Outside Address

Write the name and address on the envelope as precisely and as legibly as you can. If your writing is poor, print.

When you are writing to someone who lives in an American city be sure to use the zip code as it is an essential part of the address. The zip code should appear on the same line as the city and state. Zone numbers are used in many foreign cities and are also an integral part of the address.

The address may be written with each line indented a few spaces:

> Mr. Harvey S. Simpson
> 4 Hillside Lane
> Clinton, OH 28000

or with a straight margin on the left:

> Mr. Harvey S. Simpson
> 4 Hillside Lane
> Clinton, OH 28000

Either form is correct.

Correct Use of "Esquire"

The use of "Esquire" has virtually gone out of general use in the United States—except among a few conservative members of the older generation and among lawyers and justices of the peace. When "Esq." or "Esquire" follows the name, "Mr." *never* precedes it. "Esq." is frequently used in business correspondence from one lawyer to another. It may also be used by anyone else writing to a lawyer, unless the letter is to the lawyer and his or her spouse, when "Mr. and Mrs. Hathaway" is correct. "Esq." is also considered correct today in writing to a woman lawyer. The salutation of a letter, regardless of the form on the envelope, is "Dear Mr. (Miss or Ms) Hathaway."

To a Married Woman

No note or social letter should ever be addressed to a married woman—even if she is a widow—as "Mrs. Mary Town." Correctly and properly a widow keeps her husband's name, always. The correct form is "Mrs. Robert Town." The only exception is if you do not know the husband's name. In that case it is better to write to "Mrs. Mary Town" than to "Mrs. Town." When a married woman does not assume her husband's name, correspondence for both of them is addressed "Ms Alison Peters and Mr Jason Cohen."

To Unmarried Couples

Correspondence to men and women living together who are not married are addressed

Ms Jane Stuckey
Mr. Hugh Sidney

or if they prefer, simply

Jane Stuckey
Hugh Sidney

Note that the names appear on separate lines.

When a Married Woman Is a Doctor

Even though a married woman may be known both professionally and socially in conversation as Dr. Mary Flint (her husband's last name), there is some confusion when it comes to addressing social correspondence to her and her husband together. If her husband is a doctor, too, it is simple—they are addressed as "The Drs. Flint," or "Drs. Mary and Simon Flint." If, however, he is not a doctor and she wishes to retain the title socially, letters must be addressed to "Dr. Mary and Mr. Simon Flint."

To Young People

Young girls are addressed as "Miss" socially. Both their first and last names are used on envelopes—the only time a girl is addressed as "Miss Taylor" is on the inner envelope of a wedding invitation.

Boys may be addressed as "Master" until they are six or seven. After that they are addressed without title until they are approximately eighteen. At that time they take the adult title of "Mr."

"Messrs." may not be used to address a father and son. It is correct only in writing to unmarried brothers, or to two or more business partners or members of a firm. Sisters may be addressed as "The Misses," but two unrelated women are addressed separately.

"Personal," "Please Forward" and "Opened by Mistake"

In writing to someone at his or her home address you properly assume that no one else will open the letter. Therefore it is rude to write "Personal" on it. But if you are writing a social note to a friend's business address, it is entirely correct.

"Please Forward" is correct if you know only a former address but not the current one.

It is not uncommon to open a letter addressed to someone else by mistake. It can easily happen if you live in an apartment house where letters are often put in the wrong box, or if your name is a common one. When this happens write "Opened by Mistake" and your initials on the face of the envelope, seal it with a piece of tape and put it in the mail.

The Art of Writing Letters

The ability to write a letter that people cherish and save is a gift. However, it is not true that if one doesn't have this gift one might as well not bother. Instead of thinking about yourself and the impression you may be making, think of the recipient and his or her feelings. Think about letters you have loved to receive—they are usually the ones that carry so much of the writer's personality that he or she seems to be sitting beside us and chatting with us. To achieve this happy feeling of *talking* through a letter, one must employ certain devices so as not to sound stilted. The following suggestions may help to make your letters reflect your personality:

- In a personal letter phrases typical of your speech should be used and not artificially replaced by more formal language. A son who commonly uses the expression "a super person" "or *the* hot item of the day . . ." would sound most unnatural and self-conscious if he wrote instead, "she is a lovely young woman," and "the most relevant and newsworthy event . . ."
- The use of contractions is another means of making your writing natural. Since you would most likely not say, "I do not know," for "I don't know," why write it that way?
- Occasionally inserting the name of the person to whom you are writing gives your letter an added touch of familiarity and affection. "And, Helen, guess what we are going to do this summer!" makes Helen feel as though you are really thinking about her as you write.
- Punctuation can add interest and variety to your letters, much as the change in tone of a speaker's voice adds zest and color to a story. Underlining a word or using an exclamation point after a phrase or sentence gives emphasis where you want it. A dash is effective instead of a longer, possibly more grammatical, phrase. "We went to a dance last night—what a party!" is more colorful than "We went to a dance last night, and it was a great party." Don't overdo, however—a few dashes and exclamation points add zest—too many are boring.
- Don't stop too long to think of *how* to say it. Decide what you want to say and then write it as quickly as possible; that way, it will seem as if you are truly talking to your friend.
- Finally, brevity is infinitely more interesting than lengthy rambling. As Pascal wrote, "This letter shouldn't have been so long, but I haven't the time to make it shorter."

How to Begin

The people who wonder how they will ever fill a blank sheet of paper find that the difficult part of a letter is the beginning. The instruction of an English professor who said, "Begin at the beginning of what you have to say, go on until you have finished, and then stop"—is just about as much help as the artist who proclaimed, "You simply take a little of the right color paint and put it on the right spot." Perhaps the following suggestions will be more helpful.

Your letter may be typed or handwritten, but it should never begin, "I know I should have written sooner, but I haven't anything to write about," or "You know how I hate to write letters . . ." Yet such sentences are written time and again by people who are utterly unaware that they are expressing an unfriendly and negative thought.

Instead, write, "Do you think I have forgotten you entirely? You can't imagine, Ann, how many letters I have planned to write to you." Or, "Time and time again I've begun a letter to you, but every time I thought I had found a quiet moment and corner, I was interrupted by—*something!*"

It is unfortunate when the answer to a letter has been so long delayed that it must begin with an apology, but even an opening apology may be attractive rather than repellent.

The Body of the Letter

The best letters do the following:

- Share news and information.
- Mix good with bad news—never list woes and ailments and then end abruptly.
- Respond to the questions asked by the recipient in his or her letter.
- Ask about the recipient and/or comment on news he or she has shared.
- Include only information you would be happy to have others see, or see yourself again in 15 years. This means no idle gossip, no defamatory or unattractive remarks about others, and nothing so personal that it would prove embarrassing to you or to someone else—letters have a way of resurfacing and/or reaching the hands of others.
- Include mention of people you both know, but not go on at length about someone the recipient has never heard of and couldn't care less about, unless it is someone who will continue to play a significant part in your life. Writing about Jane Jones who won the garden club award is meaningless. Writing about Jane Jones who is a significant person in your life is meaningful.

Ending a Letter

When you leave a good friend's house you don't have to invent a special sentence in order to say good-bye. Leave-taking in a letter is the same. In a personal letter, it is not necessary to use the standard forms of closing (Sincerely, Very truly yours, etc.). Just your name (handwritten if the letter is typed), "Love, Betsy" or "Fondly, Hank" depending on your relationship with the recipient, are all fine.

Don't end by saying, "Well, I guess you've read enough of this," or "you must be bored to tears by now." Don't write, "the mountains were beautiful at sunset," which means nothing personal to the recipient. If you add, "they reminded me of when we were all in Colorado together," however, you have established a connection.

Letters That Shouldn't Be Written

Letters of Gloomy Apprehension

No useful purpose is ever served by writing *needlessly* of misfortune or unhappiness—even to members of one's family. Our distress at hearing about illness or unhappiness among those we love is intensified by the number of miles that separate us from them. For instance:

"My little Betty ["my little" seems so much more pathetic than merely "Betty"] has been feeling miserable for several days. I'm worried to death about her, for there are so many cases of mononucleosis around. The doctor says the symptoms are not alarming, but doctors see so much of illness that they don't seem to appreciate what anxiety means to a mother," etc., etc.

Or: "The times seem to be getting worse and worse. I always said we would have to go through a long night before any chance of daylight. You can mark my words, the night is hardly more than begun."

Neither of these letters serves any useful purpose, and can only worry or irritate the recipients, or depress them.

The Unwise Letter

Every day the mails carry letters whose fallout would be spectacular if they fell into the wrong hands. Letters that should never have been written are continually introduced as evidence in courtrooms, and many of them cannot, in any way, be excused. Silly women and foolish men often write things that sound to a jury, for example, quite different from what was innocently intended.

However, people *will* continue to declare their feelings in writing to absent loved ones, so if you are a young person—or even not-so-young—and are determined to write a love letter, then at least put it away overnight in order to reread it and make sure that you have said nothing that may sound different from what you intended to say.

Remember: Written words have permanency, and thoughts carelessly put on paper can exist for hundreds of years.

Angry Letters

The light, jesting tone that saves a quip from offense cannot be expressed in writing, and spoken remarks that would amuse can become sharp and insulting when written.

Anger in a letter carries with it the effect of solidified fury. Bitter spoken words fade away once the cause is forgiven; written words are fixed on the page forever. Admonitions from parents to their children may very properly be put on paper—they are meant to endure and be remembered—but momentary annoyance should never be more than briefly expressed. Parents who get into the habit of writing in an irritable or fault-finding tone to their children soon find that the letters are seldom read.

One point cannot be overstressed: Letters written under strong emotion should be held for twenty-four hours and reread before being sent—or probably torn into small pieces and not sent at all.

NOTES OF APOLOGY

A note of apology should offer a valid excuse for breaking an engagement. Although you may have telephoned, a written explanation should follow.

Tuesday

Dear Janice,

I do apologize for having to send you the message about Monday night.

When I accepted your invitation I stupidly forgot entirely that Monday was a holiday and that our own guests were not leaving until Tuesday morning; Arthur and I could not very well go off and leave them!

We are disappointed and hope that you know how sorry we were not to be with you.

Affectionately,
Yvonne

Occasionally an unfortunate accident occurs, which, although it may have been entirely beyond our control, requires that we send another type of note of apology.

Dear Mrs. Johnson,

Your little boy has just told me that our dog got into your flower bed and did a great deal of damage.

My husband will build the fence around his pen higher tonight, and he will not be able to escape again. I shall send you some plants to replace those that were ruined, although I'm afraid that new ones cannot compensate for those you lost. I can only ask you to accept my apologies.

Sincerely yours,
Katherine Pennybacker

THANK-YOU LETTERS

The most important qualifications of a thank-you letter are that it sound sincere and that it be written promptly. You use the expressions most natural to you and write as enthusiastically as though you were talking.

There are times when one not only wants to express thanks for extraordinary acts of kindness but also to repay that kindness. I always answer this concern with the thought my landlady gave me when I was young and couldn't afford a sitter. She listened and checked on my baby for nothing. When I said I didn't know how I could ever repay her she said, "Oh, it doesn't work that way—you pass it on to someone else."

The following chart tells you when thank-you notes are obligatory, optional, or unnecessary.

Occasion	Obligatory	Optional or Unnecessary
Dinner Parties	Only if you are a guest of honor.	Otherwise, always appreciated but not necessary if you have thanked your hostess when leaving.
Overnight visits	Always except in the case of close friends or relatives whom you see frequently. Then, a telephone call would serve the purpose.	
For birthday, anniversary, Christmas and other gifts	Always, when you have not thanked the donor in person. Here again, a phone call to a very close friend or relative is sufficient.	It is never wrong to send a note in addition to your verbal thanks.
Shower gifts	If the donor was not at the shower or you did not extend verbal thanks.	Many women like to add a written note to their verbal thanks, but it is not necessary.
Gifts to a sick person	Notes to out-of-towners and calls or notes to close friends are obligatory as soon as the patient feels well enough.	
For notes of condolence	Thank-yous should be sent for all notes of condolence except for printed cards with no personal message.	

Occasion	Obligatory	Optional or Unnecessary
For congratulatory cards or gifts	All personal messages must be acknowledged.	Form letters from firms need not be acknowledged.
Wedding gifts	*Obligatory*—even though verbal thanks have been given. All wedding gifts must be acknowledged within three months, but preferably as the gifts arrive.	
When a hostess receives a gift after visitors have left	Even though the gift is a thank-you itself, the hostess must thank her visitors, especially if the gift has arrived by mail, so that the visitor will know it has been received.	
When a client is entertained by a sales representative		Even though the entertainment is charged to the sales representative's company it would not be remiss to send a note. It is not necessary, but might help to ensure a good relationship.

(See chapter 35 which begins on page 593 for more on acknowledging gifts.)

To Whom Are Thanks Addressed?

When a gift is sent by more than one person—a birthday gift to you from "the Joneses" for example—to whom do you write? It might be awkward to name all of the Joneses in the salutation, so you address the envelope to "Mr. and Mrs. Jones," write the salutation to "Dear Brenda and Fred," and include their children in the text: "Please thank Brian and Diane and Freddy for me, and tell them how much I like the perfume."

A bride usually writes her thank-yous to "Mrs. Jones," on the assumption that Mrs. Jones actually made the purchase, but it is equally correct for her to write to "Mr. and Mrs. Jones" if both of their names are on the card.

A dinner-party thank-you (optional) is sent to the hostess, but thanks for an overnight visit are either sent to both husband and wife, or the husband is included in the text.

For Wedding Presents

Insofar as possible, thank-you notes for wedding presents should be written as soon as the gift is received. This is not always possible, but if they are not sent before the wedding, they must be written as soon as the couple return from their honeymoon. Even for a very large wedding, when the gifts are innumerable, all thank-you notes should be mailed within three months.

The notes sent before the wedding are properly written on plain white notepaper, or paper engraved with the bride's maiden initials. Those mailed after the marriage may be written on full-size paper or notepaper, plain or marked with her married initials.

Wedding presents are sent to the bride, who often writes the majority of the thank-you notes. But she should word her letters to include the bridegroom, especially if the gifts have been sent by friends of his. Some women prefer to sign the notes with both their names. This is not incorrect, but the first way is more proper. She might write something like this:

Saturday

Dear Mrs. Beck,

How did you ever find those wonderful glasses? They are perfect, and Jim and I want to thank you a thousand times!

The presents will be shown on the day of the wedding, but do come over Tuesday morning if you can for a cup of coffee and an earlier view.

Thanking you again, and with love from us both.

Joan

More formally, the bride-to-be might write:

Dear Mrs. King,

It was so thoughtful of you and Mr. King to send us such a lovely clock. I have never been noted for my punctuality, and your gift will surely help me to improve. Thank you very, very much.

Looking forward to seeing you on the tenth.

Very sincerely,
Joan McCord

The salutation is usually addressed to Mrs. King only, but thanks to her husband are often expressed in the text. Otherwise, however, "you" is understood to mean "you both." It is equally correct, however, to address the note to "Mr. and Mrs. King."

For a present received after the wedding the bride might write:

Dear Mrs. Chatterton,

The mirror you sent us is going over our living-room mantel just as soon as we can hang it up! It is exactly what we most needed, and we both thank you ever so much.

Please come in soon to see how beautiful it looks in the room.

Affectionately,
Mary Franklin

For Gifts of Money

When a gift is a sum of money the recipient should indicate how it will be used. "Your check for $50.00 is going into our 'sofa fund,' and we can't tell you how pleased we were to receive it." If you have no such specific use to mention, you can simply say that it will be such a help in furnishing your apartment, building up your savings, or whatever. You should mention the amount just as you would mention the specific item in a thank-you note for a chair or an ashtray.

For Holiday and Birthday Gifts

Thank-you notes for holiday and birthday gifts should be written within two or three days of the time the gift is received. In the case of Christmas or Hanukkah gifts, they should be sent before New Year's Day.

In some parts of the country it is customary for children to have large birthday parties to which their entire class is invited. Some parents do not have their children open the gifts during the party for fear a child will not know how to handle a duplicate present, or how not to say "I already have this!" I do not agree with this, believing that a little instruction to the child beforehand gives him or her the skills to be graceful should these situations occur. If this is the policy, however, and the gifts are not opened during the party, thank-you notes must be sent to each child. If the presents are opened during the party, a verbal thanks by the birthday boy or girl is imperative, and a written thanks may or may not be sent as well.

Children also should be taught to write thank-you notes to grandparents, aunts, uncles, etc. who send gifts at holiday times and birthdays. This is a habit that cannot be learned too young.

For a Baby Gift

Dear Mrs. Foster,

No one else in the world can knit like you! The sweater you made for the baby is perfectly adorable on her. Thank you so much, from both of us.

Affectionately,
Danielle

Dear Mrs. Cooper,

 Thank you ever so much for the blanket you sent Lee Ann. It is by far the prettiest one she has, and so soft and warm that I wish I had one just like it!

 Do come in and see her, won't you? We love to show her off—just let us know when you can come.

      Affectionately,
      Jennifer

For Overnight Visits

When you have stayed overnight, or longer, at someone's house, it is absolutely necessary that you write a letter of thanks to your hostess within a few days after the visit. Unless, of course, your host and hostess are your closest friends with whom you are on "family" terms, or relatives with whom you frequently visit back and forth. Even in those cases a note is in order if you will not see your hosts for some time. If you are all returning to the same town, perhaps after a weekend at their summer home, you should call them on the phone a day or so later, or before seeing them again, to repeat what a good time you had.

Never think, because you cannot write a letter easily, that it is better not to write at all. The most awkward note imaginable is better than none.

Dear Hilari,

 You and Ken are such wonderful hosts. Once again, Judy and I can only tell you that there is no other house where we have such a good time and hate to leave so much. We especially enjoyed the party Saturday evening.

 Thank you very, very much for including us, and Judy joins me in sending much love,

      Stu

Dear Mrs. Farthingham,

 Last weekend was the high spot of the summer. Everything you planned was wonderful, but the best of all was the trip to the crafts fair on Sunday. I wish I could have bought almost everything I saw there.

 I truly enjoyed every minute with your family, and I thank you more than I can say for inviting me.

      Very sincerely,
      Linda

To a Stranger Who Has Entertained You

When someone has shown you special hospitality in a city you visited:

Dear Mrs. Duluth,

It was so good of you to give my husband and me so much of your time. We enjoyed and appreciated all your kindness to us more than we can say.

We hope that you and Mr. Duluth may be coming East before long and that we may have the pleasure of entertaining you at our home.

In the meanwhile, thank you for your generous hospitality, and my husband joins me in sending kindest regards to you both.

Very sincerely yours,
Katherine Starkweather

When Entertained as a Guest of Honor

Whether a neighbor has welcomed you with a coffee for other neighbors or a hostess has held a cocktail party in your honor, it is thoughtful to send a thank-you arrangement of flowers or other gift either beforehand or the next day. Additionally a telephone call or thank-you note written immediately should be made or sent to express your gratitude for the event.

Difficult Thank-Yous

The most difficult thank-you letter to write is the one you owe for a gift that you can't bear. It is all very well to say, "It's the thought that counts," but we sometimes receive gifts that are so dreadful or so inappropriate that it is impossible to believe the donor thought at all!

However, we still don't want to hurt someone's feelings—it is always possible that he or she really did like the monstrosity you received—so you must write something. You need not lie. It is quite possible to find a phrase that can be taken to mean anything the recipient wishes. Consider the following examples:

You do have the most original ideas—whoever else would have found such an unusual gurgling pitcher?

The silver and gold bowl is unique—it has become a real conversation piece in our house.

The upside-down clock is simply fascinating—I've never seen anything quite like it.

None of the statements is untrue, and yet they indicate approval, if they don't actually give it.

Printed Thank-You Cards

Commercial cards may be used for a thank-you instead of your best note paper, as long as a personal message is written on them by hand. It need only be a line or two, but it must express your own feelings—not those of the card company—and it must mention the gift or the occasion.

Engraved Cards of Thanks

An engraved card of thanks is proper only when sent by a public official to acknowledge the overwhelming number of congratulatory messages inevitably received from strangers after winning an election or having been otherwise honored by his or her state or country.

Executive Mansion is the established name of the house in which a governor lives; but if he or she prefers, all official letters may be sent from the Executive Office. For example:

EXECUTIVE MANSION [OR OFFICE]

My dear [name inserted by hand]:
I warmly appreciate your kind message of congratulation, which has given me a great deal of pleasure, and sincerely wish that it were possible for me to acknowledge it in a less formal manner.

Faithfully,
[Signed by hand]

For Those Who Receive No Thank-You

I receive innumerable letters every week asking what should be done when no acknowledgment for a gift sent weeks or months before has been received. This is no time to stand on ceremony. After three months, at the outside, you must write and ask whether or not the gift was received. If the recipient is embarrassed, that is fine—she should be, and perhaps will be more appreciative in the future. If her letter was lost she will tell you that she has written, and your mind will be at rest.

It is *inexcusable* not to thank the donor for *any* gift, and people have been driven to desperate measures to ensure some acknowledgment. One suggestion is to send all gifts insured. You then have a good reason to write and say, "Since I haven't heard from you I assume the gift I sent was lost. If this is so I would like to put in a claim for the insurance, so would you let me know as soon as possible whether you received it or not." One woman has become so annoyed with this frequent carelessness that when she sends a gift from a department store and has received no "thanks" in a reasonable length of time, she sends a postcard to the bride with two lines on the back:

I did receive the package from Tiffany.
I did not receive the package from Tiffany.

She claims she always gets results immediately, and I believe it. However, such measures may seem a bit strong—even rude, to some—and I would not suggest using them unless you *know* that your gift was received and that others, as well as you, have received no acknowledgments of their gifts. In that case, it is obviously not an error, and the bride deserves no consideration.

When the gift in question is a check, you might write, "I am quite concerned about the check I sent you for your birthday. It has been cashed and returned to me, but since I have received no word from you I am worried that it fell into the wrong hands and it was not you who cashed it. Would you let me know?"

LETTERS OF CONGRATULATION

All letters of congratulation excepted printed or form letters require an acknowledgment:

On an Engagement

Dear Pam,

While we are not altogether surprised, we are both delighted to hear the good news of your engagement. Ted's family and ours are very close, as you know, and we have always been especially devoted to him. He is one of the finest—and now luckiest—of young men, and we send you both every good wish for all possible happiness.

Affectionately,
Nancy Jackson

Dear Ted,

Just a line to tell you how glad we all are to hear of your upcoming marriage. Pam is delightful and of course, from our point of view, we don't think she's exactly unfortunate either! This brings our very best wishes to you from

Aunt Nina and Uncle Bill

In response, Pam or Ted would write a note of thanks for the best wishes extended to them.

Dear Mrs. Jackson,

It meant so much to me to receive your note. Ted's family and friends have made me feel so welcome already. We look forward to seeing you soon and again I thank you for your warm words.

Pam Brown

Dear Aunt Nina and Uncle Bill,

Thank you both for your wonderful note. I'm really happy that my favorite aunt and uncle agree with me that Pam is wonderful! We are looking forward to seeing you in two weeks at the Hansons' barbecue for us.

Love,
Ted

On the Birth of a Baby

Dear Tamara,

We were so delighted to hear the news of Jonathan Junior's birth. Congratulations to all three of you!

May I come to see you and the baby the first time that I'm in town? I'll call and let you know when that will be.

Much love,
Helen

Dear Helen,

Jon, Jonathan and I thank you for your note, and we all are looking forward to seeing you when you are in town. Jon and I want very much for two of our favorite people to meet one another as soon as possible!

Love,
Tamara

For Special Achievement

Dear Mrs. Steele,

We are so glad to hear the good news of David's success; it was a very splendid accomplishment, and we are all so proud of him and happy for you. When you see him or write to him please give him our love and congratulations.

Sincerely,
Mildred Bowen

Dear Mrs. Bowen,

How thoughtful you were to write a note about David. I shared your note with him when I spoke to him last night, and he asked me to extend his thanks with ours for your good wishes and congratulations.

Sincerely,
Amanda Steele

On A Promotion

When a newspaper article has brought either an achievement or a promotion to your attention, it is thoughtful to enclose it with your note of congratulations.

Dear Michael,

We were all so happy to hear of the confirmation of your appointment. The state needs men like you—if we had more men of your caliber the ordinary citizen would have less to worry about. Our warmest congratulations!

Jim

Dear Jim,

Thanks so much for your note. Your good wishes and congratulations mean a lot to me—your support has carried me through some challenging times before, and it will be great to know its still there as I begin this new endeavor.

Michael

For Recognition of Special Effort

Often others perform acts of kindness or professionalism beyond anyone's expectation. A letter of recognition for these acts to the person who performed them is important. A letter to that person's supervisor is a way to give additional thanks. It is sad but true that people in general are quick to complain and slow to commend. Letters of complaint flow freely by the thousands; letters of praise trickle in by twos and threes.

When you are prompted to write a letter of commendation, first do your best to get the name of the person or persons who rendered the service and the name or title of the person to whom you should write. Then describe the act or attitude that pleased you, and the date on which it occurred. A letter containing these specifics is of far more value than a more general commendation.

Brandt Tools, Inc.
4500 Main Street
Milwaukee, Wisconsin 53200

Mr. S. N. Jones, Manager
Flight Service
American Air Lines
Love Field
Dallas, Texas 75235

Dear Mr. Jones:

The normal conduct of my business takes me over a good part of the world via air travel, and from time to time there is an opportunity to write a complimentary letter about services that have been rendered.

Such a happy circumstance presented itself on January 26 on Flight 425 from Dallas to Phoenix, Arizona. The plane was full, and the three flight attendants in the coach section really did a job for you. They were not only efficient, but pleasant and cheerful to the point that it was really a pleasure to be on the flight.

The particular flight attendants involved were Sally Keene, based in Dallas, Juanita Velez of Dallas, and Gail Brooks, based in Chicago. Will you please see that my thanks are transmitted in some manner to these three women.

Yours sincerely,
Henry Dorfuss

H. Dorfuss
President

Dear Dr. Klosek:

As the school year comes to a close, I wanted to share with you my appreciation of the efforts of Mrs. Adler throughout the year. Cassie has never had a more wonderful academic experience, thanks to Mrs. Adler's sensitivity, creativity, and skill as a teacher. It is a wonderful feeling to see a child approach each school day with enthusiasm and leave the classroom feeling proud of her accomplishments and eager for more. Mrs. Adler is a true asset to Osborn School and we feel most fortunate that Cassie was in her class this year.

Sincerely,
Barbara Thomas

I often receive letters from readers who wonder whether a gift of some sort should accompany a letter of appreciation to a professional who has performed a service "above and beyond the call of duty." Again, a letter to the "powers that be" is always welcome. Additionally, a copy of the letter to the local newspaper, when the service is by members of a civic or town agency or organization, serves as a public recognition. If desired, a contribution to the organization may be a fitting gesture. For example, if the police reacted instantly to an emergency and provided support for which you are particularly grateful, a check to their Benevolent Association, Athletic League, or whatever organization the police force supports is an extra way of expressing appreciation.

Dear Commissioner Franklin,

Last week when a moving van went out of control and crashed into my car, pinning me and my children inside, it was the thorough professionalism of Police Officers Michael Flynn and Paul Degenhardt that kept us all calm during the process of freeing us from the car.

There really are no words to properly thank them or express my appreciation to you but please know that I shall always be grateful for their attentions to my children, who were terrified, and for their quick work in extricating us. You should be very proud of having two such fine officers on your force.

As a small token of our appreciation, enclosed is a contribution for your Benevolent Association which we give in the names of Officers Flynn and Degenhardt.

Sincerely,
Marjorie Wynne

LETTERS OF REFERENCE

(See also pages 188–189 for letters of reference for a domestic employee and page 235 for information on letters of reference for employees.)

When writing a letter of reference for a personal acquaintance, for a teen who has babysat, for a woman who has done housework, or anyone else who has done work for you, your personal letter takes the form of a business letter. If possible, it should be typewritten rather than hand written, and should be addressed to a specific individual rather than "To Whom It May Concern."

71 Glen Oaks Drive
Valley Cottage, NY 10989
May 28, 1992

Ms. Harriet Smithson
Director of Personnel
The Village Book Shop
232 Main Street
Valley Cottage, New York 10989

Dear Ms. Smithson:

I am pleased to address you about Christopher Ferretti who has served as a tutor to my son over the past three years. His conscientiousness in preparing lessons and his skill in explaining difficult problems have been commendable. He has always been prompt and extremely courteous and his ability to communicate areas of concern not only to my son but also to my husband and to me have been most professional.

I understand that you are considering him for a summer job in your store, and could not recommend him more highly. Please feel free to call me at 555-0964 if you have any questions.

> *Sincerely,*
> *Diane Hillman*
> *(Mrs. David Hillman)*

LETTERS OF INTRODUCTION

A business letter of introduction is somewhat different from a social one, although it carries the same implicit approval of the subject. It also implies the writer's request that the receiver pay due attention to the one being introduced. It should not be written casually or for a person who does not merit the introduction.

A businessman might write to his friend, Bob Riggs, in another city to tell him that John Simms will be in that city on such-and-such a date, and that a meeting might be mutually advantageous. However, he is far more apt to pick up the telephone and call Bob in person, giving him some background information that might be useful if a meeting is arranged. At the same time he may give John Simms one of his business cards with "Introducing John Simms" written at the top. John then gives this card to Bob's secretary when he arrives at the office and it serves as a reminder that he comes "recommended" by a mutual friend.

A business letter of introduction does not necessarily oblige the receiver to entertain the subject socially. If he wishes to, he certainly may, but generally his attention to the bearer's business is sufficient.

The social introduction is far more of a responsibility. But when you know someone who is going to a city where you have other friends and when you sincerely believe that it will be a mutual pleasure for them to meet, a letter of introduction is proper and easy to write.

The *formal* letter of introduction, delivered in person by the one being intro- duced, is a thing of the past. Most social introductions as well as business ones are arranged by a telephone call, but indirect letters of introduction are still not uncom- mon. They are far more sensible than the formal notes which were often embarrassing to both presenter and receiver, since they carried an unavoidable obligation to entertain and to be entertained whether the two took to each other or not.

Today when the Franklins are going to move to Strangetown, their friend Sue Connors may write Tracy Hartwell, who lives there, and tell her that "My neighbors, Helen and Tom Franklin, are moving to Strangetown and I think you'd like them very much." Sue is free to entertain them or not as she sees fit. However, if Sue writes, "I've told them about you, and given them your number," Tracy is obligated to at least ask the Franklins over for a drink or a cup of coffee.

If an acquaintance, unbeknownst to you, gives your number to a friend who is coming to your town and that person calls you, you are under no obligation to entertain the stranger unless you wish to. The visitor, who may well feel shy about calling a total stranger, may feel more comfortable if she extends the invitation herself: "Sue Connors has told me so much about you—wouldn't you come down and have lunch with me at my hotel?"

Letters of Condolence

Intimate letters of condolence are too personal to follow a set form. One rule, and one only, should guide you in writing such letters. Say what you truly feel. Say that and nothing else. Sit down at your desk as soon as you hear of the death and let your thoughts be with the person you are writing to.

Don't dwell on the details of illness or the manner of death; don't, especially to a mother who has lost a child, try to convince her that her loss is a "blessing in disguise." Remember that a person with an aching heart will not wish to wade through interminable sorrowful thoughts. The more nearly a note can express your sympathy, and a genuine love or appreciation for the one who has gone, the greater comfort it brings.

Forget, if you can, that you are using written words. Think merely how you feel—then put your feelings on paper.

Suppose it is the death of a man who has left a place in the whole community that will be difficult, if not impossible, to fill. All you can think of is "Steve—what a wonderful man he was! I don't think anything will ever be the same again without him." Say just that! Ask if there is anything you can do at any time to be of service. There is nothing more to be said. A line into which you have put a little of the genuine feeling that you had for Steve is worth pages of eloquence. A letter of condolence may be badly constructed, ungrammatical—never mind. Flowery language counts for nothing; sincerity alone is of value.

The few examples below are intended merely as suggested guides for those at a loss to construct a short but appropriate message.

Dear Mrs. Sutphen,
We are so very shocked to hear of the sorrow that has come to you.
If there is anything that either my husband or I can do, I earnestly hope that you will call upon us.

Alice Blake

Dear Mr. and Mrs. Conrad,
I know how little words written on a page can possibly mean to you at such a time. But I must at least tell you that you are in our thoughts and in our hearts, and if there is anything that we can do for you, please send us a message— whatever it may be.

With deepest sympathy,
Mary Newling

Or, one my husband received when Emily Post died: *We have so much sympathy for you. It must have been wonderful to have had her as your grandmother.*

Letter Where Death Was a Release

It is difficult to write a letter to one whose loss is for the best in that you want to express sympathy but cannot feel sad that one who has suffered so long has found release. The expression of sympathy in this case should not be for the present death, but for the illness that started long ago. The grief for a paralyzed mother is for the stroke that cut her down many years before, and your sympathy is really for that. You might write: *Your sorrow during all these years—and now—is in my heart; and all my thoughts and sympathy are with you.*

To Whom Are Letters of Condolence Written?

Letters of condolence may be addressed in various ways. If you knew the deceased well but do not know his or her family, the note is addressed to the closest relative—usually the widow, the widower, or the oldest child. Some like to add "and family" on the envelope, and this is permissible when you feel that you are sending your sympathy to all rather than to one special person.

When you did not know the person who died but do know one of his or her relatives, you write to that person rather than to someone who might have been more closely related. In writing to a married person who has lost a parent you may write to the one whose parent it was, or if the other partner was close to his or her in-law the letter may be addressed to both.

Letters to children who have lost a parent may be addressed to Miss Lucy Field (the daughter), with Mr. John Field (the son) underneath. The salutation would read: "Dear Lucy and John."

I am sometimes asked if one should write to the surviving member of a divorced couple when the other dies. If they have maintained a friendly relationship, and you know that the survivor is truly upset by his or her ex-mate's death, naturally you should write. In most cases, however, the divorce indicates that they no longer wish to share each other's lives, so there is little need to send sympathy. The children of the divorced couple, even though they live with the surviving member, should receive notes if they have continued to see the deceased.

Acknowledgment

Notes of condolence should always be acknowledged—by the recipient if possible. If he or she cannot do it—for whatever reason—other members of the family should write the notes. The only exceptions to this obligation are when the expression of condolence is simply a printed form with no personal message, or when the writer asks that his or her note not be acknowledged—a thoughtful thing to do when writing a close friend, or someone you know will receive a great number of condolences.

Printed acknowledgments may be sent in reply to printed expressions of condolence if any acknowledgment at all seems necessary, but they should not be used in answer to warm, personal notes. You may, of course, use those given out by the funeral director as long as you add a personal word or two to the printed "Thank You."

VISITING OR CALLING CARDS

Rarely seen today, a visiting card, when used, is presented at the time one makes a formal call or left with the maid if the person one is calling upon is not at home.

More usually, these cards are used as a gift enclosure.

Size and Engraving

Of necessity, the width of visiting cards varies according to the length of the name, but a woman's card is usually from 3 to $3^{1}/_{2}$ inches wide and from $2^{1}/_{4}$ to $2^{1}/_{2}$ inches high. A man's card is narrower, from 3 to $3^{1}/_{4}$ inches long and from $1^{1}/_{4}$ to $1^{5}/_{8}$ inches high. The cards are made of white or cream-white glazed or unglazed bristol board of medium thickness, and they are not plate-marked (with raised border).

Addresses

It is not incorrect, but it is unusual, to have an address on a social card. If you wish to do so, the address should be written out in full, with no abbreviations. Numerals may be used. The address is engraved in the lower-right-hand corner.

More often, the address is simply written on the card by hand when it is requested or necessary.

Names and Initials

To be impeccably correct, one should not use initials on a visiting card. A man's card theoretically should read "Mr. John Hunter Titherington Smith"; but when the name is awkwardly long, he may have his card engraved "Mr. John H. T. Smith" or "Mr. J. H. Titherington Smith," if he prefers. His wife's card should be the exact duplicate of his, and not read "Mrs. J. Hunter Smith" when his reads "Mr. John H. Smith." She uses "Jr." if he does, and drops it, if he does, when his father dies.

```
Mrs. William Goadby Post
```

```
Mr. William Goadby Post
```

Women's Social Cards

A married woman uses her husband's name in exactly the same form that he does. A widow should continue to use her husband's given name: "Mrs. John Foster Hughes"—not "Mrs. Sarah Hughes." A divorcée uses her own first name: "Mrs. Janice Forsythe." A single woman's name is written out in full (no initials) and from the age of ten her name is preceded by "Miss." She may drop the title and just use her name, if she prefers. A woman who uses a title, such as "Doctor", uses the title on social cards. It would read "Doctor (written out if space permits) Jean Hamilton." Her business card would instead read "Jean Hamilton, M.D."

Men's Social Cards

A man's card is engraved with his title, "Doctor" or "Mr." "Mr." is never written "Mister," but "Doctor" is preferable to "Dr."

If a man is a junior, his cards should be engraved "Mr. John Foster Hughes, Jr.," "Junior" may be engraved in full; when it is, it is not spelled with a capital j. John second, or John third may have "2nd" or "3rd" after their names, but the Roman numerals II or III are more customary.

As for a woman, a man's social card, when he has a professional title, includes the title: "Doctor Henry Gordon," "The Reverend William Goode," "Colonel Thomas Doyle," "Judge Horace Rush," "Senator James Widelands." Their professional card, on the other hand, would be written "Henry Gordon, M.D." Holders of honorary degrees do not use the title or the letters on their cards.

Husband and Wife Cards

"Joint" cards often have the couple's address on them, as they are used for more practical purposes than the individual calling card. Titles such as "Doctor" and "The Reverend" must be abbreviated because of space. "Mr. and Mrs." cards are almost always enclosed with wedding gifts, and all presents that are given by both husband and wife. They are also used with flowers going to a funeral or to a bereaved family.

Mr. and Mrs. William Goadby Post

Husband-and-wife cards are never left by the woman when she makes an official call by herself. Nor can the husband use one if he makes a call alone. On official calls, their separate cards are left, even when they go together.

A married woman doctor would have a joint card printed "Dr. Susan and Mr.
William Perry," so that the man's names are not separated or if he is a doctor too, "Dr.
and Mrs. William Perry," or "Drs. Susan and William Perry." The card may not read,
"Mr. and Dr. William Perry" since she is not Dr. William Perry.

Other joint cards when professional titles are included might read, "The
Reverend and Mrs. William Goode," "Judge and Mrs. Horace Rush," etc.

Social Cards of Office Holders

Titles may be included on personal cards, such as:

Mr. John Lake
Mayor of Chicago

But titles of courtesy have no place either in a signature or on a personal card. For
example, the American title of courtesy, "The Honorable," unlike this title given to
sons of British earls, viscounts, and barons, is never correct on an American's
personal card.

Enclosed With Flowers

Occasionally a calling card is enclosed with flowers sent as an expression of
sympathy or congratulations, especially when it is a "formality" rather than extended
to someone to whom you wish to send a more personal message. All that is required
is to write "Congratulations on your new job" or "With deepest sympathy" above
your engraved name. No message is written when the flowers are sent to "the funeral
of John Smith" at the church. The card is put in an envelope and stapled to the paper
around the flowers.

As a Baby Announcement

A miniature visiting card with your baby's name on it, attached by a ribbon to
your card, makes the nicest birth announcement possible.

As a Gift Enclosure

When sending a gift to anyone, it definitely adds a "touch" if you enclose your
own card, rather than one picked out from the selection on the counter. Although
you need not write any message at all, most people, if they know the recipient
personally, like to write a word or two at the top of the card. To a bride you might
write "Best wishes for your happiness" or "Love and best wishes to you both."

When you are enclosing a card with a gift being sent to someone you know
well, you may feel that your "Mrs. Franklin Carey" or "Mr. and Mrs. Franklin Carey"

card is too formal. It is perfectly permissible to scratch out the entire name and write "Mary and Frank" above it. Or if it is to someone who might not think of you quite that informally (a young bride, for instance), you may scratch out all but the last name and write in "Mary and Frank." However, leaving the engraved name as it is, and writing whatever you wish above it, is correct in all circumstances.

Your card is put in an envelope that is put inside the gift box. If the message on the card is very personal it may be sealed; otherwise it is not. The name (without address) of the recipient is written on the envelope when the gift is being sent from a store, but if you are mailing the package yourself that is not necessary.

Greeting and Get-Well Cards

Birthday and anniversary cards, get-well cards, and all other messages of friendship are welcome evidence of good wishes from family and friends. The wide variety of cards now available makes the choosing and sending of them a pleasure rather than a chore.

But a word of warning is in order. The very fact that they are attractive and easy to find may on occasion lead to their abuse. Elderly Aunt Margaret will enjoy her birthday card only if you take the trouble to add a little note in your own handwriting expressing something of your feelings about the day or giving her a bit of family news. A printed message, however delightful, cannot possible make up for lack of personal attention.

Get-well cards, especially when accompanied by a personal note, do much to cheer the ailing person.

I would like to quote from a letter I received recently:

While ill for some weeks I received a vast number of get-well cards. I was touched that so many friends thought of me, but I can't help my feeling of disappointment that so few contained a personal note, even one line. If one could realize how much even the shortest personal note enhances the card in the eyes of the receiver, more people would take the extra time and trouble to write something beneath the printed message.

Need I say more?

When you know someone is dying, however, a cute get-well message is obviously inappropriate. At these times, a blank greeting card in which you may write your own message, or a "Thinking of You" card is acceptable.

Holiday Cards

There is virtually no limit to the list of those to whom one may send holiday cards, with exceptions. A Christmas or Easter card to a Jewish friend is meaningless since they celebrate neither of these holidays, just as a Passover or Hanukkah card to a Christian friend is meaningless. However, a "Seasons Greeting" card, with no religious figures, messages or symbols on it, is appropriate, and appreciated in either situation. It is also fairly pointless to send a card to everyone with whom you have a nodding acquaintance, and in this day, a very expensive proposition. Instead, these cards should be sent to people you really wish to greet, with whom you do not exchange gifts, whom you may not have seen for some time, and most of all, those who do not live near you and with whom a holiday card may be your only communication.

Signatures on Greeting Cards

When cards are sent by a couple, the one who writes the names usually writes his or her own name last, although some people feel the ladies name should be first. To close friends, the last name need not be written; to others, it should be included. When signatures are printed, there is no rule about whose name should be first, but the last name is always used. "Mary and John Godfrey" may seem more polite to Mary, but "John and Mary Godfrey" does, of course, follow the conventional "Mr. and Mrs." form. When children's names are included the father's name comes first—always. For example: "John and Mary Godfrey and John Jr." Cards sent by a family having several children might be from "The John Smiths—All Five"; or from "The Smiths—John, Mary, Johnny, Marie, and Tim." There is, of course, no rule about anything as informal as this.

A title—"Mr.," "Mrs.," etc.—is never used.

When a husband and wife have each been married before and have children from both previous marriages the signatures can become very complicated if they try to include all the names. It is not incorrect to write "Pat, Jean, and Billy Smith," and "Bobby, Rich, Frank, and Carol Brown" under the parents' names, but it seems more practical if the parents sign "Bob and Sue" and add "and all the family" or "and children" after the signature.

Christmas Cards as Newsletters

Christmas cards are often used as carriers of news—and rightly so. They may announce a birth in the family by the signature—"Mary, Joe, and Joe Jr., born August seventh in Williamstown." They may carry unhappy news, too—"John and I were divorced in September, so please write me at my new address. . . ." Or a death is announced simply by the fact that a card comes from "Mary Cross" when always before it had come from "Bill and Mary." And of course, we all write brief news notes or special thoughts to people whom we have not seen, or do not see often. But there is another type of "newsletter" I would like to mention. That is the mimeographed history of the past year, which has no handwritten note added, and which often runs to four or five pages. The people who send these form letters mean well—they are trying to get all the news into this once-a-year communication, and they go to great trouble to do it. But the truth is that outside of their closest friends, most people don't really care if the baby has six teeth, or that Johnny had his tonsils out. A handwritten note on a pretty card, possibly telling of the high points—a marriage, a birth, etc., would be much more appreciated. So if you want to have one of these letters printed up, fine, but I urge you to send out cards to the majority of your acquaintances and enclose the newsletter only to those who you are sure will be interested.

A Holiday Card to Someone in Mourning

A card to someone who is in mourning will be gratefully received if in some way it illustrates the promise of peace or comfort or if its message is one of love or friendship. But please do not send a gay or humorous card shouting "Merry Christmas and Happy New Year" to one who probably feels so unhappy at this time. Whether or not those who are themselves in mourning send cards depends entirely upon their own feelings. Naturally they would not send cards to mere acquaintances, but certainly there is no impropriety in wishing their friends happiness, if they can forget their own unhappiness enough to do so. On the other hand, no one could possibly want them to do anything that could add to their difficulties or emotional burdens.

Christmas Cards to Business Acquaintances

When it is company policy to send a Christmas card to a client, it is sent to the person at the business address, in the name of the company—"The Hollister Hardware Company wishes you a Merry Christmas and a Happy New Year"—rather than to the client's home in the name of the president or other officer of the company. But if the client is known to the executive socially as well as through business, it may be addressed to husband and wife and sent to their home, even though the sender of the card may not know the client's spouse personally.

All personal Christmas cards should be addressed by hand, and even secretaries who are sending a great number out for their firm, or as the "personal business" cards of an employer, should make every effort to do so. Nor should they use a postage meter. It takes no longer to write the address by hand than to insert the envelope in the typewriter, type the address, and remove the envelope; and stamps can be affixed quickly and painlessly by using a wet sponge. A typed, metered envelope can easily be mistaken for an advertisement and be tossed, unopened, into the wastebasket. A card with a typewritten address announces "Business only." Unless the number is overwhelming, or the secretary is physically incapable of writing, the boss's cards should be addressed by hand.

BUSINESS CARDS

A standard form of business card for a salesperson or anyone not in an executive position has the name and address of the company printed in the center of the card with the employee's name in the lower left-hand corner and the telephone number in the right-hand corner. If the company has a number of telephone lines, the number listed should be the one where the individual can be reached, or where a message may be left. If all calls come in through a general switchboard it is helpful to include the individual's extension on the card. For sales purposes the ink may be colored and there may be an emblem or drawing on the card.

MY PARTY ENTERTAINMENTS, INC.
16 Centre Street
Ames, Iowa 50010

Allen Lewiston
Sales Representative   515-555-3888

An executive has his or her name in the center with the position in smaller letters under the name or in the lower left corner. The name and address of the company are put in the lower left corner and the telephone number in the lower right. The telephone number should be the one for the executive's office, not a general company switchboard number. In addition, a FAX number may be listed on the business card. The printing on an executive's card is engraved or thermographed on good quality paper.

Business cards are approximately three and one-half by two inches. They carry the name by which a person is commonly known in the business world. For instance, if a woman's full name is Elizabeth Morgan Rosetti, but she has dropped her middle name for business purposes, her card will simply read "Elizabeth Rosetti." Titles (Mr., Ms, Mrs., Miss, Dr., etc.) are never used on business cards.

Business cards are never used for social purposes. An executive does not enclose one in flowers to a sick staff member or issue invitations on the back of them or leave them on a social call. They are limited to the use specified by their name: business.

They may be given to a prospective client, and to someone meets on business with whom one wants to keep in contact. They may also be attached with a paper clip to the top of a business letter to someone with whom one will be conducting

---

MARSHA HOLLIS
Sales Manager

Ebb Tide Company
Columbus, Ohio 43200   614-555-7400

OR

STEPHEN VIOLA
Vice-President, Sales and Marketing

Rollins Research   Telephone 317-555-1234
Wayne, Indiana 47899   Fax 317-555-1200

---

business, or is hoping to conduct business, so that the recipient can file it in an index box or carry it with him or her.

In some European countries, business cards are exchanged automatically, the moment one meets someone else. When traveling on business overseas, it is a good idea to carry a large supply of business cards for this purpose.

ELECTRONIC COMMUNICATION

Whether a tape or video cassette, a facsimile (FAX) letter, or a letter sent from one computer to another, an electronic communication should be in keeping with all the guidelines for other social and business correspondence. The contents should never be of such a private or personal nature that you would be embarrassed were it to fall into the "wrong" hands, and the communication should be neat, legible, attractive, or audible, in the case of a tape cassette.

Audio and Video Cassettes as Letters

Particularly for grandparents and other friends and relatives who live far away, an audio tape or a video cassette is a wonderful form of correspondence. It shares the voice or the image of loved ones in a personal way that even a letter cannot reproduce. Naturally, it is important to ascertain first that the recipient has compatible equipment for listening or viewing.

Cassettes used for business purposes can save time and offer clear descriptions or demonstrations of the information being communicated. They should not be accompanied by personal asides or background music, however, which only serve to annoy and detract from the intended message. If you are recommending a lighted sign for outside your building and board members cannot travel to a location where a similar sign is in place, for example, a videotape of the sign from all angles is a convenient accompaniment to your presentation. You may talk, describing your angle or location, but you should never tell small jokes or be shooting from a car window with your car radio blaring in the background.

Facsimile Machines

The FAX has done much to make written communication an instant process. When used properly, it is a marvelous way to transmit copies of documentation that previously had to be mailed, entailing the delay of at least a day. The FAX is a communication vehicle, however, and whether used for personal or business purposes, should not be abused. Unless someone has a FAX in his or her home which makes it a more private means of communication, the equipment is usually located at a central point in an office. Transmittals can be read by anyone who happens to be walking by the machine. A FAX may be marked "confidential," but unless the recipient is standing right next to the machine to receive the pages you send, there is nothing confidential about the process.

A FAX transmission, therefore, should be to the point, be able to be a public document unless privacy is ensured, be neat, and legible. It is not an inexpensive means of communication, and a company FAX should not be used for private purposes. Although the charge is to the sender, the receiver incurs costs, as well, in paper used to receive communications. Most FAX machines today have built-in systems which provide a list of telephone numbers called for FAX transmittal. The threat of disclosure should not be the reason for not abusing this system by personal communications on company time, but knowing it exists is another deterrent, on top of your own sense of integrity, to abusing it.

A FAX is *not* a substitute for other kinds of correspondence. Putting off extending invitations until the last minute and then sending them by FAX is not acceptable, for example, nor is using a facsimile machine a suitable substitute for delivering a report or other communique unless it was requested in a rush. Again, there is a charge to the receiver even though the delay is your fault, and it does nothing for your professional image to have your report submitted late on FAX paper instead of on time in the form you would ordinarily use. And, because a FAX is not a private means of communication, it should not be used for personal invitations or messages of any kind.

The first page of any FAX should list the telephone number and/or FAX number of the sender, the name of the intended receiver, and the number of pages being sent, so that the receiver knows he has gotten everything you have sent. When sending a FAX to someone within a corporation, it is important to include the full name, title and location of the recipient so that it may be delivered directly to that person by the one who takes it from the machine.

Electronic Mail by Computer

E-mail is another means of instant communication, and again, should not include subject matter you would not be comfortable having anyone else see. Although directed specifically to one or a group of individuals as indicated by the sender, E-mail is not necessarily confidential or private. It should not be used for frivolous correspondence, as a cost is generally incurred by the receiver for computer time.

As carefully as is possible, E-mail transmittals should follow the form of typewritten memos and be succinct and professional.

THE FORM OF A BUSINESS LETTER

Business Stationery

A firm's business stationery should be carefully chosen, as the impression it makes may be widespread. It should be conservative, attractive, and of good quality, to indicate that the firm itself has those characteristics.

The most appropriate company stationery is a single sheet, white or off-white, measuring approximately eight by ten inches. This fits into the standard file, and folded into thirds, into a regular business envelope.

When it is to be used by various people in a company it carries the name of the firm, with the address and telephone number, at the top. If the company has a logo or emblem it regularly uses, this symbol is also included on the letterhead.

Many large companies have paper printed (or engraved) for their executives. The executive's name and position are printed in the upper-left-hand corner on the company's stationery. In this case the secretary does not type the executive's position after his or her signature.

Both men and women executives often have their personal office stationery in addition to the company stationery. The paper is engraved with the executive's name and the firm's address, without title unless he or she is a doctor, commander, etc. If necessary the secretary may include the executive's position in the firm when typing the name below the signature. A woman's title does not appear on the paper but does on the envelope—"Miss," "Mrs.," or "Ms."

On business envelopes the return address should always be on the face of the envelope.

Contents

Letters from business offices depend so thoroughly on the nature of the concern that little need be said except that they be clear, concise, and to the point. If you know exactly what you want to say and give considerable thought to the initial statement of your most important point you cannot go far astray. And when you have said what you intended to say, stop. A meandering last paragraph can destroy the entire effect of the letter.

Recipient's Address

A correct form for business letters shows the receiver's address at the left, below the level of the date and two lines above the salutation, exactly as it appears on the envelope.

June 7, 1992

Mr. James Johnson
Smith, Johnson & Co.
20 Broadway
New York, New York 10027

Dear Mr. Johnson:

Another correct form is to line up the date, recipient's address, salutation, and closing and signature all along the left margin.

Salutation

In most cases when writing a letter, you follow the practice of names you have established in person. For instance, if you address the vice-president of marketing as "Jim," you are expected to open your letter with "Dear Jim." If he remains "Mr. Wallace," your letter must begin, "Dear Mr. Wallace."

Occasionally you meet someone for the first time, and although you use first names, you really do not know each other well enough to use the first name in a letter. In that case you may open your first letter with, "Dear Mr. Wallace."

The question often arises about when one may properly change from addressing someone by the title and last name to the first name. If your correspondence leads to personal meetings and continued business relations, you may use that person's first name in correspondence as soon as you are invited to do so in conversation. When your business relationship continues only by correspondence, you may broach the subject as one executive I know does. After corresponding with Mr. Newton for some time, she begins one letter with *Dear Isaac, if I may:*. Mr. Newton's reply would set the tone for your continued correspondence; a reply addressed *Dear Cheryl* indicates that Mr. Newton does not object to this change, and may in fact welcome it; whereas a reply addressed *Dear Ms Peters* would tell you he prefers to maintain a more formal relationship.

When writing to an executive whose name you do not know, you should first call the company and ask for his or her correct name and title, if it is possible to do so. This enables you to personally direct your correspondence. If you cannot do this, then you may write "Dear Sir or Madam," or you may address the person by the job: "Dear Editor." This may be cumbersome, as in "Dear Complaint Department Manager."

In this case, you may skip the salutation entirely, insert a line which synopsizes your letter, and follow with the body of the letter:

Barton Business Tools
3323 Third Avenue
New York, New York 10017

Re: Order Number 6345, Catalog 55

On September 30th, our firm placed the order referenced above but to date. . . . etc.

This is the least preferable style, but it does solve the dilemma when the addressee is unknown to you.

The salutation on a business letter is followed by a colon instead of the comma used on a personal letter.

Closing

The close of a business letter should be "Yours truly" or "Very truly yours." "Sincerely" and "Best regards" are also correct. "Respectfully" is used only by a tradesman to a customer or by an employee to an employer. "Yours" is often used on informal office correspondence.

Signatures

In signing a letter, it is proper to use the same form you used in the introduction. If you opened with "Dear Jim," you sign your name "Alice." If you opened with "Dear Mr. Wallace," you sign "Alice Simmons." You never sign your last name and title—"Miss Simmons" or "Mr. Adams." In either case your secretary, or you if you type your own letters, will have followed accepted business form and typed your full name below your signature if you are using your company's letterhead. If you are not using company stationery, your company's name comes below your signature. For instance:

Very truly yours,

Alice Simmons
ARJO SPECIALISTS, INC.

The telephone has virtually replaced all other forms of communication and with the frequency of its use has come the frequency of its abuse. One can be held captive on the telephone as easily as in person by a garrulous friend or associate. And what adult is there who hasn't become enraged at getting a constant busy signal when calling home or someone else's home where children and teens abound?

Every day new telephone tricks are thought of—the creditor who calls via an electronic system and asks you to wait for one of their employees to be free to speak with you—the 900 number that costs you anywhere from 50 cents to $9.00 a call to find out if you won a free weekend in the Poconos or to hear Santa Claus tell a story.

The only solution to the nightmare that telephones can become is manners. One not only must practice them, but insist on them as well, both at home, and in the office.

15
On the Telephone

Personal Calls

When you talk on the telephone, whether in your home or in an office, the quality of your voice and your ability to express yourself clearly and concisely are of utmost importance. The person at the other end of the line cannot, after all, see your facial expressions or gestures, and the impression received depends entirely on your voice.

The telephone is designed to carry your voice at its natural volume and pitch. It is not necessary to shout. In fact raising your voice, especially during a long-distance call, will only distort it. The telephone transmitter should be held about one inch from your lips and the earpiece close to your ear. Speak clearly and distinctly, with the same inflections that you would use in a face-to-face conversation. If you must put the telephone down during the conversation, do it gently, and when you hang up, do not slam the receiver down. The person at the other end may still have the phone close to his ear, and the sudden sharp bang can be quite deafening.

Answering Your Telephone

The best way to answer the telephone at home is still "Hello." "Yes" is abrupt and sounds a bit rude, but "This is Mrs. Jones's house" leaves the door standing open wide, and "Mrs. Jones speaking" leaves you without a chance to retreat.

This is not nonsense. It is a really important aspect of modern telephone
etiquette. In all big cities telephones are rung so persistently by every type of stranger who wants to sell something to Mrs. Householder, to ask a favor of Mrs. Prominent, or to get in touch with Mr. Official (having failed to reach him at his office) that many prominent people are obliged to keep their personal telephone numbers unlisted.

The Caller

I cannot emphasize strongly enough how helpful and courteous it is to give one's name as soon as the person at the other end answers your call. *What* name you give depends on how well you know, or are known to, the person who answers. But if your call is a legitimate one and you therefore have no reason to hide your identity, *give your name at once*. Here are some of the ordinary forms:

To a maid or secretary: "This is Mrs. Franklin. Is Mrs. Harvey in?"

To a child who answers: "This is Mrs. Franklin. Is your mother in?"

When you recognize the voice answering: "Hello, John. This is Helen. Is Sue there?"

When the person you are calling answers: "Hi, Sue, this is Helen," or "Hello, Mrs. Brooks. This is Helen Franklin."

An older person calling a younger one says: "This is Mrs. [or Mr.] Bailey."

A young person calling an older man or woman says: "Hello, Mrs. [or Mr.] Knox. This is Janet Frost."

Who Is Calling, Please?

Unfortunately not everyone does give his or her name and the caller may simply respond to your "Hello" by saying, "May I speak to Mrs. Franklin?" or "Is Mrs. Franklin in?" In this case, you may simply say, especially if you recognize the caller's voice, "Just a moment, please," if the call is for someone else, or "This is Mrs. Franklin," or "This is she." Most people, however, prefer the person who answers to ask who the caller is before coming to the phone. It used to be considered rather "snoopy" if a maid said, "May I tell her who is calling?" or a child said, "Who is this, please?" But with the widespread use of the phone today, and the variety of reasons for calls, a slight warning is often very helpful to the person being called. For example: Mrs. Franklin is upstairs when the telephone, which is downstairs, rings. It is the president of her club, asking how many people have accepted the invitation for the Christmas dance. If her daughter, who answers, doesn't get the caller's name, Mrs. Franklin runs down, answers, runs back up to her desk to get her lists, and back down again. If her daughter had said, "Mom, it's Mrs. Harrison for you," Mrs. Franklin would have taken the lists down the first time.

So, if it sometimes seems a little rude to ask the caller's identity, it stems from the caller's rudeness in not identifying himself.

When a child is alone in the house, it is not a matter of courtesy—it is a matter of safety. Many calls are made just to find out whether a house is empty, or whether there is an adult at home. If the child who answers does not recognize the voice that asks for "Mr. Householder," she (or he) *must* say, "Who is this, please?" Then, if the name is unfamiliar and the caller does not further identify himself, she does *not* say, "He's not home." She says instead, "He's busy just now" or "He's not available just now—may he return your call?" "Not available" is an excellent excuse for a child to give when his parents are out because it is true and yet it *implies* that they are there but can't come to the phone for the moment. Under no circumstances should children ever admit that they are alone in the house.

Invitations by Telephone

There are no rules about what you say to a friend when you call to invite him or her to a party, but there are a couple of things you should consider. You should never start out by saying, "Hi, Mary. What are you doing Saturday night?" or "Are you busy Sunday afternoon?" This maneuver puts Mary in the embarrassing position of saying "Nothing" and then not being able to refuse after being told that she is being asked to dine with the Borings or to play golf with the Shanks. On the other hand, if she answers, "I have an engagement," and is then told that she would have been invited to something she likes very much, it is disappointing to be unable to go. A young woman who says she "is busy" and is then told, "Too bad you can't come, because John Brilliant was looking forward to meeting you," cannot change her mind and say, "Oh, then I'll get out of my dinner somehow and come." To do so would be thoroughly rude to everyone concerned.

Therefore when issuing a telephone invitation, start right out with it: "Hi, Mary, we're having a few people in Saturday night for dinner and bridge. Can you and Hank come?" Mary is free to accept, knowing it is just what she would enjoy Saturday night, or to say, "I'm so sorry but we are busy Saturday," if she hates to play bridge.

In responding to a telephone invitation, it is very rude to say, "I'll let you know," unless it is immediately followed by an explanation, such as "I'll have to ask John if he has made any commitments for that weekend" or "We have tickets for the high-school play for that night, but perhaps I can exchange them for two on Friday." Without this definite sort of reason, "I'll let you know" sounds as though you are waiting for a better invitation to come along before saying "Yes."

Four Important Don'ts

When you get a wrong number, don't ask, "What number is this?" Ask instead, "Is this 555-3456?" so that you can look it up again or dial more carefully the next time.

Don't answer and then say, "Wait a minute," and keep the caller waiting while you vanish on an errand of your own. If the doorbell is ringing and you can't listen at that moment, say, "I'll call you back in a few minutes!" And do so.

Don't let too young a child answer the telephone. A lot of the caller's time is wasted trying to make the child understand a message and relay it to the right person. If there is a long silence, there is no way of knowing whether the child is hunting for Mother or playing with his dog.

Don't hang up before letting the telephone ring at least six times. Nothing is more irritating than to rush down from the attic or out of the bathtub to answer and find that the caller has hung up.

Terminating Telephone Calls

Under ordinary circumstances the person who originates the call is the one who terminates it. This is not a matter of great importance, but it is helpful to know if a call seems to be dragging on and getting nowhere. The caller simply says, "I'm so glad I reached you—we'll be looking forward to seeing you on the seventh. Good-bye," or any other appropriate remark.

The person who places the call is also the one who calls again when you are cut off in the middle of a conversation.

We have all been trapped on the telephone by a long-winded caller—a determined salesman, perhaps, or a loquacious friend. When you have made several tentative efforts to end the conversation, which have been completely ignored, you may take more aggressive measures. At the first pause, or even interrupting if necessary, you may say, "I'm terribly sorry, but I simply must hang up—the baby's crying," or "My bath is running over," or even "I'm late for an appointment now."

Another occasion on which a call should be terminated quickly is when the person who receives it has a visitor—either in a business office or at home. It is very inconsiderate to carry on a long chat while your visitor tries to occupy the time and avoid listening to your conversation. When you answer the phone and find it is not a call that can be terminated in a moment or two, you should postpone it for a more convenient time. At home you might say, "Joan just dropped in for a visit, so may I call you back in a little while?" The businessman could say, "I have a customer with me at the moment. If you will give me your number, I'll call you back when I am free."

In either case be sure that you do return the call as soon as you can.

On the other hand, if you are making a call that you know will take a considerable time, or if you want to settle down for a nice long chat, it is a good idea to say to your friend, "Is this a good time to call?" or "Have you a few minutes to chat?" If more people did this there would be fewer complaints about the "nuisance" and "invasion of privacy" of telephone calls.

Long-Distance Calls

When making a long-distance call, remember not to shout—amplifiers on the circuits will step up your voice all the way. On some overseas calls, it is also important to wait for the other person to finish speaking before you start. It can be a one-way-at-a-time circuit, and if both speak at once, both are shut off until one or the other stops talking.

Keep on the tip of your tongue what you have to say, and say it promptly. If you have several things to say, write them down and read them off.

If you call long distance often, a telephone timer is a must. It is a small second-counting gadget that rings a bell before each three minutes. If you are making a personal call and the person on the other end of the line likes to talk on and on, when you put in your call you may ask the operator to interrupt when the three minutes are up. But in these days of direct dialing, you will do well to have a timer—even a three-minute egg timer—at hand, for you may never have a chance to speak to the operator.

On a Party Line

The usual number of families sharing a party line is four, and the maximum ten. When you realize that while one person is talking no outside call can reach any other person on that line, it is obvious that each one must show consideration for the others.

Ordinarily, when you find the line in use, you hang up for three minutes before signaling again. In an emergency it is permissible to break in on a conversation and call out clearly, *"Emergency!"* and then, "Our barn is on fire," or "Johnny's had an accident," or whatever it is. But unless everyone on the line hangs up, your telephone is cut off.

Callers on a party line should limit their calls to five minutes—ten at the very most.

During the Persian Gulf War a soldier wanted to say a few last words to his wife just before his plane took off for Saudi Arabia. For fifty minutes the long-distance operator repeatedly received a "busy-wire" signal. At the last moment he remembered that while the operator is not permitted to cut in on a busy wire, her supervisor can. He quickly asked for the supervisor and briefly explained the situation to her. Calling it an "emergency" she cut in, announced a long-distance call for Mrs. Soldier, and asked those talking to hang up, please, so that she could receive it.

Obscene Calls

The best way to handle the occasional obscene call is to hang up immediately. Don't give the caller the satisfaction of hearing you become upset, or even respond-

ing. If, as sometimes happens, the call is repeated as soon as you hang up, leave the
receiver off the hook for a little while. If the caller is a youngster looking for a laugh, or a random-number-picking pervert, he will soon give up when he keeps hearing the busy signal.

If you are subjected to such calls regularly, you should, of course, notify the telephone company. They can, and will in serious cases, try to trace the calls.

There is also another effective remedy that will discourage the occasional caller. Keep an ordinary police whistle by the phone, and as soon as you hear the first obscene word, blow a hard blast right into your speaker. That caller will drop you from his list of victims there and then.

Paying for Your Calls

On a Neighbor's Telephone

Today almost everyone has his or her own telephone, but sometimes, especially in resort areas, there are people who become embarrassing and expensive nuisances by using a neighbor's telephone over and over again.

For an occasional local call, you might let it go; but for a telephone borrower who makes many long-distance calls, it is simplest as well as most accurate to show the toll list inserted in the telephone bill to the one who made these calls and ask that he or she pay for them. Local calls that are charged for individually will also be listed on the bill and should be shown to the person who made them, if you wish payment for these also.

Try to avoid making calls from a busy doctor's (or other) office, but if you must do so, pay the nurse for the call or use a telephone credit card.

By Visitors and Houseguests

Many visitors forget to offer to pay for their calls. The definite rule is this: Should a houseguest be obliged to make a local call or two, he or she would not ordinarily offer payment for it, but it is absolutely required that every long-distance call be paid for. Moreover, this is the only way in which a houseguest can feel free to telephone as often as he or she may want to. One way the guest can pay is to call the operator as soon as the call is finished and ask for "the toll charge on 212-555-9121." The necessary amount should be left with a slip, giving the date and the number called. If it is a substantial amount, the tax should be added. Or if a visitor has used the telephone a great deal during a long stay, the complete list of calls or telegrams with the amounts of each and their total should be handed to the host or hostess and paid for when the houseguest leaves. This is not humiliating, and no matter how rich the host may be, this debt must be paid.

A very satisfactory way to pay for a call is to charge it to your own home number. This may be done even though you do not have a telephone company credit card. The operator may or may not call your home and ask whoever is there to accept the charge. You must, of course, warn those at home in advance in case an operator does. This system saves you the annoyance of finding correct change or cash to pay your hostess, and saves her the inconvenience of a larger bill. Occasionally if the operator calls your home and finds no one there to approve the charge she will refuse to accept your home phone number as a guarantee, so, if you have a telephone credit card, by all means use that.

One additional note about houseguests: They should not answer the phone while visiting unless they say, "Would you like me to answer?" or the hostess says, "I'm in the tub—would you take that call, Sue?"

Call Forwarding

Call forwarding is a good way to be "reachable" when you are away from home. By having your calls forwarded to the place you will be, you are sure of being accessible to family members—especially important to parents of teens who may be out and need assistance. It is not polite, however, to assume it is all right with your host or hostess to have your calls directed to their home. Before automatically forwarding your calls, check with your host and make sure he doesn't mind—for in addition to a teen calling in need of a ride or help, everyone else calling you will be rung through to your host's telephone number. And it is your host, not you, who will be answering the telephone each time it rings.

When you do receive calls at someone else's home, keep them brief and to the point. It is discourteous to tie up someone else's telephone with your lengthy conversations.

Telephone Answering Machines at Home

A great convenience is an answering machine—it enables the caller to leave a brief message and lets the owner of the machine know who is trying to reach him. The one with the machine should make every effort to make this message brief. It is extremely annoying to call someone and have to listen to the theme song from their favorite show or a long and rambling "cute" message before the beep indicates they may leave their message. It can be costly to someone calling long distance, and is certainly an aggravation to everyone.

Simply record words to the effect of: "You have reached the Browns." (or, if you prefer not to give your name, then state your telephone number—"You have reached 818-555-3487"). "Please leave your name, number and message at the sound of the tone and we will get back to you as soon as we can. Thank you." There is no need to say "we aren't home right now" or "we can't come to the phone right now." This is obvious.

The one obligation attached to using an answering machine is that you indeed return calls when messages are left.

The person calling should be equally brief even on machines that have limitless time for messages to be left, as the recipient does not want to hear an unlimited message. State your name, the day and time you called, and your message and leave your telephone number if you need to be called back.

Many people become inhibited when confronted with a machine. No need to be. If you simply say, "Hi, Mary, this is Joan. It's 10 A.M. on Tuesday. Tonight's meeting has been postponed to next Tuesday, 8 P.M. at the community center. Call me if you can't make it—555-3946. Thanks." "Joe, it's Harry. Nothing urgent—give me a call when you have a few minutes to talk. Thanks!" It is not necessary to say "Good-bye" or sign off. "Thanks" is sufficient. When you are calling someone you don't know, state your message clearly and succinctly. "Mrs. Brown, this is Jeremy Hawthorne. I'm a friend of Betty Johnston's. Betty recommended that I call in reference to the recycling committee you are forming. I'd be delighted to join. My telephone number is 555-4978. The best time to reach me is after 6 P.M. I look forward to speaking to you."

Call Waiting

As convenient as it is to have call waiting, it is also an intrusion on the call you are on. Unless you are expecting an urgent call and say so, it is impolite to continually put someone on hold while you answer another call. This is particularly true when you have made the call in the first place.

When a call is waiting on your line, you hear the beep. The person to whom you are speaking may hear a momentary interruption and is aware you have another call waiting. If he says, "I hear you have another call—go ahead and answer, I'll wait," you should feel free to do so. Otherwise say, "I have another call, can you hold just a second? Take the second call, explain you are on another line and that you will call back shortly. Then go to your first caller, quickly finish the conversation and return the second call.

If you are expecting an important call and someone else calls, say immediately, "Kathy, hello. I'd love to talk, but I may have to interrupt you—I'm waiting for a call from the pediatrician (plumber, John, the children, etc.). This way, Kathy is fore-warned and does not take it personally that you must put her on hold or terminate your conversation abruptly.

Beepers

Many professional people wear beepers at all times, including during social events, because they truly must be constantly accessible. These people include a doctor on call, a supervisor, a parent who has a child with a serious medical condition, etc. Although there may be a few who wear beepers because it helps them feel important, most people who wear them really must. When their beepers ring, they must find the nearest telephone and respond, whether in the middle of the second aria at the opera, or a formal dinner party. Those with them should not criticize or impede their attempt to respond quickly to a call, nor should they be offended if the one with the beeper must immediately excuse him- or herself and make a call.

Those wearing beepers should turn them off instantly when in the company of others, since the insistent tone can be irritating. They should then excuse themselves, explain that they must make a call in response to the beeper, and do so. There is no need, upon returning to the group, to explain the nature of the call unless it is necessary to leave. In this case, a simple, "I'm so sorry, there's an emergency at the office," or "Forgive me, Georgia, I feel terrible leaving in the middle of dinner, but I have a sick patient being transported to the hospital," is courteous.

If you indeed are called away and have escorted another to a social event, it is important to make sure he or she is able to wait for your return and if not, that you arrange for other transportation.

BUSINESS CALLS

Telephone manners may make or break a business deal. They begin with answering the call. If central operators process incoming calls, they should be trained to speak pleasantly, giving the company name: "Packer Industries, good morning." When assistants or secretaries answer, they give their employer's name: "Miss White's office [or Betty White's office]. May I help you?" If people answer their phones directly, they need only identify themselves: "Hello. This is Betty White."

The caller responds to the central operator with a simple, "May I please have Miss White's line?" To the secretary, however, she identifies herself: "Hello. This is Mildred Pearlman. Is Miss White in?" If the executive answers her own phone, the caller may need to identify herself more fully: "Hello, Miss White. This is Mildred Pearlman. I'm with the Ogilvie Company."

If a caller fails to identify herself to a secretary, he or she will be asked, "May I ask who is calling please?" Because it is often possible for a secretary or assistant to help the caller, he or she may correctly ask, "May I ask what this call is in reference to?" or less bluntly, "Will Miss White know what this call is about?"

When you call and are asked to state your business, do not be disgruntled: the secretary is merely trying to speed up service. Also, do not be evasive: you will create ill will. Do not say you are calling on a personal matter unless you truly are: pretense will not endear you to the boss even if it does get you through.

When an executive is not in to receive your phone call, the secretary can prevent feelings of rejection or disappointment in handling the situation. A curt "She's not in" only alienates. Rather let the secretary say, "I'm terribly sorry, Ms

Pearlman, but Miss White is away from the office right now. Is there something I can do? Or may I ask her to call you when she returns?"

On the occasions when the executive is too busy to speak to the caller, the assistant's courteous manner plays an even more important role. Honesty is the best policy, for a false "She's not in" is always suspect. The assistant should explain the situation first: "Miss White is in, Ms Pearlman, but she is in a meeting and can't be interrupted right now." Then the assistant should go on to offer an alternative: "May I help you? Or is there someone else you could speak to?" If replies to both questions are negative, she may conclude with, "I'll ask Miss White to call you as soon as she is free, but as she has meetings scheduled all day, it may not be until tomorrow."

Office Telephone Etiquette

Avoid lengthy personal phone calls in the office. While personal messages are at times unavoidable, both to make and to receive, long chatty conversations are not only out of place, but also wasteful of time that belongs to the company, not to the employee. Telephone chatter annoys other people in the office who cannot help overhearing and interrupts the routine of office procedure.

Handling the Difficult Caller

Since not all callers are as polite as you wish they were, some pose especially difficult problems which require careful handling:

- *The caller who insists on speaking only with the boss.* You can take this tack: "As I told you, Miss Rogers cannot come to the phone now. I'll be happy to take a message, or if you tell me what you wish to discuss with her, I'll ask her to call you back." Or: "I'm sorry, but Miss Rogers does not speak with people unknown to her until she is aware of the purpose of their call."
- *The caller with a request above and beyond the normal,* asking for an employee's home phone number, for instance. You should explain, "I am sorry, but I am not privileged to give you that information. Perhaps you could phone her here at her office tomorrow." Whatever the request is, do not be coerced into complying with it.
- *The caller referred to you whom you would rather not see or speak to.* Rather than create an issue, you will find it easier to say, "I expect to be terribly busy for the next few weeks and really will not have time. If you leave your number, I'll try to get back to you after that." The postponement may end the matter. However, if the caller is persistent, you may have to see him if you feel obligated to the person who referred him; or if you do not, you may cut him off with, "I really haven't time to see you."
- *The hostile caller.* No matter how unfounded his anger, you will want to try

to calm him. You might say, "I am terribly sorry if I have done something to make you angry, but I really cannot help you further in this matter." In the case of service businesses, hostile calls are an everyday occurrence. The best way to handle them is, "I understand how you feel, and I apologize for the inconvenience. We will do whatever we can to rectify the matter."

"Who Gets There Last?"

There is a game played by executives of both sexes that might be called "Who Gets There Last?" One asks his secretary to put through a call to another, whose secretary answers. The latter may say, "Mr. Jones is on another line. He'll be free in a minute or two." The executive whose secretary maneuvers the other executive onto the line first so that his own secretary may say, "Just a moment, I'll put Mr. Black on the line," wins. Let it be known that only the most insecure of executives play this game, for use of the telephone to assert authority is evidence of very little authority. The more important the executives, the more likely they are to bypass secretaries and put through their own telephone calls.

ELECTRONIC ANSWERING SYSTEMS

More and more businesses today are cutting back staff positions and installing computerized systems that answer calls electronically. The voice you hear has been recorded and will not answer your questions. It will run through a list of instructions, giving you various numbers to push to reach different departments or people. Eventually, it will instruct you to push "0" for the operator if you need assistance or it will connect you with a machine which will record your message. There is little that can be done about the frustration of these systems except to listen carefully. One of the most annoying aspects is when, after spending at least two minutes pushing numbers to try to reach the person you are calling, you receive a busy signal. The best advice I can offer is to make notes when you initially place the call so that if this happens you can directly bypass the system and push the numbers for the person you are calling when you place the call again. Taking out your annoyance on the person you are calling is fairly worthless, since it is likely he or she had nothing to do with installation of the system in the first place and all you achieve is to begin your call on a hostile note.

PUBLIC TELEPHONES

When you are the caller, be courteous. This is not the time to stack up a pile of quarters and chat with your friends while you wait for an appointment, particularly when there is a line of people behind you waiting to make calls, too. Conduct your business and hang up. If you have a string of calls to make and someone is waiting anxiously to place a call, it is thoughtful to ask her if her call is urgent and short and if so, if she would like to place it, since you have several more calls to make. This is particularly thoughtful for salespeople whose offices are public telephone booths and who are the worst offenders when they make call after call, confirming and lining up appointments for the day.

When you are the person in line, it is not polite to hover over someone on the telephone. Stand enough of a distance away that you are not in earshot of his conversation. If you are so close that you can hear what he is saying, simply pretend that you can't and make an effort not to eavesdrop.

If you have a true emergency and are waiting for the telephone behind someone who is going on and on and there are no other pay phones in sight, you may signal to her and state your urgency. She is not obligated to disconnect her call, but should she be willing, it is incumbent upon you to be as quick as possible and return the use of the phone to her.

CELLULAR PHONES

Another convenience to salespeople or others who are on the road a good deal of the time are car phones. There are really only two points of etiquette for users: First, each call is expensive and is charged to the owner, so they should not be used just for fun. Second, I have seldom seen anyone use one when a third party didn't inadvertently cut in. By the nature of the system you are not using telephone lines— you are broadcasting, they are not to be considered private, and should never be used for private or confidential conversations (no telephones should—crossed wires are not uncommon at any time).

V

TRAVEL & TIPPING

*T*here are some people who find it so pleasant to make plans for a trip that they truly consider the preliminaries "half the fun." But to the joys of poring over maps and collecting suggestions from your friends must be added certain practical preparations without which travel can be a nightmare instead of an exciting adventure. Dream of castles in Spain if you will, but don't forget that you may well be footsore and weary by the time you have actually toured your first one. Comfortable shoes, a good dinner, and a decent bed may make all the difference in your enthusiasm for the next day's expedition.

If you want to get the most out of your travels, read as much as you possibly can, in advance, about the places you plan to visit. Carry travel books and stories with you, too. A diary written by someone who has taken the same trip is invaluable. Ask friends who have been there to give you tips—about what to see, names of guides, places to stay, or clothes to wear.

16
Travel for Pleasure and Business

PRE-TRIP SCHEDULE

When you have spent months or even years planning the trip of your life you certainly don't want anything to go wrong. If you make your plans far enough ahead and implement them on a specific schedule, you will not forget anything and your day of departure will find you "calm, cool, and collected." Here is a suggested schedule leading up to a trip abroad.

At Least Four Weeks Ahead

Make your travel reservations or go to a travel agency and enlist their services.

Apply for your passport if you do not have one. You can get the application blanks at most local post offices. It generally takes ten days to two weeks after your application is sent in for the passport to arrive. At peak vacation seasons it may take longer.

If you are going to a country where a visa is required, you must apply at that country's consulate as soon as you have your passport. It is not necessary—legally—to get shots for some European countries, but many people take the precaution regardless. It is good insurance to be sure that your tetanus shot is up to date, and smallpox vaccinations and yellow-fever shots are required before returning to the United States from many areas. Hepatitis shots are a good idea, but since they do not last long the shot should be given just before leaving.

Three Weeks Ahead

Make sure that your insurance is up to date and take out trip insurance if you wish to.

Get your wardrobe together and be sure that all your clothing is clean, no buttons are missing, etc.

Get your camera equipment ready. Buy new batteries for your camera. You can buy film all over the world, but sometimes they are out of the type you want, so take a supply with you.

Apply to the AAA for an international driver's license if you plan to rent a car in Europe. It is not required in all countries—your American license is accepted— but it is a good thing to have in case your plans change and you go someplace where the American license is not accepted.

Be sure that you have the luggage that you will need and that it is in reasonably good shape. If you intend to bring back a number of gifts or other purchases, you may want to take an empty canvas bag that can be folded into one of your suitcases.

Two Weeks Ahead

Get your "medical kit" together. Be sure you have a supply of the headache pills, laxatives, special prescriptions, and "travelers' tummy" remedies that work best for you. Put your pills and liquids in plastic, rather than glass, containers.

Have your eyeglasses checked and be sure to take an extra pair. Get a good pair of sunglasses if you don't have one.

Make up an itinerary of your trip to be left with your parents, your children, or anyone who might want to be able to reach you.

If you have a strong preference for certain brands of soap, cosmetics, shaving blades or lotions, etc., stock up on them now and put them with your luggage.

One Week Ahead

Cancel all deliveries and put your valuables in a safe-deposit box or other safe place. Be sure some responsible person knows what steps you have taken.

Arrange for a cab, a driver, a friend, or whatever means you will use to get to the airport. Remember to make plans for getting *back* from the airport, too. Your travel agency will know about bus or limousine service in your area.

Pack your bags—heavier articles on the bottom and lighter on top. Put breakables between layers of clothing in the center.

Get your traveler's checks and some cash in the currency of the country where you will land. Fifty dollars should be more than enough to take care of any immediate expenses—taxis, tips, etc.

311
TRAVEL
FOR
PLEASURE
AND
BUSINESS

Reservations

Using a Travel Agency

By far the easiest way to plan your trip is to go to a travel agency. Tell the agency just where you want to go and when and how—in fact give all the details you can and let them work out the best possible plan for you. This is their business, and they can do it better and more economically than you can. There is no extra cost to you, as they get their commission from the transportation company, the resort, or the hotel. A competent travel agency can of course arrange the most elaborate accommodations—from the best rooms in deluxe hotels to automobiles with chauffeurs. With equal interest the same travel agency will provide the equivalent degree of quality to those traveling on a limited budget.

Making Your Own Reservations

With virtually every hotel, motel, inn and bed and breakfast equipped with toll-free telephone numbers and FAX communication and with the variety of travel books available, you needn't use a travel agent to establish your itinerary. In fact, if you are an independent type you may not wish to use a travel agency. But, if your schedule takes you off the beaten track or to unusual destinations you may have no choice but to write for reservations. When this is the case start well in advance. If you are refused at the first hotels or inns you write to, you may have to wait days or even weeks before you have word from your alternate choice. It is not unreasonable to make the arrangements for a trip to a popular area six months or more ahead of time. The reservations *must* be reconfirmed a week or two before your departure. When you phone for reservations get the name of the reservation agent who handled your call and the confirmation or reservation number assigned to you. When you write for reservations it is also absolutely essential to request a receipt or acknowledgment (and don't forget to carry it with you) to be shown on your arrival. It is all too easy for a careless innkeeper or hotel manager to fill up the rooms with earlier arrivals and tell you cheerfully when you arrive, hot and exhausted, "But we have no record of your letter!"

Your travel reservations should be made at the same time as those for hotel rooms, and don't neglect your homebound ticket. With a little forethought you can plan your return date as definitely as that of your departure and thus prevent a last-minute case of jitters and impatience that could ruin your whole trip.

A tip to parents: When your son or daughter sets off for a summer of traveling, possibly with no more than a backpack and no planned stopping places other than a list of youth hostels (inexpensive lodgings for bicyclists and motorcyclists found in almost every country), be sure that he or she has a return reservation, either with him or held at the airline office. It is all too easy for a youngster to cable home: UNABLE TO GET SPACE UNTIL SEPTEMBER 15—three weeks longer than you had expected to finance this trip!

Travel Documents

Several weeks before your departure you should apply for your passport, visas if they are required, and health certificates. If you already have them, make sure that they are still valid and in good order. These matters have to be attended to in person, although after you have filled out the forms and paid the fee at the passport or local post office, your passport will be sent to you by mail. Your doctor will tell you where to get official health forms if he does not have them. You may have to go in person to the consulate of the country from which you wish to get a visitor's permit or visa. Everything else can be done for you; and if you are obliged to go on a suddenly planned trip a great deal of valuable time can be saved by having an experienced agent make your reservations and deliver your tickets to you.

It is advisable to get some foreign money in small bills and change to have in your hand when you land. However, it is unwise to get too much cash as it can be both costly and inconvenient to change it back into U.S. dollars when you leave the country. There are restrictions as to the amount you are permitted to take in or out of some countries, and these should be checked before you leave. It is also very important to take the bulk of your money in traveler's checks, which can be replaced if lost and are accepted everywhere as readily as cash. Major credit cards are accepted more readily than travelers checks in many European stores but it is wise to carry both checks and cards as one or the other will always be accepted.

TRAVELING WITH CHILDREN

Traveling with children who are old enough to read, write, or play games need not be a problem. By taking along a supply of papers, crayons, or one of the excellent game books that are sold just for the purpose, the time can be made to fly. Verbal games, too, such as "Twenty Questions," help to pass the hours.

When traveling by car, one way to reduce the number of times "Are we there yet?" is asked is to say at the onset, "We have several hours of driving, and I will tell you when we are half-way there, and then when we are almost there so you don't have to ask me."

When traveling on public transportation, having games and diversions on hand is just as important, since it is unreasonable to expect children, especially small ones, to be able to sit still for long periods of time. It is up to you to keep watch over them, however, and not let them roam by themselves or make excessive amounts of noise. Fellow passengers have paid for their travel tickets and even those who love children can learn to hate them quickly when trapped in a train or airplane with those who are ill-behaved.

313
TRAVEL
FOR
PLEASURE
AND
BUSINESS

On cruise ships there are usually activities for children. Although it is a break for parents to be able to send their children off to participate and have some time alone, your expectations of their continued good behavior should be made clear—cruise line personnel are not hired to be disciplinarians or intermediaries in children's squabbles. Children should not be permitted to race through corridors or to be unsupervised, no matter how much you enjoy relaxing in your deck chair without them nearby. As Robert Benchley wrote, "There are two ways to travel—first class or with children." It would be unfortunate if your children were the cause of other's feelings that they were also traveling "with children"—yours—because of their intrusion through constant noise, bickering, or untrammeled behavior.

More and more frequently, children are sent to travel unaccompanied by an adult, whether to visit a non-custodial parent, or to travel to a grandparent. Many parents expect that a flight attendant or train steward will take care of their children when they send them off alone. This is an unreasonable expectation. Travel attendants have specific jobs to do, and these do not include child care. For that reason each airline has established a minimum age for unaccompanied children. As long as that regulation is respected, there is no reason that children who are emotionally stable and unafraid should not travel by themselves. In my experience with our grandchildren, the airlines have done an excellent job of caring for them and the children have enjoyed it thoroughly. Of course, if it is not possible for a parent to accompany a very young child, then another adult should be hired as a traveling companion.

When an older child is sent on a trip alone, he or she should be told what to do and what not to do during the trip, and be given instructions for her arrival in the event that the person meeting her is not there. Unless a child has been checked in as an unaccompanied child, it cannot be assumed that a flight attendant will be able to provide companionship for a older child waiting for someone to meet him, nor should it be expected.

TRAVELING WITH OTHERS

Some couples feel that they can never travel with anyone else—that companions would necessarily curtail their freedom to do what they please or that there would be too many different interests to have all of them satisfied.

Personally, my husband and I find that traveling with another couple, at least occasionally, is stimulating. You do more things than you probably would by yourselves, you get a more varied viewpoint about the places you visit, and even the most devoted couples get a little tired of nobody's company but their own from time to time.

You *must*, however, choose your companions carefully. If you like to be up and out on the sightseeing bus by 8:00 A.M., don't travel with people who sleep until noon. If you prefer picnics in the country and simple country inns, don't go with a couple whose idea of heaven is a nightclub in Paris. Be sure that your interests and your life-styles are reasonably similar. In the case of very close friends these differences might be overlooked, but only if each is prepared to compromise, or to go their own way and meet only at specified times.

When you are traveling with another couple, there is invariably a problem with expenses. Hotel bills and travel fares can be paid individually of course, but restaurant and bar bills—and food bills if you are doing your own cooking—are more complicated. The ideal solution is a "kitty." Each couple puts in the same amount of money at the beginning of the trip and replenishes the kitty with equal amounts whenever it is necessary. All food and liquor bills (or whatever has been agreed upon) are paid for from the kitty, and whatever is left over is divided evenly at the end of the trip.

TRAVELING ALONE

Often people hesitate to travel alone because they worry that they might become the victims of others' interference. A well-intentioned, "Are you alone? Why don't you join us?" or even personal comments such as, "Too bad you don't have any friends who could travel with you," cause many to stay at home with the door locked instead of adventuring out to take advantage of the vast world around us. Should this occur and should you not wish to become instant friends with fellow travelers, a friendly smile and quiet, "Thank you, but I'm enjoying this break and need some time just to be by myself" serves to deter all but the most insistent. If someone does persist, a firm, "No, thank you. I appreciate your offer but I really prefer to be by myself right now," should do the trick. Of course if you would enjoy a tour or a meal with others, by all means accept the offer.

Dining alone needn't be uncomfortable nor should you feel you should stick with room service and avoid the dining room. Many travelers are solo and maitre d's are used to finding tables for one. If you need something to look at and the restaurant isn't dim, take a book. In some restaurants, a maitre d' might ask you if you would mind being seated with another single traveler. If you mind, say so. If you don't, you will have to engage in some conversation but you needn't feel obligated to become an instant hostess or to share the story of your life. Your checks, in this case, would be presented separately, and neither of you need wait for the other to finish.

HOTELS

At most hotels, a doorman opens the door of your car or taxi and removes your luggage to a luggage cart. If it is your own car, or if it is a rented car, he will also make arrangements to have your car parked in the hotel garage or lot. Since he is not the one who will transport your bags to your room, he should be tipped at the time of his service. For advice on tipping all hotel personnel, see pages 341–343.

To register, go to the registration desk and say "I am Mrs. George Smith. You have a reservation for me and my daughter." If the desk clerk does not find a record of your reservation at once, present your confirmation. He or she is then obliged to give you a room, or if there has been such an error made that the hotel is completely full, the desk clerk will try to find you a room in a hotel of equal quality.

Hopefully, however, your reservation is in order and you will be given a form to sign and asked for a credit card or cash deposit. In most European hotels and many first-class American hotels service is included in the bill. This means that you do not need to tip bellhops, maids, waiters, etc. If there is no sign or mention about this it is wise to inquire when you register. In any case, the desk clerk is not to be tipped.

A man registers as "John Smith, New York." He does not use "Mr." if he is alone, but with his wife he adds the title to their joint names: "Mr. and Mrs. John Smith, New York." If he is accompanied by his entire family "John Smith and Family" is acceptable. Other members of your traveling party such as a nanny, or those with a different name should be listed separately so that they may receive mail or messages.

If Mrs. Smith arrives first, she fills in the blank for both herself and her husband. When Mr. Smith arrives he says to the room clerk, "I think Mrs. Smith has already arrived and registered. What is the number of our room, please?"

As soon as you have registered, the clerk hands the key to a bellman who collects your bags from the doorman and goes to the elevators. You follow. In your room, the bellman puts down your bags, turns on the lights, and demonstrates any features of the room, such as air conditioning, the television, the bar or refrigerator, etc. In some instances, the desk clerk will give you the key directly with instruction that a bellman will deliver your bags shortly. In either case, the bellman is tipped, unless service is included in the bill.

Service

Any service that you require is requested by telephone. You tell the operator if you wish to be called at a certain time or ring the desk if you want to inquire about mail. You call the porter's desk if you have any inquiries about luggage or transportation or reservations. You call room service when you want food or drinks sent up to you, and valet or maid service if you need a dress or suit cleaned or pressed.

If you want breakfast in your room you call room service and order it—this may be done the evening before, or you can call when you awaken. Most hotels have breakfast menus in each room, and you may choose from them. Presently the waiter brings in a cart with your order on a tray, which he sets down wherever there is space. It should be completely set: damask cloth, china, glass, silverware, thermos pitchers, and possibly plate covers to keep the food hot.

It is entirely proper to open the door for the waiter, dressed in a bathrobe. He is used to carrying breakfast trays into the presence of all varieties of pajamas and negligees, and it is not necessary for even the most old-fashioned woman to be completely dressed to receive him.

After the waiter has arranged the breakfast and removed the covers from the dishes you sign the check and give it to him with a tip amounting to approximately 15 percent of the total. Most hotels will include an additional amount as a room-service charge, but this does not take the place of the normal tip to the waiter. If you wish, you may wheel the serving cart or place the tray outside your door when you have finished in order to give yourself more space in a small room and to avoid being disturbed when the waiter returns for it.

You telephone maid service to have your clothes washed unless, as is often the case, there is a bag or receptacle marked for laundry in the bathroom. Pressing is done by the regular valet or maid, but in a small hotel a woman's dress as well as a man's suit may be sent to a cleaner. If there is no regular valet service, you ask a chambermaid, "Where can I have my dress [or suit] pressed?" She answers, "I will do it for you," or tells you who will.

In many hotels there are bars and refrigerators in guest rooms. These are stocked daily and an inventory taken of what you have removed. These items are added to your bill and are paid for when you check out. If you make use of these services, a tip is left for the employee whose job it is to replenish what you use.

Some hotels have swimming pools and health "clubs." Often there is a fee for using these services. Ask the desk clerk when you register what the arrangements are. If you do use these facilities, it is generally requested that you do not take your room towels from the room. Towels are provided at the pool or exercise room for the use of guests. When going for a swim, it is expected that you will wear at least a long shirt over your swimming suit and not parade through the halls clad only in swim wear and bare feet.

Pilferage

An inexplicable urge seems to come over many otherwise decent, honest citizens when they are guests in a hotel. This is the urge to pilfer—to help themselves to articles that can be hidden away in luggage—exactly as if such things were put out as gifts to the guests from the management! Bath towels with the hotel's name on them, ashtrays, writing paper, dining-room silver, and even bed linen disappear in such quantities as to be a major expense in every large hotel. These pilferers, when accused of stealing, say, "Not at all—the management expects these things to disappear!" How any normal law-abiding person can thus excuse what is technically petty theft I cannot understand. All I can suggest is that the next time you, or anyone traveling with you, is tempted to take home such a souvenir, say to yourself or to them, "That ashtray is hotel property; if I take it home with me it will have to be replaced, and I am no better than a common thief." There is an exception: the small bottles of shampoo, bath oil, conditioner and shower cap that are found in the bathrooms of all first-class hotels and motels are there for the guests use and may be used while in the hotel or taken home if you wish.

Many hotels now offer items for sale. Terry bathrobes and hair dryers provided for guest convenience, for example, may be purchased. A form is left in each room for guests to check what they would like to buy and if they should simply decide to take the item instead, the charge for it is added to their bill. This practice has cut pilferage from hotels considerably.

Departure

When a guest is ready to leave he or she telephones the desk clerk and requests that a bellman be sent to carry down the luggage. The guest tips the bellman, goes to the desk marked "Cashier," pays the bill, leaves the key, gives a forwarding address if he or she wishes any mail forwarded, and departs. The guest with little luggage carries his or her own bag and goes directly to the cashier when ready to check out.

Most hotels have a specific check-out time, usually before noon. If you plan to stay later than the designated time but do not wish to pay for a full extra day, check out at the required time. Usually arrangements can be made for you to store your luggage until you are ready to depart.

MOTELS

Even in foreign countries motels have sprung up like mushrooms. They are becoming more and more luxurious as the competition increases, with some of them actually serving as resort hotels. As in America, the larger ones, and those belonging to national chains, are equipped with every facility for the traveler's comfort and pleasure, including swimming pools, tennis courts, sunbathing areas, video cassette recorders and movies for rent, and individual coffeemakers in each room.

Because of the immense popularity of motels as stopping places, especially in the U.S., it is wise to make reservations in advance. If after spending a night in a motel, you choose to spend the next night in a motel of the same chain, the manager will call ahead to the member motel in or nearest your next destination to reserve a room for you. Since you usually pay for this reservation at the time it is made or guarantee it with a credit card, you need not fear that your room will not be held for you, no matter how late your arrival. The larger chains will also help you plan your trip, providing road maps and lists of restaurants, entertainments, and points of interest, as well as the location of their own or associated motels.

Dress is more casual in motels than in most hotels. Since the majority of patrons are spending only one night, they are not expected to unpack their luggage, and travel clothes are acceptable. Only in very luxurious motels are jackets and ties for men expected at dinner. However, even the most exhausted traveler will enjoy dinner more and make the atmosphere pleasanter for the other diners if he freshens up and changes into clean clothes before appearing in the dining room. Some motels provide the best dining rooms in town, and residents go there as they would to any other restaurant. It would add little to their "night out" if the transients all came in straight from a long day in the car—dirty, wrinkled, and bedraggled.

Otherwise there are few restrictions on behavior other than ordinary rules of courtesy. Don't play the radio or television too loudly or entertain until late in your room (most motel guests go to bed early to prepare for an early start or a day full of business meetings). Don't take the ashtrays or towels as souvenirs. Lock the door and turn out the lights when you leave, and keep your children from running around the halls and disturbing other travelers. Speaking of leaving, be especially careful if you are making an early departure. Don't call back and forth, don't slam the room door or the car doors, and don't race your engine or leave it warming up for a long time.

BED AND BREAKFAST

Many towns offer "Bed and Breakfast" lodging, as an alternative to other guest facilities. These are generally large, private houses with rooms provided for guests. At a bed and breakfast, guests are treated as friends, sometimes sharing a bathroom with other guests and sharing breakfast family style with the owner who often serves as cook, maid, and tour guide as well. Unless previously arranged, other meals are not provided.

Courtesy dictates that you indicate your plans for the day and that if you expect to be back late, you make arrangements for a key so that you do not need to ring or knock loudly to be let in, thus disturbing other guests and forcing your host to stay up late at night waiting for you.

In addition to your bedroom, a communal room is usually available for your use for relaxation and conversation. You should pick up after yourself and not leave shopping bags or personal items lying around. Your room will be made up, but again, personal items should not be strewn everywhere and you should make every effort to be neat and thoughtful. In a bed and breakfast where a day-worker or maid is hired to tend to guest rooms, a tip is left on the dresser. If the owner serves as jack of all trades, a tip is not expected, but, since the nature of the lodging has necessitated that you have exchanged conversation with him or her, warm thanks upon departure are.

INNS

There are many charming country inns which are neither hotel nor motel, but are more full-service than are bed and breakfast establishments. Because they tend to be converted mansions or large houses, the number of guests is less than found at hotels or motels, and the proximity of bedrooms is closer. Good manners include using "indoor voices" and keeping other noise to a minimum. If bathrooms are shared, it is expected that you will not leave hair in the sink or any other traces of your personal hygiene routine, and that you do not monopolize the bathroom for extended periods of time. Full service is provided, and workers should be tipped according to their service at the time of your departure.

EUROPEAN HOTELS

Large first-class hotels in Europe—those most frequented by tourists—are essentially the same as our best hotels in the United States. Before venturing into less well traveled areas, however, be prepared for certain differences in facilities and service. For example, a service charge is often added to the bill, so that you do not need to tip maids, porters, valets, etc. Inquire when you arrive so that you will not tip for each service that is covered.

In many European hotels all services other than your actual accommodations and meals are provided by the concierge. He corresponds to our head porter but has a much wider range of responsibility and is as important as the hotel management. He presents a separate bill, or his bill appears as a separate item on the hotel bill. The concierge and his staff handle luggage and mail, including the sale of stamps. They will make all your travel reservations for you or will arrange for car rentals. They will recommend restaurants and places of interest, purchase tickets, and make the necessary reservations or arrangements.

AIR TRAVEL

Airlines offer first-class and "other" accommodations, the "other" being called many different names, from "tourist" to "economy" to "business class," depending on the moment and the promotion being offered. The basic difference, beside the offering of more space in first-class and business class is that first-class services are free, while extras such as cocktails and movies ordered in the other class are provided for a fee and generally take a little longer to be provided.

Whichever class you use, remember that flight attendants are not slaves and should not be treated as such. With few exceptions, they are doing the best they can to provide for the needs of all travelers, and will get to you as soon as they can. They are not there to load your carry-on luggage or to carry your belongings and should not be asked to do so. Flight attendants are not tipped, but if service has been exceptional, a personal "thank you" is most welcome.

Arriving at the Airport

Because of the necessity of intense security checks, you are expected to arrive at the airport anywhere from one hour for domestic flights to two hours for overseas flights in advance of your flight time. When you arrive, your luggage, if it is to be checked through and not carried on board, is taken by a porter who will give you a claim check and either put it in line to be weighed when you check in, or it will be taken directly to the plane. In either case, the porter is tipped for his service.

Security checks of both your person and whatever you are carrying are automatic. To avoid delays or embarrassment going through security, pack any metal objects in those suitcases that will go to the baggage compartment where they will be screened. If something you are wearing or carrying does set off a detector, your own good humor is essential. The process is for your own protection, and no matter how long it takes to discover that the buttons on your jacket or your earrings are causing the problem, ill temper is ill-mannered.

While in the Air

When boarding, find your seat and sit down as quickly as possible so as not to keep those behind you waiting. During the trip the flight attendants, when not serving meals or drinks, will do their best to assist you in any way they can. You can signal them with a light that you find above your head. They will bring magazines, newspapers, extra pillows or blankets, and will help by heating bottles for babies, etc.

The same rules apply in using the washrooms or lavatories on an airplane as on any public transportation. You should leave the washstand and the room in perfect order. Wipe out the basin thoroughly and dispose of trash in the receptacle provided. Neatness is the first essential of good manners. Never leave any unpleasant trace of untidiness behind.

Make your trips to the lavatory when meals or drinks are not being served. It is impossible to pass the bar cart in the aisle, and the attendant cannot wheel it all the way to the end of the cabin to let you go by.

There are three habits that are very annoying to the people in the seats behind and in front of you. The first is dropping your seat back suddenly. You have every right to recline, but before you do, glance back and be sure that the passenger behind you is not in the middle of taking a mouthful or leaning over to pick up a newspaper. Unless his or her tray is down all the time, it is more thoughtful to wait to tip back until the tray is no longer being used. The second annoyance is slamming the tray into its latch, which jars the person in the seat in front of you. It is quite possible to turn the latch with one hand while holding the tray up with other. It is *not* necessary to slam it hard or repeatedly to make it catch. The third sinner is the person who continually bumps into your seat. There are people who cannot help squirming or swinging their feet when their knees are crossed. If you are one of them request an aisle seat. You can then at least turn your knees toward the aisle, being careful, of course, not to kick anyone passing by. You are also free to get up and release your tension by an occasional walk up and down the plane.

Other Passengers

321
TRAVEL
FOR
PLEASURE
AND
BUSINESS

Those who are willing to talk—and in a plane nearly everyone is—are entirely free to do so. On the other hand, if you wish to be left alone, you can avoid conversation with the explanation, "I'd rather not talk. I'm very tired," or by pointedly burying your nose in a book or magazine and saying no more than "Un-hunh" to conversational gambits.

Most often, conversation starts over a drink or when a meal is served. People tend to open their book or newspaper or take out their knitting or their crossword when they first settle down. But when the attendant comes with drinks or the tray, books or paperwork is laid aside, and it is a natural time to start talking. Ordinarily the conversation starts most impersonally, and generally stays that way. "Isn't this a gorgeous flight—look at those cloud formations!" or "I wonder if we'll make up the time we lost waiting to take off," are all you need to determine whether your seat mate wants to chat or not. You may or may not exchange names and information about what you do, where you are going, etc., but generally conversation is more impersonal.

If a passenger is obviously inebriated or his or her behavior is so offensive as to be ruining your trip, report him or her to the flight attendant who will take care of the situation or request the help of one of the plane's officers, if necessary. If possible, the offender will be moved to a seat where he or she will not bother anyone.

Upon arrival at your destination, obey the rules. Leaping to your feet and ignoring the "seat belt" signs to be the first one off the plane is not only dangerous, it is rude to other passengers. Your scrambling to retrieve your overhead luggage and blocking the aisle does little to speed your own departure, since you will surely be asked to resume your seat by the flight attendant, but it also inconveniences other passengers, none of whom intend to linger on the plane, either.

Private Planes

Many corporations and a few individuals have their own planes and permanent or hired flight crews. Guests on these planes should be aware that, unless one of the crew members is specifically designated as a flight attendant, the crew's only responsibility is to fly the plane. Snacks or meals are brought on board and passengers are expected to help themselves. Passengers are expected to carry their own luggage and to be neat, and the atmosphere is fairly informal. Private flight crews are used to passengers having questions, and would far rather tell you where the trash receptacle can be found than to find your crumpled papers crammed into the tape player or under the seat when they clean up upon landing—another of their responsibilities.

It is extremely inconsiderate to be late to the airport when flying in a private plane. The crew is responsible for clearing flight time and your delay can cost them hours while they wait for a second clearance, given after preference to airlines. If you are detained for any reason, you should appreciate the value of their time and call ahead to say so, giving the time you expect to arrive.

After landing, clean up any litter you have created and carry your own bags, making sure to thank the crew for the flight. No tips are given to private plane crews, but thanks are, and should be extended as well to your host when the plane is privately owned.

If you avail yourself of the services of private airline companies, the same guidelines apply, although they generally provide a flight attendant to tend to your needs.

TRAIN TRAVEL

When traveling long distance by train, a porter, when available, will take your luggage to the train. It will be placed at the end of your sleeping car and will be fairly inaccessible to you during the trip, so you should keep with you those things you need to use while in transit. The porter is to be tipped. In large cities, rates are posted by the checkroom or the porter's stand. Since there may not be porters available, it is wise to restrict your baggage to pieces that you can carry yourself.

A train porter will be assigned to your roomette. He will tell you at what times meals will be served, will make up your bunk, and will tend to any other needs you have. He is to be tipped as well, at the time of an extra service, and at the end of the trip.

When you are ready to go to bed, you ring for the porter to make up your berth, by ten or ten-thirty at the latest, since he has other duties to attend to. If you are not tired at that time, you may go to the bar or club car to socialize rather than trying to entertain in your room which becomes much smaller once the bed is made up.

Dining and club cars necessitate some conversation with other passengers since seating is usually in groupings.

On train trips when sleeping accommodations are not available, there generally are club cars on which seats may be reserved. These cars are the equivalent of first-class seats on an airplane and seating is not available to passengers with tickets for regular seats, even though they may enter the club car to purchase refreshments. Attendants on these cars serve beverages and food to club car passengers and should be tipped for their service.

Commuter Trains

Commuters on the whole are a frustrated, dissatisfied group. I don't believe I have ever, in any area of the country, heard anyone rave about the commuter train service. This general air of discontent inevitably affects their manners, and as a rule there is little communication or even consideration on the trains. It is "every man for himself" in a rush to get a window or aisle seat—or any seat at all—and women have learned not to expect any special consideration whether they want it or not.

323
TRAVEL
FOR
PLEASURE
AND
BUSINESS

However, certain unwritten rules *do* exist and should be observed.

A man should offer his seat to an elderly lady or to a pregnant one. Naturally, both men and women offer their seats to crippled people or to anyone who is obviously feeble or unwell.

Many commuter trains have three seats on one side of the aisle. "First come, first served" is the rule, and late arrivals should not expect people on the roomier aisle seat to move over to the center. The last person to arrive gets the less comfortable middle seat. He or she asks the person on the aisle politely, "Is this seat taken?" The latter replies, "No," and stands up to let the other in.

Conversation is not expected or welcomed on commuter trains. Most passengers want to read their newspapers or catch up on some work for the day ahead, or simply catch forty winks on the way home. If you do happen to be traveling with someone, or run into an old friend by chance, keep your voices low so as not to disturb those near you. In spite of the above, friendships have been formed and an occasional romance started on commuter trains. I personally know two cases where commuting couples met and courted and were subsequently married—though not on the train!

If you eat or drink on a commuter train, make every effort not to spill and do take empty bags or other containers with you when you exit. No one is pleased when the beverage left in a cup put on the floor runs under his seat as the train jolts to a stop, or when he is covered with the powdered sugar flying off your doughnut.

If you are doing work or reading a newspaper, keep your elbows down and your work or paper in your lap. Experienced and polite commuters have learned how to fold a newspaper so that only the two or three columns they are reading are opened in front of them. Thoughtless train riders hold the paper open, turning pages with vigor, so that it extends over the space of the person next to them. In these situations, I have been tempted to bat the newspaper right out of the hands of my seatmate. As much as many of us would enjoy doing this just to make a point, say instead, "Excuse me, but you are leaving me very little room. Could you please hold your paper in front of you and not in front of me?"

TRAVEL BY BUS

Coach travel by bus is an alternative to train and car travel, and carries with it the same expectation of good manners as does train travel. Although you may be sitting for hours with a seatmate, do not spend the trip chatting unless you see that he or she is interested in hearing your views on any number of topics. If the bus is equipped with a lavatory, clean up after yourself. If you are traveling with a radio or tape player, wear earphones. Do not expect that your seatmate shares your taste in music, or even wants to be surrounded by sound, no matter how much you find it helps pass the time.

Do not carry on more luggage than fits above or under your seat or you will find yourself holding it in your lap for the duration of your trip. If you are traveling with snacks, you do not need to offer anything to your seatmate, but do clean up after yourself and take only things that do not have a strong smell, and that are not likely to spill or make a mess.

Seats are not assigned, but once chosen, your seat stays yours for the trip. It is a good idea to place a magazine on the seat when you get off at rest stops to indicate that it is taken. If the bus is not crowded and there are empty seats available, you may move to another seat, but it is polite to say to your seatmate, "I'm going to move across the aisle so we both have more room" so that he does not think he has offended you in some manner which can make the rest of the trip uncomfortable for both of you.

Local bus travel carries with it the same rules as does commuter train travel. Never sit in a seat reserved for the handicapped unless you are handicapped. Give your seat to someone who is frail, handicapped, pregnant or encumbered with small children. When getting off, turn to see if the person behind you needs assistance. Don't litter, and don't take up more than the one seat you have paid for.

TAXIS

Every town has its own regulations for taxis. In New York City they are hailed on the street, or, at some transportation depots, they wait in line and receive passengers by turn. Those desiring a taxi also wait in line and it is extremely rude to push ahead or assume you are in a greater hurry than anyone else, unless you have an extreme medical emergency. In this case, you ask those in line if you may go ahead of them, explaining your situation. In Washington D.C., taxis are zoned and may refuse a passenger traveling outside their zone. In Los Angeles, taxis may not be hailed but must be requested by telephone. It is a good idea, if you are traveling to another town, to find out what system is used so that you are not left floundering, surrounded by suitcases or stranded in an unfamiliar area.

In many areas, it is the practice for passengers to share taxis. There is no need to exchange more than a smile and a nod in this case. The fare is charged per passenger, and each takes care of his or her own tip. In an instance where someone asks you if he may share your cab, you have every right to refuse, if you wish. If you don't mind and he is exiting before your stop, it is expected that he gives you, not the taxi driver, his portion of the fare and an adequate tip which you will add to yours upon arrival.

TRAVEL BY CAR

Suffice it to say that any discussion of manners and car travel is prefaced by two reminders: Always wear your seat belt and insist that any passengers do, too. Never drink and drive, and never allow anyone you know to do so either.

Courtesy is essential to safe driving. The thoughtful driver constantly is aware of how his actions will affect those behind, in front of, and beside him, and is alert to what other cars are doing as well. Because of this attitude he is a safe driver. Many men and women whose behavior in all other circumstances is beyond reproach become transformed into bad-mannered autocrats behind the wheel of a car. Even calm and considerate drivers become jittery when exposed to repeated experiences with rude motorists. These otherwise safe and well-mannered people, when impatient and irritated, often become "accidents going somewhere to happen."

On long trips it is essential to make occasional stops to stretch your legs and take some refreshment. If you are accompanied by a licensed and capable driver you should, of course, take turns at the wheel. A good rule is to stop and change drivers every hundred miles or every two hours, whichever comes first.

If you are stopping at motels along the way, it is wise to make a reservation for the following evening before you set off in the morning. Chain motels all over the United States will help you estimate the distance you will cover and call ahead, free of charge, to one of their member motels to reserve a room for that night. You will find yourself much less tired if you plan to arrive at your destination by four in the afternoon to allow time for a rest, a little sightseeing if there are attractions in the neighborhood, and a leisurely dinner.

When a young couple has an older person with them, the older person should be given the front passenger seat. This is especially true in a two-door car. The more agile younger person can climb into the back much more easily than the older one.

On short trips or when traveling to social events with another couple, the couples generally sit in a car as couples, with the driver and his or her spouse or date in the front and the other couple in the back. However, when the man of the second couple has particularly long legs, the woman of the first couple may suggest that she sit in the back so that he may be more comfortable.

Getting In and Out of a Car

The custom of a man's opening the door and assisting a woman into a car is still correct—in fact some women feel slighted if the gesture is not made. However, when the car is parked on a busy street the man should not help her in and then walk into the stream of cars to get in on the other side. In this case he excuses himself for preceding her and slides in from her side. Safety for everyone concerned is far more important than obedience to an old and impractical rule of etiquette. On a wide or lightly traveled street a man enters the car on his own side after first assisting any women into the car on the curb side. Obviously passengers in the back seats should also enter from the side nearest the curb whenever possible.

A man taking a woman on a date, or on any occasion when the woman is dressed up, gets out of the car when they arrive at their destination, goes around, opens the door, and offers the woman a hand if necessary. But on ordinary

325
TRAVEL
FOR
PLEASURE
AND
BUSINESS

occasions—a trip to the store, or the beach, or whatever, the woman opens the door and gets out by herself.

In an Emergency

If in spite of all precautions you have an emergency such as a flat tire or broken fan belt, it is not only essential to your safety but is also courteous to the other motorists to pull well off to the side of the road. Raise the hood and tie a white handkerchief or cloth to your door handle, as this is the universal signal of distress. Any policeman, and often a kindhearted passerby, will stop to offer assistance. On a superhighway stay in your car until help arrives. Walking for help on such a road is dangerous.

Car Pools

Many thousands of Americans go to work in "car pools." As a practical and economical arrangement the car pool allows the other members of their families to have the car except on those days when it is their turn to provide the transportation.

For people who are about to join a car pool there are several basic rules of courtesy to be observed.

1. Be on time! If you keep the others waiting, you may cause them to be penalized for late arrival at work.
2. Don't carry quantities of articles. If you must take a package or two, don't pile them where they will obstruct the driver's view, either directly or in the rearview mirror.
3. Don't open or close windows without asking the permission of the other passengers.
4. Don't bring an extra passenger without asking the driver if there is room. For example, some drivers do not object to three in the front seat, but others might find this a considerable annoyance.
5. Ask the permission of the other riders before smoking. When you do smoke, make sure that a window is opened, if only a little, to allow the smoke to escape.
6. Don't use the rearview mirror to fix your makeup. Carry a small mirror or a compact with a mirror in your purse.
7. If you must carry an umbrella when it rains, shake it well (and your raincoat too) before getting in the car, so that you don't soak your neighbor.
8. If you are not planning to use the car pool let the driver know in advance, so that he does not go out of his way to pick you up or wait for you unnecessarily before continuing his trip.

Seating order for a car pool is determined by logic. In a four-door car, the first to be picked up sits beside the driver and the others sit in back. In a two-door car, the first to be picked up gets in the back, and the last sits in front.

327
TRAVEL
FOR
PLEASURE
AND
BUSINESS

Sharing Expenses

If a car pool rotates drivers, it is assumed that each is carrying his or her portion of the expenses when it is his or her turn to drive. If there is one driver who uses his own car, he or she must determine what fee is to be given by each of the passengers, based on the cost of gas and wear and tear on his or her car. This fee should be discussed before the car pool is formed, along with a payment schedule. It is ridiculous for each passenger to hand over money every time he gets into the car. Instead, a weekly or monthly amount should be determined and paid promptly when expected. If the price of gasoline goes up, it should be understood that the fee goes up accordingly.

A more informal form of car pool is among parents whose children attend the same school or activity. Unless one parent cannot take his or her turn, no money is involved and arrangements are made on a rotating basis. A parent who cannot participate because of job responsibilities or because he or she does not drive should offer to pay the other parents for transporting his or her child. If payment is refused, a gift should be given periodically to those who drive.

Sometimes, awkward situations are created by those who don't drive and who depend on others to transport them. Unless you can afford to share the expenses don't take advantage of a friend or neighbor by continually accepting a "lift." If you are in the position of relying on friends for transportation frequently, *be sure* you can repay them in some way. Insist on paying for the gas occasionally, or if you ride with them regularly, offer to pay a fixed weekly amount. One woman arranged with a gas station to make out a "gift certificate" and gave it to a friend who drove her frequently. If the driver refuses to accept money, then you should invite her to lunch or dinner at a restaurant, send her flowers, or buy her a present every now and then.

SHIP TRAVEL

Travel by ship can be anything from a one-week cruise to a transatlantic crossing to an around-the-world tour by freighter. The latter is fairly informal, while cruises and crossings can be very formal. If you have never taken a cruise, your travel agent will have specific information as to dress expectations, activities on board, and tipping guidelines as well as the duration at ports of call.

Clothing for a Cruise

The majority of cruises head for the Caribbean or points south, and cool cottons, shorts, and bathing suits can be worn all day. Bathing suits may not be worn in the dining room unless covered with a long shirt or coverup, but other sports clothes are acceptable at lunch and often at dinner. Other than in first-class on a luxury liner, passengers do not dress formally for dinner except for the night of the captain's dinner. Women generally wear dressy cottons, silks or pantsuits for dinner, and men wear blazers with sportshirts or shirts and ties. Nights can be cool at sea, so take a sweater or cover of some sort. A few first-class passengers on a luxury liner often dress in evening clothes—tuxedos for men and dinner dresses for women—every night except the first and last on board. This is not necessary, however, except on the night of the captain's dinner, and cocktail dresses and business suits are acceptable on other evenings. There are sometimes costume parties on cruises, often the evening of the captain's dinner. Again, your travel agent can tell you what to expect. Generally you can rent something from the purser, plan ahead and take along a favorite costume, or create one while on board.

Since cruise passengers will be making trips ashore, they should be prepared with comfortable shoes. It is not required that women cover their heads in most churches. But is could do no harm to carry a scarf in your pocketbook in case you should run into a service in progress or a church that has some restrictions. Women should wear long shorts, skirts or slacks for sightseeing tours rather than short shorts. If you plan to visit elegant restaurants or nightclubs in resort areas, long skirts or dressy pants and tops for women and summer-weight jackets for men are appropriate, although not necessary.

The same level of informality/formality is found on northern cruises, but of course warmer clothing replaces the summer-weight clothes worn in warmer climates.

Luggage

Ship cabins are generally small. You will be more comfortable in your cabin if you pack sparingly or you might find yourself surrounded by luggage. Luggage not needed en route, if you are taking a transatlantic ship and have extra luggage for when you arrive, may be checked.

On your arrival at a pier, there is a porter to put your luggage on the elevator or escalator to the boarding level. At some piers the same porter takes the luggage to the loading station. At others, a second porter takes it on from the escalator. In spite of posted signs to the contrary, porters expect tips. (*See pages 344–345 for information on tipping on board ships.*)

Small bags go directly to your cabin. Larger pieces that are checked are brought to you just before landing. You claim it at a central unloading area, similar to that found at an airport. A porter will take it to the customs counters, or you may take it yourself.

Be sure to arrive at the ship in plenty of time to be certain that your luggage is on board. Any trunks sent to the pier by express or delivered by other means will be covered by numbered checks, the stubs of which will have been given to you. These stubs should be turned in to the baggage master, or to whoever is in charge of his desk on the pier. The luggage will be stored in the hold or sent to your cabin or stateroom, as requested.

329
TRAVEL
FOR
PLEASURE
AND
BUSINESS

Boarding

After taking care of your luggage when you arrive at the pier, you will be directed to the boarding ramp. The ship's crew is generally on hand to greet you and direct you to your cabin. Generally, your cabin will contain literature on the features of your cabin and of the ship, and indicate where to find those you should contact to make arrangements such as dining room and deck chair reservations. Conveniences on board ship are usually similar to those found at better hotels, including cabin service, valet and laundry, etc. If there is no written information in your cabin, your steward can be of assistance.

Immediately after being shown to your cabin you should go to the dining room and reserve a table, if you have not done so in advance, at the sitting you wish—early or late; the times will be posted. Next, go to the main deck and see the head deck steward about a lounge chair. If you have a preference about location this is your chance to get it.

Bon Voyage Parties

You may have friends coming to the ship to wish you "Bon voyage!" It's a fine excuse for a party and a happy beginning to your trip. There are two ways of giving such a party. If you have a large, comfortable stateroom your steward will bring mixers and soft drinks, hors d'oeuvres, ice and glasses to your cabin. Often one of the guests will bring a bottle of champagne or liquor as a going-away present. If you are in a small room you may have your party instead in one of the bars or lounges. In either case, you board the ship as early as possible and make the arrangements with your cabin steward or with the headwaiter in whichever public room you choose.

Social Life on Board

If you entertain shipboard acquaintances in the same way as you entertain at a bon voyage party, the same arrangements may be made, depending on the size of your quarters. You should tip the stewards who serve such a party 15–18 percent of the bill at the time rather than add it to your regular tip at the end of the trip.

Unless your own group is very large or you request a table to yourselves, you may be seated with other people in the dining room. No formal introductions are necessary on board—you introduce yourself to your neighbors and with luck you quickly find congenial people with whom you will become fast friends for the length of the voyage. If you aren't lucky and you find yourself seated with people who are really obnoxious, you may ask the headwaiter if you may switch to the other sitting or to another table. In deck chairs around the swimming pool, in the lounges, or in the game rooms you may also open a conversation with anyone who appears to be congenial; but if a person does not respond with the same enthusiasm do not force yourself on him or her; this person may honestly wish to be left alone.

Often the cruise social director will offer opportunities for activities. If you love to play bridge and are traveling without a foursome, you may tell the social director of your interest and he or she will endeavor to find others who would like to play, too.

Depending on the ship and the length of your passage, there are other personnel, such as computer teachers, craft directors, and children's activities directors who are delighted to involve you in whatever the event of the moment may be. One caveat—the children's activities directors are just that. They are not baby-sitters, and you should not plan to abandon your children the moment you find the director. Activities are planned for specific times and you should return at the designated time to collect your children, or tell them where you will be so they can find you when they are finished.

The Captain's Table

It is an honor to be invited to sit at the captain's table, and the passenger thus honored should never refuse without a most valid reason.

People seated at the captain's table or at the tables of the other senior officers should arrive at the same time as does the officer. If he or she is delayed, wait before starting unless he or she sends word to go ahead. At other tables it is not necessary to wait for the people with whom you are seated.

On many transatlantic ships, the captain entertains at cocktails—once for first-class and once for tourist-class passengers. He may also give smaller parties for prominent persons, personal friends, or those sitting at his table as well as the large formal party for all first-class passengers that occurs on a transatlantic crossing. These invitations should always be accepted, if possible. If you are invited to one of the smaller parties and cannot attend, a written refusal is sent.

The captain is always addressed as "Captain Tompkins," and the other male officers are called "Mr," female officers are addressed as Ma'am.

TRAVELING TO OTHER COUNTRIES

The principal rule of conduct, abroad as well as at home, is to do nothing that either annoys or offends the sensibilities of others. Thus it is necessary for us to consider the point of view of all those with whom we come in contact when traveling. We must learn something of the customs that determine the attitudes of those who live in the countries we visit if we want to be accepted with warmth and understanding.

331
TRAVEL
FOR
PLEASURE
AND
BUSINESS

You will make yourself thoroughly popular in every part of the world if you show appreciation and enthusiasm for the customs and sights of the country you are in. Of course there will be annoyances—service in many places is less efficient than that to which you are accustomed; neither the food nor the climate may appeal to you; but it is not necessary to voice your disappointments in public. You need not be falsely ecstatic, but you may be politely noncommittal and attempt to find and dwell on the parts of your stay that you do enjoy.

Making Comparisons

Don't compare everything you see with the United States. We may have taller buildings, bigger automobiles, newer supermarkets, and better highways but because no one wishes to "suffer by comparison," to make such claims is the surest way of alienating your foreign acquaintances. Every country in the world has something to offer that we do not.

You may also find that you are resented just because of your nationality. Sadly, travel in some countries is less pleasant simply because the residents of the country do not harbor warm feelings for North Americans. Just as many Americans unfortunately generalize that *all* members of a different nationality are lazy or rude or whatever, those from other countries sometimes make unfavorable generalizations about Americans. If you are confronted by hostility, it is best not to engage in argument but rather to represent your own country well in your attitude and appearance.

Appearance

The first thing that the native of another country notices is your appearance. Neatness and appropriateness are the two most important features. Your clothing may be the least expensive you can find and you may be traveling with only two or three outfits. But if you choose wrinkle-resistant materials insofar as possible, unpack your clothes when you arrive and keep them clean (always carry a good spot remover and soap powder) and pressed (use valet service or your own traveling iron or steamer), you will appear well dressed. Good-looking pants suits or skirts and blouses are ideal for daytime sightseeing. Women should include a dressy suit or dress for dining out, and both men and women should take the proper clothes for any sports they intend to participate in. In resort areas you may wear the same things you would wear at any American resort. In foreign cities, clothing is generally more formal than in our cities. This is not so in the tropics, however, where the women often wear sleeveless cottons. Businessmen in hot countries do not wear shirts and ties, but a loose cotton or linen shirt-jacket, worn outside the trousers and sometimes beautifully pleated or embroidered.

No matter how you are traveling or for how long, your luggage should be neat and compact. Nothing looks worse or makes a traveler so uncomfortable as broken-down bags and numerous bundles.

Young people who are hiking or biking around Europe wear just what they do at home. They should always have with them, however, one "good" outfit (a dress for the girls; a shirt, jacket, and tie for the boys) for a visit to a private home or a good restaurant, for church, or simply to be ready for the unexpected invitation or event that may require dressing up.

General Conduct

The next thing people abroad will notice is your general behavior. Don't attract attention to yourself by talking in a loud voice. Americans have a reputation for being "loud," and it is true that foreigners, Latins especially, are brought up to admire a well-modulated voice. You will be far more attractive to people abroad if your voice carries only to those with whom you are talking. Your actions should be as inconspicuous as your voice. When you see a friend from home across the square or in a crowded restaurant, it is not necessary to shout and wave violently to attract his attention. Approach him quietly and greet him as you would ordinarily do at home.

Don't push ahead of others in lines or crowds. Most Europeans are more polite about waiting their turn than we are, and nothing can be ruder than shoving ahead of someone who is too polite to object.

Above all, don't stare. Of course you are interested when you see a Greek gentleman pull out his worry beads and toy with them, or when a peasant family approaches with mother burdened down with a heavy load while father rides the donkey. But don't stand rooted with your mouth open, obvious surprise or criticism written all over your face. Their customs are natural to them—it is not your place to judge them—and when you are in their country accept whatever you see as normal, storing it away in your memory as an interesting facet of life abroad.

Probably the best piece of advice was suggested to me by a young woman who had just returned from a most successful trip to Europe. She said, "Don't try to be different from what you are at home, but be the same as nicely as possible."

One cannot stress enough the importance, first, of knowing a few words of the idiom of whatever countries you are planning to visit, and second, of carrying a small pocket dictionary or phrase book with you. It is not necessary, of course, to take a course or buy a self-teaching system, but the following few often-used words and phrases (your grammar need not be perfect—your inflection will indicate a statement, question, exclamation, etc.) will smooth your path in any strange land:

"Yes" and "No."

"Please" and "Thank you." (Most important of all!)

"Hello." "Good-bye." "Good morning." "Good evening." "Good night."

"How much?" and "How much does it cost?"

"The check [or bill], please."

"Please speak slowly."

"I don't speak [whatever the language may be]."

"I don't understand."

"Where is . . . ?" and "How do you get to . . . ?"

"Ladies' room" and "Men's room."

"More, please" and "No more, thank you."

"Beautiful," "Wonderful," "Nice," "Kind," etc. These single words, said admiringly and sincerely about the place or people you are visiting, will warm the heart of the most skeptical native.

All phrase books will give more explicit sentences and questions on many subjects, but the above words should be learned by heart, so that they can be used quickly and easily without having to refer to a book.

On many overseas flights the airline gives out booklets about the country you are flying to. They contain practical information about currency, language, clothing, customs, etc., and are generally excellent. If you have not had time to "study up" beforehand, avail yourself of this opportunity on your flight.

Nothing pleases a native of any country, including our own, more than the realization that a visitor has taken the time and made the effort to learn a little of the country's language. If we could all remember this we would be far more eager to enter into conversation with foreigners. A great stride would be made toward furthering friendship among all peoples, and we would derive much greater pleasure from our travels.

Anyone who has walked through a little alley in a tiny town on a Greek island and seen the beaming smiles and eager response of the old ladies who sit there in the sun and hear *"Calimera"* instead of "Hello" or "Good morning" will know that this is true.

Taking Pictures

If you wish to include a close-up of a citizen of the country in your pictures, have the decency to ask his or her permission. Although an impoverished farmer may appear unusual or picturesque to you, he may be ashamed of the very costume that to you seems "typical," and the last thing he wishes is to have his poverty recorded and distributed to strangers from another land. Some tribes in Africa believe that the camera is an "evil eye," and in the bush one should be sure that pointing the camera at a child will not scare him out of his wits.

In countries where the natives still wear a national costume (which is rare in Europe except on holidays, but common in Africa and the Middle and Far East), the

333

TRAVEL
FOR
PLEASURE
AND
BUSINESS

people are accustomed to being photographed by tourists, but it is still polite to ask their permission unless you are just taking a picture of a large crowd.

Even though children may be frightened of you or the camera, their fears can usually be overcome by a smile and perhaps some token—a coin, candy, or gum. In areas where there are many tourists, children will often crowd around you, offering their services as models.

If you happen to see a tourist couple, one of whom is taking a picture of the other, offer to snap the picture for them, so that they may both be in it. This is always greatly appreciated, and we should remember to be thoughtful to fellow travelers as well as to the residents of the country in which we find ourselves.

Going Through Customs

Whenever you travel across a border to another country, you will have to go through a customs check. Customs officials have a job to do; they are not the enemy unless you are trying to smuggle the crown jewels into the country. Make every effort to help speed the process by cooperating and being patient, no matter how tired or cranky you are feeling. You will be asked to fill out a declaration listing the items and value of anything you have bought in another country. The customs officer will look at the list, charge you any duty fees accordingly, and frequently ask you to open your bags so that he or she may look through them. When finished, he or she will tell you to close your bags and will pass you through, unless there is some question about an item or items you are carrying. If this is the case, you may be able to explain right there, or you may be asked to go to the customs office for a further interview. When the customs inspection is finished, there are usually porters available to assist you to whatever form of transportation you are using when leaving the airport or pier. When porters are not available you can rent a small cart to carry your luggage. These carts are always located near baggage claims areas in airports.

TRAVELING ON BUSINESS

When you must travel on business, either domestically or to another country, it is important that you understand the guidelines of your company. Most use the services of travel agencies; some large companies have their own travel departments. Whichever you use, it is up to you to communicate all your needs, including ground transportation when you arrive, so that they can make appropriate arrangements. If you make your own arrangements, remember to adhere to your company's travel policy. Some companies do not permit employees to travel first class, for example, no matter how long the flight, and some have limits that may not be exceeded at company expense. Some have arrangements with hotels to bill the company directly, while others expect that you will pay personally and be reimbursed later. Find out, too, what the per diem permitted for meals is, what is reimbursed in gas and mileage, etc. so that you can keep scrupulous records of your expenses.

Even the best-laid travel plans often go astray; storms delay flights, traffic holds you up, cars break down, meetings run late, flights are canceled. If you suddenly find yourself delayed, the first obligation is to phone any people who are meeting you or expecting you at an appointment. If they are waiting at an airport or train station, ask to have them paged. When a delay is the airline's fault, the airline will often pay for your long-distance call; check at the ticket counter. Try to get information on the arrival of your new flight so you can relay it to the person at the other end.

335
TRAVEL
FOR
PLEASURE
AND
BUSINESS

Traveling Alone

When traveling to a branch office of your company, or to a client in another city or country, those you are meeting often expect to entertain you or to be entertained by you outside of the time you will be conducting business together. In the case of being entertained, if it is the last thing you want, either because you haven't time or are just plain tired, make it clear initially that although you would love to have dinner together after your meeting, you simply can't. It is excusable to plead fatigue or workload, as long as you are sincere in your thanks for the offer, and as long as you don't wait until the last minute to bow out. This is a courtesy to your "host" so that he knows he will be free for the evening and not obligated to entertain you.

In the event that you are to be the host, you must follow through on your invitation, no matter how tired you are. If you are in a city unfamiliar to you, you may ask your guest, whose city it is, to suggest an appropriate restaurant so that you can make reservations.

Traveling With a Business Associate

When two or more associates travel together and are equal in rank, they generally take turns picking up the tab so that one expense account doesn't carry the burden of all their expenses.

When one is senior to the other, it is customary that he or she pays the bills for meals and other expenses. If traveling by car, the owner or renter of the car usually drives, although this duty may be delegated or shared, particularly if the trip is long.

Everyone carries his or her own luggage, registers in his or her own name at a hotel, and pays his or her own hotel bill, whether equal in rank or of different levels.

When traveling by private plane on business, the senior person boards first and is given first choice of seating.

Business Travel With Your Spouse

On some business trips spouses are invited to accompany executives. In this case the company covers all expenses for both. On other trips, however, when spouses of executives go along on their own, the spouse's travel expenses must be paid for personally and the hotel bill pro-rated. If a single room costs sixty dollars and a double, ninety dollars, the company could be expected to pay the sixty dollars with the couple personally covering the thirty-dollar difference.

Spouses accompanying executives on a business trip must keep in mind that they are there to have fun on their own—sightseeing, shopping, visiting grand-children—and/or to help host evening entertainment. While they may breakfast together, their husbands or wives are not expected to entertain them at lunch or during the day. If during dinner the executive and his or her associate fall into a business discussion, a spouse can be of great help by allowing the conversation to take place and chatting with the associate's spouse.

Hosting an Out-of-Town Business Meeting

When traveling executives need to call a business meeting out of town, they will probably use the conference room or an office in the company branch where they are visiting. If this is not possible, they may rent a hotel suite and hold the meeting in the living room there.

A salesperson who needs a "showroom" on the road may rent a separate room at the hotel where he or she is staying or reserve a suite instead of a single room and use the living room for business. It is not appropriate to use one's hotel bedroom unless the bed makes up into a sofa and the room takes on the appearance of a living room.

Conducting Business in Another Country

I commend to you many of the books written for the business traveler to specific countries, and recommend that you read as much as you can before departing. Each country has its own ways of doing business that are integrally involved with social custom, and the wise business person knows ahead of time what they are. Knowing, for example, that if meeting with Japanese counterparts and they entertain you, you are expected to entertain them in return, but never at a level more elaborate, saves everyone embarrassment. Knowing that you should take flowers to a business associate in the Netherlands who invites you to his home for dinner adds to your charm (and detracts from it if you don't know). If you are a woman, knowing that many European executives will expect to be chivalrous will keep you from feeling as though you aren't being taken seriously when your chair is pulled out for you to be seated in a boardroom or all the men rise when you enter. Many Europeans still follow the social rules for handshakes in business, and would wait for a woman to offer her hand first.

It is not only good manners but also smart business sense to go prepared, and to adopt the customs of the country you are visiting, to the limit that is expected of you, but not beyond that limit. Do not, for example, when seeing Saudi businessmen embrace when meeting, think you should follow suit. They, who know each other well, would be horrified if you, a virtual stranger, tried to hug them. Your greeting would be a handshake, not a hug.

If you are a first-time international traveler for your company, it is also a good idea to talk with your boss or another executive who has been to the country you are about to travel to so that you understand such things as company policy on gift-giving, an accepted custom in many other countries, on entertaining, and on the particular people you are going to meet.

337
TRAVEL
FOR
PLEASURE
AND
BUSINESS

*J*t would be ideal if everyone who offered a service of any kind were paid so well that he or she did not need to depend on tips, but this, unfortunately, is not the case. Therefore we must remember that many, many people are dependent on a "reward" for good service, in addition to their regular salaries.

I do believe firmly, however, that the tip should be merited. Where service is bad and the personnel is deliberately rude, inattentive, or careless, the amount should be reduced. If it is bad *enough*, no tip should be left at all, and you should bring the situation to the attention of the manager. If everyone continues to tip at the same rate, regardless of the effort made to please, there is no incentive to make any extra effort at all. We are all at the mercy of the "system," but by rewarding good service more generously and withholding a gratuity when the service is bad, we can help to make tipping acceptable.

17
Tipping

IN RESTAURANTS

It is difficult to give definite rules for tipping, because it depends upon where you go and the service that is given you. That is, if you patronize luxurious restaurants, or if you have special requirements or are difficult to please, greater "compensation" is expected than if you choose simpler restaurants and receive less service.

Waiters, Waitresses and Headwaiters

It wasn't long ago that 15 percent of the bill, excluding tax, was considered a generous tip in elegant restaurants. Now the figure is moving toward 20 percent for excellent service. In ordinary family style restaurants 15 percent is still the norm. When there is a wine steward, the price of the wine is not included in the total you use as the base for determining your tip. When your waiter takes care of your wine order, the price of the wine is included. The tip is determined by the total of your bill before tax.

If you are paying cash, the tip is left on the tray on which your change is returned by the waiter after he has taken your money to the cashier.

When paying by credit card, you check the bill presented to you by the waiter and place your credit card on top of it. He takes the bill to the cashier who prepares a credit card slip. This slip, with your card and the original bill, is returned to you, often in a folder or on a tray. The charge slip usually has four lines: one showing the charges for your meal, one for the tax on that total, one blank line for you to add the tip, and a bottom line for the total of these three amounts. You are expected to enter the amount of your tip and then total the bill.

Like the waiter, but unlike the maitre d', the captain depends on tips for a living wage. Leaving him five percent in addition to what you leave the waiting staff is adequate. Or, if his service to you has been extraordinary, and he has worked side by side with your waiter, you may divide the total tip leaving 75 percent to the waiting staff and 25 percent to the captain.

The maitre d' is not tipped, nor would you tip a host or hostess, unless you are a regular patron of the restaurant, in which case you should tip $5 to $10 *once in a while* if he or she remembers your favorite wine, for example, or makes sure that you are seated and served carefully and promptly. Most restaurant owners say that tipping a maitre d' for a "good" table is fairly pointless but agree that a tip occasionally by frequent patrons is acceptable, as is a tip to the maitre d' who arranges a large dinner party or special occasion for you.

Waiting staff in buffet or smorgasbord restaurants should receive approximately 10 percent of the bill. In luncheonettes, diners, coffee shops and at counters, no tip should be less than a quarter, even if all you have is a cup of coffee and otherwise is approximately 15 percent.

Busboys

Do not tip busboys, except in the now practically extinct cafeteria restaurant when a busboy carries your tray to your table. In this event 50 cents is a standard tip.

Service Charges

A common feature of travel and dining in many other countries, the service charge is a fee automatically added to your bill to cover gratuities. It is uncommon in the United States, but when it is the practice in a particular restaurant, it is so stated on the menu and an additional tip is not expected.

Bartender and Wine Steward

When you wait for your table in the bar you may pay for your drinks as they are ordered, or the bartender may run a tab for your drinks which is then included with your dinner bill. In either case, you should leave a tip for the bartender when you are told that your table is ready.

When you are having drinks only, your tip should be between 15 and 20 percent—at the higher end if the bartender has run a tab for you.

The wine steward is tipped approximately 15 to 20 percent of the wine bill if you have received special attention (assistance in making your selection, attention to your needs and budget, and service when your glasses need to be filled again), or between 10 and 15 percent if he has simply taken your order and poured your first glass of wine. How much you give also depends on the number of bottles as well as the price of the wine. The wine steward is paid in cash. He will make himself available when he sees that you are getting ready to leave or may ask you if you want more wine when he sees that you have finished your wine. If you don't wish to order any more, you may thank him and give him his tip at that time rather than waiting until you are ready to depart.

Checkroom and Washroom Attendants

Checkroom attendants should be tipped $1 per coat, or $2 if you have also checked parcels, umbrellas, attache cases, and the like.

Washroom attendants are tipped no less than 50 cents for doing nothing more than handing you a paper towel. If they provide a special service, such as brushing off your dress or whipping out a needle and thread to catch up your falling hem, then $2 should be left. There is almost always a small plate with a few coins or a dollar bill on it in an conspicuous place to remind you, and your tip is placed here, not handed to the attendant.

Musicians

Tip the piano player or strolling musician at least $1 per special request. If several members of a large party make requests, the tip should be given per request performed. In many restaurants, strolling musicians "stroll" to each table, play a song, and then ask if you have a request. Even if you don't and all you want is for them to go away, a tip is expected. Again $1 is appropriate, whether you've asked them to play for you or not. It is not expected that you put down your fork and gaze at them as they perform, even though it seems awkward to keep eating and your instinct is to give them your undivided attention. A song can take anywhere from two to five minutes, during which time your just-delivered filet of sole is rapidly cooling. Keep eating, but do smile and say "Thank you" when they finish, as you hand them your tip. In the instance where you are right in the middle of a business transaction or an emotional moment, it is not impolite to wave them away.

Restaurant Valet Parking

Tip the parking attendant $1 in smaller cities and $2 in large cities at the time your car is brought to you, not when you arrive.

Dinner Parties in Restaurants and Catered Dinners

Some restaurants and caterers add a service charge of between 15 and 20 percent to the bill for a large dinner party. This is divided among the waiters and/or waitresses. The host is not obligated to tip an additional amount unless he wishes to for outstanding service. After a large dinner the host should, in addition, give the person in charge—headwaiter, maitre d', or whoever it may be—a separate tip of no less than $10, depending on the size and elaborateness of the party. If no service charge is added to the bill, the host gives the person in charge approximately 20 percent of the total and asks that he divide it among the waiters.

When a caterer sends one or two waiters or perhaps a bartender and waitress to serve at a dinner party at your home, they should be given their tips personally before they leave. For a dinner of ten people for which the bill might be $150, each of two waiters would receive about $15 or his share of 20 percent of the bill.

In Hotels

Hotel workers, like restaurant workers, depend on tips to augment their usually small salaries. Rather than being annoyed at having to tip the doorman who greets you, consider it part of the cost of travel and be prepared with the dollar bills you will need to hand out before you ever get to your room.

Doormen

Depending on the amount of luggage, tip $1 to $2 to the doorman who takes your bags and turns them over to a bellman. If you are visiting and have no luggage, you naturally do not tip him for simply opening the door for you. Tip him again when you leave with your luggage as he takes it from the bellman and assists you in loading it in your car or into your taxi.

When the doorman obtains a taxi for you, tip him $1 to $3 (the higher amount if he must stand in the rain for a period of time to get it). When he has your car brought to the door for you, tip him $1 to $2 at the time of this service.

Bellman

Tip between $2 and $3 to the bellman who carries or delivers your luggage to your room, or more if you are traveling with a tremendous amount of luggage. In a luxury hotel when someone from the manager's office shows you to your room, no tip should be given to this person but the bellman who is following behind with the luggage should still be tipped.

When the bellman does something special for you, such as make a purchase or bring something you have requested to your room, but not room service deliveries, he or she should be tipped $2 to $3 for every service, at the time it is provided.

Maid

For stays of one night, or more the maid should be tipped $2 per night per person in a large hotel; $1 per night per person in a less expensive hotel. Give the maid her tip in person, if she can be found. If not, put it in a sealed envelope marked "chambermaid" or, if you prefer, give the envelope to the desk clerk and ask him or her to see that the maid receives it.

Valet

Valet services are added to your bill, so there is no need to tip for pressing or cleaning when items are left in your room. If you are in when your cleaning and pressing is delivered, however, tip $1 for the delivery for one or two items, more when several items are being delivered.

Room Service Waiter

Tip 15 percent of the room service bill, but never less than $2, each time an order is delivered. This tip is *in addition* to the room service fee charged by the hotel. Give your tip in cash or add it to the bill.

Dining Room Staff

Tips for dining room staff are exactly the same as they are in any other restaurant—15 percent except in the most elegant dining rooms. If you are staying in an American-plan hotel where your meals are included in your total bill, tips are as usual, but an additional tip should be given to the maitre d' who has taken care of you during your stay. This tip ranges anywhere from $10 to $15 for a weekend for a family or group of four people to $20 to $30 for a longer stay or larger group.

Personal Services

Barbers, manicurists, beauty shop operators, and other personal service providers are tipped on the same basis as in shops outside of hotels. (*See Personal and Professional Services later in this chapter.*) Pool and sauna helpers, fitness club assistants, and other special service attendants do not receive tips unless they perform a special service.

The concierge is tipped a minimum of $5 for handling such things as airline or theater reservations for you, or up to $10 if the service provided is extraordinary, such as the obtaining of tickets for a sold-out show.

IN MOTELS

One of the attractions of a motel is that there is less need to tip than in a hotel. For a short-term stay, no tips other than those which would normally be given in the bar or restaurant or to the bellman, if there is one, are necessary. For longer stays, however, you must reward the people who wait on you over a period of time. This means leaving a tip for the chambermaid, and in larger resort motels, for the bellman, room service waiter and valet when you avail yourself of their services.

IN TRANSIT

Travel anywhere, with the exception of commuter travel, generally requires that you keep handy a pocketful of dollar bills and change. As grudging as you may feel to have to tip skycaps, taxicabs, or pullmen porters on top of paying hefty travel fares, it is usually worth it just for the convenience of getting where you have to go on time and the relief of not having to drag your luggage behind you.

Air Travel

No tip is ever given to flight attendants or flight officers on commercial flights or on private planes. Skycaps (porters) receive $1 a bag for unloading your luggage curbside and processing it through to the flight or delivering it to the airline counter. If they are tagging it for your flight and processing it directly to the flight, tip them curbside since you won't see them again. If they are taking it to the airline counter for you to send through yourself, give the tip when they carry it in and place it in line with you.

Trains

Redcaps (train porters) receive a per bag charge at a rate that is fixed and posted. Generally this charge is anywhere from 50 cents to $1 per bag. A tip of $1 is usually added to this fee.

Dining or club car waiters are tipped exactly as waiters are in any restaurant. They are given from 15 to 20 percent of the bill, and never less than a quarter if all you order is a soft drink or cup of coffee. Waiters or stewards who deliver ice, glasses, water and soda to your sleeping car are tipped 15 to 20 percent of the bill.

The sleeping car porter receives at least $2 for each person per night on an overnight trip—more if he has given additional service beyond making up the berths.

Taxis

In a large city such as New York, you should tip a minimum of 50 cents. In general, a tip to a taxi driver is about 20 percent of the fare. For a $5 ride, tip $1, for example. If the taxi driver actually assists with your luggage or packages a slightly larger tip is in order.

If, in spite of your friendly smile, your courtesy, and your adequate tip, the driver growls a nasty remark at you as you leave the cab, you have one means of retaliation. Get out on the passenger side and walk away, leaving the cab door open.

Charter Buses and Bus Tours

Charter- and sightseeing-bus drivers receive no tip. However, some chartered buses and sightseeing-bus services provide guides or driver-guides. Passengers generally tip $1 per person for this service, but it is not obligatory. On a prolonged tour, driver and guide (if there are both) are tipped $5 to $10 depending on the length of the tour, unless gratuities are included in the fare. The person in charge of a private charter sometimes asks for contributions of $1 a person as a tip for the driver.

Private Car and Limousine Service

When you have an account with a car service or are being billed, the easiest way to handle tipping is to tell the service, when you request the driver, to add the gratuity to your bill.

If you are paying for the ride when you reach your destination, then you add the tip to the fare. In a larger city, the tip is about 20 percent. In smaller cities, it is 15 percent.

On Board Ships

Dock porters, like train and airport porters, are tipped $1 per bag at the time their service is rendered.

Depending on whether you are making a transoceanic crossing, taking a barge trip through France or taking a week-long cruise in the Caribbean, there are different tipping systems on board ship and traditional times that tips are given. Some cruise lines are now adding a substantial service charge to the fare. In this case, there is no tipping unless an extra special service is provided. To be sure you know what is expected, it is best to discuss tipping amounts and procedures with your travel agent or the cruise line agent when you are booking your trip.

The first guideline is that you *never* tip the ship's officers. Thank the purser, at the end of the trip, for his courtesy. If you consult the doctor on board, you will probably receive a bill for services rendered. If you are not billed for medical

treatment, it is proper to send the doctor the amount that probably would have been
charged by your own doctor at the time you leave the ship. If you are ill enough to be
hospitalized, an extra charge will be added to your fare. It is not expected that you tip
a bridge instructor, children's activity director or aerobics instructor either, although
to do so is not improper, as it would be were you to attempt to tip an officer of the
ship.

For a very long trip, tip weekly, generally on Friday evenings. Tipping weekly
enables personnel to have cash to spend during stops in ports. If you are traveling
first-class, the following amounts are standard:

- $25 per week to your cabin steward
- $20 per week to the deck steward
- $25 per week to your dining room steward
- $20 per week to the chief dining room steward
- $5 to $8 per week to the busboy

Tips in the cabin and tourist classes are lower, in proportion to the difference
in the passage fare. A good general rule for shipboard travelers is to allow approximately 15 percent of their fare for tips. Divide about half of this allowance between
the cabin and dining room stewards and distribute the rest to others who have
served you.

On a shorter cruise, tip your cabin steward and your dining room steward
each $3 per day minimum. At the end of your cruise, put your tips into separately
addressed envelopes and hand them to each person, with a note of thanks if you
wish.

Lounge and bar stewards are tipped 15 to 20 percent of your bar bill at the
time they render their services. If you are running a tab which you pay periodically
you may tip at the time you settle your bill, but it is preferable to pay and tip as
you go.

The wine steward should receive 15 percent of the total wine bill each time
you avail yourself of his services.

Tip all service people, such as hairdressers or manicurists, as you would on
land. (*See Personal and Professional Services later in this chapter.*)

In Other Countries

In most European restaurants and hotels, and in those of many other countries, a service charge is added to your bill. You are not, in most cases, expected to
give additional tips. You do not tip the bellboy or the maid. In a restaurant you may
leave the small coins the waiter brings back in change but you should never add the
equivalent of another dollar or two.

When no service charge appears on the bill, or if you think it is too low or
"nominal," you tip exactly as you would in the United States.

Theater ushers are tipped in Europe. They are not tipped in England, but there is a charge for the program. Differences like these are the rule rather than the exception. Consult a current guidebook or talk to your travel agent for specific tipping guidelines for the countries or cities you are visiting.

At Clubs

Personnel in most private clubs, other than dining room staff, are not tipped at the time they render service. Members usually are requested to give to a Christmas fund for employees, and most give additional tips to those who have given them personal attention—the washroom attendant, locker room attendants, the head-waiter, etc. These personal tips are generally $5 to $10, depending on the type of club and the amount of service. Additional tips may be given for special services throughout the year.

Guests in clubs are not expected to tip personnel unless they are residents for a time. In that case, if no service charge is added to their bill, they tip as they would in a first-class hotel.

If a gratuity is not included in the greens fees at golf clubs, caddies receive 15 to 20 percent of the regular club charge for eighteen holes. For nine holes, the tip is usually 20 percent.

Neither the tennis pro nor pool lifeguards are tipped. If you are especially pleased by your work with the tennis pro, however, a small gift is appropriate.

At health and fitness clubs, tips may be expected by locker room attendants, and often a tip basket is visible. $1 is a usual tip. Otherwise, like private clubs, a Christmas fund may be established which is distributed to employees. Personal trainers and exercise instructors may be given a gift at Christmas but are not tipped throughout the year.

A masseuse or masseur is tipped 20 percent of the cost of the massage.

For Personal and Professional Services

Answering Service

Each operator who takes a shift on your service should receive a minimum of $10 at Christmas.

Barbers

For a haircut in a small rural area for a child, tip no less than 50 cents; but for a haircut in a city barber shop, 15 to 20 percent of the bill but never less than $1 is about average. An adult's haircut costs more than a child's and so the tip is correspondingly higher. If you are having a shampoo, shave, manicure, etc., then tip

$1 to $2 to those providing the services or 15 to 20 percent of the charge for each

service. A regular customer does not tip the shop owner for each haircut, but gives him or her a gift at Christmas.

Beauty Services

When a bevy of beauticians is involved in your appointment, it can be confusing to know who should be tipped and how much. Check the totals for each service provided when you are given the bill and use each amount as the base for your tip. Everyone but the owner is tipped and even most owners accept tips despite this long-standing guideline. Some shop owners charge more for their own services than they do for those of the beauticians who work for them, others do not. Those that do usually do not accept tips. The best way to find out is to ask the receptionist at the time you make your appointment, or when you arrive, "Does the owner accept tips?" You can also watch and see what other customers do if you are visiting a beauty salon for the first time. The range of tips for other personnel is as follows:

- Colorist—15 to 20 percent of the fee
- Hairstylist—15 to 20 percent of the fee
- Shampoo person—$1 to $3 depending on whether you have any special condition treatments or extra latherings
- Manicurist/pedicurist—$2 for simple manicures; 15 to 20 percent of the fee otherwise
- Facial, make up, waxing or other personal service—15 percent of the fee

Regular customers give the proprietor, stylist manicurist and shampooer small gifts at Christmas, as well.

In salons where there is a coatroom/changing room matron, $1 is the standard tip.

These same tipping guidelines apply to men who frequent styling salons instead of barber shops.

Car Wash

Tip $1 at a car wash. There is usually a pot at the end of the car wash which serves as a "kitty" and is shared among all the car washers, placed handily so that you can reach it from your car window.

Deliveries

The amount of the tip to delivery personnel depends on the volume of the delivery as well as on whether your house or apartment is difficult to reach. A delivery to a fifth floor walk-up apartment warrants a bigger tip than one that is carried up in an elevator, for example. Generally, however:

- A supermarket delivery person receives around $2.
- The dry cleaner, florist, pharmacy or butcher delivery person receive from $1 to $2 for a normal delivery.
- Food deliverers usually receive 10 percent or less of the bill. For a pizza, $1 is adequate if the bill is between $5 and $10. A tip for a larger order may be up to $3.
- Department store deliverers are not tipped unless they uncrate and set up your delivery. In this case, they would receive between $5 and $10 each, depending on the amount of work they do.
- Newspaper deliverers, if neighborhood children, receive $5 to $15 at Christmas, depending on the number of days you receive the paper and the quality of the service. They may be tipped a small amount—50 cents—when they collect each week or month as well, if you wish. If you do tip weekly or monthly, then a smaller tip at Christmas is appropriate. If you live in a large city or the delivery person is unknown to you and you are billed by the newspaper rather than paying a delivery person each week or month, the equivalent of one month's bill at Christmas is sent to the newspaper service and they will distribute it.

Domestic Staff When You Are A Guest

On those occasions when you visit a friend or acquaintance who has household staff, you would give or leave a tip for members of the staff. The amount would depend on the length of your stay. The following are guidelines for a long weekend to week-long visit:

- Chauffeur—No tip is given if he has driven you with your hosts to various events. If he has driven you to the airport, done errands for you, etc., however, on a personal basis, then you might give him $5 to $10 depending on the distance and amount of time he has expended on your behalf, regardless of the fact that your host has asked him to do this.
- Cook—From $10 to $15.
- Gardener—no tip required unless he or she has provided you with daily fresh flowers or another special service, in which case leave $5 to $10.
- Maid—From $10 to $15 if she has performed personal services for you, such as cleaning, unpacking, ironing, or providing meals in your room.

Garage Attendants

If you have your car parked in a garage while you go to the theater or to dinner, tip the attendant who brings your car to you $1.

If you keep your car in a garage and pay a monthly rental, attendants are not tipped each time they deliver the car. However, service may be faster and better care taken of your car if $5 is given to each employee periodically throughout the year in addition to the traditional Christmas tip.

Garbage Collection

If your garbage collection is provided by your municipality, check to see if you would be violating the law by tipping the sanitation crew. If not, or if service is provided by a private company, Christmas tips range from $10 to $15 per crew member.

Gardeners

People who cut your grass are not tipped weekly and in the case of a gardening service, usually are not tipped at all. If, however, you have hired one person to take care of your gardening needs, he or she is tipped from $10 to $25 for once-a-week service, either at the end of the season or at Christmas if he or she continues to work on your property throughout the year.

Grocery Loaders

Tip 50 cents to $1 for a normal number of bags taken to your car and loaded in the trunk; $1 to $1.50 for a very large number of bags.

Hospital Staff

No monetary tips.

The question of tipping the nurses may arise, but its answer is simple—don't. It is perfectly proper, however, to bring a box of candy or the like that can be shared by all the staff caring for the patient. Since hospitals have three shifts, three of whatever the item is should be given, clearly marked "first shift," "second shift," and "third shift." The packages should be left with the nurse on duty at the nursing station, with a word or two to the effect that "this is for all of you who have been so nice." If you only give one box of candy, it is likely that it will be consumed by whichever shift is on duty at that time, with none left for nurses and caregivers on the other two shifts.

Private nurses on prolonged duties may be given Christmas gifts or a gift on departing, but not monetary tips.

Household Helpers

Part-time helpers, such as once-a-week cleaning women and regular babysitters, are given Christmas gifts. These gifts usually are a monetary tip ranging from

$10 to $25 plus a personal gift. In the case of a regular baby sitter, the tip would be from you and the gift from your children.

Live-in helpers, such as cooks and housekeepers, are tipped during the year only when you have asked them to provide services well beyond their usual duties. Otherwise, they are given Christmas gifts ranging from $50 to one month's salary, accompanied by a personal gift—either clothing or an item for their rooms.

Nursing Home Employees

Nursing home personnel are not tipped individually for services provided. Usually a Christmas or holiday fund is established, and relatives of residents are asked to contribute whatever they can. This fund is then divided among the employees. It is fine to give a gift to special care givers, during holidays or after some extraordinary act of kindness on behalf of your parent, if you wish, perhaps with a card signed by both you and your parent.

Residential Building Employees

Christmas tips for residential building employees depend on a number of factors: the type of building, the size of the building staff, and the amount of time staff members spent helping you. In some cases building residents may also consider employee seniority in addition to any special services performed at the resident's request during the year.

Another factor is whether you tip employees throughout the year—every time the doorman gets you a taxi or receives your dry cleaning, for example. In this case, the traditional Christmas tip is smaller than if you do not tip during the year.

Depending on the size of your building and the amount of service provided by each employee, the following are tipping guidelines:

- Superintendent—Around $50 to live-in supers who do such things as take care of your deliveries, fix things for you, and help you carry heavy packages. Superintendents in luxury buildings often receive up to $100 for these services, particularly if they are not tipped throughout the year. Twenty dollars or less if the superintendent lives off-premise and provides few or no services.
- Doormen—From $35 to $50 for the most helpful doorman, and from $10 to $25 for those you never see. Special services provided by the doorman, such as feeding your cat or holding your mail when you are away, should be rewarded at the time they are provided or considered in the Christmas tip.
- Elevator operators—From $10 to $20.

- Handymen—From $10 to $20 depending on whether you tip them at the time they provide services. If so, then give them less at Christmas. If not, then their Christmas tip should be larger.

Guests staying at a friend's apartment for more than a few days may tip on departure any member of the staff who has been especially helpful.

Providing tips to those who serve you helps augment their incomes and aids their self-esteem, but giving them your respect as well is just as important. No amount of money thrown at someone as a tip makes up for rude behavior on your part. Furthermore, passing on your thanks, praise, and commendation for a job well done not only to the person himself, but to his or her supervisor, is the very nicest way of all to say thank you.

VI

ENTERTAINING & ENTERTAINMENTS

*I*nvitations can be anything from a spontaneous "We're celebrating spring, it's such a beautiful day, and wondered if you and Sam could come over at six for a barbecue!" to a formal invitation to a wedding or a ball sent four to six weeks in advance of the event. The first invitation is made in person or by telephone while the second is elegantly printed and mailed. Both have guidelines, and both require immediate replies.

Guidelines for a spur-of-the-moment invitation are that they are never worded, "What are you doing this evening?" or "Are you busy tonight?" which leave the one being asked the question uncertain of how to reply. He wants to know *why*—if the one asking is planning a viewing of three hours of videotape from her family's vacation in the mountains, he may wish to decline this opportunity. If the one asking is planning, instead, a casual dinner among friends, the invitation may be more appealing. But if the intent of the invitation isn't stated immediately, the reply is difficult. It is awkward to ask "Why do you want to know?" but often this is the only recourse. The breach of etiquette is really being committed by the one asking in not saying, "I know this is last minute, but John was just sent a case of prime steaks by a client and we'd love to share them with you—are you free to come to dinner tonight?"

Guidelines for invitations to more formal occasions are covered in the following pages. Like any other form of correspondence, the form and content of the invitation is a reflection of the sender, and it is time well spent to select invitations that convey the formality or mood of the event.

The Obligations Created by an Invitation

Wedding and shower invitations, invitations to dances or balls, and invitations to any official function, or one that you pay to attend, carry no "return" obligations. Parties in private homes, whether luncheons, brunches, cocktail or dinner parties, *do* require a return invitation.

The "pay-back" invitation need not necessarily be "in kind." A bachelor living in a hotel or tiny apartment cannot invite his boss to an elaborate dinner of the kind to which the boss invited him. He must repay, however, by taking his boss to dinner in a restaurant, or perhaps inviting him to a picnic at his beach cottage instead. An invitation to a large cocktail party means only that the next time you entertain in a similar way

18

Invitations and Replies

your host and hostess should be on your list. To be invited to a small dinner party is another matter. This invitation is more personal, more flattering, and should be returned in kind within a couple of months. The same is true of a weekend-visit invitation. Often it cannot be repaid at once, but when circumstances permit, you should invite your host and hostess to visit you. If you have no facilities to repay their hospitality in that way, you should plan to treat them to dinner and the theater, or anything that they would especially enjoy. Wedding invitations should never be used to pay back other social obligations.

One attempt to return the invitation after a dinner party is not enough. If your hosts refuse your first invitation you should try at least once, and preferably twice, more. After that, if you cannot seem to get together, you might well give up, or at least wait until some future date when they will fit into a party you are planning.

You are never, in any way, except according to your own conscience, obligated to accept an invitation. Once having accepted, however, you must go. Nothing can change an acceptance to a regret except illness, death in the family, or a sudden, unavoidable trip.

Furthermore, having refused one invitation on these grounds, you must not accept another more desirable one for the same day. You need give no excuse beyond "I'm afraid we are busy on the thirteenth," and *that* leaves you free to accept anything else that comes along. But if you have refused because you would be "out of town" and then you appear at a party attended by a mutual friend, you can certainly give up any idea of friendship with the senders of the first invitation.

When you are invited to a party and cannot go, you incur a milder obligation to return the invitation. It is not so important as if you had accepted the host's hospitality, but the *intent* to entertain you was there and should be acknowledged by an invitation in the not-too-distant future.

Anyone receiving an invitation with an R.s.v.p. on it is *obliged* to reply as promptly as possible. It is inexcusably rude to leave someone who has invited you to a party with no idea of how many people to expect.

Your reply should "match" the invitation. A formal, third-person invitation requires a third-person reply. However, a good friend who wishes to explain her refusal or to express her delight in the invitation may always write a personal note if she prefers. Those who groan at the thought of written replies should stop and think how much easier it is to follow the prescribed third-person form than to compose a lengthier letter!

When the R.s.v.p. is followed by a telephone number, do your best to telephone your answer. If you cannot get through to the host after several attempts, however, do not give up. Rather than no reply at all, he will appreciate a brief note or even a postcard saying "We'll be there" or "So sorry, can't make it."

If the invitation says "regrets only," don't send or call an acceptance unless you have something to discuss with the hostess. If there is no R.s.v.p. at all, you are not obligated to reply, but it is never *wrong* to do so, and any hostess will appreciate your effort.

When invitations are being sent out, *every* guest should receive one. This is not the place to save expenses by verbally inviting good friends and neighbors when invitations have been mailed to everyone else. Should the good friends and neighbors find out others received a more formal invitation, they will feel as though they were a last-minute, fill-in invitee, not on your original list of guests. Even best friends should reply in the same manner as everyone else when they receive an invitation.

Formal Invitations

"Third-Person" Formal Invitations

(*Information about wedding invitations and announcements, is covered in Chapter 39 which begins on page 665.*)

Formal invitations are engraved on white or cream cards—either plain or bordered by plate-mark (a raised border in the paper). Thermography is a relatively inexpensive printing process that simulates and has all but replaced engraving. Ask your printer to show you samples of both.

The size of the card of invitation varies with personal preference. The most graceful proportion is approximately three units in height to four in width, or four high by three wide. Cards may vary in size from 6 by 4½ to 3 by 4 inches. Postal regulations dictate that mailing envelopes be at least 3½ inches high by 5 inches wide. If you select invitations smaller than this size, you must obtain mailing envelopes that comply with postal regulations.

The lettering is a matter of personal choice, but the plainer the design, the safer. Punctuation is used only when words requiring separation occur on the same line, and in certain abbreviations, such as "R.s.v.p." The time should never be given as "nine thirty," but as "half past nine o'clock," or the more conservative form, "half after nine o'clock."

If the dance or dinner or other entertainment is to be given at one address and the hostess lives at another, both addresses are always given, assuming that the hostess wishes replies to go to her home address.

Traditionally, the phrases "black tie" or "white tie" were never used on invitations to weddings or private parties. It was assumed that people receiving formal invitations to these events would *know* what to wear. Today, however, the vast majority of parties are *not* formal, so the hostess who wishes her guests to dress formally must indicate this on her invitations. The phrase "black tie" should appear in the lower-right-hand corner of invitations to proms, charity balls, formal dinners or dances, evening weddings, or any event to which a wide assortment of people are invited.

Handwritten Formal Invitations

When the formal invitation to dinner or luncheon is written instead of engraved, plain white or cream notepaper or paper stamped with the house address or the family's crest is used. The wording and spacing must follow the engraved models exactly. The invitation must be written by hand—it may not be typewritten.

> *Mr. and Mrs. William Post*
> *request the pleasure of*
> *Mr. and Mrs. Andrew Prescott Jr.'s*
> *company at dinner*
> *on Tuesday, the sixth of December*
> *at eight o'clock*
> *the Englewood Field Club*
>
> *R.s.v.p.*
> *223 Glenwood Road*
> *Englewood, New Jersey 08850*

Or it may be worded:

> *Request the pleasure of your company*
> *at dinner*

If the return address does not appear on the back flap of the envelope, it must be written under the R.s.v.p.

The replies are addressed to the person, or persons, from whom the invitation comes. The full first name, rather than initials, is used, and the name of the state is also written out in full. A return address should appear on the back flap of the envelope. When a response card is sent with the invitation, it should be used for the reply, rather than a handwritten response.

Dinner Invitations

Private dinners that are formal enough to demand a third-person invitation are rare, but they take place occasionally, and there are many diplomatic, official, or organizational dinners that require formal invitations.

An engraved invitation to a private dinner reads:

> *Mr. and Mrs. Wayne Johnson*
> *request the pleasure of your company*
> *at dinner*
> *on Saturday, the fourth of July*
> *at half past seven o'clock*
> *Seabreeze*
> *Edgartown, Massachusetts*

R.s.v.p.
Box 65
Edgartown, Massachusetts 02539

If the dinner is held in honor of someone, "to meet Mr. Edgar Rice" is inserted before the address, or it may also be written by hand at the top.

The Fill-In Formal Invitation

Hostesses who entertain frequently and formally often have a supply of "fill-in" cards engraved that can be used for any occasion.

> *Mr. and Mrs. Christopher Saladino*
> *request the pleasure of*
> *Mr. and Mrs. Jonathan Fields*
> *company at dinner*
> *on Saturday, the second of March*
> *at eight o'clock*
> *43 Windsor Drive*
> *Princeton Junction, New Jersey 08850*

R.s.v.p.

If there is a guest of honor for the occasion, "to meet Mrs. Clarence Holland" is again handwritten at the top.

Invitations to a dinner party should be extended between two and three weeks ahead of time, especially during busy social seasons. They should be answered as soon as the recipient knows whether or not they can accept or must decline.

Invitations to Dances and Balls

To a Private Dance

The forms most often used are the following:

> *Mr. and Mrs. Andrew Reed*
> *request the pleasure of*
> *Miss Jacquelyn Abelson's*
> *company at a dance*
> *Monday, the first of January*
> *at ten o'clock*
> *400 Lake Shore Road*
> *Madison, Wisconsin*

R.s.v.p.

If it is a dance for young people and dates are to be included, the wording is: "request the company of Miss Jacquelyn Abelson and her escort's company at a . . . ," or "Mr. Joseph Antonio and his guest."

Titles are always used on formal invitations—for man, woman, or child. Note that while "Miss" is not used on wedding invitations, the title is always used on other invitations. If the woman prefers to be known as Ms that title may be used in the invitation:

Mr. and Mrs. John Warren
request the pleasure of your company
at a dance in honour of their niece
Ms [or Miss] Lee Warren
Thursday, the twenty-second of December
at ten o'clock
1300 Boulevard East
Tucson, Arizona

Mr. and Mrs. Jerome Roth
request the pleasure of your company
at a reception to celebrate the graduation of their son
Mr. Robert Steven Roth
Sunday afternoon, June the twenty-sixth
at four o'clock
The Essex House
New York City

Please reply to
Rothmeadows
Old Brookville, Long Island 11545

If the address to which replies are to be sent appears on the envelope, or follows "R.s.v.p." on the invitation, the ZIP code is not included in the body of the invitation.

Mr. and Mrs. Thomas Sullivan
Miss Lillie Sullivan
request the pleasure of your company
on Friday, the third of June
at half after nine o'clock
The Hunt Club
Seattle, Washington

R.s.v.p.
8 Rosewood Avenue   *Dancing*
Seattle, Washington 23200

To a Debutante Assembly

An invitation to present the debutant reads:

The Committee of the Westchester Cotillion
invites
mr. and mrs. David S. Williams
to present
miss Penelope Williams
at the Cotillion
on Friday, the ninth of September
at ten o'clock
Shenorock Shore Club
Rye, New York

To a Benefit

When the assembly is to benefit a charity or the expenses are to be covered by the sale of tickets these invitations are accompanied by a card stating the amount of the subscription, where it should be sent, etc. Names of the debutantes being presented, the committee and sometimes the patrons are printed inside the invitation.

The Governors of the Tuxedo Club
invite you to subscribe to
The Autumn Ball
to be held at
The Tuxedo Club
on Saturday, the twenty-second of October
Nineteen hundred and ninety-two
at eleven o'clock
Tuxedo Park, New York

R.s.v.p.

To a Public Ball

The word *ball* is rarely used except in an invitation to a public one—or at least a semipublic one—such as may be given by a committee for a charity or by a club or association of some sort. For example:

The Entertainment Committee of the Greenwood Club
requests the pleasure of your company
at a Ball
to be held at the clubhouse
on the evening of Thursday, the seventh of November
at six o'clock
for the benefit of
The Neighborhood Hospital

Single Ticket $25.00   *Black Tie*
Couple $50.00

Response cards, lists of patrons, and cards with pertinent information accompany these invitations.

One does not need to refuse this type of invitation. The return of the filled-in response card and the check for the tickets constitute an acceptance.

Invitations to dances and balls, like invitations to formal weddings, are usually sent four to six weeks before the event.

Invitations to Receptions and Teas

Invitations to receptions and teas differ from invitations to balls in that the cards on which they are engraved are usually somewhat smaller. The traditional form of invitation to a debutante ball, rarely seen today, used the phrase "At Home," whether the party was held at home or not. For a tea or reception the phrase "At Home" with capital letters may be changed to "will be home" with lower-case letters or "at Home" with a small *a*. The time is not set at a certain hour, but is limited to a definite period indicated by a beginning and a terminating hour. Also, except for very unusual occasions, a man's name does not appear.

An invitation to a tea for a debutante would read:

Mrs. James Townsend
Mrs. James Townsend, Junior
Miss Pauline Townsend
will be home
Tuesday, the eighth of December
from five until seven o'clock
850 Fifth Avenue

R.s.v.p.

Mr. Townsend's name would appear with that of his wife if he were an artist and the reception were given in his studio to view his pictures; or if a reception were given to meet a distinguished guest, such as a bishop or a governor. In this case "In honor of the Right Reverend William Grosvenor Ritual" or "To meet His Excellency the Governor of California" would be engraved at the top of the invitation. Suitable wording for an evening reception would be:

> *To meet the Honorable Percy Walker*
> *Mr. and Mrs. James Townsend*
> *at Home*
> *Tuesday, the eighth of December*
> *from nine until eleven o'clock*
> *850 Fifth Avenue*

R.s.v.p.

From an Organization

An example of this type of invitation:

> *The Alpha Chapter*
> *of*
> *Beta Chi Delta*
> *requests the pleasure of your company*
> *at a reception*
> *on Monday, the twenty-third of February*
> *at four o'clock*
> *at the Beta Chi Delta House*
> *2 Campus Row*

Invitation Enclosures

Answer or Response Cards

Although I still deplore the use of answer cards, believing that a reply in kind to a formal invitation is not that difficult to write, I do acknowledge that their use is widespread. The reason—so few people bother to take the time to write a response, leaving the hostess dangling as to how many guests to expect. Answer cards seem to be the only way a hostess can obtain replies.

An answer card is usually small and engraved in the same style as the invitation, with a box to check that indicates whether the invited guest will attend or not. It is not at all a good idea to have a line which reads "Number who will attend," since some of the recipients may take that to mean that they can bring additional guests, including their children or their houseguests.

Invitations to private parties usually include a self-addressed stamped envelope with the card. Subscription-dance committees may send the envelope, but generally do not stamp it.

Responding has been made so simple for the recipients of these invitations that they can hardly fail to answer them. Having returned the card, they should not send a formal reply as well, as the hostess or committee undoubtedly is keeping a filing system for response cards and does not wish to receive the answer in a variety of shapes and sizes.

Mr. Warren Harris

☐ accepts

☐ regrets

Friday, January second
Columbus Country Club

M_____

will _____ attend

Friday, January second

Maps

If your home, the club or location of the party is unfamiliar to some guests, or difficult to find, it is helpful and courteous to draw a map of the best route to take, or to write directions, have the map or instructions reproduced, and enclose them with your invitations.

Tickets

When the invitation is to an event where tickets are required, such as a commencement, these tickets may be enclosed with the invitation if you know the recipient will be coming and the invitation is a formality.

Raffle Tickets

Charity and fund-raising organizations often enclose raffle tickets with their invitations, hoping that even if the recipient cannot attend the event, he will purchase a raffle ticket and support the organization in that way.

Any of these enclosures are placed in front of the invitation which is inserted with the writing facing the flap side of the envelope so that the recipient sees the enclosures as the invitation is removed.

THE FORMAL ACCEPTANCE OR REGRET

The form of acceptance or regret depends upon the form of the invitation received, for the degree of formality or informality is generally the same. The exception is this: If you receive an invitation to a dance, or perhaps a wedding invitation, from a good friend, and you cannot accept, you may well feel that the impersonal third-person reply is too formal and unfriendly. Because you want to explain your refusal, and perhaps extend your best wishes to the guest of honor or the bride, you would prefer to write a personal note. Do it. Just as the personal note is the most flattering kind of wedding invitation, it is also the friendliest type of reply under special circumstances. However, on most occasions, for acceptances and when there is nothing special to say, the "reply-in-kind" rule holds.

On the telephone, of course, there are no problems, but for the handwritten answer there are formulas that should be used. Once learned, the formal reply is the easiest to write, because no changes or embellishments are necessary other than in the names and the dates.

Your reply is always addressed to the person or people from whom the invitation came. If it is from "Mr. and Mrs. Arthur Smith" your reply goes to "Mr. and Mrs. Arthur Smith," even though you know that Mrs. Smith alone is keeping the records.

Whether the invitation is to a dance, a dinner, or whatever, the answer is identical, with the exception of the pertinent word—that is, the following form may be used with the substitution of "a dance," etc., for "dinner."

> *Mr. and Mrs. Rothmore*
> *accept with pleasure*
> *the kind invitation of*
> *Mr. and Mrs. Peter Angeles, Jr.*
> *for dinner*
> *on Monday, the tenth of December*
> *at eight o'clock*

Also used, but not quite so formal, is this form:

> *Mr. and Mrs. Lewis Rothmore*
> *accept with pleasure*
> *Mr. and Mrs. Angeles's*
> *kind invitation for dinner*
> *on Monday, the tenth of December*
> *at eight o'clock*

Note that in the first form the full name, including "Jr." when appropriate, must be used, whereas in the second, "Mr. and Mrs. Johnson's" is sufficient.

When the wording of the invitation is:

> *Mr. and Mrs. Stuart Zeitlin*
> *request the pleasure of your company, etc.*

your reply may also say:

> *. . . accept with pleasure*
> *your kind invitation for . . .*

The formulas for regret:

> *Dr. and Mrs. Kenneth Cohen*
> *regret that they are unable to accept*
> *the kind invitation of*
> *Mr. and Mrs. Jordan Evan Anderson*
> *for Monday, the tenth of December*

> *Mr. Michael Ingber*
> *regrets that he is unable to accept*
> *Mr. and Mrs. Harris's*
> *kind invitation for dinner*
> *on Monday, the tenth of December*

"Monday, December the tenth," is sometimes used, but the wording above is better.

In accepting an invitation you must repeat the day and hour so that any mistake can be rectified. But if you decline an invitation it is not necessary to repeat the hour.

Combination Acceptance and Regret

It is entirely proper for a wife or husband to take it for granted that either one alone will be welcome at a wedding reception and to send an acceptance worded as follows:

> *Mrs. Warren Harris*
> *accepts with pleasure*
> *Mr. and Mrs. Smith's*
> *kind invitation for*
> *Saturday, the eighth of June*
> *at eight o'clock*
> *but regrets that*
> *Mr. Harris*
> *will be unable to attend*

If it were the wife who could not attend, the wording would merely transpose the "Mr." and "Mrs." If the invitation is addressed to both members of an unmarried couple who are living together, they may respond in the same way.

Reply to An Organization

Miss Elinor Schoen
accepts with pleasure
the kind invitation of
The Alpha Chapter
of
Beta Chi Delta
for Monday afternoon, February twenty-third

A women who uses "Ms" socially may use that title in her response.

Reply to a Committee

If the name of the committee or its organization is very long or complicated, you may write your reply in the following form:

Mr. and Mrs. David Tarling
accept with pleasure
your kind invitation
for a Ball
on Saturday, the first of January

Invitations From More Than One Hostess

There is no rule about the order in which the names of two or more hostesses should appear, except that the one at whose house the party will be held is usually placed first. Or if one is a great deal older her name may head the list. The invitation should make very clear where the event is to take place and where the acceptances and regrets are to be sent. For example, if a dinner is to take place at a club or restaurant, the form is this:

Mr. and Mrs. William Alan Parker
Mr. and Mrs. Henry Edwards
Mr. and Mrs. Jamison Greenstein
request the pleasure of your company
at dinner
Tuesday, the second of November
at half after seven o'clock
at
The Brook Club

R.s.v.p.
Mr. and Mrs. William Alan Parker
123 Greenwood Lane
Lakeville, Michigan 48036

If, on the other hand, it should be a luncheon to be at Mrs. Parker's house, the correct form would be this:

Mrs. William Alan Parker
Mrs. Henry Edwards
Mrs. Jamison Greenstein
request the pleasure of your company
at a luncheon
Tuesday, the second of November
at half after one o'clock
123 Greenwood Lane
Lakeville, Michigan 48036

R.s.v.p.
Mrs. William Alan Parker

Reply to More Than One Hostess

If the names of two or more hostesses appear on an invitation, the reply is addressed to the one at whose house the party is to take place; or if it is to be at a club or hotel, to the name and address indicated below the R.s.v.p. Without such indication you must address it to all of them at the hotel or club.

When you write your answer you repeat all the names that appear on the invitation, even though your envelope is addressed only to the name following the R.s.v.p., or the first name on the list of hostesses.

Mrs. Richard Roth
accepts with pleasure
the kind invitation of
Mrs. Parker and
Mrs. Edwards and
Mrs. Greenstein
for Tuesday, the second of November
at half after one o'clock

Semiformal Invitations

Visiting-Card Invitations

For an informal dance, a tea to meet a guest, or any other semiformal occasion, a woman may use her ordinary visiting card. (*See Chapter 14 for their style and form.*) Because the U.S. Postal Service will not accept envelopes smaller than 3½ by 5 inches, a size at least this large should be ordered for visiting cards or other small-sized cards. These larger envelopes, being thinner but of the color and texture of the cards, need not look unmatched. It is possible to order larger cards to fit the envelopes, but these would not be used as enclosures with gifts or as "visiting" cards.

The following examples are absolutely correct in every detail—including the abbreviations. They should be written, if possible, in black ink:

> *To meet*
> *Miss Angela Gordon*
>
> Mrs. John Kindhart
>
> *Tues. Jan 7*
> *Dancing at 9. o'ck.*
>
> 1350 Maplewood Avenue

> *Wed. Jan. 18*
> *Bridge at 2. o'ck.*
>
> Mrs. John Kindhart
>
> *R. s. v. p.*   1350 Maplewood Avenue

Semiformal Fill-In Cards

A very popular form of invitation is a fill-in card, but unlike the "formal" fill-in, it is printed rather than engraved, colorful, and comes in a variety of styles. The printed lines follow the wording of the formal third-person invitation, and you may either order them with your name already printed on them, or you may buy them unpersonalized and fill in your own name.

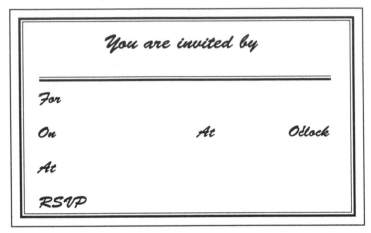

The cards are usually bordered and printed in a bright color on a white background, or they may be beige bordered in brown, yellow bordered in green, etc. The printing is apt to be modern and stylized, rather than traditional. Even though the wording is "third-person" these are *not* formal invitations and need not be answered as such. A brief note, a telephone call (if the number appears in the invitation), or your own informal with "So sorry, must regret the 17th," is all that is necessary.

Semiformal Replies On Visiting Cards

The reply on a visiting card is simply this:

accepts with pleasure!
Wednesday at 4.

Mrs. William Goadby Post

14 Water Street

Sincere regrets
Wed. Jan. 8

Mr. and Mrs. William Goadby Post

INFORMALS AS INVITATIONS

The use of informals (small folding cards, described in Chapter 14) for invitations is correct and practical. Again, the envelope must comply with postal regulations. If the card is engraved with your name, the invitation is written in this way:

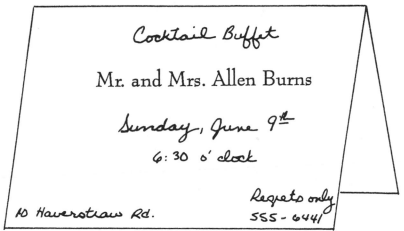

Cocktail Buffet

Mr. and Mrs. Allen Burns

Sunday, June 9th
6:30 o'clock

Regrets only
555-6441

10 Haverstraw Rd.

If the card is monogrammed or unmarked, the invitation takes the form of a brief note and must include your name, since the recipient may not know by whom it was sent. If the card is going to a close friend the signature need be only the first name; but if there should be any question whether the receiver knows from which "Lucy" the invitation came, it is safer to include the last name.

If you prefer, on all informal invitations it is correct to put "Regrets only," followed by your telephone number or address, instead of the R.s.v.p.

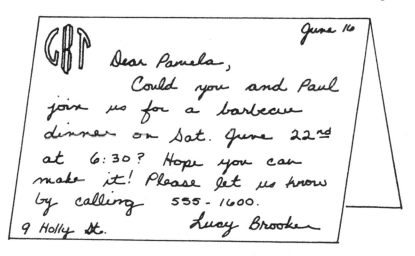

June 16

Dear Pamela,
Could you and Paul join us for a barbecue dinner on Sat. June 22nd at 6:30? Hope you can make it! Please let us know by calling 555-1600.
Lucy Brooke

9 Holly St.

INFORMAL INVITATIONS

With the exception of invitations to house parties, those sent to out-of-town guests, and those requiring a certain amount of formality, the invitation by note is almost a thing of the past. On informal occasions, the attractively designed and decorated fill-in invitations sold for every sort of entertainment are widely used. Many of these are charming and in the best of taste. The telephone is also a perfectly acceptable means of extending an informal invitation, and nothing need be said about the correct form beyond a reminder that you should be perfectly clear about the date and hour and leave your guests in no doubt about what is intended. If you feel that a written invitation is needed, that is certainly never incorrect. However, as is true with more formal invitations, the informal one should not be typewritten unless the sender is truly unable to write by hand.

Informal Replies

When replying to an informal invitation you do whatever that invitation indicates. If the R.s.v.p. appears, followed or not by an address, you may use your informal as illustrated below, or you may write a sentence on your notepaper or a postcard. All you need say is "Thanks so much—we'll be there on the 16th."

If a telephone number follows the R.s.v.p., make every effort to reach the hostess by telephone. But if the date is approaching and you have been unable to reach her, drop her a note instead.

When an invitation says "Regrets only," don't reply unless it *is* a regret. To do otherwise can be confusing to the hostess.

When there is no R.s.v.p. at all, you are under no obligation to do anything. But it is never amiss, and often very much appreciated, if you reply by phone call or note regardless.

As mentioned on page 370 the reply to a semiformal fill-in invitation should be informal, in spite of the third-person wording of the invitation.

As with formal invitations your informal reply is addressed to the person who signed the invitation.

RECALLING AND REQUESTING INVITATIONS

If invitations have to be recalled because of illness or for some other reason, the following form is correct. The card is always printed instead of being engraved—there being no time for engraving. In an emergency the message may be handwritten or given by telephone.

Owing to the illness of their daughter
Mr. and Mrs. John Huntington Smith, III
are obliged to recall their invitations
for Tuesday, the tenth of June

ASKING FOR AN INVITATION

One may never ask for an invitation for oneself anywhere. Nor does one ask to bring an extra person to a meal unless one knows it is a buffet at which one or two unexpected people could make no difference.

When regretting an invitation you may always explain that you are expecting to have weekend guests. Ordinarily the hostess-to-be says, "I'm sorry!" But if it happens that she is having a big buffet lunch or a cocktail party she may say, "Do bring them. I'd love to meet them."

Requests for invitations are almost always telephoned, so that the invitee's situation can be explained, and the hostess can also explain her "Of course" or "I'm sorry you won't be able to join us."

CHANGING YOUR ANSWER

From "Yes" to "No"

If for any reason you find you cannot attend a function that you have already accepted, it is essential that you let the hostess know immediately. If it is a seated dinner or a bridge party it is obvious that it would be most inconsiderate not to do so at once, since she will want time to invite others in your place. Even at a large catered party it is important, because the hostess pays for the number of guests expected and not for how many actually arrive. In the case of an open house or a big cocktail party, it is not so much a practical matter as one of common courtesy.

In most cases a telephone call is best, as it is quick and gives you a chance to explain your problem and express your regrets. If you prefer, however, and there is ample time, you may write a short note, giving the reason and your apologies.

From "No" to "Yes"

Sometimes a person refuses an invitation for perfectly legitimate reasons and then finds that circumstances have changed and he can attend after all. If the affair is a party involving a limited number, such as for bridge, a theater party, or a seated dinner, he must swallow his disappointment and hope to be asked again. The hostess will surely have filled his place, and it would only embarrass her if he asked to be "reinstated." However, if the party is a large reception, a cocktail buffet, a picnic, or any affair at which another guest or two would not cause any complications, he may call the hostess, explain his situation, and ask if he may change his regret to an acceptance.

19

Entertaining at Home

*T*he first considerations when you entertain at home are the space you have available for entertaining, and the degree of formality you want and can achieve, if desired, within that space. Someone who lives in a small house that has a large deck or patio would be more comfortable inviting guests to a barbecue or backyard picnic than to a formal dinner, while someone who has rooms with generous proportions could more easily give a formal dinner party.

No matter what your available space is, your next consideration is what type of party you can give comfortably and how many guests you can accommodate. Comfortably means being so organized that you spend the majority of your time with your guests, not in the kitchen. To do this, you must prepare as much as possible in advance, and plan a menu that enables you to serve as the host or hostess, not as the cook or waiter or waitress.

Eight is usually the maximum number that you can serve yourself at a sit-down dinner. You can certainly cook for as many guests as you want, but to serve a seated dinner of more than eight efficiently and quickly it is almost essential to have an assistant. For more than sixteen the services of two people are recommended—one to help at the bar, pass hors d'oeuvres, and serve dinner, the other to work in the kitchen. Greater numbers, of course, require more help.

THE SUCCESSFUL DINNER PARTY

Almost any dinner where guests are seated at a dining-room table and are served by someone other than themselves is considered a "formal" dinner today. Of course there are all degrees of formality, depending upon the dress, the table setting, the food served, and the type of service. Emily Post wrote in 1922 that "it is not possible to give a formal dinner without the help of servants." Yet today the hostess who cooks a perfectly prepared meal and serves it at a beautifully set table is considered to have given a "formal" dinner.

There are "official" formal dinners, which must follow certain rules and are given only by diplomats or people in very high public positions. In those cases rules of protocol and precedence must be rigidly followed, and there are government agencies and special books to help those who are unacquainted with the requirements. For details not included in this book, newcomers to the world of diplomacy can get the information they need through the Office of Protocol in Washington or from the famous *Green Book* published each year with all the current social information a hostess needs to know—names, titles, rules of precedence, etc.

This chapter deals mainly with the requirements for the sort of formal dinner with which most of us are familiar, and which we enjoy. By taking the suggestions that appeal to you, by eliminating the details that would be difficult for you or seem unnatural to you, and by combining the elements that are suitable to your home and your friends, you can use the information as it should be used—as a guide. Remember always, it is far less important to have matching silver or fine goblets than it is to be a warm, relaxed, and gracious party giver. Self-confidence helps you to be all these things, and a knowledge that you are doing things correctly—to the very best of your ability—will give you the assurance to entertain easily and well.

Whether your dinner party is held in a restaurant, a club, or your own home, and whether there are a hundred guests or eight, the requisites for a successful dinner party are the same. They are:

Guests who are congenial.

A menu that is well planned and suited to your guests' tastes.

An attractive table—everything in perfect condition: linen pressed, silver polished, glassware sparkling.

Food that is well prepared.

Servants (if you have them, or are hiring them for the evening) who are competent and pleasant.

A gracious and cordial hostess and host who are welcoming and at the same time enjoy their guests.

Serving Staff

If you have live-in help, they will presumably have learned to serve in the way you like best. Most of us, however, must hire temporary help for the evening when we want to entertain formally. Catering services and specialized employment agencies are resources for temporary help. Although they may be professionals at what they do, you still need to give them instructions so that they are able to assist according to your wishes. Temporary help is generally hired to cook and/or serve and clean up. It is up to the hostess to do all the other preparation, from setting the table and arranging flowers to making sure the bar is stocked and there is plenty of ice.

Catering Service/Cook

A catering service will provide all the elements of the meal with instructions as to how they are to be heated, etc., or it will provide the food and a cook. If there is to be a cook, he or she arrives early enough to learn the workings of the kitchen and to have time for preparation of the meal.

If there is no cook, the food is either picked up or delivered early enough for the hostess to do whatever finishing touches are needed.

Many catering services also provide bartenders and waiters/waitresses, if required.

Bartender

If cocktails are to be served, a bartender arrives early enough to set up the bar, see that he or she has all the necessary ingredients, and be ready when the first guest arrives.

Waiters/ Waitresses

Temporary waiters and waitresses can provide many services, which should be discussed at the time hiring arrangements are made. They may wait in the hall to direct guests, take coats, etc., they may pass hors d'oeuvres, assist the bartender in passing drinks if guests do not go to the bar themselves, and they serve at the table. They also may be expected to clean up. Depending on their duties, they arrive early enough to perform whatever their first function will be.

The bartender and waitress ordinarily do not leave until the guests have been ushered out, the last glass washed, and the last ashtray emptied. However, if they are hired on an hourly basis, the hostess may specify ahead of time that they may leave at ten or eleven, or whenever she wishes. The cook, however, unless all three work as a unit, leaves as soon as the cooking utensils and dinner service have been washed and the kitchen made immaculate.

The method of paying temporary help varies in different localities and also depends on the policy of the agency. Some caterers send a bill for their services and prefer that you do not add a tip. Others send a bill indicating that you may add a tip. If the help has been hired from an employment agency or by you personally, you simply pay them before they leave at the rate you have agreed upon, adding the appropriate tip. In any case, it is most important to establish the method and amount of payment at the time servants are hired to avoid embarrassment or unpleasantness later.

Selecting Your Guests

When making up her guest list, a hostess must try to invite and put together those who are likely to be interesting to each other. Professor Bugge might bore *you* to tears but Mrs. Entomoid would probably adore him, just as Mr. Stocksan Bonds and Mrs. Rich would probably have interests in common. Making a dinner list is a little like making a Christmas list. You put down what *they* will like (you hope), not what you like. People placed between congenial neighbors remember your dinner as delightful, but those seated next to their pet aversions will need wild horses to drag them your way again.

While a friendly difference of opinion or even a mild argument is often stimulating, a bitter controversy is embarrassing and destructive to good conversation. It is thus safer to avoid seating people next to each other who are deeply involved in, or rabidly opinionated about, opposite sides of a controversial issue.

Greeting Guests

At very large formal dinners guests are greeted at the door by a servant who takes their coats. The hostess stands in the living room, near the door. As guests enter she greets them with a smile and a handshake and welcomes them. She may simply say, "I'm very glad to see you," or "I'm so glad you could come!" but her smile is full of warmth. Her husband, who is circulating and talking to other guests, excuses himself and comes to greet newcomers as soon as he can.

Most dinners, however, are much less formal. The host and hostess stay near the door if possible, or if they happen to be in the living room, they go together to greet their guests when the doorbell rings. If the host is serving cocktails he brings them what they wish, or he sees that the waiter or bartender takes their order. The hostess introduces them to the people they do not know.

If cocktails are served, dinner should be planned for at least an hour later than the time on the invitation; twenty minutes later if drinks are not served, to allow late arrivals a moment of relaxation. During this period the hostess may slip out to the kitchen to attend to last-minute details or to be sure that her help are having no problems. She should make her absence as brief as possible so that the guests will not feel that she is overburdened.

The Late Guest

Fifteen minutes is the established length of time that a hostess need delay her dinner for a late guest. To wait more than twenty minutes, at the outside, would be showing rudeness to many for the sake of one. When the late guest finally enters the dining room he must go up to the hostess and apologize for being late. The hostess remains seated, and if the guest is a woman she merely shakes hands quickly so that all the men at table need not rise. The hostess should not take the guest to task but should say something polite such as, "I'm so sorry you had such a bad drive but I was sure you wouldn't want us to wait dinner." The latecomer is served whatever course is being eaten at the time he arrives. Of course, if that happens to be dessert the hostess would ask the waitress to bring him a plateful of the main course from the kitchen.

When Dinner Is Announced

When dinner is ready to be served, the candles are lighted and water glasses are filled. If there is no help, the first course, if it is not a hot course, is in place so that the hostess may sit down right away with her guests. The hostess announces to the group, "Dinner is ready, shall we go in?" if the group is small. If the group is large, she may ask two or three good friends to help her in moving the other guests toward the dining room so that she doesn't need to stand in the doorway and shout. If she is having difficulty getting people to respond, she may, if she wishes, suggest that her guests bring their cocktails to the table to encourage them to delay no longer just to finish their drinks.

At a very formal dinner when the table is being made ready by servants and there is a butler, the butler approaches the hostess to tell her that dinner is ready, and she then asks her guests to move to the dining room. Again, the first course, if not a hot course, may be in place. If it is a hot course, such as soup, the butler serves it after people are seated.

Being Seated

The host leads the way in to dinner with the female guest of honor whom he seats on his right. Other guests walk in with whomever they are talking to when dinner is announced. When there is no particular guest of honor among a group of friends dining together, the hostess might choose the oldest woman or one who has not visited her house for some time to sit on her husband's right. Otherwise she may seat her guests according to whatever arrangement she thinks they will enjoy the most, alternating the men and women and separating husbands and wives. If there is an uneven number of men and women she must space them as evenly as possible. She may keep her place at the end of the table unless doing so puts too many women in a row. Whatever else she may do, she still seats the honored guests at her and her husband's right. The woman next in importance sits at the host's left, and her husband, or the man of next importance, on the hostess's left.

The hostess is always the last to go into the dining room when place cards are used. If there are no place cards, she goes ahead to tell guests where to sit. Women sit down as soon as they find their places, even though the hostess remains standing until everyone is at his chair. The men hold the chairs for the women on their right. The men do not sit down until the hostess is seated. The male guest of honor, even though he has escorted the hostess in, seats the lady on his right, and the man on the hostess's left seats her.

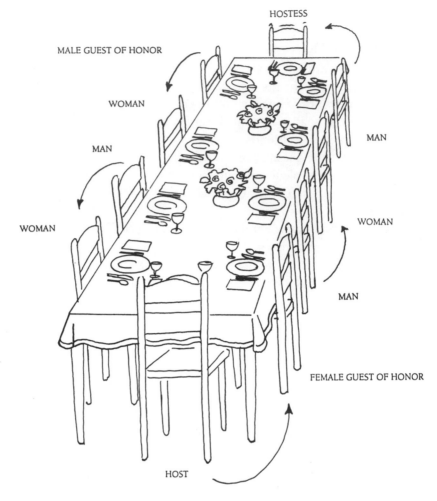

A woman is seated by the man at her left, as indicated by the arrows.

When a single woman entertains at a large dinner, she seats the female guest of honor, if there is one, at one end of the table and herself at the other end. If a man is acting as host, he is seated to the woman of honor's left. The man of honor is seated to the hostess's right, and other guests are seated alternating men and women around the table.

When you are seating three, five, or seven couples, there is no problem at all. It works out evenly, with the hostess at one end of the table (usually the end nearest the kitchen), the host opposite her, and the men and women alternating on either side. However, when you have multiples of four you must make another arrangement. To avoid seating two women and two men together, the hostess moves one place to the left, so that the man on her right sits opposite the host at the end of the table.

Other situations require variations, too. For instance, whenever it is convenient, it is thoughtful to seat a left-handed diner at a corner where his or her left arm

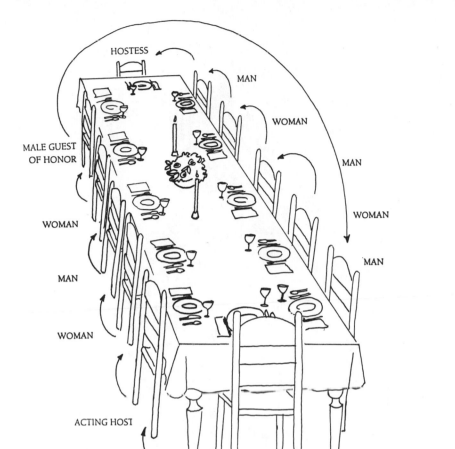

The correct seating arrangement for a group that has a hostess but no host. Arrows indicate order of service.

will not bump into the right arm of the person beside him, when they are both eating. Almost all seating problems can be worked out by common sense and an awareness of which guests will be happiest seated next to certain others.

Place Cards

Place cards are always used at very formal dinners and I find them very useful at any dinner so large that the hostess cannot easily indicate where everyone is to sit. (*See pages 422–423 for place card styles and placement.*)

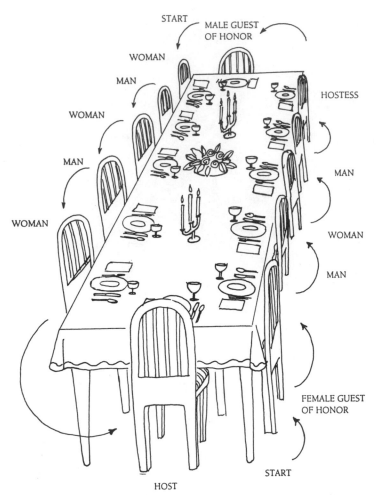

START
MALE GUEST OF HONOR
WOMAN
MAN
WOMAN
MAN
WOMAN
HOST
HOSTESS
MAN
WOMAN
MAN
FEMALE GUEST OF HONOR
START

Seating arrangement for a party of eight, twelve, or sixteen. To avoid seating two men and two women together the hostess moves one place to the left so that the male guest of honor sits opposite the host. Arrows indicate order of service.

Formal Service

At a very formal dinner served by a *large* staff, a butler always stands behind the hostess's chair, except when giving one of the men under him a direction or when pouring wine. His duty is to see that everything goes smoothly and he is not supposed to leave the dining room. At a smaller dinner he naturally does everything himself; or if he has a waitress to help him, he passes the principal dishes and she follows with the accompanying dishes or vegetables.

In any case, whether there are two at a table or three hundred, plates are changed and courses presented in precisely the same manner. No serving dishes or platters are ever put on the table except the ornamental compotes of fruit or candy.

The meat is carved in the kitchen or pantry; vegetables, bread, and condiments are passed and returned to a side table or the kitchen.

From the time the table is set until it is cleared for dessert, a plate should remain at every place. The plate on which oysters or clams are served is put on top of the service plate, and so is a plate holding fruit or cold seafood in a stemmed glass. At the end of the course the used plate is removed, leaving the service plate. The soup plate is also put on top of this same plate. But when the soup plate is removed, the underneath plate is removed with it, and the hot plate for the main course immediately exchanged for the two taken away.

If the first course is passed instead of being served on individual plates, it is eaten on the service plate. An exchange plate is then necessary before the soup can be served. That is, a clean service plate is exchanged for the used one, and the soup plate then put on top of that.

Although all dishes are presented at the left of the person being served, it is better that plates be removed from the right. If more convenient, however, it is permissible to remove them from the left. Glasses are filled and additional knives placed at the right, but forks are put on as needed at the left.

The only plates that are properly brought into the dining room one in each hand are for soup and dessert. The soup plates are put down on the service plates, which have not been removed, and the dessert plates are put down on the tablecloth. The plates of every other course have to be exchanged, and therefore each individual service requires two hands. Soup plates two at a time can be dangerous, as it is while putting down one plate and balancing the other that a mishap can occur. If only one plate of soup is brought in at a time, accidents should not happen. Also, the spoon and fork on the dessert plate can easily fall off unless it is held level. Two plates at a time are therefore not a question of etiquette, but one of the servant's skill.

At one time good service required the removal of each plate the instant the fork was laid down on it, so that by the time the last eater was finished, the entire table was set with clean plates and was ready for the service of the next course. But the protests of the slow eaters were loud and clear, and a considerate hostess now does not have the plates removed until the slowest eaters have finished.

The Food and Drink

Before Dinner Cocktails

Two or three varieties of cocktails should be offered, with the bartender or host indicating what they are. Wine should be offered too, for those who prefer it to hard liquor. There must also be soda, tomato juice or sparkling water available for those who prefer something other than liquor. Unless dinner is delayed because of waiting for late arrivals, only two cocktails need be served. There is usually wine with the meal, and the smart hostess knows that wine does not mix well with too many cocktails.

Menu Suggestions

Six courses are the maximum for even the most elaborate formal dinner. They are:

1. Soup *or* fresh fruit cup *or* melon *or* shellfish (clams, oysters, or shrimp)
2. Fish course (*or* on rare occasions, a dish such as sweetbreads instead of fish, and omitted if shellfish is served first)
3. The entrée, or main course (usually roast meat or fowl and vegetables)
4. Salad
5. Dessert
6. Coffee

Notice that the salad is served between the entrée and the dessert. This is correct in spite of the custom in almost all restaurants of serving it as a first course. Unless you know that a group of friends at a casual dinner prefer it first, salad should be served as stated here, or it may be served with the entrée, on a separate salad plate.

One should always try to choose a well-balanced menu; an especially rich dish is balanced by a simple one. Coquilles St. Jacques (scallops with a thick cream sauce) might perhaps be followed by medallions of lamb, Cornish game hens, or a filet mignon; broiled fish by a more elaborate meat dish.

Consider the appearance of the food you serve. Avoid a dinner of white sauces from beginning to end: creamed soup, creamed sweetbreads, followed by breast of chicken and mashed potatoes. Combine flavors intelligently. Don't serve all "sweet" dishes: beet soup, duck basted with currant jelly, a fruit salad, and a sugary dessert. In these examples each dish is good in itself but unappetizing in the monotony of its combination.

Wine

Tradition has always decreed that one particular wine goes with one particular food, but unless the meal is strictly formal there is no reason why the host may not choose any wine he thinks his guests would prefer. The two most important considerations in choosing a wine are not the cost or where it came from, but that it complements the food with which it is served and pleases the palates of the people drinking it.

Wine glasses are filled only halfway, never to the top of the glass. If more than one wine is to be served during dinner, there should be a glass for each wine. Wine glasses should be picked up by the stem rather than the bowl. In the case of white wine and champagne this helps to keep the wine cool, and in the case of all wines, including red wines, it enables you to appreciate the color.

There are five main categories of wine we should consider.

APERITIFS

Aperitifs include *Lillet, Dubonnet, Campari, Cinzano*, dry or sweet vermouths, and sherry. They are generally served as a before-meal drink, but sherry may be the first wine offered at dinner and also is served at lunch or supper. It is usually offered with a soup that contains sherry in the preparation during dinner. It should not be offered with cream of chicken soup or vichyssoise, but it would be an appropriate accompaniment to black bean or green turtle soup. Sherry should be put in a decanter at room temperature and poured into small, V-shaped glasses. If you don't have sherry glasses, small wine glasses or liqueur glasses are suitable substitutes. Sherry can stand being decanted almost indefinitely without spoiling.

Other aperitifs are served according to preference, either in a small old-fashioned glass with ice, or chilled or at room temperature in a small aperitif glass.

FLUTE SHERRY

WHITE WINE

Dry white wines should be served chilled in the refrigerator for several hours or even days before being used, or may be cooled in a bucket or cooler filled with a mixture of ice and cold water. The actual melting of the ice in the water will cool the wine faster than if it is immersed in cracked ice alone. Drawing the cork and turning the bottle from time to time will hasten the cooling.

Traditionally, white wines are served with "white" meats such as fish, chicken, and veal, and with fruit and salads. This is still the case, but many people drink white wine as their cocktail choice and prefer to continue drinking it throughout the meal, no matter what the entree is. Unlike red wine, white wine contains no sediment and the bottle may be upended to empty it.

GERMAN ALSAC

RED WINE

Red wines, for the most part are served at a cool room temperature. If they are too cool, they may be warmed by placing the hands around the bowl of the glass, or by being left before serving in a warm spot (but never over a burner or flame).

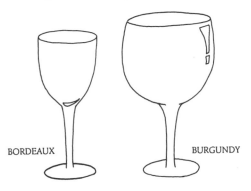

BORDEAUX BURGUNDY

Traditionally, red wines are served with beef, certain cheese dishes, pasta with a red sauce and some fowl, although, as with white wine, red wines are often drunk regardless of the entree as a wine of preference or because they have been drunk during the cocktail hour before dinner. This would be more likely with a claret, a light red wine, than with a burgundy, which is much heavier.

Rosé wines of the non-sparkling variety are in the red wine family. They are served chilled, generally with lighter entrees such as fish, veal, some chicken dishes and fruit.

The procedure for serving a fine vintage red wine is somewhat complicated but should be followed carefully if its excellence is to be appreciated. A day or two before it is to be used, the wine should be removed from the wine cellar or closet. This is done by transferring the bottle into a straw basket as gently as possible, maintaining the bottle in a semihorizontal position. Actually in the basket it should be tilted 15 or 20 degrees more toward the vertical than it was in the bin, and it is left in this position for a day at least to permit any disturbed sediment to settle.

If you do not have a wine cellar, purchase the wine several days before your dinner and follow the same procedure. The bottle should be opened an hour or so before serving. At this time, the foil is neatly cut away to prevent the wine from coming in contact with it while being poured. For the same reason a damp cloth is used to wipe the mouth of the bottle, removing any accumulated dirt and grime. The cork is then carefully pulled and placed beside the neck of the bottle in its basket in order that the host or any interested guest may note that it is undamaged. During this hour the bottle is open, the wine is given an opportunity to "breathe" and rid itself of any musty or other unpleasant odor it might have absorbed in the cellar.

It should be served in the basket, with the label showing to permit each guest to note what he is being offered. Caution must be taken when pouring the wine to avoid any "backlash" or bubbling that can result if it is handled carelessly. This would agitate the sediment, which should be resting in the bottom of the bottle. Finally, it is obvious that the last inch or so should not be poured from the bottle, since this will be murky with sediment.

When a bottle of red wine is so heavy with sediment that the procedure given above will not result in a palatable drink, it may be decanted.

SPARKLING WINES

This category of wine includes sparkling rosé wines, sparkling burgundies, and sparkling white wines, including champagne.

Champagne is, above all other beverages, that of the very special dinner party. When other wines are included, it is served with the meat course, but when it is the only wine it is served as soon as the first course has begun. Its proper temperature depends upon its quality.

Champagne that is not of especially fine vintage is put in the refrigerator for a day and then chilled further by putting it into a cooler with a little salt as well as ice. Occasionally, holding the bottle by the neck, turn it back and forth a few times. In doing this, take care not to leave the bottle in the salt and ice too long, or the champagne may become sherbet Also, when opening, be sure to wrap the bottle in a towel or napkin as a protection in case it explodes.

An excellent vintage champagne, on the other hand, is packed in ice without salt, which chills it just a little less. There are two shapes of champagne glasses, coupe-shaped and flutes. Coupe-shaped glasses usually have hollow stems, which cause the champagne to warm because of the heat of the fingers holding the stem. A flute also tends to prolong the life of the effervescent bubbles that distinguish champagne from other wines.

COUPE   FLUTE

Champagne glasses ought to be as thin as soap bubbles. Thick glasses will raise the temperature at which a really good champagne should be served and spoil its perfection. If thicker glasses must be used, the epicurean thing to do is to chill them in the refrigerator and put them on the table the moment the champagne is to be poured.

DESSERT WINES

Sauternes and other sweet wines may be served with dessert, chilled. Sweet sherry, port or Madeira are served after dessert is finished and may accompany coffee in place of liqueurs.

The Order of Service

Whether there is serving help or not, the woman of honor on the host's right is always served each dish first. If there is serving help, servers move around the table counterclockwise, serving the host last. The hostess is never served first. The diagrams on the preceding pages explain seating and service arrangements.

When there is no serving help and the host or hostess fill plates and pass them, they say "This is for you" when giving the first plate to the guest of honor so she knows she is to keep it and not pass it down the table. The second plate is passed down the table on the right side to whoever is sitting at the opposite end from the host. The rest of the guests are served in order, working back toward the guest of honor. The process is then repeated on the hosts's left side. He serves himself last.

When food is served directly from the kitchen, service is also counterclockwise with the host served last. Plates are served from the guests' left side and removed, if possible, from the right.

Since any of these procedures can take considerable time and the food will surely be getting cold, it is important that the host or hostess ask the guests to start after three or four people have been served. If the host and hostess forget to do so, one of the guests is perfectly correct in beginning to eat.

Filling Glasses

If there is a waiter or waitress, he or she goes to the right side of each guest and asks quietly, "Wine, sir [or madam]?" Glasses are filled from the right without lifting the glass from the table. If more than one wine is being served, the host or hostess should be sure that the waiter is experienced in serving wine and knows which glasses are used for which wine. The waiter watches each guest's glass carefully and refills it when he sees it is empty.

When there is no help, the simplest way to offer wine is to place the opened bottle on the table in front of the host, preferably on a coaster or wine holder to prevent any drops from soiling the tablecloth. If there are several guests, a second bottle is placed at the other end of the table and the host asks a man at that end to assist him in pouring.

Anyone who does not wish wine merely says, "No, thank you," but does not cover his glass with his hand nor does he turn his glass upside down.

Serving Bread and Condiments

Breads are passed in a flat dish or a basket. A guest helps himself with his fingers and lays the roll or bread on his butter plate. Whenever a guest has no bread left at his place, more should be passed to him. Except at formal dinners, bread and other condiments are usually passed around the table by the guests themselves. If there is a choice of two or three sauces or other condiments, placing them together in a divided dish, or on a small, easily managed tray, ensures that they are passed together and all guests are aware of the choices. As with other service, dishes are passed counterclockwise, and all should be passed in the same direction.

Salad

When salad is served at a party where there is no help, it is best that the guests pass the bowl, each one in turn holding it for the person on his right.

Presenting Dishes

When there is serving help, dishes are held flat on the palm of the server's left hand; every hot one must have a napkin placed as a pad under it. An especially heavy platter can be steadied by holding the edge with the right hand.

Each dish is supplied with whatever silver is needed for serving it. A serving spoon and a large fork are put on most dishes, or the spoon alone is used if the dish is not hard to help oneself to. With the spoon underneath, the fork is held with the prongs turned down to hold and balance the portion when both utensils are used.

Second Helpings

A sideboard or serving table, if there is room for one, acts as a halfway station between the dinner table and the kitchen. It holds plates for the next course, extra flatware, and finger bowls. All serving dishes after being passed may be left on the serving table on a warming tray in case they are needed for a second helping, or they may be taken to the kitchen and kept warm on the stove. When the hostess sees that guests are ready for another portion, she either rings for help and says "Would you please pass the meat and rice again?" or if she has no help, she gets up and gets the serving bowl and passes it.

Clearing the Table

Salad plates as well as the plates used for the entrée are removed before dessert is served. The saltcellars, pepper shakers, unused flat silver, and nut dishes are taken off on a serving tray, and at a formal dinner, the crumbs are brushed off each place with a tightly folded napkin onto a small tray or a "silent butler" held under the table edge.

When giving a dinner party without serving help dishes are removed two at a time. They are never stacked or scraped at the table. Each time something is taken to the kitchen, you may bring back dessert plates, salad and salad plates, or whatever is needed. If you wish, you may put a dessert plate at each place you have cleared as you return to take the next plate. Or as soon as you have removed the host's plate, you may put a stack of dessert plates and the dessert in front of him, and he may serve it while you are finishing the table-clearing.

If finger bowls are used, they may be brought in on plates after dessert is served or they may be placed on a small doily along with the dessert fork and spoon on the dessert plate. The diner puts the finger bowl, lifted by the doily, above his plate, and the fork and spoon each to its proper side. If no finger bowls are used, dessert may be brought in from the kitchen already on the plates and placed before the guests in the same order as was the main course. In other words, any system that speeds and smooths the changing of courses is acceptable, so that your guests do not feel that you are going to too much trouble.

To guests who offer to help you clear, you must say, "No, thank you, really it is easier to do it myself" or you will find that everyone but one or two of your guests is suddenly on his or her feet and in the kitchen. Of course a very close friend or relative may be asked in advance to help and a son or daughter should be expected to help, but your other guests should be just that—guests, and remain at the table.

After Dinner Coffee

Coffee is served in one of four ways:

1. A server passes a tray of cups, saucers, and sugar; the waiter or waitress follows with the coffeepot and pours into the cup held in the guest's hand.
2. A tray with filled cups is proffered by the server to the guests, who help themselves.
3. The tray of cups and sugar (if not too heavy) is held on the servant's left hand. The guest puts sugar into one of the cups and the servant pours coffee with the right hand.

4. At a less formal dinner, the coffee tray is placed in front of the hostess in the living room. She pours, and her helper passes the filled cup, on a tray with sugar and cream, to each guest.

Serving after dinner coffee is more complicated today than it was in Emily Post's day when real coffee was served with real cream and real sugar—no choices, no questions. As people have become more conscious about their health the choices and questions have multiplied. Real coffee; brewed or instant decaffeinated coffee; regular, flavored or herbal teas; cream, whole or skim milk; sugar or sugar substitutes can now be offered after a meal. In deciding what to offer, today's hostess considers the preferences of her guests. When giving a small dinner for friends whom she knows drink only decaffeinated coffee the choice is simple. When entertaining a larger group the hostess should offer a choice—a pot of brewed decaffeinated coffee and a pot of hot water with a selection of teas, perhaps.

After Dinner Drinks

After dinner drinks may be served with coffee. If coffee is served at the table, the bottles of after dinner drinks may be placed on the table on a tray containing a variety of glasses and each guests asked which he or she would prefer. If coffee is served in the living room, the tray containing the bottles and glasses is placed on the coffee table and a choice is offered to each guest.

You'll need four different types of glasses. Brandy snifters, either large or small, are for serving cognac or armagnac. Small, stemmed glasses are for sweet liqueurs. Regular wine glasses may be used for port, and small old-fashioned glasses may be used for white or green *creme de menthe* to be served over cracked ice.

When dinner is over there is no need to clear the dessert dishes unless your dining table is at one end of your living room. In that case, you would not want to subject your guests to the unappetizing sight of dirty dishes for the rest of the evening. You should not, however, abandon your guests and begin washing dishes after dinner is over, no matter how compulsively neat you are, nor should you permit your guests to insist on washing them. Every meal produces dishes to be washed; you have invited friends to your home to enjoy a pleasant visit, not to have them do the same chores they must do every day at home. Thank your guests for the offer but politely insist that you'll worry about doing dishes later.

Taking Leave

It was once a fixed rule that the guest of honor be the first to take leave, and everyone used to sit on and on, no matter how late, waiting for him or her to go. More often than not the guest of honor was saying to herself, "Oh, my! Are these people *never* going home?" until it dawned on her that the obligation was her own!

Today it is not considered ill-mannered for any couple or individual to rise if the hour is growing late. They simply stand up, say good-bye to the people with whom they were talking and to the guest of honor, and look for their hostess. They chat for a *brief* moment with her and the host, and then offer their thanks and good-byes, and leave.

Buffet Dinners

There are three great advantages to a buffet dinner that appeal to all of us. First, you can accommodate many more guests than your dining-room table will seat. It is important, however, to restrict the number so that there will be places for everyone to sit down, and also so that there will be room for the guests to move about freely when serving themselves and returning to the living room.

Second, lack of service is no handicap. Because a buffet is truly a "do-it-yourself" party, even the hostess without help may spend almost the entire evening with her guests.

And third, it has the informality that most of us so much enjoy. There is something about sitting in one place before dinner, going into the dining room and foraging for yourself, then coming back to the same place or finding a new place, as you prefer, that makes buffet parties so popular. Also, you are free to choose your dinner companions yourself, as you cannot do at a seated dinner.

Invitations

Invitations to a buffet dinner may be written on informals, on your notepaper, or on purchased, fill-in invitations. They are almost never in the formal third-person form. The R.s.v.p. is generally followed by your telephone number. You may telephone your invitations, too, but if you do so ten days or two weeks ahead, you might want to send reminder cards—a post card reading, "Looking forward to seeing you on the 8th, 7 p.m." a few days before your party.

Types of Buffet

Real Buffet

When guests at a real buffet have served themselves in the dining room, they simply take their plates into the living room (where there should be enough chairs for everyone), hold their plates on their laps, and set their glasses on the nearest table. Your guests will be much more comfortable and there will be much less chance of an accident if you set a small table (the folding kind that fit in a rack are ideal and easy to store) near each chair, or at least by each chair not within easy reach of a coffee or side table.

Seated or Semi-Buffet

At this type of buffet your guests may be seated at the dining table and at small tables—sturdy card tables, perhaps—in your living room, hall, or library. This arrangement is, of course, dependent on your having large enough rooms so that the tables will not be in the way before dinner or while the guests are serving themselves. If you do have the space, most men and many women prefer to be seated in this way. The tables are covered with cloths of almost any color and style. The places are set exactly as for any seated dinner, and since the guests need not carry silver, napkins, or glasses with them, a great deal of space is saved on the buffet table. The guests serve themselves as at all buffets, going for second helpings and removing their empty plates unless there is a maid to do it. If the living room is used for the small tables, the hostess must take the tables out after the meal to make room for conversational groups or whatever activity she may have planned. For a bridge party she simply clears the tables and removes the cloths, leaving them ready to be used.

The Buffet Table

The basic principle of buffet table-setting is that only necessary and useful objects are used. Unless there is ample space omit articles that are solely ornamental. Flowers in the center of the table are lovely, of course, but if it is a question of choosing between decorative flowers and edible fruit, a centerpiece of the fruit to be served for dessert is preferable.

In the same way, if the table is crowded and candles are not needed to see by, they are better left off. If candles are needed, candelabra are better than candlesticks because first, they give better light, and second, they are less likely to be knocked over by a guest reaching for a plate of food.

If the party is large it is better to leave the table in the center of the room so that two lines of guests may serve themselves at once. Then the most important dish is divided into two parts, and one platter or casserole placed at each end of the table. The plates are in two stacks beside them, and the napkins and silver neatly arranged next to the plates. Dishes of vegetables, salads, bread and butter, and sauces and condiments are on each side of the table so that the guests need to pass down only one side—greatly speeding the service and keeping them from turning back and bumping into each other.

If the table is set against the wall, place your plates and main dish at the end that makes for the best flow of traffic. This is usually the one nearest the entrance, so that the guests, after serving themselves, do not have to double back against the people coming in.

Your buffet table may be set as formally or informally as you wish. If you use a white damask cloth, silver candelabra, and an elaborate centerpiece, your buffet will appear quite formal. But you can just as well go to the other extreme and use pottery

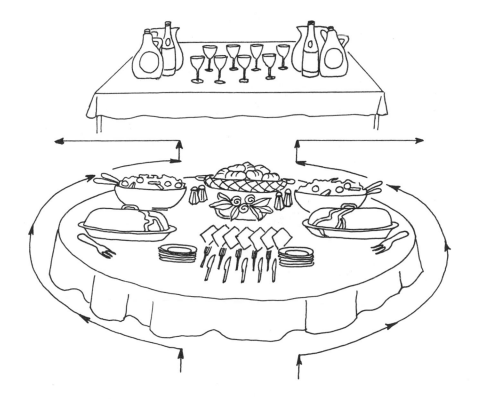

Buffet table in the center of the room. Arrows indicate traffic pattern around the table.

dishes on a checkered tablecloth with a bowl of fruit in the center of the table. What makes your table attractive is not the elegance of the utensils and decorations you use, but the combination of dishes, linen, and silver, and the way in which they are arranged.

Color plays an enormous part in the beauty of a buffet table. If you have a copper bowl or kettle to use as a centerpiece, fill it with red and yellow fruit or a combination of fall vegetables—squash, tomatoes, pumpkins for a Halloween or Thanksgiving table. Keep the autumn tints in mind: Use green, red, or russet mats and yellow pottery on a bare table. Or a green or yellow tablecloth is warm and inviting. Bright red napkins and/or china set the tone for an appealing Valentine's Day table, and of course pastel pinks, yellows, or blues are synonymous with springtime.

Whichever type of buffet you are serving, the most valuable piece of equipment you can have is one that keeps things hot. I recommend an electric hot plate or tray, because they can be used to heat your plates and keep your meal warm for an almost indefinite period of time. As long as a finished casserole is covered so that it will not dry out, it may be placed on a hot plate an hour or more before dinner and be as delectable when it is served as it was the moment it was taken from the oven. The only exception, of course, is a soufflé, which must be served at once. Furthermore,

Buffet table against the wall. Arrows indicate traffic pattern.

with an electric appliance on the buffet table, there is no need to take the dishes to the kitchen to be kept warm for second helpings. And finally, it is unnecessary to watch and replace fuel for flame-heated chafing dishes.

Beverages

Red or white wine, a punch or other cold drink, sparkling water, or beer in its cans or bottles, together with glasses, are on the sideboard or a nearby table. If it is a seated buffet, water glasses are on the tables and are filled before the guests sit down. Wineglasses should also be at the guests' places, but they are never filled in advance. The host (or a waitress) passes the wine when everyone is seated, or there may be an opened bottle of wine on each table to be poured by the man nearest to it.

If coffee is on the sideboard the guests may serve themselves at any time. Or the hostess, if she prefers, takes a tray set with cups, a coffeepot, cream, and sugar into the living room to serve after dinner.

When there are no individual stands or tables and guests must put their glasses beside them on the floor, it is wise to use iced-tea glasses or highball glasses because they are steadier than goblets. If the beverage is served with ice in the glass, it should not be put down on a table unless coasters are provided.

Beginning the Meal

When the guests have all arrived and the time allotted for cocktails (if served) is over, the hostess announces that dinner is ready and people in more or less of a queue file around the dining table. The guests go first, urged by the hostess, if necessary, but whether it is a seated dinner or a buffet the hostess should *never* serve herself first. The women as well as the men help themselves—it is fun to see what there is to eat and to take just what one wants. Sometimes, however, and quite correctly, a man may ask a woman what she would like, fill a plate, and take it to her.

A man seeing a woman sitting without a plate or with an empty one asks her, "Can't I get you something to eat?" or "Would you like more of anything?" If she says, "Yes, please" he brings her whatever it is she would like. But most likely she says, "Thank you, but I'm going into the dining room in a moment."

If people continue to sit and wait to be served, the hostess has to prod them a little, saying, "Please go into the dining room and help yourselves to dinner." If they linger at the buffet, carrying on a long conversation and blockading the table, she should suggest that they take their plates into the other room.

The only serving detail of importance in a buffet meal is the clearing away of used dishes. If the hostess has help for the evening, each plate is removed as soon as it is put down. Also, if there are servants they refill the glasses of seated guests from time to time, and the main dishes may be passed for second helpings. The servantless hostess can ask one or two members of her family—or her most intimate friends—to help her take the used dishes to a convenient table or sideboard, from which she can take them to the kitchen as unobtrusively as possible.

The Buffet Menu

It does not matter what foods you choose so long as they are well prepared and easy to eat with fork alone if your guests are not seated at tables. Beyond that, merely use a reasonable amount of common sense in selecting dishes that will be satisfying to the people invited.

There are countless delicious menus to be tried; the only limit is your imagination. If you wish to be very elaborate, or if you have a great many guests, you may wish to serve two main dishes. But choose two dishes that will be complemented by the same vegetables and condiments, or you will have more preparation than you can easily handle and not enough space on your table for all the dishes. If you do serve two main dishes, your guests may help themselves to the one they prefer, or they may take a little bit of both. They should remember, however, that it is very easy to overload a plate when there is a variety of tempting dishes. If you are a guest at a buffet don't let your eyes dictate to your stomach, and while you may try as many dishes as you want, take very small portions of each.

LUNCHEONS

Social luncheons, unlike business luncheons, are usually given for and by women. If they are held on a weekend, luncheons of course include men, but purely social weekday luncheons are more apt to be made up of people who are free in the middle of the day.

Small luncheons are sometimes held in the hostess's home; larger ones generally take place in a club, hotel, or restaurant. The number you can accommodate in your dining room or at small individual tables, as well as the amount of time you can spend on preparation and the help that is available to you, determines the choice of locale.

When men are included in the guest list, the menu generally resembles that of a light dinner. When the luncheon is for women only, the food is considerably less substantial, yet it should be as beautifully prepared and attractively presented as any formal dinner.

Invitations

The word *lunch* is used much more often than *luncheon*. *Luncheon* is rarely spoken, but it is written in books like this one and sometimes in third-person invitations.

Although invitations may be telephoned, an engraved card is occasionally used for an elaborate luncheon, especially for one given in honor of a noted person. However, a formal invitation to lunch is more often in the form of a personal note or on a "fill-in" invitation. It is rarely mailed more than a week in advance. The personal invitation might read:

> *Dear Gloria and John,*
> *Will you come to lunch on Saturday the tenth at half past twelve to meet Jane's fiancé, Bob Thomas?*
> *I hope so much that you will be able to join us.*
>
> > *Sincerely*
> > *[or Affectionately],*
> > *Elaine [Andrews]*

If it is a very large luncheon for which the engraved card is used, "To meet Congresswoman Prescott" is written across the top.

Cocktails

Cocktails may or may not be served before lunch. If they are, they differ a little from those offered before dinner. A glass of white wine or a Bloody Mary is the typical pre-lunch drink. As always, there must be sparkling water and regular and diet sodas available for those who wish it.

The Lunch Table

A lunch table may be the dining room table, several card tables, or a patio table for an al fresco luncheon. Depending on the formality of the luncheon, the table may be set with a table cloth, or with placemats. (*See pages 431–432 for luncheon table setting suggestions.*)

Beginning the Meal

When all the guests have arrived and have had time to enjoy a cocktail if it is offered, the butler or maid at a large luncheon notifies the cook, goes back to the living room, and approaches the hostess and says quietly, "Luncheon is served." At a simple luncheon, the hostess, after seeing that the table is ready, says, "Shall we go in to lunch?"

If there is a guest of honor, the hostess leads the way to the dining room, walking beside her. Otherwise the guests go in in any way they wish, except that the very young should make way for their elders. Men stroll in with the women they happen to be talking to. If alone, they bring up the rear. Men never offer their arms to women going in to lunch—unless there should be a very elderly guest of honor, who might be taken in by the host, as at a dinner.

The Service

If the luncheon is to be formal the hostess will need help, whether her own servants or temporary ones.

The formal service is identical with that of dinner. Carving is done in the kitchen, and except for the ornamental dishes of fruit, candy, and nuts, no food is set on the table. The plate service is also the same as at dinner. The places are never left without plates, except after the salad course when the table is cleared and crumbed for dessert. The dessert plates and finger bowls are arranged as for dinner.

At a simpler luncheon one can serve eight or twelve guests quite easily if the first course is already on the table. The waitress may clear the plates from card tables by standing at the corners and taking away one plate in each hand. The main course should be limited to a single dish and salad, or it will take a rather long time to serve, as the maid must pass the food in the usual way, from each person's left. The salad may be all ready in small bowls or plates, which are brought in two at a time and placed on the guests' left. If there is no first course, the salad may already be on the table. Rolls, butter, and iced water and any other beverage should also be put on the table beforehand.

When dessert is finished, the waitress carries the coffee tray to another room and if it is a bridge party readies the tables while the hostess pours the coffee.

If you are serving without the help of a maid or waitress you will be wise to make your party a buffet luncheon. The food is set out as for a buffet dinner, on the dining-room table or on any table with sufficient space. For a ladies' luncheon the fare is much simpler than for a dinner. A delicious but light and healthful meal is a wonderful respite in the middle of the day.

As soon as you announce that luncheon is served, your guests file past the table and serve themselves, taking their plates to the card tables and seating themselves wherever they wish. If you are having a course before the entrée, it should already be on the tables when your guests arrive, and they sit down and finish it before going to the buffet table for the main course. When there is no serving staff to help, the guests take their empty plates and leave them on a side table as they go to get their next course. While they are helping themselves you may remove the soiled dishes to the kitchen.

The same procedure is followed when the guests are ready for the salad or dessert. When they have finished you ask them to go to another room, or at least to leave the tables and sit on more comfortable chairs to have their coffee. This gives you a chance to clear away the glasses, silver, and cloths from the table, and if bridge is to follow, to set out the cards.

The Luncheon Menu

Two or three courses are sufficient at any but the most formal luncheon. If you serve many more than that and then move to the bridge table, you will find some of your players falling asleep over their hands! There are five possible courses, and you may select the ones you wish to serve from those listed below:

1. Fruit, or soup in cups
2. Eggs or shellfish
3. Fowl, meat (not a roast), or fish
4. Salad
5. Dessert

The menu for lunch eaten in a private house never consists of more than four courses, and two or three are the general rule.

Melon, grapefruit, or fruit cup, with or without a liqueur poured over it, is a popular first course. The latter may be served in special bowl-shaped glasses that fit into long-stemmed, larger ones with a space for crushed ice between, or it can just as well be served in champagne glasses, after being kept as cold as possible in the refrigerator.

Soup at a luncheon is never served in soup plates, but in two-handled cups. It is eaten with a teaspoon or a bouillon spoon, or after it has cooled sufficiently the cup may be picked up. It is almost always a clear soup: in the winter a bouillon, turtle soup, or consommé, and in the summer a chilled soup such as jellied consommé or madrilene. Vichysoisse is also popular in hot weather.

There are innumerable lunch-party egg and fish dishes, and they often serve as the main course at a ladies' luncheon. But when men are present, the third course should not be omitted. A second course that is substantial should be balanced by a simple meat, such as broiled chicken served with a salad, combining meat and salad courses in one. On the other hand, if you serve eggs in aspic, or escargots, first, you could have meat and vegetables, as well as salad and dessert.

While cold food is both appropriate and delicious, no meal—except on the hottest of hot summer days—should ever be chosen without at least one course of hot food. Some people dislike cold food, and it disagrees with others; but if you at least offer your guests a hot soup it is then all right to have the rest of the meal cold.

Hot breads are an important feature of every lunch—hot crescents, baking-powder biscuits, English muffins, dinner rolls, corn bread, etc. They are passed as often as necessary. Butter is usually put on the butter plate beforehand, and it is passed again, whenever necessary, until the table is cleared for dessert. Preferably it should be served as butterballs, or curls, rather than in squares.

Bread-and-butter plates are always removed immediately before dessert, with the saltcellars and pepper pots.

Beverages

Wine is often served with lunch. One wine is sufficient, and it should be a light one such as dry Rhine wine or a claret.

A chilled white wine with soda (a spritzer) may also be served in the summer, but iced tea or iced coffee is the usual choice. Tea is poured into the glasses and decorated with sprigs of fresh mint. Iced coffee should be passed around in a pitcher on a tray that also holds a bowl of granulated sugar and a pitcher of cream. The guests pour their own coffee into tall glasses that are half full of ice and accompanied by long-handled spoons. Or if your luncheon is a buffet, a pitcher of each should be available close to the buffet table. A bowl of fruit punch may take the place of iced tea or coffee and appears cool and refreshing if it is prepared with floating slices of orange and lemon and is surrounded by glasses or cups adorned with fresh sprigs of mint.

In the winter many hostesses like to have hot coffee or tea served with the meal instead of, or in addition to, serving it later.

A pitcher of iced water is welcome in hot weather or glasses of water may already be on the table if it is a seated luncheon.

After Lunch

On a hot summer day when people have been playing cards for an hour or more, a tray of cold drinks should be brought in and put down on a convenient table. One thing that hostesses frequently tend to forget is that five people out of six long for a cold drink in the afternoon more than anything else—especially after a cocktail or two and a larger-than-usual lunch.

TEAS

Afternoon teas are given in honor of visiting celebrities, new neighbors, to "warm" a new house, for a houseguest, or for no reason other than wanting to entertain your friends.

Invitations

Invitations to an informal tea are almost always telephoned. However, if the occasion is more formal, the invitation is sent on a fill-in invitation or your personal notepaper. (*See pages 357–358.*)

Tea Party Guests

When a tea is given for someone, or to celebrate something special, it is, to some extent, "formal." Women wear dresses or suits, hats, and gloves if they wish. The latter are always removed with the coat. Men wear business suits.

When there is a guest of honor, you introduce him or her to your guests as they arrive. But rather than forming a receiving "line" you and the guest of honor stand together near the door and talk for a little while with the arriving guests.

Otherwise, behavior is very informal. As a guest you may (and should) talk to anyone there, whether you have been introduced or not. You may return to the tea table as many times as you wish (or your calorie count permits), but you may *not* overload your plate at any one time. When you are ready to leave (and you are not expected to stay until the very end at a large tea) you simply thank your host and hostess, say good-bye to the guest of honor, and go.

The Tea Table

Those who have dining-room tables use them as the simplest and most comfortable place from which to serve. However, the tea table may be set up in any room that has adequate space and easy access and exit. The guests should be able to circulate freely without becoming trapped in a corner after they have been served.

Except on a glass-topped table a cloth must always be used. It may barely cover the table, or it may hang half a yard over the edge. A tea cloth may be colored, but the conventional one is of lace or white linen with needlework, lace, or appliquéd designs.

A large tray is set at either end of the table, one for the tea and one for the coffee.

One tray is used to bring in all the equipment necessary for the proper serving of tea: a pot with boiling water—with a flame under it, if possible—a full pot of tea, tea bags if the tea is not made with loose tea, cream pitcher, sugar bowl, and thin slices of lemon on a dish.

The coffee tray is simpler. The coffee is in a large urn or pot—with a flame under it. A pitcher of cream and a bowl of sugar (preferably lumps) complete the tray. If chocolate is served instead of coffee, there is nothing needed other than the pot of steaming chocolate.

The flames under the pots are not lighted before the trays are set down in order to avoid the danger of fire.

The cups and saucers are placed within easy reach of the women who are pouring, usually at the left of the tray, because they are held in the left hand while the tea (or coffee) is poured with the right. On either side of the table are stacks of little tea plates, with small napkins matching the tea cloth folded on each one. Arranged behind these, or in any way that is pretty and uncluttered, are the plates of food and whatever silver is necessary. Forks should be on the table if cake with soft icing is served. If the table is not large enough to hold all the plates some may be placed on a sideboard or a small table in a convenient location.

Tea table

Food for a tea party is quite different from that served at a cocktail party. For one thing, much of the food is sweet—cookies, cupcakes, fruitcake, or slices of iced cake are almost always offered. In addition, for those who do not have such a "sweet tooth," tea sandwiches are served. They are small, made on very thin bread, and are usually cold, although in winter there is sometimes a tray of hot cheese puffs, pastry filled with mushrooms, etc. The sandwiches are light and delicate—watercress rolled in thin bread, a cherry tomato sliced on a round of bread, cream cheese on date-and-nut bread, and crabmeat on toast are typical choices for tea-party menus.

Because nothing needs to be passed to the guests, it is perfectly possible for anyone to give a formal tea without help. If you have no maid you set out the tray with everything except the boiling water before the guests arrive, leaving the kettle on the stove in the kitchen. Greet your guests at the door, tell them where to leave their coats, and when you are ready for tea simply fill the teapot from the kitchen kettle and carry it in to the tea table.

Making Good Tea

The most important part of the tea service is boiling water and plenty of it.

To make good tea, first, half-fill the pot with boiling water, let it stand a moment or two to heat the teapot, and then pour it out. Put in a rounded teaspoonful of tea leaves or one tea bag for each person. Half this amount may be used if the tea is of superb quality. Then pour on enough *actually boiling* water to cover the tea leaves about half an inch. It should steep at least five minutes (or for those who like it very strong, ten) before additional boiling water is poured on. When serving, pour half tea, half boiling water for those who like it "weak." Increase the amount of tea for those who like it strong. The cup of *good* tea should be too strong without the addition of a little lively boiling water, which gives it freshness.

When tea has to stand a long time for many guests, the ideal way is to make a strong infusion in a big kettle on the kitchen stove. Let the tea actually boil three to four minutes on the range; then pour it through a sieve or filter into your hot teapot. The tea will not become bitter, and it does not matter if it gets quite cold. The boiling water poured over no more than the tablespoonful of such tea will make the drink hot enough.

Those Who Pour

The pouring is usually done by close friends of the party giver. These close friends are asked beforehand if they will "do the honors," and unless they have a very valid reason, they should accept. Sometimes, after half an hour, the first two are relieved by two other friends.

Each person walks right up to the table and says, "May I have a cup of tea?"

The one pouring should smile and answer, "Certainly! How do you like it? Strong or weak? Would you like cream or lemon?"

If the visitor says, "Weak," *boiling* water is added, and according to the guest's wishes, sugar, cream, or lemon. If the guest prefers coffee, he or she asks for it at the other end of the table. If you are not too busy pouring and the guest is alone, you make a few pleasant remarks; but if there are a number of people around the table you need only smile as you hand each guest a cup of tea or coffee.

RECEPTIONS

The reception today is primarily a state affair, a public or semipublic gathering in honor of a prominent person or an important event. Receptions most frequently take place on the diplomatic or civic level and are handled, like official dinners, by a household staff or a caterer.

However, there are occasions that call for a reception at home, and one that occurs quite frequently is when a groom's parents wish to give a party for their son and his bride. This generally happens when the wedding has taken place in the bride's distant hometown, and the groom's family wants to introduce their new daughter-in-law to their friends.

Receptions are rarely given for women only so liquor is almost always served as well as punch and coffee. There may be some tea-type sandwiches offered, but small meatballs, dips, various kinds of cheese and crackers, and nuts, olives, etc., are added to the menu.

The table for a reception is covered with a floor-length white tablecloth rather than the shorter tea cloth. The table is set with the platters of food, small paper napkins, plates, and forks if necessary. Alcoholic drinks are served from a bar or passed around, and coffee and punch are on side tables from which the guests help themselves.

Since receptions are almost always given in someone's honor, there is generally a receiving line, consisting of the host and/or hostess, guest of honor, and in some cases, various officials of the committee giving the reception.

Receptions—especially official ones—take themselves seriously, and guests are expected to dress and act accordingly.

COCKTAIL PARTIES

In many parts of the country cocktail parties have become the most common form of entertaining, and they can be the answer to a busy person's prayer. Along with open houses, barbecues, and picnics they provide a relatively simple answer to the rule that all invitations must be repaid. Their advantages over a dinner party are many in a society in which relatively few households have servants, and in which the cost of hiring temporary help or a caterer is beyond the reach of many. Cocktail parties require less preparation, they are less expensive than a dinner party, they are limited as to time, and you can entertain many more people at once in a small house. On the other hand, no one invited to a cocktail party feels as honored as if he had been invited to dinner, and at a large party the host and hostess cannot spend as much time with any one guest as they would if they were seated at a dinner table. Cocktail parties do provide an excellent opportunity for entertaining new acquaintances, particularly if you also wish to include the people at whose house you met your new friends, and others to whom you want to introduce them.

Cocktail parties may be as large or small, as simple or elaborate as you wish, and the ways of inviting people are varied. If the number of guests is small the invitation is almost always by telephone. For a larger party they are usually written on a printed fill-in card, or on one of the many attractive illustrated cards sold at stationers for every occasion.

When there is to be no buffet the time is usually stated: "Cocktails *from* 5:00 to 7:00," rather than "Cocktails *at* 5:00." While "RSVP" is often omitted, thoughtful guests let their host and/or hostess know whether or not they are planning to attend the party. If there is an RSVP the telephone number is usually written beside it, as this type of invitation may always be answered by telephone.

At a cocktail party you may serve literally every sort of hors d'oeuvre or appetizer that you think tastes good and looks tempting—as long as it can be eaten with the fingers. At some cocktail parties small plates are placed on the hors d'oeuvres table and guests are expected to fill these plates with a variety of appetizers. I am very much against this practice as it is extremely difficult, if not impossible to hold a drink in one hand, the plate in the other, and somehow manage to eat the hors d'oeuvres or even shake hands when both hands are full. You might serve olives or artichoke hearts (either chilled or wrapped in bacon and broiled) or tiny broiled sausages; thin bread rolled around baby hot dogs, skewered, and toasted; or small frogs' legs, broiled, with a garlic dip. Or try this: Hollow out a cabbage, put a can of Sterno in it, and beside it a plate of little frankfurters or bits of tenderloin to be speared on a pick and cooked over the flame. This is sure to be a conversation piece! Don't forget a pile of cocktail napkins—cloth or paper—on the hors d'oeuvres tray. Many hors d'oeuvres are a little greasy, and also, since plates are not used, the napkin may be used to hold an appetizer that is, for a moment, too hot to eat.

Paper napkins should be offered with the cocktails or be available on the bar, too, to wrap around the glasses. Especially at a large party, where everyone stands most of the time, it is unpleasant to have to hold an icy, wet glass, and furthermore the napkin prevents drips.

Plenty of coasters are a necessity if you wish to preserve the finish on your tables. Disposable paper ones are fine—just be sure they are in view at every conceivable resting place for a glass.

At a large party extra glasses are essential too. Guests continually put down their glasses and forget where they put them, or leave their empty ones behind when they go to the bar for another drink. You may get very inexpensive glasses—even plastic ones—for a big party, but be sure you don't run out.

What Drinks to Serve?

The two most important things about "what to serve"—whatever you decide on—are to have enough and to have the drinks mixed properly. As a general rule you should count on each guest's having at least three drinks. Since a quart of liquor will provide 21 one-and-a-half-ounce drinks, one bottle will serve approximately seven people.

Even though the occasion is called a "cocktail" party not all of your guests may choose an alcoholic beverage, so you *must* have nonalcoholic drinks available. Tomato or other fruit juices, colas, mineral water, and ginger ale are all popular substitutes. It is also thoughtful to have diet sodas available.

Bartenders and Waiters

If you are planning a cocktail party for more than eighteen or twenty people, and if you have no servants, it is wise to consider hiring a bartender for the evening. One bartender can serve between twenty and thirty people very well. If it is a really large party the services of a waiter or waitress as well will make the evening much pleasanter for you. You may prepare the hors d'oeuvres yourself in advance, even days ahead if you wish, or may hire a waitress or caterer who will both prepare and serve the food.

The bartender attends to the drinks in any one of various ways, or he may combine several means of serving. He generally stands behind a large table loaded with ice, bottles of each kind of liquor and soft drink to be served, and every sort of cocktail glass. At a big party it is essential to have two bars or the crush around one will become unmanageable. The guests go to the bar themselves and request the kind of drink they wish. A man usually asks the woman with him what she would like, and she waits at a little distance from the bar while he gives the order to the bartender and brings her the drink. If a group of women are talking together, it is perfectly correct for one of them who wishes another drink to go to ask the bartender to mix it for her, rather than to interrupt a conversation that her husband or escort might be having.

Another method of serving is for the bartender to pass a tray of drinks, already mixed, to each guest as he arrives. He may continue to do this, but it involves using an enormous number of glasses, because a fresh one must be passed each time. Therefore, after the first serving, it is more practical for him to watch carefully for empty glasses, and when he sees one, approach the guest and say, "May I bring you another drink?" The guest replies, "Thank you, I'm drinking gin and tonic," and hands him the glass to be refilled.

If you have two men to serve drinks, but only one bar, one man acts as a waiter. He may ask each new arrival for his order, go to the bar where the second man (as bartender) mixes the drink, and return with it to the guest. This method is too slow for one man alone, however, especially when a large group of people arrives at the same time.

One important note to remember: Be sure that you instruct the bartender in advance exactly how you like your drinks mixed and insist that he use a measure. If you let him measure "by eye," you may find that your liquor supply is about to run out long before you had planned. Or you may have some unexpectedly boisterous guests on your hands!

Without Help

When no extra help is hired for the evening, the host is the bartender and the hostess is the waitress. She passes the trays of hors d'oeuvres once or twice, sometimes with a close friend helping her. The food is then left in a conspicuous spot (on a hot plate or in a chafing dish if the hors d'oeuvres are hot), and the guests help themselves. She must watch carefully and remove trays or dishes even before they are empty. There is nothing more unappetizing than one remaining cold, limp shrimp, or a mayonnaise-smeared platter.

The host-bartender asks each guest as he arrives what he would like to drink. If the choice is limited he may say, "Will you have a martini or bourbon?" rather than "What would you like?" This saves them both from the embarrassment of having the guest request a drink that is not to be had. Also, he may ask the men to refill their own glasses as well as those of any women who wish another drink. He will have much more time to mix with the group and perform his other duties as host if he does not have to spend the entire evening at the bar.

If there are only a few guests the host may hang their coats in a hall closet. If there are more wraps than a closet can conveniently hold, the men and women are asked to put them in separate bedrooms (or in the same bedroom if the house or apartment is small), neatly on the beds. This scheme is far better than having them piled on chairs or banisters in the entry, and furthermore the guests have an opportunity to freshen up before they appear in the living room if they choose.

Either the host or the hostess should stay within sight of the door to greet arriving guests, but they should try to avoid being out of the room where the party is held at the same time. They should not go to the door to greet their guests with drinks in their hands.

Inebriated Guests

The circumstances under which someone takes too much to drink, and how it becomes evident, are far too varied for the host or hostess to be able to deal with every eventuality. However, there are a few important steps to take when a guest becomes obnoxious or embarrassing at your party. First, if the offender becomes truly drunk, enlist the aid of the person or people he or she came with in getting the overindulger home or in helping should he or she be feeling sick. Of course, the drunken person may have come to the party alone. If it is a man, ask your husband or a male friend to help you deal with him. If it is a woman, deal with her yourself, unless you need someone's help in assisting or carrying her to a bedroom or a taxi. If the reveler is merely on the way to becoming loud, try to keep this guest from having any more to drink—to the point of saying you think perhaps he or she has had enough, and asking, "How about a cup of coffee?" When a drunk becomes insulting or offensive, as sometimes happens, try to smooth it over with the *victim*, explaining that "Jim [or Joanne] has had a little too much to drink, and really doesn't know what he [or she] is saying." And get Jim or Joanne diverted, and away from the bar.

Most important, never let anyone who has had too much to drink get behind the wheel of a car. If there is no one to do the driving, you should see that a mutual friend sees him or her home safely, call a taxi or put him or her to bed in your home. For the safety of other travelers as well as his or her own, you must go to any lengths to prevent this person from driving.

Overstaying Your Welcome

Cocktail parties rarely begin—or end—at the hour stated on the invitation. Although the hosts must be ready on time, the guests may—and do—arrive as much as half an hour after the start of the party. Invitees who do not drink, or only drink a little, may stop in very briefly out of courtesy and friendship. However, a late arrival should not mean a late departure. Every experienced hostess knows that she must expect some of her guests to linger a half hour or so beyond the indicated time, but that is as much as she should be expected to endure. She may even take steps to hurry the last survivors out. The best way to get guests to leave is simply to remove the liquor and close the bar. Once the guests finish the drinks in their hands and find no more being served, the party will soon be over. As a safety valve, in case there are diehards who linger on regardless, a smart host and hostess make plans to go to a restaurant for dinner after the party with a few friends. This provides the excuse to say, "It was such fun to see you, but I'm afraid we must get going—the Forsythes are waiting for us. . . ."

"Pay-Back" Parties

People who have been invited to a great many parties and haven't the time or the energy to give a number of small parties sometimes repay their obligations by inviting everyone to whom they are indebted at once. The guests are not chosen for compatibility, there are not enough places to sit down, the crowd is likely to be such that no one can move freely from group to group (or table, or bar), and the noise level reaches a deafening pitch. If you are a popular guest and incur social obligations with any frequency try to make the effort to give small parties from time to time and avoid the necessity of a yearly "pay-back."

Cocktails Before a Dance

A pleasant form of entertaining is to have a group of friends for cocktails before a dinner dance or any other function that they would enjoy attending. Invitations are sent out on informals, fill-in cards, or any printed cocktail-party invitation card, but they must state: "Cocktails before the dance at the Black Rock Golf Club, 6 o'clock," as well as the place and date. It is also necessary to add "RSVP," because the hostess usually makes the reservations for those of her guests who wish to go on to the other event.

It is also correct to extend the invitations by telephone. In that way the hostess knows immediately how many will be joining her at the club or dance and can make the reservations sooner. An invitation to this type of party should not be accepted if you do not intend to go on to the later party. Unless a hostess specifically says, "Please join us first even though you can't come to the club afterward," it is not up to you to make this suggestion in most cases. Only to very close friends might you say, "We'd love to stop by for one drink, but we are going to dinner at the Browns'."

When you are the guest you must pay the cost of admission, dinner, drinks, and anything else at the later party unless your hostess specifically says or writes that she expects you *as her guest.* If you are not a member of the club involved, you must find out in advance whether you may sign as a member of another club or pay in cash. If neither is permitted, then you must ask your host if you may sign his name and add your initials to enable you to pay him your share when he receives his bill.

Cocktail Buffets

A cross between a cocktail party and a buffet dinner party, the cocktail buffet is the choice of many for entertaining all except the smallest and most informal groups. Because there is usually enough food presented that the guests need not have dinner afterward and therefore are expected to linger longer, the invitation frequently states only the hour of arrival. In many sections of the country this is likely to be a little later than a simple cocktail party, often at six thirty or seven. It should be made very clear that the gathering is a "cocktail buffet," so that the guests realize that they will be served some substantial food and need not make other plans for dinner.

The menu may vary from simple to very elaborate, but even the simplest must provide more than just hors d'oeuvres. The least that one can expect is a platter of cold meat—ham, chicken, or roast beef—slices of buttered breads, accompanying dishes such as sliced carrots, celery, olives, raw cauliflower, and possibly some sandwiches. This minimum type of buffet may be eaten standing near the table without a plate. The meat can be placed on a slice of bread and eaten like a sandwich, and the raw vegetables picked up and dipped in a sauce if one is served. Often a smoked ham or turkey is placed whole on the table, and when the platters of meat are running low, the host, or any of the guests, may carve additional slices as they are required.

The table should be covered with a tablecloth, and napkins must be available. If there is room a centerpiece of flowers or fruit is attractive, but it is better to leave it off and use a decorated cake (or even one of the main dishes) in the center rather than crowd the table.

For a more elaborate buffet you might include one or more hot dishes, generally casseroles that can be kept warm on an electric hot plate or served in a chafing dish over a flame. In this case, of course, there must be stacks of plates and rows of forks. If the main table becomes too crowded, the hot dishes and plates may be put on the sideboard or on a side table. The main difference between this type of cocktail buffet and a buffet dinner is that only one real course is served, although cookies or cake may be offered with coffee.

If you do not wish to go into the added complication of plates and silver you may choose a hot dish such as bite-sized meatballs or frankfurters, tiny hot potatoes dipped in salt, and hot bread or rolls with a cheese fondue, all of which may be speared with a toothpick. Tacos are hearty and can be bought frozen. Fritonga, a South American mixture of fried bits of meat, banana slices, potatoes, and popcorn, will give you a reputation for originality. Chicken wings dipped in batter and deep-fried are delectable too. Use your imagination and you will delight your guests, but don't experiment on them—try out your new ideas on family or your best friends beforehand!

BYOB and BYOF Parties

"BYO" means "Bring Your Own"—bottle or food, as the case may be. Such parties serve a real purpose, but they also can and do cause resentment, so one should be very careful in planning this sort of entertainment.

Let's talk first about "BYOB" parties. These are almost invariably given by young people who are on a tight budget and could not possibly entertain a group of friends if they had to provide *all* the refreshments. So they call their friends, invite them over, tell them that they will provide the food and mixes but the guests are asked to bring whatever they want to drink. When a written invitation is sent, all that is necessary is to put "BYOB" in the corner and the rest is understood.

The bottles brought to these parties are *not* intended to be gifts for the host and hostess. They simply make it possible for the group to get together without anyone's incurring an enormous expense. Therefore each couple may initial their bottle and take home any liquor that is left. The bottles are "pooled," however, at the party, and if one couple runs out of Scotch, for example, they are offered some by one of the other Scotch-drinkers.

Guests do not take their own mixers. These are provided by the host, who should also have soft drinks available.

Bring-your-own-dinner or bring-a-dish parties are usually given for much the same reasons as BYOB parties. The host and hostess want to get their friends together and have a good time, but they can't afford to do it all, so they ask everyone to chip in. This is perfectly all right, with a big "IF." That is, *if* it is made clear *when the invitation is extended* that it is a chip-in party. The misunderstandings and resentments occur when a guest accepts an invitation and is *then* told that he or she is expected to bring a casserole or perhaps to contribute ten dollars "toward expenses."

A hostess who arranges this sort of evening is not "giving" the party—she is "organizing" it. There are several ways of doing it. She may call several people and say, "Let's get a group together. We'll all bring one dish, and I'll have a keg of beer on hand." Or she may do it "on her own" by sending written invitations asking each person to provide a specific dish. In this case she would write "Come to a Pot-Luck Dinner" or a "Chip-in Dinner" at the top. Unless she has specified a dish *and* a bottle, she should provide the liquid refreshments. However she goes about it, the important thing is that she make it quite clear that she is not "giving" the entire party— *before* the guest is trapped. The invitees are then free to refuse the invitation if they are unwilling or unable to contribute.

In spite of the obvious advantages of this type of entertaining, it cannot take the place of the party you truly "give" for your friends. As long as you can afford to provide even the simplest food and drink, you should accept the entire responsibility. A host or hostess should *never*, for a private party, ask for contributions of money to help defray expenses. The only time this is permissible is when the group—official or unofficial—gives a party to celebrate a special event (a testimonial dinner, for example) or to raise funds for a cause, and either sells tickets or asks for donations. Again the amount requested must be clearly stated on the invitation, and guests should never be asked to contribute—without warning—at the party.

BARBECUES

A barbecue is an informal way to entertain just a few special friends or a large group, depending on your available space and your barbecue equipment. Ideally, two people host a barbecue, since one has to tend the grill while the other sees to bringing the other dishes from the kitchen.

Setting the Barbecue Table

Since the setting is informal, disposable plates, cups and utensils are appropriate. There should be tables and chairs for everyone, or at least comfortable places to sit. Centerpieces can be fresh flowers arranged in unusual containers, such as copper kettles or earthenware jugs.

For an evening barbecue, there should be plenty of light, both for the chef to
see what he is cooking and for guests to be able to maneuver easily. Floodlights directed into the trees give a beautiful effect, as do colorful paper lanterns or candles placed in hurricane lamps. Citronella candles are an excellent idea for a summer night, since they keep insects away.

If the evening becomes cool, be prepared to move guests into the house after dinner or they will soon start to leave.

The Barbecue Menu

The main dish—meat, fish or fowl—is prepared on the grill. Unless specified, the others are prepared in advance and kept on the stove indoors or brought out to sit on a corner of the grill where the temperature must be neither too hot nor too cold.

Beer, any soft drink, and wine all go well with the informality of a barbecue. In hot weather, iced tea, iced coffee, and icy sangria are delicious. Pots of coffee should be kept hot on the grill for serving either during or after the meal.

Cocktails may be served, but since the food is hearty, elaborate hors d'oeuvres are not necessary. A few dishes of nuts or potato chips scattered about are sufficient.

A side table loaded with a variety of condiments is a nice idea. As each guest fills his plate (the host usually cuts and serves the meat) he passes by this table and helps himself to ketchup, mustard, relish, sauce, or whatever may be offered.

PICNICS

Although picnics can be utterly delightful when well managed, they can be perfectly awful when bungled! Therefore here are a few general directions for the benefit of those who want to have a really outstanding picnic.

What Kind of Picnic?

There are several ways of organizing a picnic.

The first is to give the picnic yourself, inviting the guests by telephone. If they accept, tell them the hour, where to meet, and possibly ask them to bring a blanket or backrest if the party is large and you do not have enough for everyone.

Or you may call and say, "Mike and I are trying to get a group together for a picnic Saturday night. We'll bring the steaks, and we're asking each couple to contribute one dish. Would you rather bring dessert or salad?" Others might be asked to bring the condiments, chowder, corn, or the drinks.

Lastly, a group of friends may simply arrange to picnic together, each family bringing their own food and cooking it over a community fire. It is fun to see what the others have prepared, and often there is considerable trading and sharing. "I'll trade you a chicken leg for a lobster claw," or "Do try some of this special steak sauce that Susie taught me to make." This sort of picnic is especially good if children are included, as each mother knows best what her young ones will eat most happily.

Being Host or Hostess

If you wish to entertain friends by taking them on a picnic, your first task is to consider your guest list very carefully. Nothing is so dampening to the enjoyment of a picnic as the presence of one or more faultfinders who never lift a finger but sit and complain of the heat, of the wind, of a possible shower, of the discomfort of sitting on the ground, or of their personal sufferings caused by mosquitoes or flies. On the other hand, if you select your company from friends who really enjoy picnics, not only will they make everyone forget blowing sand and inquisitive ants or hungry mosquitoes, but most likely they will work like beavers.

Knowing that you have a congenial group and considering the ages and preferences of your guests—whether adults and children or just adults—you now decide whether you are going to provide an already prepared outdoor lunch or supper, meaning that you will take only things that are ready to serve—sandwiches, or cold chicken and salad, and a thermos of liquids, for example—or whether you are going to build a fire and cook.

Next you must choose the location. If you live near the mountains you may decide to climb or drive to a site that has a beautiful view, but if there are children in the party be sure there is a field nearby for games or races, or a stream in which they may swim. It should scarcely be necessary to remind you to select a site that you know something about—because you or your friends have picnicked there before. Be sure that the ground is not swampy, that it is not more mosquito- or ant-infested than anyplace else, and that it is not covered with poison ivy.

If you choose a beach remember to make some preparation to shield both your guests and the food they are to eat from blowing sand. For this nothing is better than some five-foot garden stakes and a few yards of burlap with a wide hem at each end through which the stakes are inserted. Thrust the stakes into the sand to form a windbreak. If you are going to be on the beach all day, an umbrella is a must for those who are not well tanned or accustomed to the sun.

If you are giving a large picnic and including a number of people who are not necessarily picnic addicts, it is important to select a site that is easy to get to or away from. You may have a Jeep or "beach buggy" that allows you to reach a remote part of the beach with no effort at all, but if not, don't expect your average guest to tramp through miles of soft sand carrying blankets, beach towels, and backrests.

Having made up your mind as to what to eat and where to cook it, you should plan as carefully as you would if you were inviting people to dine with you at home. You wouldn't ask guests to lunch at your house at one o'clock and then not serve until three; nor would you give them fish or chicken that was raw on one side and charred to a cinder on the other. There is no more reason to do this at an outdoor meal than at an indoor one.

Hot or Cold?

The very simplest type of picnic is a "continental" picnic, straight from the farmers of Europe. It consists of a loaf of bread, a piece of cheese, and a bottle of wine. If the cheese and wine are good and the bread fresh, this menu has all the advantages of being delicious and nourishing, requiring no preparation, and costing next to nothing. However, in spite of the ease of getting together and carrying the ingredients of a continental picnic, most Americans prefer to expand the menu in varying degrees. Using the three items above as a base, you may add whatever you wish—fruit for dessert, little tomatoes as a vegetable, tins of sardines or meats, and so on.

In fact if you have the necessary equipment you may have an entire buffet spread on a folding table. But most people prefer a simpler picnic, and the main requirement is that the food be the best of its kind. Cold fried chicken, or cold boiled lobster, accompanied by coleslaw or lettuce brought in a damp cloth and mixed with dressing when the group is ready to eat, bread and butter, and fresh fruit for dessert make a meal that is truly "fit for a king."

Many men enjoy cooking meat over an open fire, and they generally have more assistance and suggestions than they need from their male guests. If the host— or the hostess—likes to do it, there is nothing more delicious than meat or fish cooked over coals. Whole potatoes or corn, wrapped in foil and roasted in the coals, and a mixed green salad make the best accompaniments, along with as many condiments such as mustard or ketchup as you can fit into your baskets. Cold sliced watermelon, or perhaps fresh strawberries, already sugared, might finish the meal.

Your plates for a "hot" picnic must be more substantial than uncoated paper. Plastic or enameled ones are really the most satisfactory, even though they must be taken home to be washed. Plastic bowls or cups for chowder are more leakproof and easier to hold than paper cups. As long as you are bringing the utensils for this type of meal, there is no reason not to accompany your main dish with a salad already mixed in a big bowl and breads kept warm by several layers of foil wrapping.

Good strong coffee in a thermos and plenty of beer and soft drinks kept cold in a tub of ice should be on hand for the singing around a roaring fire that should be a part of every evening picnic.

Tailgate Picnics

Tailgate picnics have come into being with the universal popularity of the station wagon. They are particularly suitable on two occasions. First, if you are making a long trip and do not wish to take too lengthy a break for lunch, you may pull over to the side of the road (preferably in a "rest area" if you are on a big highway, because of the receptacles provided for garbage, etc.), let down the tailgate, spread your picnic out on it, and eat, in no time at all.

The other occasion that has gained tremendous popularity is the lunch before a college football or baseball game. Call your classmate who lives in another town— "How about meeting us at the Number Two parking lot at the stadium, before the State-Hometown game in October? We'll bring the food, and you bring the drinks, and we'll have a reunion!" Having arranged the meeting place specifically, you load your whole family into the station wagon and enjoy the game and a chance to catch up on all the news of old friends after a sumptuous meal cooked on your folding grill. In fact many of those friends may turn up in the same parking lot. Tailgate picnics have been such a success at colleges that the custom has caught on before professional games too.

The tailgate takes the place of a folding table, and the only other pieces of necessary equipment are the grill and a piece of plastic to lay on the tailgate, which is likely to be dusty or sandy.

Of course, it is not necessary at all to have a station wagon to have a delightful picnic with your friends before a game or at any other time. A folding table and your own ingenuity can more than make up for lack of a tailgate.

Clambakes

The preparations for a clambake are quite specialized; but if you know how a seaweed oven is made (practically, as well as theoretically), and you have a loyal friend who is willing to spend the whole day helping, nothing is more in keeping with a holiday at the seaside. To be successful, however, you or someone on your beach must have experience in preparing and timing the baking of corn on the cob and potatoes as well as the clams and lobsters. Therefore, since most seashore resort areas have clambake specialists who will do the entire bake for you, it is far wiser for the unpracticed amateur to avail himself of their services.

Leaving the Picnic Site

No matter where your picnic has taken place, be sure not only to tidy up before you leave so that no trace will be left, but to be careful, while you are eating and opening papers, not to throw them carelessly aside where they will blow away. Many of our highways have pleasant wayside parks for picnickers, equipped with rustic tables, safe drinking water, and incinerators. On the property of a private owner, the least payment you can make is to be sure that you do nothing that might despoil any of his property.

Most important of all, *never* leave a fire without being absolutely certain that it is out. In the woods water may be poured on the logs until there is no sign of steam,

or if you have a shovel or other means of lifting them, the embers may be carried to a
nearby pond or stream and thrown in. On the beach a fire should also be put out with water. *Never* cover the coals with sand, as they will retain the heat for hours, and someone walking by with bare feet, unable to see the remains of the fire, may step on the hot sand and receive a terrible burn.

OPEN HOUSE

An open house is literally what the name implies. The door is open to all those invited at any time between the hours stated on the invitation. Today most open houses are held to celebrate a holiday—New Year's Day, perhaps, or Christmas Eve.

When invitations are issued in church or club announcements the host is saved from having to invite the entire membership individually. Personal invitations are generally sent out on informals or commercial cards bought for the occasion.

Because an answer is never expected, refreshments are simple and the sort that may be expanded or not set out all at once. Dips, sandwiches, bowls of nuts, and a punch—rather than individual drinks—are good choices. People drop in to greet their hosts, and friends wish each other a "Happy New Year" or "Good luck to you in your new home." They generally stay no more than a half hour to an hour.

If the open house is to celebrate a holiday the decorations are generally appropriate to the season. At Christmastime the tree would be trimmed and whatever other decorations you might wish to use would be arranged as beautifully as possible. Eggnog, grog, or wassail is the traditional drink at a Christmas open house. For a Fourth of July party, red, white, and blue streamers, balloons, or bouquets might add a note of gaiety. But if the open house is not held to celebrate any particular holiday no decorations are necessary other than some vases of pretty flowers or greens.

The food and beverages may be arranged on the dining-room table if you have enough plates of cookies or sandwiches so that it will not look bare. If your refreshments are restricted to one or two plates of food and a punch bowl they should be set out on any conveniently placed table in the hall or living room, or on a side table in the dining room. You may wish to surround a bowl of eggnog with holly twigs or a fruit punch with flowers, but otherwise only the attractive arrangement of glasses, Christmas napkins (cloth or paper), and food is necessary to assure the charm of your refreshment table.

BRUNCHES

Brunch—a combination of breakfast and lunch that relies on both breakfast and lunch dishes for its menus, although it is held closer to the usual hour for lunch—is a pleasant sort of informal, even casual, entertaining. It is not unusual to find brunches being given on the day after a large party, especially if there are many out-of-town guests who have come for the "big" occasion. However, no such excuse is necessary if you find the late-morning hours convenient for you and your friends.

In any event informality is the rule. In the country, slacks or simple dresses may be worn by the women, or if the host is having the party beside his swimming pool, people may come in shorts and bring their bathing suits. In the city any daytime clothing—dress or slacks—is correct for a woman, and a man usually wears a sports jacket rather than a business suit.

Invitations may be telephoned ahead of time, but this kind of gathering is so casual that the host often simply says to his friends as they are leaving someone else's party, "Why don't you come over around eleven-thirty tomorrow for a late breakfast?" or "Would you all come for brunch after church tomorrow?"

Bloody Marys are often served, as well as martinis and other cocktails. But tomato juice or consommé must also be offered without the liquor for friends who prefer it that way.

The food is arranged on a buffet table less elaborately set than for lunch or dinner, but attractively and conveniently laid out. Breakfast and lunch dishes are combined. For example, a platter of scrambled eggs surrounded by bacon or little sausages may be accompanied by hot rolls, toast, sautéed potatoes, and broiled tomatoes. Or platters of waffles may be served with maple syrup or with creamed chicken for guests who prefer a heartier meal. Pitchers of fruit juice and pots of coffee should be on a table beside the buffet.

CARD PARTIES

In giving a card party, whether of two tables or of ten, the first thing to do is to plan the tables carefully. The tables may all be different—one with good players, another with beginners, one where the stakes are high, another where they play for nothing—but you must do your best to put those who play approximately the same kind of game at the same table. In addition to skill it is important to remember temperament. Don't put people who take their game seriously (and "play for blood") with those who chatter unceasingly and keep asking, "Whose bid is it?" or "What's trump?" One poor player can spoil the whole evening—or afternoon—for the three who play well.

However, when a group of friends play together regularly, and they have approximately the same degree of skill, they may prefer to draw for partners and tables in order to have the opportunity of playing with different combinations of people. They may also move around—changing tables and partners after four hands, two rubbers, or whatever they decide upon. Each player keeps his own individual score. The game is just as much fun but far less "cutthroat" than the conventional play tends to be.

And now your preparations: It seems scarcely necessary to say that the pack of cards on each table must be fresh and that the pencils laid beside the score pads must be sharp. And yet I have played with grubby cards and kept score on odd little scraps of paper in the most beautiful homes! On each table you leave a slip of paper with the names of the players who are to sit there, or you may simply tell each guest at which table he is to play. It is important to see that each table is comfortably lighted. Poorly placed light that is reflected from the shiny surface of the cards is just as bad as darkness that makes red cards indistinguishable from black ones. If you have any doubt about the light, sit in each place, hold the cards in your hands, lay a few on the table, and see for yourself.

Refreshments

The kinds of refreshments you offer your card-playing guests depends, of course, on the time of day. While small sandwiches and tiny cakes accompanied by tea or coffee might be suitable when served at four o'clock to a group of women, they would hardly please the men at an evening gathering. Then, if you have not served dinner, a selection of cold meats and cheeses and a variety of breads for do-it-yourself sandwiches, served with coffee and beer around eleven o'clock, would be more appropriate. In either case, however, the food may be attractively arranged on the dining-room table, and having served themselves, the guests either return to the cleared card tables or take their plates to more comfortable chairs in the living room.

A dessert card party is a happy compromise for the hostess who may feel that she cannot provide a full luncheon or dinner for her guests, yet wishes to do more than simply invite them to play cards. When the group is small and she has a dining-room table large enough to seat them, dessert may be served in the following way: The dining table is set for the dessert course only. Individual place mats are set with a dessert plate, a lunch napkin on the plate, a fork at the left and a spoon at the right, and a glass of water. When the guests are seated, the hostess passes the dessert, and while they are finishing, she pours coffee, and it is handed around the table. After coffee they begin playing on tables already set up in the living room.

If there are more guests than she can seat, the dining table may be set as a buffet, using a tablecloth or place mats or round paper or lace doilies under the stack of plates and the dishes on which the dessert is served.

The guests serve themselves and take their plates to the living room to eat. The hostess may or may not ask them to sit at the card tables, which have already been set up and readied for bridge. They help themselves to coffee, and if they wish to start playing immediately, they may take their cups with them to the bridge tables.

Prizes

If it is customary in your community to play for prizes, then you must select a first prize for the highest score made by a woman and a first prize for the highest score made by a man. At a party of women only, a second prize is usually given. All prizes should be attractively wrapped before being presented. Those who receive the prizes must, of course, open the packages at once and show some evidence of appreciation when thanking the hostess.

Reading, Discussion, Musical and Craft Groups

When neighborhood groups include both men and women they usually meet in the evening at a time agreed upon as convenient for everyone. But a group of women interested, for example, in reading French together may find that an afternoon or even a morning meeting is the only solution to the problem of family schedules. The convenience of the members determines the hour, and the place the meeting is held is usually rotated among the members.

Refreshments are served after the activity of the meeting, and of course the kind depends on the hour, the preferences of the group, and the inclination of the hostess-of-the-day. Coffee and sandwiches, Welsh rarebit and beer, cider and doughnuts, would all be appropriate after an evening gathering. Earlier in the day coffee and rolls or tea and cookies might very well be adequate.

Otherwise there are no rules for such groups—except to be firm with those who don't try to keep in tune or with the gossipers who wander from the topic under discussion.

The hostess at whose house a craft or sewing group meets should have a supply of different-sized thimbles, extra needles, and several pairs of scissors and spools of thread. What is sewed depends upon the purpose of the group, which may be to make garments for a nursery, hospital, or other organization. It may have no object other than to meet socially, in which case the members sew for themselves— doing needlepoint, quilting, hooking rugs, even knitting. Sometimes a sewing circle is a lunch club that meets weekly or fortnightly at the houses of the various members. They sew from eleven until about one and then have a sit-down or buffet luncheon. More often coffee and light refreshments, such as coffee cake, cookies, or doughnuts, are served approximately halfway through a session that may run from ten to twelve or from two to half past four.

The Most Formal Table Setting

The one unbreakable rule for a formal table is that everything must be geometrically spaced: the centerpiece in the actual center, the places at equal distances, and all utensils balanced. Beyond this one rule you can vary your arrangement and decorations to a wide degree.

Tablecloths

If the tablecloth is of white damask, which is best for a truly formal dinner, a pad must be put under it. (If you do not have a felt pad cut to the dimensions of your table, a folded white blanket serves very well.) Damask is the most conservative tablecloth, suitable in any dining room from English or French style to contemporary furnishings. Embroidered or lace-inserted tablecloths are appropriate for low-ceilinged, old-fashioned rooms. Either lace or linen goes over the table without felt or other padding.

When a damask or linen cloth is used, the middle crease must be put on so that it is an absolutely straight and unwavering line down the exact center from head to foot of the table. If it is an embroidered cloth be sure the embroidery or monogram is right side up.

The tablecloth for a seated dinner should hang down approximately eighteen inches. It should *not* extend to the floor as it does on a buffet table.

No matter how concerned you are about soiling your beautiful—possibly heirloom—damask cloth, *never* cover it with clear plastic. Not only does it have an unpleasant, slippery surface, but the beauty of the cloth cannot possibly show clearly, and you might just as well buy an imitation plastic cloth and keep the other in the drawer! With today's cleaning processes, there are few spots that cannot be removed, and those who are fortunate enough to have lovely table linens should not hide them away, but should use them, for their own enjoyment and to the delight of their guests.

Napkins

A truly formal damask dinner napkin matches the table-cloth and is approximately twenty-four inches square. Whether your napkins are that size or not, they are folded in the manner described below.

Very large napkins are folded three times in each direction to make a smaller square. The two sides are then folded under, making a loosely "rolled" rectangle. The napkin is not flattened down completely. Care must be taken so that the monogram shows at the lower left corner of the rectangle, or if the initials are at the center of one side of the napkins, that they appear in the center third of the "roll."

Napkin folded to form a loosely rolled rectangle allowing monogram to appear in lower left hand corner. Napkin folded diagonally allowing monogram to show in the center point.

Smaller napkins may be folded in the same way, making only two folds to form the smaller square. Or the smaller square may be folded in half *diagonally*, and the two points folded under, leaving the monogram showing in the center point.

Napkins are placed in the center of the service plate with the monogram facing the diner. They are put at the side only when a first course is put on the table before seating the guests. To put the napkins at the side of the empty plate simply in order to display the plate is incorrect for formal table-setting. The old custom of wrapping a roll in the napkin was most impractical and, fortunately, is passé. When the diner flicked open the napkin he generally also flicked the roll right onto the floor.

Place Cards

Place cards are about three-quarters of an inch high after folding by two and a half inches long, usually plain or bordered in silver or gold. Decorated cards, while suitable on such special occasions as Christmas or a birthday, are out of place on a formal table. Some hostesses have their cards monogrammed in silver or gold, and a family that uses a crest may have the crest engraved at the top.

The courtesy title and surname—"Dr. Idzik," "Mr. Thompson,"—are used at official dinners except when there is more than one guest with the same surname, in which case "Mr. George Anderson" and "Mr. Howard Anderson," for example, should be used to make the distinction. At a party of friends or relatives first names are used, or if necessary to differentiate, "Helen M." and "Helen G." The writing should be large enough to be seen easily by the guests. (*For proper titles for govern-ment officials and diplomats, see the chart beginning on page 37.*)

Place cards may be put on top of and in the center of the napkin, but if unsteady there, they may be placed on the tablecloth above the service plate at the exact center of the place setting.

Menu Cards

Menu cards are most often seen at official dinners or banquets, but once in a while one sees them at a formal dinner in a private home. Usually there is only one, which is placed in front of the host, but sometimes there is one between every two guests.

The menu card never includes obvious accessories such as celery, olives, rolls, jelly, chocolates, or fruit, any more than it would include salt and pepper or iced water.

Silver

The silver used at a formal dinner should be sterling, or at least should appear to be sterling. Gold is used at the White House, but it is not so appropriate as silver for private parties.

It is not necessary that *all* silver match, although all forks or all spoons or all knives should be of the same pattern. Dessert silver, which is not on the table but is brought in with the dessert plates at a formal dinner, need not match the dinner forks, and after-dinner coffee spoons are frequently entirely different. Knives and forks should match, unless you happen to have a set of knives with crystal or carved-bone handles that may be used with any pattern.

Crystal

Each place should be set with the number of glasses which will be used during the meal, with the exception of the dessert wine glass, which is put on the table after the dessert is served. Water goblets are placed closest to the center of each setting, with the wine glasses to the right in the order they will be used.

China

China, too, may be mixed, but *all* the plates for each course at one table should match. For example, all the service plates must be of one pattern, although the dinner plates, while matching each other, may be entirely different. Silver or glass butter plates and glass salad or dessert plates may be used with any fine china. The most important consideration is that each item be of the same high quality as the others. It is entirely incorrect, for example, to use heavy pottery salad plates with fine china dinner plates, just as it is to use paper napkins with a damask tablecloth.

The Centerpiece

The first piece to be put on the table once the cloth is in place is the centerpiece. As its name implies, it must be in the exact center. It must never be so high that the diners cannot see over it, but its length and width are limited only by the size of your table. It can be composed of a wide variety of things—fresh flowers being the most common and surely one of the loveliest. "Cheap" plastic artificial flowers are out of place, but lovely glass, china, or silk imitation flowers or fruit are appropriate. Carefully arranged fruit makes a beautiful centerpiece, and ornaments that need neither fruit nor flowers can be effective too. Two of my own particular favorites are a covered china tureen decorated with charming shells and fish, and a pair of large crystal fish, which I use with glass candlesticks.

Candles

Candles for the most formal dinner should be white, and brand-new. Only if you are skilled with a candle-tip shaper and there is no evidence of smoke or drips, might a used candle be permissible.

Candles are lighted before the guests come to the table and remain lighted until they leave the dining room.

When the centerpiece is in place, a pair of candlesticks is placed at each end, about halfway between the centerpiece and the end of the table, or candelabra at either end halfway between the places of the host and hostess and the centerpiece. The number of candles depends upon whether the dining room is otherwise lighted or not. If the candles alone light the table, there should be a candle for each person. You will need two or four candelabra, depending on the length of the table and the number of guests. If there are two candelabra at each end, they are spaced evenly between the centerpiece and the host's and hostess's places. But if the candles are merely ornaments, two or four candles will be adequate for a table of up to eight. Candlesticks or candelabra must be high and the candles as long as the proportion can stand, so that the light does not shine into the eyes of those at the table.

Finishing Touches

Dishes or compotes filled with candied fruit, thin chocolate mints, or other edible trimmings may be put at the corners, between the candlesticks or candelabra and the centerpiece, or wherever there are equally spaced vacancies on the table. They are left there through the entire meal and are sometimes passed around after dessert is finished. Nuts may be put on the dinner table either in large silver dishes or in small individual ones at each of the places, but they are removed with the salt-and-pepper shakers after the salad course. The colloquial description of eating "from soup to nuts" does not apply to a formal dinner. After-dessert "nuts and raisins" belong only on the family dinner table—especially at Thanksgiving and Christmas.

Flowers are also often seen in two or four smaller vases or epergnes, in addition to the larger arrangement in the center.

Pepper pots and saltcellars should be at every place or between every two places. For a dinner of twelve there should be six (and never less than four) salts and peppers. Open saltcellars must be accompanied by tiny silver serving spoons, which sometimes have a gold bowl—gold is not so easily damaged by the salt.

Most hostesses prefer that their guests do not smoke at least until coffee is served, and no ashtrays or cigarettes are placed on the table. When this is so, the guests should have the good sense and courtesy to refrain until after dinner.

The Individual Places.

Next comes the setting of the places. The distance between places at the table must never be so short that guests have no elbow room and the servants cannot pass the dishes properly. When the dining-room chairs have very high backs and are placed so close as to be almost touching, it is difficult for even the most skillful server

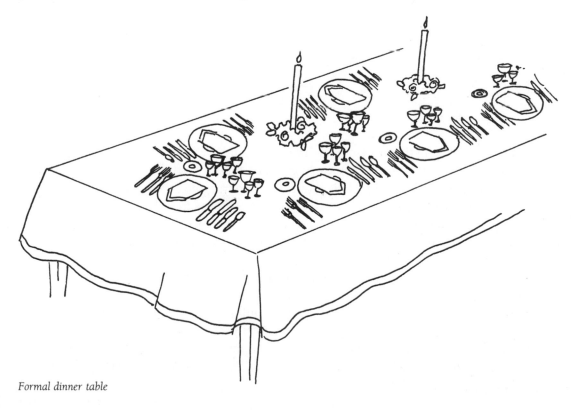

Formal dinner table

not to spill something on someone. On the other hand, people placed a yard or more apart will find a shouted conversation equally trying. About two feet from plate center to plate center is ideal. If the chairs have narrow and low backs, people can sit much closer together. This is especially true of a small, round table, the curve of which leaves a spreading wedge of space between the chairs at the back even if the seats touch at the front corners.

The service plates, with the pattern properly positioned so that the "picture" faces the diner, are first put around the table at equal distances. The silver is placed in the order of its use, with the implements to be used first farthest from the plate. The salad fork is placed next to the left of the plate, then the meat fork, and finally the fish fork, which will be used first. Just to the right of the plate is the salad knife, next is the meat knife, and on the outside is the fish knife, the cutting edge of each toward the plate. Outside the knives are the soup spoon and/or fruit spoon, and beyond the spoons, the oyster fork if shellfish is to be served. Note that the oyster (or shellfish) fork is the *only* fork ever to be placed on the right.

Formal place setting

No more than three of any implement are *ever* placed on the table (with the exception of the oyster fork's making four forks). Therefore, if more than three courses are served before dessert (rare, these days), the fork for the fourth course is brought in at the time it is served. Or the salad knife and fork may be omitted in the beginning and may be brought in when salad is served.

Dessert spoons and forks are brought in on the dessert plate just before dessert is served.

Although for many years butter plates were never seen on formal tables, this rule is rapidly being forgotten. Today there are few people who do not prefer their bread or roll with butter, and the idea of putting a buttered roll, or a dry one for that matter, directly onto the tablecloth is totally contrary to the aims of etiquette. Therefore, no matter how formal the dinner, the use of a butter plate is now correct. The butter plate is located above the forks at the left of the place setting. The butter

Formal table set for two

knife is laid across it, slightly diagonally from upper left to lower right, with the sharper edge of the blade toward the edge of the table.

The wineglasses chosen depend of course upon the menu, but their table-setting arrangement is according to size, so that little ones are not hidden behind large ones. Therefore the goblet for water is placed directly above the knives at the right of the plate; next to it, at a slight distance to the right, the champagne glass, in front and between these two, the claret or red-wine glass, or the white-wine glass; then, either in front of this or somewhat to the right again, the sherry glass. Or instead of grouping the glasses on the table, some prefer to have them placed in a straight row slanting downward from the goblet at the upper left to the glass for sherry at the lower right.

Such an array as this is scarcely ever seen except at a public dinner, which is more properly classified a banquet. At the private dinner two or three glasses in addition to the goblet are usual—one for sherry, one for claret or possibly a Burgundy, and one for a light white wine.

THE INFORMAL TABLE

Whether you call your dinner party "informal," "semiformal," or "casual," you have much more latitude in planning your table setting than you do for a formal dinner. There are a few overall considerations that should be given attention, based on your available space, the style of your home, the theme of your party, and the tastes of your guests. Outside of the restrictions imposed by that list, you may give your imagination and your creativity free rein in setting your table.

Table Coverings

While there is no reason not to use a white damask or lace cloth for a semiformal dinner, you should add color in the other table appointments to give the table warmth and interest and to take away the formal atmosphere. The color may come in the napkins, the centerpiece, and your choice of china or pottery.

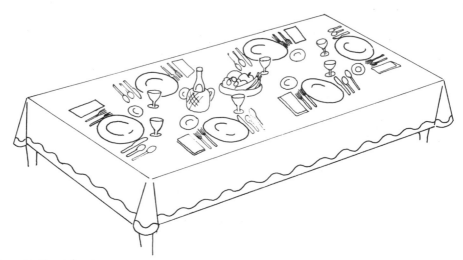

Informal table set for six

More often, the table is covered with a gaily colored or patterned cloth, or with place mats. If you have pretty linen, lace, straw or woven mats with napkins that match or complement them, they are ideal for informal dinners, and there are even lovely plastic sets that are appropriate too. Whatever covering you choose, be sure that your centerpiece and china go well with it. Strive for an unusual or individual look that will make *your* table stand apart.

Candles are used on informal tables just as they are at formal dinners, but usually in candlesticks rather than candelabra. They may be of any color that goes well with the tablecloth or mats, but must be high enough so that the flame is above the eye level of the diners. The hostess (sometimes one of the guests helps her) extinguishes the candles as she leaves the table. Some brave souls pinch the flame quickly between thumb and forefinger, but I prefer to cup my hand behind the flame and blow it out!

The centerpiece, too, may show your originality. A Thanksgiving turkey made of a large crooked-neck squash with smaller gourds for neck and head and pineapple leaves for tail feathers makes a real conversation piece. A dried-flower arrangement on a brown tablecloth with orange or beige napkins is stunning. Wide red ribbons crisscrossing a white tablecloth and a centerpiece of large red crepe-paper poppies brighten a winter or Valentine's Day table. In short, don't rely on the usual bowl of flowers—pretty though it is. Look through magazines for ideas if you are not creative yourself, and give your dinner guests a happy surprise.

Place Settings

As at a formal dinner everything on the table should be symmetrically and evenly spaced. The main difference between the formal and informal place setting is that for the latter there is less of everything. There are fewer courses served, so fewer pieces of silver are set out.

Generally only one—at the most, two—wines are served, so a water goblet and one (or two) wineglasses are all that are necessary. Frequently wine is not served at all, and iced-tea glasses or simply tumblers for water or mugs for beer are used. If bread or rolls are to be served, a butter plate should be used. If you do not have butter plates to match your dinner plates try to buy a set of glass ones. It is less than appetizing to have one's bread or roll get soggy and messy because it has slid into the juice or salad dressing on your dinner plate, or to see the pat of butter on the edge of the warm plate melting rapidly down into your meat or vegetables before you can spread it on your bread.

For more or less the same reason, serve separate salad plates if your menu includes any dishes with gravy. Salad may be put on the same plate with broiled steak or chops or chicken, perhaps, but an unappetizing mess results when it is combined with lamb stew!

The typical place setting for an informal three-course dinner would include:

2 forks—one for dinner at the far left
          one for dessert or salad to the left of the plate
dinner plate—not on the table when guests sit down
salad plate—to the left of the forks
1 knife—next to the plate on the right—for steak, chops, chicken, or game birds, it may be a steak knife
2 spoons—dessert spoon to the right of the knife
          soup spoon at the far right

Notice that the silver to be used last is next to the plate.

1 butter plate with butter knife—if you have them
1 water goblet—or tall tumbler
1 wineglass—if you plan to serve wine
ashtray—if you do not mind your guests smoking at the dinner table
napkin in the center

Informal three-course dinner place setting, as the diner arrives to be seated

If you plan to serve coffee with the meal, the cup and saucer go to the right of the setting, with the coffee spoon on the right side of the saucer.

Service plates are not used at an informal dinner, except under the stemmed glass used for shrimp cocktail, fruit cocktail, etc., and under soup plates. It may be a true service plate, or it may be simply another dinner or dessert plate—whichever size and style is most appropriate.

The dinner plate should not be on the table when your guests sit down, because it should be very warm when the food is served. If you have help, the maid passes the hot plates around before she starts serving. If you are having a seated buffet the stack of warm plates is on the buffet table.

The dessert spoon and fork (or if you prefer, just a spoon) need not be beside the plate. They can be brought in, as at a formal dinner, with the dessert plate, or they can be placed, European style, above the center of the place setting, horizontally, with bowl and tines to the left.

You may use any materials that appeal to you on your informal table. Wooden salts and pepper grinders, pewter plates, wooden salad bowls, ironware, pottery, and stainless-steel "silver" are all fine. However, each item must be in keeping with the others. Don't combine plastic wineglasses with fine bone china, or plastic plates with delicate crystal glasses. You may, however, use wooden salad bowls with pottery or "everyday" china plates, or glass salad plates with stoneware dinner plates. The secret is not in having everything of one design, but in creating, out of a variety of patterns and colors, a harmonious whole.

When your guests arrive at the table, the butter should already be on the butter plates, the water glasses filled, and the wine (if served) in a cooler beside the host or in a decanter on the table. Salad is often served with the main course instead of as a separate one, and as mentioned above, rather than putting a crisp cool salad on a hot plate or one swimming in gravy, a salad plate or a bowl should be set at the left of each place.

Ashtrays, salts and peppers, and condiments in serving dishes—not the jars they came in—must all be in place, conveniently spaced around the table.

If the host is serving the meat and vegetables, the stack of warm plates may be in front of him along with the foods to be served and the necessary implements. If there is a course already on the table, however, the hostess or maid must bring the entrée in from the kitchen after the plates have been removed.

A course to be served before the entrée should be on the table when the guests come in to dinner. Long-stemmed glass bowls containing fish or shrimp should have a plate under them. Both are removed to make way for the hot plates of the main course. If your first course is soup the most practical soup dishes are little pots with lids, which will keep the contents hot while the guests are seating themselves.

In some houses the salad-dressing ingredients are arranged in a set of bowls and bottles that, with the salad bowl, are put in front of the hostess, who mixes the dressing herself. A few drops of this or shakes of that, according to the taste of the hostess, lend an excitement to a dressing that can never be duplicated in a store-bought bottle.

The same idea exactly has made certain internationally known restaurants famous—the headwaiter, or the proprietor himself, cooks and mixes something before your eyes. The ducks of the Tour d'Argent, the noodles of Alfredo's in Rome, or Japanese sukiyaki seem to acquire a special flavor by the visible preparation. In short, preparing a dish at the table (which many hostesses think of as a handicap) may easily become a special feature of your hospitality.

LUNCHEONS

The Table

Candles are not needed on a lunch table, but are sometimes used as ornaments. They should never be lit in the daytime. The plain white tablecloth that is correct for dinner is not used for luncheon, although colored damask is acceptable. Far more often, the lunch table is set with place mats made in any variety of linen, needlework, lace, or plastic. A runner, matching the mats but two or three times as long, may be used in the center of the table.

The decorations are practically the same as for dinner: flowers or an ornament in the center, and two or four dishes of fruit or candy where they look best. If the table is very large and rather too bare without candles, four small vases with flowers matching those in the centerpiece—or any other glass or silver ornaments—may be added.

The places for a large formal luncheon are set as for dinner, with a service plate, a fork, a knife, or a spoon for each course. The lunch napkin, which should go well with the tablecloth, is much smaller than the dinner napkin. Generally it is folded like a handkerchief, in a square of four thicknesses. The square is laid on the plate diagonally, with the monogrammed (or embroidered) corner pointing down toward the near edge of the table. The upper corner is then turned sharply under in a flat crease for about a quarter of its diagonal length; then the two sides are rolled loosely under, with a straight top edge and a pointed lower edge and the monogram displayed in the center. Or it can be folded in any simple way one prefers.

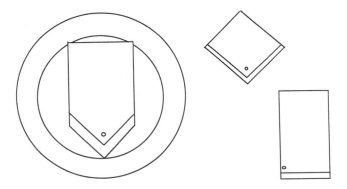

Ways to fold luncheon napkins

If it is a large luncheon, guests are often seated at several card tables, and place cards are used just as they are at dinner. Card tables are covered with square tablecloths, either white or colored. A small flower arrangement makes the prettiest centerpiece.

Luncheon place setting

FAMILY STYLE DINING

Practicality is the keynote in setting the table for family meals.

Seating arrangements at table depend on the convenience of the family. One parent may sit nearest the kitchen door with young children who may need help seated nearby. The other parent sits at the opposite end of the table. If there is a male guest he is seated on Mother's right, a female guest on Father's right.

Kitchen Dining

Some families, even though they have a dining room, prefer the coziness and convenience of the kitchen when dining by themselves. If space permits, it is grand to have an end of the kitchen set apart, furnished and decorated so that the children feel the importance of good manners at the table, no matter where it may be. In our country's past the kitchen served early settlers as living room, dining room, and cooking area, and certainly from Mother's point of view it was practical. Aside from the convenience in serving, she was right with the family, not only during the meal, but while preparing it.

When eating at the kitchen table an extra effort should be made to make the room neat and attractive before the family sits down.

Even a kitchen table should be nicely set for dinner—the one hour of the day when families can get together "socially." There should be place mats or a tablecloth (a pretty plastic one is most practical) or even paper place mats; spotless utensils, though they may be stainless steel; and pretty, colorful glasses and plates, even though they were bought at the "five-and-ten." In times past the family dinner was an institution. It was the time when children learned table manners, the art of listening and conversing, and many other courtesies. Unfortunately few families today take advantage of this opportunity because their schedules do not permit it and in some households, because television has been allowed to lure the youngsters away from the seated dinner; it is a great loss.

The Bare Essentials

A minimum number of utensils is put at each place—only those absolutely necessary. Since there is usually only one course and dessert, there may be only three pieces of silver—a fork, a knife, and a spoon for the dessert. Of course if you are having soup or fruit first, utensils for those foods must be added. You do not need to bother with separate salad forks, although individual salad bowls should be set out, even at the family table. Butter plates and knives may be omitted, although if you have a dishwasher the extra plate is more than worth the trouble of putting it in the rack.

TV dinners and other prepared dishes should not be eaten from the containers, but should be spooned out onto warm plates.

Milk glasses should be filled before the meal, or the milk should be served in a pitcher. However, ketchup, jellies, pickles, etc., may be served in their jars if no guests are present. The jars should be on saucers, and each should have its own separate serving spoon or fork on the saucer.

Paper napkins are perfectly correct for family meals. However, if you prefer cloth napkins you may wish to conserve on your laundry by using napkin rings.

Family place setting

These, too, are correct for family meals. Each member has his own ring, marked so that he can recognize it. He folds his napkin at the end of the meal and puts it back in the ring, which is removed from the table until the next meal. Napkins should be changed after two or three meals—some families change each morning or evening. Of course if a napkin gets badly soiled, it should not be used again.

Napkin rings are not used by guests, with the exception of a relative or close friend who is making a prolonged visit. Occasionally they are put on a table as part of the decor at an informal party, but the guests do not replace the napkins in them after dinner.

The rings are usually placed at the left of the setting, but they may be put in the center, especially if they are broad, flattened ones.

Place Settings

Since no china or silver that will not be used need be placed on the table, the following settings must be reduced to fit your menu.

Breakfast

More so than at other meals, there is a wide difference in the tastes of breakfast eaters. Some people prefer to eat no breakfast at all—or perhaps a piece of toast and a glass of milk. Many take only a cup of coffee and a glass of juice, while others eat a hearty morning meal and watch their calories at lunchtime. Others like a more substantial meal, sometimes two or three courses, including fruit, cereal, and eggs. Unlike other meals, breakfast may, and should, be prepared "to order." That is, if one member of the family truly dislikes eggs, that person should be given a dish of cold cereal, but others should not therefore be deprived of their scrambled eggs and bacon.

In setting the breakfast table, you put out just those utensils that will be needed by each person.

A variety of cold cereals, milk, cream, sugar, salt and pepper, and jams or jellies may be placed in the center of the table or on a convenient side table, but whoever is doing the cooking serves the hot food directly onto the plates and places them in front of those sitting at the table. If your table is large enough, a lazy Susan or turntable is most convenient and makes each item easily accessible to everyone.

The setting is as follows:

Fork at the left of the plate.
Knife at the right of the plate.
Spoon for cereal at the right of the knife.
Teaspoon for fruit or grapefruit spoon at the right of the cereal spoon.
Napkins, in rings or not, at the left of the place setting.
Coffee cups with spoons on the saucers or mugs at the right of each plate if the coffee is served from the kitchen. If it is served by Mother at the table, cups and saucers, or mugs, and coffeepot are beside her place.
Glass for milk or water, to the right and above the spoons.
Butter knife across the bread-and-butter plate, which is to the left and above the fork (optional).

Lunch

For the busy woman who does not work outside her home, lunch usually consists of a sandwich, a bowl of soup, or a salad. She may eat it at the dining-room or kitchen table, or she may bring it to the living room or patio on a tray. When children are home for lunch, they usually eat in the kitchen. If the man of the house has lunch at home, he will probably want a more substantial meal, and the table is set in accordance with the food to be served. In the average household—unless the main meal is eaten at midday, in which case the table is set as for dinner—no more than three courses are ever served for lunch, and even that number is most unusual.

The setting is as follows:

Meat fork at the left of the salad fork.
On the right, a meat knife; and at the right of this knife, a soup or dessert spoon, if necessary.
Butter plate and knife above the fork at the left.
The dessert fork or spoon may be brought in with the dessert plate if you prefer.
Glass for a beverage above the knife.
Napkin at the left of the place setting.

Dinner

If the food is to be passed, the warm dinner plates are at each place on the table when the family sits down, or they are stacked in front of the head of the household if he or she is to serve. However, many women prefer to serve the plates directly from the stove in order to avoid the use of extra platters and serving dishes. The table setting for dinner is similar to that for lunch:

At the left of the plate, the dinner fork.

At the right, the dinner knife next to the plate, then the soup spoon or the oyster fork or the dessert spoon (if necessary) on the outside.

Glass or goblet for a beverage at the right above the knife.

Butter plate to the left and above the fork, with the butter knife laid on it diagonally from the upper left to the lower right.

Salad plate (if necessary) at the left of the fork.

Napkin at the left of the setting.

Coffee mug or cup and saucer with a spoon at the right. If you are using mugs for coffee during the meal, the spoon goes to the right of the mugs.

The Mealtime Tray

Although few people in the ordinary household are served breakfast on a tray, there are many occasions when a member of the family is ill and must remain in bed for his meals. An attractive tray with a flower in a little vase or with a brightly colored napkin and tray cloth can do much to aid a lagging appetite and a sagging spirit. Also, dinner is frequently eaten from a tray taken to the living room or den when a favorite television program is in progress.

For all meals the tray is covered with a tray cloth, a doily, or a place mat of some sort. The setting is the same as the individual place setting at the table insofar as space permits. Because of lack of room, the dessert plate and the coffee cup and saucer are usually brought when the main meal is finished. The dinner plate should be heated. A piece of foil laid over the food will keep it warm while the tray is carried to its destination.

Individual breakfast sets for trays were often given as wedding presents but today are more often purchased for someone confined to bed. They generally include an egg cup, a cereal bowl, two or three plates and a cover, a coffee cup and saucer, sugar bowl, cream pitcher, and small coffeepot. They come in colorful patterns or lovely solid colors and by the very charm of their appearance make the morning more cheerful.

*A*lthough the day of the great house staffed by a horde of servants is almost gone, the simple house with a relaxed hostess and enthusiastic guests can be the setting for a house party that is just as successful as the elaborate affair of the past.

The size of the house party today is limited mainly by the number of available beds. However, for a hostess who has no help, it is certainly easier to cook, serve, and keep the house in order with two guests than it is with eight, a fact she should remember even after she has counted the beds.

OVERNIGHT INVITATIONS

Invitations are generally telephoned, but if your guests live far away they may be written:

June 15

Dear Rebecca,

Jason and I are hoping that you and Alan and the children can spend the weekend of the fourth with us in Edgartown. If Alan could leave the office a little early on Friday the second, there is a 6:00 P.M. ferry that would get you here in time for dinner, and there are ferries leaving the island at 5:00 and at 8:00 on Sunday. The fishing should be great, and the children are counting on Jessica and Michael for the annual picnic. Please come—we have wanted to show you the island for so long.

Much love,
Annette

With the rising popularity of winter sports, more and more people are acquiring lodges in the mountains, and ski weekends are becoming almost an institution in all sections of the country where there are nearby slopes. An invitation might be on this order:

January 4

Dear Joan,

The forecast is for snow and more snow, and Dick and I are hoping that you and Bill will spend the weekend after next skiing with us at Stowe. Come as early as you can on Friday the eighth, and stay until Sunday night so as not to miss a minute of it. The Hortons are coming, too, so maybe you could drive up together. To find us, you turn off Interstate 89 on Route 100, drive exactly three-tenths of a mile past the Standard Church, and we are the house on the right.

No formal clothes, only your ski outfits, and slacks to change into. Plenty of woollies and flannels—it's cold!

We're counting on you, so do say "Yes."

Love to you both,
Barbara

In your letter or on the telephone, be sure to give the details of transportation, or the route if your guests are coming by car. If they will be arriving by public transportation, you must tell them to let you know at what hour they will arrive so that you can meet them at the station or airport.

To make it easier for guests to know what to bring, it is wise to indicate what the activities will be: "We're planning a deep-sea fishing expedition on Saturday," "The Joneses have asked us to a beach picnic on Sunday," or "There is to be a black-tie dance at the club on Saturday."

Since hostesses for weekend parties or house parties have to do more planning than dinner hostesses, it is essential that prospective guests answer the invitation promptly. If it is a telephoned invitation, don't say, "I'll have to find out about thus-and-so. I'll let you know next week." If you can't give a definite answer or promise one within a day or two, it is better to refuse. Let the hostess fill your place with someone else. You may, of course, say, "May I call you back tomorrow?" or "on Monday," or whatever, but never leave it indefinite or until a day or two before the weekend. Written replies, too, should be sent promptly, and should include the time of your arrival and your means of transportation: "Dear Joan, What a wonderful invitation. We plan to drive up by car, and should arrive about 7 o'clock Friday (the 12th). Can't wait to see you. . . ."

Guests who are coming and going by public transportation should have their return reservations confirmed. No matter how successful the house party, it should end when the hostess expects it to (which should be made clear in her invitation), and no guest should overstay his welcome because he suddenly finds there are no spaces left on the Sunday-night plane.

(For suggestions about gifts for hostesses, see page 575.)

Rooms for Your Guests

An Appealing Guest Room

Although it may seem that not a great deal can be done to make a guest room out of one that is used every day, many of the suggestions made in the following section describing the permanent guest room can be adapted—to the comfort and convenience of your visitors.

439
HOUSE
PARTIES
AND
WEEKEND
VISITS

It is by no means idle talk to suggest that every hostess try her guest room by spending a night in it herself. If she doesn't do this she should at least check the facilities thoroughly. If there is a guest bathroom that is not used frequently, she should check the drains to see that there is no stoppage and make sure that the toilet flushes properly. If a man is to use the bathroom she should see that there is a receptacle for used razor blades and a well-lighted mirror in which he can see to shave. Even though it may be adequate for powdering her nose it would be safer to ask her husband to shave in the guest bathroom and then listen to what he says about it.

There must, of course, be plenty of bath towels, face towels, a washcloth, a bath mat, and fresh cakes of soap for the bathtub and on the washstand. If the bathroom will be shared with family members, then guest towels and washcloths may be hung on a rack in the guest room so your guests know they are theirs, or a towel rack may be cleared in the bathroom for their use. If you prefer to hang them in the bathroom, then be sure to point them out when you show your guests their room and the bathroom.

It is not expected but it is a nice touch to place bath oil, bath powder, and hand lotion in decorated bottles on the washstand shelf and aspirin, Alka-Seltzer, and Band-Aids in the medicine chest. A good clothes brush and a pincushion with both straight and safety pins are always a welcome sight on a bureau or dressing table, and a new toothbrush in the bathroom has saved many a guest a trip to the local drugstore.

Good beds are most important. The mattresses should be firm—many people develop serious backaches from sleeping on a sagging bed. The most desirable arrangement is to have twin beds placed together, possibly with a single headboard. This satisfies both the couple who cannot sleep in the same bed and the couple who are used to a double bed. It also serves perfectly well for two girls or two boys. If there is space, the beds may be pushed apart and a table put between them if the visitors are not intimate friends.

It is nice but not necessary to provide two pillows for each guest, one medium-hard and one soft, so that there is a choice. Two pillows are also a comfort to those who like to read in bed.

There must be a light at the head of each bed or between the beds—not just a decorative glowworm but a 75- or 100-watt bulb with an adjustable shade that provides good reading light. Each light should, if possible, be so shaded from the other that the occupant of one bed can read while the other sleeps. A reliable clock, with an alarm, is essential, or if you have one, a clock radio is best of all. And in case the visitor has not brought his own reading material, there should be magazines, a few short paperbacks, or a volume of condensed books—chosen more to divert than to strain the reader's attention.

There should be a wastebasket in the room, and an extra blanket at the foot of the bed.

Facial tissues in pretty containers should be placed on the dressing table or beside the beds, and in the bathroom.

If there is a desk in the room, the blotter should be fresh and the calendar up-to-date.

The closets should contain wooden clothes hangers with bars or pressure clips for trousers, and plastic hangers for dresses. Thin wire hangers from the cleaner's crease the shoulders of dresses and the knees of pants, and are barely adequate.

The lining in the bureau drawers must be fresh, and everything stored in the drawers by members of the family must be removed to make space for the belongings of the guests. Lightly scented sachet in the drawers is delightful. Everyone loves flowers, and vases of them dress up rooms as nothing else can. Even an uninteresting room embellished with a few wild flowers or a potted plant becomes inviting.

Guest rooms should have dark shades for those who like to sleep late.

If you have no thermos jugs to be placed by the guest-room beds, be sure that there are glasses in the bathroom, or suggest that your guest take a glass of iced water with him when he says good night.

Temporary Arrangements

Most families today do not have a room in their house that is intended solely for the use of guests. When they wish to have friends spend a night or a weekend (or more), the children are doubled up to vacate a room, or perhaps sent to spend the time with friends. If there is a library or den with a convertible sofa it is put in readiness. In a child's room toys are hidden from sight, some clothes are removed from the closet, sufficient drawer space is cleared so that the guest may unpack his or her suitcase, and the room is made sparkling clean.

The host and hostess should never move out of their own room to give it to their guest or guests. It would cause considerable confusion, since all their personal belongings are in the closet, in the drawers, and in every other imaginable place. The guest could not help but feel that the visit was an imposition that was making everyone uncomfortable, and the guest would therefore be uncomfortable too. Even putting the guest on a convertible sofa in the living room, with a screen arranged around it to afford privacy, is preferable to switching everyone about. Of course if a guest is staying only for a night or two, a child, or children (if the sofa makes into a double bed), might be moved into the living room, but they should not be expected to give up their quarters, either, if the visit is an extended one.

Unmarried Couples

I am frequently asked by parents what they should do when their sons or daughters arrive home with someone of the opposite sex with whom they have been living without benefit of matrimony. Should they put them in the same room, or insist that they sleep separately?

441
HOUSE
PARTIES
AND
WEEKEND
VISITS

Parents have a right to insist that their own standards be observed in their own home. If they have been brought up to feel that it is morally wrong to sleep with someone before marriage and they would feel guilty or uncomfortable allowing it in their house, they should make that very clear to their children *before* they come home. If the parents have accepted the situation, but do not want to meet it face-to-face, they must wrestle with their own consciences. If the son or daughter says, "Very well then, I won't come home at all," they have an even harder decision. They must decide whether their relationship and continued communication with their child is more important than upholding their standards. I cannot give an answer because it is a very individual matter of conscience—not one of etiquette. I *can* repeat that everyone has a right to insist on certain standards in their own home, and I can add that if you and your children understand each other and have a good relationship to begin with, they will hesitate to put you in a difficult position and will accept the "rules" you establish for their behavior in your home. My only advice is, whatever you decide, let them know when they call and say, "We're coming home next weekend"—not after they carry their bags upstairs.

The House With Servants

When houseguests arrive at a house staffed by a number of servants, the personal maid of the hostess (if she has one—otherwise, the housemaid) unpacks the luggage, putting folded things in the drawers and hanging dresses and the men's suits in the closet. She also sees that the clothes are pressed if necessary.

The breakfast tray is carried to the guest's room by the waitress.

A breakfast set consists of a coffeepot or teapot, a cream pitcher and sugar bowl, a cup and saucer, two plates, one bowl, an egg cup, and a cover. Hot cereal is usually put in the bowl, toast in a napkin on a plate, and eggs and bacon on a plate with a cover. Glasses for fruit juice and iced water complete the tray. The thoughtful hostess who has a morning paper sent up with her guest's breakfast tray deserves a halo. When the visitor breakfasts in the dining room, the hostess sees that the paper is near his or her place at the table.

When a guest has been told to ring for breakfast the maid goes into the room and pulls up the shades. In cold weather she closes the windows and turns up the heat. If the hostess has not done so the night before, the maid asks what the guest would like for breakfast at this time.

Anyone breakfasting in the dining room is expected to dress before going down to the table.

In the evening the guests' beds are turned down while they are at dinner. The bedspread is removed, folded neatly, and put in a closet or some inconspicuous place. The sheet and blanket are folded back on one side. The guests' nightgowns or pajamas are folded neatly on the bed, or placed on a chair with their bathrobes, and their bedroom slippers are put on the floor beside them. A small tray with glasses and a thermos of iced water is placed on the bedside table.

Tips

When you dine in a friend's house you do not tip anyone—ever. But when you go to stay overnight or longer as a houseguest, you are expected to give a gratuity to anyone who has given you personal service—unpacked your bag, pressed your clothes, etc.

In a large household, where a number of guests are entertained often, the hostess compensates the servants herself for the extra work involved, and thus ensures that they will not object to frequent visitors. Guests are informed about this and do not tip anyone except someone, as mentioned above, who has given them personal service. (*See page 348 for who and how much to tip household servants.*)

THE HOUSE WITHOUT SERVANTS

When you entertain without help, the more planning and preparation that can be done ahead, the more effortless and pleasant the result. House parties do not generally last for more than two days and nights—at most, three. With the help of a separate freezer, or even the freezer compartment of your refrigerator, your meals can largely be prepared in advance. And with a microwave oven you can reheat more easily than in a conventional oven. A casserole kept warm in the oven can be ready at whatever hour your guests arrive, early or late. A steak cooked on the beach in summer or over the coals of the fireplace in winter, served with potato chips and salad, takes little effort. And you may wish to treat your guests to a dinner in a local restaurant that specializes in food native to the region. At most summer resorts yacht clubs, hotels, or nightclubs provide dinner and dancing on Saturday night.

For lunches you may prepare the ingredients for a chef's salad, lobster rolls, chowder, and sandwiches ahead of time, ready to be mixed or spread at the last moment.

The one meal that the hostess cannot organize in advance is breakfast. Because one of the joys of a weekend away from home is being able to sleep as late as one wants, a good hostess does not awaken her guests unless there is an activity planned in which they truly wish to participate.

The hostess should get up at an early hour to precede her guests to the kitchen. She makes coffee, prepares fruit or juice, and gets together the ingredients for those who want to prepare their own breakfast—eggs and bacon for some, fruit and yogurt for others. She puts an assortment of cereals and milk on the table, which she sets with places for everyone. She may wait for her guests, or she may eat her own breakfast and be ready to help the latecomers as they arrive. If some of the group want to make an early start, to the beach or to ski, for instance, plans should be made the day before. The host and hostess may accompany those who are leaving, as long as everything is left in readiness for those who wish to sleep or relax and arrangements have been made for their joining the group later on if they wish.

There are many people who get very upset if they do not get breakfast at the hour to which they are accustomed. When you are one who wakes at dawn, and the household you are visiting has the custom of sleeping late on a Sunday morning, the long wait for your coffee can truly upset your whole day. On the other hand, to be aroused at seven on the only day when you do not have to hurry to your office, in order to yawn through an early breakfast and then sit around and kill time with the Sunday paper, is just as trying.

If there are servants in the house, the guest cannot very well appear in the kitchen before the cook has had her own breakfast, but the farsighted guest with the early habit can, in a measure, come prepared. He can carry his own little electric water-heating outfit and a package of instant coffee or tea, sugar, powdered milk or cream, and a few crackers. He can then start his day all by himself in the barnyard hours without disturbing anyone. Or, in the household without servants he may slip quietly into the kitchen and make himself a cup of coffee and a piece of toast to sustain him until the others are ready for a full breakfast. Few people care enough to fuss, but if they do, these suggestions for a visitor with incurably early waking hours can make a great difference to his enjoyment of the entire day.

Extended Visits

Extended visits are almost entirely restricted to family members—a grandmother, a bachelor uncle, or a widowed parent who comes to stay for a couple of weeks or more. These visits often take place over a holiday season, and problems arise concerning invitations you receive while your visitor is there. Should you tell the prospective hostess, let us say, that your mother is with you and ask if you may bring her? Should you just go without her? Or must you stay home?

There are several answers. When the invitation is to an open house, a cocktail party, or a church or club festivity, one more guest would cause no difficulty, and you should feel free to ask if you may bring your mother along if she wishes to go. Naturally, your visitor, whoever it may be, should be consulted first. When it is a dinner or luncheon invitation you can say, "I'm afraid we can't come—Mother is staying with us." This leaves it up to the *hostess* to suggest that you bring your mother if she wishes, but there should be no criticism or ill-feeling if she does not. One more person could disrupt her entire plan for seating, entertainment, etc. Close friends and other relatives who know that your mother is with you should not invite you without including her in this invitation. And don't forget, your older visitor will be pleased and flattered if you arrange a party or two in your own home, so that she has a chance to see your friends.

443
HOUSE
PARTIES
AND
WEEKEND
VISITS

When the visit is really a long one, you are certainly free to say occasionally, "Would you mind if we left you for a little while Saturday evening? Some old friends are going to be at the Ponds'." The wise visitor who wants to be asked again will obviously say, "Of course not—go ahead. I'll rent a good movie for the VCR that will keep me busy."

PETS

Never ask whether you may bring a pet along on a visit. Your host and hostess may be great dog-lovers but they will probably not want a strange dog who may or may not get along with their Fido, and whose manners may or may not be the best. You are putting your hostess in a difficult position if she is not enthusiastic about your request.

If she makes the suggestion, naturally your pet may go. But be sure, before you accept on his behalf, that his behavior will be exemplary. You have no right to take a dog that is not perfectly housetrained, chews things, or will not stay off furniture or legs or laps to anyone else's home.

(*For advice for guests, hosts, and hostesses, see Chapter 24 which begins on page 467.*)

PRIVATE AND PUBLIC BALLS

There are two fundamental differences between balls and dances. First, while guests at a dance are of approximately one age, those at a ball may go from high-school students to octogenarians. Second, since dances are smaller, the decorations and refreshments are simpler.

Although private balls have become almost unheard of in recent years, this book would be incomplete if a reference to them were omitted. Besides, the charity and debutante balls that have replaced private ones all over the country are similar to them in terms of customs, rules, and procedures.

22

Balls and Dances

Planning the Ball

The host and hostess who give a private ball must, of course, assume the final responsibility for every aspect of the evening, but fortunately they may enlist the aid of many and various people. The club or hotel where it is to be held will provide the servants, the food, and the drinks; or if the ball is held at home, a caterer will provide the same services. A florist will see to the decorations, and there are social secretaries available who can help with the lists and invitations. But no matter how much help they are able to amass, those giving a private ball must make the final decisions on all the details that are so important to the success of the party.

A public ball is run by a committee, whose chair is in some ways comparable to the hostess, but without the full burden of responsibility. Special duties are allotted to each member of the committee: One takes charge of invitations, one of decorations; others are appointed to be responsible for the orchestra, the food, the ticket money, etc. In the following paragraphs, you may substitute *committee member* if the ball is other than a private one.

The first thing you must do is make an appointment to see the manager of the hotel, club, or any other suitable assembly room and find out which evenings are free. It is important to select an evening not already taken by another individual or organization in order not to conflict on lists, or in a small town, on the services of caterers, florists, etc.

You then telephone and engage the best orchestra you can for the chosen evening. If it can possibly be arranged, there should be two orchestras so that when one finishes playing, the other begins. You cannot give a ball or a dance that is anything but dull if you have poor music.

Having hired the bands and engaged the ballroom and necessary extra rooms, you make out the guest list and order the invitations. They are sent out four to six weeks prior to the ball. Invitations to balls, private or public, are always formal. There are, however, many variations in good taste. (*For these forms and also for less formal invitations appropriate to the smaller dance, see pages 359–362.*)

Dress For A Ball

The traditional dress for a man going to a formal ball is white tie and tails. Nothing could be handsomer, and men who have these suits welcome the rare opportunity to wear them. However, few men own a set of "tails," and rather than rent them for the evening, they wear the less formal tuxedo. "Black tie" (tuxedo) is accepted at all balls, even though the invitation says "formal." Only if it actually says "white tie" must one make the effort to rent a tailcoat for the evening.

Women who may live most of their lives in sweat suits and jeans go "all out" for a ball. Dresses are always long and as elegant as one can afford. A ball is also the time to take your best jewelry out of the safe and enjoy it. Pants on women are not acceptable unless they are very full and styled to look like a long ball gown. Even the youngest guests should dress up as they never have before. The attraction of a ball *is* that it is very special and very elegant, and every person there should cooperate in appearance, in behavior, and in graciousness to keep it that way.

Women guests at a debutante ball never wear white, which is reserved for the debutantes.

With sleeveless, or strapless gowns, women may wear long gloves, which they leave on through the beginning of the ball but remove when they begin dancing or when supper is served.

The Night of the Ball

A receiving line is formed on the stroke of the hour specified in the invitations. It is comprised of the host and hostess at a private ball, and the committee heads at a public ball. (*Guidelines for a receiving line at a debutante ball appear later in this chapter.*)

The receiving line is formed in front of the doorway to the ballroom, not at the front door. Guests enter the hotel, club, home, or whatever the setting and check their wraps before passing through the receiving line. After shaking hands, guests enter the ballroom.

At a private ball, every man should dance with the hostess giving the ball, the hostess of the dinner he went to before the dance, and the women he sat between at dinner. Naturally, he dances the first dance with his wife or date for the evening. He should also watch during the evening to be sure she is not stuck too long with any one partner.

If a woman is sitting with one man, a second man should not come up and ask her to dance. But if she is sitting in a group, he may approach her and ask, "Would you like to dance?" She may either say, "I'd love to," or "Not just now, thanks, I'm resting." But to refuse to dance with one man and then immediately dance with another is an insult to the first. In ordinary circumstances, if a woman wants to dance, she must dance with everyone who asks her, if she does not want to dance, she must not make exceptions. At a formal dance, she should not ask a man to dance.

Cutting In

A woman who is dancing may not refuse to change partners when another cuts in. This is the worst phase of the cutting-in custom; those who particularly want to dance together are often unable to take a dozen steps before being interrupted. Possibly the current custom of dancing only with one's date the entire evening is a reaction against the old idea that to be popular a woman must be constantly cut in on.

When a man sees a woman with whom he wants to dance, he steps forward and taps the shoulder of her partner, who relinquishes his place in favor of the newcomer. The couple then dances until a third man cuts in or the music stops. The partner who was first dancing with the woman should not cut back on the man who took her from him, nor should a man continue to cut in on the same man when the latter dances with other partners.

Supper Is Served

Since most balls begin well after the dinner hour, a late buffet supper that begins after midnight and continues for an hour or more is often served. People may serve themselves whenever they feel like it, and small tables are provided so that the guests may sit down to eat. They may sit where they please—with a group making up a table, or a man and his partner may take any two vacant chairs. A woman is always taken in to supper by the man who is her escort. If there are unescorted women at the party, the host or hostess should see that an unescorted man takes them to supper or that they are included in a group.

Suppers may take the form of breakfast, or they may consist of a variety of sandwiches, platters of cold meats, and accompanying dishes. There may be hot drinks and/or bowls of iced fruit punch, or champagne.

At almost all balls there are two or more bars serving liquor and soft drinks throughout the evening, but until the supper hour no food is in evidence with the possible exception of bowls of nuts on strategic tables.

When you are ready to leave a private ball, you find the host and hostess and thank them, just as you would at a smaller party. If you are at a public ball as a member of a small party or as the guests of friends or acquaintances, you would thank them before leaving. If there is a guest of honor, you should say good-bye to him or her also.

CHARITY BALLS

With few exceptions, public balls are charity balls, given to benefit an organization or a cause. Once you arrive at a charity ball the procedure is identical to that described above unless the invitation includes dinner.

In that case you will receive an invitation, on which the cost is indicated. The committee members and the sponsors organize parties and reserve a dinner table for their own group. The host and hostess doing this generally give a cocktail party first, but their guests pay for their own tickets to the ball.

In addition to guests who pay a fee to attend a charity ball, there is an additional group of sponsors. They have nothing to do with running the ball, but they are people, selected by the committee, who are asked to make an additional contribution to increase the amount given to the benefiting charity, or to donate items that are given to each guest as a favor. Their names are always listed on the program and sometimes on the invitations. When sponsors are individuals, their names appear with their titles: "Dr. and Mrs. Eugene Wasserman," "Mr. Robert Reid," "Ms Jennifer Crown," etc.

DEBUTANTE BALLS

The phrase "presenting a debutante to society" has a quaint flavor and seems to echo a long-outdated social custom. It has been replaced by the simpler term "coming out," which today means simply a celebration of a girl's eighteenth birthday at a formal ball or party.

The most elaborate party, only possible for parents of considerable means, and becoming rarer and rarer today, is a private ball. Somewhat less elaborate is a small dance. Third is a tea dance. Fourth, and currently the most popular, is the big dance given for, or by, a number of debutantes together. Sometimes it is given cooperatively by a group of parents who get together and share the expense of a single coming-out party for their daughters. In other cases it may be given by an organization that invites a group of girls to participate. Many balls or cotillions of this kind are benefit affairs, handled by a committee representing the sponsoring charity. Thus they serve a double purpose, since the parents of the girls invited to participate are expected to give a substantial donation to the charity involved in return for the privilege of having their daughter presented at this ball. (*The correct forms for the invitations to these functions and their answers may be found on pages 359–362.*)

The Receiving Line at a Private Debut

The debutante's mother—or grandmother, or whoever is giving the party and "presenting her"—stands nearest the entrance. The debutante stands next to her, and they are the only people who formally "receive." On entering, the guests approach the hostess, who introduces the debutante to those who do not know her.

At a ball, where the guests begin coming around ten o'clock, the debutante receives for about an hour. Then she is free to join the dancing. She usually dances the first dance with her father and the next with the man (or men) she has asked to be her escort for the evening.

At an assembly or cotillion given for a group of debutantes, the receiving line is comprised of the assembly chairpeople. The debutantes, who are presented as a group later in the evening, are not a part of the receiving line.

At Supper

The debutante goes in to supper with her escort. She makes up her own table, which includes her most intimate friends. It is usually somewhat larger than the tables surrounding it, and has a card on it saying "Reserved."

The Debutante's Dress

At a ball, the debutante traditionally wears a white gown. Although a pastel color or a color in the trim of the gown is acceptable, the gown must never be scarlet or bright blue and it is never black. When the ball is an assembly or cotillion, the committee determines the color of the debutantes' gowns (almost always white), and this decision must be followed. Although the girls must wear the same color, they may choose their own style. They wear long white gloves through the time they are presented.

The mothers of the debutantes wear evening dresses in any color except white or black. Male guests wear tuxedos to debut parties, but the escorts and the fathers of the debutantes who are coming out usually wear white tie and tails.

Sending Flowers

It is customary for family members and very close friends to send flowers to the home of the debutante at the time of her coming-out party. They may be bouquets or baskets. The debutante's escort(s) may also send flowers, and may send a corsage if one will be worn, but he should ask before doing so. At assemblies, the girls generally do not wear flowers on their gowns but may pin them to their bags or wear them on their wrists.

If you are a relative or very close friend of the debutante or her family, you may give her a gift, but it is not required, nor are gifts given by other guests of the family or committee, in the case of a cotillion or assembly.

ASSEMBLIES, COTILLIONS, AND COMMUNITY DEBUTS

To come out as a member of a group and so eliminate the expense and rigors of a private ball is becoming more and more common. In fact in many large cities mothers apply years ahead to assure their daughters a place on the lists of the most prominent cotillions. While one hears constantly about the decline of the private debut, the cotillion or "mass" debut is gaining popularity and has spread to every corner of our society. If she wishes, a girl's parents may give a small debut party or tea at home and still present their daughter at one of the assemblies or cotillions.

The debutantes send in the names of their escorts as soon as they have accepted, and the committee then sends the young men formal invitations. The girls are expected to pay for their escorts' tickets if the ball is charity-sponsored. At most multiple debuts the committee does not invite guests, but each debutante's family is allowed a certain number of invitations, and they are responsible for paying for those guests whom they invite. Some committees, however, do invite extra boys—and girls—at their discretion.

There may be entertainment in the form of a dance performed by the debutantes and their fathers or escorts, or nothing more than the formal presentation, by their fathers, of the girls to the committee members who are acting as hostesses. There may or may not be professional entertainment—a singer or dancer, perhaps.

The party may be a dinner dance, but it is more likely to be a late party. When a ball is private, friends frequently give dinner parties preceding it; and when it is run by a committee, the members often have dinners for the debutantes and their escorts. This may also be done by the families of the girls themselves.

Whatever the local traditions, these "mass debuts" are a great success. By sharing the costs many families can afford far more elaborate decorations, prettier dresses, and better music than they could otherwise hope to obtain. The debutantes, if they are at all shy, are spared the nightmare of being alone in the spotlight. And any mishaps that may occur seem smaller when the responsibility is divided, whereas sharing a success with friends makes it doubly sweet.

SMALLER DANCES FOR DEBUTANTES

An afternoon tea dance occasionally takes the place of a debutante party.

Invitations are usually written on a fold-over informal, or on a "fill-in" invitation.

Since houses with rooms large enough for dancing are comparatively few a tea dance is usually given at a club or in a small ballroom of a hotel. Remember that it is a mistake to choose too large a room, for too much space for too few people gives an effect of emptiness that throws a pall on the party. Also remember than an undecorated public room needs more people than a room in a private house to make it look filled. Although a crush may be unpleasant, it does give the effect of success. Nothing is more dismal than a half-empty room with scattered guests.

The arrangements for a tea with dancing are much the same as for an evening dance. A screen of greens behind the musicians and flowers on the tables form the typical decorations.

Whether in a hotel, club, or private house, the curtains are drawn and the lights lighted as though for a dance in the evening.

Tea, coffee, tea sandwiches, and cakes are served. In addition there is usually a table nearby with pitchers or bowls of fruit juice or punch, and a bar for those who wish stronger drinks.

Guests go to the table and are served coffee or tea. They help themselves to the sandwiches or cakes, which they eat standing at the table, or if there are tables set up for all the guests, they return to the one at which they have been sitting.

The small evening debut party needs little comment, because its pattern is precisely the same as the informal dance discussed later in this chapter. As at every coming-out party the debutante and her mother or hostess stand in line and receive the guests as they arrive.

At an afternoon tea dance, the debutante and female guests wear pretty afternoon dresses and men wear dark suits and ties.

Dress for a small evening dance or dinner dance is semiformal; cocktail dresses for women and tuxedos or dark suits and ties for men.

INFORMAL DANCES

Informal dances are held for any number of reasons—to celebrate a graduation, an anniversary, a birthday, a holiday, or simply because the host and hostess and their friends like to dance. Generally the dress is "black tie"—tuxedos for the men and long dresses or evening pants for the women. There are also costume parties, for which, of course, fancy dress is specified on the invitations.

Invitations

When a dance is given to celebrate an anniversary or a birthday, or is for any reason considered to be somewhat formal, invitations are written on an informal or an engraved or printed fill-in invitation. But in most cases they are sent out on commercial fill-in party invitations with attractive drawings on the outside and spaces for writing time, address, and type of party on the inside. Remember to include at the bottom a hint about clothes. An RSVP with a telephone number beside it is the surest way of having some idea of how many will be at the party. The invitation, too, may be by telephone.

Decorating for a Dance

When the dance is held in your own home rather than a public room of any sort, the most important thing is good, "danceable" music. Next in importance is a large enough clear space and a floor properly prepared for dancing. If possible all the furniture should be removed from the room, but if not, take out whatever you can and move the rest close to the wall. The rugs should be rolled and put away, and the floor freshly waxed.

Decorations should be cheerful and imaginative rather than expensive and elaborate. A few flowers placed where they are not in the way—on a mantel, for instance—are sufficient but not very original. For more interesting ideas look through magazines or get one of the many books that are full of decorating tips. If the party is held during a holiday season, appropriate decorations such as Christmas sleigh bells or valentines on the walls always add a festive note.

Outdoor Dances

If you are fortunate enough to have a smooth terrace or a stone patio, perhaps beside a swimming pool, an outdoor dance on a summer evening is one of the loveliest ways of entertaining. There should be tables and chairs available for those who are not dancing. The bar, if you are serving liquor, and the refreshments should be nearby.

Plenty of light is important. There must be light for members of the orchestra to see their music, and the bar should be well lit for the benefit of the bartender and waiters. Your guests may be delighted to dance in the moonlight, but when they are ready to sit down, uneven ground or steps may be a hazard if not well lit. The most satisfactory lighting, because it is diffused and has a romantic effect, is achieved by placing floodlights in the trees, with some of them pointed up to reflect off the branches.

The Importance of Good Music

Probably the most important element in assuring the success of any dance is good music. Therefore, although you may save as much as you can on decorations and refreshments, spend as much as you can afford on the music. Rhythm, gaiety, and a knowledge of the taste of the age group at the party are the essential qualities that the orchestra must have. If the guests are people in their fifties, they probably will not want to dance the latest teenage fad. By the same token, teenagers would think a party a miserable failure if the orchestra played nothing but foxtrots and waltzes.

If you simply cannot hire an orchestra and are planning to use a CD player or tape deck, choose music that is specifically intended for dancing and will appeal to your guests. If you borrow CDs or tapes from your friends—and many people do in such a situation—be sure the owner's name is clearly printed on the label in indelible ink or put on with marking tape.

Who Dances with Whom?

Good manners at a dance are the same for young and old alike. Whatever the local customs about cutting in, double-cutting (that is, switching partners on the dance floor), and so on, a man must dance with his hostess, and he must dance the first and last dances with the woman he brought to the party, whether she be his wife or a date. The exception is the dinner dance, when he dances first with the woman seated beside him.

At a dance where the guests are mostly married couples, there may be a few or no extra men, and the only time to change partners may be during the intermission or when the music starts again. At this type of party there are almost always tables to which the couples return between dances. The men are expected to ask the women next to them, their wives, and their hostess to dance. If the hostess is at another table, a man should not ask her to dance until he is sure that all the women at his table have partners or at least that there is a group remaining at the table so that no one woman is left alone.

When the dance is over, every guest must, of course, find his host and hostess, thank them, and say "Good night."

Saturday Night at the Country Club

In many communities the Saturday-night dance at the local country club has largely replaced informal private dances. Usually a group of friends will attend a country club dance together after a cocktail party or similar gathering. On arriving at the club you ask to be shown to the table that your hostess at the earlier party has reserved. Or, since she cannot leave her home before all her guests have departed, the guests may gather at a table in the bar until she arrives. If you do go directly to the table, and she has not arranged to have place cards, you should leave seats free at each end or at opposite sides for her and her husband.

Generally, in deciding where to sit, husbands and wives split up, since much of the fun of a dance is to enjoy the company of different people.

As soon as possible a man should dance with the women seated on either side of him. If his wife is one of these two, and the woman on his other side has already been asked to dance, he then asks his wife for the first dance. Otherwise he waits to be sure his wife has a partner and then asks the woman on his other side for the first dance. After dancing with the women on either side of him he should try to dance with as many of the other women at the table as possible, being certain not to forget either his hostess at the cocktail party or his wife! When she gets up to dance, a woman leaves her bag, if it is a small one, on the table, or a larger bag on her chair.

When you make up a group to go to this type of party try to choose couples who like to dance. It is inexcusably rude for the men to go off to the bar or otherwise ignore the women at the table. From time to time a man may of course cut in on a woman he knows who is sitting at another table, but after that particular dance is over he should escort her back to her own table and then rejoin his original group.

At a late party you do not have to stay until the music stops, although do not leave so early that your departure will be construed as breaking up the party. Since people do not always want to leave at the same time, it is far safer to take your own car to the club than to share a ride with another couple. Even though sharing a ride may seem practical and friendly before the dance begins, it can be very disconcerting to have to stay on at a party just because your companions have decided to make a night of it.

HIGH SCHOOL PROMS AND FORMAL DANCES

Generally, the host or hostess pays for the tickets. Flowers—corsages and boutonnieres, are given according to school custom. If given, they must be worn, even if they clash terribly with what is being worn. Even when a boy asks his date what color her dress is, the choice still might be unfortunate. A girl can pin something she can't wear on her dress, onto her bag or to a ribbon to be worn on her wrist, if need be.

Dress is usually planned by the class or indicated on the invitation. A boy or girl inviting a date from another school should be sure to say whether most of the boys will be wearing tuxedos, and the girls long gowns, or the boys sport coats and slacks and the girls street length dresses, for example, so that he or she doesn't arrive inappropriately dressed.

Often the "after prom" expenses are shared—breakfast out, the day at the beach, a picnic, etc.

If a boy has asked a girl to the prom and he is footing the bill for transportation and tickets, and he has also invited her to the following day's events, she may offer to have the costs of that day be "on her." The same is true when a girl invites a boy, and in many areas is expected. The girl pays the expenses of the prom, and her date pays all extra costs, including transportation.

Socializing with business associates can provide an opportunity to talk in a relaxed atmosphere, a chance to cement relationships, and a way to get to know clients, employers, and employees better. Being relaxed, however, does not mean that business relationships become intimate or personal or that you can "let your hair down" just because you are outside the office setting. Just as your appearance, behavior and manners are used in the office as a criteria for your promotability, they are used outside the office, too. Having too much to drink, being loud or rude, and even dressing inappropriately can be strikes against you in the eyes of your employers. And if you are "the boss," it should be unnecessary to say that your professional image must be intact no matter what the social situation.

Before undertaking any business entertaining, you should be clear about your company's expense account policy. If it encourages entertaining and you will be reimbursed for genuine business socializing, then only two words need be said on the subject: be honest. I know of people who pad their expense accounts in assorted creative ways that range from listing a dinner party with friends as business to securing false restaurant receipts. The employer who suspects such shenanigans loses trust in the employee; the employer who can prove it fires the culprit. What might have been a promising career is over. Keep receipts for all business expenses, even taxicabs. Attach them to an itemized bill organized in chronological order. Do not let an expense account accumulate, but rather turn it in at the end of each month.

ENTERTAINING DURING THE BUSINESS DAY

Very often, social occasions are used not just for relaxation, but for conducting business in a more informal setting. Some such occasions include the following:

- to thank someone for a service rendered;
- to celebrate a newly closed deal;
- to win the confidence of a client or prospective client;
- to share common problems;
- to get to know someone better;
- to ask a favor;
- to propose or discuss ideas;
- to introduce other people;
- to simply get away from the office and relax.

23
Entertaining For Business

Whom You Invite

You may invite a co-worker, a client, a prospective client, a peer from another company, and from time to time, your secretary, to lunch or dinner during the business week. If you are "the boss," you may invite any members of your staff.

Never invite a superior to lunch or dinner in a restaurant during the business day. However, if someone in a superior position invites you or you and your spouse or live-in companion to a *social* occasion, you do return the invitation in some way. Following are a few guidelines that may lessen the trauma:

- Do not extend the invitation in person as you may to a co-worker. If you are a woman, write an invitation to your boss and his or her spouse; if you are a man, ask your wife to write the invitation, or write it yourself.
- If you call your boss "Mr." or "Ms" at the office, do not switch to "Bob" or "Jeanne" either in the invitation or as you speak during the evening, unless your boss suggests it.
- If you call your boss by title and last name, your spouse should follow suit.
- If you and your spouse address your boss by title and last name, you should both address his or her spouse similarly.
- You may find it easier to entertain your boss if you include a few other guests. Select people with whom they may have common interests.
- You need not reciprocate your boss's invitation in kind. For instance, you may repay a fancy dinner at a restaurant with a simple buffet dinner in your home.
- Do not put on airs when you entertain the boss. Act as you normally act; entertain as you normally entertain. Do not hire special help unless you ordinarily do; do not serve a hard-to-carve roast unless you can handle it; do not borrow chinaware or glassware which you may be fearful of breaking. In other words, be yourself, and be comfortable.
- Being gracious and interested will impress the boss far more than outdoing yourself in a way that he above all people knows you cannot afford.

Lunch Invitations

A lunch invitation is the most common in business; some executives have a lunch date every day. It should be set up ahead of time at a restaurant convenient to both you and your guest. You should make a reservation at the restaurant, requesting a quiet table, particularly if you have business matters to conduct.

Although companies no longer adhere to a strict hour's lunch, you should not extend the lunch beyond an hour and a half or two at the most since any longer period imposes on both your guest and your company. If you are accustomed to a cocktail before lunch, limit it to one, but do not feel compelled to drink. If your guest orders another, you need not keep up; order something nonalcoholic instead. If your guest continues drinking, you may politely suggest, "Perhaps we should order. We're running late."

Lunches tend to be informal even when you have a group of guests, and only rarely need you make seating arrangements. One occasion on which you would assign seats at the table is when the express purpose of the lunch is for two people to meet or pursue a discussion.

Dinner Invitations

Business dinner invitations are less common than lunches since they obviously impinge upon people's personal life. However, when executives are so busy that they cannot meet for lunch, a business dinner may be arranged. More frequently a dinner invitation will include a group of people brought together for a common cause.

Dinner invitations should be extended well in advance. An executive's secretary may either telephone the prospective guest or write him a note saying that Mr. Franklin would like to take Mr. Jones to dinner on the 27th . . . etc. Those without secretaries make the invitations themselves in the same way. The invitation should be addressed to the business person only, at his office so it will be clear that spouses are not included. A reservation should be made at a convenient restaurant—at a somewhat quiet table or, if possible, in a private room, which many restaurants have for this purpose.

You as host must be there ahead of time to greet your guests, introduce them if they are not acquainted, and seat them at the table. Place the highest-ranking guest or the one due the greatest honor at your right; the second highest, at your left. Others you may seat at random. If everybody is equal, you might simply say, "Why don't we just sit anywhere."

You should order drinks when everyone arrives; if, however, someone is late, order anyway and let the latecomer catch up upon arrival. One or two pre-dinner drinks should be the limit, but if a guest orders a third, there is very little you can do about it. Do not assume everyone wants another and order a round; it is uncomfortable for guests to have a full drink standing untouched. When you order wine with dinner, it is wise to have a bottle of red and one of white.

Frequently a dinner invitation is extended when you have tickets for an evening event. "I have tickets to the ball game next Wednesday. If you are free, I'd love to have you join me at the game and dinner first." If you want to entertain special clients, you might ascertain their particular interest—theater, music, baseball or something that your city is known for—and get tickets and plan dinner beforehand. Let the setting dictate the entertainment. When in New York clients who are theater buffs are invariably delighted to be taken to a top Broadway show, while in New Orleans clients who are jazz lovers may enjoy an evening out in the French Quarter.

Country Club Entertaining

One of the traditional ways businessmen have entertained clients is at the country club—a round of golf or a few sets of tennis. More major decisions are made, it is said, on the seventeenth hole than in the executive office. There is no reason for women to feel less free than men to entertain at a country club, nor for women to be less freely entertained there either.

When you do this kind of entertaining, you may meet at the club in the morning, play golf or tennis, eat lunch, and then part, either to return to work or to go home. On the other hand, you may both work in the morning, drive to the club—together or separately—for lunch, and then spend the afternoon together on the links or on the court. In either case it is an enjoyable and profitable way to entertain for business.

ENTERTAINING WITH SPOUSES

There are occasions that call for entertaining with spouses:

- when out-of-town businesspeople and their spouses visit in your area;
- when you return an invitation that included your spouse;
- when you want to get especially close to a client;
- when the occasion to which you are extending the invitation is a husband-and-wife affair, such as a formal dinner or a dance;
- when you and a business associate find you have become friends and want to enjoy and share that friendship with your spouses;
- when you, as boss, wish to get to know your employees personally and have them know you as a person as well.

Invitations

Frequently business associates decide to extend their relationship into semisocial situations involving spouses. When you extend such an invitation, you include your own spouse; when you accept, you accept for both of you. If you are unattached, you should invite a date when you host such a situation, and when you are invited as a guest to a husband-and-wife affair, you may ask, "Shall I bring a friend, or would you rather I came alone?"

If you are unmarried but in a living-together relationship, your companion should be treated exactly as a spouse would be. Any party, whether at the office or at a business associate's home, to which husbands and wives are invited should properly include your living-together partner. If your partner has been excluded from an invitation because of the host's ignorance of your arrangement, all you need do is ask, "May I bring Joan Whitehead, the woman I live with?" or, "I live with Bill

Adams, and I'd like to bring him. Is that all right?" Since good manners dictate that a living-together partner be invited to social occasions just as a spouse is, the answer you receive should be, "Yes, of course."

If the reply is negative, however, then you must decide whether you want to attend the affair alone or decline the invitation. If the former, you accept and go, trying not to act disgruntled. If the latter, you may politely explain, "I'm sorry, then, but I won't be able to accept. Thank you for inviting me all the same."

You must remember that there are office parties to which spouses are not invited. Bill Adams or Joan Whitehead should not be expected to attend those either.

Evening Entertainment

Most outside business entertainment which includes spouses confines itself to evening entertainment—a restaurant dinner, perhaps followed by attendance at an event. Dinner in a restaurant should be handled in the same way as any social dinner. As host, you should extend the invitation in ample time, sending a written note to the guest's home, or arranging the date in person in the office. You should make a reservation, arrive early to greet your guests, and make the seating arrangements. You should alternate men and women around the table, with the two most honored guests and their spouses on the right and left of you and your spouse.

Sometimes, instead of meeting at a restaurant, a host will suggest that guests meet at his or her home for cocktails and then proceed together to the restaurant. In this case, serving is handled as it is for any social situation, with the host assuming responsibility for getting the party to the restaurant on time.

If you plan to take your guests out after dinner, before securing tickets or reserving space, find out what they would enjoy. Don't, for instance, get a box at a baseball game if your associate's spouse hates baseball; don't reserve a table at the trendiest night club if your associate's spouse dislikes dancing. If you do not know their tastes, you might decide on light theater, which is universal enough to please almost anyone.

Personal Social Events

There are times when business and social life overlap and it is difficult to know whether to invite business associates. One such occasion is the wedding of a son or daughter. Many business executives use the occasion of a large wedding to entertain clients, prospective clients, and business associates. If you choose to do this (and I would do this only with the approval of your son or daughter even if you are paying for the entire wedding), be careful not to slight anyone by failure to extend an invitation. Naturally, you would invite business associates who are also friends without having to invite the entire department or your complete client list.

A Word About Children

Although children are rarely included in business-social invitations, there are occasions on which they may be—a company outing to the circus, a picnic, boating, or company family parties. If you are the guest, never suggest that you bring your children; let the host make the offer. And never simply show up with your children if they aren't included in the invitation, no matter how informal the event. A menu is planned and items purchased to feed the employees at an company party, not uninvited guests or an employee's children, no matter how adorable or how little they may eat.

Entertaining at Home

Home entertaining goes a step beyond outside entertaining in making business associates feel like friends as they share the relaxed atmosphere of someone's personal surroundings. When people invite business associates and clients to their homes, their spouses are automatically included. There may be an occasional breakfast or lunch for businesspeople alone in the home of one of them, but this would be for convenience or privacy rather than for a social purpose.

If you are not married but living with someone, your partner is treated the same as a spouse in home entertaining. Even though business associates may not know you live with someone, it will soon become obvious. A simple introduction as your guests enter is all that is needed: "This is Joan Whitehead [or Bill Adams]."

Guests

If you ask only a few business associates to a party, you must be sure you have not offended others. Either invite them another time or keep the invitation so private that they will not hear about it. Some employers make a ritual of inviting each member of their staff once during the year; some throw parties with small groups, while others invite the entire staff at once. What you do depends on the accommodations your home can provide and also the kind of entertaining with which you and your spouse feel most comfortable.

One of the warmest ways to entertain business associates is to include one or two with nonbusiness friends in your home. In this way you truly make them feel like personal friends about whom you care enough to share your social as well as your business life.

Greeting Guests

As your guests arrive, you will know at least one half of each couple. Greet the one you know first with a handshake and then quickly turn to the other, whose name you already know since you have phoned or mailed an invitation: "Hello, Eric [or

Susan]. I am so happy to meet you." Your spouse should be close behind you as you greet them so that you may turn and say, "I'd like you to meet my wife [husband]. Jennifer [or Michael], this is Susan Appleton, my assistant, and her husband Eric."

With introductions over and hands shaken, the host may take the guests' wraps or show them where to put them if a room is being used for that purpose. At a small party, the host should take them around the room, introducing them to the people they do not know. In a large gathering, such as a cocktail party, business associates may assume this responsibility themselves, introducing their own spouses to their co-workers.

The Role of Your Spouse

No matter how individualistic and equal-rights-minded our society has become, you cannot detach your spouse from the judgment people make about you. "How could she have married *him*?" they say, or, "What did he see in *her*?" The answers to their questions evaluate *you*. No matter how much in love you are, if you think your spouse will offend your co-workers, my best advice is not to entertain them in your home. When you return invitations, do so outside your home, where your spouse will not be the focus of attention.

When you entertain at home, your husband or wife is there to support you—to make your guests feel welcome, to help them enjoy being with you both, as well as to assist with refreshments. Since there will undoubtedly be a great deal of "shop talk," it is your spouse's job to be interested—to listen, to ask questions, to indicate the involvement of both of you in the company. Yet your husband or wife is an individual too and as such, interesting to your business associates. He or she should feel free to discuss his or her profession and personal concerns . . . but not too much about the children, please! In short, a spouse should act in such a way that when guests leave they are able to say, "What a nice couple!"

THE SINGLE HOST OR HOSTESS

If you are single and plan to invite business associates to your home, it can be helpful to ask a friend to help you host the party. Business entertaining at home is a little different than purely social entertaining in that half of the people, the business staff, know each other well, while the other half, their spouses or dates, may not know each other at all. It eases the situation to have both a host and hostess who can make the spouses feel a part of the group.

When a single woman gives a business party, she may ask a close male friend or relative to act as host. Asking a male co-worker is less advisable since it places him in a more intimate relationship with the hostess, creating possible jealousy among other staff members or even a suggested sexual relationship. One responsibility of the stand-in host is to handle drinks—to either serve them or see that guests are attended to by waiters or at a self-service bar. Another responsibility is to talk with guests, particularly with the husbands of the businesswomen, who may feel out of place. Introducing spouses and engaging them in conversations among themselves will help. Although the hostess will also be circulating to speak with guests, she may be busy making last-minute preparations and serving hors d'oeuvres and dinner.

When a single man hosts a business party, the situation reverses itself. He will undoubtedly be relieved to have a woman friend act as hostess. While the responsibility for food and drinks will fall upon him, she will help greatly by being pleasant to his business associates and helping their wives and husbands to fit in.

While it is not a rule of etiquette to have a stand-in host or hostess, it makes entertaining far easier for a single person.

WEEKEND ENTERTAINING

If you own a country place, you may wish to extend an invitation for the weekend to business associates or clients and their spouses. Unless you and your spouse know them well, however, and feel perfectly comfortable with them, a weekend can create tension; there is no escape. A weekend is easier if you have a large place with facilities such as swimming, boating, or tennis. If you do not have domestic help, you should prepare as much as possible ahead of time since a host relegated to the kitchen all day can do little to add to the guests' comfort. Planned evenings add pleasure to weekend entertaining: a country auction, summer stock, outdoor music, or a local fair is often available nearby.

If you and your spouse are invited by business associates to their country home, you can add to the weekend's enjoyment by following the suggestions in Chapter 24, "Advice for Guests, Hosts, and Hostesses" which begins on page 467.

RETURNING AN INVITATION

Business invitations need not be returned in the same way that social invitations must be. Remember that you do not return a business lunch or dinner invitation from your boss, but you do return, in some form, a social invitation. If a salesperson invites you or if, as a client, you are entertained, you are not expected to repay this business lunch or dinner, although you certainly may if you have continuing business together. Neither are you expected to repay a social invitation where you, as a client, have been entertained, even if the invitation has included your spouse or your entire family. You are expected to return social invitations from co-workers and other business associates who have extended a hand of friendship to cement a business relationship or simply because you enjoy one another's company outside the office or your business ties.

A Word of Warning

Since home entertaining merges your business and social lives, you must exert caution in undertaking it. If, as an upper management executive, you socialize regularly with your staff, you may weaken your position of authority, making it difficult to reprimand or fire someone or to pass over someone for a raise or a promotion. If, as an employee, you socialize with your boss, you may create resentment among the rest of the staff and be accused of deliberately currying favor. Home entertainment on a regular basis should be confined to peers or to clients who have become friends. The occasional home party may include anyone in the office.

OFFICE PARTIES

Office parties at which personnel let down their hair, get roaring drunk and land in trouble or in car accidents are almost over and gone. Today, fortunately, the office party has matured, by and large, into a pleasant, morale-building event.

The Christmas Party

A Christmas party, usually held on the afternoon of the Christmas holiday, is hosted by a management executive. In a larger company the heads of individual departments may host parties for their own staffs. If the director or department head is away or so antisocial as to eschew parties, a lower-level executive may host the party instead. Only in rare cases does the staff give its own party.

The host organizes the party and determines whether or not spouses are to be included. There are pros and cons. On one hand, with spouses present, the staff tends to behave with greater control; on the other hand, spouses are often ignored, feeling like misfits. Whatever the host's decision, plans will have to be made to counteract the disadvantages: a careful eye on those who drink too much on one side; on the other, a way to include spouses in conversation.

Invitations to office parties are more informal than those for social affairs. The host may send a memo, or if your office is networked an E-mail message, to each staff member. It might read like this: "The graphic services department will celebrate a good year and a Merry Christmas on Friday, December 23rd, in the office. All work stops at 3:30 sharp for cocktails and a buffet. I look forward to celebrating with you." When office parties are held in a restaurant rather than in the office, invitations should be more formal—on cards, handwritten for small groups, offset for large ones.

Details of party arrangements may be delegated to staff members—mainly the food and drinks. Some offices plan entertainment: a humorous gift or poem to be written by each member of the staff and distributed or read at the party; songs and music if some staff members have the talent and the inclination. Most parties rely merely upon conversation to entertain.

At office parties held at a restaurant, the host stands by the door, with spouse if spouses are included, and greets each staff member upon arrival. In the office the host circulates, shaking hands and greeting the staff with a "Merry Christmas!" and a personal word of thanks.

Other Office Parties

Many offices have parties for occasions other than Christmas: when someone leaves or retires, when someone is going to be married or is having a baby, or when someone achieves an outstanding honor.

Special-occasion parties of this nature may be given by the boss or by the staff and should include the entire department and any special friends the guest of honor may have in other areas of the company. While spouses are not necessarily included, the spouse of the guest of honor will often be invited to share the occasion.

An informal party may be given in the office, but more often a lunch or dinner will be planned at a nearby restaurant. A staff committee should be appointed by the boss (or by the staff if they are hosting the party) to handle details of time, place, menu, speeches and gifts if there are to be some. Bills should be given directly to the boss if he or she is hosting the party; they should be split among the staff if they are the hosts.

Parties held in the office usually begin in the afternoon, some hours before closing. Drinks and simple refreshments may be set up on desks or in a lounge or conference room if these are available.

Office Party Dress

At a party held in the work place, both men and women generally appear in the clothes they have worn all day. In fact, they may have put on a somewhat fancier dress or jacket than usual that morning in anticipation of the event. Women may elect to dress up by adding some accessories, but overdressing would be out of place.

At an office party held outside the office, both men and women may properly change from work clothes into dress clothes. Still, it is a business affair, and overly dressy clothing is in poor taste.

Office Party Pitfalls

People who drink too much at office parties do their professional careers great harm. Their lack of self-control becomes obvious to their superiors, who will think twice—or not at all—about giving them future responsibilities. They also create embarrassing situations for themselves and their associates, whom they have to face at work again. A good host keeps a careful eye on his staff during an office party; if he sees people overdrinking, he should quietly steer them away from the bar. If they fail to get the hint and return for another, he may say in private, "I think you've had enough to drink, don't you? Why don't you get something to eat and a cup of coffee."

Equally disadvantageous is the practice of becoming too intimate at office parties. With a little too much to drink and in the spirit of seasonal abandon, men and women may place themselves in regrettable situations. Personal secrets may be exchanged and amorous overtures made and accepted for which they will hate themselves in the clear light of the office workday. The safest way to avoid such embarrassment is to be aware of its possibility and stay in control. Limiting your drinking is a starting point.

For years the occasional drunk was the most visible sign of over-indulgence at an office party. Today however, a radical change in behavior could be due to the use of drugs. Those who choose to use drugs may believe they are no worse than the use of alcohol. But the fact is that alcohol is legal and, so far, drugs are not. It should go without saying—the use of any illegal substance will not be tolerated. If the host of the office party witnesses the use of drugs the offender should be asked to leave.

Groups of people at an office party may want to extend the festivities after the party is over, going to someone's house or to a local bar to drink and dance. This can be fun if warnings about overdrinking and intimacy are heeded. Attention must also be given to transportation home. Since it is not safe for most individuals to use public transportation alone at a late hour, plans should be made ahead of time for people to travel together whenever possible. If someone commutes to work from out of town, he or she might be able to arrange to sleep over at a co-worker's home.

THANK-YOU GIFTS AND NOTES

When you have been entertained for a business-related occasion where the occasion crosses from business to social, whether at a dinner, an evening out with your spouse, at a weekend house party at the home of an employer or associate, or as guest of honor at an office party, a thank-you note is in order. When you are one of many guests at an office party or where your share a meal in the ordinary course of business, your verbal thanks at the end of the occasion is sufficient. While it is never wrong to write a thank-you note you may reiterate your thanks in your next business correspondence in place of a separate thank-you.

When the occasion was a social one, your thank-you note should be addressed to your host and his or her spouse and sent to their home. Social thank-you notes are handwritten on informals or personal stationery. Business occasion thank-you notes come in several varieties. If your company honors you with a dinner celebrating your 25 years with the firm, a handwritten note on personal stationery is called for, addressed to your immediate boss, and to the president of the company if he or she attended the gathering. If you had lunch with a client you see regularly a separate note is not necessary. You would, instead, mention your thanks for the lunch in your next letter, *"Thanks again, Jim, for lunch. We really accomplished a lot. I'll have that proposal to you by next week."* When your business lunch is a first meeting, or an infrequent one, a short note is called for. It may be typed by your secretary on business letterhead: *"Julia, it was a pleasure to meet you after so many months of working together over the phone. I very much enjoyed our lunch together and hope we can do it again soon."*

"Host" or "Hostess" gifts are taken only for at-home business entertainments, whether dinners or weekend visits, never for business lunches or dinners. The practice of taking gifts to the host of an at-home cocktail party varies in different parts of the country. In many areas, no gift is taken while in others, a bottle of wine or liquor or small hostess gift is given. If new to a community, it is best to ask to avoid being the only one who shows up with a gift or worse, yet, the only one who doesn't.

When advising her readers on how to be a perfect guest, Emily Post wrote in 1922: "Courtesy demands that you, when you are a guest, shall show neither annoyance nor disappointment—no matter what happens . . . you must learn as it were not to notice if hot soup is poured down your back. If you neither understand nor care for dogs or children, and both insist on climbing all over you, you must seemingly like it; just as you must be amiable and polite to your fellow guests, even though they be of all the people on earth the most detestable to you . . . You must pretend that six is a perfect dinner hour though you never dine before eight or, on the contrary, you must wait until eight-thirty or nine with stoical fortitude, though your dinner hour is six and by seven your chest seems securely pinned to your spine . . . If you go for a drive, and it pours, and there is no top to the carriage or car, and you are soaked to the skin and chilled to the marrow so that your teeth chatter, your lips must smile and you must appear to enjoy the refreshing coolness . . ."

Words of advice from Emily Post for the hostess in 1922 included: "If a guest prefers to sit on the veranda and read, don't interrupt him every half page to ask if he really does not want to do something else. If, on the other hand, a guest wants to exercise, don't do everything in your power to obstruct his starting off by saying that it will surely rain, or that it is too hot, or that you think it is senseless to spend days that should be a rest to him in utterly exhausting himself."

Nothing has changed! The considerate guest is all that he or she was in the 1920's and more, whether invited for an hour for a cup of coffee, or for the weekend or longer. The considerate host or hostess has planned so carefully that she or he is relaxed and able to enjoy the company of his or her invited guests while neither badgering them with too much attention nor dashing, frazzled, hither and thither, making them feel like terrible burdens.

24 Advice for Guests, Hosts and Hostesses

MEALTIME GUESTS

When to Arrive

This varies so much according to locality that it is impossible to make a hard-and-fast rule. In general it is safe to say that one should never arrive early. You are almost sure to embarrass your host and hostess, who may well still be dressing or hurrying to get dinner ready. In areas where cocktails are not served, and hostesses pride themselves on the good food they serve, you should arrive at the time stated on the invitation, or within ten minutes of it. Sensible hostesses allow at least fifteen minutes' leeway for guests who meet unavoidable delays. And then there are sections of the country—generally in big cities and their suburbs—where guests are not *expected* to arrive until fifteen minutes to half an hour after the stated hour. If you are new in an area, you will find this out the first time you arrive a half hour before anyone else. Whether you approve of it or not, you are wise to bend with the wind and follow the local custom. When you entertain yourself, simply ask your guests to come a half hour earlier than you expect them to arrive. Some hostesses have followed a system evolved by widely traveled people who have lived and entertained all over the world, and which seems to me very practical. On their invitations they write: "Cocktails at 7:00, dinner at 8:30." This is a great help to guests who may not enjoy a prolonged cocktail hour and can arrive a few minutes before dinner without upsetting their hostess. It is also a help to the hostess, who can count on serving a soufflé at an exact moment, knowing her guest will *all* have arrived during the one-and-a-half-hour cocktail period.

When you arrive and remove your coat, put it where your hostess suggests—whether in a closet or upstairs in a bedroom. Don't clutter up her hall by saying, "Oh, I'll just leave it over here," and dropping it over the stair rail.

Gifts For Your Hostess

When a party is given especially for you, you should send flowers to your hostess beforehand. Other guests need not do this, although a few flowers sent later as a thank-you for a very special evening are always appreciated. Ordinarily, however, neither a gift sent later nor a note is necessary, and your verbal thanks when you leave is enough. A phone call the next day to say how much you enjoyed the evening is *always* welcome.

I am, however, constantly asked about taking a gift of food or wine to your hostess when you go to a party. As far as food goes, I do not recommend it *unless* you consult with your hostess first. It is very disconcerting for a hostess who has planned a light dessert to follow a hearty meal to feel that she must serve a rich cake or a sugary pie brought by one of her guests. A box of candy or other food that can merely be passed after dinner or kept for another occasion is far more acceptable but not necessary at all.

The custom of taking wine as a gift to a small dinner party (one bottle only serves four, or possibly six at the most) is becoming very widespread. It is not too expensive or elaborate and has the advantage that if the hostess does not wish to serve it at once because she has planned another type of wine or a different beverage, she need not do so. If your gift goes well with her meal, and she feels it would be more popular than whatever she had planned on serving, she should certainly offer it, but no guest should ever feel insulted if his hostess says, "Thanks so much, but I already have white wine chilled and I'd like to save this red wine for the next time we have steak."

It is better not to take a gift at all to a larger or formal party—especially if you do not know the hosts well. It may not be customary among their friends, and you will only embarrass your hostess and other guests who have not brought a gift.

What to Wear

Most people know, without giving it much thought, what sort of dress is expected when they are invited to a friend's house for dinner. A woman may have to decide between a long skirt and evening slacks, or a man between a sports jacket and a suit, but in most cases either would be correct, and you should wear whatever makes you most comfortable.

However, when you are invited to a comparative stranger's home for the first time, or to a party where the other guests are not the people you see regularly, the decision is more difficult. If the group is so different from your own that you are really at a loss, it is perfectly correct to call your hostess and ask just how formal the party will be. If you decide to make your own choice, there is only one thing to keep in mind. Choose a middle road—neither very informal nor too formal—and remember that it is always better to be underdressed than overdressed.

Even an invitation that suggests a certain type of dress can be confusing. Although there are variations, according to the age of the people involved and the locality, here are the most common terms and their meanings.

"White tie." The most formal evening wear—white tie, wing collar, and tailcoat. This is almost never required today, except for official and diplomatic occasions and a rare private ball.

"Black tie" or "formal." The ordinary formal evening wear—a tuxedo with soft shirt and bow tie. Formerly black, jackets today—especially in summer—may be patterned or in almost any color.

"Semiformal" on invitations to a party means "no jeans or T-shirts." Women wear dresses or "good" slacks—men wear sports shirts and slacks rather than jeans.

Other invitations may say, "Come in slacks," or something similar, and guests should do their best to comply with their hostess's request.

When Dinner Is Announced

When dinner is announced don't ignore the invitation, sitting back and sipping slowly at your full cocktail glass. On the other hand, don't jump up and fly out as if you have been kept waiting to the point of starvation. Watch your hostess, and if she seems to be edging toward the door, take one more sip and rise. She may say, "Dinner is ready, but don't hurry. It will stay hot for a few minutes." Unless she says, "Please bring your drink with you," don't. She may be serving wine or a meal that she does not feel is complemented by a cocktail.

At a buffet don't hang back and wait for someone else to start when your hostess says, "Dinner is ready." People are always reluctant to be the first one, but you will earn your hostess's gratitude—and that of other hungry but shyer guests— if you will lead the way to the buffet.

Dinner Conversation

The "turning of the table" is a long-outdated custom designed to make people divide their conversation time more or less evenly between their two dinner companions. The hostess, after the first two courses (or any time she chose), would turn from the man on her right to the one on her left, and each woman at the table was supposed to notice this and switch at the same time. This was certainly a forced means of achieving a change that should happen naturally at a convenient break in the conversation rather than at a signal! Today, conversation at the table often includes three or four people sitting near each other. If, however, you notice that one of your neighbors is left with no one to talk to, common courtesy dictates that you should either include him in your conversation or turn at a break in your discussion to talk to him for a while.

The unbreakable rule is that you must at some time during dinner talk to both your neighbors. You must; that is all there is to it!

Even if you are placed next to someone in whom you have little interest, consideration for your hostess and the other guests demands that you give no outward sign of your dislike and that you make a pretense, at least for a little while, of talking together.

There are other more flexible rules, too. A popular guest does not talk at length about himself, he is not didactic but listens to his neighbors' point of view, and he does not (at length, at least) "talk shop."

"Shop talk" can dampen any party unless everyone there is involved in the same business, sport, or hobby. Have you ever been to a party on a Saturday night, where most of the men had played golf that day? If you were not an ardent golfer yourself, you might as well have stayed at home with a good book! In short, any guest who talks continually about one subject, regardless of the listener's interest, can only be classified as a bore.

At the Start of the Meal

At a small dinner women wait until the hostess is ready to seat herself before they sit down, unless she says, "Please sit down. I have to bring in another dish." At a large formal dinner, however, men help the women on their right to be seated as soon as they get to the table.

If there is a cold first course already on the table, you must wait for the hostess to pick up her fork or spoon before you start. However, after four or five guests have been served a hot course one of them should pick up his fork and start to eat, even though the hostess may have forgotten to say, "Please start."

Smoking at the Table

So many people have given up smoking entirely, and so many others object to the odor of smoke during a meal, that ashtrays are becoming more and more obsolete at the dinner table. When a hostess indicates, by having no ashtrays on the table, that she would prefer that her guests do not smoke during the meal, the guests should comply with the unspoken request and wait until after dinner to light their cigarettes.

Second Helpings

At formal dinners guests should not ask for second helpings. If dishes are passed a second time, anyone is free to help himself, even though others do not. At an informal dinner a guest may say to his hostess, "Is there any more of that chicken? It is just delicious," and the hostess passes it to him or asks the maid to pass it around. If only one person takes a second helping, a considerate hostess will take a little too, so that her guest will not feel he is responsible for holding everyone up.

For Those Who Don't Eat Meat

No guest should ever feel it necessary to eat anything that is injurious to health or contrary to their moral standards.

If you are a vegetarian, you need not feel obliged to taste the roast. In most cases don't mention it to your hostess when you accept the invitation, because she will feel obliged to change her menu or prepare something special for you. You may tell her privately when you arrive, saying, "I am a vegetarian and I just wanted to tell you so you'll know why I'm not eating the meat." Or you may take a very little meat and leave it on your plate, since no one is required any longer to leave his plate clean. If you are concerned that your dietary restrictions will result in your not getting enough food you can always fortify yourself with a snack beforehand. If you know that *nothing* will be served that you can eat, as sometimes happens with Orthodox Jews, who eat only strictly kosher foods, you might better discuss it with your hostess beforehand. If it is a formal "public" dinner you might have to refuse the invitation, but if it is a "friendly" occasion you can tell the hostess you will bring a little dish for yourself, prepared according to your restrictions.

For Those Who Don't Drink

Nondrinkers should not necessarily feel that they must refuse cocktail parties or dinners where liquor will be served. *Many* people do not touch alcohol, and there is nothing wrong with saying, "No, thank you." If you are a don't drink for moral reasons and disapprove of drinking in general, you should refuse invitations to homes where liquor is served, but you should do so without sermonizing or expressing your disapproval. However, if you do not drink yourself but enjoy the company of your friends who do, accept their invitations happily. Every good hostess has soft drinks of some kind available, but if you are worried about it, take a bottle or two of your favorite soda along. Leave it in the car unless you find that there is literally nothing you can drink in the house.

Helping Your Hostess

No matter how much you want to help or to keep your hostess company, don't follow her to the kitchen and chatter away while she is making her last-minute preparations.

When she rises to pass something or to clear the table, don't jump up to help unless she has asked you to beforehand. You'll probably only get in her way. However, it can only be a help if you wish to offer to pass the cups around when she serves coffee after dinner.

At a dinner served by a maid (or butler) guests never try to help by handing her empty plates, stacking dishes, etc. An exception is a large restaurant table where the waiter cannot reach some of the places. In that case one of the guests, or the person beyond his reach, may take the plate from him and put it in its place. Guests do not talk to servants at a formal dinner other than to say "No thank you" or possibly to request something that the hostess is not aware of. Of course if you know a servant well and have not seen her (or him) before a small dinner, you would greet her briefly when she passes something to you, saying, "Good evening, Mary—nice to see you," or whatever you wish.

Even though a hostess has no help, do not insist on clearing the table and washing the dishes. If the dinner is formal, or you are somewhat of a stranger, you should not even make the offer. At a more casual dinner you may ask, "Can't we help clean up?" but if your hostess says, "No, I'd really rather do it later," don't pursue it. Only when you are dining with closest friends or relatives, whose kitchen and habits you know well, should you try, unobtrusively, to get one load into the dishwasher.

After Dinner

Guests do not put their napkins on the table until their hostess does. When she rises to signal the end of the meal, they do not prolong their conversation, but rise and go wherever she indicates.

If games are suggested after dinner, no matter how you feel about them, try to look as though you think it's a fine idea and help your hostess to organize the group. Very often, especially if the guests do not have a great deal in common, entertainment that a hostess would ordinarily avoid can be the means of pulling a party together and making a delightful evening out of what started out as a very dull one.

Departing

Once you have decided that it is time to go—GO! Nothing is more irritating than the guest who gets her coat, says good-bye to the other guests, and twenty minutes later is still standing in the open door giving last-minute words of wisdom to her hostess.

Try to be sensitive and aware of the people around you. Most hostesses are reluctant to try to "speed the parting guest," so make an effort to observe when your hosts—and others at the party—begin to look tired, and make the move to break it up yourself. When there is a guest of honor, it is supposedly his or her obligation to leave first. But many of them do not know this, and furthermore they may be having a better time than some of the other guests and not want to leave as early. So, fortunately, that old rule is obsolete, and with the exception of when the President of the United States is present, guests at a large party may leave whenever they wish. They should, however, remain for at least one hour after dinner, as it is hardly complimentary to the hostess to "eat and run." At a small party a couple should not leave long before anyone else seems ready to go, because their departure is very apt to break up the party.

It is a good idea for husbands and wives to agree on approximately the time they think they should go home before they go to a party. Of course the hour would be subject to change if they were both very bored, or both having a wonderful time, but it would help to avoid the problem of one feeling very tired while the other gets a "second wind." Should one wish to stay on longer than the other, they must settle their argument quietly between themselves and not embarrass other guests and their hostess by having a loud argument.

If you have gone to a party in someone else's car, it is up to them to decide when to go home. You may, of course, say quietly to them, "We're ready whenever you are." But if you think there is a chance that you will want to go home earlier than the others, you will be wise to try to get to the party on your own.

If You Want To Be Asked Again . . .

At a dinner party, if there is a hamper in the powder room, wipe off the basin with your hand towel and put it in the hamper. Otherwise fold it loosely so that others will know it has been used. Leave or put the toilet seat, and the lid as well, down.

Don't tip chair backs on their rear legs if you value your hostess's friendship.

Use coasters for your drinks and ashtrays for your cigarettes.

If you do burn a table or a rug, break an ornament, or snap the back legs of the chair, don't "hide" the damage. Apologize at once and arrange to replace the item if possible or to pay for repairs if not. If it is a substantial amount perhaps your insurance policy will cover it.

Wipe your feet carefully if it is muddy or wet outside and keep them on the floor whatever the weather. No hostess is happy with a guest who tracks dirt across the carpets or who lies back and puts his feet on the couch or an easy chair.

Don't use the telephone without permission, and then only if you charge the calls to your credit card or home number.

Don't use call waiting to forward your calls to your host's house without asking permission to do so and then only if you are an "on call" professional or are expecting an emergency or have children who are out and may need to reach you. Then, if you do get calls, keep them brief.

WEEKEND GUESTS

Arrivals and Departures

The first cardinal rule for weekend (or longer) guests is to tell your host or hostess precisely when you are arriving *and* when you are leaving. If you are driving out to a beach house after the rush hour traffic diminishes, say, "John and I are going to try to avoid the rush hour. We'll eat before we leave and plan to be with you about 8:30 if that's okay." If you don't say this, your hostess may expect you for dinner and be frantically trying to keep the roast from burning, wondering where you are. At the same time, tell her precisely when you plan to leave. If she is expecting you to stay through Sunday evening and you are going to leave after breakfast, she will have planned two more meals around your visit, or may have refused another invitation for Sunday afternoon, expecting that you would still be there.

Gifts for Your Host or Hostess

It is not only courteous but obligatory to give your host or hostess a gift—and/ or if they have children, to take presents to them.

When you take a gift with you, give it to your hostess as soon as you arrive. If you send it later, be sure to do it as soon as possible. In this case, the hostess must write you or call with her thanks so that you know it has arrived. Another option is to find the perfect hostess gift while you are visiting. During a long visit with my family, a young friend was shopping with me to select a wedding gift for someone else. I admired a demitasse set in passing which she went back and purchased while I was in another department. When we returned home, she presented it to me, much to my surprise and delight.

Communicating Your Plans

Just as it is incumbent upon you to share your arrival and departure plans with your hostess, so is it important to let her know if you have other plans. If, for example, she lives in the same town as another friend who you would like to visit, you must say, preferably in advance of your visit, "Mary, I am hoping to have time for a few hours to visit Lorraine Mignone. Is this possible, or would it disrupt your plans?" If she is positive about this, ask her what would be the best day and time for you to make your call. If you don't communicate this ahead of time and simply announce that you are leaving for a few hours in the middle of your visit, you may be spoiling an activity she had organized for your pleasure. Instead, knowing ahead that you will be occupied for a period of time gives her the opportunity to make other arrangements, whether they be taking a nap, devoting time to her children, or doing some gardening.

It is also thoughtful, if you plan to take your host and hostess out to dinner one evening during a stay of three days or more, to discuss this ahead of time rather than surprising them after you have arrived. Again, knowing ahead enables them to plan appropriately for your visit. Simply say, "Andy and I are planning to take you out to dinner while we're there—we thought that seafood place you took us to the last time we visited, if it's still as terrific as it was then, or somewhere else if you have a better recommendation. You let us know which night would be better for you and we'll make the reservations." If you don't communicate this in advance, your hostess may already have planned and prepared a special meal to have at home.

If your hostess is a good friend, when making your initial plans offer to bring a roast or a casserole to provide one evening's meal. There is no reason why the hostess should not accept such an offer. On an informal weekend, guests feel more comfortable if they can contribute and it certainly adds to the pleasure of the hostess.

Although you would not do this for a dinner party, you should communicate any dietary restrictions or allergies to your hostess of a weekend or longer so that she will not have prepared a delicious crabmeat mornay only to find that you are allergic to shellfish.

Other important communication takes place during your visit. Both guest and host need time apart from one another, and it is often easier for the guest to say "Liz, I've taken up jogging (walking, meditating) two hours every day and thought I'd get to it soon, unless there is something I can do to help you or there is something we should be doing, in which case I can jog later." This gives her the opportunity to say, "Good for you! Now's a fine time—I have about 50 phone calls to make and I'll make them while you're out," or to say, "Oh, I thought you might like to go with me to the farmer's market—it's a real attraction around here. Would you like to come and then do your running about 4:00 or so?" This kind of exchange lets her know she will have a two-hour break from feeling that she must entertain you, while giving her the option to take advantage of it at that moment or later.

If you run into other friends in the area and they invite you and your hosts over for a swim or to play tennis, you should never accept the invitation and then relay it to your hostess. It is better to leave the "door ajar" and say, "May I call you back?—I'm not sure about Janet's plans."

Helping Your Host and Hostess

Even when staying in a house with many servants, remember that each has a share of work to do. If the maid offers to press a dress that has become mussed in packing, accept her offer and later give her a gratuity—but you should not ask this service unless the pressing is really necessary.

If the hostess does her own housework you must make your bed, pick up your room and offer to help in preparing the meals, clearing the table, and cleaning up in the kitchen. You must be particularly careful to keep your bathroom immaculate, especially if you are sharing it with other people. Don't leave a ring in the tub, a rim of dried shaving soap in the basin, hair anyplace, or dirt on the soap. A wise hostess leaves a sponge on the basin to help her guests leave a clean bathroom, but if she doesn't, either ask for one or use a paper towel or toilet tissue to wipe up after yourself—never your washcloth.

When sharing a bathroom, don't leave your cosmetics or shaving gear spread all over the available space.

And don't use more than your share of hot water if others are planning to bathe, or use any towels but your own. Finally, leave the toilet seat—and preferably the lid too—down.

The morning of the day you are going to leave, ask your hostess what she would like you to do with your bed linen. She will probably say, "Oh, just leave the beds," but don't! Unless she especially says, "My cleaning service is coming in later to make up the beds," remove the sheets, fold them, place them at the foot of the bed, and pull the blanket and spread up neatly so that the bed will look "made." If you make it up with your sheets in place, it is all too easy for a busy hostess to forget, and then turn down the beds for the next guest, only to find the dirty sheets still on. Or if you take her at her word and leave the bed untouched she is almost forced to do something about it after you leave, when she might rather be doing something else. If you are very close friends and a frequent visitor, make the bed up for her with fresh sheets. But if you are only casual friends your hostess will feel that this is an imposition on you and it will make her uncomfortable.

Remember that very wise adage, "Neither a borrower nor a lender be." Try to take everything you need with you. But if you *must* borrow, return the article as soon as you no longer need it—in as good, or better, condition than when it was lent to you.

If you borrow a book from your hosts, don't "dog-ear" it by turning the corner of the page down. Find a piece of paper or something similar to use as a bookmark. Don't go home with a book you have started, without your host's permission. If he does suggest that you take it home, return it promptly unless he tells you explicitly that he does not want it back.

If you use the telephone for long-distance calls be sure to pay for them. You can:

- ask for the charges and pay your host in cash;
- use a credit card if you have one;
- reverse the charges; or
- charge the call to your home number.

In any case, do not monopolize the telephone.

Mornings and Bedtime

Whether it is easy or not, you must conform to the habits of the family with whom you are staying. You take your meals at their hours, you eat what is put before you, and you get up and go out and come in and go to bed according to the schedule arranged by your hostess. And no matter how much the hours or the food or the arrangements may upset you, you try to appear blissfully content. When the visit is over, you need never enter that house again, but while you are there you must at least act as though you are enjoying yourself.

One way to while away the hours when your hosts are still sleeping and you are awake or they have gone to bed and you aren't tired is to take a good book with you and read it in your room if no one has offered you the run of the house during those hours. Other ways to keep occupied are to take your stationery and write all those letters you never have time to write otherwise or to work on the needlepoint you love to do but never seem to get to.

If you are particularly good friends and you know you keep different hours than your hosts, you may say that you would like to get up early and tour the town during quiet hours, or whatever, assuring your hosts that you don't want them to get up with you. One young friend of mine and her family spent a miserable weekend visiting friends who had a wonderful house designed to keep guests busy for hours, including a swimming pool. Her hosts indeed slept until noon, while she and her children were up by 7:00. The house had an alarm system that was set, so they were virtual prisoners in the house for five hours, gazing out the window at the sparkling pool (and hungry, to boot!).

She might have said, "Allison, the boys are really early risers and I don't want them to disturb you—is there a way we can go out for a while in the morning without setting off the alarm?" If the answer was affirmative, she should also ask if it would be all right if they used the pool.

As to hunger, again with close friends, simply ask if it is all right to have juice and make toast or whatever when you are visiting with children. Whereas your growling stomach can wait, unless you have a condition that mandates you eat regularly and early, children's tummies can't wait. If requesting this would make you uncomfortable or you are visiting people who are not close friends, then be sure you travel with portable snacks, like granola bars and bottled juices, or whatever, so your children's hunger pangs can be staved while you wait for breakfast time.

If You Want To Be Asked Again . . .

Any party—whether of four hours' duration or a whole weekend—will be a success if the guests are enthusiastic, congenial, and considerate. If they are none of these, there is nothing the hostess can do to save the occasion. So, while it is her responsibility to try to choose guests who will have fun together and cooperate to make the party a success, it is the guests' responsibility to help her.

The welcome houseguest in addition to all the characteristics listed above is, above all else, adaptable. You must always be ready for anything—or nothing. If the plan is to picnic, even if you can't bear picnics, you like them during this visit and you prove it by enthusiastically making the sandwiches or the salad dressing or whatever you do best. If, on the other hand, no one seems to want to do anything, you find a book to be absorbed in, or a piece of sewing or knitting, or you walk on the beach by yourself, all the while exclaiming what a fun, relaxing, or whatever kind of time you are having.

Popular and sought-after guests *never* stay longer than planned. The length of the visit should be clearly stated by the hostess and interpreted literally by her guests. When you are inviting Aunt Sally for the Christmas holiday your invitation should say something like this: "Dear Aunt Sally, Bob and I—and the children—are counting on you to spend Christmas with us. We could pick you up on Friday the 23rd, and take you back on Wednesday the 28th, and we are making all sorts of plans so you can see the rest of the family . . ." If from past experience a hostess knows that certain guests are apt to try to extend their visit, she should make plans for the day after they are to leave so that she can tell them that if the problem arises.

In short, for both guest and hostess, it is far better to end a visit while everyone is still enjoying it.

Overnight visits require written thank you notes within a day or two of your return home. The only exceptions are when your hosts are relatives or close friends with whom you visit back and forth frequently, or they are friends or neighbors with whom you travel to their vacation home and back. Even then a call the next day to say, "We're still talking about what fun the weekend was!" is appreciated.

FOR HOSTS AND HOSTESSES

It definitely takes work to entertain successfully. If you do your work in advance, however, with thorough planning and preparation, the dinner or weekend party is bound to be pleasurable not only for your guests, but for you as well. There is nothing more uncomfortable for guests than to feel their host and/or hostess are exhausted by entertaining them or that their presence is an intrusion. If you are going to entertain, then you must be present to do so, not locked in the kitchen cooking and cleaning, or dashing madly through the house emptying ashtrays or polishing sinks. If you want your guests to be relaxed, you must be relaxed, too.

Mealtime Parties

Put yourself in the place of your guests. If you have invited them for a dinner party, plan your day so that you are ready at the hour of the invitation. Don't expect that everyone will be late and rush to the door with your hair half-dried or with a dust rag in your hands when they arrive on time.

Have the table set in advance, and plan meals that do not require that you spend the entire cocktail hour in the kitchen.

Seat guests next to those with whom they will have something in common. If children will be at the dinner party, don't seat the president of a corporation between two of them—as much as she may love children, their conversation will naturally be limited. If one of your guests is a staunch Republican and another a radical left-winger, you probably should not even have them at the same dinner party. But if you do, wisely separate them during dinner. Although a lively argument may be interesting, you have no way of knowing if "lively" will turn angry.

Be clear in your invitation as to the formality of the occasion. Don't write "casual" and wear satin and diamonds yourself.

Make a point of circulating among your guests and introducing strangers to one another, staying with them long enough to get a conversation launched.

Keep an eye on guests' drinks, offering a second cocktail if the cocktail hour is long enough, so that they don't have to ask.

Remember that guests look to you to "raise your fork" first during dinner and do so promptly so that they may begin eating, or be sure to say, after the first three or so guests are served, "Please begin eating," so that their food doesn't cool while they wait for you to be served or to serve yourself.

If you don't eat meat there is no reason for you to serve it at a dinner party. There are all sorts of wonderful dishes that don't involve meat, and most people won't notice its absence. Don't warn your guests in advance if you'll be serving an unfamiliar food, however, as telling them could prejudice them against it before they take their first bite.

(For other tips for successful dinner parties and entertainments, see Chapter 19 which begins on page 375.)

Weekend Visits

The best possible advice I can give to hosts and hostesses who are entertaining overnight or longer guests is to communicate clearly.

Make your initial invitation clear. State the dates and times the invitation covers, and include your plans so that they know how to prepare. If you will be having a formal dinner party during their visit, say so so they bring appropriate clothing. The same is true if you are suggesting golfing or boating, or swimming at your club. If you are inviting city friends for a weekend of sailing or camping, however, you should indicate what equipment you already have on hand and provide as much as you can since your guests should not be expected to buy those things for one weekend's use.

Communicate during the visit, as well. Show guests not only where their room, bathroom, towels and other items are, but also where the refrigerator is. Assuming you feel this way, they should be made to feel comfortable helping themselves to snacks, juice, or whatever. If something is off limits, say so. "Please don't wait for me to offer—help yourself to anything you see except the strawberries—they're for dessert tomorrow night."

Share your plans. "Sunday is our lazy morning to sleep in—if you get up first, the English muffins are in the bread drawer and the coffee maker will be all ready to go—just push the start button." "We were thinking about going to the club at about two tomorrow for a swim and then staying for the buffet. How does that sound to you?" Then be sure to share whatever the dress code may be, whether you have a cabana or locker room, etc. so your guests know how to prepare. "I have to go to a meeting Monday morning, so am leaving you on your own. The car keys are right here if you want to go out—I should be back about 11:30."

When good friends are visiting, don't be afraid to ask for help, and don't, in your anxiety to be sure they relax and have a good time, refuse their offers. Most guests sincerely want to help and feel uncomfortable if constantly rebuffed or if left to sit while you do all the work. "Brenda, would you read the children a bedtime story while I get dinner ready?" "Tom, would you man the grill for a few minutes?"

(*For other guidelines for successful weekend visits, see Chapter 21 which begins on page 437.*)

DEALING WITH THE UNEXPECTED

Uninvited Guests

"Drop-in," or unexpected, visitors, if you can judge by the mail I receive, cause as much confusion and ill-feeling as anything else I know of. People are thrown completely off-balance by the arrival of someone they have not expected—especially when it happens, as it often does, at the most inconvenient times.

Other than the normal requirement of being courteous to *any* visitor, you have no actual obligation to an unannounced visitor. If you are not busy and have no other plans, naturally you should ask him to stay, and entertain him as you would any guest.

But when he arrives just before mealtime, you have several choices. If you are having a stew or a meal that will stretch, and you value his friendship, ask him to join you. If the meal cannot possibly feed an extra person (or two, if the visitors are a couple), explain that you were about to eat and could he—or they—stop by later? He may say that he has already eaten, in which case ask him to sit down with you and have a cup of coffee or some after-dinner drink.

If guests arrive uninvited when you have other plans for the evening, say so. Your first obligation is to the people with whom you have made the plans. Tell the visitors that you are so sorry but the Joneses are expecting you for dinner (or whatever), and ask them to call you the next time they are in your neighborhood—thereby hinting that you would like some advance warning. Or if you wish, make a definite date to get together with them soon.

Of course, if your "plan" was just to run over to your sister's for a cup of coffee, and the drop-in visitors are your oldest friends whom you have not seen for years, you will undoubtedly want to call your sister and postpone your date until another evening. If she knows the guests too, you might ask her if you may bring them along, but you should not do that without warning her.

The same holds true when visitors "drop in" when you already have invited guests. You may ask the unexpected callers to have a drink or a cup of coffee if you are just sitting and chatting, but if you have invited a couple to play bridge, for example, your obligation is to them. Continue the game, asking the newcomers if they would like to join you and "kibitz." Only if the invited guests *insist* on stopping the game should you do so.

Single Women

Although single women are far less reluctant to go to a party by themselves than they used to be, there are still many—especially older women—who hesitate to do so. Either they feel left out of the generally marriage-oriented conversations or they are nervous about going and coming home by themselves.

Thoughtful hostesses are aware of this and ask a couple who pass near the single woman's home on the way to pick her up and to take her home. And you, if you have one or more single friends, will be showing real consideration if you ask them to go with you to parties to which they are also invited.

Lingering Guests

When a hostess feels that a party has passed its peak, but a few diehards don't seem to be ready to go home, what can she do? Must she sit and suffer or can she "speed the parting guest"?

She can, and she should.

The first, and usually the most effective, way to end a party is to close the bar.

The host may offer "one last nightcap," and then—quite obviously—put the liquor away. The hostess may, more subtly, glance at her watch or hide a yawn. If these measures don't work, you can drop a broader hint. You might say, as Johnny Carson once suggested, "Would you mind dropping the kids off at school on your way home?" Or more seriously, copy Peg Bracken's story about the kindly professor who said loudly to his wife, "Well, my dear, don't you think it's time we went to bed so these good people can go home?"

When one of your guests makes a tentative suggestion that it is time to go home before you want the party to break up, you should make that clear, too. It is far friendlier for a host to say, "Oh, don't go—it's Saturday night, and we can all sleep late tomorrow morning," than to jump up and bring in the coats the minute someone says, "Well, it's getting late. . . ."

A house-party hostess may perfectly properly go to bed before her guests. All she need do is say something like this: "If you all don't mind, I'm going to bed because the baby will be crying for her bottle by six . . . but stay here as long as you want and help yourself to a beer or whatever you want. Just turn out the lights when you go up. . . ."

Liquor Problems

Hosts who are doing their own bartending frequently run into a problem with their guests who want to mix their own drinks. Although the guests may simply be trying to be helpful, they often are more hindrance than help, especially if the host feels they are apt to be heavy-handed in pouring their drinks. Without being insulting, the host can hardly tell his friends to stay out of the bar. But he can control the situation somewhat. He can go to the bar *with* the men, and ask them to get out the ice or the mix or whatever while he pours the liquor himself. He can avoid having more than one bottle of any liquor in evidence. He can make it very obvious that he uses a jigger to pour drinks, and he can *hand* the jigger to his friends before they pour themselves.

When it becomes obvious that one of the guests has had too much to drink, the host or the person tending bar should not serve him more liquor. He may become insulted and abusive, but that is preferable to having him become more intoxicated.

As the host you are responsible for seeing that a drunken guest is taken home. You may ask a good friend to take him or her, you can go yourself if the inebriated person's home is close by, or you can call a cab, give the directions, and pay for it. The person's car keys should be taken away if he or she is not willing to go with someone else. If he or she has reached the stage of almost passing out, two or three of the other guests should help him or her to a bed to sleep it off overnight. If the offender has a spouse or a date present, the host and hostess should offer this person accommodations too, or see that he or she gets safely home.

Unexpected Gifts

Although this subject was discussed earlier in this chapter, it is worth mentioning from the hostess's side of the fence.

When a dinner guest arrives with an angel-food cake or an apple pie without having warned you in advance, you are put "on the spot." There is undoubtedly an obligation to serve it—to share it with the other guests. This is fine—if you have no dessert made, or if it could be served in addition to your dessert. But if you do have a very special dish ready to offer to your guests, the unexpected gift, like unexpected guests, need not be given priority. You are quite free to say, "Thank you so much—it looks wonderful. But I had promised a specialty of mine for tonight, so may I keep this to enjoy tomorrow?" Guests who have not "cleared" their intentions with their hostess beforehand should never be hurt when their gift is not served at the dinner. After all, they presumably brought it for their hostess's enjoyment, and she should feel free to use it as she wishes.

Sometimes you may be given two or three cakes or boxes of candy, or whatever. In this case it would be unreasonable to cut into, or open, all of them, so choose the one that seems to go best with your meal and appeal most to your friends, and offer that one.

The same rules apply to a gift of wine. If it goes with your menu and you do not have another beverage planned or another wine chilled, serve it. Otherwise thank the donor and tell him how much you will enjoy his gift at another meal.

THE HOSTESS'S RECORD BOOK

One of the best ideas I can offer a hostess who entertains at all frequently is to keep a notebook in which you record the names of the guests at your parties, the dates the parties were held, and the menus you served. With this record, you will not serve the same people the same veal tarragon three times in a row, nor invite the Joneses every time you invite the Smythes. In addition you can make a note of foods that some of your friends particularly like or dislike, or to which they are allergic.

*S*ince you will undoubtedly be called upon to make a toast on either a business or social occasion, I am including the subject of both here.

The custom of toasting goes back almost as far as history itself. Ancient warriors drank to their pagan gods, Greeks and Romans drank to gods too, and early Norsemen drank to each other. Almost every culture practiced toasting in some form, and the custom gradually evolved into today's toasts to love, friendship, health, wealth, and happiness.

One story has it that the term itself originated in England in the seventeenth century, when it was customary to float a bit of toast on a drink. A well-known belle of the day was in the public baths (in Bath, where then, as now, the waters were considered salubrious). Her lover scooped up a little of the bath water, added the customary toast, and having drunk to her health, offered the glass to a friend. The friend commented that he didn't really want the water but he'd enjoy the toast.

25
Toasts

THE MECHANICS OF MAKING A TOAST

Men, frequently, and women, occasionally, are called on to make a toast, and it can be a perplexing experience for those who are not accustomed to it. The best solution is simply to say exactly what you feel. Toasts never need be long, and if you do panic when called on unexpectedly, you can get away with something as brief as "To Joe, God bless him," or "To Carol—a wonderful friend and a great boss."

But if you wish to appear more poised and more eloquent you must add a few remarks—a reminiscence, praise, or a relevant story or joke. The toast should, however, always be in keeping with the occasion. A touch of humor is rarely out of place, but toasts at a wedding should be on the sentimental side, those in honor of a retiring employee nostalgic, and so on.

On ceremonial occasions there is generally a toastmaster, and if not, the chairman of the committee or the president of the organization proposes the necessary toasts at the end of the meal, and before any speeches. At less formal dinners anyone may propose a toast as soon as wine or champagne is served. The toasters need not drain their glasses. A small sip each time allows one to drink numerous toasts from the serving.

Many people do not touch alcohol, including wine, at all, even for toasts. These non-drinkers should not turn their

glasses upside down. They may, of course, refuse the wine when it is passed and
merely rise empty-handed or raise the empty glass when the toast is drunk. However, I feel it is less conspicuous (and implies less criticism of the drinkers) if they say to the waiter, "Just a little, please," and then raise the partly filled glass to their lips without drinking. Or if it seems expedient they may ask the waiter quietly to bring them a soft drink. Years ago one was not supposed to toast except with an alcoholic beverage, but today one may participate in the toast with whatever liquid is available. In any case, one must rise and join in the spirit at least—it would be extremely discourteous to remain seated.

Replying to a Toast

The person being toasted does not rise or drink the toast. Instead a man rises and drinks to his toasters in return, either saying, "Thank you," or proposing his own toast to them. While a woman is perfectly free to make toasts if she wishes to, her reply to a toast is simply a smile and a nod in the direction of the speaker. She may also raise her glass toward him in a gesture of "Thanks, and here's to you, too."

SOME SAMPLE TOASTS

The following toasts are intended only to give you some ideas for various occasions. They must be changed to fit the particular circumstances, of course, and a word or two of your own feelings will always add a personal touch.

Toast to a Retiring Employee or a Member of the Firm

"It is often said that nobody is indispensable, and that may sometimes be true, but for all of us there will never be anyone who can replace Joe. Although we will miss him greatly, we know how much he is looking forward to his retirement, and we wish him all the happiness he so richly deserves in the years to come."

OR

"I know that every one of us here tonight thinks of Lucy [Mrs. Smith] not as an employee [employer] but as a friend. When she leaves we will suffer a very real loss both in our organization and in our hearts. At the same time we rejoice that she will now be able to enjoy the things she wants to do, so let us rise and drink a toast to one of the finest friends we have known."

Toast to a Guest of Honor at a Testimonial Dinner

"We are gathered here tonight to honor a man who has given unselfishly of his time and effort to make this campaign so successful. Without the enthusiasm and leadership that Bob Jones has shown all through these past months, we could never have reached our goal. Please join me in drinking a toast to the man who more than anyone else is responsible for making it possible to see our dream of a new hospital wing finally come true."

OR

"Ladies and gentlemen, you have already heard of the magnificent work our guest of honor has accomplished during her past two years in Washington. Right now we would like to tell her that no matter how proud we are of her success in her chosen career, we are even more pleased to have her home with us again. It's great to have you back, Mary!"

Foreign Toasts

Since the custom of toasting originated in Europe, and is still more widely practiced there than here, well-traveled Americans are bringing home toasts from abroad. A knowledge of the most common of these can be very useful, but if you are not sure of the pronunciation use the equivalent English toast instead. The following examples all mean, translated, "To your health."

French—*A votre santé.*
Spanish—*Salud.*
German—*Prosit.*
Swedish—*Sköal.* (This is often taken to mean that the toasters must empty their glasses, but that is not necessarily so in the U.S.)
Yiddish—*L'Chayim.*
Irish—*Sláinte.*
Italian—*Salute.*
Russian—*Na zdorov'e.*
Polish—*Nazdrowie.*

Engagement Party Toasts

This is the conventional announcement made by the father of the bride-to-be at a dinner. After seeing that all glasses at the table are filled, the host rises, lifts his own glass, and says, "I propose we drink to the health of Joanne and the man she has decided to add permanently to our family, Paul Baldwin."

OR

"Now you know that the reason for this party is to announce Mary's engagement to John. I would like to propose a toast to them both, wishing them many, many years of happiness."

OR

"Mary's mother and I have always looked forward to meeting the man Mary would choose to marry. She lived up to all our expectations when she picked John.

We want you all to know how pleased we are to announce the engagement tonight.
Please join me in wishing them a long and happy marriage."

Everyone except the future bride and groom rises and drinks a little of whatever the beverage may be. They congratulate the young couple, and Paul is called upon for a speech. He must stand and make at least a few remarks thanking the guests for their good wishes.

Wedding Rehearsal Dinner Toasts

A Bridegroom's Father's Toast at the Rehearsal Dinner

"I would like to ask you to join me in drinking a toast to two wonderful people without whom this wedding could never have been possible: Veronica's mother and father, Mr. and Mrs. Brown."

OR

"I don't need to tell you what a wonderful person Lynn is, but I do want to tell you how happy Brett's mother and I are to welcome her as our new daughter-in-law. To Lynn and Brett."

A Best Man's Toast at the Rehearsal Dinner

"Alex and I have been friends for a long time now, and I have always known what a lucky guy he is. Tonight all of you can see what I mean when you look at Marie. Please join me in a toast to both of them. May this kind of luck continue throughout their lives together."

OR

"Here's to Dave, who is truly the best man—and the luckiest too—and to Annamarie, who made him that way."

Wedding Reception Toasts

Here are some toasts you can amend to fit the occasion when you are given the honor of making a toast at a wedding reception.

A Best Man's Toast to the Bridal Couple at the Wedding Reception

"To Mary and John—a beautiful bride, a wonderful man—and the happiest couple I ever hope to see!"

OR

"To Mary and John—may they always be as happy as they look today."

A Bridegroom's Toast to His Bride at the Wedding Reception

"I'd like you all to join me in a toast to the woman who's just made me the happiest man in the world."

OR

"All my life I've wondered what the woman I'd marry would be like. In my wildest dreams I never imagined she would be as wonderful as Mary, so please join me in drinking this first toast to my bride."

Anniversary Toasts

The following are intended to give you ideas in writing your own toast. Change them to fit the particular circumstances and always add a few special words to give your toast your personal touch.

"Many of us who are here tonight can well remember that day twenty-five years ago when we drank a toast to the future happiness of Ann and Roger. It is more than obvious that our good wishes at that time have served them well, and therefore I would like to ask that all of you—old friends and new—rise and drink with me to another twenty-five years of the same love and happiness that Ann and Roger have already shared together."

OR

"John, I'd like to propose a toast to you and Emma on your fiftieth anniversary. It has been a wonderful party tonight, and all of us wish you both health, wealth, and the years to enjoy them."

The basic principles of conduct at any public entertainment are the same: Do not draw attention to yourself by noisy or conspicuous behavior. Do remember that others in the audience, as well as the performers, are entitled to your consideration.

26
Public Entertainments

THE THEATER

Arriving at the Theater

On arriving at the theater the host (or hostess) holds the tickets in his hand so that the ticket-taker may see them, but he allows his guests to pass in ahead of him. If the usher is at the head of the aisle the host gives the usher the stubs and steps back. The women in the party precede the host down the aisle. If, however, the usher is already partway down the aisle, the host may lead the way until he reaches the usher. If the party is large the host or hostess should tell the guests ahead of time in what order they are going to sit, so that they may arrive at their row in more or less that order, avoiding a great deal of shuffling about and confusion in the aisle.

A man should sit on the aisle. When there are two couples, one man should go in first, followed by the two women, and finally the other man. Each woman generally sits next to the man who is not her husband.

When the party is larger a woman does lead the way into the row, and the others alternate, men and women, leaving the host, or one of the men if there is no host, on the aisle.

In the case of a man and a woman alone, she of course, goes in first, and he follows, sitting on or nearest to the aisle.

When the Performance Is Over

The first man to leave the row naturally stands in the aisle for a moment, so that the woman who follows can walk with him, or if the crowd makes two abreast impossible, precede him. In nearly all situations a woman goes first. Only when the crowd is really dense does a man go first to make a wedge for her. In a theater party of six or more, the first man should let the woman who sat next to him go ahead of him, but he does not wait to follow the others.

Dressing for the Theater

It is perfectly correct for both men and women to wear daytime clothes to the theater. During the week many members of the audience are likely to be businesspeople who have been at the office all day and have not had the opportunity to change clothes. They hardly wish to see their dinner and theater partner arrive dressed in elaborate clothing.

On the rare occasions when a hostess plans a large theater party, perhaps to celebrate an anniversary, she may wish to make the evening more gala by requesting that the men wear "black tie." The only other time that more formal dress is required is on the opening night of an evening performance, when one attends by special invitation. Then the women wear cocktail or dinner dresses and the gentlemen wear tuxedos.

Courtesy at the Theater

Be on time. If you are with a party, it is terribly unfair to others to make them miss the beginning of the performance because of your tardiness. If you are unavoidably late, wait at the back of the theater until the first scene or act is over and slip into your seat quickly and quietly.

This is a time for hats off and small hairdos. Afros and other large hair styles obstruct the view of the persons seated behind you. If you don't want to change your hairstyle, then request tickets for the back row of whatever section you are seated in.

"Excuse me, please," is the natural thing to say when having to disturb anyone in order to get to or leave your seat in a theater, and if someone is obliged to get up to let you pass, you add "Thank you," or "I'm sorry." Should you by any chance have to pass someone a second time, you say, "I'm sorry to disturb you again," and "Thank you" as they let you go by.

When climbing in and out of a row of seats, face the stage or front and press closely to the backs of the seats you are facing, being careful not to drag your coat or purse over the heads of those seated in front of or behind you.

When you are seated you must give others enough room to pass. If the seats are far enough apart so that you can do this by merely turning your knees sideways, so much the better, especially if the play has started. But if there is so little space that passersby have to step over your knees, you must stand and sit down again—quickly! Remember that during every second you stand, you are cutting off the view of all who are seated behind you.

Quiet please! Don't whisper, rustle, rattle, or talk. If you have a coughing or sneezing fit that just won't stop, excuse yourself and leave the theater until you have it under control. If you are accompanied by a child who can't be quiet, exit with the child. The price of theater tickets today is so exorbitant that people are less pleased than ever to miss what is happening on stage because of the noise made by others.

If one wishes to go out to the lobby between acts to smoke, stretch, or purchase refreshments, his or her companion(s) usually goes along, but this is not required and the other person(s) may certainly remain seated in the theater or simply stand in place.

THE OPERA

The general rules are the same as those for the theater.

Seating in a Box at the Opera

Three or four couples often subscribe to a box at the opera together, sharing the cost and enjoying each other's company during the season. So that each member of the group may enjoy the better seats and no two men be always relegated to the back row (especially if it is an off-center box that does not offer a full view of the stage from all of its seats), these friends may agree to switch their seating arrangements around, even though it violates the old rule of "no gentlemen in the front row."

Between the Acts

Both women and men may visit friends in other boxes between the acts. They may also go out to enjoy the refreshments that most opera houses provide or simply to "people-watch." Everyone should return as soon as the signal is given for the raising of the curtain, for it is very annoying to have people coming in after the performance has resumed, not only to the audience but to the performers as well.

The Audience's Conduct

It should not be necessary to point out that there must be no conversation during the overture or the performance. An enthusiastic audience may applaud at the end of an aria, and of course, after each curtain, but not for the entrances or exits of a performer.

Dressing for the Opera

Clothing is very much the same as that worn to the theater, but one may occasionally see tuxedos and dinner dresses. One never sees tails on other than an opening night, but men who have the opportunity to change from business clothes sometimes put on a dinner jacket, especially those sitting in the boxes.

THE BALLET

The rules for theater- and opera-goers apply to audiences at the ballet. Absolute silence is imperative, and applause is withheld until a complete dance or scene is over. Individual performances are applauded at the end of the ballet.

THE SYMPHONY

Applause

The conductor and guest soloists are always applauded when they walk out onto the stage. Clapping stops as soon as the conductor steps onto the podium and raises his baton. Applause for the music is held until the end of each selection, when the conductor turns toward the audience and bows.

Silence

Since a concert is entirely auditory rather than visual entertainment, silence in the audience is of utmost importance. In addition to not talking during the performance, one should not hum or "keep time" with fingers or feet, rustle programs or candy wrappers, wear jangling jewelry, open or close a purse with snaps, or indicate approval or disapproval with gasps, groans, sighs, etc.

ROCK CONCERTS

While opera and symphony concerts can bring out the most elegant manners among audience members, rock concerts can bring out the worst. It is to be presumed that those who pay to see and hear a favorite group perform would prefer to see the group—not the hindquarters of the enthusiast in front who is standing on his seat— and to hear the performers on stage, not the voice of a fellow audience member singing along. There is no reason why attendance at a rock concert should mandate that audience members drink and smoke, either, although it seems that many feel this is perfectly acceptable behavior. It is not. Not only do the artists on stage deserve respect from the audience, members of the audience deserve respect from one another. No matter how compelled one is to sing along, to clap out the rhythm, to shout, whistle, and scream during a favorite song, or to dance in the aisles, one should think about how annoying this is to others and to the performers. Those on stage did not come to audition you. Fellow audience members did not pay a hefty ticket price to hear you. Naturally, when a member of the group invites the audience to sing along, or to clap in time, it is expected that you will do so if you wish.

THE MOVIES

Finding Seats at the Movies

The order in which a couple goes down the aisle in a movie theater is unimportant. When there are no ushers a man and woman go down the aisle together. Either one might say, "There are two—shall we take those?" The other agrees or suggests two farther down.

If you come in after the movie has started wait at the rear until your eyes have become adjusted to the darkness. By doing this you may avoid stumbling into the center of a row only to find that there are not the necessary vacant seats, having to back out, and tripping over unsympathetic spectators.

Audience Pests

If those behind you insist on talking, it will do you no good to turn around and glare. If you are young they pay no attention, and if you are older you may discover that most young people think an angry older person the funniest sight on earth. The only thing you can do is say amiably, "I'm sorry, but I can't hear anything while you talk." If they persist you can ask an usher to call the manager. However, perhaps the simplest thing to do, if there are other seats available, is to move.

W hether a sports spectator or a participant, the rules of common courtesy enhance your enjoyment of the event, not to mention that of those around or with you. From nursery school on, children are taught about being good sports, yet their parents can be the worst offenders, booing, name-calling and screaming at sports events, or throwing their tennis rackets to the ground, steering their boats too close to others, or becoming red with rage at their partner's "stupidity" during a bridge game. Just because the event is competitive or active does not mean manners are dropped. To the contrary. Watch college team players—football captains shake hands before the coin toss and basketball and hockey players line up and shake hands with their opponents after the game. Fans should be as courteous!

AS A SPECTATOR

At a sports event you need follow few rules other than those of ordinary courtesy. Arrive on time so that you do not disturb others in reaching your seat. You are expected to cheer for your team or your favorite player, but don't shout insults at the opposing team, as you may very well find yourself in a fight with your neighbor, and you will gain little by being escorted to the nearest exit by an usher or a policeman. Try to refrain from jumping up in moments of crisis; the people behind you are interested in seeing too, and you will be deluged with shouts of "Down in front!" If you smoke and are attending an outdoor event hold your cigarette or cigar in such a way that smoke does not blow into someone's face. And last but not least, don't shove! If you have an appointment following the game, slip out quietly a minute or two before the end. If you leave when the game is over, walk slowly *with* the crowd, not *through* it, to the exit.

AS A PARTICIPANT

The basic requisite for good manners at any game table or sports area is that age-old quality *sportsmanship*, and the quality that more than any other gives evidence of true sportsmanship is absence of any show of temper. After all, if you can't take sports with grace and good temper, you shouldn't go in for them. Cursing your faults or your luck, excusing, complaining, and protesting against unfairness won't get you anywhere—except in trouble. To hide your ill humor is the first rule of sportsmanship. This does not mean that you may never—by expression or gesture—show either satisfaction or chagrin. It simply means that at all times your emotions are under control.

The next rule is always to give your opponent the benefit of the doubt. Although the particular point in question may seem very important at that moment, never argue with the umpire. If he rules a line ball on the tennis court is out, it is out. Do not turn toward the spectators with an expression that says, "He must be blind!"

Another shortcoming of an unsportsmanlike player is the practice of understating ability before a match. It is a commonplace occurrence to hear a man who is actually perfectly satisfied with his skill say, "I am not much of a player," or "I know I'll be terrible today—I've got a 'bad' arm!" He is not necessarily being dishonest; he may be motivated by a subconscious effort to create admiring surprise if he plays well and to save face should his game be off. The only time a player may justifiably discuss his or her skill—or lack of it—is when poorer play would be a source of annoyance to a group of competitors playing.

One last example of bad sportsmanship is the person who complains of illness after losing a match: "I had such a pain in my side [or knee, or back]! I don't know how I ever got through the game!"

Sportsmanship can be acquired by following a few simple rules: Keep your mind on the game, not on your feelings. If you win, don't at once begin to consider yourself a star. A gloating winner is detested even more than a bad loser. But when you lose, don't sulk, or protest, or long-windedly explain. If you are hurt, don't nurse your bruises if they are minor. Get up and good-naturedly get ready for the next play. This is playing the game—and it is good sportsmanship.

It is worth teaching your children these rules, and the way to teach them is to play games with them. They will learn not only sportsmanship, but also tolerance, patience, and cooperation. Of course *you* must set the example. It is up to *you* the parents to show your children how to be modest winners and philosophical losers.

There are fixed rules for playing every game—and for conduct in every sport. The details of these rules must be studied in the books of the game, learned from instructors, or acquired by experience. And if you tend to get annoyed or bored with the number of rules there seem to be, remember this: If there were no rules, there could be no competitive sports at all.

Above and beyond the "rules" there are certain "manners" that must be observed too. In many cases they are as traditional and as important to the practice of the sport as are the rules of play.

It would be impossible to discuss good manners in every game played by sports-loving Americans. Nor is it necessary, as most are governed by a combination of very strict rules and common courtesy.

I have chosen five sports, however, in which good manners *beyond* the rule book are most important. They are boating, tennis, golf, skiing, and running. I have chosen them for three reasons. First, because of the enormous number of people who enjoy them. Second, because their popularity has increased so tremendously in very recent years that there are more people who do not know the rules. And third, except for tennis, adherence to the rules of etiquette is essential for safety when enjoying the sport.

Boating

If you are the proud owner of a new boat, be it sail or power, and especially if it is your first venture in ownership, you must learn thoroughly and completely the rules of safety on the water. These rules and regulations can easily be obtained from the United States Coast Guard, and there are many excellent books available on all aspects of boating. After complying with the rules affecting other boats, the captain may establish the routine for his own boat in as rigid or as relaxed a way as he wishes. But since there are certain procedures that have come to be regarded as most correct and most practical, every guest should be acquainted with these conventions before accepting an invitation to go cruising.

On all but the most elaborate yachts or houseboats, space is very limited. Therefore one takes along as few clothes as possible. If you are going on an extended cruise, you must find out where and in what circumstances you will be going ashore. You may attend receptions, parties, or dinners in five different ports; but remember that because the people ashore will not have seen you in the other ports, and the people on other boats understand the space problem, the same outfit will serve for several trips to shore. Most captains keep foul-weather gear on their boats, but before you sail be sure that he has enough, and if not, bring your own.

If you are a smoker you must remember to throw your match or your cigarette overboard to leeward—the side away from where the wind is coming from.

Although many boat owners do not object to hard shoes on board, it is only polite to find out how your captain feels. If he does object, carry your party shoes in your hand until you reach shore, where you may change into them. Remember that regular rubber soles are slippery. If you are to be on board a boat that will be "heeling" (tipping with the wind) or one small enough to pitch about in a rough sea, you should have grooved, nonskid sneakers especially made for sailors.

All clothing must be packed in canvas bags or duffel bags, never in a hard suitcase. The latter is impossible to stow away, whereas the canvas ones can be squashed into a minimum of space.

If cruising on a luxurious yacht, you treat the crew exactly as you would the servants in a house on land. They should be regarded with friendliness and respect, and if a steward has taken care of you and your clothing, you may leave him a tip, just as you would a chambermaid, before going ashore.

Other rules are simply those of good manners anywhere. Remember that the skipper is boss, and as much for safety as for politeness, his word is law. He, after all,

is the one who knows the limits of his boat and also the capabilities of his guests or
crew, and he has planned for the greatest enjoyment (and in racing, the greatest chance of success) that he possibly can.

As the proud new owner of a yacht—whether a houseboat, a cabin cruiser, or a sleek yawl or sloop—you must observe certain rules of courtesy both in harbor and at sea. Some are interrelated with safety, and others are just plain good manners—designed to make boating more of a pleasure for you and everyone else. Here are some of the things a considerate—and popular—skipper does:

He doesn't warm up his engines more loudly and for longer than necessary when he is getting off to an early start.

He observes the "no-wake" signs, especially when passing close to boats tied up at docks.

He is careful not to spray neighboring boats when hosing down his decks at a marina.

He keeps the noise level reasonable at evening festivities on his boat and sees that they do not go on too late, when tied up close to other boats.

He gives trolling fishermen a wide berth so as not to cut their long lines.

He slows down when passing small fishing boats at anchor, so as not to rock them or scare away the fish.

Unless absolutely necessary, he does not discard any trash at sea, but keeps it in plastic containers to be disposed of on shore.

He keeps ship-to-shore telephone conversations as short as possible and remembers that everything he says can be heard by everyone else on the circuit.

Because of the close community living on board a boat, consideration for the other people with you is of utmost importance. Before you make any move, ask yourself if you will disturb one of the others, and try to be constantly aware of the special habits and likes and dislikes of your fellow cruisers.

Tennis

Although manners of *any* kind are sadly lacking among our nation's top players and in international tournament play, good manners on the local tennis courts are generally the rule. However, one does see enough violations of etiquette to make them worth mentioning. More often than not tennis is a partnership game, and one cannot, as in golf or skiing, play alone. Therefore the most important rules of etiquette are those which deal with considerate manners between players.

First of all, never question the ruling of the linesmen or referee. You may think your ball landed "in" by a foot, but he is in a better place to see each line, and his decision must be final.

If your ball bounces out of your court and into the occupied court next to you, wait until those players have finished the point. Don't call "Ball, please," or dash over to retrieve it while their ball is still in play.

Change sides on every odd game if the sun or wind give an advantage to one court. This is a requirement in tournament play, and even in a friendly game the offer should be made.

Children and beginners should not sign up for courts (at many clubs they are not allowed to) on weekends or other days that are the only ones on which the businesspeople can play. If those happen to be the only times available to the novice as well, he or she should arrange to play early in the morning or late in the afternoon.

When you arrive at the hour for which you have signed up and find the players on the court are playing what are probably the last points, wait patiently without pacing, bouncing balls, or glaring at them. In fact it is polite to say, "Go ahead and finish. We don't mind waiting a few minutes." And when you are the one on the court, don't try to finish if you are not near the end of a set. Never finish out more than the game you are playing, and if that does not end the set, leave the court anyway.

At the end of a match it is not necessary to hop over the net as the players do in the movies, but do go up to the net, and shaking hands with your opponents, congratulate them for the good game if they won, or thank them for the excellent match if they lost.

White is still often the required color for tennis clothing. When it isn't clean, neat, modest shorts or dresses, whether all white, a soft color, or a combination of both, are correct on every court in every locality.

Golf

Golf was originally considered (and with reason) a rich man's game. Today, however, with the appearance of the thousands of public courses that eliminate the necessity of joining an expensive club, millions of people are enjoying the game. For those who have recently started to play, there are—above and beyond learning to hit the ball correctly—some important rules of etiquette to be learned.

Golf places a particularly severe strain upon the amiability of the average person, and in no other game is serenity more essential. It is safe to say that those who lose their tempers are almost certain to muff shots and lose the match.

Golf players, of course, know the rules and observe them; but it sometimes happens that casual strollers walk out on a course to watch the players. If they know the players well, that is one thing, but they have no right to follow strangers. A diffident player is easily put off the game, especially if those watching are so discourteous as to make audible remarks. Those playing in tournaments expect an audience, and therefore erratic and nervous players ought not to sign up for tournaments—certainly not two-ball foursomes where they will handicap a partner.

Let us consider those rules which help to eliminate danger on a crowded golf course.

Never, under any circumstances, hit your shot until the group ahead of you is out of range. On weekends there is generally a starter on the first tee who will tell you when to drive, but if not, you *must* wait until those who teed off before you have hit their second shots and are definitely beyond the limit of a drive. And this rule is followed on every one of the eighteen holes. The only exception occurs when the group ahead feels that they are holding you up and signals to you to "go through." In this case, at least wait until they have moved to the edge of the fairway, and also be sure that they are all watching your ball in case it should go astray.

If you hit a wild shot that goes toward a player on another fairway, or if someone appears unexpectedly from behind a bush where he was searching for a ball, shout "Fore!" at the top of your lungs. Although he will not have time to locate your ball in flight and dodge, your shout will generally cause him to throw his arms over his head and possibly avoid serious injury.

On a blind hole (a hole where the green is not visible from where you are hitting), send a caddy or another player to the point at which he can see the area where your ball may be expected to land. If there are still other golfers in range, he holds up his hand to signal you to wait, and then, when it is safe for you to hit, waves and steps to the edge of the fairway.

While waiting on a tee for your turn to drive, look around before taking a practice swing. Not only may you hit someone with your club, but if you are swinging toward someone else you may blast him painfully with bits of stone or turf from the ground. This is true while playing other shots as well—your caddy or companions may be closer behind you than you think—and it is always safer to look before you swing.

In addition to these rules affecting safety on the golf course, there are many that add to the pleasure of the player and the orderly progression of the game.

Never speak, rattle your clubs, or move when another player is making his shot. This is especially true on the green, where intense concentration is required, but it can be disturbing on any part of the course. Even though you may think you are far enough away from the player whose turn it is to hit, the wind may carry a sound right to him, or he may catch your movement from the corner of his eye in the middle of his backswing.

One matter of convention rather than etiquette should be mentioned because it is important to the smooth functioning of the twosome or foursome: The person whose ball is farthest from the pin, or hole, plays first. Around the putting green there are certain golf rules that apply to special situations, but in an informal match the ball farthest from the hole is played, even though it is not on the green, or putting surface. A player whose ball stops close to the hole has the option of "putting out," or tapping it in, to save the time involved in marking the spot, moving his ball, waiting for the others to play, replacing the ball, and then sinking the putt.

A foursome is obligated to allow a twosome to "go through," or pass them, if there is an empty hole ahead of them. This "if" is important, because when there are players directly in front, the twosome will be prevented from moving on, there will be a pileup of six or more players on the same hole, and those behind will have an even more lengthy wait. In the case of a foursome following a foursome, or a twosome following a twosome, the first one obviously holding up the second, it is very rude of the slower one not to allow the others to go through.

It is customary for the player who has had the lowest score on the previous hole to "tee off," or drive, first on the next hole. If two or more are tied for the "honor," as this privilege is called, the one who had the lowest score on the last hole on which there was a difference plays first. In the case of teams, all members of the team that won the last hole go first and usually keep the same order no matter which one of them had the low score.

The final three rules relate to the proper care of the course. It should hardly be necessary to say that divots (pieces of turf dug up by the club head) should be replaced, but if one walks over a course after a busy weekend, it becomes apparent that golfers' education has been sadly neglected in this area. Equally important is the need for repairing the little pits made in a soft green by a high approach shot.

After playing a shot out of a trap (or bunker), the player must rake the sand to eliminate his footprints and the hole made by his club. If he has a caddy, the caddy must do it. In the event that there is no rake by the trap, he should do his best to smooth the sand with the head of the club.

In addition to these rules, all golfers will continue to enjoy the sport more if tempers are restrained and everyday rules of courtesy are observed.

Skiing

The number of people who have recently become enthusiastic about skiing in winter makes this sport comparable to golf in the summer, and as in golf, many of the rules of etiquette for skiers have developed from a need for safety regulations. In fact, on the ski slopes, except for the ordinary rules of good behavior and consideration for others, almost all the etiquette is derived from an effort to eliminate dangerous situations.

Never ski alone. Even the most expert skier in the world can have an accident—in fact the best skiers may have the most serious falls, as a result of their speed—and cold and emptiness are no respecters of skill if one falls on a lonely trail when no one knows his whereabouts.

Never ski on a closed trail. The commonest reason for blocking it off is that it is considered too dangerous for skiing at the time. Some daredevils, thinking that nothing is too difficult for them, are occasionally tempted to ski a trail that has been marked "Closed." First and foremost, this is foolish, as the ski patrols have no obligation to patrol that slope and in case of accident the skiers are far from help. Second, the trail may be closed in order to keep the snow in condition for a time later in the season or for a special competition. In the latter case using the trail indicates a lack of consideration for the management of the area as well as for the skiers who are to use it when it opens.

Never ski on a trail or slope that is too difficult for you. All ski areas mark their trails "Novice," "Intermediate," or "Expert," or possibly a combination of two— "Novice-Intermediate." If you have been skiing only a short time, don't assume that because in other sports you are as good as your friend Sally, who has been on the slopes since she was three, you are capable of accompanying her to the top of the mountain to try the new expert trail. Not only are you likely to break a leg, but you will infuriate the true experts who are entitled to use the trail and who will hardly appreciate rounding a curve at high speed only to find a novice "snowplowing" down the middle of the trail in front of them.

The other side of the coin must be mentioned too. If you are an expert, high-speed-loving skier, stay off the novice and intermediate slopes as much as possible. There is no need to make them more crowded than they ordinarily are, and nothing is more terrifying to a beginner than a hurtling skier rushing past him or even, as I have seen so often, running over the tips of his skis or actually knocking him down.

Skiers cannot be put on little tracks labeled "10 mph," "20 mph," "40 mph," and so forth, however, and there are certain to be occasions when a faster skier must pass a slower skier on a narrow trail. In order to warn him (or her) that he is about to pass, he calls "Track, right" or "Track, left," indicating that he will pass on that side, thereby warning the slower skier to pull to the other side—or at least not to make a sudden turn toward him as he passes.

If, because of a miscalculation, or for any reason whatever, you do knock another skier down, STOP! Apologize and make absolutely sure that he or she is not injured before you continue on down the hill.

If he appears to be having difficulty in regaining his feet, it is only common courtesy to go back to assist him. If he is unable to move or get up or is in pain, do not fly off hysterically looking for help, but stay with him, doing whatever you can to make him more comfortable, such as undoing his harnesses, until another skier approaches. Then, and only then, having asked the new arrival to stay with the injured person, should you go as fast as you possibly can to the nearest ski patrol. Never try to move the fallen skier. If he is suffering from a broken bone you may cause a much more serious injury if you move him incorrectly. The ski patrol are trained to do this and will have the proper equipment with them when they arrive.

Remember that the mountain may be very large, and it is very difficult to find another person at any given time. When you are a member of a group of family or friends it is wise to set a specific place and time at which to meet for meals, to go home, or just to "check in."

Otherwise, good manners for skiers are simply a matter of employing consideration for others at all times. Don't ridicule the novice even jokingly, and don't boast of your own skill. When the line waiting for the lift is long, don't shove ahead of those already waiting, but take your place patiently and cheerfully. If you are skiing alone, offer to pair up with another "single" on the double lifts, so that no chair goes up unoccupied. If you are with a group, don't hold the better skiers up by insisting that they wait for you, and if you are one of the more expert skiers, don't insist that the beginners accompany you where they are not capable of staying in control.

Skiing is a wonderful sport, both for physical thrills and for the social life that is a part of it. But more than in almost any other sport, consideration of others and good manners are essential to the enjoyment and safety of everyone.

Running

Runners whose track is public pathways should stay to the right. Although runners have the right of way and other pedestrians should step to the side of the path or sidewalk to let them pass, those who exercise in pairs or groups should run single file when others are strolling or walking nearby. It is extremely rude to run two or three abreast, virtually forcing others off the sidewalk.

CARD GAMES

The same rules of good manners apply to players of bridge, gin rummy, hearts, poker—mixed or stag—or any other game.

Irritating mannerisms should be avoided like the plague. If there is one thing worse than the horrible postmortem, it is the incessant repetition of some jarring habit by one particular player.

Common offenses are drumming on the table with one's fingers, making various clicking, whistling, or humming sounds, massaging one's face, scratching one's chin with the cards, or holding up the card one is going to play as though shouting, "I know what you are going to play! And my card is ready!"

Many people whose game is otherwise excellent are rarely asked to play because they have some such silly and annoying habit. Don't spoil your chances for many a pleasant evening by allowing yourself to be unaware of those habits.

If luck is against you, you will gain nothing by sulking or complaining about the awful cards you have been holding. Your partner is suffering also, and you can scarcely expect your opponents to be sympathetic.

Don't try to defend your own bad play. When you have shown poor judgment the best thing you can say is, "I'm very sorry, partner," and let it go at that.

Playing for Money

The intelligent card player makes it a rule never to play for stakes that it will be inconvenient to lose. Of course there *are* people who can take losses beyond their means with perfect cheerfulness and composure because they are so imbued with the gambler's instinct that a heavy turn of luck, in either direction, is the salt of life. But the average person is equally embarrassed at winning or losing a stake that matters, and the only answer is always to play only for what one can easily afford.

Because of this every hostess owes her guests protection from being forced into paying for stakes that can embarrass them. If you invite a stranger to play bridge with friends who always play for certain stakes, you should say when you invite him, "The Smiths and Browns and Robinsons are coming. They all play for a cent a point. Is that all right?" The one invited can say either, "I'm sorry. My limit is a tenth of a cent," or "They must be way out of my class! But ask me again when you are having people who play for less."

VII

CELEBRATIONS
AND CEREMONIES

BABY SHOWERS

Some people feel that baby showers are best given after the happy event takes place because there is always a faint chance that something can go wrong, and nothing could be sadder for the bereaved mother and father than to have to put away or return the unused shower gifts. However, they are more commonly held before the baby is due so that the mother will have the use of the shower gifts as soon as the baby is born.

Showers may be given for second babies, but they should be restricted to either *very* close friends and family or to people who were not invited to showers for the first baby. They are appropriate if the mother has moved to a new area and has a new circle of friends or if a number of years have past since the first baby's birth.

Showers for Adopted Babies

It is not only correct, but a nice thing to do, to give a shower for the mother of an adopted baby. It is exactly the same as any baby shower, except that on the invitations you should include the correct size for baby clothes, since the child is not necessarily a newborn.

Showers for Single Mothers

Fortunately, the stigma of being "born out of wedlock" is nowhere near as black today as it used to be. Those who find themselves in this situation frequently need more support and love from their families and friends at this time than they ever will again. Therefore it is perfectly acceptable to give a small shower for an expectant single mother, or for one whose baby is already born. If she wishes, however, the shower should be restricted to close friends and relatives.

Grandmother Showers

When a women's club or social organization learns that one of their members is about to become a grandmother the others may wish to give her a "grandmother shower." It is usually held during or at the end of their regular meeting or get-together, with some special refreshments served and a few extra minutes devoted to the opening of the gifts. However, it may be given in the usual way—by a close friend or group of friends of the grandmother-to-be as an afternoon tea or a morning coffee.

The main distinction between a grandmother shower and any other is that the gifts are not for the use of the recipient. Often they are gifts for the baby or the new mother, which are given through the grandmother. They may also be articles to be used by the grandmother when she is caring for the new baby—diaper pins, a bassinet, a teething ring, bibs, etc.

Whatever the arrangements, the grandmother shower is a delightful way to honor a friend and to make the prospective grandmother feel an important part of the coming event.

Office Showers

Quite frequently the staff at an expectant mother's office will get together to give her a shower. These showers may be held after work at the office, in a restaurant, or in a staff member's home. While they are usually restricted to female co-workers, that is not necessarily so, especially in a small office where everyone might be included. Co-workers may also give a shower for an expectant father. It is usually arranged, however, by the women, and generally takes place in a small office where everyone is congenial.

Everyone invited chips in on the cost of the food and drink as well as bringing a gift. In some cases a collection is taken up and one large gift such as a crib is presented, rather than smaller individual ones.

ANNOUNCEMENTS

The first announcement of the birth of a baby is usually made to friends and relatives as soon as the proud father or delighted grandparents can get to the telephone. Sometime before the blessed event actually takes place, or immediately thereafter, the parents may, if they wish, visit a stationer's and select an announcement card to be sent to their relatives and to those of their friends who are close to the family. After the birth and as soon as the name is determined, the father notifies the stationer, and in a few days the cards are ready.

One of the nicest types of birth announcement consists simply of a very small card with the baby's name and birth date on it, tied with a pink or blue ribbon to the upper margin of the "Mr. and Mrs." card of the parents.

A large variety of commercially designed announcement cards with space for the baby's name, date of birth, and parents' names to be written in by hand are also available, and as they are much less expensive they are very popular. Some are in the best of taste, but those which include unnecessary data and foolish phrasing or coy

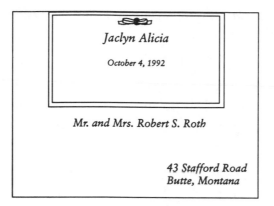

Birth announcement

designs are better left on the rack. Other parents design their own announcements, and if you have the talent these cards are the nicest of all.

To announce the birth of twins, have both their names printed on the small card, and if they are a boy and girl, use pink and blue ribbons. Or have a card printed, saying, "Mr. and Mrs. William DeRosa announce the birth of twins," or "twin daughters," followed by the names.

Commercially designed birth announcement

The arrival of a birth announcement carries *no obligation*—it does not mean that the recipient need send a gift. Parents sometimes hesitate to send cards for fear that that will be the reaction, and there will always be people who think it does require a gift. But they are wrong, and this should not discourage new parents from taking this pleasant way to let friends know about the happy event.

It *is* thoughtful, however, for those who receive announcements to send a note of congratulation to the new parents. Depending on your relationship, your message may be sentimental or humorous. Few of us could top the advice sent to a new mother by Arlene Francis: "Don't take any wooden nipples."

Announcements are sent for second and third (and additional) babies just as they are for the first.

Announcement of Adoption

It is a fine idea to send a card announcing an adoption to your friends and relatives. A card such as this will bring reassuring comfort to the child later on, should he or she ever doubt his place in the hearts of the family who chose him.

> *Mr. and Mrs. William Cipriano*
> *are happy to announce*
> *the adoption of*
> *Richard*
> *age, thirteen months*

Or if announcements are sent during the legal proceedings, the wording may be changed:

> *Mr. and Mrs. William Cipriano*
> *are happy to announce*
> *the arrival of*
> *Richard*
> *December fifteenth, 1992*
> *age, two months*

If you choose to use a commercial birth announcement for your adopted child, choose one in which you can easily insert the words *adopted* or *adoption* in the

Every Child Comes with a Message
That God is Not Yet
Discouraged of Man
—TAGORE

Kenneth, Hilari, Jonathan and David Cohen
are proud and happy to announce
the adoption of

a daughter and a sister   a son and a brother
Jessica Susan   *Shawn Michael*
born January 18, 1987   born November 29, 1989

arrived from Chile—December 12, 1992

Adoption announcement

wording, and one appropriate to the child's age. In other words don't select a card with a picture of a stork with a baby in its mouth to announce the arrival of your two-year-old adopted son. Again, if you can design a card appropriate to the situation, that will be the best announcement of all. One of the nicest I've ever seen was this card sent by a family who already had a son and a daughter.

It is not uncommon today for a single person to adopt a child. He or she may send out announcements in the same style as those above, or of course they may write personal notes or design their own cards. If a man selects a formal announcement, he should use his title—Mr. or Dr.—and a woman should use Miss or Ms or her professional title, if applicable.

A Single Woman's Announcement

When a mother and father are divorced before a baby's birth, the mother may, for a variety of reasons, wish to send out announcements. It is still a happy event for her, in spite of her marital situation. She does not, since she is no longer married, use "Mr. and Mrs." She should use whatever name she plans to be known by—probably "Mrs. Mary Johnson." In most cases, however, the new mother would prefer to write personal notes in which she could explain her new status as well as announce the baby's birth.

Women who are widowed during their pregnancy may also wish to send announcements, and they certainly may do so, but a widow should use "Mrs. James Johnson," not "Mr. and Mrs."

There are today some women who have no desire to get married, but wish to give birth to and raise their own child. If this is her choice and she is happy with it, the mother certainly may send announcements. Again, she uses the name and title she goes by ("Miss" or "Ms") if the cards are printed; otherwise she, too, writes personal notes.

Office Announcements

The picture of the puffed-up father strutting around offering cigars to everyone in sight is a thing of the past, but men should announce the happy event the first time they are in their office after the birth. They may, if they happen to smoke cigars themselves, pass a box around, but it is no longer the "expected" thing it used to be. In addition to a man's verbal announcement to his co-workers, his wife should send written announcements to his boss and to those closest to him in the office.

Newspaper Announcement of Birth

In the week following the birth, the parents may send a release to the local newspapers announcing the event: "Mr. and Mrs. Roberto Marino of 202 Parker Avenue, Tuscon, announce the birth of a son, Barry, on July 10, 1992, at Doctors'

Hospital. They have one daughter, Megan, four. Mrs. Marino is the former Miss Theresa Viola." Or: "A daughter, Sharon Lea, was born to Mr. and Mrs. Jason Karp of 19 Maple Avenue, Hillsdale, on February 9 at St. Joseph's Hospital. Mrs. Karp is the former Miss Barbara Rosenfeld of New Haven, Connecticut." The same announcement may be sent to the editor of the church or synagogue newsletter or bulletin.

PRESENTS AND VISITS

Anyone who wishes to send a gift to the baby may do so. It may either be addressed to the parents at home or brought with you if you visit in person. It is thoughtful to bring something for the new mother too. *For gift suggestions, see Chapter 33.*

Since the average stay in the hospital after a normal birth is rarely more than two days, and visiting hours and numbers of visitors are limited in most maternity wards, the majority of people who want to see the new mother and child must wait until they return home. If you do plan to visit in the hospital, call the mother first and find out during which visiting hours she expects to have few, or no, visitors. Later, when she is home, call to find out what time will be most convenient so that you do not interfere with naps, feedings, etc. Friends *should* do the calling first—they should not expect the busy new mother to call all her friends and relatives to say, "We're ready for visitors."

Thanks for Presents

When a baby is on the way—especially a first baby—friends and relatives rally round to help the expectant mother in any way they can, and to cheer her through the tedious months of her pregnancy.

Friends give her showers, mothers who no longer need their bassinet or high chair fix them up and lend them, and others whose pregnancy is past lend maternity clothes.

For these favors no concrete repayment is expected. However, it would be courteous and friendly of the new mother to invite her shower hostess for lunch with one or two friends, or perhaps to take the hostess and her husband out to dinner. A small gift such as a potted plant or a box of homemade cookies would show your appreciation for the baby furniture or the clothes, although a gift is not obligatory. The one requirement is that when you are finished with the maternity clothes they be returned to the lender (if they are still wearable) or passed on to another friend who is pregnant. The one who lent the clothes first may well say, "Keep them or give them away—I wore them until I was sick of the sight of them!" but she *might* be looking toward another pregnancy herself, and she should have the chance to refuse to take them back.

If a friend arrives at the hospital or the house with a gift for the baby, and the mother thanks her warmly at the time, she need *not* then write a note. However, when gifts are sent or delivered when she is not at home, a note—or a phone call to close friends—is in order.

The note may be handwritten, or on a thank-you card with a personal message. It should be signed with the mother's name, *not* the baby's. Everyone knows the baby can't say "Thank you" himself, and cards that say, "Baby . . . thanks you . . . ," are painfully "cute."

CHRISTENINGS AND BAPTISMS

Invitations

Usually, christening invitations are given over the telephone—or to out-of-towners, by personal note.

> *Dear Paula*
> *We are having Arlene christened on Sunday at 3:00 in Christ Church.*
> *Would you and Peter come to the ceremony at the church, and join us afterward*
> *at our house?*
>
> *Love,*
> *Julie Ann*

Or a message may be written on the "Mr. and Mrs." card of the parents, or on an informal, saying simply, "Arlene's christening, St. Mary's Church, Jan. 10, 3 o'clock. Reception at our house afterward." All invitations to a christening should be very friendly and informal.

The Child's Clothes

The baby's christening dress is provided by the parents, not the godparents. It is often one that was worn by the baby's mother, father, or even one of his or her grand- or great-grandparents. Everything the baby wears on this occasion should be white, although this is merely a custom and not a church requirement. The traditional christening dress is long, made of sheer, soft material with lace and hand-embroidery trim, and worn with delicate long petticoats. It is not necessary to go to the expense of buying a traditional christening dress if there is no family heirloom; any long, or even short, plain white dress will do. However, some very pretty christening dresses are available in the new synthetics, which are quite inexpensive.

Older children or even adults who are baptized dress nicely but do not wear white or other special clothing, unless they belong to a denomination that baptizes by total immersion or has those being baptized wear white robes.

Godparents

If your faith requires godparents they should be asked before the day of the christening is set. They may be asked to serve when the baby's arrival is announced to them, and in some cases they are asked even before the birth. It is perfectly correct to send a note if the godparent lives at a distance, or he may be asked by telegram: "It's a boy! Will you be godfather?" And of course an invitation by telephone is equally correct.

One must never ask any but a most intimate friend to be a godparent, for it is a responsibility not to be undertaken lightly and also one difficult to refuse. Godparents are often chosen from among friends rather than relatives, because one advantage of godparents is that they add to the child's stock of "relatives." But when a child is born with plenty of relatives, they are sometimes chosen from among them.

The obligation of being a godparent is essentially a spiritual one, therefore the godparent should be of the same faith as the parents. The godparent is supposed to see that the child is given religious training and is confirmed at the proper time. Beyond these obligations he is expected to take a special interest in the child, much as a very near relative would do. He remembers his godchild with a gift on birthdays and at Christmas until the child is grown—or perhaps longer if they remain close. Godparents who live far away and have lost contact with the child and his or her parents need not continue to give presents after the threads of friendship are broken.

If there are other children in the family, the godparent might choose a gift that could be enjoyed by all of them, but he need not give individual gifts to the others. Each of them has his own godparents to take care of him.

Godparents do not, as is sometimes thought, have any obligations to give financial assistance or to adopt children who lose their parents. This responsibility is the guardian's—not the godparent's. Naturally, since they are—or were—close to the parents, they will offer to help in any way they can, but their actual obligation is spiritual only.

If a godparent is unable to be present, a proxy acts for him or her at the ceremony, the consent of the real godparent having first been given. It is considerate for the real godparent to send a note to the minister authorizing the proxy.

Godparents for Catholic children must be Catholic, according to the rules of the church, and Catholics are not allowed to serve as godparents for children of other faiths. Other denominations do not have these restrictions.

Godparents always give a christening gift to their godchild. (*See page 567 for suggestions.*)

What the Guests Wear

The guests at a christening or baptism wear what they would wear to church. The mother and sponsor or godmother may be given corsages.

The Church Ceremony

The minister is consulted about the hour for the christening before the guests are invited. In most Protestant churches, baptisms are held during the regular church service, or directly after. In many Catholic churches, a special baptism ceremony is arranged, either for just one baby or for many babies being christened together. Customs vary among churches. In some, the godmother holds the baby. In others, which do not require godparents, the father holds the baby. The minister instructs the parents and godparents as to what the ceremony involves, and it is a good idea, as well, to ask for a copy of the ceremony from the service book to practice the responses the participants make.

Baptism is a sacrament of the church for which no fee is ever required. A donation, however, is presented in an envelope to the clergyman after the ceremony, commensurate with the elaborateness of the christening. When the minister is a close friend of the family, a personal gift is often given as thanks—an addition to a collection or hobby he may have, an article of clothing, an accessory for his desk, or something else that shows appreciation for his friendship and participation in the baptism.

A House Christening

If permitted by the church to which the baby's parents belong, the house christening is a most satisfactory ceremony—because a baby whose routine has not been upset by being taken to a strange place at an unusual hour is more apt to be good.

The arrangements for a house christening are quite simple, the only necessary decoration being the font. This is always a bowl—usually of silver—put on a small, high table.

Most people prefer to cover the table in a dark fabric such as old brocade or velvet—a white napkin suggests a restaurant rather than a ritual and is therefore an unfortunate choice. Flowers may be arranged around the bowl in a flat circle.

At the hour set for the ceremony, the clergyman enters the room, the guests form an open aisle, and he takes his place at the font. The godmother, or the father if there are no godparents, carries the baby and follows the clergyman; the other participants walk behind, and they all stand near the font. At the proper moment the clergyman takes the baby, baptizes it, and hands it back to the godmother or father, who holds it until the ceremony is over.

After performing the ceremony the clergyman, if he wears vestments, goes to a room that has been set apart for him, changes into his street clothes, and then returns to the living room as one of the guests.

The Christening Party

Although it is not at all necessary, a reception is often held to celebrate the christening or baptism. This reception varies in elaborateness among different ethnic groups more than among different religions, but my personal feeling is that the simpler the ceremony is, the better it is. When possible, an at-home reception for close family and friends enables the baby to be put to bed for a nap and the parents to relax and enjoy their guests. It may be a brunch directly following the ceremony, or a gathering for christening cake, generally a white cake elaborately iced, and champagne or punch.

Guests eat the cake as a sign that they partake of the baby's hospitality and are therefore his friends, and they drink the punch to his health and prosperity.

Gifts are usually taken to the baby, since those invited are presumably very close to the family. (*See page 567 for gift suggestions.*)

JEWISH CEREMONIES FOR NEWBORNS

A healthy male child is initiated into the Jewish community on the eighth day after birth through the ceremony of circumcision, known as *brith milah* in Hebrew and *brit* in Yiddish. Only if medical considerations warrant may the *brit* be postponed. The circumcision is accompanied by a religious ceremony during which the boy is named. After the ceremony, which generally takes place at home (since few infants are kept at the hospital more than two or three days), there is a joyful meal—often a brunch, as the *brit* is usually held early in the day. If the parents choose to have the *brit* performed before the child comes home from the hospital, they should check the hospital's facilities and policies regarding the use of a room for the *brit*, whether or not refreshments may be served, and the number of guests permitted.

Relatives and close friends are invited to the *brit* by telephone since the time between birth and the ceremony is short. When the *brit* is held in a synagogue, family members and guests dress as they would for a service; tradition requires that all men wear yarmulkes or hats, but the rules of the synagogue, be it Orthodox, Conservative, or Reform, prevail for women. Non-Jewish female guests might check with a member of the baby's family or telephone the synagogue to find out if head coverings are required. If the *brit* is held at home men will wear hats, but custom determines whether or not women will be present for the ceremony and if they do or do not wear a head covering.

Girls are named in the synagogue on the first Sabbath that falls closest to thirty days after birth, when the father is called up to the Torah. The mother may be present, as well as the child. In some Reform congregations boys are also named in the synagogue (in addition to being named at the *brit*) when both parents are present, and a special blessing is pronounced by the rabbi. The mother may be hostess at the reception following the service. Friends and relatives may be invited to attend the religious service during which the baby will be named.

The ceremony of redemption of the firstborn, the *pidyon haben*, which takes place only if the firstborn is a boy, is performed when the baby is thirty-one days old. According to ancient custom described in the Bible, the firstborn son was dedicated to the service of God. It became customary for a *cohen* (a descendant of the priestly tribe) to redeem the child from his obligation, entrusting him to the care of his father for upbringing in the Jewish faith. The *pidyon haben*, consisting of a brief ceremony and a celebration, is held in the home. Informal notes of invitation are sent about ten days beforehand to close friends and relatives.

*T*here are a few special occasions as a child grows and matures that commemorate his or her religious and academic achievement, or simply a "landmark" age. While it certainly is not mandatory that parties be given to mark each of these achievements, some recognition, if just a hug or a personal note, should be given. With the exception of a sixteenth birthday party, each represents commitment and hard work on the part of the young person—surely laudable in a decade where many believe they should simply be *given* what they deserve and that the effort required to *earn* achievement and recognition is hardly worth it.

One note for celebrants invited to religious services of other faiths—while it is not expected that you recite creeds, genuflect or do anything that is contrary to your own faith, it is expected that you rise and sit when others do, and that you follow along and participate in all aspects of the service that are not contrary to your own beliefs.

FIRST COMMUNION

First Communion for a Catholic child takes place when the youngster is six or seven. It is the first occasion on which he actually receives the Host, and is an important event in his religious life. The child goes through a simple course of instruction, to learn both the meaning and the ritual, and his class takes First Communion together.

Although some families celebrate the occasion with elaborate festivities, most, because of the youth of the participants, restrict the celebration to relatives and perhaps a few close friends. These attend the service, and if they are also Catholics, participate in the Mass. The little girls wear white dresses, some with elaborate veils and headpieces, and in other congregations, simpler white costumes. The boys wear dark suits with white shirts and ties.

Usually a small party is held for the young celebrant at the parents' home, or the family may go to his or her favorite restaurant for a dinner party.

Immediate family members give meaningful gifts of a lasting nature.

For Protestant children, First Communion takes place at an older age, usually between 11 and 14, depending on the denomination. Girls generally wear nice dresses and boys shirts and slacks with or without a jacket and tie. Most often, the ceremony is held during a regular church service with the entire congregation participating.

Celebrations are at the discretion of the parents and gifts are given only by immediate family members, if at all. If guests are invited to a Communion party, then a gift is taken. Others may send cards if they wish to recognize this important event in a child's life.

CONFIRMATION

Catholic children are generally confirmed when they are eleven or twelve, Protestants a year or two older. However, if one was not confirmed as a child, it may be done at any age, and there is a special confirmation for those who change their faith.

The candidates for confirmation in all faiths undergo a period of instruction. Those who complete these lessons satisfactorily are confirmed by the church minister, a bishop, or another high church dignitary in the manner of a graduating class. The service, which in the Protestant church is held at a regular Sunday service, and which in the Catholic church is separate from the regular Mass, usually is attended by members of the families and close friends of the young people.

Some churches hold an informal reception after the ceremony, at which the parents and friends may have a chance to meet and chat with the visiting churchman who performed the confirmation.

Afterward the family and a few friends usually gather at the house for lunch, and those who wish to, give the newly confirmed youngster a gift. This is often of a religious nature—a Bible with his or her name engraved on it, a prayer book, a gold cross, a medal, or a charm of a religious nature is an appropriate choice.

Catholic girls wear white dresses and sometimes a short veil. Some Protestant clergymen request that the girls wear white, but most only ask that they wear simple, modest dresses in quiet colors. This is up to the discretion of the minister. In both Protestant and Catholic churches, the boys wear dark-blue or dark-gray suits or jackets and ties with nice slacks.

Confirmation is a religious occasion rather than a social one. It is the moment when the young person himself confirms the vows that were made for him by his godparents at the time of his baptism. It is a thoughtful and serious event and therefore is celebrated joyfully—but with restraint.

BAR MITZVAH

For a Jewish boy the ceremony that compares to the Christian confirmation is the Bar Mitzvah. There is a corresponding ceremony for girls of thirteen in some Conservative and Reform congregations, the Bat Mitzvah. The following paragraphs might apply to either a Bar Mitzvah or a Bat Mitzvah, but the girls' ceremony is not usually so widely celebrated—nor so elaborately—as the boys'. In the Orthodox and Conservative branches, and in some Reform congregations, the Bar Mitzvah takes place on the first Sabbath (Saturday) after the boy becomes thirteen. As in the Christian church, candidates have undergone a period of religious instruction prior to the ceremony. Other Reform congregations have replaced the Bar Mitzvah with a "confirmation" service at which both boys and girls are confirmed, sometimes at an older age than the traditional thirteen. A Jewish boy's Bar Mitzvah or confirmation celebrates his acceptance as an adult member of his congregation.

The Bar Mitzvah differs from the Christian confirmation in that, in addition to being a deeply religious occasion, it is always celebrated socially as well. It is one of the most important events in the boy's life, and the family generally makes every effort to make it as wonderful an occasion as they can. The religious ceremony, which takes place on Saturday morning, may be followed immediately by a gathering in the social rooms of the synagogue. This is open to any member of the congregation who wishes to offer congratulations.

The party—luncheon, dinner, or reception—that follows later in the day usually includes all the close friends of the parents as well as friends and classmates of the boy. Only those who receive invitations may attend.

Invitations may be engraved in third-person style if the party is formal; they may be handwritten notes or they may be telephoned if it is not. Often many more people are invited to the reception than can be accommodated at the synagogue, so the invitation must be quite explicit as to the hour, the place, and the occasion. It must, like other invitations, be acknowledged promptly, and in kind.

For the ceremony, guests wear the clothes that they ordinarily choose for a religious service. And if the party is a luncheon, they go directly to it without changing. If the celebration is later in the day, they change into clothes more appropriate for an evening party. If the affair is formal or "black tie," this should be specified on the invitation. Otherwise the women wear cocktail dresses or long skirts and the men wear dark suits.

Everyone invited to a Bar Mitzvah is expected to send, or take, a gift. (*See page 572 for gift suggestions.*)

The boy must, of course, write thank-you letters promptly for each and every gift.

The reception itself is just like any other. Dinners and luncheons may be sit-down or buffet, and the party may be held at home or in a club, hotel, or restaurant. There may or may not be an orchestra, but if many young people are invited, they will enjoy dancing after the meal is over.

Mr. and Mrs. Stuart Zeitlin
joyfully invite you
to worship with them
at the Bar Mitzvah of their son
Saul David
Saturday, the fifth of December
Nineteen hundred and ninety two
at ten o'clock in the morning
Congregation Ben David
3802 Newbridge Road
North Bellmore, New York

RSVP
2549 Howard Road
East Meadows, New York

Bar Mitzvah invitation

SWEET-SIXTEEN PARTIES

A sixteenth birthday is a big milestone—really the division between childhood and young adulthood. Therefore it is often celebrated more elaborately than other birthdays, with a sweet-sixteen party. Although there is no rule about it, it seems to be a female prerogative, and few boys have sixteenth birthday parties—even under another name.

Sweet-sixteen parties are usually given by the girl's parents, although a grandmother or aunt could certainly do so, and a group of friends—with the parents' approval—often proposes a surprise party.

Invitations may be telephoned, but they are usually written on decorated, fill-in commercial invitations, which can be found, if you wish, specifically for sweet-sixteen parties. They are almost always sent in the girl's name rather than her mother's. For a mixed party a girl may send invitations to all her classmates—boys and girls—or else may send them to the girls only and write on them, "Please bring a date if you want to." If she knows the date's name she sends him an invitation too.

All invitations should have "RSVP" on them, followed by a telephone number. Telephoning a response seems easier to phone-prone youngsters than writing a reply, and this will elicit more and quicker answers.

The party is sometimes held in a club or hall if it is large, but more often it is held at home.

Sweet-sixteen parties may be for girls only, and sometimes take the form of a "slumber" party. When they are mixed they are often, but not necessarily, dances. They *can* be almost anything; a brunch, a hayride, a theater party, a weekend house party, or a swimming-pool party, for example.

Entertainment

While some groups of young people would rather dance than do anything else, others like more variety at their parties. It is as good idea to break up the dancing with some games. Active games like "pool," carpet bowls, and Ping-Pong are fine if you have the facilities, but some "mental" games, like "Trivial Pursuit," are fun too. Charades give youngsters a chance to "ham it up," and there are many others that are good for a laugh. Put out eight or ten dishes of common substances and see how many the blindfolded guests can identify. Or cut out advertising slogans from magazines and have the young people write down what products they think they advertise. Offer some prizes, and you will find that games—alternating with good music—will make the evening fly.

Refreshments

If you are serving a meal—luncheon or dinner—the menu should simply be the favorite food of the birthday girl, although nothing so exotic that it will not appeal to the majority of the guests. But for an after-dinner party a hearty snack should be served about 11:00 P.M. A big tray of hamburgers on rolls, a tasty pasta salad, a stack of waffles, pizzas, or crisp fried-chicken pieces are sure to make a hit. For a noontime brunch a platter of scrambled eggs and sausages, English muffins, and, again, waffles are popular. Teenagers almost all like sweets, so cakes, ice cream, cookies, fruit punch, and all sodas should be available in quantity.

Dress

There is no rule—the dress depends on the type of party. The young hostess can help her guests tremendously by specifying on the invitations, "jacket and tie," "jeans," "long skirts," "slacks," or whatever she wishes.

Gifts

Gifts are expected at a sweet-sixteen party, and they are usually somewhat more elaborate than for other birthdays. Each person who receives an invitation "on his own" should take a present, but when a girl invites a boy to go with her, she selects a gift to be presented from them both.

Look for specific gift suggestions in Chapter 33.

Gifts are opened at the party. If there are just a few guests the packages may be opened as each one is presented, but if it is a big party and lots of people arrive at one time, the gifts are set aside and opened at one time with everyone looking on. The hostess, who thanks each donor as she opens the gift, does not need to write thank-you letters later.

GRADUATION

Invitations and Announcements

Attendance at schools and colleges has grown so fast that the facilities of these institutions cannot handle the crowds of parents and friends who would like to attend the graduation festivities. Years ago graduates could invite their entire families, and often friends too. Today almost every educational institution limits the number of visitors each student may invite—often to no more than four. The invitations are usually provided by the school, but if they are not, the parents or the graduate himself may write them, have them printed, or issue them by telephone. The graduate and his or her family must select the recipients very carefully so that there will be no hurt feelings. If, for instance, both sets of grandparents would like to be included, the ones who receive the invitations must be chosen with great tact. If there are no valid reasons for choosing one over another, names might be drawn out of a hat—perhaps the fairest solution of all. The ones who do not attend the ceremony should be included at any other festivities that take place.

The Class of

Nineteen hundred and ninety-three

of

Consequogue High School

requests the honor of your presence

at its

Graduation Exercises

Sunday afternoon, June twenty-fourth

four o'clock

Main Auditorium

Consequogue High School

Langhorne, Pennsylvania

The restriction on the number of invitations allowed has led many parents to send graduation announcements. This is all right as long as the list is restricted to close family, who would otherwise be invited to the ceremony, and to friends of long standing. These announcements are intended only to spread the good news and *should* carry no obligation at all. But the current rage for giving gifts for every occasion has made announcements appear to be a request for yet another donation. So the list should include only those who would *want* to send presents, or you may write at the bottom, "No gifts, please."

The announcements are generally printed formally, but if the graduate is creative there is no reason why he should not design and make his own. Many young people prefer to do this or to buy informal illustrated cards, feeling that it seems more natural to them and less foreign to their life-style.

When the school distributes announcements, as some do, the graduate's name is written in the appropriate space in black ink. A male graduate uses "Mr." on his card; a girl uses "Ms" or "Miss." A married student uses her married name on the card of announcement, but if she is sending any to schoolmates or to people who do not know she is married, she may add the name by which she is known in parentheses under the married name.

If for any reason a student does not graduate with his class, but must make up a credit or take an exam over, he may not send out his announcements at the time his class graduates, even though they have been printed. He should keep them and may write in a new date and send them when he has met the necessary requirements. Those who complete their courses and "graduate" at midterm or anytime other than the normal end of the school year also send their announcements and celebrate the event then—not the preceding or following June.

Clothing

Clothing varies with the activities planned, of course, but it is much the same as for similar social events elsewhere. Guests are usually sent a program well in advance, either by their son or daughter or by the college, and can determine then what may be needed.

Since most graduations take place in May and June and it is apt to be very warm, mothers and girl friends will look prettiest and be most comfortable in cool summer dresses for the baccalaureate and commencement services. A dress with a matching jacket or sweater is an ideal choice, in case it does turn cold or damp. Naturally, if any of the parties are formal, the men attending must wear tuxedos, and the women long dresses or evening pants costumes.

Hats are not required at either the baccalaureate service or commencement, but if you wish to wear one it is perfectly correct. Since those behind you will want to have a clear view of the proceedings, you should either choose a close-fitting hat or remove it as you would in the theater.

Presents

Graduation presents are unlimited in variety, but the closer the giver is to the graduate, the more elaborate the gift. Parents may give a fine watch, jewelry, an automobile, or even a trip to Europe. If these gifts are beyond their means, anything that is lasting and of the best quality that they can afford is always appreciated. A nicely bound book on a favorite subject, for instance, or a good pen-and-pencil set can be a source of much pleasure.

Although it is not obligatory it is a very nice gesture for parents of a graduating senior to have small gifts for his or her roommate and closest friends.

(For other specific gift suggestions, see Chapter 33 which begins on page 561.)

Thank-You Notes

A note of thanks, written by hand, must go to everyone who has not been at the commencement but who has sent a gift. This note need not be long, but it should express appreciation and be written as promptly as possible.

Dear Aunt Annamarie,

I can't thank you enough for the check you sent me, which will be such a help toward my summer in Europe. I'm looking forward to seeing you in the fall to tell you all about the trip.

With much love,
Claudia

OR:

Dear Uncle Carlos,

Thank you so much for the pen-and-pencil set. Mother must have tipped you off that I really needed them! I was disappointed that you couldn't make the graduation, but I'll drive down to see you and thank you in person as soon as possible.

Thanks again,
Antonio

Graduation Parties

Private parties are frequently held to celebrate high-school graduations, but rarely for college graduations. Occasionally a young man or woman's family will give a small dinner or a reception when he or she receives a graduate degree, but in most cases the graduation gift is the only special acknowledgement of the occasion. This section, therefore, is primarily devoted to high-school graduation celebrations.

Invitations should be sent out at least three weeks ahead if you wish to be sure that your particular friends will be there. Several other members of the class may be planning parties, too, and some may have selected the same night you have. If your class is not too large it is wise to try to talk to other seniors and coordinate your plans so that not everyone chooses graduation night, or the following Saturday, for the parties.

The lively illustrated invitations available at all stationers are ideal for the occasion, since very few of these parties are "formal." Write at the top, "In honor of Sue's graduation," because your parents—rather than you—give the party. You may write "R.s.v.p." at the bottom, followed by a telephone number, or you may prefer to write "Regrets only." Either of these impose easier or fewer obligations on your friends than "R.s.v.p." followed by an address. If your party is to be catered, so that you must know the number of guests coming, and you know that people in your group are slow to reply, you may enclose a response card.

There are very few "rules" about graduation parties—your party should be whatever you and your friends enjoy most. It may be a dance at home or in a club or hall, it may be a dinner party at home or in a restaurant, or it may be an after-dinner party, a barbecue, or a picnic. Your guest list may be made up mostly of relatives if you have a large, close-knit family, or it may be all your classmates and only enough adults to organize the party and help with the food, drinks, etc.

It may be held on graduation night, or anytime thereafter, but it should *not* be held before you have received word that you are to graduate. If you are having many adults, choose a Friday or Saturday night, so that they will not have to go home too early in order to be ready for work the next day.

Although relatives would undoubtedly bring gifts to a small, intimate party, guests at a big celebration should not be expected to bring presents. If a few do, the boxes should be unwrapped somewhat privately with only the donors present, so that other guests will not feel that they were remiss in not giving a gift too. Or the presents may be set aside and opened after the party, for the same reason. If everyone brings gifts they should all be opened at one time with the guests sitting around and watching.

Whatever type of party you plan, you and your parents should stand near the door and greet the guests. This is not a formal receiving line, but the party is in your honor, and the guest of honor, whatever the person's age, should be standing where the arrivals can greet and congratulate him or her.

If the party is a seated family dinner, and if the graduate is a girl, she sits on her father's right; a boy would sit on his mother's right—the places "of honor." As guest of honor you may choose who sits on your other side, and where the other guests sit. If, at a larger party, there are a number of small tables, you should feel free to choose the people you want to sit with you. You may want your parents there, or you may prefer to sit with a group of your best friends.

Otherwise graduation parties are just like all others, and they are generally great successes because the occasion is such a happy one.

ANNIVERSARY PARTIES

Anniversary parties may be given in honor of any anniversary, but the first, fifth, tenth, twenty-fifth, and fiftieth are those most generally celebrated. The parties given for the first three are usually informal, not distinguishable from any other reception except that there would be toasts to the bride and groom, and close friends would bring gifts. The twenty-fifth and fiftieth anniversaries, however, are given much more importance, and certain customs—almost rituals—are followed. Therefore this chapter will deal principally with the latter two.

When it is convenient the party should be given on the actual date of the anniversary. But should the couple prefer to have it on a Saturday night, for example, it is perfectly all right to move it forward or back a few days. If the husband or wife is ill or absent at the time, an anniversary may be celebrated several weeks after the true date. When the illness or the absence is prolonged, it is preferable to celebrate the anniversary the following year. There is no rule that says one must recognize the twenty-fifth rather than the twenty-sixth.

Who Gives the Party?

Early anniversary parties are always given by the couple themselves. By the time they reach the twenty-fifth they may well have grown children who wish to make the arrangements, but it is perfectly correct for them to do so themselves if the young people do not or cannot. When a couple do not have children close friends sometimes prepare the celebration. Fiftieth-anniversary celebrations are almost invariably planned by the family of the couple.

Invitations

The form of the invitations depends entirely on the degree of formality of the party. They may range from an informal telephone call to an engraved "third-person" invitation. In between lie the most common forms—handwritten notes, or the necessary information written on an informal or a fill-in card. Formal invitations for a twenty-fifth anniversary are often bordered and printed in silver; those for a fiftieth, in gold.

The following are some sample invitations.

When the couple are giving the party themselves:

1970–1995
Mr. and Mrs. Harvey Langdon
request the pleasure of your company
at a reception
in honor of
their silver wedding anniversary
on Saturday, the eighth of December
at eight o'clock
Barrymore Country Club

R.s.v.p.
12 Corning Road

On an informal (name engraved):

```
┌─────────────────────────────────────────┐
│                                          │
│           1970 – 1995                    │
│                                          │
│        Mr. and Mrs. George Blinn         │
│         Cocktail Buffet                  │
│       March 10 at 6 P. m.                │
│       120 Harbor Road.                   │
│                                          │
│    R. s. v. p.                           │
│                                          │
└─────────────────────────────────────────┘
```

When the children of the couple give the party:

Dear Anne [or Mrs. Franklin],

Will you and Joe [or Mr. Franklin] join us for dinner at the Rosemont Club on Saturday, May 4, at 7:00 P.M., to help us celebrate Mom and Dad's twenty-fifth anniversary? Hoping to see you then,

> *Helen and Bill*
> *[or Helen and Bill Porter]*

Or if they have a card printed:

In honor of the
fiftieth wedding anniversary of
Mr. and Mrs. Henry Muller, Sr.
Their Son and Daughter
request the pleasure of your company
for cocktails and dinner
on Tuesday, the fourth of July
at seven-thirty o'clock
10 Glenwood Road

R.s.v.p.

Planning the Party

The party may be held in the home of the couple, in the home of the person planning the party, in a church parish house, or in a room of a hotel, restaurant, or club.

If the party is a dinner or a small reception, the guests are primarily family, members of the wedding party, and closest friends. If it is to be a large reception or an open house, the list may include business acquaintances, church and club members, and in very small communities—everyone in town.

Refreshments

The refreshments depend on the type of party being given. If it is a meal—a luncheon or a dinner—the hostess simply chooses whatever menu she thinks will please the couple and the guests most. Since the later anniversaries attempt to recreate the wedding day to some extent, the food might be the same as that served at the original wedding reception.

If the party is a cocktail party, hors d'oeuvres are served, and a wedding cake may be cut and passed with a round of champagne for toasting the couple before the guests leave.

At an afternoon reception or an open house, the menu varies according to the formality of the party and the pocketbook of the host and the hostess. The refreshments may consist of sandwiches, snacks, and punch, or a complete buffet—cold ham, turkey, sliced fillet of beef, and chafing dishes filled with hot snacks or hors d'oeuvres. Whatever the other food, as close a replica of the couple's wedding cake as can be made is often a feature of the menu.

Drinks may range from tea and coffee at an afternoon reception to wine, champagne, or mixed drinks at an evening affair. Soft drinks should always be available for those who prefer them. Punch made with or without liquor is often

1944 — 1994

The Children of

Joan and John Forrest

request the honor of your presence

at the

Fiftieth Anniversary

of the marriage of their parents

on Saturday, the twenty eighth of August

nineteen hundred and ninety-four

at eight o'clock

Dinner and Dancing

Mandarin Oriental Hotel

San Francisco, California

served at open houses and other daytime parties. When the family does not object to alcoholic beverages a glass of champagne is the traditional drink for toasts—at any hour of the afternoon or evening. Otherwise the toasts may be made with punch or whatever drinks are available.

Decorations

Decorations need not be elaborate, but the twenty-fifth anniversary party should feature white and silver ornaments and flowers, and the fiftieth, gold (or yellow) and white. Flowers make the loveliest decoration of all, and the "bride" should always be presented with a corsage.

Music

There need not be any entertainment, but a strolling musician adds a touch of romance, and he or she can be asked to play the couple's favorite tunes, wedding music, etc. If the host and hostess wish to hire an orchestra or provide records, dancing will be all the entertainment necessary.

The Receiving Line

One of the distinguishing features of an anniversary party is the receiving line. Except for a somewhat elderly couple celebrating their fiftieth, the couple stand near the door and greet the guests. Their children may join them in the line, and if the party is given by someone else, that person always heads the line as hostess.

Older couples who tire easily, or who may not be well, may be seated in a central spot—in front of a fireplace, for example. The guests, after greeting the hostess near the door, move on to find the honored pair and offer their congratulations.

The Main Table

The table should be as much like the bridal table at the couple's wedding reception as possible. The "bride and groom" sit together at the center of a long table or in the places facing the guests if the table is a round one. The bridesmaids and ushers, if any are present, are seated next to them; their husbands or wives are also included at the table. The couple's children are seated with them, the oldest son on the "bride's" right and the oldest daughter on the "groom's" left. Their husbands and wives, their older children, and brothers and sisters of the couple are arranged in whatever way they will enjoy most.

When the party is given by a married son or daughter of the anniversary couple, the host and hostess sit at either end of the table, or at a round table, opposite

the "bride and groom." But the couple always sit together rather than having the
"bride" sit on the host's right and the "groom" on the hostess's right as would other guests of honor.

The table is decorated with white flowers, or for a fiftieth anniversary, gold or yellow flowers. If there is room the wedding cake may be in the center of the table, but if it is large it is more convenient to place it on a side table.

Pictures

Because the event is such a memorable one, all anniversary couples enjoy having candid pictures made of their party. They are generally taken by one of the guests, although a professional photographer may be hired. These pictures, put into an album, make an ideal present for the couple, either for the anniversary itself or for the next Christmas. A picture of the whole family, including children and grand-children, also makes a perfect anniversary gift.

Gifts

For specific gift suggestions and a chart listing anniversary gifts, see Chapter 33.

Opening Gifts

When gifts are brought to the anniversary couple—as they should be, if "no gifts, please" was not written on the invitations—the opening of the packages is a feature of the party. After everyone has arrived, or perhaps after dinner while the guests are enjoying their coffee, everyone gathers around, and the couple open the gifts and thank the donors. One of their children, or anyone they choose to designate, helps by taking care of the wrappings, making a list, collecting the ribbons, etc. The couple do not need to write notes later to those they have already thanked, unless they wish to do so.

Older Couples

Some couples who are celebrating their fiftieth anniversaries are so elderly or infirm that they must be given special consideration. If they are given a party, they should not be asked to stand to greet their guests, but should be seated in a central spot where people can pass by comfortably to offer congratulations. In most cases it is best to plan to have the celebration in their home, or perhaps in the home of one of their children, rather than in a restaurant or hall.

Don't plan a surprise party unless you know that the shock or surprise will not be too much for the couple's health.

If the couple is not up to any party at all, a lovely thing to do is to arrange a card shower. A daughter or son sends out cards saying that the parents' anniversary will be celebrated by a card shower, and would the "guest" attend by sending a card. No other gift is expected, but the couple will be delighted with the messages of love and congratulations carried in the cards.

Some couples who marry late in life may feel that they will never reach their golden anniversary and ask whether they may have a big celebration on their thirty-fifth or fortieth. Of course they may! There is nothing "magical" about the fiftieth, and a couple may celebrate any anniversary they choose to. It is tradition only that makes the fiftieth the "big" one.

Widows and Widowers

The nicest thing you can do for people who are recently bereaved, if you live close enough, is to take them out to dinner, or have them to your home that day. This will give them something to look forward to and keep them from being lonely and sad.

For those farther away, to whom you have always sent a card, write a letter instead or send a friendship card, not a congratulatory type. You need not mention the bereavement or the anniversary other than to say, "We want you to know we are thinking of you today."

When one member of a couple is ill, or perhaps in a nursing home, the other will not feel like celebrating alone. But family and friends can make it a special occasion in the same way mentioned above—by taking him or her out to dinner, or having a few close friends for dinner in their home.

When There Has Been A Remarriage

Couples who divorce and subsequently remarry each other celebrate the anniversary of their *first* marriage, counting their twenty-fifth as twenty-five years from that date and forgetting the intervening years of separation.

REAFFIRMATION OF MARRIAGE VOWS

Some couples want to reaffirm their marriage vows on their twenty-fifth or fiftieth anniversaries. They may have—insofar as it is feasible—a duplicate of their wedding service if their church or synagogue and minister or rabbi agree. Many will not perform a "second" wedding ceremony but most will conduct a simple reaffirmation of vows.

In either case, as many members as possible of the original wedding party gather for the service. If it is permitted that a formal ceremony be held, then the best man and maid of honor are present, if possible, and they stand with the couple. If there are children from the marriage, they sometimes stand with the couple as well.

The "bride" should not wear her wedding dress, nor should the couple and attendants walk up the aisle. Women guests wear dresses appropriate to the hour of the day, and men wear business suits in the daytime and either suits or tuxedos, whichever is indicated, in the evening.

After the service, everyone may be invited to the couple's home for a reception, and a replica of the wedding cake may be served as dessert, or with coffee and champagne. Toasts by members of the "wedding party" and the couple's children are in order.

HOUSEWARMINGS

When you have put a great deal of time and effort into making a lovely home you are naturally as eager to show it off as your friends are to see it. The nicest way to do so is to call your friends and ask them to a housewarming. Or you may invite them informally whenever you want. Invitations on informals or commercial fill-in cards are suitable too. Because the object of the party is to show your guests the house, it isn't a bad idea to have two or three small parties at which you will have to give the tour only a few times. If you have too many people at once, you may spend the entire time leading groups from one room to another.

A housewarming is generally a cocktail party or a cocktail buffet. It may be as simple or as elaborate as you wish, but it is fun to keep the style of your house in mind when you plan your decorations. For instance, if it is an Early American type, a brown tablecloth set with copper or pewter may be more appealing than lace with crystal or silver.

(*For gift suggestions, see page 572.*)

FAREWELL PARTIES

Farewell or "going-away" parties are like any others in most ways, but there are one or two things to be remembered when the move is permanent. First, the guests of honor cannot be expected to reciprocate by giving a party and inviting those who have entertained them. Therefore, more than in other cases, they should do more than say "Thank you," and should show their appreciation by sending flowers or a small gift to their hostess.

If you are planning a party for someone who is leaving town for good, coordinate your efforts with other friends. I know a popular couple who moved away from my hometown recently, and there were *thirteen* parties held for them! By the time the departure date arrived, their exhausted friends could hardly wait for them to go! So if you find that your friends are being overly feted, plan something different—take them to the theater, or a hockey game, or whatever they will miss most in their new locale.

While friends are expected to take farewell gifts to one party, they should not be obligated to take gifts to several. This

31
Special
Celebrations

should be made very clear on the invitations. (*For gift suggestions, see page 568.*)

RETIREMENT PARTIES

Retirements are recognized in a variety of ways, usually by the company or organization from which an individual is retiring. When the recognition is formal, it is celebrated at a luncheon or dinner party with the retiree's immediate family members invited to join people from the department or company. Although these parties may take place in the company dining room or auditorium, most usually they are held in the private room of an outside restaurant or a club. Other guests may include those who are involved in the professional life of the retiree.

Sometimes the retirement of a particularly prominent person takes the form of a roast, with speakers called upon to comment on the career of the retiree, generally with a great dash of humor thrown in, as well as remarks of sincere appreciation and recognition by the department head, company president, or even the chairman of the board.

Other organizations, particularly publicly supported, volunteer and service groups, recognize retirements at their annual meeting, or at a regular meeting where a portion of the agenda is set aside to honor the retiree. There are no refreshments, but the accomplishments of the retiree are noted and applause and thanks are extended to the person or people being honored.

Retirement parties rarely are given by other than professional associates, the people most involved in the retiree's work life.

(*For retirement gift suggestions, see page 571. For toasts appropriate for a retiree, see page 485.*)

ADULT BIRTHDAY PARTIES

Spouses, children, and sometimes close friends may want to celebrate a "big" birthday, such as the 30th, 40th, 50th, etc. of the birthday person.

There are virtually no limits on the kind of celebration this may be, from a barbecue or picnic to a formal dinner dance at a club or restaurant. The only real requirement is that at some point during the party, the host or hostess ask for the attention of the assembled guests and offer a toast to the birthday person. Often guests wish to make their own toasts, read a poem or verse prepared especially for the guest of honor, or make a speech about the birthday person.

Invitations may be printed, fill-in, or even telephone calls, depending on the formality of the event. Because it is a birthday party, it is assumed that gifts are to be taken, unless the invitation indicates "no gifts please."

Unlike a children's birthday party where the gifts are usually opened during the party, the guest of honor may elect to open them after, depending on the formality of the occasion and the other activities occurring. For example, at a dinner dance at a club, there is little opportunity for guests to gather around and watch the birthday person open his or her gifts, while at a family backyard barbecue, the opening of gifts would be a part of the planned activities for the celebration.

On the subject of gifts, it should be said that the most frequent awkwardness about gift-giving to an adult at his or her birthday party has to do with the type of gift to give—a "real" gift, or a "gag" gift. It can be embarrassing when gifts are opened and yours is the only "over the hill" present among luxury items given by everyone else. If you are not certain which direction to take, call the host and ask. If the host is the spouse or a child of the birthday person, they will be hesitant to direct you and are likely to say, "Oh, don't bring a gift!" rather than, "Yes, people are bringing nice presents, not gag gifts." If this is the case, ask if you may have the names of one or two others invited to the party so that you can check with them instead.

CHILDREN'S BIRTHDAY PARTIES

A friend who herself is childless recently took on the charge of planning and running her young niece's fifth birthday party. She had elaborate decorations, hired a clown/magician to entertain the children, planned a wonderful lunch and ordered a spectacular birthday cake. It took her hours, but everything was, to her thinking, perfect. Soon it was time for the children to be picked up by their parents. They seemed reluctant to leave, and she was congratulating herself on a job well done when one of the children, by now impatient, approached her and asked, "Where's my party bag?"

Not having a clue as to what a party bag was but knowing that somehow she had made an error, she was beside herself because of this oversight.

The point of this illustration is that customs vary from community to community, and before launching into an elaborate party for a small child, it may be wise to call a seasoned children's birthday party-giver (another parent) and ask about local expectations. The very worst custom in some communities is parental competition over their children's birthday parties. If Janie has a pony, Tammy has two ponies. If Sam has a children's ferris wheel, Andrew rents a mini amusement park. The truth of the matter is that children simply enjoy being together, and the younger they are, the less formal the entertainment they need.

Aside from games, themes, and other entertainment, the menu is an important consideration as is the opening of gifts.

Some parents do not let their children open their gifts until everyone has gone home, partly because they want to keep all duplicates intact so they can return or exchange them. I believe that children should open their gifts in front of their friends, for several reasons. First, it is one of the moments of the party where they are in the limelight. Second, other children are often excited about the gift they are giving and are anxious to see him or her open it and express pleasure. Third, it is an opportunity for children to use their best manners and they can be told ahead of time how to handle the duplicate gift or the peculiar one.

And finally, when the gift is opened and the donor thanked personally at the time of the opening, a thank-you note needn't be written. Children, with few exceptions, are less than enthusiastic about writing thank-yous, and if the presents are piled up and set aside to be opened later, the birthday child must then write a personal note, mentioning the gift by name, to every donor.

Surprise Parties

Since surprise parties can take countless forms, in honor of birthdays, new babies, anniversaries, etc., all that need be said about them is that you must be *sure* the guest of honor would absolutely love to have you do this, and that you have a fail safe plan to get him or her to the party.

Otherwise, surprise parties take the form of any other kind of party mentioned in these chapters.

*I*t is sometimes said that the purpose of all the details one must attend to when a family member dies is to give the grieving person a focus and a direction when he or she is otherwise incapable of doing anything but mourning. That may well be, for there are indeed many details to attend to.

The Death Certificate

The death certificate is filled out and signed by the physician in attendance at the time of death. If the death was sudden or caused by an accident, or if for any other reason there was no doctor in attendance, he or she should be called anyway. The doctor will either come to the house, if the death occurred at home, or will call the county medical examiner or coroner. Either will ascertain the cause of death and sign the certificate. This must be done immediately because no other steps can be taken until the death certificate is properly signed.

Organ Donations

If the deceased has signed an organ donation permission form, or has indicated that he or she would want his or her organs donated, the doctor or funeral director should be so notified immediately or the telephone number on the organ donation card that the deceased signed should be called. If the situation is such that the body must be delivered to a hospital right away so that organs may be removed for transplants, this and the return of the body to the funeral home is coordinated by the funeral director.

Notifying Family and Close Friends

Family members and close friends of the deceased or of the family must be notified as soon as possible, by telephone. Each person called may be asked to call another family member. For example, a close cousin may be called and asked to notify his brothers and sisters. If funeral arrangements are known, it is helpful to share them at the time the calls are made to preclude the need of making a second round of calls to pass on this information.

32

At Times of Loss and Grieving

The Funeral Director and the Clergy

The next most immediate matter is that of contacting a funeral home and a minister or rabbi. If the deceased person or his or her family belonged or belongs to a church or synagogue, the family may call the office for information about funeral directors in the area and the clergyman will recommend one who will suit their needs. The family doctor can also provide this information.

The funeral director will go to the hospital or come to the house as soon as possible after he is called and remove the body to the funeral home. Whoever is in charge for the family discusses all the arrangements with him at that time, telling him how simple or elaborate a funeral the relatives wish and how the details that the funeral director will enumerate are to be handled. The type of casket must be chosen as well as any floral arrangements for the casket. If the service is to be held at the funeral home or in the home of the deceased, the day and hour must be settled. If it is to be held in a church or synagogue, the minister or rabbi must be consulted immediately to fix the time. If the family is not affiliated with a place of worship, the funeral director or a friend can recommend a clergyman or woman of any faith the family chooses to perform the service.

A note should be added that although most funeral directors are reputable and sympathetic, there are some who prey on the emotions of the survivors by implying that a disservice is being done to the deceased if anything less than the most expensive casket is purchased, if anything fewer than several cars are hired to be part of the cortege, etc. It is wise to have a clear-headed friend of the family in attendance to be sure such decisions are not made on an emotional basis that result in purchases well beyond the financial means of the survivors.

The choice of burial or cremation has hopefully been made by the deceased while living and shared with the family or minister. In fact, although difficult for many people, a great service is done for those who eventually survive us if we take a few minutes and write personal preferences and instructions in the event of our deaths. These instructions should include our wishes for the disposition of our bodies or ashes and such things as the kind of funeral service we would prefer, hymns and verses we would wish to have be a part of the service, etc. Knowing the wishes of the deceased is a great relief and aid to those who are otherwise uncertain as to what decisions to make.

If the deceased is to be buried or his or her remains put in a mausoleum, but the family has not pre-purchased a grave site or mausoleum space, the funeral director will make these arrangements with the cemetery of the family's choosing.

If the deceased is to be cremated, the disposition of his or her ashes, after the funeral service, can be taken care of by the funeral director, or the ashes are given to the family for disposition.

Clothing for Burial

The person who has been put in charge of arrangements, with the help of someone who may know of the deceased's special preferences or a favorite piece of suitable clothing, delivers the clothes to the funeral director, who will specify what clothing is needed. Members of some faiths, Orthodox Jews among them, still prefer to bury their dead in shrouds, but most religions have no restrictions on clothing for a burial. Dresses should be in solid, subdued colors, of a style that might be worn to church. Young girls are usually buried in white, and children in their Sunday-school clothes. Men are also dressed as for church; generally the family chooses a dark suit. Wedding rings are usually left on, but other jewelry is removed.

For Jewish funerals, the body is washed and dressed in white linen grave clothes which symbolize purity and dignity. These clothes are available from the burial society of the synagogue or from the funeral director. A prayer shawl is then placed over the shroud of a man. All jewelry except for a wedding ring is removed.

Notifying an Attorney

The next step is to notify an attorney, preferably the one who drew up the will of the deceased. If neither that person nor anyone in the firm is available, or if there is no known will, then any other attorney who is reputable may be called.

Newspaper Notices

There are two kinds of newspaper notices: a paid notice, arranged by the funeral director, and an obituary, written by a newspaper staff member. In the case of the former, a family member or spokesperson should discuss with the funeral director what should be included. For example, the tendency to write "devoted sister" or "beloved father" may not represent the wishes of the family, and this should be stated. The notices usually contain the date of death, names of the immediate family, hours and location where friends may call on the family, place and time of the funeral, and frequently a request that a contribution be given to a charity instead of flowers being sent to the funeral.

A man's notice might read:

MILLER—*Paul B., on December 17, 1992. Beloved husband of the late Mary Stuart Miller. [Devoted] father of Catherine Miller Sutphen, Frederick and John Miller. Friends may call at 636 Jones Rd., Englewood, N.J., on Friday, December 19, 2–5. Funeral service Saturday, December 20, 11:30 A.M., Christ's Church, Englewood.*

The word *suddenly* is sometimes inserted immediately after the deceased's name to indicate that there had not been a long illness, or that the death was by accident.

Instead of "Friends may call at [private address]" the phrase "Reposing at the Memorial Funeral Home" is commonly used.

A woman's notice always includes her given and maiden name for purposes of identification. The same is true when married daughters and sisters are mentioned.

> Harris—*Sarah Gerb, on May 13. [Beloved] wife of Isaac, loving mother of Rebecca, Jonathan, and Samuel, [devoted] sister of Anna Gerb Gold and Paul Gerb. Services Thursday, May 14, 2 P.M., at Star Funeral Home, 41 Chestnut St., Pittsburgh. In lieu of flowers, please send contributions to the United Jewish Appeal, or your favorite charity.*

The deceased's age is not generally included unless he or she is very young, or the age is needed to establish further identification. It is usually added after the names of young children.

Daughters of the deceased are listed before sons, and their married names are used.

Occasionally the notice reads "Funeral private," and neither time nor place is given. Very intimate friends are given this information, either by telephone or on the personal card of the relative or friend in charge:

> *"Sam's funeral will be at Christ Church, Monday at eleven o'clock."*

Others are not expected to attend.

An obituary is telephoned, sent by FAX, or delivered to the newspaper. It may be written by a family member and submitted, although it is the option of the newspaper as to whether or not it is printed. Generally, a reporter calls a family member or representative to verify facts.

"In Lieu of Flowers"

When "in lieu of flowers" or "family and friends are making contributions to . . ." appears in the death notice, everyone except a most intimate friend or relative is expected to follow the suggestion, if they would have otherwise sent flowers.

The family has it put in because they honestly feel the contribution will help them to feel that some good has come from their loss, and thus they are comforted. A check is sent to the charity with a note saying, "This donation is sent in loving memory of Mrs. Roy Haskell, of 10 Park Place, Mount Vernon." If the family members who should receive an acknowledgment did not live with the deceased, mention the name and address to which the acknowledgment should be sent: "Please send the acknowledgment to Mrs. Haskell's daughter, Marie Zimmerli, at 400 West Broadway, Port Station, NY." The address of the sender should also appear on the note. The charity sends an acknowledgment, which serves to let the donor know the contribution has been received, and is also for use in claiming a tax deduction. The charity also sends a notice of the contribution to the family of the deceased. The charity's acknowledgment to the sender *in no way* takes the place of a thank-you note from the bereaved family—one of whom must write in person to express their appreciation.

Occasionally a notice reads, "Please send a contribution to your favorite charity." You are free to choose whichever one you wish, but it is thoughtful to select one that might also mean something to the bereaved family.

When you write a condolence note to a bereaved person or family you may, if you wish, mention that you have sent a contribution as they requested. This will ensure that they know of it in case the charity is lax in sending notices to the family or an error has been made.

The amount of the contribution is, of course, up to you. However, you should *not* give less than you would have paid for a flower arrangement, and in view of the tax deduction you should really give more.

If no "in lieu of" appears in the notice, you should send flowers, since it indicates that the particular family feels they would derive the most comfort from the beauty of the flowers, and this is surely their prerogative.

Although people may not want a mass of flowers at the funeral, a lovely plant or flower arrangement may always be sent to the family a few days after the burial as an indication of your continuing sympathy and love. Sometimes friends do this instead of funeral flowers or contributions; others do it in addition to one or the other. Cards accompanying these flowers or plants should not mention the recent loss, but may simply say, "With love from us all."

Gifts of cash should never be sent directly to the family in place of flowers or a charitable contribution. However, a group—fellow employees, club or lodge members, or just neighbors—may take up a collection for a bereaved person who is in financial difficulty. This is a generous gesture and can be a great help in defraying funeral expenses.

Sending and Receiving Flowers

If there is a notice in the papers requesting that no flowers be sent, you send none. Otherwise they are addressed to "The funeral of Mr. James Snow," either at the funeral home or at the church. When you did not know the deceased, but only his close relatives, flowers may be sent to them at their home. An enclosed card, on which you write, "With deepest sympathy," or if appropriate, "With love and sympathy," is addressed to "The family of Mr. James Snow," or to the one you know best.

If you hear of the death sometime later, you may still send flowers to the family of the deceased at their home. In fact, these flowers, arriving after the confusion and misery of the first days, are often appreciated more than those which arrive promptly.

To avoid confusion, whoever is making the arrangements for the family should appoint one person to take charge of flowers, and he or she must carefully collect all the accompanying cards that are sent to the house or funeral home. This person writes a description of the flowers that came with the card on the outside of each envelope if this has not been done by the florist or the funeral director. The cards are delivered to the bereaved family after the funeral. For example:

Large spray of Easter lilies and greens
Laurel wreath with gardenias
Long sheaf of white roses—broad silver ribbon

Without such notations the family has no way of knowing anything about the flowers that people have sent. Moreover, these descriptions are invaluable when writing notes of thanks.

If some friends have sent potted plants or cut flowers to the house, their cards are also removed and noted for later acknowledgment.

Acknowledgment of Sympathy

When impersonal messages of condolence mount into the hundreds, as may be the case when a public figure or perhaps a prominent business executive or a member of his family dies, the sending of engraved or printed cards to strangers is proper:

The Governor and Mrs. State
wish gratefully to acknowledge
your kind expression of sympathy

OR:

The family of
Harrison L. Winthrop
wish to thank you for
your kind expression of sympathy

If such cards are used, a handwritten word or two and a signature must be added below the printed message *when there is any personal acquaintance with the recipient.* In no circumstances should such cards be sent to those who have sent flowers or to intimate friends who have written personal letters.

Perhaps as the result of the use of cards in these rare but permissible cases, a most unfortunate practice has sprung up. Some funeral directors supply printed cards, and the mourner feels that he need only sign his or her name to them. This is a poor return, indeed, for beautiful flowers or even a sincere and comforting note. The bereaved may use these cards, but he or she *must* add a brief personal note below the printed message.

A personal message on a fold-over card is preferable to any printed card, and it takes but a moment to write "Thank you for your beautiful flowers" or "Thank you for all your kindness."

If the list is very long, or if the person who has received the flowers and messages is really unable to perform the task of writing, some member of the family or a near friend may write for her or him: "Mother asks me to thank you for your beautiful flowers and kind message of sympathy." No one expects more than a short message of acknowledgment, but that message should be *personal* and written by hand!

Acknowledgments should be written for all *personal* condolences, for flowers, for Mass cards, for contributions, and for special kindnesses. They need *not* be made for printed condolence cards with no personal message added, or for calls at the funeral home.

Letters must also be written to the honorary pallbearers and those who may have served as ushers.

The Gravestone

When a person is buried in a cemetery, a marker is put in place until a gravestone can be ordered. The ordering of the stone can be done directly with a gravestone company, or it can be arranged through the funeral director or the cemetery office.

For most of us the gravestone we choose for our loved one is the only permanent memorial that will exist. Therefore, it, and the inscription on it, should be chosen with great care. The worst mistake one can make is to rush into ordering an ornate stone with sentimental carvings and a flowery inscription, which may later seem in poor taste or objectionable. For example, one might wish in the emotion of the moment to write something about the deceased being "the only love" or "the greatest love" of the spouse. This could conceivably cause considerable anguish to a future husband or wife.

The wisest course is to choose as handsome and appropriate a stone as one can, and refrain from ordering terribly ornate decorations. Almost invariably, the simplest constructions—be they monuments, buildings, or any work of art—are those which endure and continue to please forever. The inscription, too, should be simple and sincere. "Beloved husband of Jessica" expresses true devotion without excluding other members of a present, or future, family. Titles are not used for either men or women, with some exceptions. A man who spent his life at sea might wish to have "Captain Ahab Marner" on his stone, and the names of men of high military rank or on active service are generally preceded by their titles.

The relationship of wife and husband is usually included, although not necessarily. Today, no other legend or information usually appears, and perhaps it is too bad. Years ago, most interesting poems and inscriptions were written for loved ones. My particular favorites are three gravestones in New England. The center is

inscribed (let us say) "Captain Cyrus Miller." Next to him lie the remains of
"Elizabeth, his wife." And on the stone on his other side the legend reads, "Sarah, who should have been!"

Today, however, a typical inscription reads

1900–1995
Helen Jones Schaeffer
beloved wife of
John Simon Schaeffer

Whatever you choose, remember that you must consider the feelings of the living. While a memorial is, in part, a solace to the bereaved, it is something that will be seen and shared with others. Surely the one who has died would not want a memorial that could ever be anything but an honor to him and a pleasure to those he leaves behind.

In cemeteries where it is permitted, some people plant a veritable flower garden around a grave. Others prefer to have only grass and to bring fresh flowers or potted plants regularly as an evidence of their continuing love. This can become quite a chore, however, as the first grief diminishes, because garden flowers need constant care or they become a straggling weed patch in short order. A very satisfactory solution is that of using evergreen shrubs and ground cover, which look beautiful all year round with little attention.

Many cemeteries offer a maintenance contract for the appearance of graves for which they bill an annual fee. Before signing such a contract, be sure to observe the way other graves are maintained.

Other Memorials

Many bereaved families wish to make a material gesture to honor their dead. For the very wealthy this may take many forms, from the building of a monument to the donation of a piece of equipment to the hospital that cared for the deceased. This type of memorial does not need a great deal of discussion in this book, because its very nature requires that it be considered carefully, and because time will be required for extensive planning before it can be done. The advice of other people will be involved, and that will put an automatic restraint on those who might otherwise be overcome by their emotions.

THE ROLE OF FRIENDS WHEN A DEATH OCCURS

Immediately on hearing of the death, intimate friends of the deceased should go to the house of mourning and ask whether they can be of service. There are countless ways in which they can be helpful, from assisting with such material needs of the family as food and child care, to helping with notifications and details of the funeral, making phone calls, and answering the door. When you hear of the death of a less intimate friend, you call at the home or funeral parlor according to the directions contained in the newspaper notice. At the house, you visit briefly with the family. At a funeral home you sign the register and offer the family your sympathy in person. If by chance you do not see them, you should write a letter to the family at once. Telephoning is not improper, but it may cause inconvenience by tying up the line, which is always needed at these times for notifying members of the family and/or making necessary arrangements.

Honorary Pallbearers

The member of the family who is in charge sometimes asks six or eight men who were close friends of the deceased to be the pallbearers. This may be done when they come to pay their respects, or by telephone. When a man has been prominent in public life, there may be eight or ten of his political or business associates as well as six or eight lifelong friends. Members of the immediate family are never chosen, as their place is with their family.

There are almost never any pallbearers at the funeral of a Christian woman, but in the Jewish faith both men and women may have pallbearers.

One cannot refuse an invitation to be a pallbearer except for illness or absence from the city.

Honorary pallbearers serve only at church funerals. They do not carry the coffin. This service is performed by the assistants of the funeral director, who are expertly trained. The honorary pallbearers sit in the first pews on the left, and after the service leave the church two by two, walking immediately in front of the coffin.

Ushers

Ushers may be chosen in addition to, or in place of, pallbearers. They serve at women's funerals as well as those of men. Although funeral directors will supply men to perform the task, it is infinitely better to select men from the family (not immediate family) or close friends, who will recognize those who come and seat them according to their closeness to the family, or according to their own wishes.

When there are no pallbearers the ushers sit in the front pews on the left and march out ahead of the coffin as pallbearers would. If there are pallbearers the ushers remain at the back of the church.

At the Funeral Home

More often than not, the body of the deceased remains at the funeral home until the day of the funeral. In that case some members of the family receive close friends there, at specified hours, rather than at home. The hours when they will be there to accept expressions of sympathy should be included in the death notice in the newspaper. People who wish to pay their respects but who do not feel that they are close enough to intrude on the privacy of the bereaved may stop in at any time and sign the register provided by the funeral parlor. Their signatures should be formal, including their title—"Dr. and Mrs. William Cross" or "Ms Deborah Page," and not "Bill and Joan Cross" or "Debbie Page"—in order to simplify the task of anyone helping the family to acknowledge these visits. Close friends who feel it is unfriendly to sign "Mr. and Mrs." may use their first names but must put "Mr. and Mrs. William Cross" in parentheses after "Bill and Joan Cross." A visitor who sees and personally extends his sympathy at the funeral home need not write a note of condolence, unless he wishes to write an absent member of the family. Those who merely sign the register should, in addition, write a note. The family need not thank each and every caller by letter, but if someone has made a special effort or if no member of the family was there to speak to him, they may wish to do so.

The visit to the funeral home need not last more than five or ten minutes. As soon as the visitor has expressed his sympathy to each member of the family, and spoken a moment or two with those he knows well, he may leave. If the casket is open, guests are expected to pass by and pay their respects to the deceased, but if this is too difficult or repugnant to someone, he need not do so. Unless one's religion has specific requirements, the question of whether or not the coffin will be open is entirely up to the family. The funeral director will follow their instructions.

In general, visitors should follow the religious customs of the bereaved family when they make their visit. However, they need never do anything that is contrary to their own faith. For example, if there is a crucifix over the coffin of a Catholic, a Jew need not kneel, and a Protestant need not cross himself. An attitude of respect and sincerity can be indicated by standing a moment with bowed head and saying an appropriate prayer silently.

In speaking to members of the bereaved family, who are generally seated (the men may prefer to stand) in a different part of the room or even in another room adjacent to that where the coffin lies, what you say depends entirely on your relationship to the family. Acquaintances and casual friends need say no more than "I'm so sorry" or perhaps "He was a wonderful person." Closer friends might ask whether there is anything they can do to help or say that "We are going to miss John so much, too." Visitors should not ask about the illness or the death, but in some cases widows or widowers feel a need to talk about it. If they do bring the subject up, their friends should offer as much comfort as possible by listening and discussing it.

In reply to visitors' comments, the family members need say only "Thank you for coming," or "Thank you so much," or "You're very kind."

Visiting friends who happen to meet at a funeral home greet each other just as they ordinarily would. If a stranger is present, and introductions are made, the response is the usual one—"I'm very glad to meet you." Naturally, laughing and giggling are in very poor taste, but a short chat about subjects other than the unhappy reason for the meeting is perfectly correct.

Visitors should not smoke when they pass by the coffin, nor in the same room where the coffin is lying, unless the bereaved family are smoking in another part of the room. If the relatives are receiving in a separate room, which is often furnished as a living room, visitors may smoke if the policy of the funeral home allows it. However, if the family members are not smoking, visitors should ask if it would bother them before lighting their cigarettes. In most cases the visits are so brief that there is no need (or excuse) for smoking until the call is over.

Who Attends the Funeral

All members of the family should find out when the funeral is to take place and go to it without waiting to be notified. If the newspaper notice reads "Funeral private," a friend does not go unless he has received a message from the family that they wish him to come. If the hour and location of the service are printed in the paper, that is considered an invitation to attend. It is entirely up to you to decide whether you knew the deceased or his family well enough to wish to be at his funeral. But it is certainly heartless not to go to the public funeral of a person with whom you have been closely associated in business or some other interest, to whose house you have often been invited, or whose family are your friends.

A divorced man or woman may go to the funeral of the ex-wife or ex-husband if cordial relations have been maintained with the family of the deceased. He or she may make a brief visit to the funeral home, and may go to the church service, sitting in the rear and not attempting to join the family. If the deceased had remarried, and there was bitterness and ill feeling, the former spouse should not attend, but should send flowers and a brief note of condolence. If one member of a divorced couple who have young children dies, the surviving parent should be with the children at the funeral unless he or she has severed relations with the ex-spouse in which case grandparents would take care of them.

Clothing

It is no longer considered necessary to wear black when you go to a friend's funeral unless you sit with the family or have been asked to be one of the honorary pallbearers. However, you should choose clothes that are subdued in color and inconspicuous.

CHRISTIAN FUNERALS

At the Church

Some people find the church funeral most trying because they must leave the seclusion of the house and be in the presence of a congregation. Others find the solemnity of a church service—with the added beauty of choir and organ—helpful.

As the time appointed for the funeral draws near, the congregation gradually fills the church. The first few pews on the right side of the center aisle are usually left empty for the family and those on the left for the pallbearers, but this may be reversed if the vestry or waiting rooms are on the left.

Friends enter the church as quietly as possible, and if there are no ushers, they seat themselves wherever they wish. Only a very intimate friend should take a position far up on the center aisle. Acquaintances seat themselves in the middle or toward the rear of the church.

The trend today is to have the casket closed. Protestants may follow their own wishes; at a Catholic service it is obligatory that the casket be closed.

At most funerals the processional is omitted. The coffin may have a floral piece or a blanket of flowers on it. In some churches it may be covered with a pall of needlework, or for a member of the armed forces, it may be draped with the flag. The coffin is placed on a stand at the foot of the chancel a half hour before the service. The family usually enters through the door nearest the front pews.

However, if the deceased is very prominent, or if the family wishes a processional, it forms in the vestibule. If there is to be a choral service, the minister and choir enter the church from the rear and precede the funeral cortege. Directly after the choir and clergy come the honorary pallbearers, two by two; then the coffin; and then the family—the chief mourner first, walking with whoever can offer the most comfort to him or her.

Usually each woman takes the arm of a man. But two women or two men may walk together, according to the division of the family. For example, if the deceased is one of four sons and there is no daughter, the mother and father walk together immediately after the body of their child, and they are followed by the two elder sons and then the younger, and then the nearest woman relative. It is important that the people in deepest grief should each be placed next to the one whose nearness may be of the most help to them. A younger child who is calm and soothing would be better next to his mother than an older one who is more nervous.

At the chancel the choir takes its accustomed place, the clergyman stands at the foot of the chancel steps, the honorary pallbearers take their places in the front pews on the left, and the casket is set upon a stand previously placed there for the purpose. The actual bearers of the casket walk quietly to inconspicuous stations on the side aisles. The family and pallbearers occupy the front pews; the rest of the procession fills vacant places on either side. The service is read when everyone is seated. Upon its conclusion the procession moves out in the same order it came in, except that the choir remains in its place.

If the family wishes, one of the male relatives may stop at the back of the church to thank those who have attended the services. He need say nothing more than "Thank you for coming," with perhaps a special word for close friends, but the gesture will certainly be warmly received.

Outside the church the casket is put into the hearse. The family enters automobiles waiting immediately behind. If there are a great number of floral pieces they are put into a separate car; if no separate car is needed flowers are placed in the hearse with the casket. Flowers are sometimes taken by a different route and placed beside the grave before the hearse and those attending the burial service arrive.

At the House

Occasionally a family chooses a house funeral. It is simpler and more private, and it eliminates the necessity for those in sorrow to face people. The nearest relatives may stay apart in an adjoining room where they can hear the service yet remain in seclusion.

Years ago there seldom was music at house funerals, because at that time nothing could substitute for the deep, rich tones of the organ. Now, however, phonographic recordings of organ and choir music are excellent and readily available and may be used as a beautiful addition to a house funeral.

Arrangements are usually made to hold the service in the living room. The coffin is placed in front of the mantel, perhaps, or between two windows, at a distance from the door. It is usually set on stands brought by the funeral director, who also supplies enough folding chairs to fill the room without crowding.

At a house funeral the relatives can either take their places near the casket or stay in a separate room.

All the women keep their coats on if it is cool. The men carry their overcoats on their arms and hold their hats in their hands.

Only a very small group of relatives and intimate friends goes to the cemetery from the house.

At the Funeral Home or Chapel

In recent years the establishments of funeral directors have assumed a new prominence. There is always a chapel in the building, actually a small and often very beautiful nonsectarian church. There are also retiring rooms and reception rooms where the families may remain undisturbed or receive the condolences of their friends.

Services are conducted in the chapel just as they would be in a church, although sometimes there is a private alcove to one side so that the family need not sit in the front pews.

The Burial

Those who wish may join the cortege to the cemetery. At the cemetery, the coffin is normally placed graveside, the flowers which were sent to the funeral home or church are placed around it, and mourners stand in a circle around the coffin. The minister says the prayers that are a part of the Rite of Burial. Often the funeral director will arrange for each mourner to be given a flower. After the spouse or closest family member of the deceased has tossed his or her flower onto the coffin, others follow suit, paying their last respects and quietly walking back to their cars to depart the cemetery. A cortege is not formed to leave the cemetery and people may linger quietly or depart immediately as they wish.

Less frequently, the coffin is lowered into the prepared grave before prayers are said, and the flowers, rather than shovelfuls of earth, are thrown onto it by departing mourners.

Cremation

Many people whose religions allow it prefer the idea of cremation to burial. The service is exactly the same as that preceding a burial. The family may or may not, as they wish, accompany the body to the crematorium. If they do, a very short service is held there also. However, many ministers incorporate the burial prayers into the funeral service, thus eliminating any need for the family to go to the crematorium.

The ashes are later delivered to the family to be disposed of in any way that the deceased would wish (as long as it is not contrary to any law). Often, however, the urn is deposited in a building or section set aside in the cemetery or churchyard, and sometimes it is buried in the family plot.

A MEMORIAL SERVICE

When there is an immediate cremation, when a funeral takes place at a distance from the home community, when the deceased has died in another country or when there are no remains, a memorial service is held instead of a funeral. This service usually takes place within a week or two of the death. Notice of the service is put in the obituary column of the paper just as a funeral notice is.

There are obviously no pallbearers, but there may be ushers and there are often special printed bulletins. A register for those who attend to sign may be put in the narthex of the church.

The service generally consists of verses, prayers, and hymns, and a eulogy delivered by the minister and/or a family member or close friend.

An alternative to a memorial service is a "Service of Thanksgiving for the Life of John Doe." The service is simple, consisting of two or three tributes or eulogies given by friends or relatives, a prayer by the minister, and perhaps two or three hymns or musical offerings that were favorites of the deceased. The bulletin prepared for a service of thanksgiving is a variation of the usual bulletin that would be prepared for a regular church service. The cover of the bulletin lists the name of the deceased and often their birth and death dates:

> *A Service of Thanksgiving*
> *for the Life of*
> *Peter Mark Lattimer*
> *January 1, 1925–July 24, 1991*

In addition to listing the order of service the inside of the bulletin provides information for those who attend, "Interment took place in St. Patrick's Cemetery on July 26," as well as allowing the family a way to invite people to visit following the service, "Following the service, all are invited to join the family for lunch [for coffee and cake] at 100 Andrews Road, Cos Cob." At the memorial service for the father of one of my daughters-in-law the bulletin included a separate sheet for remembrances which said, "If you have any remembrances of Peter that you wish to share with the family, please write them below and place in the basket at the rear of the church. They will be most welcome." The service was as lovely as a funeral can be and the opportunity to share memories with the family added a special touch.

Regardless of which service you choose, usually only altar flowers are used, which may be ordered by the family of the deceased, or given by friends or associates. If additional flowers are sent, they are arranged as bouquets and placed in the chancel.

The family, which exits from the front pews first, may form a receiving line at the back of the church. Guidelines for what to say are the same as described earlier in this chapter for visitors who call at a funeral home. If they wish, family members may ask the minister, at the end of the service, to invite everyone to the home of a family member or close friend where a reception is being held. Or they may extend private invitations to particular friends passing through the receiving line if they do not wish to invite everyone in attendance.

JEWISH FUNERALS

Although there are restrictions as to when a funeral may not be held, it should be held as close to death as possible, since embalming the body is forbidden and since prompt burial is considered a mark of respect. If family members must travel a great distance to the funeral or if the death occurred away from home, the funeral might be delayed up to three days in order to allow relatives to be present. Ideally, the service takes place early in the day in the chapel of a funeral home, rarely in the sanctuary of a synagogue.

Orthodox tradition decrees that the casket be a plain wooden box, constructed with wooden pegs, and neither varnished nor carved. At the funeral, it is draped with a plain cover, supplied by the funeral home or the synagogue. No flowers are on the casket or used in the chapel. Rather than ordering flowers, friends and relatives make a donation to a charity in the name of the deceased.

Conservative practice generally follows this tradition, but Reform ritual permits a more elaborate casket and permits flowers. If you are unsure if flowers will be permitted and the newspaper notice does not specify, call the officiating rabbi or funeral home for guidance.

The coffin at an Orthodox and Conservative Jewish funeral is left closed so there is never a viewing of the body. The Reform ritual sometimes permits viewing of the body.

The funeral service includes a reading of Psalms by the rabbi, a eulogy by the rabbi or by a close friend or relative, and the recitation of the memorial prayer. The family may request that a cantor chant the Psalms or other parts of the liturgy.

After the memorial prayer, the family leaves the chapel first, directly behind the coffin as it is carried to the hearse for the burial service at the cemetery. All who will go to the cemetery form a cortege with their cars and follow the hearse to the cemetery.

At the graveside, the first memorial prayer, or *Kaddish*, is recited. Male mourners drop a handful of earth into the grave, followed by all other men present who wish to participate. It is customary to remain until the coffin is covered or even until the grave is filled.

A memorial service may be held later if the funeral takes place at a distance from the home community.

AFTER THE FUNERAL

Fees and Donations

No fee is ever asked by the minister or rabbi, but the family is expected to make a contribution in appreciation of his services, and they should do so. The amount may be anything from $25 for a very small funeral or memorial service to $100 or more for a very elaborate one. A check may be presented to him or her either before or after the funeral, or it may be mailed a day or two later with a personal note of thanks for his or her services.

If an organist plays during the service, he or she receives a fee from the family. The minister, sexton or office assistant who participates in the plans for the service should be consulted as to the organist's fee.

If a cantor is part of a service, he or she receives a fee, as well. The rabbi should be consulted to arrange for the services of a cantor and about the proper amount for the fee.

A Gathering of Family and Friends

A Post-Service Wake

The custom of having a roaring wake after the funeral service often helps those who are accustomed to it to get their minds off their tragedy, but others feel that it shows neither sadness nor respect for the deceased. However, it is a time-honored tradition among some ethnic groups and in some localities, and where this is so, wakes are beneficial and therapeutic to those who participate. If some friends or mourners resent the seeming gaiety, they should stop in and pay their respects to the bereaved family, but they need not stay to drink or take part in the "festivities."

In most cases a quiet luncheon or reception at the home of one of the relatives takes the place of a real wake. If it is held at the house of the immediate family, other relatives and close friends often provide the food. Members of the family who may not have seen each other for some time have a chance to talk, and it provides a meeting place and a meal for those who have come from out of town.

Sitting Shivah

The seven days following a Jewish funeral and burial represents a period of mourning known as sitting *shivah*. (*Shivah* is the Hebrew word for seven.) It begins immediately upon the return of the family from the cemetery. During this time, a condolence call is made to the home of those in mourning to express sympathy to the bereaved. Friends usually wait until at least the third day after the funeral, leaving the first three days for mourning among close relatives.

Most people call in the evenings or on the Sunday of the week of the death, although regular meal hours should be avoided for calls, so that the family is neither interrupted nor made to feel obligated to invite visitors to the table. It is permissible to call ahead to see if it is a convenient time to call. Calls are not made from Friday afternoon to after dark on Saturday, which is the Sabbath.

When calling on an Orthodox household, one should knock and enter, not ring the doorbell. The door is usually left unlocked so that no one needs to attend the door. If the door is locked, then naturally you would have to ring the bell or knock.

The purpose of the *shivah* visit is to console the bereaved and to express sympathy. Visitors are not usually served food or beverages, and should refrain from frivolous chatter or behaving as though at a party, greeting others, talking loudly, etc. It is appropriate to recall the deceased, if possible, and/or express sorrow for the loss of the mourners. A *shivah* visit does not need to last more than a quarter of an hour. Upon departing, a few words of support, such as "May God comfort you," may be said.

The Behavior of the Family

As soon as possible after the funeral the life of the family should return to its normal routine. There are many things that must be attended to at once, and while these may seem like insurmountable chores to a grieving husband or wife, the necessity of having to perform them, and in so doing to think of others rather than oneself, is in reality a great help in returning to an active life.

The return of the close relatives of the deceased to an active social life is up to the individual. He (or she) may start, as soon as he feels up to it, to go to a friend's house, to a movie, play, sports event, classes, or meetings. He may wish to avoid large gatherings for a time, but little by little he increases the scope of his activities until his life has returned to normal. A widower or widow may start to have dates when he or she feels like it, but for a few months these should be restricted to evenings at the home of a friend, a movie, or some other inconspicuous activity. After six months any social activity is permissible. One year is generally considered the appropriate "waiting period" before remarrying, but there are many valid reasons for shortening that time. It is up to the people involved, but they should, in making their decision, consider the feelings of their ex-in-laws, their children, and others close to them.

Those who consider themselves in mourning do not go to dances or other formal parties, nor do they take a leading part in purely social functions. However, anyone who is in public life or business or who has a professional career must, of course, continue to fulfill his or her duties. The fact that so many women have gone into business or are following careers is another cause of the lightening of mourning and the shortening of its duration. In sum, each year the number increases of those who show the mourning in their hearts only by the quiet dignity of their lives.

The Jewish faith provides a period of modified mourning for thirty days after the funeral. (Although the period of mourning for Orthodox and Hasidic Jews can extend for one year). During this time, an Orthodox mourner particularly may not marry, attend entertainments of a festive or even a religious nature, or travel on business. However, mourning is not permitted on the Sabbath. After the thirty-day period, all outward signs of mourning end and normal activities are resumed.

Children

On no account should children be put into black at any time. They wear their best clothes to a funeral, and afterward, whatever they ordinarily wear.

Very small children under five or six should perhaps not be taken to funerals. Older children should be seated with their family, close to someone who can give them the most comfort.

Many people are uncertain about whether children who have lost a parent should participate in their usual school activities and after-school entertainments. The answer is "Yes." They should take part in sports and in school concerts or plays. However, older children may not wish to go to a purely social party within two or three weeks, or even longer, after the death of a parent. The normal routine of small children should not be upset—more than ever they need to romp and play.

Disposition of Possessions and Heirlooms

No one can possibly foresee which of the children will want or need each piece of furniture or tableware in the home, and include all the instructions for dividing up such articles in his will. However, thoughtful parents can help their children immensely by writing a letter, which although not binding, will serve as a guideline, and which members of the family will be glad to follow. Since it is not binding, as a will is, the suggestions can be ignored if circumstances have changed since the letter was written. But it is most helpful to survivors who hardly know where to begin, if they have a word from the deceased along these lines: "I would like Sally to have the dining room table, since she has a room big enough for it. James needs a sturdier sofa, so I would like him to have the chintz sofa from the den," and so on. A mother may allot jewelry in the same manner.

If this has not been done, the most practical method is to call a family council. Each member should list his choices in order. They draw straws to decide who gets first choice, second choice, etc., and then continue around in turn. Toward the end, when there may be wide inequities in the value of the remaining items, the person choosing the lesser might be given a second choice. When two people have chosen the same article in the same "round," they might agree to draw straws again. An effort should be made not to break up sets of china or matching furniture.

These situations can be a real disaster, but if they are handled sensibly, unselfishly, and unemotionally, they can serve to draw family members closer together than they have ever been before.

VIII

GIFTS, GIVING & THANK-YOUS

*O*ne young mother I know laments frequently that a disproportionate amount of her discretionary income is spent on gifts. Her three children collectively attend approximately 40 birthday parties a year. Her office staff numbers four and she gives each a Christmas gift. The larger office takes collections, (almost daily, she says), for flowers for employees who have babies, are ill, have experienced a death in the family, or are promoted. Her husband's family is huge, and has never been able to discontinue the lavish giving of gifts for birthdays and during holidays. Her children's teachers each receive "teacher gifts," not only at Christmas, but also at the end of the school year. And she and her husband are frequently entertained, requiring a series of hostess gifts. The list is endless, as it is for most of us.

There are ways to limit the number of gifts we all give and receive, but there are still occasions where they are mandatory. This chapter discusses gifts and giving in general, with suggestions for types of gifts for each occasion. These are only suggestions, and your own creativity, thoughtfulness and imagination can expand on these suggestions so that each gift you give is meaningful to the recipient and is received with true pleasure.

Before discussing specific gift suggestions, there are categories of gifts that are appropriate for many different occasions and events.

GIFTS OF MONEY

Although giving money is sometimes a lazy way of avoiding the trouble of choosing a gift, there are occasions when a check is the most welcome present of all. There are many elderly couples with a limited income who love the opportunity of shopping for some long-desired object, and there are few teenagers who don't relish the idea of a little extra cash.

For people who dislike the idea of giving cash or a check, a gift certificate is a good compromise. One couple I know took the trouble to send for a gift certificate in the leading department store of the town to which their neighbors were moving, and presented it at their going-away party. Somehow the thoughtfulness of this gesture made the gift seem far warmer and more personal than a check.

When a great number of checks or gifts of cash are received, as at a wedding reception or a big anniversary party,

33

Gifts for Special Occasions

the envelopes need not be opened at the time. At smaller parties, or when just a few envelopes are given, the recipient opens them and thanks the giver, but does not mention the amount in front of others.

(See page 586 for information on giving money as a wedding gift.)

A Money Tree

Although in most circumstances I consider gifts of "pure" money in poor taste, a fiftieth anniversary can be an exception. The idea of giving is, of course, to please the recipient, and it is undeniably true that many older couples, perhaps living on a small pension or Social Security, appreciate cash more than gifts, which they neither need nor have room for. For them, a "money tree" is acceptable and practical.

The person giving the party sends a note with the invitation saying something on this order: "We are planning a money tree for Mother and Dad, and if you would like to add a twig, please send whatever you wish to me at the above address." An artificial tree or a dry branch is hung with rolled-up bills or checks, tied with colorful ribbons, and the cards are collected separately to be given to the anniversary couple. The amounts of the checks are not disclosed to the other guests.

A money tree is absolutely not appropriate for a wedding, a graduation, a birthday, or for any other event where someone is giving a party for himself. It may be suggested in those rare occasions when a family has lost their home due to fire or other disaster, for example, and friends want to help them get a new start, or when a group is sponsoring a refugee family who arrive with little but the clothes on their back.

FLOWERS AS PRESENTS

Flowers may be sent by almost everyone to almost anyone. There are certain times when sending them—if you can possibly afford it—is obligatory. These occasions include funerals, debutante parties, dinners at private homes in Europe, and others where local custom demands it. Flowers may be used in place of, or in addition to, the "gifts for many occasions" which begins on page 564 of this chapter.

Some thoughtful people are constantly sending flowers; other people seldom do. Most of us send them much less often than we might because we think those we can afford to buy are not good enough. This reminds me of our daughter, who as a teenager received, at times, corsages and gifts of flowers. I can truthfully say the one she treasured most was a single red rose from a boy whose knowledge of how to please a girl was well in advance of his years.

Flowers make the best gifts for a dinner hostess. Ideally, they should be sent ahead of time, so that the hostess may have them on display when the guests arrive. If you are taking them with you, it is best to have them already "arranged" so that your hostess does not have to leave her guests to put them in a container. Should you want to take a few flowers from your own garden, which are easily arranged, you might even say as you give them to your hostess, ' Show me where there is a vase, and I'll put them in water for you"—especially if a number of other guests are arriving at the same time.

In Europe it is customary to take cut flowers to a hostess, and if you do not do so, you should send flowers, with a thank-you card, the next day. This is also much appreciated in our own country.

When you are the guest of honor at a private party, you should send your hostess a flower arrangement the day of the party.

Now that it is possible to order flowers from a local florist and have them delivered in a distant town or city by an associated florist there, there is no excuse for not remembering birthdays, anniversaries, and other special occasions in this way. Those careless or lazy people who "just don't think" to get a package off in time need only pick up the telephone and make a local call to give pleasure to someone far away.

For many years flowers were not considered an appropriate gift for men. In recent years, however, the attitude has changed, and men are no longer ashamed to show their appreciation of beauty—gifts to a man who is ill, who is opening a new office, or as a birthday gift. If you fear that he may think a flower arrangement too "feminine," don't hesitate to give him a plant or terrarium. The latter, especially, requires little care and is ideal for a man's apartment or office.

BIRTHSTONES AS GIFTS

Jewelry containing birthstones are lovely birthday presents. Birthstones are also used as a substitute for the diamond in engagement rings. These are the traditional choices:

JANUARY—*Garnet*. (Its rather dark glow makes a pleasing engagement ring.) The *zircon*, a white, crystal-clear stone, makes a very attractive ring and closely resembles a diamond, particularly when square-cut and kept brilliantly clean. But because it does look like a diamond, there is a chance that a bride might fear that people will feel she is trying to fool them into thinking it really is a diamond. There is also a beautiful steel-blue variety.

FEBRUARY—*Amethyst*. (A big one with a square cut is effective.)

MARCH—*Aquamarine* first, then *bloodstone* or *jasper*. (A square-cut aquamarine is very popular and a really beautiful substitute for a diamond.)

APRIL—*Diamond*. (The stone of stones, but very expensive.)

MAY—*Emerald*. (Also very costly if perfect in color and without a flaw.)

JUNE—*Pearl*. (Nothing is more becoming to a woman with lovely skin.)

JULY—*Ruby*. (Of very high value when of the desirable pigeon-blood color.)

AUGUST—*Sardonyx, peridot* (a rare and beautiful stone), or *carnelian.*

SEPTEMBER—*Sapphire.* (A favorite engagement ring of the past and always beautiful.)

OCTOBER—*Opal.* (The opal is believed to be the stone of good fortune for those born in October, but unlucky for those not born in this month.)

NOVEMBER—*Topaz.*

DECEMBER—*Turquoise or lapis lazuli.*

GIFTS FOR MANY OCCASIONS

Anniversaries

Gifts are almost always taken to a couple celebrating an early anniversary because they are usually in need of household articles of every sort. But when a couple have been married twenty-five years or more, they probably have all the material things they can use. If they wish, it is perfectly correct to say "No gifts, please" on the invitations. Guests receiving those invitations should *not* take gifts to the party, since this is embarrassing to the anniversary couple and to those guests who abided by the request. Very close friends or relatives, who really wish to give the couple a remembrance, and perhaps know of something they especially want, should take their presents to the couple's home at some time before the party.

Among the loveliest ways to say "No Gifts" I have seen appeared in a letter to advice columnist Ann Landers. The letter dealt with a simple yet elegant way to request no gifts on the occasion of a fiftieth wedding anniversary:

Mr. and Mrs. William Carson
invite relatives and friends to attend
a worship service and reception
honoring
Elizabeth and Daniel Bailey
in celebration of their 50th wedding anniversary.
Your love and friendship are cherished gifts.
We respectfully request no other.

No one giving a twenty-fifth-anniversary party should *ever* write "No silver" or "No silver gifts, please." That is simply a clear hint that while the couple do not want silver they *do* expect other gifts.

Nor is it ever proper for a hostess to request a gift of money for herself, so a couple giving their own anniversary party cannot, in good taste, suggest to their friends that they would like gifts of cash. In most circumstances it is incorrect to include a request for money on the invitation to an anniversary celebration. If, however, the people giving the party have planned a special group present such as tickets for a vacation trip, a new television set, or a fine painting, it would be proper to enclose a short note with the invitation explaining what has been planned and asking the guests if they would like to make a contribution in place of bringing an individual gift. Each guest who contributes should sign the card accompanying the gift.

For couples who might resent gifts of money, and in fact do not want personal gifts at all, there is yet another solution. A card is enclosed with the invitation, reading, "In place of gifts, please, if you wish, send a contribution to Mother and Dad's favorite charity—the XYZ Research Foundation." The check may be sent with a note saying, "Please accept this contribution in honor of the fiftieth anniversary of Mr. and Mrs. John Doe."

When gifts are given they need not necessarily be of the traditional material allotted to each anniversary. But many people feel that it is more meaningful if they are, and the following list has been modified to include modern materials in some cases. When an article of the original material cannot be purchased, something similar but not identical may be chosen—for example, a stainless-steel or pewter platter instead of a silver one would be acceptable (and perhaps preferred) on a twenty-fifth anniversary. For all anniversaries a lovely flower arrangement or a plant that can be set out in the couple's garden is always appropriate.

Here are the traditional anniversary gifts:

1. Paper or plastics
2. Calico or cotton
3. Leather or simulated leather
4. Silk or synthetic material
5. Wood
6. Iron
7. Copper or wool
8. Electrical appliances
9. Pottery
10. Tin or aluminum
11. Steel
12. Linen (table, bed, etc.)
13. Lace
14. Ivory
15. Crystal or glass
20. China
25. Silver
30. Pearls
35. Coral and jade
40. Ruby
45. Sapphire
50. Gold
60. Diamond

Other gifts you might consider include: a photo album (to be filled later if possible with pictures taken at the party); a framed family portrait; a bottle of champagne or wine for the couple to enjoy; or any book related to the couple's hobbies or interests. If you know of the party far in advance you might consider enlisting the aid of the couple's relatives to gather photos of the couple and their family taken over the course of their marriage. Arrange the photos in a collage-type frame, perhaps leaving a space blank to insert a photo from the anniversary party. When the couple has a video tape recorder and enjoyed taking home movies of their children as they grew, enlist the help of those children to obtain the best of those home movies. Take these films to a camera store and ask that they be transferred to videocassettes. Your thoughtfulness will be remembered each and every time the couple views this tape without the hassle of setting up movie projector and screen.

A "Conference Call"

A lovely gift to a couple whose children are scattered and far away is a "conference call." The person giving the party can arrange with the telephone company to connect the lines so that all members of the family can talk together at an appointed hour. This could, in many cases, be the most wonderful gift the couple receive.

Marking Gifts

Gifts of silver are still often given on twenty-fifth anniversaries. A couple's children, for example, may get together and give their parents a beautiful silver tray, a bowl, a coffeepot, etc. These gifts should be marked to commemorate the occasion. The two simplest and most satisfactory forms are:

1970–1995
to
Mom and Dad
from
Arlene and Michael
Joann and Paul

OR:

To Mom and Dad
on their twenty-fifth anniversary
from
etc.

Once in a while, the children giving a party for their parents present mementos of the occasion to all the guests. These gifts, too, are monogrammed. Mementos such as paper match boxes or coasters could be marked and distributed:

JSP and HTP

OR:

Jean and Harry Porter
October 10
1970–1995

Baby Gifts

Since babies grow so quickly any article of clothing is always a welcome present. Other useful items include blankets and comforters; even towels and washcloths come in handy. Close relatives might consider a silver fork and spoon, or even baby's first piggy bank. If you are imaginative, personalize a scrap book with the baby's birth date and fill the first few pages with photos of the parents, grandparents, and baby's first home. You might even consider saving the newspaper from the day the baby was born; think how interesting it will be for the parents and child to look at in the future.

If you visit the new mother and baby in the hospital it is thoughtful to bring a small gift for the new mother—a potted plant, a book you know she would enjoy, or her favorite perfume, for instance.

When there is a big brother or sister, it is thoughtful to take or send a very small present for him or her, as well as for the baby. It is hard enough for young children to learn to share mommy or daddy, let alone to see piles of presents being given to the interloper. A card acknowledging how lucky the baby is to have such a wonderful older brother or sister does a lot to eliminate jealousy and build self-esteem.

Religious Ceremonies for Newborns

Those invited to a christening or *brit* usually take a gift to the baby since they are presumably close to the family. The gift should be a lasting memento of the occasion, so the gift may be engraved. Typical gifts include a silver picture frame or a silver comb and brush set.

Godparents give the baby as nice a present as they can afford. The typical gift is a silver mug or porringer, inscribed, for example:

Barry Marino
December 5, 1985
From his godfather
John Strong

Other typical presents are a silver fork and spoon, a government bond, or a trust fund to which the donor may add each year until the child is grown.

Bon Voyage Gifts

Books, small games, a trip diary, and guidebooks to the place being visited are all lovely gifts for a bon voyage party, as are a passport folder, money-exchange guide, or a travel kit of cleaning and laundry products. If the guests of honor are taking a cruise, arranging with the wine steward to have champagne or wine served as a surprise during the voyage is an especially welcome gift. Most travelers would welcome a supply of extra film, but a special treat is including the prepaid processing mailer that allows the travelers to be greeted by their photos when they return home.

Every traveler needs a certain amount of small-denomination bills and loose change for tips and cab fare when they first arrive at their destination. One woman I know gives friends the equivalent of twenty dollars' worth of bills and change in the currency of the country they are visiting. This thoughtfulness speeds travelers through airport and hotel check-in without their having to take time to exchange their money. For those traveling with electric hair dryers or traveling irons, a set of electric current convertor plugs is a handy gift.

Birthday Presents

For a "Sweet Sixteen"

Birthday gifts for a sweet sixteen include a charm bracelet with one charm; a pair of earrings; any book on the girl's special interest or hobby; personalized stationery; perfume; a scarf, belt or other fashion accessory; cassettes; wall posters or other decorative ornaments for the girl's room.

For Teenage Boys

Clothing, sports equipment, and records or tapes of a favorite rock group are generally a good choice for a teenage boy. Other ideas include wall posters, a video game, or a computer software program.

For a Wife or Husband

Any little present you know he or she wants but has avoided buying because *you* maintained that it was foolish or extravagant.

For an Older Couple

Providing travel tickets for a special vacation is a lovely and thoughtful gesture but not always practical. Welcome gifts include a newspaper or magazine subscription, a gift certificate, a plant, or any book of interest to the couple.

For Friends

The gift you present to a friend for his or her birthday depends on the closeness of the friendship and the depth of your feeling for one another.

For Everyone

Anything you have knitted, baked, constructed—in short, *made*—yourself!

Business Gifts

Office gifts are a way of saying, "Thank you. I appreciate what you are doing." The common occasions for office gift giving are Christmas, pre-vacation, birthdays, engagements, weddings, house warmings, baby births, retirements and sometimes the completion of a long and harrowing project. A Secretary's Week has been instituted, probably by a florists' association, which it is difficult for an employer to overlook.

From an Employer

Employers may give gifts on any of these occasions, although more commonly they will limit them to a few. At Christmas time they may distribute small gifts to all members of the staff, or in the case of men who still cling to bits of male chauvinism, only to female members. Whether they follow this practice or not, male and female executives are expected to give their secretary a gift—candy or perfume if they have not been together long, a more substantial gift such as a pocketbook or a piece of jewelry if they have. Executives with a male secretary follow the same procedure, giving items such as a silk tie, a toiletries set or a wallet. Although a gift certificate may lack the personal touch, many secretaries are grateful for an opportunity to select their own gifts.

To an Employer

In general, employees do not give gifts to their employers. However, a secretary who has worked for the same executive for many years may want to give him or her a Christmas present which will surely be appreciated. The gift should not be too expensive or personal—a desk item, scarf, tie, etc. If the executive is married, it is appropriate to select a gift suitable for the executive's spouse as well—a plant, a vase or bottle of wine.

More often joint gifts may be given by the entire staff to their boss at Christmas or on any other special occasion. Many people find this the easiest way to reciprocate to the boss who distributes individual presents, since it might be expensive and embarrassing to shower the boss with individual gifts.

Joint Gifts to a Co-worker

When an office staff wants to recognize a fellow member with gifts, it is common practice for them to collaborate on a joint gift. People contribute what they wish, the boss included, and no one must be coerced into paying. Those who have contributed sign a card, attaching it to the gift, which one or two of them have purchased for the group. Some offices also establish a gift fund to which everyone contributes the same amount. Joint gifts for staff members are paid for out of this fund.

Gifts Between Co-Workers

Individual gifts that peers choose to give each other should not be exchanged in the office, since associates may notice and feel slighted. A lunch together is a good opportunity for exchanging gifts. If one of your co-workers gives you an unexpected gift, even though your initial response may be to rush out and buy one to reciprocate, do not. The gift will obviously look like an afterthought and cause an embarrassing situation. Say a warm "Thank you," and perhaps tuck away in your mind the thought of getting the person a gift the next time an occasion rolls around.

From Sales and Other Service People

Frequently sales and service people at Christmastime give gifts to the people with whom they do business, which may range from a personalized desk calendar to a case of imported champagne. When you accept a small gift, you accept the "Thank you for your business" that accompanies the gift; but when you accept an expensive gift, you also accept a silent obligation to continue doing business with them. Many companies have policies that forbid employees to accept any but the smallest gifts, while some forbid the acceptance of any gifts. Therefore, you should check your company's policy beforehand and be prepared with a polite "Thank you for the thought, but the company does not allow gifts of this kind." Even if your company has no such policy, you may want to avoid the obligation that goes with a gift: all you need do is express your appreciation and add, "But I really cannot accept such an expensive gift."

To Clients

When you are in the position of selling or delivering a service to a client, you will face the question of giving Christmas gifts. Before making a purchase, check the policy of the client's company or store, for it may limit or prohibit gifts. Even if there is an open policy, select a small gift: it delivers a message of gratitude without obligation or possible embarrassment.

When Someone Retires

Company policy usually determines the type of retirement gift given to employees. These may range from an item that adds to the employee's collection or hobby to the standard gold watch. Watches and other items of silver or gold (such as a silver tray) are usually engraved with the retiree's name and dates of service to the company. The gift commemorates years of service, regardless if those years were spent in the mailroom or the boardroom.

Thank-Yous for Business Gifts

A thank-you letter is a must for any gift you receive from an individual, whether your employer or peer. Even when you receive a joint gift from ten or twelve staff members, individual thank-you notes would be appreciated. However, with that many or more people collaborating on a gift, you may write one letter of thanks and either circulate it through the office or post it on the bulletin board. If your office is equipped with an electronic mail system you may use it to thank many co-workers at once. However, if everyone who contributed to your gift is not networked to the electronic mail system do not the system to send your thanks. All thank-you letters should be written immediately, not only because they acknowledge appreciation of the gift, but also because the longer you wait, the more difficult they become.

A bonus given at the end of the year is not considered a personal gift, even though your employer may announce it to you. It is a present from the company, requiring a thank-you to your boss but no letter.

Debutante Gifts

Gifts are given to a debutante only by family and very close friends. They are not expected of others invited to the coming out ball or dance. Sometimes the escort or escorts of the debutante are expected to give her flowers or a corsage. When there is a cotillion or assembly and a committee organizing the ball, the committee determines whether the debutantes will wear flowers.

Among gifts appropriate for debutantes are flowers delivered to her home, simple "good" jewelry, an ornament for the debutante's room, a white leather picture frame for her debut portrait, perfume, and good stationery.

Farewell Gifts

In choosing a gift, try to think of something that will serve as a memento to the ones going away. A picture of their home, of their friends, or candids of the going-away party will be treasured. A subscription to the local newspaper will help them to keep up with news of their old friends. And a gift certificate for a store in their *new* locality will prevent their having to pack one additional item.

To help keep in touch choose a gift of stationery printed with the new address. Inquire if the telephone company offers gift certificates that will help good friends stay in touch.

College Graduation Gifts

Typical gifts include: money, gift certificate, savings bond, shares of stock, an initial deposit in a new savings account, a clock or clock-radio, a personal television or small computer, a desk lamp, books (especially those useful in his or her chosen career, or standard reference works), a subscription to the trade journal in his or her chosen field, luggage, a piece of camera equipment, sports equipment, stereo components, or a piece of jewelry (such as a ring or a watch). If the graduate has a car your gift might be an engraved key ring, or a leather case for maps and registration.

Housewarming Gifts

The guest generally takes a small gift to a housewarming. It need not be expensive, but it is better to find something that will be of permanent use rather than flowers, which will only last a short time, or paper napkins, which will soon be used up. A few pretty guest towels or place mats, a framed print for the wall, a brush for the fireplace are a few possibilities.

Other gift ideas include an address book listing the names, addresses, and phone numbers of recommended local services and stores; seeds or bulbs for the garden; a subscription to the local newspaper; leather or silver stamp holder (made even nicer when filled with postage stamps); or personalized return address labels.

If the new neighbors are from far away, anything that will help them orient themselves to the neighborhood and surrounding area is bound to be appreciated. Gather together a local road map, local transportation schedules, brochures on local activities and points of interest, registration forms for pet licenses, parking permits, anything you can think of that will make moving in easier and make your new neighbors feel welcome and at home.

Religious Confirmation, First Communion, or Bar Mitzvah Gifts

Any of the following are acceptable: prayer book, religious charm or pendant, a gift of money, jewelry, a fine book, or a pen and pencil set. Select your gift based on your closeness to the youngster.

GIFTS FOR OTHER SPECIAL PEOPLE

Doctors, Lawyers and Other Professionals

Generally no gift is given to professionals consulted for their professional services. There are occasions, however, when a patient or client wants to express special thanks for extraordinary consideration or services rendered. In these cases, any of the following are appropriate: a desk set, a food specialty (such as a home-made cheesecake or a deluxe box of cookies), an accessory to a favorite sport (such as golf balls, tennis balls, etc.,) or a special bottle of wine or favorite liquor. There are also many specialty items, such as figurines and statues of doctors, for example, and "Americana" type prints and paintings for their offices. Other gift suggestions include decorations for patient or client rooms, such as a mobile for the ceiling to be hung above an examining table, or an attractive table top ornament.

Nurses

Gifts of money should never be offered to nurses, whether hospital or private duty. Personal gifts, such as articles of clothing or accessories may be given to a private-duty nurse who has served over a period of time. Gifts of food that can be shared by everyone at the nurses station may be given, but in multiples of three, one for each shift on duty. (If only one box of cookies is delivered, it is likely that it will be consumed by the shift on duty at that time with none left for personnel who serve on the other two shifts.) Cookies, candy, or fruit are some suggestions. They are delivered to the nurses' station, either periodically during a long hospital stay, or at the end of the stay, by the patient or by his or her family. Each package should be marked, "first shift," "second shift," "third shift" with a note thanking the staff for their kindness.

For Sick People and Hospital Patients

Let the severity of the illness and the length of the hospital stay guide you in selecting a gift. Light reading matter (both in weight and content), a crossword puzzle book, an autobridge game, or a portable video game makes a suitable gift for old or young. If the patient is to be laid up for a lengthy period, a new dressing gown, bed jacket, or pillow-type bedrest can be a real day-brightener. Before bringing any food gift check with the patient's doctor.

Teachers

If the custom is to give holiday or year-end gifts to classroom teachers, it is meaningful to the child to help shop for the gift and if old enough, to write his or her own note to accompany the gift. Sometimes, parents of children in a class donate to the price of a combined present in place of individual gifts. Gifts for teachers may be a leather-bound book or any other professional book, or something more personal, such as an accessory or item of clothing, or a desk clock or a picture for the wall. Other suggestions include homemade jellies and jams, Christmas cookies, a tie or scarf, a tree ornament, or other kind of ornament.

The same suggestions are appropriate for other teachers, such as tutors, music or dance teachers, etc.

Nuns

Your choice of a gift may depend in part on whether or not the nun will be wearing her habit. Those nuns who elect not to wear habits would be most appreciative of a check, cash, or a gift certificate to a local department store. Other gift suggestions include white linen handkerchiefs, religious pictures or statues, books (including light novels), a magazine subscription, black gloves, small luxury items (such as lotions, powder, and bath accessories), cookies and candy, or a warm shawl.

Newly Ordained Priest, Minister, or Rabbi

Any of these would make suitable presents: leather diary or address book, pen-and-pencil set, magazine subscription, wristwatch, wallet or briefcase, or a gift certificate to a local department store.

A Girlfriend or Boyfriend

Typical gifts include a key case or wallet, flowers or a plant, a pair of tickets to a rock concert, a piece of jewelry, imprinted stationery, a picture frame with the giver's picture, any clothing accessory (such as gloves, a scarf, or a belt, but no item of "personal" clothing), or a book, video tape or CD of especial interest. Perhaps the nicest gift of all is one specially and personally made.

Household Staff

Holiday gifts are given to household staff, usually as an accompaniment to a cash gift equivalent to a week's or month's salary, depending on the hiring arrangements. (A once-a-week cleaning service would receive an extra day's pay, while a live-in housekeeper might receive a bonus of a month's pay.) Suggestions include items for their rooms, if they live in, or articles of clothing, soaps, perfume, travel accessories, or items related to a special interest they may have.

A nanny or au pair, in addition to a cash gift from the parents, would receive a present from the children, again an item for her room or a personal gift of clothing or accessories.

Personal Care Personnel

Health club personnel, personal trainers, tennis pros, and other "teachers" do not receive tips, but do receive personal gifts, whether food, liquor, or accessories or gifts of clothing.

A beautician, if visited monthly or more frequently, receives a gift at Christmas time, which may be a festive box of Christmas cookies, a boxed set of personal care items, or an accessory or ornament.

GIFTS AS A THANK-YOU

For a Dinner Invitation

In some areas a gift is taken to a host or hostess who has extended an invitation for dinner. In other localities gifts are not expected. Gifts need not be taken to large cocktail parties or receptions, unless it is to honor a special occasion.

Gifts may be flowers, homemade cookies or jam, a box of candy, or bottles of wine, liquor, or liqueur. If gifts of food are taken, it should be made clear that they are not intended for the meal being served. Instead, a gift of croissants and jam "for breakfast tomorrow" or a bottle of champagne "for your next special quiet time together," or a box of cookies "for the children to enjoy tomorrow" may be taken. There is nothing more disconcerting for a hostess than to have a guest show up with her prize angel food cake and the expectation that it will be served for dessert when she has planned chocolate souffles or fruit and cheese.

For a Weekend Visit

It is obligatory that guests who spend a weekend or longer send or take a gift for their host and/or hostess. Flowers may be sent in advance with a note that reads, "We are so looking forward to seeing you," or the day after departure with a note, "It was great . . . we miss you already!" or words to that effect, including a simple "Thank you! We loved every moment." A gift may be taken, which may be wine, liquor or liqueurs, candy, household ornaments, a unique appliance (such as a coffee grinder for coffee lovers, or a videocassette rewinder for movie buffs), a vase, etc.

The length of the visit and the elaborateness of the entertainment determines the elaborateness of the gift. You may take the host and hostess to dinner or to another entertainment, or take the fixings for one evening's meal which you prepare and serve as a thank you for their hospitality.

GENERAL GIFT ETIQUETTE

Opening Presents at a Party

Half the fun of giving and receiving presents at any party is to see and enjoy what everyone else brought. The nicest way to do this is to have all the presents collected in one place until everyone has arrived, at which time the guest of honor opens them. Whether a gift is an inexpensive gag present or a more expensive article is not important. The recipient reads the cards enclosed, particularly if they are funny ones, and shows enthusiasm for each gift. It is important to include a card even with a gift you deliver personally because many people like to collect and save the cards they receive at these times as mementos of the occasion. If anybody has given money instead of a present, the amount should not be mentioned but the recipient may well say something like, "This is a really welcome contribution toward the china we are saving for," or whatever else may be appropriate.

On occasions when gifts are not necessarily expected, but two or three people bring them regardless, they are opened in the donor's presence but without drawing the attention of other guests. This might happen, for instance, when a couple brings a gift to a dinner hostess. She must show her appreciation, but making a display of the present could embarrass guests who did not bring one.

Unwanted Gifts

Many people are far more sensitive than their friends suspect. For this reason it is important never to choose a gift that might be construed as a show of criticism. A present of a cookbook can be most welcome, provided your friend knows that you have enjoyed her cooking and—even more important—you know she likes to cook. This same cookbook might well be resented if given shortly after a disastrous dinner at which the food was all but inedible.

Presents requiring constant care when given to people who are not interested or able to give that care can be a real disaster. Foremost among those are live birds or fish or other animals. The well-meaning family friend who gives a young child a puppy or kitten without first clearing the matter with his parents will not long remain a family friend.

Then there are the white elephants that seem to grow in every gift shop. Before buying any present in this category think to yourself, "What will she do with it? Does he have a place for it?" and if you can't find an answer, don't buy it.

Ostentatious gifts are in very poor taste. The gift that has obviously stretched the purse strings of the sender, or is not in keeping with the lifestyle of the receiver, is a gift that gives no pleasure at all.

Meanwhile people get into a pattern of exchanging gifts with friends or relatives and then find it difficult to stop, even though their relationship has changed to the point where the exchange of gifts has become a meaningless nuisance. I can only say, "Be frank." Well ahead of the occasion (Christmas, birthday, or whenever the gifts habitually arrive), either write or say to the person, "I've loved your gifts, but what with the economy like it is [or the new baby, or redecorating the house, or whatever seems a good reason] let's just send cards this year. Write us your family news—that will be the best present of all."

When someone arrives at your door with an unexpected Christmas present, you are "on the spot." Unless you have a supply of small gifts ready for such an emergency (not a bad idea in some localities!) you can only say, "Thanks so much—but you really shouldn't have done this," to indicate that you do not expect to start an annual exchange of gifts.

"No Gifts, Please"

When an invitation says "No gifts, please," the request should be honored. If you are very close to the sender or the guest of honor, you may take or send a gift to his or her home before or after the party. But to take it to the celebration is only embarrassing to the host or hostess and rude to the guests who *have* complied with the request.

Gift Wrappings

Just as a picture needs a frame, a gift needs an attractive wrapping—as well as a card—to go with it. Most department and gift stores provide special gift wrapping free or at a slight extra charge. For those who have neither the time nor the inclination to wrap their own presents, this is a great boon. On the other hand, devising a clever or entertaining way to present a gift can add to the fun of giving it. In many cases an unusual or attractive package adds greatly to the present itself. Wine bottles packaged in picnic baskets or homemade cookies packaged in an attractive reusable metal container are examples of this. The original packaging you do yourself, however, can be even more entertaining or useful. A friend of mine camouflaged his Christmas present of ski poles for his teenage daughter as a poinsettia plant. The handles of the poles were stuck into a pot filled with sand, and red-and-green construction paper was used to make the petals and leaves to complete the illusion.

In recent years we have been made to realize the importance of saving our natural resources and therefore the importance of not using paper extravagantly and needlessly. I have received many letters suggesting ways to conserve paper and I pass a few on to you!

The first and most obvious—reuse wrapping paper. Instead of ripping it off packages, remove it carefully, fold it, and store it where it can be laid flat, or roll it.

Use pretty boxes that do not require an outside wrapping of paper. To decorate plain boxes, you can paste colorful cards or decorate packages with the variety of stickers that can be purchased at most card stores.

Inventive packages can be made by using brown paper bags, colorful shopping bags, and even newspaper. Pieces of thick, colorful leftover yarn serve well as ties, instead of paper ribbons.

At Christmas one or two large boxes can be wrapped for each member of the family, and the smaller packages placed in them, unwrapped.

Consider using decorated shopping bags which can later be reused.

Marking Gifts

Discussion of a gift's appearance leads to the question of whether to personalize or monogram it. The obvious drawback is that once an article has been initialed it can never be returned. Therefore, before you have anything of value marked, be sure it is something you know is wanted and also that it is the right size, color, and style. If you *are* sure of this, then initials are a handsome addition to many gifts.

It is always possible, also, for the receiver to have the gift marked later. If free engraving is offered with the purchase, it will be honored at any time later. If there is a change, however, you should have the bill for the marking sent to you, and be sure that the recipient knows this.

When handkerchiefs or other articles that may be marked with a single letter are given as a gift, the initial of a woman's first name is used, whereas the initial of his last name is used for a man.

(*For details on marking silver, glass, linen, etc., see pages 566–567.*)

Presents From Two or More

There are many occasions when it is perfectly permissible to send a joint present.

The staff in an office may contribute to a single present for a co-worker.

Friends invited to a birthday or anniversary party may be asked to contribute to one big present rather than give individual gifts.

Engaged or living-together couples may give joint wedding and birthday gifts, but may wish to give individual presents to members of their own families on Christmas.

Two people or two couples may get together to give a weekend hostess something nicer than they could afford individually.

On the other side of the fence, you may sometimes give one present *to* several people. Godparents who hesitate to give a gift only to a godchild who has brothers or sisters, stepparents, and many others face this problem. Rather than give a present to each of the children in the family, you may give *one* gift—a game, play equipment, etc.—that can be used by all.

"What Do You Want for Christmas?"

When someone asks you what you want for Christmas, or for a wedding present, or for *any* occasion, don't say, "Oh, I don't know," or "I'd rather *you* picked something out." Many people honestly have very little imagination about gifts, and in your own interests they need help. Unless you know it is within their means and easily available, don't mention a specific item. But suggestions such as "You know I love to cook, and *all* kitchen gadgets fascinate me," or "John and I just redecorated our apartment—any plant would be perfect," can be very helpful to the person who is puzzling over a gift for you.

Returning and Exchanging Gifts

If a gift arrives broken, take it, with its wrappings, to the shop where it was purchased. If it comes from another city, return it by mail, accompanied by a letter explaining how it arrived. Any good store will replace the merchandise on reasonable evidence that it was received in a damaged condition. Do not involve the donor in this transaction; do not even let him or her know what happened if you can possibly avoid doing so. Of course, when an *insured* package arrives damaged in the mail, you must inform the sender so that he can collect the insurance and replace the gift.

Exchanging gifts received on occasions other than weddings require a little tact. A present should not be exchanged just because it doesn't happen to be exactly what you want. If it is a duplicate, it would be thoughtful to call the giver and say, "Mary, I happen to have two bottle warmers already. Would you mind terribly if . . . ?" or "Sue, I adore the sweater you sent but it's a thirty-two and I take a thirty-six. I'm going to try to find one as nearly like it as possible in my size." Then in your thank-you note tell Mary or Sue how much you are enjoying what you got as a replacement.

Gifts given to prospective nuns or priests who decide, just before taking their vows, against a religious life should be returned also. The situation is similar to that of a broken engagement.

Almost all of the events surrounding weddings involve gifts, whether from friends and family, from the bride and groom to their attendants, or to each other. The gift suggestions in this chapter are based on traditional customs. However, there are several based on traditional customs. However, there are several ethnic groups which have slightly different customs, giving what traditionally would be a wedding gift as a shower gift and giving money as a wedding gift, for example. In other groups, the groom's family gives lavish gifts of jewelry to the bride at an engagement party, participating in putting necklaces around her neck or bracelets on her wrist as she opens them, at the party.

Therefore, these suggestions are a base from which to begin, but when you are uncertain of custom when invited to a wedding of friends or acquaintances of a different ethnic background than yours, ask someone you know will be another guest, or a friend of the same ethnic background.

34
Gifts for Engagements and Weddings

ENGAGEMENT GIFTS

Presents are expected only from close relatives and intimate friends and are almost always intended especially for the bride:

Towels for bathroom or guest towels
Luggage for honeymoon
Bed linen such as a set of sheets and pillow cases (*For guidance on marking linen see pages 611–612.*)
Jewelry
Lingerie
Place mats
Bar or kitchen towels
Table linen
China figurine
Silk flower arrangement

When the Bride Gives the Groom an Engagement Present

Probably because the giving of an engagement ring is his particular province, the bride-to-be very rarely gives her fiancé a ring. If she chooses to give him a gift, the more usual presents include such articles as a pair of cuff links, a watch, a key chain, or if he smokes, a cigarette lighter.

SHOWERS

There are three hard-and-fast rules about shower gifts.

1. The gift is presented to the guest of honor at the shower. It is never sent from the store. If, however, the donor cannot attend, the wrapped package is left at the hostess's house ahead of time.
2. The gift must be accompanied by a card, so that the guest of honor knows from whom each present comes as she opens it.
3. Presents must be opened at the shower, and each donor thanked personally then and there. The bride may write thank-you notes later if she wishes, but it is not necessary unless the donor was not there to receive her personal thanks.

Shower gifts should not be elaborate. They should be useful, appropriate, and as original as the donor can make them. Traditionally, shower gifts were handmade for the occasion, and such gifts are still the nicest of all, but unfortunately many of us today do not have the time or the ability to create a handmade gift.

Money-tree showers should be avoided, since the shower gift is meant to be a memento of the giver, and money can hardly fulfill that requirement. In the rare case in which a couple is not going to have a home immediately after their marriage, a money tree would be acceptable. The guests of honor do not disclose the amounts in the envelopes on the tree.

Second-Marriage Showers

Every effort should be made to make a shower for a second marriage one that will be really helpful to a couple who may already have all of their basic necessities. Liquor showers, food showers, garden showers, and ticket (to some entertainment) showers are often more appropriate than the traditional kitchen or linen showers.

WEDDING GIFTS

Typical wedding presents include almost anything ornamental or useful for the furnishing of a home or the setting of a dining-room table. Naturally, the less you know about the future living plans of the bride and groom, or their tastes, the more necessary it is to choose a gift than can be used by anyone living anywhere.

Here is a list of gifts in various price ranges, which would be usable in almost any style of home:

Set of folding tables on rack

Wooden salad bowl

Mirror for entry or hall

Large pepper grinder or salt-and-pepper sets

Crystal vase

Food processor

Framed print or photograph

Electric hot tray

Wastebasket

Lamp

Hors d'oeuvres tray

Set of glasses

Items of the silver or china selected by the bride

Carving set

Microwave cookware

Answering machine

Unless you know that your gift is something the bride wants, and that it will not be duplicated, it is safer not to have it monogrammed or marked. The exceptions are articles of her selected pattern of silver, or monogrammed glasses she has asked for. Other gifts that are improved by monogramming are leather or silver cigarette boxes, leather picture frames, silver trays, etc. These would be articles she would not be likely to exchange, since she can always use more than one.

Second-Marriage Wedding Gifts

Select an ornamental "nonpractical" gift when both members of the couple have all the basic household necessities. There are also items that one can *never* have too many of, such as unusual place mats, or such things as wineglasses or on-the-rocks glasses. No matter how many the couple had originally, glasses inevitably get broken and they will surely be able to use a new supply.

It is not necessary in choosing a second-marriage gift to worry much about permanence as a memento, as one does for a first-time gift. Things which can be greatly enjoyed once by the newlyweds such as theater, concert, or opera tickets or a gift certificate for an elegant restaurant dinner make great presents. Here are some other suggestions that cannot help but please even the couple that "has everything":

A plant, tree, or shrub, for their garden or terrace

A selection of fine wines or champagne

If they are collectors, anything that might add to their collection

A picture frame with a picture that will mean something to them—of themselves, their children, their wedding, etc.

If they enjoy cooking, ceramic or copper molds are both useful and decorative

A subscription to a magazine related to their special interests

A gift package of gourmet food selections

A painting or lithograph—*if* you know their tastes

If either one has small children, sitter service for a specified period (either yourself or hired)

Gift-Giving When a Living-Together Couple Marries

Since the couple probably has most of the necessities for their home, checks or gift certificates may be more welcome than gifts. Whether you are or are not expected to send a gift at all depends even more than usual on your closeness to the family.

The kind of gift may differ sharply too. With all the toasters, electric blankets and cookware already in use, what is left to give? There are always the special things they would not buy for themselves—a painting, elegant wineglasses, new china, a start toward a set of silver flatware. Ask their parents for suggestions or make mental notes as you visit their home. Select a gift, if you are doubtful, that is returnable and let the couple know that they may return it with your blessing. For the couple who has fully furnished their home, you might consider the gifts listed above for second marriages.

Gift Giving for the Couple Who Elopes

A person receiving an announcement of an elopement, either in the name of the parents or without their names, is in no way obligated, nor even expected, to send a present. If, of course, out of love or affection for either the bride or the groom or their families, one wishes to give them something, it will be an especially appreciated gesture.

PERSONAL GIFTS

Bridal Attendants' Gifts to Bride or Groom, or Both

After-dinner coffee spoons, each engraved with the initials of one attendant
Silver tray, pitcher, or picture frame engraved with attendants' names
Coffee table with copper plaque engraved with attendants' initials

From Bride to Bridesmaids

Either at the bridesmaids' luncheon shortly before the wedding or at the rehearsal dinner, the bride gives each bridesmaid her present. A typical gift is a bracelet with a monogrammed disk, a pin, or other jewelry, and according to the means of the bride, may have great value or scarcely any. The gift to her maid or matron of honor may match those given the bridesmaids or be slightly more elaborate. If it is something that can be engraved, such as a small silver picture frame, the date and the initials of the bride and groom or the bridesmaids' initials commemorate the occasion.

From Groom to Ushers

The bridegroom's gifts to his ushers are usually put at their places at the bachelor dinner—if one is held. If not, they are presented at the rehearsal dinner or just before leaving the church. Silver or gold pencils, belt buckles, key rings, wallets, billfolds, and other small and personal articles are suitable. The present to the best man is approximately the same as, or slightly handsomer than, the gifts to the ushers.

The Bride and Groom Exchange Presents

The custom of the groom giving the bride a present in addition to the wedding and engagement rings has more or less fallen out of style. If the groom does wish to give his bride a gift, he goes shopping alone and buys the handsomest piece of jewelry he can afford.

The bride need not give a present to the groom, but she sometimes does if she chooses. Her gift is something permanent and for his personal use—ranging from cuff links to a watch or ring.

GUIDELINES FOR GUESTS

Having sent your acceptance—or your regrets—you should next turn your thoughts to whether or not you will send a gift to the bride.

If you are not an intimate friend of the bride or groom or of their families and if you are not invited to the wedding reception, you need not send a present, unless you know that there is to be no reception. Of course, a gift always may be sent if you wish to, whether or not you receive any invitation at all. Obviously, the more personal the invitation the greater the obligation to send a gift. An invitation by written note definitely indicates that you are considered an especially close friend, and you will therefore certainly want to send a present. And you must always send a present to one who is marrying into your immediate family.

It used to be considered obligatory to send a gift, even though you could not attend the wedding. This is still true when the principals are friends whom you see from time to time, or who live nearby. In the days when that "rule" was made, people did not move around as they do today, and invitations were sent *only* to those within a reasonable distance. Today people often send invitations to their entire list of acquaintances (perhaps using a Christmas card list), not thinking about the obligation they impose. So, if you live in California and receive an invitation to a wedding in New Jersey from people you haven't seen in ten years, *don't send a gift*. If you are a customer, a client, or a patient of someone you meet *only* professionally, and you have never met the bride or groom, *don't send a gift*. The bride's parents *should* have sent you an announcement instead of an invitation—carrying no obligation—and the fact that they were thoughtless excuses you from "having to" send a present.

This does *not* mean that you should not send a gift to a bride whose family you will see in the near future, even though you are at a distance when the wedding takes place. For example, the daughter of people you see every summer at your vacation home, who has grown up with your children, gets married in December. The fact that you are hundreds of miles away does not relieve you of the responsibility of sending a gift, if you receive an invitation to both wedding and reception. If you don't, you will surely receive a cool "reception" yourself when you meet next summer.

"Joint" Gifts

Engaged couples, or an unmarried couple living together, may give a "joint" gift—one gift from both of them.

Others who may do this are:

The staff or co-workers from an office, unless they have each received a separate invitation.

A woman and her date, when the invitation has indicated that she may bring an escort. In a sense he is *her* guest rather than the bride and groom's, so he should not be obligated to give a gift to someone he does not know. Therefore she would select and pay for a gift to be given from them both. He may offer to pay a share of it if he wishes to.

A man and *his* date—the same as above.

When and Where Gifts Are Delivered

Gifts are generally delivered to the bride's home or the home of her parents before the day of the wedding. They may be delivered in person, or they may be sent directly from the store where they were purchased. Those sent by mail or from a store are addressed in the bride's maiden name. When gifts are sent after the wedding takes place, they are addressed to "Mr. and Mrs. Newlywed" at their new address, or in care of the bride's mother.

When you do not know the bride's address and it does not appear on the invitation, either under an RSVP or on the envelope flap, it may be very difficult to discover where presents are to be sent. If you have no way of getting her address, or her family's, the only solution is to send gifts and responses in care of the club, hotel, hall, or whatever is given as the site of the reception.

In some localities and among certain ethnic groups it is customary to take your gift to the wedding reception rather than send it ahead of time. Checks are usually handed to the bride and groom as you go through the receiving line, but gift packages are placed on a table prepared for them, as soon as you arrive. If there is a large number of presents, the bride and groom do not open them until a later date, so that they will have time to enjoy the other festivities. If there are only a few, however, they may open them after the receiving line breaks up. One of the bride's attendants should help, disposing of wrappings and keeping a careful list of the gifts.

Choosing the Gift

There is no "formula" to determine the amount you should spend on a wedding gift. The size or elaborateness of the wedding should have nothing to do with the amount you spend or give. Your decision should be based on a combination of two things—your affection for the bride, the groom, or their families, and your financial capability. No one should ever feel that he must spend more than he can afford; not only is it impractical, but it is ostentatious and therefore in poor taste. On the other hand, one should not give a "piddling" gift to a bride whose family are old friends. That would surely make you look "cheap." Having set the appropriate amount you want to spend in mind, you must think carefully about what the couple might most like or need, taking their situation into account. If they are young, just starting out, and have few possessions of their own, a practical gift is indicated. If they have been living independently from their families for some time and have acquired all the basic necessities, something purely ornamental, which they might not buy for themselves, is a better choice.

Remember this: Even though the couple are going to be living in the simplest manner, in the tiniest apartment for the present, someday they will have a larger place and the surroundings to use more elegant things. Although your gift of a silver serving dish may not be exactly what they need right now, it is something they can put away for that later day. Couples moving to larger apartments or houses have tremendous expenses to begin with, and having a supply of wedding presents to be brought out and enjoyed, and which will save them additional expense in furnishing the home, is a real thrill.

When a bride has registered her choices of gifts at a neighboring store (or stores) you will be wise to avail yourself of this assistance, especially if you do not know her, or her tastes, well. You are under no obligation to select anything from her list, especially if she has not chosen items within your price range. However, you will do well to study her selections whether you buy one of them or not. They will indicate to you the style, the materials, the colors that she likes, and you will be able to select something that you are reasonably sure will please her.

Money as a Wedding Present

The custom of giving money as a wedding present is a long-established tradition in many communities. Even at those weddings where most guests give presents, close relatives and intimate friends of the bride's or groom's parents sometimes prefer to give money. To set maximums or minimums on a sum given as a gift is against every principle of etiquette. The sum you give is *in no way* supposed to help pay for the wedding and should never be based on the presumed "cost per head." In some groups it is accepted and expected that one gives, for example, twenty or fifty dollars or more as a gift. If this is the custom in your area, you must go along with it or risk criticism. Otherwise, for anyone to say "You must give thus-and-so" is entirely wrong.

A check given before the wedding is made out in the bride's maiden name, or if the couple have opened a joint account, it may be written to both the bride and groom. Occasionally a grandparent or godparent may intend a gift especially for the groom, and may make the check out to him alone. A check to be presented at the reception may be made out to the bride's married name if she is taking his name as her own, or to the couple jointly.

Bonds or shares of stock also make wonderful wedding gifts because of their lasting and (hopefully) increasing value. If sent before the wedding the bond may be in the name of the bride alone or it may be in both names: "Albert C. Foster and Emily Johnson." After marriage all bonds and securities given to the couple are made out to "Albert C. Foster and Emily J. Foster."

Delayed Presents

If for some reason your present is not sent until some time after the wedding, a note should accompany it, giving the reason for the delay. Late presents are sent to "Mr. and Mrs. Newlywed" at their own new address. If you do not know their address, they may be sent in care of the bride's family.

Presents from the Bridegroom's Friends

You seldom send a present to the bridegroom. Even if you are an old friend of his and have never met the bride, your present is sent to her—unless you send two presents, one in courtesy to her and one in affection to him. Sometimes friends of the bridegroom do pick out things suitable for him, such as a decanter or a rather masculine-looking desk set, which are sent to her but are obviously intended for his use.

When You Receive No Acknowledgment for a Gift

If after several months you have not received a thank-you note from the couple, you need not hesitate to write them and ask whether your present ever arrived. You must word your letter carefully, not implying that you are criticizing them for not writing, but making it clear that you only wish to know what happened so that you may send another gift if the first was lost in the mail. They, too, may have been wondering why a present from you had never arrived, and your letter will serve to clarify the situation for you both. And if they have not thanked you through laziness or thoughtlessness, they deserve the embarrassment your letter will cause!

GUIDELINES FOR THE BRIDE AND GROOM

Using a Bridal Registry

Just before or immediately after your invitations are mailed, you should go to the local stores where you would like to register your choice of gifts. You and your groom should select your china, silver, and glassware patterns, so that they may be registered, too. Your choices should cover a wide range of prices, and as much variety in types of gifts as possible, to allow your friends more leeway in picking a gift.

Then, when someone asks you what you would like, you need only say, "I've listed a number of choices at the Gift-in-Hand. They'll be glad to show you the things on my list." If your friend cannot get to the stores where you are registered, or there are no appropriate stores in your area, you should answer the same question with a generalization rather than mentioning a specific item. "We prefer stainless steel or pewter to silver," or "We're planning to furnish our apartment in the art deco style," or "Our living and dining room will be Early American," will help your friend make a choice, without committing her to paying more or less than she wants to.

You may *never* make any mention of a gift on your invitation. Even though you know some of your friends can't afford to give you one, you must call or write them and and ask them not to, rather than writing "No gift, please," on their invitation (as can be done in other circumstances). Wedding guests expect to give gifts, and usually want to, even though they spend a minimum amount or make the gift themselves. Unless you *know* they will not resent the implication that they cannot afford it, you should not even suggest "No gift." Nor should a bride indicate on her invitation that she would prefer money to a gift. No matter how legitimate the reason, you must spread the word through friends and relatives rather than have the request come from you.

Recording Gifts

As soon as the invitations are out you should get a book to keep a list of the gifts as they arrive. You'll find a section in *Emily Post's Wedding Planner* devoted to keeping track of the gifts you receive, or you may purchase one of the books specially designed for this purpose. Although you may use any lined notebook and make the columns and heading yourself, an attractive bride's book serves not only as a record, but as a lovely memento of the wedding. The usual form is this:

No.	Date Rec'd	Article	Sent by	Sender's Address	Where Bought	Thanks Sent
3	7/2	Salad bowl	Mr. and Mrs. George White	11 High Street, New Haven	Tiffany	7/2
4	7/3	8 fruit plates	Aunt Susan	Long Mile Road New Canaan	Holloway Gifts	7/4

Sheets of numbered stickers come with the book. One is placed on the bottom of each gift as it arrives, and the corresponding number is written in the book. Only one sticker goes on each set of things—on one plate of a set of eight, for example.

Displaying Gifts

Nothing could be nicer than displaying your wedding gifts, showing your appreciation and delight in them.

If your reception is to be at home, they should be in a room easily accessible to all the guests. If they are only to be seen by friends who drop in before the wedding, they may be in a back bedroom, a basement playroom, or anywhere you have room for them.

Gifts are rarely displayed at the club, hotel, or hall where a reception is held. Instead, relatives and friends are invited to the home beforehand, specifically to see the gifts.

Furniture is removed from the room chosen for the display, and tables, or sawhorses with smooth boards across them—are set up around the walls. They are covered with plain white cloths—either damask or linen tablecloths or sheets. The sides are usually draped with net or tulle caught up here and there with bows and ribbons, and possibly silk flowers. The ribbons and flowers may be white or they may be in a color to match the color scheme of the wedding. The sheet or cloths should hang down to the floor so that boxes for the presents on display may be hidden underneath.

To do justice to the kindness of the people who have sent gifts, you should show your appreciation by placing each one in the position of greatest advantage. Very valuable presents are better put near to others of similar quality—or others entirely different in character. Colors should be carefully grouped. Two presents, both lovely in themselves, can completely destroy each other if the colors are allowed to clash. Sometimes china is put on one table, silver on another, glass on another, but I think a more attractive arrangement can be made by combining textures and shapes. A "cheap" piece of silverplate should not be left among beautiful pieces of sterling, but should be put among china ornaments or other articles that do not reveal its lack of fineness by too direct comparison. To group duplicates is another unfortunate arrangement. Eight salad bowls or six gravy boats in a row might as well be labeled: "Look at this! What can she do with all of us?" They are sure to make the givers feel a little chagrined, at least.

Displaying Wedding Gifts

When the wedding gifts are numerous and valuable it is a good idea to hire a policeman or detective to guard the house while everyone is at the wedding and reception. Thieves have been known to watch for just such an opportunity and to pull up with a "caterer's" truck and make a clean sweep while the bride and groom are exchanging their vows.

Should Cards Be Displayed?

There is no definite rule as to whether or not the cards that are sent with the gifts are removed. Some people prefer to leave them on, which certainly saves members of the family from repeating many times who sent this and who sent that, especially if the couple has received an unusual number of presents. On the other hand, other couples feel that it is a private matter between themselves and the giver and do not wish the world to know how elaborate a gift someone was or was not able to send, or perhaps wish to avoid odious comparisons!

Displaying Checks

Ordinarily it would be in very bad taste to display gifts of money. But because it would not be fair to a generous relative or intimate friend of the family to have it supposed that he or she sent no gift at all, it is quite proper to display checks with amounts concealed. This is done by laying them out on a flat surface one above the other so that the signatures alone are disclosed. The amount of the one at the top is covered with a strip of opaque paper, and then a sheet of glass laid over them all, to prevent curious guests from taking a peek.

You may also write on plain white gift enclosure cards "Check from Mr. and Mrs. Harold Brown" and display such cards neatly.

Exchanging Wedding Presents

Some people think it discourteous if the bride changes the present chosen for her, but they are wrong. A bride may exchange all duplicate presents, and no friends should allow their feelings to be hurt unless they have chosen the present with a particular sentiment. You should never, however, exchange the presents chosen for you by your own family or by your groom's unless you are specifically told to do so.

Whether or not you mention the exchange to the donor depends on the circumstances. If she (or he) is a close friend, and will be in your house frequently, you will probably wish to tell her. Or if you do not know where a present was purchased, you must ask the one who gave it and tell her why, if you wish to exchange it. But if the gift came from a mere acquaintance, or someone far away, it is perfectly all right to simply write and thank her for the present she sent, making no mention of the exchange.

When a gift arrives by mail, broken, you should immediately look at the wrapping to see if it was insured. If so, notify the person who sent it at once so that he or she can collect the insurance and replace it. If it is not insured, you must decide whether to call attention to it or not. If it is a very special gift from a very special person, you should probably do so. But if it is a small present from someone you barely know, it could be an imposition to mention it, as he would undoubtedly feel he had to buy you something else.

When the broken gift is delivered directly from the store, you should take it back as soon as possible. All reputable stores will replace merchandise that arrives damaged. You need not even mention it to the donor, as it is unnecessary to bother him or her about it at all.

Returning Wedding Gifts

Gifts are never returned to the donor, *except* when a marriage is canceled or immediately annulled.

When wedding plans are canceled, gifts that have already been received must be returned. If it is an indefinite postponement but the couple intend to be married as soon as possible, the gifts are carefully put away until the time the ceremony takes place. If there is doubt as to whether it will take place at all, the bride after six weeks to two months must send back the gifts so that the donors may return them.

(For a sample letter of explanation when the engagement is broken see page 608.)

35
Acknowledging Gifts

hatever the gift, be it the gift of time and friendship or twelve place settings of your china, it must be acknowledged. Thanks take many forms but all share one common guideline—that they be prompt. This is particularly true when gifts have been sent in the mail or delivered by a store so that the sender knows that they have arrived safely.

Gifts are discussed in several chapters of this book, since gift-giving is such an important part of our culture. In most of the discussions there is some mention of the importance of acknowledging the gift. I believe that this message cannot be repeated too many times. All too often, someone spends a considerable amount of time selecting a gift, only to wonder why he bothered, since the recipient seemingly cared so little for it that he didn't bother to mention it at all.

With the exception of shower gifts that are opened in front of the donor when verbal thanks that are all that is required, all wedding-related gifts must be acknowledged with a written thank-you.

Saying thank you is one of the common precepts of good manners—it always has been, and it always will be! If you are not sure when a thank-you note is obligatory or optional see the chart on pages 265–266. But always remember that it is never wrong to write a thank-you note.

ACKNOWLEDGMENT CARDS

There are three times in particular when printed acknowledgment cards are used: after the death of a prominent person when scores of sympathy notes, gifts of flowers or donations to charities are received, when a public official is elected and receives a "landslide" of congratulatory messages, and when a bride has such a large or public wedding that she simply cannot write personal thank-you notes.

In the case of the acknowledgment of sympathy and of the receipt of a wedding gift, she should additionally write notes to personal friends and family.

If circumstances demand it, a printed acknowledgment card for wedding gifts would read:

Mr and Mrs Joseph Amendolia
gratefully acknowledge the receipt of
your wedding gift
and offer their sincere thanks

Quite frequently the bride and groom are away at college, or are working at a distance from where the wedding will be held and where the gifts will be sent. Because the RSVP gives the bride's mother's address, the presents are sent there, too. Even though the mother may open the gifts and send the bride daily lists, so that she can keep up with the thank-you notes, there can be considerable confusion and delay. Therefore in this case I would recommend this thoughtful solution, suggested to me recently. The bride's mother has cards printed (they need not be engraved), saying, "This is to assure you of the safe arrival of your thoughtful gift. Ileane and Martin will express their gratitude when they have received it from my custody." Although Ileane will have a lot of letter-writing to do when she gets back from her honeymoon, her notes will be more sincere, because she will have seen the gifts herself.

THANK-YOU NOTES

For Wedding Gifts

As mentioned before brides must send a separate handwritten letter for each present they receive. If humanly possible, they write each letter of thanks on the day the present arrives. If not, the list will soon get ahead of them, and the first weeks of their marriage will be taken up with note-writing. A note of thanks is also sent to those who send congratulatory telegrams on the day of the wedding. There is no excuse for not having all thank-you notes written within three months of the wedding—at the most.

It is not possible to overemphasize the rudeness of a couple who sends a printed or even an engraved card of thanks with no personal message added. If you prefer a card that says "Thank you," or has a poem or message on it, choose one that is simple and dignified, and then add your own note, mentioning the specific gift and how you feel about it or intend to use it. Since you *must do this* in any case, it seems foolish to go to the expense of buying cards that come to much more than a box of plain notepaper.

Many brides order paper with their maiden initials on it to be used before their marriage, and other paper with their married initials for afterward. Any of the papers described in Chapter 14 are appropriate, whether plain or bordered, white or colored.

Since most wedding gifts are sent to the bride, she usually writes *and* signs the thank-you note. But there is no reason the groom should not share this task. I'm sure there are many relatives and friends of the groom who would be delighted to receive a thank-you note from him rather than from a bride who is a relative stranger to them. It is not incorrect to sign both of your names, but it is preferable to sign your name and include your spouse in the text: "Bob and I are so delighted with . . . etc." or "Fran and I . . . etc."

Thank-you notes for gifts from married couples are often addressed to the wife only, on the premise, I suppose, that it was she who selected and bought the gift. However, when the present comes from "Mr. and Mrs." or "Hal and Donna," I feel that it is warmer to send your thanks to "Mr. and Mrs." or "Hal and Donna." However, it is equally correct to write; "Dear Mrs. Hancock, I want to thank you and Mr. Hancock so much. . . ."

Every note, no matter how short (and it may be very short), should include a reference to the present itself. While you need not lie about your feelings about the gift, you must try to make some comment that shows your appreciation of the thought and effort spent in choosing it. When you have received a ghastly pin-cushion covered with sequins and fake flowers, you need not say it is "lovely" or "pretty." But it *can* be "unique," "a conversation piece," or even "interesting." After being sure it is on display the first time the donor comes to your home, you can put it away and hope that its absence will go unnoticed.

For Other Gifts

Thank-you letters are not necessary for presents that have been given in person on a birthday, at a house party, a shower, or other similar occasions. Although it is in no way wrong to write a note, sincere verbal thanks at the time you receive the gift are sufficient. Nor do thank-you or "bread-and-butter" letters themselves require any reply: That would be inviting a never-ending exchange of correspondence. A thank-you *gift* sent with, or in place of, a bread-and-butter letter should, however, be acknowledged if only so that the sender will know it has been received. Sending printed cards of thanks is inexcusable, unless a personal note is added.

(For examples of thank-you letters, see Chapter 14.)

A Newspaper "Card of Thanks"

In certain localities, most especially small towns and rural areas, it is not only permissible but expected that recipients of a large number of gifts or kindnesses put a public "thanks" in the paper. Here is a typical "card of thanks."

CARD OF THANKS
We wish to express our thanks
to all those unselfish people
and organizations from whom we
received cards and gifts on the
occasion of our fiftieth wedding
anniversary
Sincerely,
Mr. and Mrs. Joseph Horne

When this is done it is not necessary to send written thanks to each and every donor and card-sender. But it would be most unappreciative not to write a personal note to those close to you who have gone out of their way to give something very special or to assist or participate in your celebration in any way.

These "cards of thanks" are published for occasions such as funerals, retirement parties, anniversaries, birthdays, political campaigns, professional advancements, and any other events that result in special kindnesses, assistance, gifts, or contributions.

OTHER THANK-YOUS

When a friend sends you a box of baby clothes for your newborn, no matter how tired you may be, send her an immediate thank-you note. You needn't send her a thank-you gift, but letting her know how much you appreciate the loan will make her glad she made the effort to find and send you the clothing.

When someone gives you a job reference, interviews you for a job, or provides his or her professional expertise in response to your request, send a thank-you note.

When friends take you to dinner to celebrate your birthday, even if they are your very best friends, send a thank-you note (or at least call the next day and be profuse with your thanks for a wonderful evening).

When a stranger rescues your dog and returns him safely to your door, obtain his name and send a thank-you note.

In other words, the list of opportunities is endless. Your appreciation, beautifully expressed, surely brightens the day of the one who committed the act of thoughtfulness or did the good deed in the first place.

For Gifts of Time or Thoughtfulness

Although friends give of themselves with no expectation of thanks, it is important to acknowledge how much their gift meant to you. If neighbors have cared for your children so you could visit an ailing parent in the hospital, or taken in your newspaper when you went away for the weekend, for example, a warm "thank you" is definitely in order, sometimes accompanied by a small token of your thanks, such as a gourmet food item or a plant for their garden.

When co-workers help you out of a jam by pitching in and collating your report, or staying late to assist you in finishing a project, heartfelt thanks are essential, sometimes accompanied by treating them to lunch or buying flowers for their desk, for example. If you routinely help one another out in times of overwork, then verbal thanks are all that is necessary, since you will be returning the favor shortly.

When your entire staff puts in the extra effort needed to make an important deadline the grateful supervisor can say "thank you" in different ways. Treating the staff to fresh bagels or rolls one morning is one way. Another, which can have long-term benefits to the employee, is to write a memo thanking the individual and sending a copy to the Personnel department. If your department budget contains no money for overtime, and company policy allows it, consider offering staff members compensatory time-off as your way of saying thank you.

IX

WEDDINGS

Whether a couple is very young and just out of school, or is older and has been living together for some time, the decision to become engaged is both serious and exciting. It is to be presumed that before this decision is made the couple has discussed their feelings on a variety of topics so that they know what goals they share, and where they differ. Being united in planning for their future together enables them to answer the questions others may ask when they announce their engagement.

36
Engagements

THE LENGTH OF THE ENGAGEMENT

A long engagement is invariably a strain on all involved. The ideal duration is from three to five months, although those planning elaborate weddings where clubs or halls, bands and caterers are sometimes booked a year in advance may have to decide upon a longer engagement.

INFORMING OTHERS

Once the couple has discussed their plans, they naturally want to share their happiness with others. Parents are usually informed by their own children. They should never be "surprised" by the introduction of a person they have never heard of before, however. If a couple feels their relationship is leading toward marriage, it behooves them to be sure they create opportunities for their "intended" to meet their parents a few times before announcing their marriage plans. If this is impossible because they live on opposite coasts or even separate continents, then the couple should be sure to mention their special relationship in phone conversations and letters before telling of their engagement. Except within certain ethnic groups, it is no longer necessary for the future groom to ask his future father-in-law for the bride's hand in marriage.

When it is impossible for a mother to go to meet her son's fiancee, and if they have not spoken on the phone, a letter should be written to her. The general outline is:

Dear Mary,
　　John has just told us of his great happiness, which, of course, makes us very happy, too. Our one regret is that we are so far away [or whatever else] that we cannot immediately meet you in person.

We do, however, send you our love and hope that we shall see you very soon, here if not there. Perhaps John can arrange to bring you here for a visit in the near future.

Sincerely and affectionately,
Martha Jones

If one or both members of a couple have been married before, they should personally inform their ex-spouses that they intend to remarry. If there are children involved, the children should be told first or at the same time. In either case children should be told by the parent who is about to remarry, not by their other parent. Hopefully, children have had the chance to spend time with their mother's or father's future husband or wife so that they do not feel threatened by or hostile to this news.

When parents disapprove, no matter what the relationship they are disapproving of, the engaged couple faces a dilemma. If they have made up their minds to marry in spite of this disapproval, they tell their parents when the wedding will take place and that they hope they will be there. If the parents care about their future relationship with their children, they will swallow their feelings and attend. They will gain nothing, and very possibly lose their child for good if they refuse.

Families Become Acquainted

When parents of the bride and groom live near enough to meet each other before the wedding, tradition decrees that the groom's family calls the bride's family to introduce themselves, express their happiness, and arrange a meeting. If it is not possible for them to meet, they still should call or write so that an initial introduction is established.

If for any reason the groom's family does not contact the parents of the bride, her father and mother should not stand on ceremony, but should make the first move themselves. This should be a happy time for the couple. Both sets of parents should act with spontaneity and in a spirit of friendship, regardless of who makes the first contact.

When the bride's parents are divorced, the groom's parents should get in touch with each of the bride's parents, separately, calling first the one with whom the bride is or has been living or is closest to. When a groom's parents are divorced, the one with whom he is closest should contact the bride's parents. Again, if he or she does not do this, the bride's parents should get in touch with first one and then the other.

After the bride's and groom's parents have been informed, the engaged couple shares their news with other family members and friends before formal announcements are made. When brothers and sisters haven't had the opportunity to meet the bride or the groom, they often suggest get-togethers to welcome the new almost-member of their family. A thank-you note sent by the bride and/or groom after such an occasion helps to cement these new relationships.

The following letter, written by a bride after paying a first visit to her husband's aunt and uncle, won her the approval of the whole family:

Dear Aunt Anne,

Now that we are home again I have a confession to make. Do you know that when Dick drove me up to your front door and I saw you and Uncle Bob standing on the top step—I was simply paralyzed with fright.

"Suppose they don't like me," was all that I could think. The reason I stumbled coming up the steps was that my knees were actually knocking together. And then you were both so sweet to me and made me feel as though I had always been your niece—and not just the wife of your nephew.

I loved every minute of our being with you, just as much as Dick did, and we hope you are going to let us come again soon.

With best love from us both,

Your niece,
Nancy

THE ENGAGEMENT RING/WEDDING RINGS

It is doubtful that the man who produced a ring from his pocket the instant that the woman said "Yes" ever existed outside Victorian novels. In real life it is both correct and wise for *him* to consult *her* taste. The fiancé may go alone to the jeweler, explain how much he can afford, and have a selection of rings set aside. He then brings his fiancée to the store and lets her choose the one she likes best. More often they simply go to the store together and select the ring.

She might choose a traditional diamond ring, or she might prefer a ring with her birthstone. If there are family heirlooms to be chosen from, the man may show them to his fiancée and have her selection set to her taste.

Today many women choose to use larger semiprecious stones, beside which a tiny diamond loses some of its appeal.

An aquamarine is first choice as a solitaire diamond's substitute. Amethysts, topazes, and transparent tourmalines are all lovely as selections for an engagement ring.

The engagement ring is worn for the first time in public on the day of the announcement. In the United States it is worn on the fourth finger (next to the little finger) of the left hand. In some foreign countries it is worn on the right hand. It is removed during the marriage ceremony and replaced immediately afterward, outside the wedding ring. *An engagement ring is not essential to the validity of the betrothal.* Some people confuse the engagement ring with the wedding ring and believe the former is as indispensable as the latter. This is not the case. The wedding ring is a requirement of the marriage service. The engagement ring is simply evidence that the couple definitely plan to marry. A man may give his fiancée a ring no matter how many times he has been married before.

Countless wives have never had an engagement ring at all. Others receive their rings long after marriage, when their husbands are able to buy the ring they have always wanted them to have. Some brides prefer to forgo an engagement ring in order to put the money it would have cost toward furnishing their future homes. A daughter may wear her deceased mother's engagement ring, but not her wedding ring.

The wedding rings may be selected at the same time as the engagement ring. If they are not, then they are selected and ordered during the engagement period.

Shortly before the wedding, it is not only customary but important that the bride go with the groom when he buys the wedding ring. Since, hopefully, she intends to wear it for a long time, she should be allowed to choose the style she prefers. No ring could be in better taste than the plain band of yellow or white gold or platinum.

If the bridegroom is also to receive a ring the bride buys a plain gold band to match hers but a little wider—or it may be any type of ring he prefers and she is able to buy. A man's wedding ring, like a woman's, is worn on the fourth finger of his left hand.

The wedding ring may be engraved with whatever sentiment the bridegroom chooses. On the broad rings of many years ago, it was not unusual to have a quotation of twenty-five letters or more, as well as initials. Today, however, only the initials and date are usually engraved.

Handcrafted rings of intricate design are popular too, and are sometimes made by the couples themselves. These can be very beautiful and are more meaningful than the most expensive diamond-studded band.

Announcing the Engagement

If the couple wishes, their engagement may be announced formally, at an engagement party and/or via a newspaper announcement.

No announcement should *ever* be made of an engagement in which either member is still legally married to someone else—no matter how close the divorce or annulment may be.

The Engagement Party

The bride's family usually gives the engagement party. However, if they cannot afford it, or if the bride's parents are dead, or perhaps live far away, the groom's family may do so.

The guest list is unlimited, but the majority of engagement parties are

restricted to relatives and good friends. Occasionally—and it is not improper—the
party is a huge open house or reception, including all the friends of both families.

Although the engagement party may be of any type that the bride and her mother prefer, it is most often a cocktail party or a dinner. The news may be told by the bride herself, or by her mother as the guests arrive and find the fiancé standing with their hostess. There is no formal receiving line, but his presence beside the family, being introduced as the guests arrive, needs no further explanation. Perhaps, if the party is a dinner, the engagement is announced by the bride's father, who proposes a toast to the couple. Little announcing is necessary by the time dinner is served, however, when the woman is wearing a brand new ring on the fourth finger of her left hand.

To those who ask about using a novel way to announce an engagement, it can be said that there is really no logical objection to whatever may be pleasing to you. Whether you let a cat out of a bag with your names written on a ribbon around its neck, float balloons with your names printed on them, display a cake decorated with the couple's initials inside two hearts, or use place cards in the form of telegrams containing the announcement, there is not a rule in the world to hamper your own imagination.

The Newspaper Announcement

An engagement may be made public through a newspaper announcement. It is not in good taste to send engraved or printed announcements. The article usually appears in the newspaper two or three months before the proposed date of the marriage, although the wedding plans need not have been completed. If the circumstances warrant, the announcement may appear up to a year before the wedding date, or as little as a week ahead. Announcements may be put in the paper by any couple who wish to be sure that all their acquaintances know of their happiness. Widows and divorcées, in some cases, may prefer to make their news known privately, and that is perfectly correct; it is entirely up to them.

The only time a public announcement is not in good taste is when there has recently been a death in either family, or if a member of the immediate family is desperately ill. In these cases the news is spread by word of mouth, although a public announcement may follow some weeks later.

The announcement of the engagement is generally made by the bride's parents or her immediate family. The information should be clearly written out and sent to large city newspapers three weeks or more ahead of the date you wish it to appear. In local newspapers a week or ten days is usually sufficient. The letter is addressed to the society editor or the society news department of the paper. Be sure to include telephone numbers in your letter so that the information can be verified. The bride's family should ask the parents of the groom if they would like to have the announcement appear in their locality. If the groom's family says yes, the bride's mother should send the same announcement to the papers they specify. If the bride's parents do not suggest this, it is quite proper for the groom's mother to put the announcement in her local papers—*in the name of the bride's parents.* If either family wishes to have a picture appear, a glossy black-and-white print must accompany the written information. This picture used to be of the bride alone, but today it may also be a picture of the couple. The date on which you would like the news to be published should be given to all the newspapers at the same time so that the notices will appear simultaneously.

Although each newspaper has its own special wording, the information included and the general form will be as follows:

Mr. and Mrs. Howard Adams of Briarcliff Manor, New York, announce the engagement of their daughter, Miss Katherine Leigh Adams, to Mr. Brian Charles Jamison, son of Mrs. Richard Jamison of Minneapolis, Minnesota, and the late Mr. Jamison. A June wedding is planned.

Miss Adams was graduated from New York University and is a communications assistant for the National Broadcasting Company. Mr. Jamison was graduated from the University of Minnesota. He is at present associated with Moore Associates advertising agency in New York City.

Although the identification of the bride and groom and their parents may vary, the information as to schools and employment remains the same. Following are some situations that require different wording in the announcement:

WHEN ONE OF THE BRIDE'S PARENTS IS DECEASED:

The announcement is worded the same whether made by the mother or the father of the bride.

Mrs. [Mr.] Allan Robert Rogers announces the engagement of her [his] daughter, Miss Joanne Lynn Rogers, to Dr. William Kelly . . . etc. Miss Rogers is also the daughter of the late Allan Robert [Joyce Green] Rogers . . .

WHEN A PARENT OF THE GROOM IS DECEASED:

Mr. and Mrs. Mark Steglitz announce the engagement of their daughter, Miss Sandra Steglitz, to Mr. John Williams, son of Mrs. Adam Carter Williams and the late Mr. Williams . . .

WHEN THE PARENTS ARE DIVORCED:

The mother of the bride usually makes the announcement, but, as in the case of a deceased parent, the name of the other parent must be included:

Mrs. Lucinda Castronova announces the engagement of her daughter, Miss Valerie Castronova . . . Miss Castronova is also the daughter of Mr. Julio Castronova of Worcester, Massachusetts . . .

WHEN DIVORCED PARENTS ARE FRIENDLY:

On occasion, divorced parents may remain good friends, and their daughter's time may be divided equally between them. If this is true, they may both wish to announce the engagement.

Mr. James Gibson of Philadelphia and Mrs. Christopher Morris of Palm Beach, Florida, announce the engagement of their daughter, Miss Carla Gibson . . .

WHEN THE PARENT WITH WHOM THE BRIDE LIVES IS REMARRIED:

Mr. and Mrs. Douglas Skolnick announce the engagement of Mrs. Skolnick's daughter, Miss Marcy Rectenwald, to . . . Miss Rectenwald is also the daughter of Mr. Franklin Scott Rectenwald of Lake Tahoe, Nevada . . .

WHEN THE BRIDE IS ADOPTED:

If the bride has been brought up with the family since she was an infant and has the same name as her adoptive parents, there is no reason to mention the fact that she is adopted. If she joined the family later in life, however, and has retained her own name, it is proper to say:

Mr. and Mrs. Abbott Smythe announce the engagement of their adopted daughter, Miss Karen Reardon, daughter of the late Mr. and Mrs. Carlton Reardon . . .

WHEN THE BRIDE IS AN ORPHAN:

The engagement of an orphan is announced by her nearest relative, a godparent, or a very dear friend. She may also announce her own engagement, impersonally:

The engagement of Miss Maryann Hayes (daughter of the late Mr. and Mrs. Samuel Hayes) is announced, to Mr. Jay Pomranze . . .

WHEN THE BRIDE IS A WIDOW:

The parents of a young widow would announce her engagement in the same way as they did the first time she was married, using her current name:

Mr. and Mrs. Allan Wheat announce the engagement of their daughter, Mrs. Jasper Fountain [or Anne Wheat Fountain] . . .

WHEN THE BRIDE IS A DIVORCÉE:

The parents of a young divorcée would announce her engagement as would the parents of a young widow, using her former husband's last name if she continues to use his name, or her maiden name, if she has changed her name back following a divorce:

> *Mr. and Mrs. Thomas Hauranek announce the engagement of their daughter, Mrs. Amanda Bieler [or Amanda Hauranek Bieler] [or Amanda Sue Hauranek] to . . .*

WHEN THE BRIDE IS AN OLDER WOMAN:

An older woman, whether marrying for the first time or a divorcée or widow, may announce her own engagement, or may forgo a newspaper announcement and notify friends and relatives by note or telephone. If she chooses to announce her engagement in the newspaper:

> *The engagement of Miss [or Mrs.] Diana Trainer to Mr. Salvator Iannuzzi has been announced . . .*

WHEN THE GROOM'S PARENTS ANNOUNCE THE ENGAGEMENT:

Occasionally a situation arises in which the parents of the groom would like to announce the engagement. For instance, when a man in the service becomes engaged to a girl from another country, her parents may not have the knowledge or means to put an announcement in the paper in his home town. Rather than announce it in their own name, the groom's parents should word the notice:

> *The engagement of Miss Inger Strauss, daughter of Mr. and Mrs. Heinrich Strauss of Munich, Germany, to Lt. John Evans, son of Mr. and Mrs. Walter Evans of Chicago, is announced.*

Timing

Whether the newspaper announcement appears before or after the engagement party is a matter of the couple's choice and local custom. If they wish to surprise their guests, naturally the party is held the day before the news appears in the paper. However, it is equally correct to have the party follow the announcement, right away or even days or weeks later.

ENGAGEMENT PRESENTS

A bride-to-be generally receives a few engagement presents, given either by her relatives, her intimate friends or those of her parents, her godparents, or by members of her fiancé's family as a special welcome to her. It is never necessary for other friends to give engagement as well as wedding presents. For engagement gift suggestions see Chapter 34.

BEHAVIOR OF THE ENGAGED COUPLE

Of course, all the world loves a lover, but the most attractive way for a couple to show their affection is by open approval of each other's actions, not by public physical displays.

Engaged men and women should not show an interest in *a particular member* of the opposite sex. If they are separated, they need not sit home alone, but neither should they have "twosome" dates. They should not see the same person frequently or let an occasional meeting lead to others of a more intimate nature.

During this period, it is most important that you do not avoid the company of others. Naturally you will want to spend a great deal of time alone together, and those hours will be your favorite ones, but it is essential that you get to know each other's friends. When one member of a couple is incompatible with those who have been a part of the other's life, the marriage has one strike against it at the start.

WHAT TO CALL YOUR FIANCÉ'S PARENTS

During the engagement period, the bride-to-be may, if she does not know them well, continue to refer to her future in-laws formally. If she has known them for many years and is accustomed to calling them by nicknames, or possibly "Aunt" and "Uncle," she should go on using those terms. Otherwise, as she becomes closer to them, she might shorten the formal "Mr. Olafson" to "Mr. O."

If the parents wish their future son- or daughter-in-law to call them by their first names, they should say so and this wish should be respected. This generally is done at some point after the wedding. Some derivative of "Mother" and "Father" may be used if the parents suggest it.

This question is truly a sensitive one, and thoughtfulness must be observed on both sides. If a nickname does not come about naturally, or if the woman does not wish to use names that her husband-to-be uses for his parents, or he for hers, tact is required to avoid too much formality—or too little respect. I once met a woman whose mother-in-law had lived with her and her husband for ten years, and they had been married for twenty years. She still called her "Mrs. Hillman," which seemed decidedly odd and extremely formal. The best solution for her would have been, and is for all couples, to initiate an open discussion. Simply say, "What would you like me to call you?" If this just seems too difficult, then reverting to the shortened "Mr. and Mrs. O." seems a satisfactory compromise.

A Broken Engagement

In the unfortunate event of a broken engagement, the ring and all other gifts of value must be returned to the former fiancé. Gifts received from relatives or friends should also be returned with a short note of explanation:

Dear Nancy,
*   I am sorry to have to tell you that Jack and I have broken our engagement.*
Therefore I am returning the towels that you were so sweet to send me.

*   Love,*
*   Elizabeth*

A notice reading: "The engagement of Miss Caroline Muller and Mr. John Ryan has been broken by mutual consent," may be sent to the newspapers that announced the engagement.

If the man should die before the wedding, his fiancée may keep her engagement ring. However, if it happens to be an old family heirloom and she knows that his parents would like to have it remain in the family, she would be considerate to offer to return it. She may keep any gifts that were given her by friends.

A Hope Chest

Years ago, most mothers started making and embroidering linens for their little girl's future trousseau almost from the time the child was born. Today, with little leisure time and less knowledge of the art of sewing, mothers go out and buy their daughters an "instant" trousseau when they become engaged. Hopefully the current rage for sewing, crewel work, embroidering, and crafts of all sorts will see a return of the hand-embroidered towels or the beautiful hand-sewn lingerie of earlier times. My daughter is fortunate to have a skilled mother-in-law who presented her with beautifully monogrammed sheets as an engagement gift—a present that could never be duplicated by machine.

Since there had to be a place to keep the lovely linens they had worked so hard over, those early-day mothers bought for their daughters trunks or boxes in which to store the articles until the girls married. These were known as hope chests. Today parents rarely buy a hope chest for their daughter before she becomes engaged, since there is nothing to put in it. But when the time comes, and the sheets, towels, table linen, etc., are piling up, it is the prerogative of the bride's family—not her fiancé's—to provide the hope chest. It is not a necessity—a closet shelf or an empty bureau drawer or two will do just as well, but a good-sized chest, perhaps a carved Chinese chest or a lovely-smelling cedar chest, will be treasured by the bride long after the contents have been removed to other places.

THE BRIDE'S TROUSSEAU

A Personal Trousseau

A trousseau, according to the derivation of the word, was the "little trusse" or "bundle" that the bride carried with her to the house of her husband. The dozens of frilly pieces of lingerie and lacy table linens that were once considered indispensable have been replaced by articles that are regarded as necessary by our modern standards.

There is no rule about how many pieces of lingerie or what kinds of clothes a bride should have in her personal trousseau. It depends entirely on her financial situation and the life that she and her groom will be leading. She should, however, plan to begin her marriage with a wardrobe sufficient to last her for one season, and preferably for one year. A bride need not feel that her wardrobe must consist entirely of new things; she should keep all of her old clothing that she particularly likes, as long as it is in serviceable condition. The three new articles that every bride should have if she can possibly afford them are her wedding dress, her going-away costume, and a nightgown and negligee for her honeymoon.

The Household Trousseau

While it is impossible to itemize the bride's personal clothes, it is quite possible to make practical suggestions for household necessities. The lists below include minimum amounts of linen, china, crystal, and silver for the young bride who will live in a small house or apartment. Even though she may be able to afford larger quantities, she should remember that closet and storage space will undoubtedly be very limited until she and her husband can have a larger home. Naturally the bride who starts out with bigger quarters, and expects to entertain on a larger scale, must add to these lists whatever she feels will be necessary.

Unlike many younger couples, previously divorced or widowed brides and grooms very likely have doubles of household items, since both are entering this marriage from their own homes and after years of accumulating items during their previous marriages. They will want to consolidate and will have to make decisions about whose china or flatware, for example, they will use, or whether they wish to give away or sell what they already own and make a fresh start with new items. For them, these lists are a guideline for checking among their possessions to make sure that what they already own is in good repair and for determining what else they might need.

Bed Linen

4 sheets for master bed (or, if master beds are twin size, 4 for each)
4 sheets for each single bed

2 pillowcases for each single bed
2 quilted mattress pads for each bed
1 lightweight blanket for each bed
1 electric blanket, or 2 woolen blankets and 1 comforter for each bed
1 bedspread for each bed (unless guest beds are convertible sofas) extra
   pillows for guests
Optional:
1 blanket cover for master bed, preferably permanent press (Blanket covers for
   guest beds are also nice but not necessary)
extra pillows for guests

Colored and patterned sheets are pretty, but, except for those to be used in the master bedroom, white may be more practical. Solid white or those with simple colored, scalloped borders can be used with any color scheme, whereas the more elaborate ones may be restricted to use in one room. Monogrammed sheets are, of course, lovely and luxurious.

Bath Linen (for one-bathroom apartment)

4 large bath towels
4 matching hand towels
4 washcloths
4 guest towels, linen or terry cloth
2 bath mats
1 shower curtain

The quantity need not be doubled for an additional bathroom, since towels can be interchanged or used in various color combinations.

Table Linen

If you have a formal dining room:

1 damask, linen, or lace tablecloth, large enough to fit a table that can seat
   eight people (at least 72 by 108 inches)
8 matching dinner napkins
2 or 3 52-inch-square tablecloths to fit card tables for additional seats at
   dinner parties or for bridge
12 linen or cotton (preferably permanent press) napkins in several colors to go
   with odd plastic mats, etc.
2 sets (4 or 6) of hard-surface plastic mats for every day
1 set (6 or 8) of more elaborate hard-surface mats for informal entertaining
24 cocktail napkins, paper or cloth

You may not feel that you will have any need for a damask cloth in the foreseeable future, but remember that it is ideal for a buffet table as well as a sit-down dinner. When you use a cloth with a pad under it, every inch of space on the table is useful, which is not true when hot plates must be placed on individual mats or trivets. Also, a tablecloth inevitably adds a touch of elegance when you wish to depart from your usual informal way of entertaining.

Even though you may have no dining-room table for the present, damask will remain fresh and unspoiled for years. Accordingly, while you may not feel you can afford to buy your future formal table covering yourself, it makes an ideal gift from a relative or godparent.

Marking Linen

Katherine Leigh Adams, who will marry Brian Charles Jamison may have the linen initialed with her married initials, KJ or KJA or her future husband's last initial, J. Often the single initial embellished with a scroll or pretty design is more effective than three initials, and the cost may be less. The bride who chooses to keep her own name may have her last initial and that of her husband divided by a dot or design: A.J

Towels are marked at the center of one end, so that the monogram shows when they are folded lengthwise in thirds and hung over a rack.

Long rectangular tablecloths are marked at the center of each long side, midway between table edge and center of cloth.

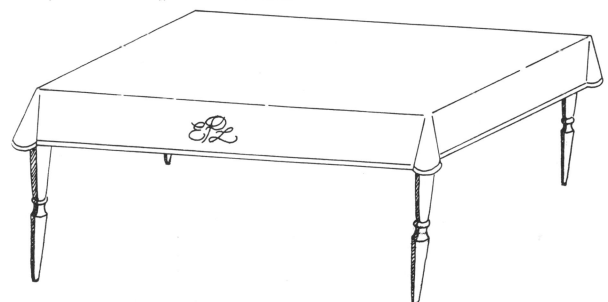

Small square cloths are marked in one corner midway between center and corner, so that the monogram shows on the table.

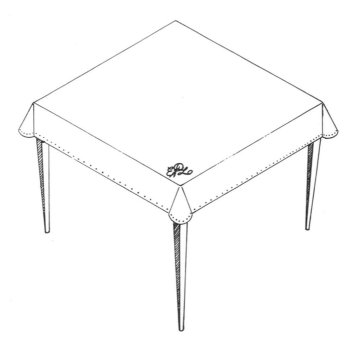

Dinner napkins are marked diagonally in one corner or centered on a rectangular fold.

Sheets are monogrammed so that when the top is folded down, the letters can be read by a person standing at the foot of the bed. Pillowcases are marked approximately two inches above the hem.

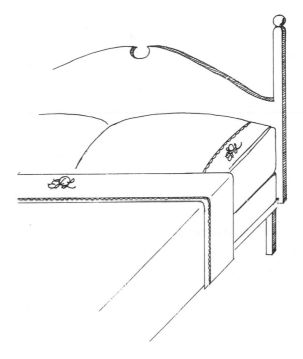

China

Today the stores are filled with colorful sets of pottery, plastic ware, and china in every variety imaginable. The problem is not to find sufficiently attractive tableware but to decide among the many to choose from. There is, however, one important thing for a couple to keep in mind. That is the matter of replacements. They should remember that in the case of a pattern not easily replaced, breakage will leave them handicapped. Therefore it is always wise to ask if a pattern is in open stock, meaning that the pattern is usually stocked by the store and pieces are available singly. Another useful hint is that soap-bubble-thin glass, or glass that is very finely chased or cut, naturally goes best with delicate porcelains, whereas the heavier glassware is best suited to pottery and plastics.

The one requirement for a table set entirely with china is that it be in harmony, meaning that it have some matching detail such as texture or perhaps a repeated note of color. In other words, dinner plates of one variety, bread-and-butter plates of another variety, centerpiece of another, dishes for sweets of another, and candlesticks of still another would look like an odd-lot table selected at random unless all those pieces match in the ways suggested.

The following lists are what the couple should *basically* have to start out with. If their funds are limited and if they are not given enough dinner and dessert plates, for instance, to complete eight or twelve place settings, they may add a piece or two as often as they can, completing one place setting at a time rather than buying two or three more dinner plates and still having an incomplete setting.

Everyday Dishes

The bride will need a complete set of 4 or 6 settings of inexpensive china, pottery, stoneware, or unbreakable plastic ware, which also comes in most attractive patterns. This set should include:

dinner plates
dessert plates (used also for salad)
cereal dishes (used also for soup, puddings, fruit)
cups or mugs
saucers if cups are chosen
cream pitcher and sugar bowl

Dishes for Entertaining

The bride may prefer to be given complete place settings. A typical place setting includes:

dinner plate
salad plate (may double as a dessert plate)
bread and butter plate
cup
saucer

Optional:

soup cup (two-handled, for both clear and cream soups)
cream pitcher and sugar bowl
platters and vegetable dishes
demitasse cups
gravy boat
sauce bowl

Or she may prefer to receive sets of 8 or 12 dinner plates, dessert plates, butter plates, etc., in different patterns, as long as they are compatible.

If the bride prefers variety to a uniform set of china, she must choose her accompanying items carefully. Glass, silver, pewter, wood, and easy-to-care-for stainless steel may be combined with any china to make a charming dinner table. To go with the varied dinner and dessert plates, she will need:

8 or 12 glass or silver butter plates
8 or 12 glass salad plates (the crescent-shaped ones are pretty and take up less
   space on the table)
12 cups and saucers in any pattern

8 or 12 demitasse cups and saucers in any pattern

2 platters and 3 vegetables dishes of silver or stainless steel

1 cream pitcher and sugar bowl of silver, glass, or stainless steel

Other useful items (which may be of any material or style that the bride prefers) are:

4 salts and peppers (silver, glass, stainless steel, wood, china, or a combination of silver and wood)

1 salad bowl and servers (wood or glass)

1 bread dish (silver or wicker)

1 gravy or sauce boat (silver or china)

condiment dishes (glass, china, or pottery)

1 water pitcher (any material)

1 teapot

1 silver coffeepot or a presentable coffee maker (such as stainless steel or glass, whether electric or not) that may be brought from the kitchen for serving after-dinner coffee

8 or 12 small bowls for serving ice cream with sauce or a "runny" dessert (glass dishes look very pretty on a plate with a colorful pattern showing through)

3 or 4 pots and casseroles, in which food is cooked and served in the same dish

1 electric warming tray (an invaluable aid when entertaining without help)

4 trays (wood, metal, or plastic)

Glasses

Glasses are so easily broken, and good glasses so expensive to replace, that a bride who wishes to have a matching set for any length of time should have far more than she actually needs to start out with.

In order to save her expensive glass for parties, she should have for everyday use and for casual entertaining:

6 tumblers

8 or 12 old-fashioned or "on-the-rocks" glasses

8 or 12 wineglasses

8 or 12 iced tea or highball glasses

6 or 8 Pilsners or beer mugs

Beyond this, she should have, depending on the number of place settings she has decided upon:

goblets

liqueur glasses

stemmed sherbet glasses

champagne flutes

Silver

Many brides request that they be given pewter or stainless steel platters, serving dishes, or similar items rather than silver, as they require little care and are more durable although nothing can replace a set of beautiful sterling flat silver on the dinner-party table. Often the parents of the bride or the groom choose the flat silver as their gift to the couple. There are innumerable patterns; the bride whose home is "traditional" may choose one of the older, more ornate patterns, and she who leans toward "modern" will probably prefer a very plain design. Each has its advantages. The modern, undecorated piece is easier to clean, but it also shows wear and tear more quickly and is sometimes marred by scratches. Whichever is chosen, remember that it is probably the silver you will use all your lives, and possibly your children after you, so it is safer to select a pattern that is not extreme in any way—neither too severely modern nor so ornate that it easily appears outdated.

As with china, it is wise to complete one place setting at a time rather than have twelve forks and no knives.

The necessary silver for one place setting is:

1 large fork
1 small fork
1 large knife
1 dessert spoon (can double as soup spoon)
1 teaspoon
1 butter knife

In addition, assuming that the bride hopes eventually to have complete service for twelve, the following items are necessary. They need not be in the same pattern as the above list:

12 soup spoons
3 serving spoons (tablespoons in the chosen pattern may be used)
2 serving forks
12 after-dinner coffee spoons
2 gravy or sauce ladles
4 extra teaspoons (for sugar, condiments, etc.)

Optional, and often received as wedding presents:

oyster forks
salad or fish forks (broad tines)
sugar tongs
butter server
ornamented spoons for jellies or jams
cake knife

pie server
steak knives

If the flat silver is monogrammed, a triangle of block letters, last-name initial below and the first-name initials of bride and groom above, goes well on a modern pattern. When Jennifer Lynn Smith marries Daniel Charles Corcoran the monogram would be:

If a single initial is used, it is the last-name initial of the groom.

If the bride or groom has inherited silver, or silver marked with maiden initials or family initials, and the couple wants to add to it, the same initials should be used.

Any initialing should be simple and legible in style. Elongated Roman goes well on modern silver, and Old English on the more ornamental styles.

Monograms on flat silver have always been placed so that the top of the letter is toward the end of the handle. In other words, when the piece is on the table, the monogram is upside down as seen by the diner at that place. People have asked me why it should not be inscribed so that the letters are legible to the user, rather than to someone across the table who probably could not see it in any case. This seems quite reasonable and, despite the fact it is not the customary way, I see no reason why, if you prefer, you should not have your silver marked in that position.

A wedding gift of silver may be marked if the giver is absolutely sure that it is something the bride truly wants and that no duplicate will arrive, but generally it is safer to leave it unmarked so that it can be exchanged if desired.

Additional Practical Equipment

It is not necessary to list the ordinary pots, pans, utensils, and gadgets for your kitchen. The variety and number are limited only by the space you have to store them, and the type and amount of cooking you plan to do. The following items, however, are particularly useful, and should be included in your kitchen equipment if at all possible:

> 4 wooden or plastic trays (for meals enjoyed in the living room, or for a meal eaten in bed)
> electric hot plate (the most valuable appliance in my household!)
> electric blender and/or food processor
> electric oven-broiler or toaster
> kitchen scales
> folding steps (for reaching high kitchen shelves)
> a wok (if you like Chinese cooking)
> fondue set
> chafing dish

A wedding, be it large and elaborate or small and simple, is one of life's most important occasions—beautiful, meaningful, and traditionally a couple's day of days. This means the *groom's* day as well as the bride's. There used to be an old saying, "A man never knows how unimportant he is until he attends his own wedding." When that is true, the chances are he will soon be attending his own divorce. Marriage is a partnership, and from the beginning all major decisions should be made by both partners.

The groom's family should be consulted and informed about all that goes on, insofar as is possible. However, if the bride's family is giving the wedding, it is their prerogative to make final decisions, taking the feelings of the groom's family into consideration.

Above all, the wedding plans should comply with the wishes of the couple. It is *their* day—not their parents'. It is sad to see a mother and her daughter at swords' points at the very time that should be the happiest in their lives. Two areas are generally the most sensitive—the formality of the wedding and its size. The life-style of many couples today may be quite different from that of their parents, and many want their weddings to reflect their life-style. A great many couples want small, private ceremonies, while their parents, having planned and saved for years for a huge celebration, want to make the most of the occasion for social, and even at times business, reasons. There must be compromises, of course, but the important thing for everyone to remember is that the people who should be happiest of all with the wedding plans are the bride and groom. Even if her mother and father are "picking up the tab" they should be doing it for their daughter's pleasure, and not as an excuse to impose on the couple the type of wedding that *they* think it should be.

There are so many details involved in even the simplest wedding that careful planning and preparation are essential if everyone is to enjoy the day itself. For a large wedding, expert help of all kinds should be arranged for well in advance. Without adequate preparation Father may be irritated, Mother jittery, and the bride and groom ready to cancel the whole thing. This chapter and those that follow are dedicated to helping you avoid such needless unhappiness.

The details involved can seem overwhelming at times. To help you plan a trouble-free wedding you may find *Emily Post's*

37
Planning the Wedding

Wedding Planner useful. Designed to be carried with you, this planner offers guidance in selecting the professionals who will help make your wedding your day of days. In addition, it provides a place to keep track of the many names, numbers, and details you'll need at your fingertips.

Let it be said at the outset that the following discussion of wedding plans will be based on the most elaborate wedding possible. Very few will want or be able to have such an affair, but only by including every detail can the complete pattern be given. Then you follow as many of these suggestions as you find pleasing and practical for you.

THE FORMALITY OF THE WEDDING

There are three categories of weddings—formal, semiformal, and informal. The formality necessarily is related to the location of the ceremony and reception, the size of the wedding party, and the number of guests. While a wedding in a church or synagogue may range from most formal to least formal, a ceremony held in a house always lends itself more to informality—unless the house is a mansion. There are infinite variations, but the table below demonstrates the main differences among the three categories.

Many of the items are interchangeable and must be adapted to fit each individual situation. However, the list should give you some assistance in knowing what you are talking about when you tell your clergyperson or your caterer that you want a "formal," a "semiformal," or an "informal" wedding.

	Formal	*Semiformal*	*Informal*
Bride's dress	Long white gown, train, veil optional	Long white gown, veil optional	White or pastel cocktail dress or suit or afternoon dress (sometimes, very simple long gown)
Bridesmaids' dresses	Long or according to current style	Long or according to current style	Same type of dress as worn by bride
Dress of groom and his attendants	Cutaway or tailcoat (*see chapter 6*)	Sack coat or tuxedo (*see chapter 6*)	Dark business suit or jacket
Bride's attendants	Maid or matron of honor, 4–10 bridesmaids, flower girl, ring bearer (optional)	Maid or matron of honor, 2–6 bridesmaids, flower girl, ring bearer (optional)	Maid or matron of honor, 1 or 2 children (optional)

	Formal	*Semiformal*	*Informal*
Groom's attendants	Best man; 1 usher for every 50 guests, or same number as bridesmaids	Best man; 1 usher for every 50 guests, or same number as bridesmaids	Best man; 1 usher if necessary to seat guests
Location of ceremony	Church, synagogue, or large home or garden	Church, synagogue, chapel, hotel, club, home, garden	Chapel, rectory, justice of the peace, home, garden
Location of reception	Club, hotel, garden, or large home	Club, restaurant, hotel, garden, home	Church parlor, home, restaurant
Number of guests	200 or more	75 to 200	75 or under
Provider of service at reception	Caterer at home, or club or hotel facilities	Caterer at home, or club or hotel facilities	Caterer, friends and relatives, or restaurant
Food	Sit-down or semi-buffet (tables provided for bridal party, parents, and guests); hot meal served; wedding cake	Buffet (bridal party and parents may have tables); cocktail buffet food, sandwiches, cold cuts, snacks, wedding cake	Stand-up buffet or 1 table for all guests; may be a meal or snacks and wedding cake
Beverages	Champagne; whiskey and soft drinks (optional)	Champagne or punch for toasts; whiskey and soft drinks (optional)	Champagne or punch for toasts; tea, coffee, or soft drinks in addition
Invitations and announcements	Engraved	Engraved	Handwritten or telephoned invitations; engraved announcements
Decorations and accessories	Elaborate flowers for church, canopy to church, aisle carpet, pew ribbons, limousines for bridal party, groom's cake (given to guests in boxes), engraved matchbooks or napkins as mementos, rose petals or confetti.	Flowers for church, aisle carpet, pew ribbons, rose petals (other items optional)	Flowers for altar, rose petals

	Formal	Semiformal	Informal
Music	Organ at church (choir or soloist optional); orchestra for dancing at reception	Organ at church (choir or soloist optional); strolling musician, small orchestra, or records for reception; dancing optional	Organ at church; records at reception optional

CHOOSING ATTENDANTS

At the average wedding there are generally two to six bridesmaids and ushers, in addition to a maid of honor and/or a matron of honor, and a best man. Even though it is sometimes difficult to make a choice, there should not be two maids of honor or two matrons of honor. When one of two good friends must be selected, the other serves as a bridesmaid. There may also be one or two flower girls, one or two ring bearers, and pages. Young relatives who are between the ages of eight and fourteen (approximately) can serve as junior ushers or bridesmaids. There need not be an even number, since it is perfectly all right for one junior usher or one junior bridesmaid to walk alone in the procession.

The bride's attendants may or may not be married, but whether they are "matrons" or not, they are always known as "bridesmaids"—not "bridesmatrons." It is better not to choose a woman who is noticeably pregnant, unless she and the bride are totally comfortable about it. The bridesmaids should be reasonably close to the bride in age. Much older relatives or friends might help serve at the reception or have other "duties," but they should not be numbered among the bride's "maids."

Although the bride need not have any bridesmaids she must have one attendant or maid of honor. The picture of her father or the best man holding her flowers while she and the groom exchange rings is, to say the least, ludicrous!

There should not be more bridesmaids than ushers in the wedding party, but there are often more ushers than bridesmaids. In deciding on the number of attendants a good rule of thumb to follow is "one usher for every fifty guests." The number of bridesmaids may then be chosen accordingly.

The bride's closest sister is almost always asked to be maid (or matron) of honor. If she has no sister near her age, she chooses her best friend, or perhaps a cousin. The groom selects a brother or good friend for a best man, and some grooms ask their fathers to stand up with them. It used to be suggested that the bride and groom include in their wedding party, whenever possible, those in whose weddings they have served. This becomes less and less practical as society becomes increasingly mobile, and as people marry at a greater range of ages and friendships change.

Of course it is nice to include them, assuming they are old friends, but it is no longer a primary consideration.

As ushers and bridesmaids are chosen from relatives or very close friends, the invitation to serve is extended in person or by telephone. If they live far away they may be asked by note. They should be contacted as soon as the engagement is announced, to allow plenty of time to choose replacements if someone must refuse. However, unless there is a very good reason, no one should ever turn down the honor of being an attendant, especially as a maid or matron of honor. If the problem is one of expense, this should be explained to the bride or groom honestly. He or she will probably be able to help with transportation costs, to assist with the purchase or rental of the costume, or otherwise help to defray expenses, so that the friend will be able to accept. If at the last moment one of the ushers or bridesmaids is forced to withdraw, the bride or groom may ask another friend to fill in. Friends should not be offended by this, but rather, flattered that they are considered close enough to be called on in an emergency.

Relatives of the Bride and Bridegroom as Attendants

Unless attendants are limited to one or two, a brother of the bride is usually asked by the groom to be an usher. The bride returns the compliment by asking the sister of the groom who is nearest her own age to be bridesmaid.

When the homes of the bride and bridegroom are at such a great distance apart that none of the groom's immediate family can make the journey to the wedding, it is not unusual for him to choose (if he has no brother) his father or even stepfather as his best man. In such situations the ushers are chosen from among the friends of the bride.

Married Attendants

When a married friend or relative is asked to serve as an attendant, it is not necessary to ask his or her spouse, as well, unless, of course, both partners are close friends of both the bride and the groom and both would be asked in any event. The one not serving as an attendant is, of course, invited to the wedding and if possible, sits at the bridal table during the reception.

THE BRIDE'S ATTENDANTS

My mail of late includes an increasing number of letters from brides who ask if their mothers may serve as their matrons of honor, or if they may escort them up the aisle instead of their fathers, because they are estranged from their fathers, or have been brought up solely by their mothers.

There is nothing that prohibits a bride's mother from serving as matron of honor, but her "job" as mother-of-the-bride has many of its own responsibilities attached to it, and is a moment of honor for the mother. I really prefer to see the mother of the bride enjoying her role and leaving the honor attendant roles to sisters, close younger relatives, or friends.

As to mothers serving as escorts or walking their daughters up the aisle, there is no reason, other than tradition, that they cannot do this. Both parents walk with their children in a Jewish wedding ceremony, and although parents no longer "give" their daughters away, the symbolism of a daughter leaving her parents' home for that of her husband is carried out when the mother serves as escort.

Many brides, however, still prefer to have their mothers be the last escorted into their pew at the ceremony and they may ask a close family friend, uncle, grandfather, brother, or in the case of an older woman, a grown son, to serve as their escort. It is also acceptable for brides to walk alone, if that is preferred. When a bride has lived with her mother and stepfather and is very fond of him yet has also remained devoted to her own father she has a difficult choice. Traditionally the perogative of escorting her belongs to her natural father and using that as a guideline may help her to choose and avoid hurt feelings on the part of her stepfather.

Maid and/or Matron of Honor

The maid or matron of honor's most important duty is to act as a consultant and assistant to the bride. She should take as many duties and as much responsibility off the shoulders of the bride as possible—especially on the wedding day. She walks just in front of the bride in the procession (unless there are flower girls and ring bearers), she holds the bride's flowers during the ceremony, and she also hands the groom's ring to the bride if it is a double-ring ceremony. She helps the bride adjust her train and veil when she turns to leave the church. If there happen to be a maid *and* a matron of honor, the maid takes precedence and is in charge of the flowers and the ring at the altar.

She signs the wedding register as the bride's witness.

The maid of honor stands on the groom's left in the receiving line and sits on his left at the bridal table. She may or may not make a toast to the couple. She helps the bride change into her going-away clothes and helps the bride's mother put her wedding dress away. Although it is not obligatory she usually arranges to give a shower for the bride, with or without the help of the bridesmaids.

She is also in charge of choosing the gift that will be given to the bride from all the bridesmaids together, and collecting the money to pay for it.

Bridesmaids

Bridesmaids have few specific duties other than forming the procession, and if the bride wishes, standing in the receiving line. They also act as "deputy hostesses" at the reception.

Any of them may give a shower, or they may all give one together. They also may entertain the bride and groom in any other way they wish.

They are responsible, as mentioned under "Expenses," for paying for their own costumes, and also for seeing that they are properly fitted and that they have the necessary accessories. It is unfortunate but true that occasionally a woman has to refuse the joy of being in the party because a complete bridesmaid's outfit costs a sum that neither she nor her parents can provide. But it is also true that seldom is the bride herself in a position to pay for six or more sets of dresses and accessories even if she wishes to make an exception to the rule. Therefore a considerate bride tries to choose clothes that will not be too expensive. Department stores as well as specialty shops offer enchanting ready-to-wear models that can be ordered to fit almost any budget. Ideally the bride should choose a model that will be useful to the bridesmaids after the wedding.

Junior Bridesmaids

Junior bridesmaids are young girls, generally between eight and fourteen, who are too big to be flower girls and too young to be regular bridesmaids. They attend the rehearsal, of course, and usually the rehearsal dinner (for a little while, at least), but are not necessarily included in other festivities.

Flower Girls

Flower girls used to scatter petals before the bride, but more often today they simply carry old-fashioned baskets of flowers, or bouquets.

They walk directly in front of the bride unless there is a ring bearer, in which case the flower girl precedes him.

Flower girls are usually young relatives of the bride or groom, although sometimes the bride chooses the daughter of a close friend. The little girl should be between three and seven years old.

The flower girl's dress is paid for by her family. It should be similar to the bridesmaids' dresses, but modified in style, if necessary, to be more becoming to a child.

Flower girls must attend the rehearsal, of course. Whether they go to some of the showers and the rehearsal dinner—for a short time—depends on their age and the wishes of their parents.

Ring Bearers

Ring bearers, like flower girls, should be between three and seven.

The ring bearer carries the ring on a firm white velvet or satin cushion. If it is the real ring, it should be fastened on the cushion by a single thread, and the best man should be aware of this. It is actually safer to have a facsimile on the cushion, while the best man and maid of honor carry the real rings.

Other Small Attendants

Train bearers, as the name implies, hold the bride's train. They, too, must be very little boys and dressed in white. Unless they have rehearsed their part thoroughly, the train trailing smoothly by itself is really safer than a train in the hands of small children whose behavior is apt to be uncertain. Pages, too, are small boys who walk in the procession, but do nothing else.

A boy who is too big to be a ring bearer and too young to be a junior usher can be made responsible for running the ribbons along the ends of the pews. When there are two boys one takes the right side of the aisle, the other one the left, and they stand beside the front pews during the ceremony.

Remember, when planning your wedding party, that no matter how charming and cute they are, the presence of too many children is distracting. Even when they are well behaved (and sometimes they are not!) they may steal the show from the bride.

THE GROOM'S ATTENDANTS

The Best Man

No matter how small the wedding, the bridegroom always has a best man, just as the bride has a maid of honor. In civil ceremonies, before a justice of the peace, the best man and maid of honor are replaced by two "witnesses." This is required by law. Generally the closest brother of the groom is best man unless he is a great deal older or younger. But this is not an unbreakable rule. When the groom has no brother he would probably choose his closest friend; or if deciding upon this is difficult, he perhaps chooses a cousin, or a brother of the bride. Frequently a son who is very devoted to his father will ask him to serve as best man.

At some point before the wedding, the best man consults the ushers about a "joint" present for the bride and groom, and he is responsible for ordering it and collecting the money. He presents the gift to the groom, usually at the rehearsal dinner.

The duties of the best man vary with the circumstances—the plans for the wedding and the honeymoon, the amount of time he has free to place at the groom's disposal before the ceremony, and so on. The important thing is that he relieve the groom of as many details and as much responsibility as possible. Any or all of the following suggestions will smooth the groom's way and add to the couple's enjoyment of their wedding day. The best man should take care of as many of these situations as he possibly can.

He may help the groom pack for his honeymoon, and he sees that the clothes the groom will change into after the wedding are packed in a separate bag and taken to where the reception will be held.

He makes sure that the groom is properly dressed and perfectly groomed. It is his job to get him to the church on time, too.

He is responsible for the wedding ring and must be sure that the groom gives him the ring before the ceremony, to be kept in his pocket until it is time for it to be placed on the bride's finger. If there is a ring bearer who will carry the actual ring, the best man sees that it is carefully attached to the cushion.

In Christian ceremonies he enters the church with the groom and remains at his side during the entire ceremony, producing the ring at the proper moment. In Orthodox and Conservative Jewish ceremonies he precedes the groom in the wedding procession. Ordinarily he walks out with the maid or matron of honor immediately behind the bride and groom. If he does not walk out with her, however, he leaves through a side door while the procession goes down the aisle. He quickly goes around to the front of the church to give the groom his hat and coat. Sometimes the sexton takes charge of the groom's hat and coat and hands them to him at the church door as he goes out. But in either case the best man always hurries to see the bride and groom into their car, which should be waiting at the entrance to the church. If a chauffeur is not present to drive the newlyweds to the reception, the best man performs this duty too.

He signs the wedding certificate as the groom's witness.

The best man is responsible for giving the clergyman his donation on behalf of the groom. He may do it before the ceremony while they are waiting to enter the church, or if he is not driving the bride and groom to the reception, he may return to the vestry immediately after the recessional to deliver the envelope. If the donation is given in the form of a check, it is made out to the minister himself rather than to the church.

If the father of the bride has reason to suspect that the circumstances of the groom or his family do not permit them to make a contribution commensurate with the elaborateness of the occasion, he may, if he wishes, make an additional contribution on his own later.

At the reception the best man does not stand in the receiving line but mingles with the guests and helps the bride's family in any way he can. When the bride and groom sit down at the bridal table, he sits on the bride's right, and it is his responsibility to make the first toast to the newlyweds. He reads aloud any telegrams or messages that have been received and keeps them to be given to the couple later. He is the first man to dance with the bride after the groom, her father, and her father-in-law.

When the bride and groom are ready to leave the reception he helps the groom change and takes care of his wedding clothes. He makes sure that the groom has his tickets, his money, his credit cards, his car keys, and anything else that he will need.

He escorts the groom's family to the room where their son is dressing, for their farewells.

The best man is also in charge of whatever transportation the couple plans to use to leave the reception. If it is by car he has the car hidden—with the newlyweds' honeymoon luggage already in it—to protect it from practical jokers. If they are using the car to get to a station or airport he often drives them there himself. In any case he leads the couple through the waiting guests to the door, and when they have pulled away in a shower of rice or rose petals he may breathe a sigh of relief and join the rest of the wedding party in a final celebration.

The Ushers

One who is experienced or close to the family is appointed head usher. He is responsible for seeing that the others get to the church at the appointed time, assigning them to special aisles if the church is large, and designating the ones who will escort members of the two families. He himself escorts the bride's mother in and out of the church, unless she has a son among the ushers, or she prefers to walk out with her husband.

As mentioned earlier, there should be one usher to every fifty guests (approximately), and they are responsible for seeing that the guests are all seated before the ceremony starts. Two ushers are assigned to putting the white carpet down the aisle just before the procession starts, and two others lay the ribbon along the ends of the reserved pews after the occupants are seated.

Ushers do not stand on the receiving line, but they do sit at the bridal table when there is one.

They are expected to contribute to a "joint" gift to the groom.

Junior Ushers

Junior ushers are between eight and fourteen years old. They dress like the other ushers and walk behind them. Sometimes, when there are two junior ushers, they are appointed to be in charge of the white carpet or the ribbons.

FINANCIAL CONSIDERATIONS

Whatever size or style of wedding you choose, it is the careful, thoughtful planning and the atmosphere—not the cost—that makes it beautiful. It is not how much you spend but how you spend that matters. While a large, elaborate wedding may cost thousands of dollars, there are many ways in which you can save without stinting. Very often the simplest wedding is the most tasteful. The following list is intended only to explain the traditional division of expenses. Many of these items may be omitted entirely without making your wedding any the less beautiful and meaningful.

There are many variations not only in ways to save, but also in how the costs are divided. Today the bride and groom often pay their own wedding costs, particularly when the wedding is a second one for either or both. The groom's family often offers to pay a share and it is quite acceptable for the bride's parents to accept this offer, especially if the groom and his family would like a larger or more elaborate reception than the bride's parents can afford. Use these pages as a guide, and make your own adjustments.

Expenses of the Bride and Her Family

Services of a bridal consultant and/or a secretary

Invitations, announcements, and enclosures

The bride's wedding dress and accessories

Floral decorations for ceremony and reception, bridesmaids' flowers, bride's bouquet (in some areas given by groom)

Formal wedding photographs and candid pictures

Videotape recording of wedding

Music for church and reception

Transportation of bridal party to ceremony, and from ceremony to reception, if hired cars are used

All expenses of reception

Bride's presents to her attendants

Bride's present to groom, if she wishes to give him one

The groom's wedding ring, if it is to be a double-ring ceremony

Rental of awning for ceremony entrance and carpet for aisle, if desired and if not provided by church

Fee for services performed by sexton

A traffic officer, if necessary

Transportation and lodging expenses for pastor or rabbi if from another town and if invited to officiate by bride's family

Accommodations for bride's attendants, if required

Bridesmaids' luncheon, if one is given by the bride

Expenses of the Groom and His Family

Bride's engagement and wedding rings

Groom's present to his bride, if he wishes to give her one

Gifts for the groom's attendants

Accommodations for groom's attendants, if required

Boutonnieres for the groom's attendants

Ties and gloves for the groom's attendants, if not part of their clothing rental package

The bride's bouquet in areas where local custom requires it

The bride's going-away corsage

Corsages for immediate members of both families (unless bride has included them in her florist's order)

The minister's or rabbi's fee or donation

Transportation and lodging expenses for the minister or rabbi if from another town and if invited to officiate by the groom's family

The marriage license

Transportation for the groom and best man to the ceremony

Expenses of the honeymoon

All costs of the rehearsal dinner, if one is held

Bachelor dinner, if he wishes to give one

Transportation and lodging expenses for groom's parents

Bridesmaids'/Honor Attendant's Expenses

Purchase of apparel and all accessories

Transportation to and from the city or town where the wedding takes place

A contribution to a gift from all the bridesmaids to the bride

An individual gift to the couple

A shower and/or luncheon for the bride

Ushers'/Best Man's Expenses

Rental of wedding attire

Transportation to and from location of wedding

A contribution to a gift from all the groom's attendants to the groom

An individual gift to the couple

A bachelor dinner, if given by the groom's attendants

Out-of-Town Guests' Expenses

Guests who come from a distance pay their own transportation and lodging expenses. The parents of the bride or groom should assist their relatives and friends by making reservations or sending them hotel and motel information, and may offer to pay any expenses they wish to assume, but are not at all required to do so. They may also accept the offers of local friends and relatives to provide accommodations for out-of-town guests in their homes.

Exceptions to Tradition

As mentioned before, there are many acceptable exceptions to these guidelines. They might be completely reversed in the case of a young girl who is an orphan or who comes from another country. In those circumstances, the groom's family could well arrange and pay for the entire wedding.

In some areas, and among certain ethnic groups, the groom traditionally provides the liquor or champagne for the reception. In others, the groom is expected to buy all the flowers for the wedding party. On occasion, because the bride is wealthy and the bridesmaids are not, she may pay for their wedding costumes or their transportation costs. But these are local customs or special situations, and for the majority of people the division of expenses listed above is considered essentially correct.

There is, however, one gradual but noteworthy change occurring. Perhaps because of the increased cost of giving a wedding, or perhaps simply because the groom and his family take a more active part in the planning and preparations than they used to, they are more and more often sharing some, or all, of the expenses with the bride's parents. In some cases the groom simply wants to include more friends and relatives than the bride's family can afford, and rather than leave out people close to him, he (or his parents) offer to help, sometimes by paying for the liquor, other times by renting a hall or whatever seems best. This is no longer considered "insulting" to the bride and her family, and in many cases it has resulted in closer ties between the families. The offer should, however, come from the groom and his parents; the bride's family should not ask for assistance. If their budget is limited, they should simply restrict the wedding arrangements to what they can afford.

When the groom's family assumes a fair share of the costs, they become co-hosts with the bride's parents. Therefore, the wedding invitations should go out in their name too.

Planning a Budget

A carefully prepared budget, based upon what you and your parents can afford, will spare you the nightmare of impractical plans that must be constantly changed—or unnecessary debts. Whether you are planning an elaborate wedding with 300 guests or a simple ceremony with 30 friends present in your own home, a realistic budget will help you make your preparations more smoothly and happily.

A budget for a large wedding should include your allotments for each of the expenses listed on the next page. The budget for a simple wedding should include the items that you cannot provide yourself and intend to purchase, and also the way in which you will take care of other requirements. For example:

Photographs—Uncle John will take them for us as his wedding gift.

Wedding cake—Aunt Doris baking it as her gift.

With imagination and good planning, a beautiful wedding can be held within any limits. Whatever you plan, keep to your budget, or the worry and insecurity will get your marriage off to a bad start.

Costs for large formal weddings can range from tens of thousands of dollars to just a few thousand dollars, depending on the number of guests, the elaborateness of the wedding, and local costs and customs. This table shows the items that must be budgeted for. Amounts are not included since they change so rapidly. When making up your budget, put down what you think you can allow and adjust the figures as you get estimates from the professionals involved.

The best way to plan is to begin with your fixed costs, such as the minister's or rabbi's and organist's fees, gifts for your attendants, postage, wedding rings, etc. Subtract that total from your available funds and see what amount you have to work with. This will give you a guide as to how much you have left for variable costs, such as limousines, a photographer, and the rehearsal dinner and reception.

Budget Categories

Bride's gown
Bride's accessories
Invitations/enclosures
Announcements
Postage
Flowers for ceremony
Flowers for reception
Bride's bouquet
Flowers for bride's attendants
Corsages
Boutonnieres
Organist's fee
Cantor/vocalist/instrumentalist fee
Music for reception
Sexton's/facility fee
Minister's or rabbi's fee
Limousines for bridal party
Photographer
Videographer
Bride's gifts for attendants
Groom's gifts for attendants
Bride's ring
Groom's ring
Marriage license
Accommodations for bride's attendants
Accommodations for groom's attendants
Rehearsal dinner (per person cost)
Bridesmaids' luncheon
Bachelor's dinner

Reception expenses (per person cost)
Wedding cake

PLANNING THE CEREMONY

When, Where, and How Big?

As soon as the couple decide approximately when they want to get married, they must find out on exactly which day their church or synagogue and the clergyman who is to perform the ceremony will be available. If it is to be a large wedding they must also coordinate the time that the church is free with the time at which the caterer or hotel or club will be available.

Next the couple must decide on the precise time of day that will be best for the ceremony. Religion, climate, local custom, and transportation schedules may be important factors, as well as the bride and groom's plans for their wedding trip. Also, due consideration should be given to the convenience of a majority of the relatives and friends who will want to come.

In the South most weddings are held in the evening when the heat of the day is over, although that is not so important a consideration as it once was since the advent of air conditioning. Many Catholic weddings that include a Nuptial Mass are held at noon. Protestant weddings most often take place in the late afternoon. This is the most satisfactory time if an evening reception is planned, because it can follow the ceremony immediately. A noon wedding leaves an awkward gap between ceremony and reception, which guests are somewhat at a loss to fill, unless, of course, a luncheon reception is held.

Remember, too, that if the reception comes at a customary meal hour, substantial food is usually provided. In this case the number of guests invited to the reception may be restricted by the expense.

Having settled on the day and hour, the bride and groom next determine the number of guests who can be provided for, considering the type of reception intended, the size of the bride's house or club, and the amount that her family can afford to spend.

The number of guests invited to the ceremony is unlimited—determined only by the size of the church, chapel, or synagogue.

Checklist for Discussion with Minister or Rabbi

☐ Date, time and length of ceremony
☐ Place of ceremony: church, chapel, synagogue, wedding facility
☐ Number of guests church or synagogue will comfortably hold
☐ Whether your service will be traditional or whether you may write part of it yourselves

☐ Whether, when, and how photographs and/or videotape may be taken before, during and/or after the service

☐ If a second minister or rabbi will be participating and how arrangements should be made

☐ When to make appointment with organist to select music and/or if there may be instrumental or vocal soloists

☐ What kinds of floral arrangements/decorations are permitted; how to arrange access for a florist; the disposition of flowers after the ceremony

☐ Whether there is a room for dressing prior to the service if you require one

☐ If you should arrange for the services of a traffic officer

☐ Whether rice, rose petals, bird seed, etc. are permitted to be thrown outside the building

☐ If you want an aisle carpet or runner, whether one is provided

☐ For a Christian ceremony: Whether or not communion will be part of the service

☐ For a Jewish ceremony: Who will provide the chuppah and if it may be decorated with flowers

☐ What fees are required for the use of the facility; the organist; the cantor; for additional musicians; for the sexton; for the minister or rabbi

Be sure to make a reservation for the rehearsal at the time you make the reservation for your wedding ceremony and to set the dates for your counseling appointments with the minister or rabbi, if required.

When the couple is not being married in the bride's own church, she may wish to have the clergyman from her home parish officiate. Or perhaps she or the groom has a relative or godparent who is a minister, and they would like him to marry them. This can be arranged quite easily, with the two clergymen participating in the service. On some occasions the clergyman of the church where the wedding takes place turns the service over to the visitor completely, but this is unusual. The donation is still given to the "host" minister, and an additional "gift" is given to the one who officiates, which may be either money or a "concrete" gift—perhaps a small wedding picture of the bride and groom in a good leather frame. Naturally, if the visiting clergyman is a relative or personal friend, the gift is more appropriate than the money. His expenses would, of course, be paid by the bride's family (or the groom's, if he came at their request).

PLANNING THE RECEPTION

The bride and groom either must decide where they want their reception and thus determine the number of guests, or they must first determine how many guests they plan to invite and then find the reception site that best suits this number, as well as the style and type of reception they want to have.

Working with a Caterer

To hold a reception in your home, or the home of a friend or relative, no matter what the size of the reception, entails a good deal of work. A very small party can of course be handled entirely by you, with the help of your mother and some friends. By preparing food in advance and freezing it, by keeping the menu and the decorations as simple as possible, the home wedding can be both inexpensive and, within reason, easy to manage. But to have more than twenty or thirty guests with any degree of pleasure and relaxation for you, you must have professional help. For a reception of more than thirty guests, this means a caterer. Depending on your requirements and the size of his or her firm, a caterer will provide food, the wedding cake, the serving staff, crystal and china, tables and chairs, and some will provide tents, dance floors, and innumerable other services.

The best way to find a reliable caterer is to ask people who have used their services. You may, of course, look in the yellow pages and at advertisements in local magazines and newspapers, but if you do, check references and if possible, sample their food and see their equipment.

If you use a caterer, either for a wedding at home or at another site, be absolutely sure that every service to be provided and the *total* itemized costs are given to you in a contract. As with any contract, read it carefully and make sure you understand and agree to all terms and costs before you sign.

Specifically, be sure the following points are covered:

- Detailed menu and how it will be served
- Beverages—open bar, champagne, soft drinks
- Wedding cake
- Number of serving staff
- Whether gratuities are included
- Number and set up of tables and chairs
- Delivery charges
- Deadline for guest count
- Overtime charges
- Coat check facilities
- Tents or marquees
- Whether glass and china are insured against breakage
- Whether taxes are included in estimate

A Reception at a Club, Hotel, or Catering Hall

Hotels, restaurants, private clubs and catering halls generally offer wedding "packages" depending on the time and elaborateness of your reception. When selecting a reception site outside of your home or other than a site requiring an outside caterer, such as an historic building or garden, make a list of initial questions to ask the restaurant or club manager.

- Is a wedding package offered?
- If so, what does it include and what does it cost?
- Are substitutions permissible?
- What food and drinks will be served at the cocktail hour? During the reception? Will brand name liquors be served? If not, how much more would the cost be to serve them? Will there be an open bar for the cocktail hour? For the entire reception?
- What does a sample place setting consist of?
- May you sample food and observe a party arranged in the room which may be selected for your reception?
- Will the establishment provide printed directions to the site for you to include with your invitations?
- Is insurance against china and crystal breakage included in the costs stated? If not, is it required and at what cost?
- What are your choices of table linen colors?
- May you see a book of wedding cakes they provide and sample the type you want? May you provide your own wedding cake (baked by a friend or at a bakery)?
- Is there a florist the restaurant or club manager uses and recommends and if so, does he or she have a book you may look at to select arrangements? If you prefer to provide your own decorations, how can this be arranged?
- May the reception be extended an extra hour? At what time do servers go on overtime pay? What would the overtime charges be?
- Are all gratuities included in the stated costs?
- Is there a special rate for providing food and beverages for the musicians and photographers?
- Is there a room available for formal portraits to be taken if they aren't taken at the ceremony site? Is there an additional charge for use of this room?
- What are the parking arrangements for guests?

Be sure to have all these details spelled out before signing a contract. Also, be sure to make note of dates by which you should communicate specific details to the club or restaurant manager—such as the final guest count, arrangements for an outside florist or baker to deliver flowers or wedding cake, whether you plan to have a groom's cake, and so on. You should also see how tables will be set up; if you want a bridal table, how many guests will the other tables seat comfortably; where will speakers be located if music will be amplified; whether you require a table where guests may pick their table assignments or a table for gifts; and where a receiving line may be placed.

A Sit-Down Reception

When the reception takes place at home, the caterer brings all the equipment, and the necessary people to set it up, the morning of the wedding. Additional help may arrive later, but well before the hour of the wedding.

In the country a tent is erected on the lawn the day before the wedding. Under the tent there is a platform surrounded by small tables, and at one end a large one is reserved for the bridal party. A second table, called the "parents' table," is reserved for the immediate families of the bride and groom, the clergyman, and a few special friends.

Place cards are put on the bridal table and the parents' table, but they are not necessary on the small tables. All the guests, except the few placed at the reserved tables, sit with whom they like. Sometimes they do so by prearrangement, but usually they sit where they happen to find friends.

The menu is limited only by the preference of the bride and groom. There may be bouillon or vichyssoise, lobster Newburg or oyster cocktail. The main dish might be beef stroganoff with wild rice, sweetbreads and mushrooms, or creamed chicken in pastry shells.

Any variety of vegetable, aspic, or salad may be served.

Dessert is usually ice cream or sherbet accompanied by little cakes or cookies, and slices of wedding cake.

At this type of reception the traditional beverage has always been champagne. However, many people also offer other liquors, and soft drinks or punch must be available. For families who do not wish to serve any alcohol a fruit punch is the best choice.

A Buffet Reception

For the stand-up, or buffet, reception a long table is set in the largest room of the home or club. It is covered with a plain white damask cloth. The centerpiece is generally a bowl of white flowers. Piles of plates (preferably white, or white and gold), stacks of napkins, and rows of spoons and forks are symmetrically arranged on the table. This table should be situated so that the guests pass on directly to another table to help themselves to food, or if there is room, the plates of food may be arranged on the same table. Even though it is not a seated dinner, there is a table for the bridal party and one for the parents. There are also a number of tables with cloths and centerpieces, but no place settings, to which guests may carry their plates from the buffet.

The wedding cake is usually the feature of the buffet, placed at the center of the table with the centerpiece of white flowers behind it or two floral pieces flanking it. If space is limited, the cake may be nearby, on its own small round table. There are usually two or three cold dishes and at least one hot dish served, with appropriate accompaniments. There should also be finger rolls and sandwiches, substantial yet small enough to eat easily.

There may be dishes filled with fancy cakes or "petits fours" chosen for looks as much as taste. There may also be compotes of peppermints, caramels, and chocolates. Ice cream is the typical dessert, served with a slice of wedding cake.

Liquor and soft drinks are served from a bar or a table arranged as a bar. Glasses of champagne are passed around to the guests on trays.

A Very Simple Reception

While a home reception that takes place after a noon or early evening wedding should provide a substantial luncheon or dinner, a reception held after an afternoon wedding need not include a meal and can be, in fact, very simple. All that is required is a beverage with which to drink the newlyweds' health, and a wedding cake. A slightly more elaborate reception would include tea and coffee and thin sandwiches.

The table decorations are white, or in a pastel color matching the dresses and flowers of the bridesmaids. Although a number of small tables may be set up in the downstairs rooms of the house, the food is more often set out on the dining table, and the guests eat standing or with plates on their laps. The bridal table, if there is one at all, is necessarily placed in the largest room, or in summer, possibly, on the porch or in the garden. If the bride has only one attendant she chooses a few of her best friends to sit at her table.

The Wedding Cake

The one essential ingredient of every reception is a wedding cake. Many years ago it was made of dark fruitcake, but today wedding cakes are almost always a white cake or a pound cake. They are usually ordered from a bakery or caterer, or from the hotel or club where the reception is held. If the bride or groom has a friend or relative who enjoys baking, there is no reason why she should not bake the cake, if the wedding is not too large.

The bride's cake or wedding cake is usually in tiers and is covered with white icing. The flowers and curlicues need not be white, but may be colored to match or blend with the bridesmaids' costumes. The cake is sometimes topped with little bride-and-groom dolls, or a little "wedding bell," but I prefer flowers—those made of frosting, artificial flowers, or real ones.

The Groom's Cake

A nice custom that has become less prevalent because of the expense, but still seen at some weddings, is that of having a separate fruitcake called a "groom's cake" cut and put into individual white boxes tied with white satin ribbon and ornamented with the combined initials of the bride and groom. These boxes are stacked on a table close to the front door, and each departing guest is expected to take one. When a member of a family cannot attend the wedding a second box may be taken home to him or her. Otherwise it is very bad manners to take more than one's own box.

Although the cost of ordering such a cake may be prohibitive the charm remains, and it might be an unusual and thoughtful wedding gift (after consulting with the bride) from a family friend who is skilled in the art of baking—or very rich. When made as a gift the individual pieces of cake need not be put into expensive boxes, but may be wrapped in white paper and tied with white or silver ribbon, possibly with a little flower or greenery through the knot.

In some parts of the South the groom's cake is a chocolate cake that is set up on a table separate from that of the bride's cake. It is not cut by the couple and served as is the bride's cake, but a waiter slices it and guests who prefer chocolate cake are free to help themselves to it at any time. The groom's cake, like the bride's cake, is provided by the bride's family.

Meeting with the Florist

The services of a florist should be requested as soon as the wedding date is determined. The florist should be told what will be required—flowers for the wedding party, boutonnieres, corsages, flowers for the ceremony site and possibly the reception. Specific details, such as colors and style, should be confirmed as soon as you know the style and colors for your gown, those of your bridal party, your mothers' and grandmothers' dresses, container sizes for the ceremony site, and table linen colors during the reception, if the florist is providing decorations and centerpieces.

In most parts of the country all flowers, including her own bouquet, are part of the bride's responsibility. She sometimes provides corsages for the two mothers and grandmothers, but in most cases the groom orders these and the one that the bride will wear when they go away.

In certain geographic areas it is customary for the groom to buy the bride's bouquet. When this is true, the corsage may form the center of the bouquet or arrangement, and it is removed before she throws the bouquet to her bridesmaids.

The groom provides the boutonnieres for the best man, the ushers, his and the bride's fathers, and himself.

To simplify ordering and floral deliveries, both the bride's and the groom's orders may be placed with the same florist. If the bride and groom are paying the costs of their own wedding, it makes no difference since the entire order will be paid on one bill. If the couple's wedding costs are being paid according to the traditional division of expenses by their parents then the florist can be instructed as to how to divide the bill.

One of the key considerations when determining your flower order is the season of the year. However much you love lilies of the valley, they are practically impossible to buy except in the spring. Don't set your heart on one variety; let your florist help you choose a flower that will be appropriate not only to your wedding, but to the season, as well.

Deciding your flower order should be a pleasurable experience and one into which you put your creativity and careful thought. Your choice of flowers and their sweet, fresh appearance and fragrance symbolize new beginnings.

Bridal Party Flowers

The bride should wait until she has selected her wedding gown and those of her attendants before placing the precise order for their bouquets, and should, if possible, have a picture of the gowns and fabric swatches to enable the florist to make the most appropriate recommendations. Flowers carried by the bride and her attendants are an accessory which must complement the gowns and contribute to the overall look of the wedding. A cascading bouquet, for example, looks best with a long gown. It appears out of proportion with a shorter dress. A small nosegay, on the other hand, is too small against a long gown with a train, but looks well with a short dress or a simple suit. You should have the mood you want to convey in mind as well, whether Victorian, exotic, sophisticated or traditional. You must decide if you want a colorful bouquet or one entirely in white. Either is lovely, but both should include a combination of flowers in a variety of sizes to give balance.

The texture of your and your bridesmaids' gowns is important, too. Camellias and gardenias with their shiny dark leaves are beautiful against a satin or brocade dress. Eyelet and cotton are better complemented by daisies or sweet peas. Chrysanthemums, stock, or carnations carry out the fluffier look of tulle or organza. Calla lilies, large orchids, and gladioli are good choices for a tall bride; tinier blossoms— lilies of the valley, violets, sweetheart roses—arranged in a smaller bouquet or cascade are better for the petite bride.

White orchids are generally arranged with other flowers. Orchids are a "formal" flower and therefore look best with a formal wedding gown. An arrangement or orchids is appropriate for decorating a prayer book or a satin purse. Calla lilies are possibly the most formal of all bridal flowers. They are stunning when carried by a bride wearing a satin or velvet gown with simple lines. They are often arranged against a background of dark, shiny leaves to provide contrast.

A bouquet may be made up so that the center flowers may be removed and worn by the bride as a corsage when she leaves for her honeymoon. The remainder of the bouquet is thrown to the bridesmaids. Sometimes a bride who wants to keep and preserve her own bouquet will order another, "tossing" bouquet for this tradition.

Formal Bouquets

If the style of your wedding is formal with long gowns for you and your attendants, you might choose either a cascade or a crescent styling with a draped effect. Orchids, roses, gardenias, camellias, stephanotis, lilies of the valley, and other lilies are lovely choices for more formal bouquets, complemented by seasonal flowers. A large nosegay or a free form bouquet of formal flowers can also be a lovely choice.

If your gown has waistline detailing, a crescent bouquet or an over-arm bouquet that won't cover waistline beading or appliqué would be a good choice.

A shiny satin or brocade gown is well-complemented by flowers with shiny, dark green leaves such as camellias and gardenias.

FORMAL

INFORMAL

Informal Bouquets

If your wedding is less formal, a loose garden bouquet is appropriate. Garden flower bouquets could include tulips, freesia, irises, astors, small daisies and roses, or a selection of seasonal fall blossoms for an autumn wedding. Other choices would include a nosegay or oval-shaped arrangement, or one or a few seasonal flowers wrapped with a ribbon. Daisies, violets, roses, and other smaller flowers can make a beautiful bouquet.

Attendants' Bouquets

Usually the maid of honor carries the same bouquet as the bridesmaids, although her special role may be highlighted by using different, complementary colors of the same flowers or a different style. Attendants' flowers should be of a similar style and mood to those of the bride.

Floral Headpieces

Flowers worn in the hair of the bride's attendants should be ordered with the bouquets so that they are well-coordinated. Be sure to choose long lasting flowers that will not wilt during the ceremony and reception. They may wear a wreath of flowers, or just a few flowers attached to a comb to be worn at the back or side of the head. The bride may also wear flowers in her hair in lieu of a hat or a veil, or they may be attached to the veil. If this is the case, the veiling should be given to the florist. You might consider using silk flowers for headpieces, identical or complementary to the real flowers used in the bouquets. Most florists carry silk flowers and are able to create headpieces for you.

Flowers for the Flower Girl

A child attendant should carry a delicate bouquet—either a miniature version of those of the bridesmaids or one more suited to her size in complementary flowers. Often flower girls carry a small basket of flowers instead of a bouquet.

Corsages

Once the color and style of the bride's and groom's mothers, and stepmothers, has been determined, coordinating corsages should be ordered for them. It is thoughtful to ask them if they have a favorite flower and if they prefer a corsage to be pinned at the shoulder, waist, or handbag, or to be worn on the wrist. Flowers for grandmothers should be something rather neutral, such as clusters of tiny white orchids or a single gardenia—something in a creamy color that will be complementary to any dress. In addition, a small floral accessory, such as a corsage or a flower for the wrist, may be given to a friend who attends the guest book and to a friend who serves as a soloist during the ceremony.

The Groom's Boutonniere

Select one flower from your bouquet for your groom's boutonniere. Often this is stephanotis, lily of the valley or another smaller flower. This tradition comes from a romantic custom of yesteryear when the bride would remove one blossom from her bouquet and pin it on her groom as a symbol of her love.

Other Boutonnieres

Ushers, other groomsmen, fathers and often grandfathers all wear boutonnieres. Brothers of the bride or groom who are not in the wedding may wear a boutonniere, as well, which is a very nice way to show them that they are important to you. These boutonnieres should be different than that of the groom's, and may be a single carnation or another flower selected from the bridesmaids' bouquets.

Decorations for the Ceremony

Flowers for the ceremony are as elaborate or as simple as you choose. Your minister's or rabbi's advice can be most helpful in choosing those for the altar and chancel, or for the chuppah, pulpit and candelabra. Whether or not you have flowers on the ends of the pews depends on the size and formality of the wedding. If your florist is not familiar with the site of the wedding, it would be helpful if he or she visited the site before your consultation to know which size and style of floral arrangements best suit the location.

These flowers may be all white with greens, or they may be bright or pastel colors. Either is appropriate, as long as they complement the colors of the site and of the clothing worn by the bridal party.

If your guest list is small but your church or synagogue is large and no chapel is available, you can counteract the feeling of emptiness by placing a hedge of potted plants or a row of greens along the back of the last pew to be used, forming a border. The part within the boundary is brilliantly lighted—the rest of the church or synagogue relatively dark. The bridal party, rather than walking down a long, dimly lit aisle, would enter from a side door. Another alternative, even simpler, is to use chancel choir stalls for guests, lighting only that section of the church.

A candlelight ceremony in the evening or very late afternoon can be very beautiful with ivy twined around the candelabra and white satin bows decorating the ends of the pews. If you prefer, flowers, greens and candles may be used together, but do not overdo the flowers, or the result will be confused and give the appearance of a hodgepodge of elements.

You should discuss with your minister or rabbi what you would like done with ceremony flowers after the service. They may be left behind if there is to be a service the next day, or they may be delivered to special friends or relatives who are infirm and unable to attend your wedding. They may also be delivered to a hospital or nursing home so they can be enjoyed. Often your florist, for an additional fee, will take care of this for you, or a church or synagogue member will make these deliveries, at the request of the minister, priest, or rabbi.

Decorations for the Reception

Decorations for receptions invariably consist of flowers and greens, sometimes white but more often mixed with colors chosen to blend with the colors of the bridal party.

A buffet table may have a bowl of flowers as its centerpiece, or, if space is limited, the center of the table may be used for the wedding cake. Often, when there is a seated-bridal-party table, the cake is placed in front of the bride and groom. If the cake is tall, however, it is better to put a low flower arrangement there, so that the bridal couple is not hidden from the guests. Depending on the length and shape of the table, there may be one or two more arrangements at each side. Candles or candelabra may be used at an evening or after-dusk reception but should not be on the tables for a morning or early-afternoon reception.

When the guests are served a sit-down dinner, there are generally small flower arrangements on each table. At less formal receptions, even though there may be tables where the guests form their own groups to rest or enjoy the buffet, there need not be centerpieces. However, if the cost is not too great, flowers on every table add greatly to the beauty of the scene.

Other than the flowers on the tables, the only decoration is a bank of greens against which the receiving line is formed. Or the bridal party may stand in front of a fireplace, decorated with nothing more than a bowl of flowers at each end. When there is no focal point in a room, the line may be formed against the longest unbroken wall space, and a tall stanchion topped with a vase of flowers may be placed at either end.

Decorations for a Home Wedding

There are so many variables in weddings at home that it is almost impossible to describe the decorations. In general, they consist of a screen or backdrop of greens or a dark drapery behind the improvised altar, and vases of flowers in the windows, on newel posts, and on occasional tables. If the room has a fireplace, this makes an ideal setting for the ceremony. The fireplace may be filled with greens, and the mantel decorated with green roping or an arrangement of greens or flowers.

An altar may easily be made up by covering an ordinary table with a white silk, lace, or damask cloth, or by an altar cloth borrowed from your church. Whether or not there is a cross or other religious objects on the altar depends on the service, on your faith, and on the officiating clergyman. More commonly there is simply a kneeling bench for the couple, possibly with an altar rail behind it, covered with greens or a drapery. A tall stand containing a flower arrangement at each end of the rail makes a lovely frame for the ceremony.

If the house is large enough to permit it, stanchions decorated with flowers may be used to support the ribbon marking an aisle to the altar. This is not necessary, but it adds to the beauty and elegance of a home ceremony.

Flowers for the home wedding, then, are used in whatever profusion and whatever manner the bride will enjoy—and her budget will permit.

Other Accessories

Accessories, as well as flowers, must be ordered in advance. If a canopy or awning is to be used at the church entrance, the sexton must arrange for it to be put up the morning of the wedding day. The carpet that is usually laid down the aisle of the church after the bride's mother is seated, to protect the bride's train, must be ordered, either from the church or the florist. Tents or marquees are provided by the caterer or a special rental service for a home garden, or by the club where the reception is to be held. They must be put up a day or two in advance.

Many brides like to provide mementos of the wedding in the form of cocktail napkins imprinted with the couple's names. They are passed with sandwiches or hors d'oeuvres and also with glasses of cold drinks, which tend to drip on a warm day. These printed accessories should be ordered six weeks or two months ahead of the wedding date if the bride wishes to be sure of their delivery.

PLANNING THE MUSIC

To me, a wedding is not a wedding unless the procession enters the church to the strains of Wagner's "Wedding March" ("Here Comes the Bride") and leaves the church to the stirring tune of Mendelssohn's "Wedding March" from his *Midsummer Night's Dream*. However, some churches consider that this music is too secular, and some couples have their own special favorites that they wish to have played instead. There are many triumphal hymns or marches of a more religious nature that may be substituted for the traditional processional and recessional. Your organist will help you choose selections for a church ceremony. If you are being married at home, and plan to use CDs or tapes for music, ask your organist or choirmaster for suggestions and then listen to the pieces in your local music store before making your choice.

At a church ceremony, organ music is almost always played while the guests assemble. The selections should be joyous, but they may not be "popular" music. In most churches, such traditional love songs as "I Love You Truly" or "Oh, Promise Me" are acceptable as background music, but in others they are not considered suitable. They have also become trite from overuse, and there are many other more original and more religious choices. A selected list might include:

"Jesu, Joy of Man's Desiring" by Bach
"Ave Maria" by Schubert
Chorale Prelude, "In Thee Is Joy" by Bach
"The Lord's Prayer" by Malotte
"Liebestraum" by Liszt
"Biblical Songs" by Dvořák
"Joyful, Joyful, We Adore Thee" by Beethoven
"The King of Love My Shepherd Is" by Hinsworth

Most of these are also excellent choices for a soloist. If you are having a choir sing at your wedding, choose the music with the help of the choir master.

Music at the reception may be provided by anything from a ten-piece band to a CD or tape player. At some very formal weddings there are two orchestras, one playing rock or country music for the young people and the other playing more conventional music for the older guests. At other receptions, a strolling accordionist or guitarist provides the background music. The choice is yours, but no matter how small and simple the party, music in some form adds greatly to the festivity. The selections are up to you and your groom. A steady diet of loud modern music is not appropriate, as it is distasteful to many of the older guests, but if you have a dance orchestra, the softer, slower tunes should be interspersed with current favorites. The bride and groom usually dance their first dance to a traditional tune, even though they may enjoy more modern numbers later. The popularity of any piece of music changes so fast that it would be impossible to recommend specific songs. Make your own choice, but give due consideration to the preferences of your guests as well as to your own favorites.

WEDDING PICTURES

The Formal Photograph

Sometime before the wedding, often at the final fitting of the bridal gown, the photographer takes the formal wedding pictures of the bride. If photographs are to be sent to the newspapers, they must be taken well in advance to allow time for choosing the ones to be used, the final printing, and mailing to the papers two to three weeks before the wedding day.

A small print of this formal picture in a silver frame, with or without date and the initials of the couple engraved on it, makes a charming present from bride to bridesmaid.

Candid Photographs

If the candid shots on the wedding day are to be taken by a professional, he must be engaged far ahead of time, especially if the wedding is to be in June. If you are fortunate enough to number a skilled amateur photographer among your friends, he will surely be delighted to record the event. He cannot, however, provide as complete coverage as a skilled professional. If an amateur covers the entire day and uses quantities of film, the bride's family must certainly pay for the supplies and the printing, which, especially if color film is used, can be exorbitant. But if he uses a roll or two at the reception of his own volition and not at the specific request of the bride, this is not necessary, and often camera enthusiasts present these pictures as a wedding present to the bride.

A candid album starts with the bride's leaving the house before the wedding and continues through the day—her arrival at the church with her father (or whoever is giving her away), the wedding party's departure from the church after the ceremony, the bridal party and receiving line at the reception, shots of the bride and groom dancing, the guests, the toasts, the cutting of the cake, throwing the bouquet, and finally, the departure of the happy pair on their honeymoon.

Pictures of the actual ceremony taken with electronic flash are in very poor taste because they detract from the solemnity of the service. The photographer should be informed of this beforehand. But once the service is over and the bridal procession is coming down the aisle, the camera may start to work, and pictures of the radiant bride and groom who suddenly realize that they are "Mr. and Mrs." are often among the best souvenirs of all.

Members of the bridal party who wish to have duplicates of the wedding pictures for their own scrapbooks may have them made at their own expense.

The bride's family are under no obligation to give a set of wedding pictures to the groom's family. They should, however, show them the proofs and arrange for them to order those they want, *at the groom's family's expense*. However, if the bride's family can afford it and the groom's cannot, it would be a thoughtful gesture to send five or six of the best pictures to the groom's parents, especially if they could not be at the wedding. They might also arrange to have a tape made of the ceremony and the toasts at the reception to be sent to parents or grandparents who were unable to attend.

Videotapes

As mentioned before, whether the wedding ceremony may be videotaped must be discussed with the minister or rabbi. Generally, videotaping is a quieter process than the snapping of photographs, and many clergymen and women permit it as long as the videographer is unobtrusive and remains in a balcony or corner out of sight of the guests. As do still photographers, videographers continue with the wedding party to the reception and tape all or a portion of the reception as well.

If you are planning to have your wedding videotaped and your clergyman or woman agrees, contact several video studios and make appointments to see video-tapes of weddings they have covered. Look carefully not only at the actual quality of the tape, but also how it has been edited. Is the editing smooth or are there jumps, dark portions and gaps? Is the sound clear? Does it cover the things you would want covered at your ceremony and reception? Ask key questions before signing a contract, and make comparisons since prices vary widely.

WHEN THERE IS NO RECEPTION

When the marriage takes place in a church and there is to be no reception afterward the bride and the groom often receive in the vestibule of the church with their parents and the bridal party. The guests stop for a moment and offer their good wishes as they leave the church.

BELATED RECEPTIONS

It sometimes happens that a couple get married privately, far from home, perhaps where they are at college, or even in another country. If they return home shortly after their marriage, the bride's family may wish to give them the reception they did not have after their wedding. The reception may include all the trimmings of the ordinary reception following the wedding. If the bride wore a wedding gown for the ceremony, she may wear it again at the reception, so that her friends and relatives may see how she looked and feel more a part of the marriage. Invitations may be engraved, in the form shown on page 673.

RECEPTIONS IN RESTAURANTS

If possible, it is best to choose a restaurant that can provide a private room for the reception. Otherwise the party is apt to become a public spectacle and object of curiosity for the other patrons.

Although some large receptions are held in the private "ballroom" of the restaurant, most restaurant receptions are small ones. A restaurant is often chosen for dinner after a civil marriage, or after a marriage attended only by the families and a few friends.

It is up to the couple to find out ahead of time what facilities are offered, and to order or reserve exactly what they wish. It is also best to order the meal ahead of time. This avoids any question of how costly a meal the guests should order and eliminates any complications in paying the check. The bride and groom may order wine or champagne for the group, and the guests may order cocktails and pay for those themselves if they wish. Or the hosts (the bride and groom, or her family) may pay for all the liquor. There should always be a wedding cake, no matter how simple, and there are always toasts to the newlyweds. Otherwise the party is much like any other restaurant dinner, and unless the restaurant has a dance orchestra the couple leave when dinner is over.

RECEPTIONS AT THE CHURCH OR SYNAGOGUE

A reception held in the social rooms of the church or synagogue, or in the parish house, offers a fine solution to the bride who lives in a very small house or apartment, and who cannot afford to pay for a hall or hire a caterer. In some rural areas where elaborate facilities are not available, all receptions are held in the church hall.

PLANNING THE NEWSPAPER ANNOUNCEMENT

Most newspapers request announcement information at least three weeks before the wedding. The announcement generally appears the day following the ceremony. Since most newspapers receive more wedding announcements than they can print, the sooner yours is sent, and the more clear and concise the information, the better your chance of having it published.

Each paper will use as much of the information as it wishes, and in its own words. In general, you should provide the following:

- The bride's full name
- The bride's parents' name and town of residence
- Bride's parents' occupations
- Bride's maternal and paternal grandparents
- Bride's school and college
- Bride's occupation
- Groom's full name and town of residence
- Groom's parents' name and town of residence
- Groom's parents' occupations
- Groom's maternal and paternal grandparents
- Groom's school and college
- Groom's occupation
- Date of wedding
- Location of wedding and reception
- Names of bride's attendants and relationship to bride or groom, if any
- Names of groom's attendants and relationship to bride or groom, if any
- Description of bridal gown
- Description of attendants' gowns
- Name of minister or rabbi
- Name of soloist, if any
- Where couple will honeymoon
- Where couple will reside (town) after wedding

A typical announcement reads like this:

Miss Deirdre Mary Jordan was married yesterday to Mr. Thomas Charles Coleman. The marriage was performed at St. John's Church on the Green, Larchmont, New York, by the Reverend Marvin E. Henk.

The bride is the daughter of Mr. and Mrs. Michael Thomas Jordan of Patchogue, New York. Her grandparents are Mr. and Mrs. John Jordan of New York City and the late Mr. and Mrs. Robert McEvoy of Brooklyn, New York.

Mr. Coleman is the son of the late Mr. and Mrs. Howard William Coleman of Larchmont. His grandparents are Mr. and Mrs. William Coleman of River Forest, Illinois and the late Mr. and Mrs. Charles Markham of Evanston, Illinois.

Mrs. Coleman wore an ivory gown of marquisette over silk and carried a bouquet of white roses, lilies of the valley, and stephanotis. Her long veil of Alencon lace had been worn by her mother and her grandmother.

Miss Katherine Tognino served as maid of honor. The bridesmaids were Miss Regina Jordan and Miss Meg Jordan, sisters of the bride. Christine and Catherine Ferrari, nieces of the groom, were junior bridesmaids.

Mr. Coleman's best man was his brother, Mark Coleman of Rye, New York. The ushers were Jeffrey Keller, Douglas Campbell, and Norbert Rudell.

Mrs. Coleman graduated from New York University and is a sales service officer with The Bank of New York. Mr. Coleman attended Wagner University and is a free lance writer.

After their wedding trip, the couple will live in Larchmont.

This completes the necessary requirements, with the exception of a description of the bridesmaids' gowns, included only when space permits.

A newspaper announcement of the wedding is also a way in which a bride who intends to keep her own name may make it known. In the second paragraph, following "The bride," she would add "who will keep her own name." In the rest of the announcement, "Mrs. Coleman" would be changed to "the bride" or "Ms Jordan."

The Bride's Timetable

The best organized weddings are the ones where every detail has been thought of in advance. Thinking of those details is only the first step, however. Keeping a master check list, whether this one or one you write yourself, ensures that nothing is left to chance. If you plan to be married in June in a large metropolitan area you may have to start to implement your plans as much as a year ahead. Otherwise you will find your first choice for the church, reception site, caterer, etc. is already spoken for. In less crowded areas, however, the following timetable should suffice.

Your timetable and your master check list should be kept in a convenient place where you can consult it regularly, checking off items as they are attended to and adding even more details that may be special to your plans.

Three to Six Months in Advance of Your Wedding:

☐ Decide on the type of wedding and reception you want
☐ Consult your clergyperson to select the date and hour of your wedding
☐ Determine the location of your reception and reserve the club, hotel, restaurant or hall if it is not to be at home
☐ Engage a caterer if your reception is to be at home
☐ Determine the number of guests you are able to invite
☐ Choose attendants and ask them to serve
☐ Make out your guest list and ask the groom and his family to send you theirs. Tell them approximately how many guests they may invite

☐ Order invitations and announcements

☐ If you wish, order notepaper for thank-you notes, some monogrammed with your current initials and some monogrammed with your married initials for later on

Three Months in Advance of Your Wedding:

☐ With your fiancé, make appointments for counseling with your minister or rabbi and for discussing music, decorations and procedures during the ceremony with the minister or rabbi, sexton and organist

☐ Order your gown and those of your attendants

☐ Make an appointment with a photographer for your formal portraits and reserve his or her time for the day and time of your ceremony and reception

☐ If you plan to have live music at your reception, hire the band or the musician, or a disk jockey if you plan to have taped music for dancing

☐ If your wedding will be at home, make arrangements now for repairs, painting, cleaning, etc.

☐ Begin shopping for your personal and household trousseaus

☐ Select china, crystal and silver patterns

☐ Select gifts for your bridesmaids and a gift for your groom if you intend to give him one

Two Months in Advance of Your Wedding:

☐ Hire limousines, if necessary, for transporting the bridal party to the ceremony and from the ceremony to the reception

☐ Notify your attendants about their fittings and accessories. If possible, have shoes dyed in one lot

☐ List your selections at local gift and department store bridal registries, with your groom if possible. Tell your mother and your maid of honor where you are registered so that they can tell guests who ask them

☐ At the time of, or soon after the final fitting of your wedding dress, have formal bridal photographs taken

☐ Make detailed arrangements with the manager of your reception site or caterer including menu, table arrangements, decorations, linens, parking, and so on

☐ Make medical and dental appointments, and a hairdresser appointment if you intend to have your hair done on the day of your wedding

☐ Address and stuff wedding invitations

☐ Make housing arrangements for out-of-town attendants and obtain hotel and motel information for guests from out of town

- [ ] With your groom, select wedding rings
- [ ] Mail invitations four to six weeks in advance of your wedding
- [ ] Remind your groom or the best man to arrange fittings and reserve any rented formalwear for himself and the groomsmen

One Month in Advance of Your Wedding:

- [ ] Check with your groom about his blood test and the marriage license
- [ ] If you are displaying wedding gifts, begin setting up tables for them
- [ ] Record all gifts and write thank-you's as they arrive
- [ ] Make a list of your honeymoon clothing and be sure it is cleaned, pressed and ready to pack
- [ ] Check on all accessories for you and your attendants
- [ ] Make final arrangements with all professionals who are working with you—florist, photographer, reception manager or caterer
- [ ] If you are changing your name, do so on all documents such as driver's license, credit cards and bank accounts, etc. Both you and the groom should obtain and complete change of address forms at the local Post Office
- [ ] Check your luggage to be sure it is adequate and in good condition
- [ ] Check on the advisability of a floater insurance policy to cover your wedding gifts—especially if you are displaying them
- [ ] Arrange the details for a bridesmaids' luncheon if you wish to give one
- [ ] Address your announcements, stamp them, and give them to your mother or a friend to mail the day after your wedding
- [ ] Make the arrangements for a place for your bridesmaids to dress
- [ ] Plan the seating for the bridal table and parents' table(s) at your reception and make out place cards for them
- [ ] Send your wedding announcement to the newspapers with your wedding portrait if you wish
- [ ] Notify your wedding party of the time of the rehearsal

Two Weeks in Advance of Your Wedding:

- [ ] Confirm hotel, motel or other lodging arrangements for your bridal party
- [ ] Confirm flower order and deliveries with florist

One Week in Advance of Your Wedding:

- [ ] Pick up gifts for your attendants
- [ ] Give final count of guests to reception manager or caterer

☐ Reserve afternoon to have friends and family visit to view your gifts, if on display

☐ Plan quiet dinner for just you and your fiancé

☐ Plan light refreshments for your attendants if they will be changing at your house

The Morning of the Wedding:

☐ Have hair done, or shampoo and arrange it yourself

☐ Make sure any orders not being delivered are picked up (flowers, food, etc.)

☐ Eat breakfast—no matter how nervous you may be

Two Hours Before the Ceremony:

☐ Have your attendants arrive at your house to prepare to dress and to assist you with any last minute details

☐ Meet your attendants at the hotel, if you will be changing there instead, or one hour before at a reserved room at the place your ceremony will be held

One Hour Before the Ceremony:

☐ Apply make-up and dress, making sure to cover face before dressing so as not to get make-up on your gown

☐ Ushers should arrive at place of ceremony at least 45 minutes before to plan duties and to seat any early arrivals

One Half Hour Before the Ceremony:

☐ Groom and best man arrive at place of ceremony

☐ Background music starts

☐ First guests arrive and are seated

☐ If you have dressed at home, you and your attendants go to church or synagogue and wait in private room

☐ Best man checks last-minute arrangements with minister or rabbi and gives him or her the fee

Fifteen Minutes Before the Ceremony:

☐ Family members and honored guests (godparents, for example) arrive and are seated "within the ribbon" or in the pews near the front

Five Minutes Before the Ceremony:

- ☐ The groom's mother and father arrive and she is escorted to her seat, followed by her husband
- ☐ The bride's mother is escorted to her seat in the front row
- ☐ The white carpet, or aisle runner, is rolled down the aisle
- ☐ The bride's father takes his place with his daughter
- ☐ The attendants take their places in the proper order for the processional
- ☐ At precisely the time stated on the invitation, the music starts and the ushers lead the procession down the aisle

A young bride being married for the first time is likely to choose a long white or off-white bridal gown. Whether or not it has a train depends on the formality of the wedding and on the bride's own taste. A bride over forty may wear a long dress if she wishes, but a pale pastel shade is often more becoming to skin tones than white. Most mature brides do not wear a veil, and divorcees or widows being married for the second time definitely should not wear a veil unless their religion decrees it.

38
Clothes for the Bridal Party

THE BRIDE

The traditional and most formal bridal material is satin, but few brides wish to wear such a warm material on a summer day. Therefore, although satin is a favorite choice for fall and winter, other materials have become more popular for the rest of the year.

Suitable fabrics for autumn and midwinter weddings are brocade, velvet, and moiré. In the spring, lace and taffeta are lovely, and in midsummer, chiffon, organdy, marquisette, cotton, piqué, and linen. An infinite variety of synthetic materials has added to the bride's choice for every season.

In the case of an informal marriage ceremony, such as a civil ceremony before a justice of the peace or a second marriage when there is not to be a large celebration, the bride chooses the prettiest dress she has or can afford to buy that will be appropriate to whatever the couple plans after the wedding ceremony.

(Refer to the chart at the end of this chapter to see at a glance the correct attire for every type of wedding.)

Borrowing a Dress

Often a friend or a relative is delighted to lend her wedding dress, particularly to someone she knows will take good care of it. There is no reason not to accept an offer of a loaned gown, as long as you indeed take extraordinarily good care of it and return it freshly cleaned and in perfect condition. If you do borrow a gown, you should show your appreciation with the loveliest gift you can give—preferably something for your friend's home, or a personal gift for her.

Renting a Dress

Many areas now have bridal and evening rental stores where a bride may rent her dress, just as the groom and ushers rent their costumes. If the dress is fresh, becoming, and in perfect condition, this can be a practical and satisfactory alternative to buying an expensive, one-time dress.

The Veil

The face veil is rather old-fashioned and is usually omitted, although it may be required in some churches. The long lace veil falling down the back from a mantilla or the veil of tulle reaching to the waist at the back is far more popular.

If the bride does choose to wear a veil over her face coming up the aisle and during the ceremony, it is always a short, separate piece about a yard square. Mounted on a foundation, it need merely be put on a bride's head in front of her headdress. It is taken off by the maid of honor when she gives the bride's bouquet back to the bride at the conclusion of the ceremony, or if it will not destroy the headdress, it may simply be thrown back over the head.

Heirloom veils of lace are very beautiful, but they limit the bride's choice of gown. They are no longer white, and the dress must be of ivory or ecru to match. If ivory is becoming to the bride and she is happy with the color, that is fine, but she should never be made to feel that she had to wear her grandmother's veil, if it means she cannot have the white marquisette gown she had always dreamed of.

Shoes and Gloves

The bride's shoes are usually of white satin (if the gown is satin) or peau de soie. She should be sure that they are comfortable because not only does she walk up the aisle in them, but also she has to stand in them at the reception. Pumps are more appropriate than open sandals.

If she chooses to wear short, loose gloves she merely pulls one glove off at the altar so that her ring can be put on. But if she wears elbow-length or longer gloves, the underseam of the wedding finger of the glove may be ripped open, and she need only to pull the tip off to have the ring put on. I find this unattractive, and wasteful, and prefer that no gloves be worn at all.

Jewelry

If the bridegroom has given the bride a piece of jewelry as a wedding gift, she wears it if she possibly can, even though it may be composed of colored stones. Otherwise she wears neutral-colored jewelry such as a pearl necklace or possibly a pin of pearls or diamonds—sometimes given to her by the groom's parents or a grandmother.

Makeup

If the bride customarily wears makeup, naturally she will wear it for her wedding, but applied skillfully and in moderation. Nothing could be more inappropriate than the bride and her attendants coming down the aisle of the church made up as though they were in the chorus line of a musical comedy.

Today some brides hire a makeup artist to apply their makeup and that of their attendants. These professionals can help the nervous bride look her best throughout the ceremony and reception.

THE BRIDE'S ATTENDANTS

The costumes of the bridesmaids are selected by the bride. She may consult her maid of honor or the bridesmaids if they live nearby, but she does not if they live at a distance, and in any case the final choice is hers alone. Six women almost certainly will have six different opinions, so it is generally safer for the bride to make the selection by herself.

Since her attendants pay for their dresses in most cases, the bride has an obligation to them to consider the price very carefully. She should also try to select dresses that can be used later, either as they are or with some modifications. She must consider the sizes and shapes of her attendants and try to select an easy-to-wear style and a color that will be becoming to all and unflattering to none.

She does not buy jewelry for the bridesmaids, but suggests to them what might look best—a strand of pearls, a gold chain, or whatever it might be.

The bride picks a headdress that will be the most becoming to the majority of the girls. If some have long straight hair and others have short curly hair, a simple bow pinned at the back of the head is perhaps safest. Wide-brimmed "garden" hats are flattering to almost everyone too. She may ask the girls with long hair if they would mind wearing it up for the occasion, but she does not tell them how they "must" wear it.

Bridesmaids' dresses are always identical in texture and style, but not necessarily in color. For example, the first two might wear deep red, the next two a lighter rose, and the next two a still lighter color, while the maid of honor would be in palest flesh-pink. All-white bridesmaids' dresses tend to detract from the bride's costume, but when color is added in the sash or trim, or in the flowers the girls carry, an almost all-white wedding can be entrancing, especially in a garden with a background of dense greens.

The material for the bridesmaids' dresses should complement the material of the dress of the bride. In other words, if the bride chooses austere satin, the bridesmaids should not be dressed in organdy or ruffled lace. They should also match the bride's dress in degree of formality and to some extent in style.

The dress of the maid or matron of honor is usually different from that of the bridesmaids. It is similar in style but different or reversed in color. For example, for an autumn wedding the bridesmaids might wear deep yellow and carry rust-and-orange chrysanthemums, and the maid of honor might wear rust and carry yellow chrysanthemums. Occasionally her dress is identical to the others, but her flowers are quite different.

Since the bridesmaids' backs are often turned toward the congregation during the ceremony, the backs of the dresses should be interesting and pretty. The hemline should be an inch or more above the ground, so that there is no chance of the wearers' tripping on the church or chancel steps.

Whether or not the bridesmaids wear gloves is a matter of the bride's preference. If they are particularly becoming to the costumes, short white gloves are most appropriate in the daytime, as are full-length kid gloves in the evening, but gloves are not necessary at all.

The bride should ask her attendants to get their shoes well ahead of time, and to give or send them to her. She then has them all dyed at the same place and at the same time, so they will be identical in color.

Headdresses may be anything from the big leghorn hat mentioned above to a wreath of artificial flowers, a mantilla, or a simple bow. Becomingness to the majority of the bridesmaids and appropriateness to the style of the dresses are the main considerations. Since a headdress of real flowers will inevitably droop in time, this is the one area where artificial flowers are acceptable.

The bridesmaids almost always carry flowers—most often falling sprays held in front of them, or sheaves that they hold on their outside arms. Those walking on the right side hold them on the right arm with the stems pointing downward to the left, and those on the left hold their flowers on the left arm with stems toward the right.

To achieve an old-fashioned appearance, bridesmaids sometimes carry muffs in winter, or in summer, round bouquets, or flower-filled baskets or hats made into baskets by tying their wide brims together with ribbons. These are carried with both hands directly in front.

Fresh flowers are almost always used for the decorations and the bouquets. If artificial flowers are used, they should be of silk and of the best available quality.

YOUNG ATTENDANTS

Flower girls may be dressed in quaint, old-fashioned dresses with bonnets, or they may be dressed in clothes similar to those of the bridesmaids but in a style more becoming to a child. They usually wear small wreaths of artificial flowers on their heads, but some wear no headdress at all, or have ribbons or flowers braided into long hair. They carry small bouquets or baskets of flowers, although they no longer—as a rule—strew them before the bride.

Very small boys—ring bearers, pages, or train bearers—wear white Eton jackets with short pants. When they are a little older they may wear navy-blue suits instead. If the boy's suit is white the shoes and socks are white; if it is navy, he wears navy socks and black shoes.

Junior bridesmaids wear dresses exactly like those of the older bridesmaids, although they are sometimes of a different color. Their flowers may be, but are not necessarily, different from the others.

Junior ushers dress in the same style of clothing as the other ushers.

The Groom and His Attendants

Attire for the male members of the wedding party follows a definite pattern from which little deviation is permitted. In temperate climates, formal evening clothes mean a black tailcoat and matching trousers, stiff white shirt, wing collar, white tie, and white waistcoat.

Semiformal evening clothes means a black or midnight-blue dinner jacket (tuxedo) and matching trousers, piqué or pleated-front white shirt with attached collar, black bow tie, and black waistcoat or cummerbund. In hot weather a white dinner jacket and black cummerbund are used. Evening clothes should never be worn during the daytime.

Formal day clothes are appropriate for daytime weddings and should be worn whenever a wedding is scheduled before six o'clock. The daytime equivalent of the evening tailcoat is a black or Oxford-gray cutaway coat worn with black or gray striped trousers, pearl gray waistcoat, stiff white shirt, stiff fold-down collar, and four-in-hand black-and-gray tie or a dress ascot tie.

Less formal daytime clothes are the same except that a suit-style dark gray or black sack coat is substituted for the cutaway, the shirt is soft instead of stiff, and only a four-in-hand tie is worn.

In warm climates or very hot summertime in more northern climates, a formal daytime wedding is usually not attempted. In the informal wedding, although the bride may still wear a simple bridal gown, the men switch to lightweight suits or to dark gray or navy blue jackets with white trousers, white dress socks and white dress shoes, or black dress socks and black dress shoes. They may also wear white jackets with dark gray trousers. Shirts are soft white with attached collar, and ties should be four-in-hand with a dark, small, neat pattern.

The groom may send each usher specifications of what he will wear and ask him to rent the correct clothing. However, for the sake of uniformity, it is better if he asks for their sizes, including their shoe sizes, and then orders the outfits himself from a rental agency. Shoes may be rented if everyone does not own the same dress shoes. The best man may take care of this task for the groom if it is convenient for him to do so. The attendants, in any case, pay the fee. In the past, ushers' gloves and ties were given to the attendants by the groom so he would know that they would match perfectly, but today formal wear rental stores generally have these items in

WAISTCOAT

TAILCOAT

TUXEDO

SACKCOAT

CUTAWAY

stock and they are part of the rental fee along with the rest of the clothing. The groom provides his attendants' boutonnieres.

When the Groom Is in the Service

When our nation is not officially at war, military regulations ordinarily allow a member of the armed forces to choose whether or not he wears his uniform when he is off the base or off duty. Therefore officers and enlisted men—with their fiancées' help—may decide whether they wish to be married in uniform. A professional serviceman will undoubtedly choose to wear his uniform, and since his friends are probably regular servicemen too, they will also be dressed in uniform. A reserve officer or enlisted man has a more difficult decision. If his ushers are chosen from among his civilian friends he must decide whether to give the wedding party a coordinated appearance by dressing in civilian clothes himself or to ignore the look-alike question to show his pride in his service by wearing his uniform. The wishes of his bride should be considered in reaching this decision.

Whatever the groom chooses to do, the ushers should be dressed alike. If some are civilians and some are servicemen, those in the service should be asked to conform to the civilians on that occasion, since it cannot be the other way around.

THE MOTHERS OF THE BRIDE AND GROOM

The bride's mother should be the first to decide on what she will wear—how long, what style, and what color. She should then tell the groom's mother what her decision is, so that the latter may plan her outfit accordingly. The bride and her mother may go so far as to *suggest* to the other mother what they think might be becoming to her—they may *not tell* her what she is to choose. It certainly looks more attractive—makes a prettier "picture"—if both women are dressed similarly, especially since they stand together in the receiving line. But if the groom's mother feels uncomfortable in the type of clothing chosen by the bride's mother, or knows that it is unbecoming to her, she should feel free to select a dress in which *she* will feel attractive and happy.

If either the bride or the groom has a stepmother to whom they feel close and she will be at the wedding, it is thoughtful for the bride, once she knows what her own mother and the groom's mother will be wearing, to pass this information along to the stepmother. This allows her to avoid dressing in an identical color, which could be embarrassing to all, and gives her a guideline as to the style and length of the dresses the mothers will be wearing.

The elegance of the dresses should be keyed to the elaborateness of the wedding. Long skirts and dresses are considered appropriate for any wedding from noon on. And long dresses may vary greatly in formality—from shirtwaist tops and skirts to brocade evening gowns.

The dresses of the mothers should not be of the same color as those of the bridesmaids. They should not try to look like members of the wedding party. Nor should they both be wearing the same color. The shades should be carefully chosen to go with the overall colors of dresses and flowers, and so that the two mothers' dresses will not "clash" with each other. Prints are youthful-looking and pretty for a summer wedding, but if one mother chooses a print dress, the other should wear a complementary solid color. Neither mother should wear black. If one is in mourning, she should wear off-white, gray, or lavender, to avoid any suggestion of sadness on this happiest of days.

At very formal weddings, the mothers should wear gloves, which are kept on while they are in the receiving line. They should also wear something on their heads—whether a small artificial-flower arrangement, a hat, a veil, or a bow.

As a rule, the mother of the bride leaves her wrap in the vestibule with those of the bridesmaids. However, if she knows that the church is likely to be cool, and if she has an attractive fur piece, she carries or wears it. Otherwise someone may put a light wrap in the pew for her before she herself comes up the aisle. In other words the bride's mother should not wear or carry anything that might spoil the effect of her dress.

THE FATHERS OF THE BRIDE AND GROOM

There is no hard-and-fast rule governing the clothes of the bride's father, but since he will be escorting his daughter down the aisle behind the ushers, the party will have a more unified appearance if he elects to wear the same outfit they do. And in fact he almost invariably does dress like the other men.

At a formal wedding the bridegroom's father may, and generally does, wear the same type of clothes as those worn by the bride's father. He has, however, no official part in the ceremony and therefore may wear a dark suit if he is more comfortable in informal clothes.

The question sometimes arises whether a mother may wear the same dress for the weddings of two or more of her children. Of course she *may*, if her budget is limited, but if it is at all possible to buy a new dress, the children who marry later will appreciate her looking as stylish and as special for their weddings as she did for the first.

DRESS FOR BRIDAL PARTY AND GUESTS

663
CLOTHES
FOR THE
BRIDAL
PARTY

	Most Formal Daytime	Most Formal Evening	Semiformal Daytime
Bride	Long white dress, train, and veil; gloves optional	Same as most formal daytime	Long white dress; short veil and gloves optional
Bride's attendants	Long dresses, matching shoes; gloves are bride's option	Same as most formal daytime	Same as most formal daytime
Groom, his attendants, bride's father or stepfather	Cutaway coat, striped trousers, pearl gray waistcoat, white stiff shirt, turndown collar with gray-and-black-striped four-in-hand or wing collar with ascot, gray gloves, black silk socks, black kid shoes	Black tailcoat and trousers, white pique waistcoat, starched-bosom shirt, wing collar, white bow tie, white gloves, black silk socks, black patent-leather shoes or pumps or black kid smooth-toe shoes	Black or charcoal sack coat with gray striped trousers, dove gray waistcoat, white pleated shirt, starched turndown collar or soft white shirt with four-in-hand tie, gray gloves, black smooth-toe shoes
Mothers and stepmothers of couple	Long or short dresses; hat, veil, or hair ornament; gloves	Usually long evening or dinner dress, dressy short cocktail permissible; veil or hair ornament if long dress; small hat, if short; gloves	Long or street-length dresses; gloves, head covering optional
Women guests	Street-length cocktail or afternoon dresses (colors are preferable to black or white); gloves; head covering optional	Depending on local custom, long or short dresses; if long, veil or ornament—otherwise, hat optional; gloves	Short afternoon or cocktail dress; head covering for church optional
Men guests	Dark suits; conservative shirts and ties	If women wear long dresses, tuxedos; if short dresses, dark suits	Dark suits

	Semiformal Evening	Informal Daytime	Informal Evening
Bride	Same as semiformal daytime	Short afternoon dress, cocktail dress, or suit	Long dinner dress or short cocktail dress or suit
Bride's attendants	Same length and degree of formality as bride's dress	Same style as bride	Same style as bride
Groom, his attendants, bride's father or stepfather	Winter, black tuxedo; summer, white jacket; pleated or piqué soft shirt, black cummerbund, black bow tie, no gloves, black patent-leather or kid shoe	Winter, dark suit; summer, dark trousers with white linen jacket or white trousers with navy or charcoal jacket; soft shirt, conservative four-in-hand tie; hot climate, white suit	Tuxedo if bride wears dinner dress; dark suit in winter, lighter suit in summer
Mothers and stepmothers of couple	Same as semiformal daytime	Short afternoon or cocktail dresses	Same length dress as bride
Women guests	Cocktail dresses, gloves, head covering for church optional	Afternoon dresses, gloves, head covering for church optional	Afternoon or cocktail dresses, gloves, head covering for church optional
Men guests	Dark suits	Dark suits; light trousers and dark blazers in summer	Dark suits
Groom's father or stepfather:	He may wear the same costume as the groom and his attendants, especially if he is to stand in the receiving line. If he is not to take part, however, and does not wish to dress formally, he may wear the same clothes as the men guests.		

THE GUEST LIST

Four lists are combined in sending out wedding invitations. The bride and the bridegroom each make a list of their own friends, in addition to the list of the bride's family and that of the groom's family.

The bride's mother discusses with the groom, or if possible with his mother, how the list is to be divided between them. If the families are old friends and live in the same community, the invitations should be divided more or less equally between them. At least half of the names on the two lists would undoubtedly be the same, and therefore each family would be able to add several more in place of those which are duplicated. But if they have never known each other well, and their friends are unknown to each other, each list would have to be limited to half the total.

On the other hand, if the groom's family live in another place and not more than a few will be able to come, the bride's mother will be able to invite as many people as will result in the total number of spaces available. Both mothers may risk being a little overliberal because there are always a few who, having accepted, are then prevented for one reason or another from coming.

When some refusals are received, the bride's mother may send out additional invitations to replace those guests, up until two and a half weeks before the wedding.

It is most important for future harmony that the family of the out-of-town groom estimate *realistically* the number of guests who will make the trip to the wedding. When the bride's mother tells them the total number that can be invited and how many acceptances she expects on her side, they should make every effort to stay within the total. It is up to the out-of-town family to respect the requests of the bride's family in this matter, as they may not be aware of the limitations of space or expense that are factors in the number of invitations to be sent.

INVITATIONS

The wording of formal traditional engraved invitations and announcements is as fixed as the letters of the alphabet. The third-person form has been used for countless years, and the replies are written in exactly the same style. The

39
Invitations, Announcements and Replies

invitation is usually sent in the name of the bride's parents, since they pay most of the expenses and are the "hosts," but if the groom's parents are assuming a full share of the costs, the invitations should be in their name also.

Invitations to a formal wedding are mailed four to six weeks beforehand; those to a small wedding may be sent as late as ten days before the ceremony.

The Style of the Invitations

Your stationer will show you several grades and shades of paper from which you make your selection. Ivory, soft cream, and white are all correct. If you can afford it, you will do well to choose the heaviest-weight paper. It may cost a bit more, but its fine appearance and feel make it worth the extra expense. Whether the paper is flat or has a raised plate mark or margin is up to you. Either the large double sheet, which is folded a second time to go into the envelope, or the smaller double sheet, which goes in unfolded, is correct. The tissues inserted by the engraver used to be necessary to avoid blotting or smudging but improved printing and engraving techniques have made them obsolete, and you may discard them if you wish.

The invitation to a reception following the church ceremony is usually engraved on a card to match the paper and engraving of the church invitation.

The stationer will show you a number of typeface also. Shaded Roman, antique Roman, and script are very popular. Simple styles are in better taste than ornate and flowery engraving. If the bride's father's family has a coat of arms, she may properly have it, or a crest only, engraved without color at the top center of the invitation. If you cannot afford engraved invitations, less expensive thermographed ones are equally acceptable.

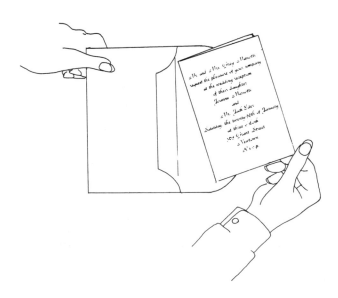

Stuffing the Envelopes

One of the unique conventions about wedding invitations is that there were always two envelopes. The invitation (folded edge first) and all enclosures were put in the inner envelope, facing the back flap. This envelope was then placed unsealed in the outer envelope, with the flap away from the person inserting it. Both envelopes were always addressed by hand.

While it is still perfectly correct to order both envelopes, it is also correct to omit the inner one. In the interests of economy and conservation, and because today we prefer the simplest and most practical customs, the inner envelope now seems superfluous.

Besides the invitations, several cards may be placed in the inner envelope (or outer envelope, if you omit the inner one). They all face the flap, and all are placed in front of the invitation itself—facing the person inserting them—or, if it is a folded invitation, within the fold.

Pew Cards

Small cards with "Pew Number—" engraved on them may be enclosed with the invitations going to those family members and close friends who are to be seated in the reserved pews. The people receiving them take them to the church and show them to the ushers who escort them.

Similar cards are sometimes engraved "Within the ribbon," meaning that a certain number of pews are reserved for special guests but no specific pew is assigned.

Pew cards are often sent separately after the acceptances or regrets come in, so that the bride knows how many reserved pews will be needed and can assign the right number of seats.

Pew numbers were formerly sent on visiting cards, but today they must be written on a card (printed with the name of the bride and groom) that is large enough to meet postal regulations.

Admission Cards

Except when a wedding is held in a cathedral or a church that attracts sightseers, admission cards are not necessary. To ensure privacy in those circumstances, each guest is asked to present his or her card at the entrance. It is engraved in the same style as the invitation and reads:

Please present this card
at
The Washington Cathedral
Saturday, the tenth of June

"At Home" Cards

If you and your groom wish your friends to know what your new address will be, you may insert an "at home" card. These cards traditionally read:

At home [or, Will be at home]
after July twelfth
3842 Grand Avenue
Houston, Texas 77001

Many people receiving these cards, however, put them away, intending to enter them in an address book or file. Some time later they come across the card, only to find they cannot remember who will be at home at 3842 Grand Avenue after July twelfth. Therefore, even though you are not married at the time the invitation is sent, I recommend that your cards be engraved:

Mr. and Mrs. Brian Jamison
will be at home
(etc.)

This also provides an opportunity for the woman who plans to keep her own name to let her friends know. Her at-home card would read:

Janet Stock and David Burns
will be at home
(etc.)

Response Cards

It is regrettable that it is necessary to write these paragraphs, but the custom of enclosing response cards with wedding invitations is so widespread that it must be discussed.

The custom has arisen, I am afraid, out of sheer necessity. Too many people are lazy, thoughtless, or ignorant of good behavior and simply will not take the time or make the effort to answer invitations. When a caterer is hired, or the reception is held at a club or hotel, those in charge want to know the exact number of guests as soon as possible. While a rough estimate may be made from the quantity of invitations mailed, the more precise estimate must await the replies. Therefore, in an effort to get this information to the caterer in plenty of time, brides and their mothers often feel that the responses will arrive more quickly and surely if cards are enclosed.

While I thoroughly deplore the lack of appreciation shown by guests who would not otherwise bother to answer promptly, I am forced to accept the practicality of the cards in certain areas, or among certain groups where they have long been expected and accepted. If you have decided to include response cards, let them be most useful and in the best possible taste. Response cards are the smallest cards accepted by the postal service, engraved in the same style as the invitation. You may include self-addressed envelopes if you wish, preferably stamped. The cards should be in the following form:

M_____

_____ *accepts*

_____ *regrets*

Saturday, January fifth

Bristol Hotel

Abingdon

They should *not* include "number of persons _____" Those whose names appear on the outer and inner envelopes are the *only* ones invited, and other members of the family—children, especially—are not necessarily included. If you use the cards, each couple invited should receive a separate invitation, and the children or single people who are invited should receive their own invitations. When "number of persons" appears, people are inclined to think this means that other members of the family may attend, and you will find yourself with three times the number of guests you expect.

Maps and Travel Information

It is very helpful, if the wedding is in the country or in an area unfamiliar to some of the guests, to have a small map drawn to enclose with the invitations going to friends unfamiliar with the location. The map should include the best approaches to the church and/or site of the reception from every direction.

The Inner Envelope

If you choose to have an inner envelope, it bears only the names of the people to whom the mailing envelope is addressed. A married couple's inner envelope is addressed to "Mr. and Mrs. Anderson" with neither the first names nor address. When an invitation is sent to several young children, the inner envelope is addressed to "Judith, Stuart and Shaun." If the outer envelope is addressed to the parents and a young daughter, her name is written on the inner envelope below her parents' name: "Miss Ann Kennedy." Intimate relatives may be addressed on the inner envelope as "Aunt Kate and Uncle Fred" or "Grandmother."

The Outer Envelope

Wedding invitations are always addressed to both members of a married couple, even though the bride may know only one, or knows that only one will attend. Invitations to an unmarried couple are addressed to Mr. John Burns and Ms. Mary French, with each name appearing on separate lines.

No abbreviations are used in addressing wedding invitations. A person's middle name may or may not be used, but if it is, it must be written out in full. "Street," "Avenue," and the name of the state may not be abbreviated.

Children over thirteen should, if possible, receive separate invitations. Young brothers and sisters may be sent a joint invitation to "The Misses" or "The Messrs. Jones." If there are both boys and girls, the address may read:

The Messrs. Jones
The Misses Jones

"Miss Mary Jones" or "The Misses Jones" may be written below "Mr. and Mrs. Franklin Jones," but "The Messrs. Jones" should receive a separate invitation.

Although it is generally not considered in the best of taste to address an envelope to "Mr. and Mrs. Franklin Jones and Family," there are circumstances when relationships are so complicated or children so numerous that this seems to be the only solution. It should be done only, however, when every person living under the same roof is intended to be included in the invitation, and only when the children are young. Each adult in the family should receive their own invitation.

When a bride and groom feel that they can accommodate a few extra people, they may address envelopes to their single friends: "Miss Sheryl Smith and guest" or "Mr. Robert Black and guest." If you are using inner envelopes, this should go only on the inner one, but if you are not, it may appear on the outer envelope, or you may indicate that a guest is welcome by a personal note included with the invitation: "Dear Sheryl, we would be delighted to have you bring a date if you would like to."

Return Addresses

Regardless of the many years during which it has been considered bad taste to put return addresses on wedding invitations, it is past time to change the rule. There are two excellent reasons. First, the U.S. Postal Service requests that all first-class mail bear a return address. Second, it provides an address to which invited guests may send replies and gifts, especially when no R.S.V.P. appears on the invitation.

Some addresses are embossed on the back flap of the envelope without inking. They often go unnoticed, however, and the envelope is discarded before the receiver realizes that no other address appears. Therefore I see no reason why you should not order the return address to be engraved legibly on every mailing envelope.

Conventional Wording and Spelling

Some of the specific rules regarding formal wedding invitations are as follows:

1. The invitation to the wedding ceremony in church reads: "Mr. and Mrs. Howard William Adams request the honour"—traditionally spelled with a "u"—"of your presence . . ."

2. The invitation to the reception reads: "Mr. and Mrs. Robert John Carlson request the pleasure of your company . . ."

3. Invitations to a Roman Catholic wedding may replace the phrase "at the marriage of" with "at the marriage in Christ of . . ." They may also add, beneath the groom's name, "and your participation in the offering of the Nuptial Mass."

4. No punctuation is used except after abbreviations, such as "Mr. or Mrs." or when phrases requiring separation occur in the same line, as in the date.

5. Numbers in the date are spelled out, but long numbers in the street address may be written in numerals.

6. Half-hours are written as "half after four," never "half past four."

7. Although "Mr." is abbreviated, and Junior may be, the title "Doctor" is more properly written in full.

8. If the invitation includes the handwritten name of the recipient, the *full* name must be written out. The use of an initial—"Mr. and Mrs. Robert S. Roth"—is not correct.

9. The invitation to the wedding ceremony alone does not include an R.s.v.p.

10. On the reception invitation, "R.S.V.P.," "R.s.v.p.," and "The favour of a reply is requested" are equally correct. If the address to which the reply is to be sent is different from that which appears in the invitation itself, you may use "Kindly send reply to," followed by the correct address.

Invitation to Church Ceremonies

The most formal wedding invitation, rarely seen today, has the name of the recipient written by hand:

Doctor and Mrs. John Joseph Saladino
request the honour of
Mr. and Mrs. David S. Williams
presence at the marriage of their daughter
Julie Anne
to
Mr. Timothy Ellis Frost
Saturday, the first of October
at twelve o'clock
St. John's Church

Mr. and Mrs. Michael Charles Jordan
request the honour of your presence
at the marriage of their daughter
Deirdre Mary
to
Mr. Thomas Charles Coleman
On Saturday, the thirtieth of May
nineteen hundred and ninety-two
at eleven o'clock
St. John's on the Green
Larchmont, Texas

R.S.V.P.
250 West 20th St.
Chelsea, Texas 55667

The traditional wedding invitation is issued by the bride's parents. Note that although the bride's name is not preceded by "Miss," the groom's is preceded by "Mr."

The most common form, equally correct, is:

Mr. and Mrs. Thomas Michael Tobin
request the honour of your presence
at the marriage of their daughter
Lydia Marie
to
Mr. Alec Barron Jenner
Saturday, the twelfth of June
at half after four o'clock
Village Lutheran Church
Jonesboro

Reception Invitations

When the guest list for the church is larger than that for the reception, a separate card is enclosed with the wedding invitation for those who are to be invited to the reception. The most commonly used form is:

Reception
immediately following the ceremony
Knolls Country Club
Lake Forest
The favour of a reply is requested
Lakeside Drive, Lake Forest, Illinois 61300

Invitations to the Reception Only

On some occasions the wedding ceremony is private, and a large reception follows. This frequently is the case in a second marriage. The invitation to the ceremony is given orally, and the wording of the reception invitation is:

Mr. and Mrs. Greg Mariotti
request the pleasure of your company
at the wedding reception
of their daughter
Joanne Mariotti
and
Mr. Jack Eder
Saturday, the twenty-fifth of January
at three o'clock
563 Grant Street
Newtown
R.s.v.p.

When All Guests Go to Both Wedding and Reception

The cards illustrated above may also be used when every wedding guest is invited to go on to the reception, but it is more common to issue a combined invitation, as described below.

When the reception follows a house wedding, or a ceremony in a hotel or club room, no separate invitation is necessary since all attending would be expected to stay on.

Wedding and Reception Invitation in One

When all the guests invited to the wedding are also to be invited to the reception, the invitation to both may be combined:

Mr. and Mrs. Clay Francis Newberry
request the honour of your presence
at the marriage of their daughter
Elizabeth Christine
to
Mr. Benjamin Steven Clark
Friday, the second of October
at half after five o'clock
Church of the Redeemer
San Francisco
and afterward at the reception
Bay Shore Country Club
The favor of a reply is requested
14 Adams Road
San Francisco, CA 99000

Wedding Held at a Friend's House

Even though the wedding and reception are held in a friend's house, the invitations are written in the name of the bride's parents or sponsors:

Mr. and Mrs. Eugene Braden Shanks, Jr.
request the honour of your presence
at the marriage of their daughter
Ann Lea
to
Mr. John Jefferson O'Dell
Saturday, the eighth of May
at eight o'clock
at the residence of Mr. and Mrs. Thomas Lockyer
Evanston, Illinois

R.s.v.p.

When the Bride's Mother Is Divorced

On formal correspondence, a divorced woman formerly used her maiden name and her last name rather than her first name (Mrs. Stephenson Barnes). Although this is technically correct, most divorcées today use their first names rather than their maiden name, and few people would know who "Mrs. Stephenson Barnes" was.

Therefore it is now acceptable for a divorcée to send out her daughter's invitations as "Mrs. Virginia Barnes."

Mrs. Virginia Barnes
requests the honour of your presence
at the marriage of her daughter
(etc.)

When Divorced Parents Give the Wedding Together

In the event that relations between the bride's divorced parents are so friendly that they share the wedding expenses and act as co-hosts, both names must appear on the invitation. The bride's mother's name appears first:

Mr. and Mrs. Matthew Corwin Brown
and
Mr. and Mrs. Robert C. Shields, Jr.
request the honour of your presence
at the marriage of
Laura Jean Shields
(etc.)

If, however, the bride's parents are not sharing expenses, yet the bride wishes both parents' names to appear, a different situation exists. If the bride's mother is not contributing to the cost of the wedding the bride's father's name appears first on the invitation and he and his wife host the reception. The bride's mother is then only an honored guest at the reception.

When the Bride Has One Living Parent

When either the bride's mother or father is deceased, the invitation is issued only in the name of the living parent.

Mrs. [Mr.] John Whelan
requests the honour of your presence
at the marriage of her [his] daughter
Margaret Ann
(etc.)

However, there are circumstances when the bride very much wants to include the name of the deceased parent. This is acceptable, as long as the invitation does not appear to be issued by the deceased.

Deborah Ellen Keyes
daughter of Mary Ann Keyes and the late William Keyes
and
James Bryant Huseby
son of Mr. and Mrs. Silas James Huseby
request the honour of your presence
at their marriage
Tuesday, the twenty-first of November
(etc.)

When the Bride Has a Stepfather

When the bride's mother has been widowed or divorced and has remarried, the invitations are worded:

Mr. and Mrs. Raymond Jones Harper
request the honour of your presence
at the marriage of her daughter (or, Mrs. Harper's daughter)
Kelly Elizabeth Quimby
to
(etc.)

If the bride's own father has no part in her life and her stepfather has brought her up, the invitation reads:

Mr. and Mrs. Raymond Jones Harper
request the honour of your presence
at the marriage of their daughter
Kelly Elizabeth Quimby
(etc.)

When the Bride Is an Orphan

"Miss," "Ms" or "Mrs." is rarely used before the bride's name. The following two cases are exceptions.

When the bride has no relatives and her wedding is given by friends, the invitation reads:

Mr. and Mrs. Thomas Allen Harrell
request the honour of your presence
at the marriage of
their niece
Miss Rosemary Londen
to
Mr. Karl Andrew Rauch
(etc.)

A bride and groom who send out their own invitations would also use a title ("Miss," "Mrs."):

The honour of your presence
is requested
at the marriage of
Miss Dawn White
to
Mr. Michael Jordan
(etc.)

[OR]

Miss Dawn White
and
Mr. Michael Jordan
request the honour of your presence
at their marriage
(etc.)

Couples who have been living together, or more mature couples, may prefer to send out wedding invitations in their own names, and not use social titles.

Mary Ann McMillan
and
Franklin Anders Nielsen
invite you to share with them
the joy of their marriage
Saturday, the nineteenth of March
nineteen hundred and ninety-two
at half after five o'clock
First Baptist Church
Shreveport, Louisiana

If the bride has brothers or sisters, or other relatives, the wedding may be given by them, and the invitations are sent in their names:

Mr. Timothy Hennessy
requests the honour of your presence
at the marriage of his sister
Stephanie Kristin
(etc.)

[OR]

Mr. and Mrs. Steven Wise
request the honour of your presence
at the marriage of their niece
Susan Schiff
(etc.)

When the Bride Is a Young Widow or Divorcée

Invitations to a young widow's second wedding may be sent by her parents exactly as were the invitations to her first marriage. The only difference is that her married name is used:

Doctor and Mrs. Barry Farnham
request the honour of your presence
at the marriage of their daughter
Carolyn Farnham Flood
(etc.)

A divorcée's second wedding ceremony may read the same way. The bride's name would be the one she is using, either her maiden name with her ex-husband's last name, or, if she has dropped her ex-husband's name, with her own middle and maiden name.

If the Bride Is a More Mature Widow or Divorcée

A more mature woman whose parents are dead, or a divorcée who has been independent since her divorce, would generally send out her own invitations.

A widow's invitation would read:

The honour of your presence
is requested
at the marriage of
Mrs. George Saunders Simon
and
Mr. Craig Forsythe Douglas
(etc.)

A divorcée's invitation would read:

*The honour of your presence
is requested
at the marriage of
Mrs. Ann Rogers Duker
(etc.)*

If she prefers, she may drop the title and have her name read simply "Ann Rogers Duker."

When a bride's and groom's grown children are giving their wedding, the invitation may be issued in their names, with the bride's children listed before the groom's. When there are several children involved their names are given in age order, from oldest to youngest, in each family.

*Mr. and Mrs. Andrew Romeo
Mr. and Mrs. Daniel Jordan
Mr. and Mrs. Frederick Ingram
request the honour of your presence
at the marriage of their parents
Susan Brown Jordan
and
David Andrew Ingram
Sunday, the Second of September
at three o'clock
at the St. James Club
Cos Cob, Connecticut*

When the Bride Has a Professional Name

If the bride is well known by a professional name and has many professional friends to whom she wishes to send invitations or announcements, she may have her professional name in parentheses engraved below her real name on those invitations:

*Pauline Marie
(Pat Bond)
to
Mr. Carl Louis Finelli*

This is done by having "(Pat Bond)" added to the plate *after* the other invitations for those who know the bride only by her real name have been printed.

Military Titles

When the groom is a member of the Army, the Navy, the Coast Guard, the Air Force, or the Marine Corps, or is on active duty in the reserve forces, he uses his military title.

Officers whose rank is captain in the Army or lieutenant, senior grade or higher in the Navy have the title on the same line as their names:

Colonel Frank Burson
United States Army

Those with lower ranks have their name and title engraved in this form:

John McMahon
Ensign, United States Navy

In the case of reserve officers on active duty, the second line would read, "Army of the United States" or "United States Naval Reserve."

First and second lieutenants in the Army both use "Lieutenant" without the numeral.

A noncommissioned officer or enlisted man may have his rank and his branch of the service below his name or not, as he wishes.

Henry Delucia
Corporal, Signal Corps, United States Army

[OR]

Marc Josephson
Seaman Apprentice United States Naval Reserve

High-ranking officers of the regular armed forces continue to use their titles, followed by their branch of service, even after retirement, with "retired" following the service:

General George Harmon
United States Army, retired

When the father of the bride is a member of the armed forces, either on active duty, a high-ranking retired officer, or one who retired after many years of service, he uses his title in the regular way:

Colonel and Mrs. James Booth
request the honour of your presence
(etc.)

When the bride is on active duty both her rank and the branch of military is included in the invitation. The name of the bride appears on one line with her rank and the branch of the military on a separate line:

marriage of their daughter
Joanne
Lieutenant, United States Navy

Other Titles

Medical doctors, dentists, veterinarians, clergymen, judges, and all other men customarily called by their titles should have them included on their own wedding invitations, and on the invitations to their daughters' weddings.

Holders of academic degrees do not use the "Dr." unless they are always referred to in that way.

Women use their titles only when the invitations are issued by themselves and their grooms.

The honour of your presence
is requested
at the marriage of
Doctor Laurie Neu
and
Mr. Norbert Rudell
(etc.)

Otherwise, she is, "their daughter, Laurie."

The bride's mother preferably does not use the title "Dr." on her daughter's invitation. If she and her husband feel strongly that she should, the wording has to be, "Dr. Mary and Mr. Henry Smith request . . ."

The Double-Wedding Invitation

Double weddings almost always involve the marriage of two sisters, and the form is:

Mr. and Mrs. Henry Smart
request the honour of your presence
at the marriage of their daughters
Cynthia Helen
to
Mr. Steven Jones
and
Linda Caroline
to
Mr. Michael Scott Adams
Saturday, the tenth of November
at four o'clock
Trinity Church

The elder sister's name is given first.

In the rare event that two close friends decide to have a double wedding, the invitation reads:

Mr. and Mrs. Henry Smart
and
Mr. and Mrs. Arthur Lane
request the honour of your presence
at the marriage of their daughters
Cynthia Helen Smart
to
Mr. Steven Jones
and
Mary Alice Lane
to
Mr. John Gray
(etc.)

When the Bridegroom's Family Gives the Wedding

When the bride comes from another country, or from a great distance without her family, the groom's parents give the wedding and issue the invitations. This is also true if the bride's family disapprove of the wedding and refuse to take any part in it.

Mr. and Mrs. John Henry Pater
request the honour of your presence
at the marriage of
Miss Marie DuBois
to
their son
John Henry Pater, Junior
(etc.)

The announcements, however, should be sent by her own family, if possible, or by the groom's family including the name of the bride's parents.

Including the Groom's Family in the Invitation

The bride's family ordinarily arranges and pays for the wedding and reception. They are, therefore, the hosts, and the invitations are issued in their name. However, there are occasions when the groom's family shares in, or pays the major part of, the wedding expenses. In such a case it seems only fair that their names appear on the invitations, since they are actually co-hosts. The wording would be:

> *Mr. and Mrs. Charles Goodman*
> *and*
> *Mr. and Mrs. George Gonzalez*
> *request the pleasure of your company*
> *at the wedding reception of*
> *Julia Goodman*
> *and*
> *Roberto Gonzalez*
> *(etc.)*

A form followed in some foreign countries, and sometimes by foreigners living here, provides for a double invitation—the bride's on the left and the groom's on the right.

Mr. and Mrs. Bruno Cairo	*Mr. and Mrs. Robert Conti*
request the honour of your	*request the honour of your*
presence	*presence*
at the marriage of their daughter	*at the marriage of their son*
Maria	*Francesco*
to	*to*
Mr. Francesco Conti	*Miss Maria Cairo*
(etc.)	*(etc.)*

Alternatives to Traditional Invitations

Many people today find the traditional third-person wording too distant and formal for their tastes. This is not unreasonable, given our informal life-style, and it has led to the composing of some very beautiful personal invitations. The invitation may be engraved or thermographed just as formally as a traditional one, or, when the wedding is to be simple and untraditional, it may be printed on paper with a design or border, often in a color carrying out the color scheme of the wedding itself.

Here are samples of invitations that are in very good taste yet seem warmer than the traditional form.

Illustrated is a very simple example written in the bride's hand:

> Andrea Sargent and Eric Dawson
> invite you to
> celebrate their marriage
> on
> Sunday, October
> the twelfth
> at four o'clock
> 144 Elkton Road, Elkton, Maryland
>
> R.S.V.P.

The invitation sets the tone of the ceremony, and a traditional wedding should have the formal, "third-person" style of invitation. However, weddings that make no pretense of being traditional may be as original as the couple and/or the bride's parents can devise as long as they are dignified and attractive and sincerely reflect the sentiments of the bride, the groom, and their families. Among the most lovely and meaningful is this example, written as a letter from the bride's parents.

Our daughter, Sandra, will be married to John David Graham, on Saturday, the eleventh of August, nineteen hundred and ninety-four, at eleven o'clock in the morning. Their vows will be spoken at Middle Collegiate Church, Savannah, Georgia.

We invite you to worship with us, witness their vows, and be our guest at the Reception and Buffet which follow at the Hanover Inn, Savannah.

If you are unable to attend, we ask your presence in thought and prayer.

Mr. and Mrs. Frank N. Davis

My own particular favorite:

Our joy will be more complete
if you will share in the marriage of our daughter
Susan Hall
to
Mr. James Bogard
on Saturday, the fifth of June
at half after four o'clock
6 Sesame Lane
Oldtown, Massachusetts
We invite you to worship with us,
witness their vows and join us
for a reception following the ceremony
If you are unable to attend, we ask your
presence in thought and prayer.
Mr. and Mrs. Hugo Stone
(or, Anne and Hugo Stone)
R.S.V.P.

When the invitation is to come from both sets of parents, it might be worded:

Judy and Mitchell Ackerson
Blanche and Daniel Goldman
would be honoured
to have you share in the joy
of the marriage of their children
Leah
and
Jonathan
This celebration of love will be held on
Sunday, the ninth of September
at five o'clock
Temple Shalom
St. Louis, Missouri
A reception will follow the ceremony
at the Palisades Lodge
Palisades Parkway
Kindly send reply to:
Mr. and Mrs. Mitchell Ackerson
(address)

A bride and groom who want to write their own invitations yet would like a touch of formality might use the following form:

Beth Holland and Christopher Saladino
invite you to attend
their marriage
on
Saturday, October the twenty-first
at three-thirty
The Hopewell School
Richmond, Virginia
A reception on the grounds will follow the ceremony
R.S.V.P.
Ms. Beth Holland
87 Grace Street
Richmond, Virginia 23223

Personal Invitations

Invitations to very small weddings and those to second marriages are often issued in the form of a personal note. Even though a bride is sending engraved invitations, she may, if she wishes, write personal ones to people to whom she feels especially close. This is the most flattering invitation possible. A typical note would read:

> Dear Aunt Sally,
>
> Dick and I are to be married at Christ Church on June tenth at four o'clock. We hope you and Uncle Jim will come to the church, and afterward to the reception at Greentree Country Club.
>
> With much love from us both,
> Jeanne

Invitation to a Belated Wedding Reception

When a reception is not held at the time of the wedding, the couple or their parents often have one later, possibly when the newlyweds return from their honeymoon. Although the party is held to celebrate the wedding, a true reception follows the ceremony, and the wording must be slightly changed.

Mr. and Mrs. Raymond Gregg Mariotti
request the pleasure of your company
at a reception
in honor of
Mr. and Mrs. Jack Nelson
(etc.)

A less formal invitation may be issued by using fill-in printed cards and writing "In honor of Joanne and Jack" or "In honor of Mr. and Mrs. Jack Nelson" at the top.

ANNOUNCEMENTS

Announcements are not obligatory, but in many cases they serve a useful purpose. They may be sent to those friends who are not invited to the wedding because the number of guests must be limited, or because they live too far away to make the journey. They may also be sent to acquaintances who, while not particularly close to the family, might still wish to know of the marriage. Announcements carry no obligation at all, so that many families send them rather than invitations to friends who are not expected to attend or to send a present. They are never sent to anyone who has received an invitation to the church or reception. Announcements are mailed as soon as possible after the wedding, preferably the next day. However, in the case of an elopement, or for some other reason, they may be mailed up to several months later.

Traditionally, announcements were always sent in the name of the bride's parents. The wording was as follows (and this is still perfectly correct):

Mr. and Mrs. James Brennan Welch
have the honour of
announcing the marriage of their daughter
Amy Sue
to
Mr. Scott Francis Crown
Saturday, the fifteenth of June
one thousand nine hundred and ninety-three
Albuquerque, New Mexico

There are several variations, equally correct. You may use "have the honour to announce," or merely the word "announce." The year is always included. The most formal wording is "one thousand nine hundred and ninety-two," but "nineteen hundred and ninety-two" is not incorrect.

However, I see no reason why today, when the attitude toward marriage that it is a "joining" rather than a "giving" of a woman to a man, the announcements should not go out in both families' names. Although the privilege has always been accorded to the bride's family, it seems to me that when the parents of the groom are also proud and happy, it would be equally appropriate to have announcements sent in this way:

Mr. and Mrs. Marshall Lee Lindskog
and
Mr. and Mrs. Joseph Frederick Planta
announce the marriage of
Marsha Jane Lindskog
and
Murray Joseph Planta
on . . .

Since announcements, unlike invitations, are intended to dispense information, surely the inclusion of the name of the groom's parents is informative as well as symbolic of their joy and approval.

The variations in circumstances, names, and titles follow those described previously for wedding invitations. In general, the wording used for the wedding invitation becomes the basis for the wording of the wedding announcement.

For example, announcements for a young widow's or divorcée's second

Mr. and Mrs. Lincoln Burgess

and

Mr. and Mrs. Thomas Wynne

announce the marriage of

Jennifer Lynn Burgess

and Paul David Wynne

Thursday, the twentieth of May

Mormon Tabernacle Church

Salt Lake City, Utah

When the wedding invitation is issued in the name of both sets of parents, the announcements are also. When this style of wording is used, the groom's name is not preceded by "Mr." as it would be when the invitations are issued in the name of the bride's parents alone.

marriage are the same as for a first wedding:

Doctor and Mrs. Barry Farnham

and

Mr. and Mrs. Nigel Withers

announce the marriage of

Carolyn Farnham Flood

and

Nigel Withers, Junior

(etc.)

When couples who have been living together send out wedding invitations in their own names their announcements are issued in the same way, that is, without social titles:

Mary Ann McMillan

and

Franklin Anders Nielsen

announce their marriage

on Saturday, the nineteenth of March

nineteen hundred and ninety-two

Shreveport, Louisiana

The announcement of the marriage of a widow of more mature years reads differently:

Mrs. George Saunders Simon

and

Mr. Craig Forsythe Douglas

announce their marriage

on Saturday, the fifth of April

one thousand nine hundred and ninety-one

at Vernon Valley

New Jersey

A divorcée and her new husband announce their marriage:

Mrs. Ann Rogers Duker

and

Mr. Peter Henwood Norton

announce their marriage

on Tuesday, the tenth of May

(etc.)

The bride who is an orphan and her bridegroom announce their marriage the same way, or, if the wedding was given by a relative or friend, the announcement, like the wedding invitation, begins with the names of those who hosted the wedding:

Mr. and Mrs. Thomas Allen Harrell
announce the marriage of
Miss Rosemary Londen
(etc.)

"At home" cards may be included with announcements.

CHANGES IN WEDDING PLANS

When the Wedding Is Canceled After Invitations Are Mailed

If the decision to cancel the wedding is a last-minute one, invited guests must be notified by telephone or telegram. If there is time, printed cards may be sent out:

Mr. and Mrs. Roy Lanza
announce that the marriage of
their daughter
Denise
to
Mr. Jeffrey Stelmach
will not take place

Telegrams would read, "Regret to inform you wedding of Denise Lanza and Jeffrey Stelmach has been canceled." Or, to closer friends, "Regret that Denise's and Jeff's wedding has been called off."

If the message is relayed by telephone, friends and relatives may be asked to help make the calls. It is easier for them to parry questions than it is for the bride or her mother, who are undoubtedly upset about the situation.

When the Wedding Date Is Changed

When it is necessary to change the date of a wedding and the new date is decided upon after invitations have been printed but before they are mailed, it is not necessary for the bride to order new invitations. Instead, she may do one of three things:

She may enclose a printed card, if there is time, saying, "The date of the wedding has been changed from March sixth to April twelfth."

If the guest list is small, she may telephone the information or write a personal note.

If the date is so soon that there is no possibility of having cards printed, she may neatly cross out the old date and insert the new one by pen.

When the wedding is postponed, not canceled, and there is time to have an announcement printed, it would read:

Mr. and Mrs. Clarence Scallion
regret that
owing to a death in the family [optional]
the invitations to
their daughter's wedding
on Saturday, December fifth
must be recalled

[OR]

Owing to the death of
Mrs. Clarence Scallion
the marriage of her daughter
Ann
to
Mr. Kevin Denning
has been postponed

THE PROBLEM OF CHILDREN

One of the greatest and most common problems is that of restricting the number of children attending the reception. In large families with dozens of cousins, nieces, and nephews, the costs may swell astronomically if they are all invited. And yet some relatives feel so strongly that their children should be included that they threaten to refuse the invitation if the children are left out.

There is no easy answer. It would be most unfriendly and in the poorest of taste to write "No children" on the invitations. There are two things you can do to discourage the youngsters' attendance. You may enclose a note to those who are most understanding, explaining that costs and space prevent your asking all children under a certain age. You may also talk to close friends and relatives, explaining the problem and asking them to help by spreading the word.

Having done this, you must make no exceptions. Outside of your own children or your own brothers and sisters, you must refrain from inviting one child under your age limit, or the hurt feelings incurred will far outweigh the money saved.

ACCEPTANCES AND REGRETS

Informal Replies

Wedding announcements require no acknowledgment, although many people thoughtfully send a note or congratulatory card in reply.

Invitations to the marriage ceremony do not necessitate an answer, unless the invitation has arrived in the form of a personal note. In that case it should be answered at once, also by handwritten note.

Replies to informal invitations need not be in the traditional third-person style. If the invitation is in a semiformal style the answer might be written in that form, with the wording varied to fit the phrasing of the invitation. For example:

> *We will be happy*
> *to share your joy*
> *and participate in*
> *the marriage of your daughter*
> *Nadine Fitzgerald*
> *on Friday, the twenty-seventh of June*
> *Anne and Howard Jones*

Other, less formal invitations may be answered by a short personal note, or even by telephone when that seems most appropriate. All invitations, no matter what the style, should be answered *as promptly as possible.*

Traditional Replies

The traditional third-person form of reply seems to baffle and dismay many people, but actually, once learned, it is far simpler than any other. There is no reason to give excuses or regrets, and the only change in wording is the name of the person who issued the invitation and the date.

The formal reply should be written on plain or bordered, monogrammed or unmarked, letter paper or notepaper in appropriate ink. The lines should be evenly and symmetrically spaced on one page.

The wording is:

ACCEPTANCE:

> *Mr. and Mrs. Robert Gilding, Jr.*
> *accept with pleasure*
> *Mr. and Mrs. Smith's*
> *kind invitation for*
> *Tuesday, the first of June*

Mr. and Mrs. Richard Brown
regret that they are unable to accept
Mr. and Mrs. Smith's
kind invitation for
Tuesday, the first of June

The alternative form is equally acceptable:

the kind invitation of
Mr. and Mrs. Roger James Smith
for Tuesday, the first of June

This form is preferable if "Mr. and Mrs. Smith" is followed by "Jr."

There are a myriad of events which may be celebrated as part of a wedding—none is necessary, but each is festive and surely adds to the excitement and later to the memories the bride and groom have of the days leading to their wedding day.

WEDDING SHOWERS

A wedding shower is a gathering of friends in honor of a forthcoming marriage. It is a celebration distinguished by the "showering" of gifts on the guest of honor. A morning coffee, a luncheon, a cocktail party, or a buffet dinner—all are suitable. A shower may be held on any day of the week that is convenient for the guest of honor, the hostess, and the majority of the guests.

Wedding showers should be held from two weeks to two months prior to the wedding. If the shower takes place too close to the wedding date, it may be very inconvenient for the bride, who has so much to do during those last busy days; if too early, there could be a change in the wedding plans.

Invitations

Invitations are almost invariably written on commercial fill-in shower invitations, which are available in an infinite variety of styles. They may also be short personal notes, or in the case of an older woman giving the shower, they may be written on her informal card. In some cases they are even telephoned or issued in person, as might happen when a woman asks her coworkers to a shower.

The name of the guest of honor and the type of gift expected should be included with every invitation. In the case of a kitchen or bathroom shower for an engaged couple, their preference in color should be noted, so that gifts will fit in with their decorating plans. Lingerie-shower invitations for a bride should include her sizes.

Who Gives the Shower?

Almost anyone who wants to "do something" for someone may give a shower. The one rule is that *immediate* family—meaning mothers, mothers-in-law, and sisters—should not, under ordinary circumstances, give showers. This is because it

40
Wedding Events

seems very "commercial" and in poor taste for someone so close to the couple to issue an invitation that, in effect, says, "Come—and give my daughter and her fiancé a present." Somehow it seems much less greedy when the invitation comes from someone less closely involved.

But even then there are *extra*ordinary circumstances. For example, when a bride comes from a foreign country, or even from the other side of our own country, and will be married in her groom's hometown but knows no one there, the groom's sisters might well give her a shower. Etiquette is meant to make life easier—not to impose unnecessary or impractical rules, and when the circumstances warrant it, the "almost" can be dropped and "anyone" may give a shower. It is also perfectly correct for two or three friends to get together and act as cohostesses for a shower, as when two or three attendants give a "joint" shower for the couple.

Guests

Ordinarily, only close friends and relatives are invited to showers, since the invitation automatically means a gift. Also, showers were traditionally sentimental occasions, and only those most intimate with the bride were included. Now, unfortunately, shower lists sometimes seem to include everyone invited to the wedding.

No one should be invited to a wedding shower who is not also invited to the wedding. It is extremely presumptuous to ask people to a shower—meaning they *must* bring a gift—if they are not close enough to the bride or groom or their families to be included on the wedding list. Nor should anyone who does not know the couple being honored be invited, not even the closest friends of the hostess. Again, it would be an imposition to expect them to give a gift to someone they have never met.

There is one exception to the above. When a wedding is very small—restricted to family only, and perhaps with no reception—the couple may be given a shower to which friends are invited who would have been included at a larger wedding. The shower, in this case, almost takes the place of the reception, and the shower gifts are given instead of (rather than in addition to) wedding gifts.

Except in the case of surprise showers, the guest of honor is consulted about the guest list. This is very important in cases where there may be several showers, because only the bride or the couple being honored can divide up the list of friends and relatives so that no one is invited to more than one or two. The hostess, however, decides on the *number* of guests, since she will be paying the bills. Attendants, who are generally included on several lists for wedding showers, should be told by the guest of honor not to bring gifts to each party, or they may keep expenses down by giving "joint" presents.

Otherwise there are no rules about who should or should not be invited. Some showers may be restricted to family members only, some to young people only, and others may be a mixture of young and old, friends and relatives.

One final word about guest lists. The huge showers mentioned above that include almost everyone invited to the wedding are in the *poorest* taste. The entire idea of an intimate party is lost, and they are no more than a demand for more gifts. As such, they are an unforgivable imposition on those invited.

Opening the Gifts

The present-opening is the high spot of all showers. When everyone—or almost everyone—invited has arrived, the guests are expected to gather round while the guest of honor opens the packages one by one and thank each giver. As mentioned above, cards should be enclosed, because otherwise each giver must say more or less sheepishly as each present is unwrapped, "That's from me."

One of the bridesmaids should sit beside the bride and make a careful list of the gifts and who gave them.

In some localities all the presents are delivered to the hostess several days beforehand. She leaves the packages as they are, but puts each in a uniform outer gift wrapping so that the whole stack of packages will be alike. When all are wrapped, the presents are piled on a table in another room or behind a screen, or perhaps in the living room.

Decorations

No decorations are necessary except a centerpiece for your table and an inventive or attractive way of arranging the gifts. For some showers, the hostess gives a gift that holds the other presents, and decorates it appropriately with bows, flowers, or whatever she wishes. For example: a laundry basket, a big picnic ice chest, or even a piece of luggage.

The future bride, and sometimes the bride's mother and future mother-in-law, are given a corsage by the hostess, although this is not obligatory.

Refreshments

There is no rule about the refreshments other than that they be appropriate to the hour and to the tastes of the guests. Cocktails may be served or not, depending on the inclination of the hostess and the habits of her guests. Wine, too, may be served if the hostess wishes. However, soft drinks or iced tea or coffee should always be offered for those guests who prefer not to drink—especially at noon. At a late-afternoon shower, the menu is typical tea fare—sandwiches, cake or cookies, tea, and coffee. A punch, mixed drinks, and beer are generally offered at evening showers.

Showers are rarely dinner parties, but they may be "dessert" parties, or they may be held later in the evening. If a substantial dessert is served when guests arrive, no additional food need be offered. But if guests arrive after dinner at home, they should be served a light "supper" later in the evening.

Entertainment

No entertainment is necessary, since the opening of the presents is the "featured entertainment" of the occasion. However, in some areas local custom dictates that games be played. The choice of games is entirely up to the hostess, who knows what is popular in her locality.

Prizes for games should not, as some people think, be handed over to the guest of honor. She has already received a gift from all the guests, and it makes the game more fun if everyone has a chance at the prizes.

When You Cannot Attend

When you are invited to a large shower for someone you do not know, or know well, and you refuse the invitation, you do *not* need to send a gift. If, however, the shower is a small and intimate one, and you are a good friend of the bride and/or groom, you are expected to give a gift even though you cannot attend. You should take the gift, with your card on it, to the hostess's house at some time before the shower takes place. The hostess usually explains to the guest of honor the reason for your absence.

Types of Wedding Showers

There are many kinds of showers, but the uninitiated may be confused by some terminology. "Round the Clock" shower guests are given an hour of the day on their invitation and bring a present appropriate for that hour. For example, if the hour is six in the evening, a guest might bring a set of cocktail glasses.

A "Recipe Shower" is a lovely idea because it allows the couple's friends to express their love without a commercial connotation or a large expenditure. With every invitation the guests receive a sheet of paper and are asked to make up a menu including their favorite recipes. These papers are collected as they arrive and are put into a notebook or recipe folder provided by the hostess. At some recipe showers, the guests also bring very small gifts—similar to those for a wishing well (described below)—in addition to the recipes.

A proxy shower is one given for a bride who cannot be there, generally because she lives too far away. This is perfectly correct, but it poses some problems for the hostess who is responsible for sending the gifts on to the bride.

The hostess usually asks the guests to bring their gifts unwrapped so everyone can see them, and she provides a variety of wrapping paper and ribbons for the guests to wrap their gifts in after they have displayed them. She may offer a prize for the prettiest package. She then packs the gifts into large cartons and mails them to the future bride.

At most proxy showers, a telephone call is put through to the bride or the couple so that they can talk to their friends or a card or note is made up with short messages from each guest present.

An invitation to a shower with a wishing well notes "wishing well" in the corner or at the bottom. This means that, in addition to bringing a regular gift, each guest brings a tiny present, such as a wooden spoon, a bottle of detergent, a miniature sewing kit, etc., which she puts into a cardboard replica of a wishing well. The wishing well gifts are wrapped and tied in ribbons, but they have no cards and are therefore anonymous. At some wishing well showers, the hostess asks the guests to write a poem which they wrap around their gift and which is read by the bride when she pulls the gifts from the wishing well.

Returning Shower Presents

Insofar as possible, bridal-shower presents should be returned if the marriage is called off. They are given to the bride or the couple with the intent that they be used in their new home, and the reason for giving them is gone. Naturally, monogrammed articles, or anything that has been used, cannot be given back, but every effort should be made to return the gifts that are unused.

The easiest way is to mail them, with a note enclosed, saying, "I appreciated your thoughtful gift so much, but since John and I (or Joanne and I) have broken our engagement, I will not be needing it and am returning it with thanks."

If the friends insist that you keep their gifts you may do so. If you become engaged again at a future date, ask the friends who gave you gifts the first time not to do so again, since the original present may still be unused.

THE BRIDESMAIDS' LUNCHEON

In many American communities the bridesmaids give the bride a farewell luncheon (or it may be a tea) in addition to the regular showers.

There is no special difference between a bridesmaids' luncheon and any other lunch party except that the table is more elaborately decorated, often in white or the bride's chosen colors for the wedding. The bride may give her bridesmaids their presents at this time, and if they are giving her a single present from all of them, this would be the occasion for the presentation.

If the bride and her attendants are working there may not be a convenient time to have a luncheon. Instead, her bridesmaids may arrange for a cocktail party after work, or for a dinner in a restaurant.

THE BACHELOR DINNER

Bachelor dinners are not held so often as they used to be, especially if the ushers are scattered far and wide or if they, as well as the groom, are working until the day before the wedding. If there is a dinner it is generally held in the private dining room of a restaurant or in a club. Traditionally the groom and the ushers had a good deal to drink, and ended the party by breaking their glasses.

The breaking habit originated with drinking to the bride's health and breaking the stem of the wineglass so that it "might never serve a less honorable purpose." This highly impractical custom is never, so far as I know, practiced today. The only remaining tradition is that toward the end of the dinner the bridegroom rises, holds his glass aloft, and says, "To my bride!" The men rise, drink the toast standing, and that ends the party.

Aside from toasting the bride and possibly some more-than-usual reminiscing, the bridegroom's farewell dinner is exactly like any other stag dinner.

Bachelor dinners used to be given by the groom's father, but that is rarely so today, unless he also happens to be the best man. Instead, the ushers generally get together to organize the party, or it may be hosted by the groom's fraternity brothers or co-workers.

PARTIES FOR OUT-OF-TOWN GUESTS

In order to take care of out-of-town family and guests who may arrive two or three days before the wedding, and also to relieve the bride's parents of extra meals and housework, friends of the family frequently give luncheons and dinners for the early arrivals as well as members of the wedding party who live nearby. Invitations should be sent a week or so after the wedding invitations go out, even though replies are not yet in. Receiving the invitation to the party may jog the memories of those who have forgotten to answer the wedding invitation. These parties are likely to be much less formal than the actual wedding festivities and may be given at home, in a club, or in a restaurant. In warm weather they may be in the form of an outdoor barbecue or swimming party; in the winter a sleigh ride or skating party could be organized for the young people, and a cozier fireside buffet for their elders. Whatever the party, the attendants, the families of the couple, their own close friends and friends of their parents may be included. To make it clear that it is not a shower, it is permissible to write "This is not a shower!" or "No gifts" on the invitations.

LUNCHEON BEFORE THE WEDDING

When the wedding is held in the afternoon a small luncheon for the bridal party may be held on the day of the wedding, again to relieve the bride's mother of extra responsibility. It is usually given by a relative or a friend of the bride's family and may be as simple or elaborate as the host and hostess wish. The bride and groom may not even attend. There is an old superstition that the bridegroom should not see his bride before the ceremony on the day of the wedding—but this is an outmoded idea, and they usually come for a short time, probably not together, but with their own families.

THE REHEARSAL

The only people who attend the rehearsal are the bride and groom, their attendants, and the bride's parents. Since the groom's parents have no active part in the ceremony, there is no reason that they should be present. If they *do* attend, having been urged to do so by the bride, they should be observers only and not complicate decisions by expressing their opinions—unless asked.

Although most of us are familiar with the traditional marriage service, we do not realize the number of details that go into its planning if all is to go smoothly on the day of the wedding. Therefore it is essential that the bride, the groom, and all the attendants listen carefully and give the clergyman their full attention. When the service is *not* traditional and has been composed by the couple themselves, even more care must be taken in the rehearsing, since it is unfamiliar to those who will participate.

Dress and Manner

People taking part in the rehearsal or attending as observers should remember that they are in a house of worship and dress accordingly. The women should wear dresses rather than slacks or shorts, and the men should wear jackets and ties except on a hot day, when a neat sports shirt would be acceptable. One clergyman I know quite justifiably sent two bridesmaids home to change from shorts to skirts to preserve the dignity of his church and the ceremony.

In manner as well as dress, the bridal party should recognize the importance of the occasion and attend the rehearsal seriously, and make every effort to make the ceremony flawless. This means that they arrive on time, listen to instructions carefully, and avoid horseplay of any kind.

Years ago it was supposed to be bad luck for the bride to take part in the rehearsal, and her role was played by a stand-in. Fortunately, we are no longer so superstitious, and today the "rehearsal" bride is the "real" bride. Although the clergyman tells the couple the order in which the words of the service come and what their responses will be, the actual service is not read, and they do not repeat the responses or vows.

The organist is present at the rehearsal so that the pace and spacing can be practiced. The order of the procession is established, and the attendants walk up the aisle two or three times until all goes smoothly.

The bride and groom decide how they would like the attendants to stand at the chancel. However, they should ask for the minister's advice about this, since he will know from past experience what looks best in his church.

The manner of pairing off and leaving the chancel is arranged, but it is not necessary to practice the recessional, since the bride and groom lead off at their own pace (not running so fast that the congregation can hardly get a glimpse of them) and the others follow at a natural walk.

THE REHEARSAL DINNER

The wedding rehearsal is generally held in the late afternoon of the day before the wedding. It is almost always followed by a dinner party, which has come to be known as the "rehearsal dinner." Because of complications in the clergyman's schedule or the inability of some of the attendants to arrive by that afternoon, the rehearsal must sometimes be held later—either after the dinner or the following morning. But the party is held in spite of that, and is still the "rehearsal dinner."

It has now become an accepted custom all over the country, although it is not obligatory, that the parents of the groom give this party. This is an extremely nice gesture—a slight repayment to the family of the bride for all the courtesies extended throughout the wedding activities to the family of the groom. If they come from another city they may ask the mother of the bride to reserve a room in a club or restaurant for the dinner and consult with her on the number of her family who should be included so that they can make the reservations in advance. They contact the manager by telephone or by letter to make the preliminary plans. Then, when they arrive for the wedding, they go at once to see the facilities and make the final arrangements. If the groom's family does not, or cannot, give the rehearsal dinner, it is arranged by some member of the bride's family or by a close friend.

The Invitations

Invitations are generally written on informals or fill-in cards, or they may be simply handwritten notes. They may be telephoned, but since there are often out-of-town guests, the written invitation serves as a reminder of the time, address, etc.

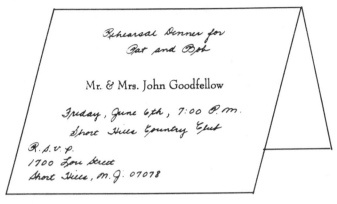

Rehearsal Dinner for
Pat and Bob

Mr. & Mrs. John Goodfellow

Friday, June 6th, 7:00 P.M.
Short Hills Country Club
R.S.V.P.
1700 Low Street
Short Hills, N.J. 07078

OR:

Dear Joan [or: Mrs. Franklin],

Ken and I are giving a rehearsal dinner for Pat and Bob on Friday, June 6, at 7:00 P.M. It will be held at the Short Hills Country Club, and we hope you and Bill [Mr. Franklin] will be with us. We will look forward to hearing that you can come.

Affectionately   [Sincerely],
Doris [Hansen]

1700 Low Street
Short Hills, New Jersey 07078

The Guests

All the members of the bridal party (with the exception of very young flower girls, pages, or ring bearers), the immediate families of the bride and groom, and out-of-town relatives who have arrived for the wedding are invited. If facilities and finances permit, a few very close friends are often included, especially those who come from a distance. If the clergyman is a personal friend, or comes from out of town, he and his wife should also be invited.

Husbands, wives, fiancés, and live-in companions of the attendants go to the rehearsal dinner, but "dates" are not included.

The Seating

For a large dinner a U-shaped table makes an ideal arrangement. The bride and groom, the bride seated *on his right,* sit at the outside of the base of the U with their attendants beside them. The best man sits beside the bride, the maid of honor

beside the groom. If there are many in the bridal party, some are seated opposite the bridal couple. The bridegroom's parents—or whoever are host and hostess—sit at either end of the U. The mother of the bride is seated on the right of the groom's father, and the bride's father sits on the groom's mother's right. Other members of the party are seated along the arms of the U in whatever way seems to make for the most congenial dinner partners. Grandparents are seated near the parents, and younger people may be grouped together.

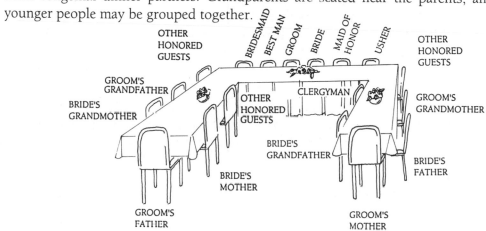

The rehearsal dinner is generally given by the groom's family and is as elaborate or as simple as they wish. This diagram suggests an arrangement for a good size party. For a larger party, simply extend the arms of the U to accommodate more guests. The overriding consideration is to arrange the seating so that dinner partners will be most congenial to everyone.

At a smaller dinner a rectangular table is best. The bride and groom sit together at the center of the one long side, their attendants beside them, the host and hostess at either end, and other guests between.

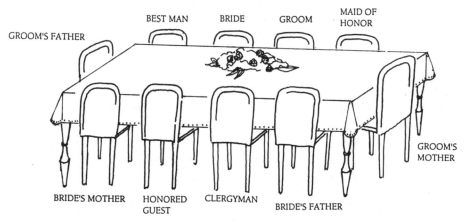

When a rectangular table is used for a rehearsal dinner, the bride and groom are seated on one long side and face their bridal party with family members all around.

During the Dinner

The rehearsal dinner makes a perfect occasion for the presentation of the couple's gifts to the bridesmaids and ushers. In return, the attendants' gifts are often presented at the same time by the maid of honor and the best man, accompanied by a short speech or toast.

The host—generally the groom's father—makes the first toast, welcoming the guests and making some remarks about his happiness at the forthcoming marriage. This is followed by a return toast by the bride's father, and by numerous toasts proposed by the ushers, and anyone else who wishes to get to his or her feet.

The attendants' toasts, while sentimental to some extent, may be filled with anecdotes and jokes about past experiences of the bride and groom. Sometimes the bridesmaids make up a poem to be read, and limericks fit the bill well. One young man, after an exposé of some of the groom's collegiate shenanigans, ended his toast: "So here's to my ex-roommate and his new roommate."

Entertainment and Decorations

Music and dancing are not at all essential, and many rehearsal dinners offer no more than the meal and a pleasant gathering. Others are far more elaborate. A strolling violinist or accordionist may play romantic background music, or there may be a full orchestra and after-dinner dancing.

The bride and groom generally leave at a reasonable hour to try to get a good night's sleep, but the guests may stay on to enjoy the festivities until the small hours if the host suggests it. Ushers and bridesmaids should remember that they have a responsibility to fulfill the next day, and refrain from either overindulging in champagne or staying so late that they look exhausted.

Decorations are simple. No matter how large the party may be, bowls of flowers on the tables make the only ornamentation.

The Menu

Rehearsal dinners usually start with a short "cocktail hour," giving the families a chance to chat, and strangers to meet. Cocktails may be served, but punch and soft drinks are offered to those who do not drink. Hors d'oeuvres are as simple or elaborate as the hosts wish.

When the wedding is large and formal, the style of the rehearsal dinner is too, and the meal compares to that of any formal dinner. However, such an elaborate and expensive menu is in no way necessary. If the wedding is informal and nontraditional, the menu should be also. The setting would be different too, of course, and these choices would be more appropriate when the setting was an outdoor barbecue or a buffet in the family game room.

Wine is usually served with dinner, with a round of champagne for the toasts.
Or champagne may be served through the entire meal. To accompany the less formal menus, beer, iced tea, sangria, or whatever appeals to the couple should be the choice.

ENTERTAINING AFTER THE RECEPTION

In some areas it is an accepted practice that the bride's family invite out-of-town guests home for dinner or a late snack after the reception. But unless it is customary in your community, it is not necessary or expected. The bride's parents have had as much or more than they can do already, and are not expected to do further entertaining—unless they wish to.

Occasionally a few close friends are asked to dine with them, possibly because they have not had time to visit during the prewedding hours, or possibly because the bride's family simply does not yet wish to be alone to face the inevitable letdown of their daughter's departure.

In cases where some of the out-of-town friends and relatives cannot leave before the next day, a relative of the bride's family may help out by inviting them to an informal dinner when the wedding festivities are over early.

The Groom's Parents' Celebration

When the bride and groom are married in her hometown, and the friends of the groom and his family, who live far away, cannot attend, his mother and father, in order to introduce their new daughter-in-law to their friends, give a "reception" for them the first time they come to visit after their honeymoon. Or they may do this if the couple come to visit a short time before the wedding takes place.

The invitations are generally "fill-in" cards or informals, with "In honor of Betty and Hank" or "to meet Betty King" written in at the top. Since they do not come from the bride's family they should not be inserted with the wedding invitations or announcements. They should be mailed separately, ten days or two weeks before the date of the party.

As there was a wedding reception at the time of the marriage, this second reception does not attempt to compete with the first. There is no wedding cake, and the bride and groom and their attendants do not wear their wedding clothes. However, if the bride wishes the guests to see her wedding gown, she may receive in it and then change after everyone has arrived.

The party can be as elaborate as the groom's parents wish, but it is usually a tea or a cocktail buffet. The host and hostess stand at the door with the newlyweds and introduce the bride to everyone who has not met her. Her parents should be invited, but they should not be made to feel that they *must* attend, especially at a great distance.

The tea or buffet table is covered with a white or pastel cloth, and the flowers may be similar to those at the wedding. Beverages consist of mixed drinks, punch, and soft drinks. Beer may be served, but champagne is rarely offered, unless one round is served for toasting the couple. The toast is offered by the groom's father, and welcomes the bride to his family. There may be either an orchestra for dancing or a strolling musician, or neither. If wedding pictures have been completed, they should be on display.

nywhere from one to two hours before the ceremony is to begin, the bridesmaids and the bride begin to dress. The bridesmaids all dress in one place—usually at the bride's home or in a dressing room at the ceremony site. If they dress at the ceremony site, an aunt or good friend of the bride's mother should be there to see that everyone's outfit is complete and in order.

The bride is usually assisted by her maid of honor and her mother. Her bouquet, those of her attendants, and the corsages for her mother and the grandmothers are delivered to the house and are distributed there. The corsage for the groom's mother is sent to her where she is staying or is delivered to the church.

41
The Ceremony and Reception

DRIVING TO THE CEREMONY

When it is time to go to the church, the cars are waiting. The bride's mother drives away in the first, usually alone. She may, if she chooses, take her younger children or one or two bridesmaids with her; but she must reserve room for her husband, who will return from the church with her. The maid of honor, bridesmaids, and flower girls follow in as many cars as may be necessary.

The bride's car leaves last, timed to arrive at the church only a minute or two before the ceremony is to start. She drives to the church accompanied only by her father. This same car stands in front of the church until she and her husband—in the place of her father—drive to the reception. If limousines are not rented to transport the bridal party, close family friends are asked to act as "chauffeurs."

MEANWHILE, AT THE CHURCH

Forty-five minutes to an hour before the time of the ceremony, the ushers arrive at the church, having dressed at their homes or wherever they are staying. The head usher is responsible for seeing that they all get there on time. Their boutonnieres, sent by the groom, should be waiting in the vestibule unless the best man has distributed them beforehand. Each man puts one in his buttonhole and puts on his gloves.

Those of the ushers who are the most likely to recognize

the closest friends and members of each family should be assigned to the center aisle, if there are so many invited that the side sections will be used.

According to tradition the parents of the bride and the groom were not to be seen until they walked down the aisle to their pews. However, at several weddings my husband and I have attended in recent years, the groom's parents were outside the church, greeting and chatting with arriving guests. This was especially nice for the friends who had come from the groom's parents' town and knew very few of the bride's guests. We were so impressed with the friendliness of the act that we did it ourselves at our son's wedding and were amazed at the pleasure our friends expressed at finding us outside the door. Having expected to arrive at a strange church (not even sure it was the *right* church) amid a sea of strangers, they really appreciated our welcome, and I highly recommend the idea to other parents of the groom.

Reserved Pews

The parents of the bride always sit in the first pew on the left, facing the chancel; the groom's parents in the first pew on the right. If the church has two aisles, her parents sit on the left of the right aisle, and his on the right of the left aisle, so that they are both in the center section of the church. (*See page 711*).

Behind these front pews several pews on either side of the center aisle are reserved for the immediate families of the couple. The people to sit there may have been given or sent pew cards to show their usher, who otherwise might not recognize them or know where to seat them. Sometimes pew cards are not sent, but the ushers are given a list of guests to be seated in the first few pews, and those people should mention to the usher that they are to sit in a reserved pew. People seated in this way are said to be "in front of the ribbon." Formerly a ribbon was actually put across the aisle behind them and raised at one end by the usher to allow guests to pass into the reserved section. Now, however, these special pews are designated by a bouquet or white bow on the end, and the aisle is not closed. Just before the procession starts, a ribbon is laid over the ends of the pews parallel to the aisle, starting with the *back* pew and ending at the last reserved pew. This task is assigned to two of the ushers, who are also responsible for removing it after the ceremony. The families are escorted out first and leave for the reception quickly, while the other guests must wait until the ribbon is removed.

The reserved pews should be "evened up" when one family needs a goodly number and the other very few. Let us say the bride needs seven pews and the bridegroom three (as often occurs when he is from a distant part of the country and few of his family or friends can be present). Then the ushers should be told that behind the first three pews those with pew cards are to be seated evenly on both sides.

Seating Widowed Parents

Widowed parents of either the bride or the groom should not necessarily be expected to sit in lonely splendor at their child's wedding. If there is no one that they would care to have by their side, then that is their choice. But if they would like to have with them a very old friend, or someone that they are dating regularly, or perhaps a fiancé(e) or a live-in companion, that person should be invited and, if the parent wishes, sit with him or her at the church—unless of course the bride or groom would resent his or her presence. The guest would not participate in any way, such as standing in the receiving line, unless he or she were about to marry the widowed parent and had already become very close to the bride or groom. The parent could request, however, that this friend be seated at the parents' table. Unless the bride or groom actively dislikes their parent's companion (and their wishes should be respected if they ask that he or she not attend), every effort should be made to treat the companion as an honored guest.

Seating Divorced Parents

When They Are Friendly

Because it is obviously better for the children when friendliness rather than bitterness exists between divorced parents, most couples who separate today try to maintain at least a civil relationship. If this has been possible, not only the couple's parents but also their stepparents (if one parent—or both—has remarried) are present at the church and reception.

The bride's mother and stepfather sit in the front pew on the left side of the aisle. If her mother has a "second" family, those stepbrothers or stepsisters are seated in the second pew. The bride's grandparents, aunts, and uncles on her mother's side are seated behind them. The bride's father (after escorting her up the aisle) sits with his wife and their family in the next pew. The groom's parents and stepparents follow the same order on the right side of the aisle.

When They Are Not Friendly

In the entire subject of etiquette, there is perhaps no situation that brings more unhappiness than the wedding of a daughter whose parents are divorced and bitterly estranged. This is especially true for the bride who loves her father and his family as much as her mother and her family, because in most cases, unless she has always lived with her father, the wedding is given by her mother.

It is true that she drives with her father to the church, walks with him up the aisle, and has him share in the marriage ceremony. After giving his daughter away, he sits in the pew behind the immediate family of her mother. His second wife sits with him if the bride wishes, but if there is great bitterness involved, the stepmother sits farther back in the church with a relative or friend. If the relationships are truly impossible, the father may see no more of his daughter on her wedding day, because he will avoid unpleasantness by not going to the reception at all. But if he is sent an invitation, both he and his ex-wife should make a great effort to "bury the hatchet" for that day, to make it as happy as possible for their daughter.

When the Wedding Is Given by the Bride's Father

When the wedding is given by the bride's father and stepmother while her own mother is also living, it is usually because the daughter has made her home with her father instead of her mother.

If the bride has remained close to her own mother, her mother sits in the front pew. If she has remarried and if she and her ex-husband are friendly, her new husband joins her there, but if there is bitterness, he sits farther back. The father gives the bride away and then takes his place in the second pew with his present wife and their family. If, however, the bride's stepmother has brought her up, and she has had little or no contact with her mother, her stepmother and her father would sit in the first pew.

The Guests Arrive at the Church

The ushers show all guests to their places. An usher offers his *right* arm to each woman as she arrives, whether he knows her personally or not. If the vestibule is very crowded and several women arrive together, he may give his arm to the oldest and ask the others to follow. More often, he asks them to wait until he can come back or another usher is available.

The usher does not offer his arm to a man unless he is quite old and it is obvious that he needs assistance. If the older man is accompanied by a younger, the latter follows so that they can be seated together.

There is an increasing feeling among wedding guests that it is incompatible with the concept of marriage for a woman to be escorted down the aisle by an usher while her husband trails along behind—like the proverbial "fifth wheel." The alternative is to have the usher lead the husband *and* wife, walking together, to their pew, and "usher" them both into it. Personally I am in favor of this. I think it is much more in keeping with the spirit of the occasion to have husbands and wives walk together.

Those who want their weddings to be strictly traditional must have the ushers escort the women in the time-honored way. But if you are more interested in the meaningfulness than the tradition, I see no reason not to instruct your ushers to escort or lead both husband and wife, as they would at a Sunday service. Instead of offering an arm to the woman as a couple arrives, the usher would simply look at both of them and say, "Please follow me."

The ushers ask those guests whom they do not recognize, or who may be friends of both bride and groom, whether they wish to sit on the bride's side—the left—or the groom's side—the right. If they fail to ask, the guest may offer the information: "I am a friend of Mary's—may I sit on her side?"

Just as the reserved pews are divided more or less evenly, so should the rest of the church be. Nothing looks sadder than the bride's side filled to the back, and a mere handful of people scattered along the aisle on the groom's side. As soon as the bride's side is reasonably full, ushers should say to guests, "Would you mind sitting on Jim's side? There are much better seats still free there."

If the usher thinks a guest belongs in front of the ribbons even though she fails to show him a pew card, he asks, "Have you a pew card?" If she has, he shows her to her place. If she has none, he asks which side she prefers and gives her the best seat vacant in the unreserved part of the church.

Ushers are not supposed to escort guests in total silence, even when they are strangers. A few casual remarks are made—in a low voice, but not whispered or solemn. The deportment of the ushers should be natural, but dignified and quiet, for they are in church. They should not trot up and down the aisles in a bustling manner; but at the same time they must be swift and efficient, in order to seat everyone as expeditiously as possible.

The guests without pew cards should arrive early in order to find good places. It is an unwritten law that those who make the effort to get there in time to have a place on the aisle, from where the "view" is decidedly better, need not move farther into the pew to make space for later arrivals. The latecomers slide past those already there and take the next best place available.

A Church With Two Aisles

In a church with two main aisles the guests are seated according to aisles and not according to the church as a whole. All the seats on the right aisle belong to the bride's family and guests. The left aisle belongs to the bridegroom.

The bride's mother is seated in the front pew at the left of the bride's aisle— exactly as she would be in a center-aisle church. On the other side of the church the bridegroom's mother occupies the front pew on the right of the groom's aisle.

For the processional the bride's (right) aisle is chosen because people naturally turn to the right to watch the procession enter rather than to the left. After the ceremony the bride and groom come down the groom's (left) aisle. The aisles are necessarily chosen in this way so as to place the immediate families in center pews. If the bride's mother were to choose the left aisle, this would seat her in a side pew instead of a center one.

However, if the church is very large and the wedding small, the right aisle alone may be used. Then the bride's family sits on the left of this aisle and the groom's family on the right, and the marriage takes place at the head of this aisle.

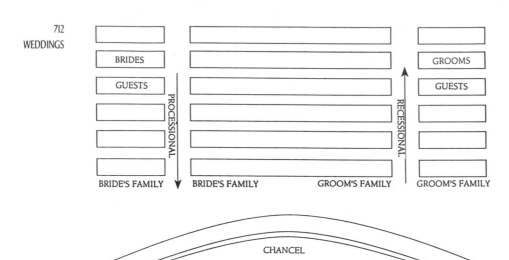

Arrangements in a church with two main aisles

The Last Few Minutes

The Bridegroom Waits

In a Christian ceremony the bridegroom and his best man arrive at the church and enter the side door about fifteen minutes before the wedding hour. They sit in the vestry or in the clergyman's study until the sexton or an usher comes to say that the bride has arrived. They then wait for and follow the clergyman to their places.

At many Jewish weddings the bride (and sometimes the groom also) receives the guests in a room in the synagogue before the ceremony takes place.

The Last Five Minutes

The groom's mother and father enter the church five or ten minutes before the ceremony is to start. As the bride's mother drives up, an usher hurries to tell the groom of her arrival, as the bride and her father should be close behind. Grandparents and any brothers or sisters of the bride or groom who are not to take part in the wedding are now taken by ushers to their places in the front pews. No one is seated after this except the parents of the bridal couple.

The groom's mother goes up the aisle on the arm of the head usher and takes her place in the first pew on the right; the groom's father follows alone and takes his place on the aisle. Or as described above, the husband and wife may walk in together, following the head usher. The same usher or a brother or cousin of the bride escorts the bride's mother to the first pew on the left. When the bride has a stepfather who is not giving her away, he follows her mother and the usher in the same manner as the groom's father.

If the bride's mother is uncomfortable sitting alone in the front pew until her
husband joins her after giving their daughter away, she may ask her parents or another close relative to sit with her. They would be escorted in immediately before the mother of the groom.

When the bride or the groom has no parents, the closest relatives—grandparents, sisters or brothers, or an aunt and uncle—would be given the first pew. A bride who is an orphan chooses a guardian or perhaps the person who is giving the wedding to sit there. Whoever is chosen is ushered in last, since that person represents the bride's parents.

If a carpet is to be laid, it is already arranged in folds so that two ushers may now pull it quickly down the aisle. At the last moment the white ribbon is draped over the ends of the pews from the back of the church to the nearest reserved pew on each side of the center aisle. Having done this, the ushers return to the vestibule and take their places in the procession. The beginning of the wedding music should sound just as they return to the foot of the aisle.

To repeat: No person should be seated after the entrance of the mother of the bride. Nor must anyone be admitted to the side aisles while the mother of the bride is being ushered down the center one. Her entrance should not be detracted from by late arrivals scuttling into their seats behind her. Guests who arrive late must stand in the rear or slip unescorted into a back pew.

The Bride Arrives

At a perfectly planned wedding, the bride arrives exactly one minute after the hour in order to give the last arrival time to find a place. This is too much to ask in today's heavy traffic, however, and I can only point out that it is better for the bride to arrive five minutes early than five minutes late. If she has a few minutes to spare, she waits in the vestibule or a convenient room. At the appointed hour the procession forms in the vestibule, and a signal is given to the groom and the clergyman that everything is ready.

THE CEREMONY BEGINS

The sound of the music chosen for the processional is the cue for the clergyman to enter the church, followed by the bridegroom and the best man. The clergyman goes up the steps to the chancel and turns to face the congregation. The groom stops at the foot of the chancel steps and takes his place at the right side of the aisle, as indicated in the diagram on page 715. His best man stands on his left, slightly behind him. They turn toward the procession coming down the aisle.

As the music for the processional starts and the first ushers step forward, the mothers rise and turn to watch the procession as it comes down the aisle. The rest of the congregation follows their lead. Everyone remains standing until the clergyman asks the congregation to be seated—usually after an opening prayer or address.

The Procession

The procession is arranged according to height, the two shortest ushers leading. Junior ushers walk behind the adults. Junior bridesmaids come next, if there are any. If not, the bridesmaids come directly after the ushers, two and two, also according to height, with the shortest in the lead. If there are only two or three, they walk singly. After the bridesmaids, the maid or matron of honor walks alone; flower girls follow, then the ring bearer, and last of all, the bride on the right arm of her

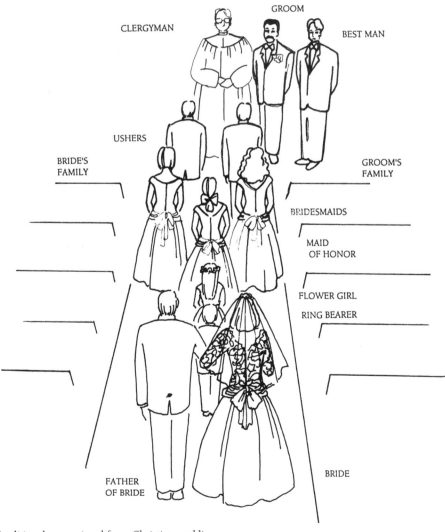

Traditional processional for a Christian wedding

father. If there are both maid and matron of honor, the maid of honor immediately precedes the bride.

The space between each couple or individuals should be even—approximately four paces apart. The attendants should walk slowly and steadily, and the "hesitation step," which used to be obligatory, is rarely seen as it tends to make the pace uneven or jerky. Posture is most important too. At the rehearsal the attendants should be reminded to stand straight and tall, as nothing looks worse than a bridesmaid or usher slouching down the aisle.

The bride (unless she has page boys who carry her train) always brings up the rear, walking on her father's *right*. This position puts her on the proper side to join her groom, and it is the honorary position, as well as being traditional and correct.

When the ushers reach the foot of the chancel they divide. In a small church the first two go up the chancel steps and stand at the top, one on the right, the other on the left. The second two go a step or two below the first. If there are more, they stand below. Chalk marks made on the chancel floor can be a great help to little children in remembering their positions.

In a big church the ushers go up farther, standing in front of the choir stalls with the line sloping outward so that the congregation may see them better. The bridesmaids also divide, half on either side, and stand in front of the ushers. The maid of honor's place is on the left at the foot of the steps, opposite the best man. Flower girls stand beside or behind the maid of honor, and the ring bearer stands next to the best man. In some cases the bridesmaids line up on the left side and ushers on the right, rather than dividing. The bride and groom make the final decision on what they think looks best, but they should take advantage of the

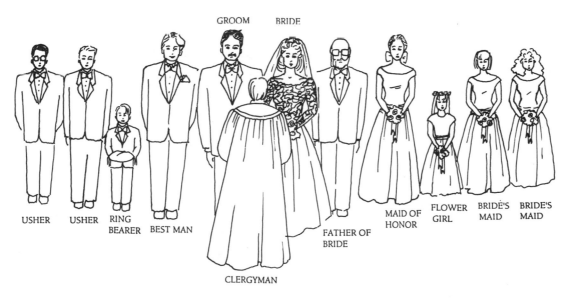

GROOM   BRIDE

USHER   USHER   RING BEARER   BEST MAN   FATHER OF BRIDE   MAID OF HONOR   FLOWER GIRL   BRIDE'S MAID   BRIDE'S MAID

CLERGYMAN

Christian ceremony, at the altar

clergyman's experience and recommendations, since he has seen many more weddings than they.

As the bride approaches, the groom steps forward to meet her. She lets go of her father's arm, transfers her flowers to her left arm, and gives her right hand to the groom, who rests it on his left arm. If this is uncomfortable for either, they may stand hand in hand or side by side. They are then facing the altar.

In a Protestant ceremony her father remains by his daughter, on her left and a step or two behind her. The clergyman stands a step or two above them and reads the betrothal. When he says, "Who giveth this woman to be married?" the father steps forward. The bride turns slightly toward him and gives him her right hand, which he puts into the hand of the clergyman and says distinctly, "I do," or "Her mother and I do." Frequently the bride gives her father a brief kiss at this point to indicate her gratitude and affection. He then takes his place next to his wife at the end of the first pew on the left. The clergyman, holding the bride's hand in his right one, takes the bridegroom's hand in his left one and very deliberately places the bride's hand in the bridegroom's.

When the bride has neither father nor any very near male relative she may choose to walk up the aisle alone. At the point in the ceremony where the clergyman asks, "Who giveth this woman to be married?" her mother remains where she is standing in her place at the end of the first pew on the left and says very distinctly, "I do." There is no rule against her going forward to take the place of the bride's father. In fact some brides who've been brought up entirely by their mothers ask if their mothers may escort them up the aisle. I see no reason that they should not if that is what makes the bride happy.

In a Roman Catholic ceremony the father of the bride joins her mother in the front pew as soon as the bride is joined by the groom. He does not give his daughter away.

Some clergymen signal the guests to be seated as soon as the members of the bridal party are in their places. Others wait until this point in the ceremony.

The clergyman turns and walks toward the altar, before which the rest of the marriage is performed. The bride and groom follow, the fingers of her right hand on his left arm.

The maid or matron of honor moves forward too, until she stands behind the bride, slightly to her left. The best man takes the corresponding position behind the groom and to his right. The flower girl and ring bearer follow, also, still in the same relative positions. The bride hands her bouquet to the maid of honor, and the bride and groom plight their troth.

When it is time for the ring, the best man produces it from his pocket, or from the ring bearer's cushion, the minister blesses it, and the groom slips it on his bride's finger. Since the wedding ring must not be put outside the engagement ring, the bride wears the engagement ring on her right hand during the ceremony. Afterward she puts it back on her left hand, outside her wedding ring.

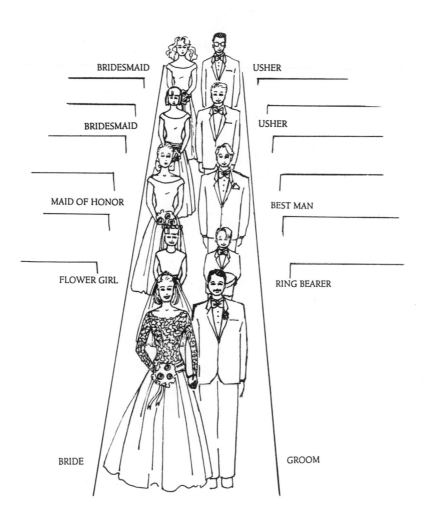

BRIDESMAID USHER

BRIDESMAID USHER

MAID OF HONOR BEST MAN

FLOWER GIRL RING BEARER

BRIDE GROOM

Traditional recessional for a Christian wedding

When it is a double-ring ceremony the maid of honor gives the groom's ring to the bride after she has received her ring from the groom. The ring is blessed, and the bride places it on the groom's finger, saying, as he did, "With this ring I thee wed." The ceremony proceeds with a blessing and a prayer, and the clergyman pronounces the couple "husband and wife."

After the Ceremony

At the conclusion of the ceremony the minister congratulates the newly married couple. The organ begins the recessional. The bride takes her bouquet from her maid of honor, who then lifts the face veil, if one is worn. If they have decided to do so, the couple kiss. With her bouquet in her right hand, the bride and groom turn, the bride puts her left hand through her husband's right arm, and they descend the steps, followed by the flower girl and ring bearer and the maid of honor walking with the best man. Then the bridesmaids and ushers pair off and follow two by two. If it is winter, one of the ushers or the best man will have put the groom's coat in the vestibule before the ceremony so that he need not go back to the vestry or waiting room for it, and someone has the bride's coat ready for her at the door.

The bridesmaids and ushers may walk out in pairs although they entered separately. Doing so adds to the symbolism of the occasion following the pattern of the bride and groom who arrived separately and leave together after the marriage has taken place.

The photographer, who remains at the back of the church during the ceremony, can now snap away the happy couple as they come back down the aisle. Photographs should not be taken during the ceremony, as the clicking and flashing is distracting and detracts from the dignity of the proceedings. Videotaping when done quietly and without harsh strobe lights may continue during the ceremony, if it is allowed by the minister.

The automobiles are waiting at the entrance in the reverse order from that in which they arrived. The best man helps the newlyweds into the bride's car, and it leaves first; next come those of the bridesmaids; next, that of the bride's mother and father; next, that of the groom's mother and father. If limousines have not been hired, the best man acts as chauffeur for the bride and groom.

If one or both sets of the parents are divorced, they should not be required to ride with their ex-spouses unless they wish to. Rather than incurring the additional expense of hiring individual limousines for each parent and his or her new spouse, the two mothers and their husbands might ride in one car, the two fathers and their wives in the other. If none of the parents has remarried, the solution might be that of Prince Charles and Princess Diana—her mother and his father in one car; his mother and her father in the other.

To return to the church for a moment: As soon as the recessional is over, two ushers return to escort the bride's mother first, then the groom's mother to the door. If the bride's and groom's mothers prefer to walk with their husbands, they may do so, following the usher who has come to escort them. At most weddings only the two mothers of the couple are escorted by the ushers, and the husbands or escorts of the other women walk out with them. Meanwhile other guests wait until the ribbons along the ends of the pews are removed by the two previously designated ushers, and then go out by themselves, starting with the front pews and working back. The best man hurries back to the vestry and if he has not done so before the ceremony, gives the clergyman his fee. If an altar boy has assisted in the ceremony, he offers him a small "tip" of three or four dollars.

As soon as the ushers have escorted the family out and removed the ribbons they, too, hurry to the reception in order to be on hand for the photographs. Their cars or means of transportation should be in a convenient place so that they will not be held up by departing guests.

A Receiving Line at the Church

When there is no reception, or when many of the guests at the church are not invited because it is to be a very small family reception, the bride and groom may greet their friends at the church. Instead of going directly to the cars they form a line in the vestibule, on the steps, or outside the door. The line consists of the bride's mother, the groom's mother, the bride on the groom's right, and the bridesmaids.

This is never done if there will be people at the reception who are not invited to the church. However, it may *take the place of* a line at the reception when all the guests invited to the reception are also at the church.

Since most clergymen do not approve of pictures being taken during the service (and the bride and groom should not encourage the photographer to do so), some couples go back into the church when the pews are empty to reenact parts of the service for the benefit of the photographer. This is perfectly all right as long as they do not insist on pictures of each and every step in the ceremony. It is *most* inconsiderate to keep the guests who have gone on to the reception waiting for a long time, especially if there is no comfortable place for them to sit or stand. Therefore pictures in the church should be restricted to half a dozen or so—one or two of the procession, one of the bride's father giving his daughter away, the exchange of rings, the kiss at the end, etc.

JEWISH WEDDINGS

Whether Orthodox, Conservative, or Reform, marriages may not take place between sundown Friday and sundown on Saturday. Therefore most Jewish weddings take place on Saturday evening or Sunday. There are also holy days, and most of the days between the second day of Passover and the holiday of Shabuoth, during which Jews may not marry. These restrictions and many others, some of which are dictated by individual rabbis or local custom rather than Rabbinic law, should be thoroughly discussed with the rabbi who is going to perform the ceremony.

Jewish weddings are often held in synagogues, but both service and reception may be held in halls, clubs, restaurants, or hotels. Frequently the bride and her family, and sometimes the groom too, receive their guests in a private room before the ceremony.

Jewish brides and their attendants wear the same clothes as those described in Chapter 38. The only exception is that at Orthodox and Conservative weddings, attendants as well as guests wear yarmulkes. These are always available at the back of the synagogue. At a very formal wedding male members of the bridal party wear top hats. They may be taken off after a Conservative wedding ceremony but must be worn during both ceremony and reception at Orthodox weddings.

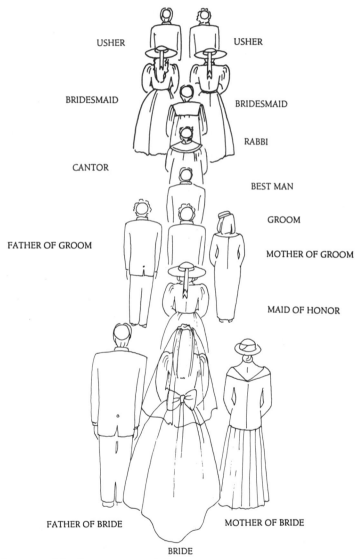

Jewish Processional for Conservative or Orthodox ceremony

At Orthodox and Conservative ceremonies, the ushers lead the procession, followed by the bridesmaids. Next comes the rabbi (accompanied by a cantor, if one is participating in the ceremony), then the best man, and next the groom, walking between his mother and father. The maid of honor follows them, and the bride, between her parents, comes last. Orthodox brides are always veiled. The marriage takes place under a canopy called a *chuppah*. This canopy used to be held over heads of the principals as they walked down the aisle, but today it is fixed in place at the front of the hall; in a synagogue it is in front of the Ark. The canopy is usually a richly ornamented cloth, although it may be made of, or decorated with, flowers.

The bride and groom, the maid of honor, and the best man—and, if there is room, the parents—stand under the *chuppah*. The rabbi faces them, standing by a table covered with a white cloth, on which there are two glasses of wine.

The Orthodox service is mostly read in Hebrew, although certain parts are in English, or the native language of the couple. The rabbi first blesses the wine and gives it to the groom. He takes a sip and hands it to the bride. A document in Aramaic is read, giving the pledge of fidelity and protection on the part of the groom and indicating the bride's contribution to the household. The groom places a plain gold ring on the bride's right index finger, which she removes to the conventional fourth finger, left hand, after the ceremony. He repeats, "Thou art consecrated unto me with this ring, according to the law of Moses and Israel." The rabbi then addresses the congregation about the sanctity of marriage. Finally, after the Seven Blessings are given, the couple drinks from the second glass of wine. At the conclusion of the ceremony the goblet is broken by the groom to symbolize the destruction of the temple in Jerusalem, which serves as a reminder that one must never lose sight of the past, even on happy occasions.

BRIDESMAIDS   FATHER OF BRIDE   MOTHER OF BRIDE   MAID OF HONOR   BRIDE   RABBI   GROOM   BEST MAN   MOTHER OF GROOM   FATHER OF GROOM   USHERS

Jewish ceremony under the chuppah

The Reform service is very much like the Christian service. The processional and recessional are the same, and the bride is escorted by her father. The service is in English, and there is no chuppah. The bride and groom do, however, adhere to the Jewish tradition of drinking wine from the same cup, and to certain other parts of the Jewish service.

The recessional is led by the bride and groom. They are usually followed by the two sets of parents, the maid of honor with the best man, the rabbi (and cantor if there is one), and finally the bridesmaids and ushers.

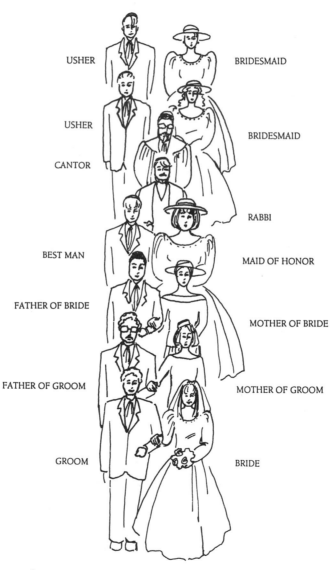

Jewish recessional

The reception after a Jewish wedding is like that following a Christian marriage, except that more importance is given to the "feast." It is usually as lavish as the bride's family can afford. A blessing is always said over the food.

Roman Catholic Ceremonies

Many Catholic weddings are centered around a nuptial mass, and traditionally these took place between eight and twelve in the morning. In many churches, a nuptial mass may now take place in the afternoon.

In marriage ceremonies that do not include participation in a mass, the service is quite similar to the Protestant ceremony. In this case the bridal couple go to their church and take Communion together earlier in the day.

Roman Catholic weddings may be held at any time of the year. The marriages are announced by banns, proclaimed from the pulpit three times, or they may be published in the church calendar prior to the wedding. Therefore, plans must be made at least that far in advance. This is a common practice for some Protestant denominations, as well.

The bride's father escorts her up the aisle but does not give her away. As soon as she has given her hand to the groom, the bride's father joins his wife in the front pew. Other details, such as whether or not the bridal party will stand within the altar rail, are determined by individual churches. The priest will discuss these practices when he talks to the couple and at the rehearsal.

While the Catholic Church prefers that both the best man and maid of honor be Catholics, at least one must be. The other attendants need not be Catholic, but they are instructed in how to genuflect, and other procedures, before the ceremony.

Catholics may serve as ushers and bridesmaids in a Protestant wedding.

When a nuptial mass follows the marriage ceremony, the bridal party is usually seated—in the choir stalls, perhaps, or sometimes the two front pews are reserved for them. The bride and groom are seated on two chairs before the altar. There is generally a kneeling bench. The maid of honor and the best man remain in the sanctuary with the bride and groom. Otherwise, the processional, the arrangements during the ceremony, the recessional, and most other details are like those described for a Protestant wedding.

When a non-Catholic marries a Catholic there are other regulations to be considered. Some are universal, others are imposed at the discretion of the officiating priest. In any case, they will be explained to the couple when they confer with the priest before the wedding and the participants must abide by the church's rules. Very often couples of different faiths have two ceremonies, that of one faith following immediately after the other. Another alternative is to have the clergy of each faith present to perform different parts of the ceremony.

CEREMONIES OF OTHER RELIGIONS

The three most widely practiced faiths in the United States, Protestant, Jewish, and Catholic, are covered in this book, but there may be occasions when the opportunity arises to attend the wedding of friends of other faiths or nationalities. I recently attended a wedding in a Greek Orthodox church where the bride and groom, with the help of their priest, had prepared a lovely program for each wedding guest which explained the order and the meaning of various traditions and practices that would take place during the ceremony. This helped make the ceremony more meaningful for those of us who had not attended a Greek Orthodox wedding before and allowed us to participate more fully.

Another time I attended a beautiful Egyptian garden wedding where the bride and the groom, dressed in lovely ornamental costume, were brought various bowls into which they placed their feet during the wedding ceremony. The service was conducted in both Arabic and English so those non-Arabic-speaking guests would be able to follow along and understand the symbolism of the bowls and the customs.

In both cases, although the actual ceremonies were different, according to their own religious beliefs, the treatment and seating of guests and the following receptions were very similar to those of Protestant, Catholic and Jewish weddings. These pages, therefore, may serve as a guide to brides and grooms of several faiths, enabling them to adjust areas where customs are different, and use as a reference those areas where there are similarities.

A guest invited to a wedding of a faith not covered in detail here should not hesitate to admit to not knowing all that may be required of a guest and asking if there is anything he or she should know in advance of attending the wedding. It is perfectly all right to call the host, or the bride or groom, whomever you are closer to, or to call a church, temple, or synagogue office and ask. Your enjoyment and experience will be all the richer when you feel confident that you have not over-looked something that may be expected of you.

For example, a guest attending a Jewish wedding for the first time may think he must buy a yarmulke in order to follow religious regulations and attend. It is reassuring to know that most synagogues have a box of yarmulkes outside the entrance to the sanctuary, and yarmulkes are provided when the wedding takes place at a catering hall or club, as well, when they are required of male guests. It is expected that, out of respect, all male guests will wear a yarmulke when it is required, but it is not expected that they will go out and buy one so both thoughtful-ness and religious requirements suggest that they be provided.

Non-Catholic guests are not expected to genuflect or to cross themselves during a Catholic ceremony, or to recite a creed or confess to a faith that is not their own. They are expected, however, to rise and be seated with everyone else, out of respect for the religion. This is true of any place of worship you enter as a wedding guest. When unsure, simply follow the lead of other guests.

THE RECEPTION

Photographs

As soon as the bride and groom and all the attendants have arrived at the place where the reception is held, the formal pictures of the bridal party are taken. Although this may cause some inconvenience to guests who arrive from the church very quickly, it is the only possible time. If it is put off until later, the bridesmaids' costumes and hairdos will not be so fresh and neat, and the newlyweds and their parents may be showing the strain of having stood in the receiving line.

The photographer should be told in advance to be as quick as he can, and the attendants should be asked to hurry to their places without delay so that the receiving line may be formed as soon as possible.

Pictures are taken of the bride and groom with the bridesmaids, with their ushers, and with the entire wedding party. They are photographed with each set of parents, and with both. If either bride or groom has stepparents, they are included in the photographs, too. However, a parent who has remarried does not appear with his or her new spouse in the *same* picture with the ex-mate, even though they are all friendly.

The Receiving Line

As soon as the pictures are taken, the bridal party forms the receiving line, in whatever room or location provides the best "flow." The bride's mother stands at the beginning of the line to greet the guests and to introduce them to the groom's mother, who stands next to her. Then come the bride and groom, with the bride on the groom's right. The maid of honor stands next, and finally the bridesmaids, if they are to take part. In order to speed up the procedure of going through the line, and because both guests and bridesmaids find it difficult to think of anything to say to so many strangers, I, personally, am in favor of leaving the bridesmaids out of the line. The two fathers may join the line if they wish, but they need not do so and usually prefer to mingle with the guests. If the groom's family comes from another town, however, his father may well join the line so that he may be introduced to relatives and friends of the bride and her parents. If he does stand in line, so should the father of the bride. Flower girls and ring bearers never stand in the receiving line.

Divorced parents do not stand in the receiving line together. If the bride's mother and stepfather are giving the wedding, she alone or both are in the line—but not the bride's father. If her father and stepmother are giving the wedding, they, as host and hostess, stand in line, and the bride's mother is merely an honored guest. If neither has remarried, only the bride's mother should be in the line unless he is giving the reception. In that case the estranged wife would not act as hostess, but the godmother of the bride, or an aunt, or even a very close family friend would receive

| MOTHER | FATHER | MOTHER | FATHER | BRIDE | GROOM | MAID OF | BRIDESMAID | BRIDESMAID |
| OF BRIDE | OF BRIDE | OF GROOM | OF GROOM | | | HONOR | | |

The receiving line

in her place. When the groom's parents are divorced, his mother joins him in the line, and neither his father nor his stepfather need be there, which eliminates all complications.

At very large formal weddings there may be an announcer, who stands next to the bride's mother and asks each guest quietly for his name as the guest approaches. He then repeats the name aloud. This can be very helpful when the wedding is so large that the bride's mother does not know a number of the people invited by the groom's family.

The guests shake hands with the mothers of the bride and groom, and either shake hands with or kiss the newlyweds, depending on their relationship with them. They tell the bride how beautiful she looks and wish her happiness, congratulate the groom, and pass on to say "Hello" to the maid of honor, and the bridesmaids if they are in line.

The bride's mother is responsible for introducing each guest to the groom's mother (and father) and, when necessary, to the bride. She (the bride) then turns and introduces her new husband to the guest. The groom, naturally, leans forward to introduce his wife to *his* friends when he sees them approaching. However, long conversations are out of place, since they delay everyone behind, so remarks other than greetings and introductions are kept to a minimum.

The bride and groom need say no more than "Thank you," "I'm so glad to see you," etc., to the guests. The bride, if she remembers what a guest sent as a gift, might mention how much she liked it, but this does not take the place of her thank-you note.

There is a trend today toward eliminating receiving lines entirely—especially at small weddings. And it is true that they are, for the most part, somewhat boring, tiring, and stiff. In spite of that, at a large wedding they provide the only means for all of the guests to offer their congratulations to the couple, who otherwise might never get to speak to some of their friends at all. Therefore I think they are a "necessary evil" at a large wedding. At a small one, where there are few (or no) introductions necessary, and where the bride and groom can circulate and spend a little time with all their guests, the reason for the line is eliminated. But if the bride decides not to have a receiving line at her wedding, she must be sure that the groom and his family meet everyone there. To do this she and her new husband, and her parents, should stand near the entrance to greet the guests as they arrive. The groom's parents should remain nearby, so that she can introduce them at once to anyone who has not already met them.

Because even the best-planned receiving line involves a lengthy period of standing for all but the first guests to arrive, it is thoughtful to have beverages and a tray of hors d'oeuvres passed to those just getting into line. They may take their glass of champagne—the usual offering—with them until they near the receiving line. A table should be placed in a convenient spot so that the guests can easily put down their empty glasses. If possible, a few tables with chairs should be placed near the entrance to the room where the line forms. If the wait is going to be long, a waiter can be posted near the door to suggest that late arrivals take a glass of champagne and sit at one of the tables until the line reaches a more reasonable length.

A waiter is always standing near the end of the receiving line to offer champagne or punch or whatever beverage is being served to those who have passed through. They take a glass and move on to the next room, the tent, the lawn, or wherever the rest of the festivities are to take place.

The Guest Book

Although it is not obligatory, many couples like to have their guests sign a register or guest book, to be kept as a permanent memento of their wedding day.

The book is placed on a table covered with a white cloth, near the entrance. A relative or friend of the bride is asked to take charge. As the guests arrive and join the line she reminds each one (or one member of each couple) to sign the book. Unlike a register at a funeral home, the names will not be used as a list to whom notes must be sent, so guests may sign in any way they wish, although last names must be included. Contemporaries of the bride and groom will undoubtedly sign "Beth and Bob Hanson," while older couples who do not know the bride personally might sign "Mr. and Mrs. John Wilson." If a space is provided for "remarks," they should be sentimental or serious rather than joking. "May you always be as happy as you are today," or "The most beautiful wedding I've ever seen," are typical entries.

The Bride's Table

When the last guest has passed through the receiving line, or perhaps after the bride and groom have mingled with their guests and danced, the bridal party is seated at the bride's table. It is a rectangular table set against one side or end of the room, and the bride and groom sit at the center of the long side, facing out so that the guests can see them. No one is seated opposite them. The bride sits on the groom's right, with the best man on her right; the maid of honor sits on the groom's left; and the bridesmaids and ushers alternate along the same side of the table. Husbands, wives, and fiancés of the attendants also sit at the bride's table. If there are too many people to fit along one side, the table should form a "U," so that they may sit at the two arms rather than obstruct everyone's view of the bride and groom. The bride or her mother has put place cards on the table earlier in the day.

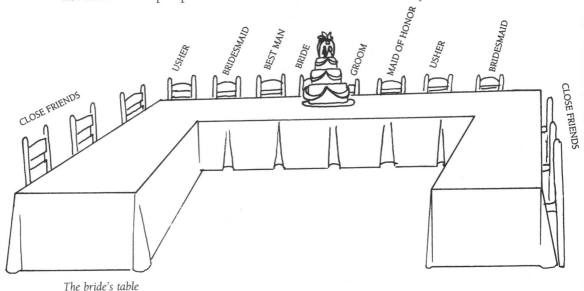

The bride's table

The wedding cake is sometimes used as a centerpiece on the bride's table, but since it is usually quite tall and tends to hide the bride and groom from the guests, the cake is more often placed on a small round table at one side or a little way in front of the bridal table. Flowers almost always form the centerpiece, and if the table is long, two more arrangements are placed near either end. Although the tablecloth is always white, the flower arrangements may be chosen to complement the color of the bridesmaid's dresses.

With No Bridal Table

Many couples prefer to wander about and mingle with their guests rather than being seated at a formal table. There should always, however, be a table reserved for the bride and groom and their attendants so that they are assured of a place to sit down and rest their feet.

The newlyweds may go to the buffet table just as the other guests do, or in some cases a waiter fills a plate and brings it to them where they are seated. The bridesmaids and ushers need not all sit with the bride and groom at the same time but may go to dance or see their own particular friends as they will. However, at some point the best man must round them all up and bring them together to join him in a toast to the couple. The attendants should also gather around when the bride and groom cut the cake.

The Parents' Table

The table of the couple's parents differs from other tables only in its larger size and the place cards for those who have been invited to sit there. The groom's mother always sits on the right of the bride's father, and opposite them the groom's father is on the right of the mother of the bride. The other places at the table are occupied by grandparents and godparents. If there are more grandparents than the limited space can accommodate, a separate table should be arranged for them and their close friends nearby. Although they have no official part in the wedding, they should at all times be treated as honored guests.

At some receptions there are separate tables for the parents and relatives of the bride and groom. I find this very unfriendly and contrary to the atmosphere of "uniting" that a wedding should create.

The parents' table is the only one other than the bridal table where place cards are used. Other guests sit wherever they wish, joining friends or introducing themselves to strangers already seated at a table.

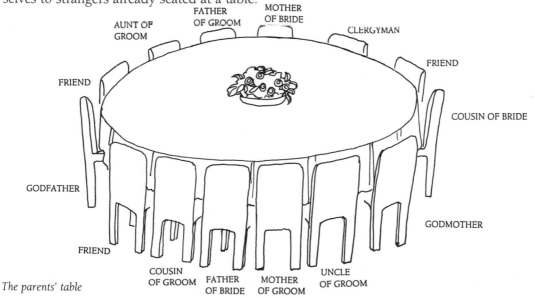

The parents' table

Divorced parents of the bride or groom are never seated together at the parents' table. If they are reasonably friendly, the parent giving the reception will invite the other, but will seat him or her at a separate table. Stepparents are included at the parents' tables, assuming that they get along with their stepchild—the bride or groom. If there has been great bitterness, it is best that the parent who is not giving the wedding, and his spouse, not attend the reception at all even though they go to the marriage ceremony. If the bride or groom insists, the father or mother might come for a short time, but to avoid possible unpleasantness his or her spouse should tactfully stay away.

A Master of Ceremonies

I find the custom advocated by many caterers and wedding specialists of having an announcer or "MC" most unfortunate. These individuals run the wedding like a circus—the ringleader announcing each event and herding people about as he might at a sideshow. The charm and intimacy of a private party are destroyed. In certain localities the wedding party and the parents are introduced as they walk into the hall. Where this is the custom, that is fine, but the introductions may be made by the disk jockey, orchestra leader or perhaps the headwaiter, who may also make any other *necessary* announcements. It is totally *unnecessary* to hire a master of ceremonies to "run" the wedding, making the whole affair seem commercial and over-organized.

A bridal consultant, who sees that things run smoothly, can be a great help. But her presence should be almost unnoticed, and she should do her "organizing" behind the scenes.

The Toast to The Bride and Groom

At a sit-down bridal table, champagne is poured as soon as the party is seated. The glass of the bride is filled first, then that of the bridegroom, and then on around the table, starting with the maid of honor at the groom's left. The best man proposes a toast to the bride and bridegroom. It is usually a very short toast, and somewhat sentimental. All except the bride and groom rise, raise their glasses, and drink the toast. Then the groom stands and replies with thanks and a toast to his new wife. Other toasts may be offered by anyone who cares to propose one. Telegrams that have arrived for the newlyweds are usually read aloud at this time. At a large reception only those at the bridal table join in the toasts, but at a small one all the guests may join in drinking together to the couple's health and happiness. (*See pages 487–488 for sample toasts.*)

Dancing at the Reception

If a regular sit-down dinner is to be served, the first course is passed shortly after the bridal party sits down, and the dancing does not start until after dessert has been eaten. However, if the reception follows an afternoon wedding, and the meal is not to be served until a little later, there would be some dancing before the bridal party goes to its table. At a buffet reception the bride and groom may start the dancing as soon as they have had a chance to recover from standing in the receiving line.

All the guests watch and applaud while the bride and groom dance the first dance. Her father-in-law asks her for the second dance, and then her father cuts in. The bridegroom, meanwhile, dances with his mother-in-law and then his mother. Next, the bride's father asks the groom's mother to dance, and the groom's father asks the bride's mother. As the groom dances with the maid of honor and the ushers with the bridesmaids, the guests may start cutting in, and dancing becomes general. Insofar as possible, all the male guests try to get a dance with the bride.

Cutting the Cake

At a sit-down bridal-table dinner the cake is cut just before the dessert is served, so that slices can be passed with the ices or ice cream. If it is a buffet dinner, the cake is cut later, often shortly before the couple leave the reception.

The bride, with the help of the bridegroom, cuts the first slice from the bottom tier with a silver cake knife. Sometimes she cuts two slices, one for her groom and one for herself, and they each feed the other a bite of these slices. After this the tiers are separated and cut into slices and passed to the guests. The bride and groom and the bridal party are served first. The small top layer with its decoration is set aside for the bride and groom to keep.

They're Off!

Sometimes the bride and groom continue dancing or chatting for so long that those who had intended to stay for the "going away" grow tired and leave. Therefore the wise bride and groom depart before either they or their guests are too exhausted. When they decide it is time to go the bride signals to her bridesmaids, who all gather at the foot of the stairs. About halfway up, she throws her bouquet, and they all try to catch it. In order to show no favoritism she turns her back and throws the bouquet over her shoulder. The one who makes the catch is supposed to be the next married. If the bride has no bridesmaids, she collects a group of friends and throws her bouquet to them. If there are no stairs, she throws the bouquet from whatever spot is most convenient. The bridesmaid who catches the bouquet keeps it.

Sometimes if a very close relative is too ill to attend the wedding, the bouquet is sent to her.

The bride goes to the room where she will change, followed by her mother and her bridesmaids, who stay with her while she changes into her traveling clothes. The groom goes to the room reserved for him and changes into the clothes that the best man has ready for him. His immediate family, as well as hers, collects to say good-bye. The bride's mother gives her daughter a last kiss. The bridesmaids and ushers hurry out to have plenty of paper rose petals ready, and everyone knows the couple are on their way. A passage is left free between the guests, whose hands are full of confetti or petals.

Preceded by the best man, the couple run out through the hall, into the car, and they're off!

Many young couples devote a good deal of thought and planning to making their going away unusual and dramatic. Every sort of departure has been tried—on skis, in sleighs, on horseback or in horse-drawn carriage, and even in a helicopter! But the most memorable I have ever seen took place when the reception was held at a yacht club on a beautiful June evening. The bride and groom left on a handsome boat, polished and shining with all flags flying. They pulled away from the pier while the horns of other boats tooted, and a carpet of rose petals floated on the water. It was truly an ending never to be forgotten by the bride and groom or by any who were there to see them go!

A Thought for the Bridegroom's Parents

At the end of the reception and as soon as she is in her traveling dress, a considerate bride sends a bridesmaid or someone else out into the hall and asks her husband's parents to come to say good-bye to her. This small gesture pays many dividends in ensuring the bride a warm place in her new in-laws' hearts.

Gifts Brought to the Reception

In some areas it is traditional for guests to bring their wedding gifts to the reception rather than send them to the bride ahead of time. A table is made ready for the packages, and each guest leaves his present there as he arrives. In some localities the gifts are opened at the reception; in others they are opened when the bride and groom return from their honeymoon.

When gifts are opened at the reception, great care must be taken that each one is listed properly so that the couple will have an accurate record for their thank-you notes. One of the bridesmaids should be assigned to keep this list and to collect the cards or see that they are kept in the bride's book. Another helper should be appointed to collect and discard the wrappings.

When there is a great number of gifts, I feel that the bride and groom will enjoy them more, and will also have more time to enjoy their friends and the other festivities, if they do not try to open them at the reception.

Among some ethnic groups it is customary to present a check as a wedding gift. This is usually handed to the bride in an envelope as the guest goes through the receiving line. The bride sometimes has a white silk or satin purse hanging on her arm into which she puts the checks, or there may be a prettily decorated box or basket for them on a table near her. The envelopes are not usually opened until later.

INNOVATIONS ON TRADITION

Many changes in wedding tradition have occurred in the past two decades. Some are so widespread that they are hardly innovations anymore, but I am frequently asked by brides and their mothers whether they are acceptable. Below are some that not only are acceptable, but to me, welcome additions which can make a wedding day even more meaningful to participants and guests alike.

Changes in the Service Itself

Addition of a favorite poem or passage to the ceremony. An example is a lovely sonnet by Elizabeth Barrett Browning.

> *When our two souls stand up*
> *erect and strong,*
> *Face to face, silent, drawing*
> *nigh and nigher*
> *Until the lengthening wings*
> *break into fire. . . .*

The optional changing of the word *obey* to *cherish*. The word *obey* was eliminated in the Presbyterian Book of Worship over twenty-five years ago, but it is still included in the services of many faiths, and the change to *cherish* must be requested.

Vows written by the couple themselves, either in addition to or replacing the traditional ones. An example I particularly like is, "I will be slow to anger and quick to forgive."

The change in the promises the couple makes from "until death us do part," to "I promise to be true to you in good times and bad," a far more realistic vow.

"I now pronounce you man and wife" is changed to "I now pronounce you husband and wife."

In many cases the guests are expected to participate too. So that they will know when, and what their responses should be, programs are prepared and handed out as the guests arrive.

The Music

It is scarcely necessary to mention that the traditional wedding march has been replaced by any number of selections more religious in nature. This is a matter that every couple planning to be married in church must discuss with the organist. Many couples have a friend who plays and/or sings their selections or music that he has composed especially for the ceremony. Guitars are most often played but recorders, flutes, harps—almost anything—have been used to provide the music too. At a wedding I attended recently the groom himself sang a song he had written for his bride.

The Parents' Part

In answer to the clergyman's question, "Who giveth this woman . . . ?" the bride's father includes her mother by saying, "Her mother and I do."

Christian brides are being escorted by their father *and* mother, as Jewish brides and grooms have been since time immemorial.

Brides who have been brought up by their mother are having her, rather than a male relative or friend, escort them up the aisle.

The bride stops as she is leaving the church and gives a flower from her bouquet to her mother and to the groom's mother. The groom kisses the two mothers and shakes hands with the fathers.

The bride places the flowers from the altar on the grave of a deceased parent after the reception. The bride who told me about doing this said that in the few moments at her father's graveside she felt that she had received his blessing.

Surroundings

I am very much in favor of outdoor weddings when it is possible and practical. Any place that offers beauty and privacy, is accessible, and has special meaning for the bride and groom is appropriate, provided their faith permits. Our church has a very beautiful enclosed garden, and my daughter and her fiancé chose to be married there rather than inside the church.

Many couples may simply prefer to be married in the familiar surroundings of their own home—however small. This too is most appropriate. One lovely wedding I attended was held in a tiny New York apartment. The young minister, saying that "a marriage affects the whole community, and therefore I feel that the community—represented by you—should have a part in the marriage," asked the thirty or more guests to form a circle and hold hands. The bride and groom, their parents, and the minister formed a part of the circle. The service was traditional except that the maid of honor and the best man passed bread and wine around the circle as a simple "Communion." The best man, a poet, read a poem he had composed for the couple. Although we, the older guests, felt a little strange at first, we came away feeling that it had been a particularly beautiful wedding and that we truly had taken part.

The Reception

Champagne used to be an essential part of the wedding reception. Today it is usually only one beverage of many offered, or it is omitted entirely. Brides and grooms tend to offer, instead, the beverages (and the foods) they know that their friends will like. Beer, wine, Bloody Marys, sparkling water, whiskey, and all manner of soft drinks have become not only acceptable but as popular as the traditional champagne.

Wedding cakes are no longer necessarily "white cake," but may be chocolate or whatever the couple likes.

The receiving line is often omitted. Most nontraditional weddings are not so large and certainly not so "structured" as traditional weddings. The bride and groom, using the time they would have spent standing in line, circulate among the guests. The advantage of a receiving line is that everyone there has a chance to offer happiness and congratulations to the bride and groom. Therefore, if no line is formed, the couple *and* their parents must make a special effort to talk to each and every guest.

Instead of traditional favors such as paper matches with the couple's initials, boxes of groom's cake, etc., one couple wrote me that they had written a message to their guests thanking them for coming and adding to their happiness, and had it printed on small cards and distributed to their friends with the slices of wedding cake. It was a nice thought, and the cards served as a sentimental memento of the wedding.

HOUSE WEDDINGS

The bride-to-be and her fiancé do not always choose to be married in church—for any number of perfectly good reasons. A house wedding requires as much attention as any other, for it should be as perfect in its way as the loveliest church ceremony.

A house wedding usually involves somewhat less expense but a good deal more work for the bride's family than does the church wedding. Of course, if a caterer is hired, the expense may be as high and the work as little as if it were held in a church or hotel. It also has the disadvantage (which may also be an advantage!) of limiting the number of guests. The ceremony is exactly the same as it is in a church, except that the procession advances from the stairs or hallway through an aisle of white ribbons or stanchions to the improvised altar. Chairs for the immediate families may be placed within a marked-off enclosure, but if the room is small, space is merely kept free for them to stand in.

In the country a house wedding may be performed in the garden, with the wedding procession under the trees, and tables set out on the lawn. Alternative facilities should be prepared in the house in case of rain.

When the couple's faith requires that they kneel during the wedding ceremony, a cushioned bench is provided for their use. It is often backed by an altar rail. The bench is usually six or eight inches high and between three and four feet long; at its back, an upright board on either end supports a crosspiece of the altar rail. It can be made in the roughest fashion by any carpenter or amateur, since it can be hidden under leaves and flowers or a drapery of some sort. Either end of the altar rail is usually decorated with a spray of white flowers.

At a house wedding, the bride's mother stands at the door of the room in which the ceremony is to be held and receives people as they arrive. But the bridegroom's mother takes her place near the altar with the rest of the immediate family. The ushers are purely ornamental, as no one is escorted to seats. The guests simply stand wherever they can find places behind the aisle ribbons. Just before the bride's entrance her mother goes forward and stands in the front row on the left.

In a house the procession usually starts from the top of the stairs. In an apartment it starts in the hall or a room off the living room. The wedding music, provided by a small orchestra, piano, or records, begins, and the ushers come in two by two, followed by the bridesmaids, exactly as in a church, the bride coming last on her father's right arm. There are seldom many bridal attendants at a house wedding—two or three ushers, and the same number of bridesmaids—unless the house is immense. The clergyman and the groom and best man have, if possible, reached the altar by another door. If the room has only one door, they go up the aisle a few moments before the bridal procession starts.

At an even simpler wedding, the clergyman enters, followed by the bridegroom; the bride then enters with her father, or alone; and the wedding service is read. The bride and groom should each have one attendant, however, and they simply step forward and join the couple standing before the clergyman.

After the ceremony there is no recessional. The clergyman steps aside, an usher removes the prayer bench if there is one, and the bride and groom turn where they stand and receive the congratulations of their guests.

When there are no garden flowers to be had, a suitable background can be made by hanging a curtain of wine-red or deep-green velvet or any other plain fabric across a flat wall space. Against this, the colorful clothes of the bride's attendants (if she has any) and her own white dress and veil are effective. The refreshments may consist of nothing but soda or fruit punch, wedding cake, and a few varieties of sandwiches placed on a small table covered with a white cloth.

One round of champagne is often served in addition to punch and soft drinks for the traditional wedding toasts.

There may be a bride's table set up in the dining room, but more often there is a buffet table, and the bride and groom mingle with their friends, moving from one group to another. If the house is very large, or the reception is held in the garden, tables with centerpieces of flowers and cloths to complement the color of the bridesmaids' dresses are set up. The guests get their food from the buffet and sit at whatever table they wish, or wherever they find a free chair. In this case, as at a reception in a hall or club, there is a table reserved for the bridal party, and often one for the parents and their special guests.

Everyone invited to a house wedding ceremony stays on for whatever type of reception is held. It may be no more than punch and wedding cake, or it may be a complete meal and dancing, but there is a single guest list and no one goes to the first part without staying for the second.

The bride may wear the conventional long wedding dress for her home wedding, or she may prefer to wear a cocktail dress or even a simpler afternoon dress. The man wears the appropriate corresponding clothing as described in Chapter 38.

EVENING WEDDINGS

All through the South, and sometimes in the West, many weddings are celebrated at eight or nine o'clock in the evening.

The details are, in general, the same as those for the morning or afternoon. In large southern cities the bride and bridesmaids may wear dresses that are perhaps more elaborate and more "evening" in type, and the bridegroom and ushers wear full evening clothes. Guests, both men and women, dress in evening clothes.

At simpler ceremonies, especially in smaller communities, the guests wear exactly what they would wear to evening service in church—a good dress for a woman and a dark daytime suit for a man.

Because of the lateness of the hour a full meal is not often served. Refreshments consist of sandwiches, cake, champagne or punch, and frequently coffee.

THE EARLY-MORNING WEDDING

Among Roman Catholics an eight-o'clock morning wedding is not unusual, and other couples choose to be married at dawn on a beach or a hilltop. The beginning of the new day is symbolic of the beginning of a new life. Still others choose the early morning because they must catch a plane or ship that leaves early in the day.

The bride wears a simple daytime dress, usually the one she will go away in. She may carry a bouquet of moderate size or a prayer book or wear a corsage. She wears no gloves. Her attendants dress like her. The groom and his best man wear business suits or light-colored trousers and blazers. A reception follows the ceremony, featuring a breakfast or brunch menu. A round of champagne may be served for toasts, and Bloody Marys are frequently offered.

Occasionally the reception is held later in the day. This is not too satisfactory, however, because out-of-town guests may be at a loss for something to do or a place to spend the intervening hours.

MARRIAGE AT THE RECTORY

Couples who do not wish to, or cannot, be married in church, but whose clergyman can perform the ceremony, are sometimes married in the rectory.

The bride and bridegroom go together and are met at the parsonage by the members of their families and any friends who have been invited. The clergyman takes his place, and the service is read. Afterward those present congratulate the newlyweds and that may be all. Or they may go to the house of the bride or of a witness or to a restaurant to have lunch or dinner together. At such a marriage the bride rarely wears a white wedding dress and veil, but it is entirely proper for her to do so if she chooses.

When the bridal party goes to a restaurant for a meal following the ceremony, it is usually paid for by the bride and groom, or the bride's parents. On occasion, however, the six or eight people present agree ahead of time to "give" the party for the newlyweds.

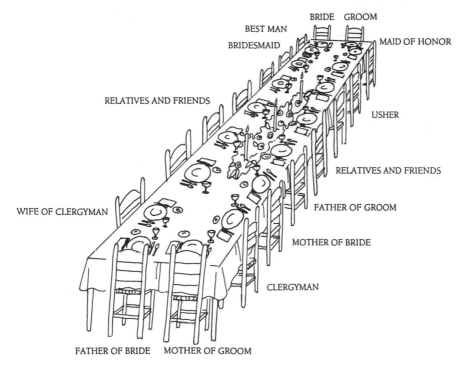

Small seated lunch or dinner following a simple wedding

CIVIL MARRIAGES

The general procedure is exactly the same as that for a marriage at the rectory. However simple and informal the plans, there are always two guests, either relatives or friends, who act as witnesses as well.

The traditional wedding dress and veil are not suitable in the circumstances, but the bride will certainly wish to wear the prettiest daytime dress or suit she has or can afford to buy.

A restaurant dinner or small party at home usually follows the ceremony.

THE BLESSING OF A CIVIL MARRIAGE

When a couple has been married in a civil ceremony, and have had the approval of their church, they may later wish to have a religious ceremony held in a church or chapel to bless that marriage. There is such a service in the *Book of Common Worship*. It is similar to the marriage service, except that the minister says, "Do you *acknowledge* [rather than *take*] this woman . . ." and makes other appropriate changes. No one, of course, gives the bride away, nor does the groom give the bride her ring again.

It is a lovely ceremony and most satisfactory for those who wanted but could not have a religious wedding originally.

The service is attended only by the family and closest friends, and there are no attendants. It is, after all, a blessing rather than a celebration of the marriage. The bride wears a street dress, and the groom, a dark suit. She may carry a bouquet or wear a corsage. There may be music, and the altar is decorated with flowers.

If a reception follows the ceremony, it may be as simple or as elaborate as the couple wish. Presuming the blessing takes place shortly after the civil marriage, the reception may have all the trimmings of any other wedding reception.

Religious Ceremony Following a Civil Marriage

Many couples who are married in a civil service wish to remarry later in a religious ceremony. This is perfectly proper—in fact a desirable thing to do. Both wedding and reception (if one was *not* held after the civil marriage) can be exactly like that of any other wedding, with one exception. The bride should not wear a veil—the traditional symbol of the "virgin bride"—but she may wear white—the symbol of purity.

If a long time has elapsed between the two ceremonies, so that the couple can no longer be considered bride and groom, the ceremony should be very simple— limited to family and close friends. The reception, too, should be intimate—a dignified celebration reflecting the religious aspect of the occasion.

Elopements

When the bride's parents have approved of the elopement before the marriage or when they have decided after to make the best of what has happened, they may send out announcements in their name. Should the parents be unalterably opposed, however, and wish the world to know it, they do not send out announcements. The newlyweds, if they wish, send them out themselves.

If the bride's mother and father give a belated reception sometime after the marriage, it is generally an informal affair attended by close friends and relatives. This is often done to introduce an out-of-town bridegroom. The invitations are telephoned or sent on informals. If written, they should include the bride's married name—"In honor of Mr. and Mrs. Harvey Kirk, Jr.," or "In honor of Nancy and Bill." If the parents are truly enthusiastic about the marriage and wish to show it, they may give a much more formal reception, including a wedding cake, engraved invitations, etc.

The Double Wedding

Most double weddings involve two sisters. The two bridegrooms follow the clergyman and stand side by side, each with his best man behind him. The groom of the older sister stands nearer the aisle. The ushers—half of them friends of the first, and the other friends of the second bridegroom—go up the aisle together. Then

come the bridesmaids of the older sister followed by her maid of honor, who walks
alone. The older sister follows, holding her father's arm. Then come the bridesmaids
of the younger sister, her maid of honor, and last, the younger bride on the arm of a
brother, uncle, or other close male relative.

The first couple ascend the chancel steps and take their place at the left side of
the altar rail, leaving room at the right side for the younger bride and her bridegroom. The father stands just below his older daughter. The younger daughter's
escort takes his place in a pew with his wife or family.

The service is read to both couples, with the particular responses made twice.
In a Protestant ceremony the father gives both brides away—first his older daughter
and then the younger. Then he takes the place saved for him beside his wife in the
first pew.

At the end of the ceremony the older sister and her husband turn and go down
the aisle first. The younger couple follow. The bridesmaids and ushers of the first
sister pair off and follow; the attendants of the second walk out last.

Each couple should have the same number of attendants. All the ushers
should be dressed alike. The bridesmaids' dresses, while not necessarily all the same,
should harmonize.

Seating the Parents at the Church

One difficulty of a double wedding is the seating of the parents of the two
bridegrooms, who must either share the first pew or draw lots for the occupation of
first or second. This question they must decide for themselves.

Occasionally the brides are cousins, in which case the front pew on the bride's
side must be shared by both mothers, the older sitting in the aisle seat.

The Reception for a Double Wedding

If the brides are sisters, there is only one hostess—their mother. Therefore she
(and her husband if he wishes) stands first in the receiving line. Next to her is the
mother of the older sister's husband, and then the older sister and her groom. The
younger sister's mother-in-law comes next, and then the younger couple. Both maids
of honor follow them, but since there are so many in the line, the bridesmaids should
be excused. The three mothers could stand together at the head of the line, but if the
two grooms' mothers stand next to their own children, they are in a better position to
introduce their new daughters-in-law to their special friends.

At a sit-down wedding reception the seating of the bridal parties depends on
the numbers. If there are many attendants, it is best to have two tables, next to or
facing each other, and arranged in the usual way. If, however, there are not too many
in the parties, they may be seated at the same table. One couple would be placed at

either end of the same side, or if they prefer, opposite each other at the center of each long side. The bride always sits on the right of the groom. The maid of honor in either case would be on the groom's left and the best man on the bride's right. The other attendants would alternate—either on the same side of the table as their newlywed couple, or at the same end where their particular couple is seated.

Each couple should have their own wedding cake. They cut the cakes one right after the other so that each may watch the other perform that ceremony.

All three sets of parents should be seated together at the same table. It is up to the brides' mother to discuss with her daughters' new mothers-in-law how many other relatives should be included with them.

In all other ways the reception is identical to that of a single wedding.

MILITARY WEDDINGS

The only way in which a military wedding ceremony differs from a civilian one is the arch of swords through which the bride and groom pass at the end of the ceremony. This occurs only when the bridegroom is a commissioned officer. As soon as the service is over, the ushers line up on either side of the aisle at the foot of the chancel steps, and at the head usher's command, "Draw swords!" hold their swords up (blades up) in such a way as to form an arch. The couple pass through, and at the command, "Return swords!" the ushers return them to their sheaths. They then turn and escort the bridesmaids down the aisle.

On a nice day the arch may be formed outside the entrance to the church. In this case the ushers quickly leave by a side door and rush around to the front of the church to form the arch. Only the bridal couple passes through.

Should there be some civilian ushers in the party, they line up also and merely stand at attention while the arch is formed.

MARRYING YOUR LIVING-TOGETHER PARTNER

Couples who have lived together and decide to marry may certainly have a traditional ceremony and reception if they wish. If they are more mature in years, they may wish to forgo a large, formal wedding and instead celebrate with a smaller ceremony and reception. They might issue invitations in their own names rather than the names of their parents, if they choose third person formal invitations. Others may feel that nothing is really changing, and simply marry quietly, letting friends and relatives know by personal note.

Announcements are made in the way that best suits the couple. If there has been a formal wedding, engraved announcements are mailed to those who are not invited to the wedding. Again, the bride and groom may decide to send the announcements in their own name rather than those of their parents, particularly if the couple is more mature in years.

UNWED MOTHERS AND PREGNANT BRIDES

I am frequently asked whether a bride who had a child before her marriage, or one who is about to, should wear a bridal gown and have an elaborate wedding. The answer is not an easy one. It depends on the bride's own feelings, her honesty, and how much she cares about what other people think or say. The last is, perhaps, less important, and yet few of us do not have some desire to conform and to be thought well of.

As discussed later in "Second Marriages," the face veil is the accepted and traditional symbol of virginity. Therefore unwed mothers and pregnant brides should *not* wear a veil. This in no way brands them as different, because many other brides do not choose to wear face veils in any case.

The white dress is another matter, and an unwed mother must decide for herself. There is no reason that she should not have a real wedding gown, especially if her future husband wants her to, but she should choose her dress with great care. She may modify the virginal effect by adding color to the trim and in her flowers or by choosing a definite off-white. She will still look as "bridey" as can be but she will be less open to criticism. The pregnant bride may, of course, wear a long gown, in off-white or pastel, but the style should be more becoming to her condition than would most traditional wedding dresses.

These marriages should be kept relatively simple so that the couple does not appear to flaunt their situation in society's face. The bride may certainly be given a shower or two, as long as they are restricted to intimate friends. There may be attendants, a reception, photographs, and newspaper announcements. Invitations follow the rules for any wedding. In sending out announcements after the wedding, the date is never falsified—even when a baby is to arrive six or seven months later. Most people will have forgotten the wedding date, and it is better to be honest than to try to hide what can't be hidden.

When announcements are sent by the bride's parents the indication that they have accepted and are happy about the marriage can be a great help to the bride and groom, who may be going through a very traumatic experience.

In fact the understanding of the bride's parents is terribly important. It can be disastrous if they force their daughter to marry a man she is not really in love with, just to "make an honest woman of her." A marriage carried out on that basis is almost surely headed for divorce. But when the couple are truly in love and *want* to get married, their parents' support will bring the two generations closer than they have ever been before.

Above all, it should be remembered that this is a *happy* occasion, and one to be celebrated. The fatherless child is getting a father, and the mother will have his support and help in bringing up her baby. Whatever her problems and mistakes have been, they are on the way to being over. So, the wedding should be dignified, beautiful, and in quiet good taste, and the reception should match it—with gaiety and an air of celebration added.

*E*tiquette for those who have been married more than once has changed radically since Emily Post wrote her original book. No longer are large church weddings, gala parties, or even white bridal gowns taboo.

The second marriages of widows and widowers and divorced people are similar in most respects, but there are certain differences that should be noted, and they will be pointed out in the following paragraphs.

Widows and widowers, in most cases, should wait a year or so after the first spouse's death before remarrying. This is simply a matter of showing respect for their spouse's memory, and because the survivor is at least mentally "in mourning." Also, widows and widowers should not rush into a marriage that might seem attractive at the time because of loneliness. Divorced persons, on the other hand, may marry the day the divorce becomes final, although they, too, are risking an unhappy marriage "on the rebound." No matter how certain a man and a woman are about their plans to marry, they may *not* announce their engagement before one or the other is legally divorced from the first mate. A woman may accept, *but never wear, in public,* an engagement ring while her "fiancé" is still—if only for another day or two—another woman's husband.

Divorced couples may plan the kind of wedding they want, but it is not in the best of taste to try to outdo a large first wedding. If a white bridal gown is the choice, the divorcée can add a colored ribbon or sash to temper a maidenly appearance. Colored flowers rather than white contribute an appropriate air.

If the groom is divorced and the bride is marrying for the first time, she should feel no restrictions on the degree of festivity with which she may do it—a newspaper announcement, an engagement party, presents. If, however, a divorced woman with children is marrying, she will probably feel more comfortable in announcing the engagement informally—telling family and close friends and writing notes to other friends. This is no longer a hard and fast rule, and if she longs for more fanfare, she may plan for it.

Please remember that the first ones to know of a coming remarriage should be the children, if any. If they have shared the growing relationship, the marriage will seem a normal evolution. If your children are young, it can be explained in this

43

For
Those
Who've
Been
Married
Before

way: "Mommy [or Daddy] still loves you more than anyone in the world. Maurice [or Margery] loves us both so much that he [she] wants to get married and live with us forever."

745

FOR
THOSE
WHO'VE
BEEN
MARRIED
BEFORE

It is important to communicate to children that the new spouse is not displacing their noncustodial parent: "You and Daddy [or Mommy] will be the same as before. You'll still be his [her] child, just as you are mine—that will never change. Maurice [or Margery] will be a different kind of person in your life."

After the custodial parent has explained the upcoming marriage, the prospective stepparent should join the conversation to reinforce all that has been said.

As soon as the children have been told, the custodial parent should tell the other parent as well. He (or she) should do his (or her) best to answer any questions that may arise.

A WIDOW'S OR DIVORCÉE'S ENGAGEMENT RING

When a widow becomes engaged to marry again, she stops wearing her engagement ring from her first marriage, whether or not she is given another. She may continue to wear her wedding ring, if she has children, until the day of her second marriage. She and her new fiancé must decide together what they wish to do with her old engagement ring. If she has a son she may wish to keep it for him to use someday as an engagement ring for his future bride. Or the stones may be reset and used in another form of jewelry—by herself or her daughters.

A divorcée does not continue to wear her engagement ring on her "wedding" finger, and she may, if she wishes, have the stones reset into another piece of jewelry.

EXPENSES

When a young woman whose first marriage ended abruptly after the sudden death of her husband, or who, perhaps, was divorced shortly after an elopement, remarries, her family often gives the wedding and pays the expenses just as they would for a first marriage. This is especially true if she returned home to live. If, however, their daughter has had one large and expensive wedding, they should in no way feel obligated to give her another. They may help as much as they want, of course, but the wedding should impose no strain on their budget. In most cases the bride and groom plan and pay for the major part of the wedding themselves.

THE CEREMONY

The wedding service itself is exactly the same as that of a first wedding. But the surroundings are usually much simpler. The bride (unless she had no real wedding the first time) has very few attendants. There is always a maid (or matron) of honor; often a flower girl or ring bearer (if she has a child or grandchild) and sometimes one or two relatives or very close friends to serve as bridesmaids. The groom has a best man and as many ushers as may be necessary to seat the guests.

A young widow or divorcée who has been living with her parents may be escorted up the aisle by her father, but a more mature woman walks alone, preceded by her maid of honor. At a private ceremony there is no procession at all, and the couple merely enter together, usually from a side door, and walk behind the clergyman to the chancel.

Children of either divorced or widowed parents should be included in the wedding party as long as they want to—as flower girl and ring bearer if they are young, as junior bridesmaid and usher if they are older. However, the approval of the noncustodial parent should be obtained if the children are to act as attendants, since to stand with one parent against the wishes of the other may cause the children to feel disloyal to that parent.

Whether they serve as attendants or not, children *should* attend their parent's marriage, unless there is great resentment of the new husband or wife. They will adjust to the new family situation much more readily if they feel they are part of the formation of that family. I recall a three-year-old who pleaded with his mother to be allowed to accompany her and her new husband on their honeymoon. "I'll sit very quietly on the end of the moon," he explained. While the choice is up to you, I feel that if you and your new husband plan a honeymoon, you should plan it without children. It can be explained as a way for you to get to know each other better before becoming a new kind of family. However, since leaving children after such a major change in their life occurs can be nothing short of traumatic for them, many couples do postpone the honeymoon until children gain security in the new family pattern. Certainly those who decide on an immediate honeymoon should keep it short.

The Bride's Dress

Neither a widow nor a divorcée should wear a face veil at her second wedding, since it is the symbol of virginity. Wearing white, the symbol of purity, is another matter, but since a second marriage should not try to be a replica of a first, it is best to choose off-white, a pastel, or perhaps white lace over a colored underskirt.

A groom who has not been married before may well wish to see his bride in a "bridal gown," even though she is widowed or divorced. To please him she may wear a long white "bridey" dress with color in the trim and carry a bouquet of mixed colors rather than all white. She may wear a bridal hat or headdress, but not a veil. Her attendant's dress matches the style of her own, and her groom's costume is also dictated by hers. He may wear the semiformal sack coat with striped trousers if she wears a long dress, or a business suit if she is in a cocktail dress or suit.

When the Marriage Cannot Take Place in Church

747
FOR
THOSE
WHO'VE
BEEN
MARRIED
BEFORE

Some faiths do not allow second marriages to take place in the church if either party has been divorced. In some cases the clergyman is permitted to perform the ceremony in the bride's home; in others he may not officiate at all, and if the couple wishes a religious ceremony they must find a clergyman from another faith to perform it. There are situations when a civil marriage is the only possibility, but it may always be followed by as elaborate a reception as the couple wishes.

The procedure for a second marriage performed at home is exactly the same as that described on pages 736–737.

THE RECEPTION

While simple receptions are usually given—especially if there was an elaborate one following the bride's first marriage—there is no rule that they must be small. If the groom has not been married before, the couple may want to have all the "trimmings" for the benefit of his family and friends. In any case the reception, which is, after all, simply a party to celebrate the marriage, may be as large or as small as everyone concerned wishes. At a large reception there is a receiving line so that everyone may meet both bride and groom; at a simpler party the line is not necessary. Although there is no rule about such details as monogrammed matchboxes, napkins, etc., they are usually omitted, but a wedding cake is always a feature.

INVITATIONS AND ANNOUNCEMENTS

When the guest list is restricted to family and close friends, invitations are usually issued by phone, or by personal note to those at a distance. If, however, the wedding is quite large, or a large reception is planned after a small ceremony, engraved invitations may be issued.

Both bride's family and groom's family may send engraved announcements to as many people as they wish, either in the bride's parents' name or in the name of both parents. The couple themselves may also send the announcements. (*See pages 677–679.*)

Announcements of a second marriage may also be sent to the newspaper. They are similar to those of a first marriage except that there are no details about attendants or the bride's dress. The name of the former spouse and previous marital status of both bride and groom may be but aren't necessarily included.

A typical announcement might read in part:

> *The wedding of Mr. and Mrs. Herman Berg took place on January fourteenth at the Third Congregational Church, Binghamton, N.Y. Mrs. Berg is the former Nancy McLeod Corey. [She is the widow of Mr. Jonathan Corey*

of Sioux Falls, Iowa.] [Or: Her first marriage to Mr. Jonathan Corey terminated in divorce.]

The announcement may then go on to mention the occupation of Mr. Berg (and Mrs. Berg, if applicable), and where they will be living. In some papers that are not pressed for space, the parents of the couple may also be mentioned.

When a widow or widower remains very close to the parents of his or her first spouse there is a question about whether or not to invite them to the second wedding. Since they are fond of him or her they are undoubtedly delighted that their daughter- or son-in-law has found happiness and that the children (if any) will have a stepparent, but at the same time it may be hard for them to see someone taking the place of their own child. The widow or widower should tell them personally that she would love to have them at the wedding, but does understand if they would find it sad or uncomfortable to be there, and leave it up to them.

Ex-in-laws are rarely invited to a divorcée's marriage, because there might well be some embarrassment or resentment on the part of the new spouse and his or her parents. But if everyone involved is friendly, and there are grandchildren to consider, the former in-laws might be invited.

GIFTS

Although family members usually give a gift to a bride being married for the second time, friends, other than those closest to her, need not do so. If it is the first marriage for the groom, his relatives and friends will surely *want* to give them gifts. Although it is not in good taste to put "No gifts" on a wedding or reception invitation, the word should be spread by family members and good friends that the couple certainly do not expect gifts from friends invited to the reception—especially if they have attended a previous one for the bride.

OLDER COUPLE'S WEDDING

Life used to begin at forty but now it frequently seems to begin at fifty, sixty, seventy, or even eighty. Recycled married life, that is. And why not? Why should people who lose a spouse at fifty or sixty feel that companionship or marriage is a thing of the past? More and more often we hear of older people forming new relationships, sometimes with benefit of matrimony, sometimes without. Whichever road they choose I'm for it, and I wish them all the best!

Problems Older Couples Face

It is hard to believe that unselfish, devoted children could stand in the way of a widowed parent's happiness, and yet it happens time and again. Usually the children *believe* that they are acting in their parent's "best interests" when they discourage them from forming a serious relationship, but often there are latent jealousies, greed, or resentments that are the underlying causes for their objections. Some of the reasons children give for trying to prevent a parent from marrying again are:

749
FOR
THOSE
WHO'VE
BEEN
MARRIED
BEFORE

> "Aren't you too old to start a new sex life?"
> "He [or she] is just after your money."
> "How can you ever put anyone in Dad's [or Mom's] place?"
> "He's all right, but how can you stand his children?"

To counter these questions and charges, it is vitally important that the widowed parent does not suddenly "spring" an unknown stepparent on the children. He or she should make every effort to have both families meet. And the parent should never consent to marriage before meeting the fiancé's children.

Once these formalities are over and the couple has definitely decided to marry, they should let their children know at once. Each should talk privately to his own family, openly assuring them that the new love in no way replaces the deceased father or mother but is merely a new and happy progression. Children should be assured that their inheritances will be safe, the will redrawn so that they will not be left out. Even though the fiancé may be completely honorable and have no designs on the parent's estate, his or her children may, and legal papers should be drawn up to ensure the family's well-being.

A great deal of emphasis should be placed on the fact that this marriage will not break up the existing family relationship or come between the parent and the children. Even adult children, on whom the bereaved parent may have been depending since the death of the spouse, are often unexpectedly jealous and resentful when their mother or father finds someone else to turn to.

The Older Couple's Wedding

Weddings of older couples, most of whom are parents and grandparents, are every bit as happy as those that of twenty-five-year-olds, but they are also a little different.

Attendants

First, there are no attendants in the usual sense. Instead, there may be a handsome man in his forties giving his mother away, or a thirty-five-year-old son handing the ring to his father. Or there may be a four-year-old granddaughter and a six-year-old grandson serving as flower girl and ring bearer. Then again, there may be a sixty-year-old sister of the bride and seventy-year-old brother of the groom acting as maid of honor and best man. In other words, attendants are *who* you want, and how many you want, but not the parade of bridesmaids and groomsmen you see at a first-time wedding. At a large formal wedding, however, the groom must have enough ushers to seat the guests.

Invitations

Although there is no rule against engraved invitations, older couples generally prefer to write their own notes. Most adult marriages are fairly small, and it does not take much time to write:

> Dear Sue,
>   Jack Green and I are being married in my house on Saturday, August 16th at 6:00 P.M. I do hope you and Ed will come and stay for a buffet supper after the ceremony.
>
>   Affectionately, Joan

If, however, Mayor John DuPont is marrying Senator Grace Hatch and all their constituents are invited, engraved invitations are sent out in their own names:

> The honour of your presence
> is requested
> at the marriage of
>   . . . etc.

Even though the couple does not want or expect wedding gifts, they should not put "No gifts" on the invitations. They may spread the word through friends, and most people know that only *very* close friends and relatives need give second-marriage gifts in any case.

Clothing

Older women simply do not look their best in frilly organdy ruffles, yards of billowing tulle, or unrelieved white. A simple long or short dress, in a style and a color that is most becoming to the bride, is a far better choice than a virginal wedding gown. Hats or hair ornaments are optional. The bride either carries a bouquet of flowers or wears a corsage on her shoulder or pinned to her purse.

The groom ordinarily wears a business suit, but if the bride is wearing a long dress and the wedding is formal, he wears a sack coat and striped trousers, or a tuxedo in the evening.

The attendants dress in the same style as the couple.

The Ceremony

The mature bride is not given away by anyone. She either walks up the aisle alone at a formal wedding, or at an informal ceremony, comes in a side door with the clergyman, her groom, and their attendants. An exception is when a bride is being "given away" by an adult son. In this case, at a formal wedding they would walk up the aisle together.

The Reception

The reception is as large or as small as the couple wishes. One of the advantages of being an adult is knowing what you want and having the experience to get it. The food, the drinks, the music, the cake, and so on are all chosen to suit their tastes and they need have no worries about flaunting tradition.

751
FOR
THOSE
WHO'VE
BEEN
MARRIED
BEFORE

"The Honour of Your Presence . . ."

As soon as you receive an invitation, to the ceremony and reception or to the reception only, and see that it includes an R.s.v.p., you must reply at once. It is both inconsiderate and impolite not to do so. Remember that the family will have to make definite preparations for every guest who has failed to send a refusal just as they do for those who accept. Failure to reply causes extra trouble *and* expense.

"And Family"

An invitation reading "and Family" includes each and every member of the family living under the same roof—and this means every child from walking and talking age up to great-grandparents. Married daughters or sons who live in their own houses are not included because if invited they are sent separate invitations.

In general, however, you should not take small children unless you are willing to look after them. Well-behaved children are very welcome at a wedding, but children out of hand can be most annoying to everyone and detract from the solemnity of the occasion.

Above all, you may *never* take a child to a wedding unless he is specifically invited—either by name on the inner envelope of your invitation, by his own invitation, or by the "and Family" on your envelope.

"And Guest"

If your invitation has "and Escort" or "and Guest" on it, you are obviously intended to bring a friend of your own choosing. However, you should let the bride know if you intend to do so, giving her the name and address of your friend. Although it is not absolutely necessary, she *should* then send your "date" an invitation.

Single, "unattached" men and women should not assume that they may take an escort. Steady dates or fiancés are usually invited, and if not, the female guest may ask the bride if she may bring her fiancé, and the male guest may do the same. Otherwise a wedding is not a "dating" occasion. Single men and single women should have no reluctance about attending alone. They

44
Especially for Wedding Guests

will find other friends there, and as a matter of fact a wedding reception is apt to be a good place to meet other "singles."

AT THE CHURCH

On entering the church you go to the back of the center aisle and wait until one of the ushers comes up to you. If you are a member of either family or a very close friend of the bride or the groom, you tell him your name. If you have been sent a pew card, you show it to him. At a wedding without pew cards he may ask your name and look on his "in-front-of-the-ribbons" list in order to seat you. If you say nothing to indicate that you should be seated in front, he will ask you whether you are a friend of the bride or of the groom, in order to seat you on her or his side of the aisle. In any case a woman puts her hand on the inside of his proffered arm, and he escorts her to a seat. A man alone walks beside the usher, or if he comes with a woman, he follows the usher and the woman unless there is room for the three of them to walk abreast. As discussed on page 710, many people object to the husband or escort tagging along like this, and I hope that brides and grooms will start to instruct their ushers to say "Please follow me" to a couple, who may then walk together, with the wife on her husband's right.

When two women arrive together, one enters with the first usher to reach her, and the other waits for another usher. If a large crowd arrives at once, however, they may walk in side by side, with the usher preceding them.

If you arrive at the church late, after the bride's mother has been seated, you should slip quietly into a rear pew. If the procession has formed in the vestibule, you may either go to a side aisle or wait until they have all entered the church before seating yourself on the center aisle. Occasionally someone attends a wedding to which he or she has not been specifically invited. This is not wrong, if the person has a good reason for being there, but he too should sit at the back and not allow himself to be ushered in—taking a space that would otherwise be filled by an invited guest.

If you arrive early enough to be seated on the aisle, you need not move over and give your choice place to later arrivals. Either stand or swing your knees to the side to let them pass by. Even though a woman enters the pew before the man she is with, they may switch places so that she (if she is shorter) may have the aisle seat and see the procession with an unobstructed view.

At a wedding it is all right to smile and nod to people you know—even to talk in a low voice to a friend sitting next to you. But when you find yourself among strangers you just sit quietly until the processional starts.

When you are in a church of a religion other than your own observe those in front of you: Stand if they stand, kneel if they kneel, and sit if they sit—as long as it is not contrary to your beliefs.

When the service is over and the recessional has passed by, those in the pews farther back must wait in their places until the immediate families in the front pews have left. If you wait until those around you start to leave, you will be sure of not making any mistake.

From Church to Reception

When you are invited to the reception—if it is to follow the church ceremony—you are expected to go directly from the church to wherever the reception is to be held. But do give the bridal party a little while to arrange for wedding pictures and form the receiving line. No provision need be made for taking any of the guests from the church to the house. You go in your own car, with a friend, or if the distance is short, you walk.

At the Reception

When you arrive at the reception you leave your coat in the dressing room or checkroom and take your place at the end of the queue waiting to go through the receiving line. Should there be an announcer you give him your name with your title—"Mrs. Harry Zuckerman," "Miss Susie Smythe," or "Dr. James Bernard"—and he repeats it to the bride's mother, who, as hostess, is first in the line. Ordinarily, if you are a stranger to her, you shake hands, introduce yourself, and she says she is so glad you could come, or something of that nature. She then introduces you to her husband, if he is in line, and you pass on to say "Hello" to the groom's mother, who is presumably the one whose list you were on. She introduces you to the bride (and groom, if necessary) and you wish the bride happiness, and congratulate the groom. When you are a friend of the bride or her mother you say a word or two about how lovely the ceremony was, and she then introduces you to the groom's mother. You shake hands with each of these people as you speak to them.

Above all, be brief in order not to keep those behind waiting longer than necessary. If you have anything particular to tell the bridal party, you can see them later when there is no longer a line.

In the excitement of the day the bride and groom may easily forget the names even of their best friends, and they are quite likely not to remember Great-Aunt Jennifer, who last visited ten years ago. Therefore it is thoughtful for a guest (even a distant relative) to mention her name even though she thinks the couple knows her. Never choose this moment to play "Guess who I am?" as some inconsiderate people do.

If you have been invited to bring a friend who is unknown to the bride and groom, you should introduce the friend to them both, as well as to their mothers.

You say a few words to any of the bridesmaids with whom you are acquainted. Otherwise you walk on with a smile and perhaps a "Hello" if you happen to be looking directly at one of them who looks at you. But there is no chance, or need, to stop and really talk to those you do not know.

If you are alone you look around for friends of your own after going through the line. If you see no one you know, the best thing to do is make your way to wherever refreshments are being served. You ask the bartender to serve you a drink, or you help yourself to whatever food you want if there is a buffet. You can linger and nibble as long as you like or just sit down and watch people. And you may speak to anyone else who is alone and looks willing to be spoken to.

If you are alone and are seated at a table with veritable strangers, introduce yourself to those at the table. It is helpful to identify yourself, too: "I'm Kathleen McNeila, an old friend of Christine's mother." If there are not place cards directing you to a specific seat, you may sit down at an unoccupied table and let others join you, or you may approach a table where several people are sitting and say, "Is this seat taken?" If it is not, say, "May I join you?" or "Do you mind if I sit here?" and then introduce yourself.

When You May Leave the Reception

When you want to leave a large reception, you just do so, although it is customary to stay at least through the cutting of the cake. It is not necessary to attract attention to your going, but if the bride's mother is not otherwise occupied, you should approach her and thank her just as you would for any party. If you know the bride or groom well and they are not dancing or surrounded with well-wishers you should also bid them good-bye and wish them *bon voyage* if they are leaving for a honeymoon trip.

Wedding Gifts

Generally, wedding gifts, are sent to the bride in advance of the wedding. If for some reason you have not done this and are taking your gift to the reception, do not hand it to the bride as you are proceeding through the receiving line. Instead, look for a small table that is usually set up for gifts, or ask a waiter or club manager where you may leave your gift.

If your gift is a check to be given to the bride or groom at the reception, which is the custom with several ethnic groups, you may deliver it as you pass through the receiving line, place it in a receptacle for this purpose or keep it with you until you are ready to leave, and then look for the bride or groom, whichever you know best. They will often give you a favor as you leave.

If you have neither sent nor taken a gift but plan to send it in the immediate future, do not be apologetic or mention it or offer reassurance that the gift will soon be on its way. This is inappropriate and sounds as though your admission to the reception is based on your delivery of a wedding gift.

Index